Practical Cross-Platform Charts and Graphics with ASP.NET Core MVC

Advanced Cross-Platform Chart and Graphics
Programming for Real-World Web Applications
Using C#, ASP.NET Core MVC, and JavaScript

Jack Xu, PhD

UniCAD Publishing

Practical Cross-Platform Charts and Graphics with ASP.NET Core MVC

Editor: Anna Xu

Contact:
jxu@dxudotnet.com
Visit us at our website: www.drxudotnet.com

Published by UniCAD Publishing.
New York, USA
ISBN-13: 978-0-9793725-8-2
ISBN-10: 0-9793725-8-5

Publisher's Cataloging-in-Publication Data

Xu, Jack
Practical Cross-Platform Charts and Graphics with ASP.NET Core MVC– Advanced Cross-Platform Chart and Graphics Programming for Real-World Web Applications Using C#, ASP.NET Core MVC, and JavaScript / Jack Xu
– 1st ed.
p.cm.
ISBN 978-0-9793725-8-2

1. C# Programming. 2. Charts and Graphics. 3. ASP.NET Core. 4. MVC. 5. Web Development. 6. .NET Applications. 7. JavaScript. 8. d3.js. 9. Three.js. 10. SQL Database. 11. Entity Framework. 12. Cross-Platform
I. Title. II. Title. III Title: Practical Cross-Platform Charts and Graphics with ASP.NET Core MVC

For my wonderful family

Contents

Introduction

Overview

Welcome to *Practical Cross-Platform Charts and Graphics with ASP.NET Core MVC*. This book will provide all the tools you need to develop cross-platform chart and graphics web applications using C#, ASP.NET Core MVC, JavaScript, and Visual Studio 2017. I hope this book will be useful for .NET programmers and web application developers of all skill levels.

We have all heard the saying "a picture is worth a thousand words", and charts and graphics are some of the most informative pictures. Charts and graphics play an important role in every web application. They make data easier to understand, add interest to websites, and have wide applications in our daily life. The scientific, engineering, mathematics, and financial communities always have a need to present data and results graphically. In recent years, web browsers have become a great platform to create powerful web applications with more features and high performance, which allows us to incorporate the beautiful charts, graphics, and animations easily into web applications.

APS.NET Core is a new web framework from Microsoft, which is an open source and cloud-optimized web platform for developing modern web applications that can run on Windows, Linux, and Mac. The platform includes the MVC Core framework, which combines the features of MVC and Web API into a single web-programming framework.

As a .NET programmer or a web developer, you may ask a question – what is the significance of the new ASP.NET Core Framework? To answer it, we need to consider the original .NET Framework. For many .NET developers, you may have confusions about this huge framework at some points. You need to decide between ASP.NET Web Forms and ASP.NET MVC for web applications, decide between Windows Forms and WPF for window applications, and decide between the Entity Framework and ADO.NET for database development. For some experienced developers the choices are obvious, for most it is not that easy, while it is more difficult for .NET beginners.

ASP.NET core is based on .NET Core, which is a cross-platform version of the .NET Framework without the Windows-specific API. It is a completely new framework that is simper and easier to work with. ASP.NET Core MVC, built on the new ASP.NET Core platform, provides the functionality of the original ASP.NET MVC Framework. ASP.NET Core MVC applications can run on .NET Core or on the full .NET Framework. The platform provides an optimized development framework for applications that are deployed to the cloud or run on-premises. It consists of modular components with minimal overhead, so you can optimize your applications to include just the NuGet packages you need. The benefits of such a smaller platform include tighter security, reduced servicing, improved performance, and decreased maintenance costs.

ASP.NET Core MVC follows a pattern called model-view-controller (MVC). This architectural pattern separates an application into three main components: the model, the view, and the controller. This is a standard design pattern that many developers are familiar with. The model component is the part of the application that implement the logic for the application's data domain. *Model* objects often retrieve and store model state in a database. For example, a *Product* object might retrieve the price information from a database, operate on it, and then write updated information back to a *Products* table in the database. *Views* are the components that display the application's user interface (UI). Typically, this UI is created from the model data. An example would be an edit view of a *Products* table that displays text boxes, drop-down lists, and check boxes based on the current state of a *Product* object. Finally, *controllers* are the components that handle user interaction, work with the model, and ultimately select a view to render that displays UI. In an MVC application, the view only displays information; the controller handles and responds to user input and interaction. For example, the controller handles query-string values, and passes these values to the model, which in turn might use these values to query the database.

The MVC pattern helps us create web applications that separate the different aspects of the application (input logic, business logic, and UI logic) while providing a loose coupling between these elements. It specifies where each kind of logic should be located in the application. It is clear that the UI logic belongs in the view, the input logic belongs in the controller, and the business logic belongs in the model. This separation helps us manage complexity when we build an application, because it enables us to focus on one aspect of the implementation at a time. The loose coupling between the three main components of an MVC application also promotes parallel development. For example, one developer can work on the view, a second developer can work on the controller logic, and a third developer can focus on the business logic in the model.

It is also important to distinguish between the MVC design pattern and the ASP.NET Core MVC implementation. ASP.NET Core MVC follows the standard MVC pattern and, in doing so, provides a greatly improved separation of concerns when compared to Web Forms. In fact, ASP.NET Core MVC implements a variant of the MVC pattern that is especially suitable for web applications. Many of the ASP.NET Core MVC API methods and coding patterns follow a cleaner, more expressive composition than was possible with earlier platforms. With ASP.NET Core MVC, developing advanced web applications is easier than ever before.

Nowadays, most modern web browsers support for new technologies that can be used to create web applications with beautiful 2D and 3D chart and graphics. They use the GPU to achieve maximal performance for web applications. The progress in the development of various client-side graphics packages allows you to create graphics easily that run directly in client's browser. These graphics packages include SVG (scalable vector graphics), WebGL, d3.js, three.js, etc. SVG is an XML-based vector image format for two-dimensional (2D) graphics with support for interactivity and animation. The key features of SVG include 2D shapes, text, and embedded raster graphics with many different painting styles. With powerful scripting and event support, SVG can be used as a platform upon which to build graphical rich web applications and user interfaces. In this book, I will show you how to use SVG to create various 2D graphics in ASP.NET Core MVC applications.

D3 (or d3.js) is a JavaScript library for manipulating documents based on data. It helps you bring data to life using HTML, SVG, CSS, and JavaScript. D3 allows you to bind arbitrary data to a document object model (DOM), and then apply data-driven transformations to the documents. D3 is one of the most powerful and flexible data visualization frameworks out there. It facilitates the generation and manipulation of web-based vector graphics with full access to the underlying SVG elements. Moreover,

D3 turns the static SVG graphics into feature-rich visualizations and offers everything you need to make a 2D visualization out of the box. In this book, I will describe the detailed procedure on how to use D3 and SVG to create the interactive chart and graphics in web applications based on the cross-platform ASP.NET Core MVC Framework. In particular, with the client computers and browsers being powerful and fast enough, there really is no need any more to generate charts and graphics on the server. I will also walk you through creating various D3 charts and graphics using the data from server side.

SVG and D3 provides you full control and flexibility for creating charts and graphics in your web applications. However, you need to put a lot of effort if you want to create applications with complex charts and graphics. Fortunately, with the progress in the web development, you do not need to reinvent the wheels from scratch – there are many good client-side JavaScript-based graphics and chart libraries, from which you can choose for your applications. In this book, I will introduce you several such charting libraries: including Google Charts API, Chart.JS, and TechanJS. Google Charts API, based on SVG and D3, is a pure JavaScript charting library, which allows you to enhance web applications by adding interactive charting capability. It provides wide variety of charts, including line, bar, area, pie charts, etc. Chart.JS is a small open-source charting library that uses the HTML5 canvas for rendering charts. It is perfect for small projects. TechanJS is also a JavaScript library built on D3 for creating interactive financial charts for web applications. I will explain how to create various 2D charts using Chart.JS and Google Charts API, as well as the stock charts using TechanJS in ASP.NET Core MVC applications. In creating these charts, I will use a JSON interface to pass the data from server (or database) to the client-side charts.

As I mentioned, most modern browsers also support for creating beautiful 3D graphics and animations that use the GPU to achieve maximal performance. This technology is called WebGL, supported by the latest web browsers. Traditionally, 3D graphics has been restricted to high-end computers or dedicated game consoles, and required complex programming. However, as PC and mobile devices, and more importantly, web browsers have become more sophisticated, it has been possible to create and display 3D graphics in web applications. With WebGL, you can create 3D scenes that run directly in your browser without the need for any plugins or libraries. This book will provide an overview of WebGL and take you, step by step, through basics of creating 3D graphics applications based on ASP.NET Core MVC Framework.

In practice, creating 3D graphics using WebGL requires complex programming. If you want to do anything more than the most basic tasks with WebGL, you need to put series effort and literally hundreds of lines of code. This is unacceptable for rapidly developing applications on web time. Depending on the requirement of your project, you are faced a choice: creating your own helper library to ease the pain, or using libraries already out there. Fortunately, there are a number of JavaScript libraries available, which wrap the WebGL internally and provide a convenient JavaScript API. You can use these libraries directly to create 3D graphics for your web applications without having to understand the complex features of WebGL. One of the most mature and feature-rich of such libraries is Three.js. Three.js provides a large number of easy-to-use APIs that allow you quickly to create complex 3D charts and graphics in your browser. In this book, I will provide you various recipes that you can follow to create beautiful 3D charts and graphics with Three.js for your ASP.NET Core MVC applications. At the same time, I will also introduce a Google sponsored 3D chart package named Graph3d, which can be used to create simple 3D surface charts.

In addition to MVC controllers, ASP.NET Core also offers Web API controllers that are used to provide access to an application's data. Web API is a framework that makes it easy to build HTTP RESTful services that can reach a broad range of clients, including browsers, mobile devices, and traditional desktop applications. In this book, I will also demonstrate how to create Web API applications and how to use the data from Web API services to create various charts, including 3D surface charts for European options and stock charts.

As you may have already noticed, a plethora of ASP.NET MVC programming books is currently available in bookstores. The vast majority of these books are general-purpose user guides and tutorials that explain the basics of ASP.NET MVC and how to use it to implement simple web applications. Users who want to develop web applications with advanced charts, graphics, and other interactive features, however, require a book that provides an in-depth introduction specifically to MVC Core cross-platform chart and graphics development.

I write this book with the intention of providing a complete and comprehensive explanation of ASP.NET Core MVC chart and graphics programming. This book pays special attention to create suitable JSON interfaces for different JavaScript libraries, which allow you to create a variety of graphics and charts on the client browser using data from the server-side data sources, such as mathematical functions and database. Much of this book contains original work based on my own programming experience when I was developing commercial Computer Aided Design (CAD) packages and chart applications for quantitative analysis in the financial industry. With ASP.NET Core MVC Framework and various client-side JavaScript chart and graphics libraries, you will find how easy it is to create web applications with complex 2D and 3D charts and graphics.

Practical Cross-Platform Charts and Graphics with ASP.NET Core MVC provides everything you need to create your own advanced web-based chart and graphics applications using C#, ASP.NET Core MVC, and JavaScript. It shows you how to use MVC Core Framework and JavaScript libraries to create a variety of web applications with advanced chart and graphics features that range from simple 2D shapes to complex 3D surfaces and interactive 3D models. I will try my best to introduce you to the ASP.NET Core MVC chart and graphics programming in a simple way – simple enough to be easily followed by a .NET programmer or a web developer who has basic prior experience in developing .NET or web applications. From this book, you can learn how to create a full range of 2D and 3D chart and graphics for your web applications.

What this Book Includes

This book and its sample code listings, which are available for download at my website at www.drxudotnet.com, provide you with:

- A complete, in-depth instruction on practical cross-platform chart and graphics programming with C#, ASP.NET Core MVC Framework, and JavaScript. After reading this book and running the example programs, you will be able to add various sophisticated charts and graphics to your web applications.

- Ready-to-run example programs that allow you to explore the charting and graphics techniques described in the book. You can use these examples to understand how the chart and graphics algorithms work. You can modify the code examples or add new features to them to form the basis of your own projects. Some of the example code listings provided in this book are already sophisticated web applications that you can use directly in your own real-world projects.

- Many C# classes and JavaScript helper functions in the sample code listings that you will find useful in your web chart and graphics development. These classes and helper functions include mathematical functions, color maps, chart and graphics wrappers, and the other useful utility functions. You can easily extract these classes/functions and plug them into your own web applications.

Is This Book for You?

You do not have to be an experienced .NET programmer or an expert in web development to use this book. I designed this book to be useful to people of all levels of .NET and web programming experience. If you have some prior experience with the programming language C#, MVC, HTML, or JavaScript, you will be able to sit down in front of your computer, start up Microsoft Visual Studio Community 2017 with ASP.NET Core 1.1 MVC, follow the examples provided in this book, and quickly become proficient in web chart and graphics programming. For those of you who are already experienced .NET and web developers, I believe this book has much to offer as well. A great deal of the information about chart programming in this book is not available in other ASP.NET MVC tutorial and reference books. In addition, you can use most of the example programs directly in your own real-world application development. This book will provide you with a level of detail, explanation, instruction, and sample program code that will enable you to do just about anything related to web chart and graphics development based on ASP.NET Core MVC Framework.

.NET developers and technical professionals can use the majority of the example programs in this book routinely. Throughout the book, I will emphasize the usefulness of chart and graphics programming to real-world applications. If you closely follow the instructions presented in this book, you will easily be able to develop various practical web chart applications, from 2D charts to a sophisticated 3D graphics. At the same time, I won't spend too much time discussing programming style, execution speed, and code optimization, because a plethora of books out there already deal with these topics. Most of the example programs you will find in this book omit error handlings. This makes the code easier to understand by focusing on the key concepts and practical applications.

What Do You Need to Use This Book?

You will need no special equipment to make the best use of this book and understand the algorithms. To run and modify the sample programs, you will need a computer capable of running either Windows 7, 8, or 10. The software installed on your computer should include Visual Studio 2017 (Community version is fine) with ASP.NET Core MVC 1.1 or higher. If you have Visual Studio 2015 with ASP.NET Core MVC 1.0, you can also run most of the sample code with few modifications. Please remember, however, that this book is intended for Visual Studio 2017, ASP.NET Core MVC 1.1, and that all of the example programs were created and tested on this platform, so it is best to run the sample code on the same platform.

How the Book Is Organized

This book is organized into ten chapters, each of which covers a different topic about ASP.NET Core MVC chart and graphics programming. The following summaries of each chapter should give you an overview of the book's content:

Chapter 1, *Overview of ASP.NET Core MVC*

This chapter introduces the basics of ASP.NET Core MVC and reviews some of the general aspects of MVC programming. It uses two sample MVC Core applications to illustrate the procedure of MVC Core programming.

Chapter 2, *Graphics Basics in SVG*

This chapter represents SVG graphics basics. It covers the graphics coordinate systems used in SVG, and demonstrates how to create basic 2D shapes. It also discusses the colors, pains, colormaps, tiles, and textures.

Chapter 3, *Dynamic SVG Graphics with D3*

This chapter introduces the D3 JavaScript library for manipulating documents based on data. It uses sample code to demonstrate how to use D3 to create various 2D graphics objects in ASP.NET Core MVC web applications.

Chapter 4, *2D Charts with D3*

This chapter illustrates how to use D3 to create various 2D charts, including line charts and certain special or application-specific charts in ASP.NET Core MVC applications. It consists of a variety of special charts that display statistical distributions of data or discrete data, including bar, stair-step, stem, error bar, and area charts. It also demonstrates how to create charts in other coordinate systems, such as pie and polar charts.

Chapter 5, *2D Charts with Chart Libraries*

This chapter introduces two charting libraries: Chart.JS and Google Chart API. These two packages based on different graphics layers: Chart.JS uses HTML5 canvas for rendering charts, while Google Chart API are based on SVG and VML for older IE versions. It consists of several examples that show how to create a variety of 2D charts using these libraries.

Chapter 6, *Stock Charts*

This chapter illustrates how to create a variety of stock charts using two different JavaScript libraries: Google Charts API and TechanJS. Google Charts is a powerful charting package that provides a variety of chart types, including stock candlestick charts. TechanJS is a JavaScript library built on SVG and D3 for creating interactive financial charts.

Chapter 7, *3D Graphics with WebGL*

This chapter covers the basics of WebGL. WebGL takes advantage of the graphics hardware to accelerate the rendering and enables the display and manipulation of 3D graphics on web pages based on JavaScript. This chapter demonstrates how to use WebGL to create simple geometry primitives and an animated 3D cube object.

Chapter 8, *3D Graphics with Three.js*

This chapter introduces a powerful 3D graphics library – Three.js. It presents the basic procedures on how to use Three.js to create 3D graphics, including defining the scene, setting camera, specifying the materials and lights, and creating geometry and mesh.

Chapter 9, *3D Charts*

This chapter shows how to use Three.js to create simple 3D surface charts and parametric charts with a specified colormap and a UV mapped texture in client side. It then illustrates how to use the server-side data to create various custom 3D geometries and UV maps, which can be used to create 3D charts. The chapter also introduces a JavaScript 3D charting library named *Graph3d* and shows how to use the library to create simple 3D charts.

Chapter 10, *Chart with Web API*

This chapter covers the basics of ASP.NET Core Web API that is used to provide access to an application's data. Web API is a framework that makes it easy to build HTTP RESTful services that can reach a broad range of clients, including browsers, mobile devices, and traditional desktop applications. The chapter demonstrates how to create Web API applications and how to use the data from Web API services to create various charts, including 3D surface charts, 3D charts for European options, and stock charts.

Using Code Examples

You may use the code in this book in your own applications and documentation. You do not need to contact the author or the publisher for permission unless you are reproducing a significant portion of the code. For example, writing a program that uses several chunks of code from this book does not require permission. Selling or distributing the example code listings does require permission. Incorporating a significant amount of example code from this book into your applications and documentation also requires permission. Integrating the example code from this book into commercial products is not allowed without written permission of the author.

Customer Support

I am always interested in hearing from readers, and I would enjoy hearing your thoughts about this book. You can send me comments by e-mail to `jxu@DrXuDotNet.com`. I also provide updates, bug fixes, and ongoing support via my website:

`www.DrXuDotNet.com`

You can also obtain the complete source code for all of the examples in this book from the website.

Chapter 1
Overview of ASP.NET Core MVC

ASP.NET Core MVC is a new open-source and cross-platform framework for building modern web applications. ASP.NET Core applications can run on .NET Core or on the full .NET Framework. Microsoft released the original ASP.NET MVC Framework a decade ago, which reflected the emerging trends in web application development, such as HTML, CSS, and JavaScript standardization, RESTful web services, and effective unit testing. At that time, the ASP.NET MVC Framework was created on top of the existing ASP.NET platform, which included a lot of low-level functionality that was already well known and understood by ASP.NET developers.

As the MVC Framework grew in popularity, Microsoft started to take some of the core features and add them to Web Forms. The result was increasingly odd, where the original features of MVC were extended to support Web Forms. At the same time, Microsoft started to expand ASP.NET with new frameworks for creating web services (Web API) and real-time communication (SignalR). The new frameworks added their own configuration and development conventions, each of which had its own benefits and oddities, and the overall result was a fragmented mess.

In order to address this issue, in 2015, Microsoft announced a new direction for ASP.NET MVC Framework, which would eventually produce ASP.NET Core MVC. This is a completely new framework. It is simpler, easy to work with, and free of the legacy code from Web Forms. Since it is based on .NET core, it supports the development of web applications on a range of platforms and containers.

New Features in ASP.NET Core MVC

ASP.NET Core has a number of architectural changes that result in a much leaner and modular framework. With ASP.NET Core, you gain the following foundational improvements:

- A unified story for building web UI and web APIs.
- Integration of modern client-side frameworks and development workflows.
- A cloud- and docker-ready environment-based configuration system.
- Built-in dependency injection mechanism.
- New lightweight and modular HTTP request pipeline.
- Ability to host on IIS or self-host in your own process.

- Built on .NET Core, which supports true side-by-side application versioning.

- Ships entirely as NuGet packages.

- New tooling that simplifies modern web development.

- Build and run cross-platform ASP.NET applications on Windows, Mac, and Linux.

- Open source and community focused.

You can build both web UI and web APIs using ASP.NET Core MVC:

- You can create well-factored and testable web applications that follow the MVC pattern.

- You can build HTTP services that support multiple formats and have full support for content negotiation using custom or built-in formatters, including JSON and XML

- Razor provides a productive language to create views.

- Tag Helpers enable server-side code to participate in creating and rendering HTML element in Razor files.

- Model binding automatically maps data from HTTP requests to action method parameters.

- Model validation automatically performs client and server side validations.

ASP.NET Core MVC Framework is also designed to integrate seamlessly with a variety of client-side frameworks, including JQuery, AngularJS, KnockoutJS, and Bootstrap.

Your First Web Application

Let us start by creating a new ASP.NET Core MVC project. In this project, we will build a web application that performs basic stock data access using Entity Framework. We will use migrations to create the stock database from our model. We usually call this project the code-first application.

Creating a New MVC Project

I assume that you have already installed Visual Studio 2017 and ASP.NET Core Framework on your computer. Open Visual Studio 2017 and create a new ASP.NET Core MVC project.

File > New > Project….

From the left menu select *Installed > Templates > Visual C#*. Complete the *New Project* dialog as shown in Figure 1.1.

Note that we choose the *.NET Core* in the left template pane and tap *ASP.NET Core Web Application* (*.NET Core*) in the center pane. We name the project "*FirstMvcApp*" and the solution "*Chapter01*". Tap *OK* to bring up the *New ASP.NET Core Web Application (.NET Core) – FirstMvcApp* dialog, as shown in Figure 1-2.

In the version selector drop-down box tap *ASP.NET Core 1.1* and choose *Web Application* from the template window. Click *OK*.

Visual Studio uses a default template for the MVC project you just created. Now, you have a working application by entering a project name and selecting a few options. You can also see a number of files and folders displayed in the Solution Explorer window, as shown in Figure 1-3. This is the default project structure for a new MVC application created using the *Web Application* template.

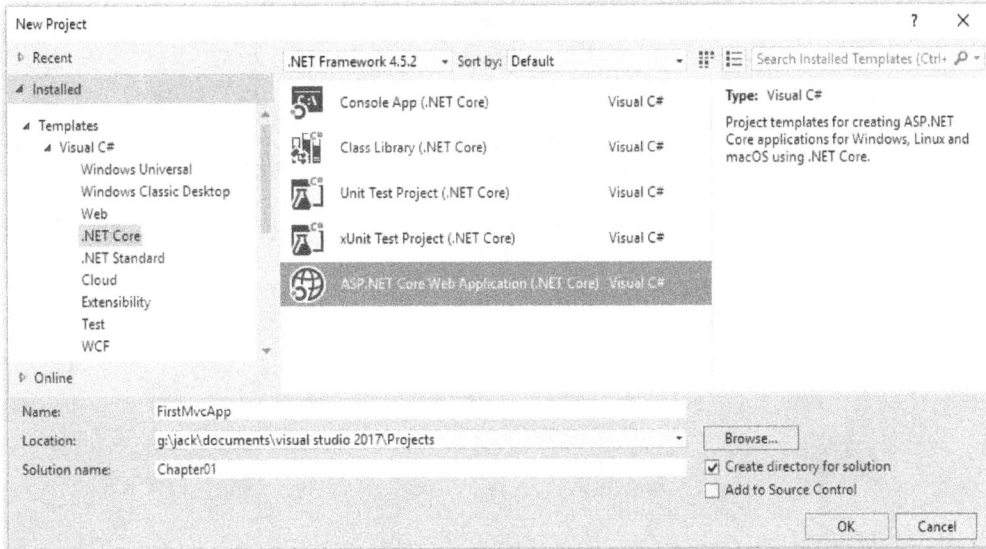

Figure 1.1. New Project dialog in Visual Studio 2017.

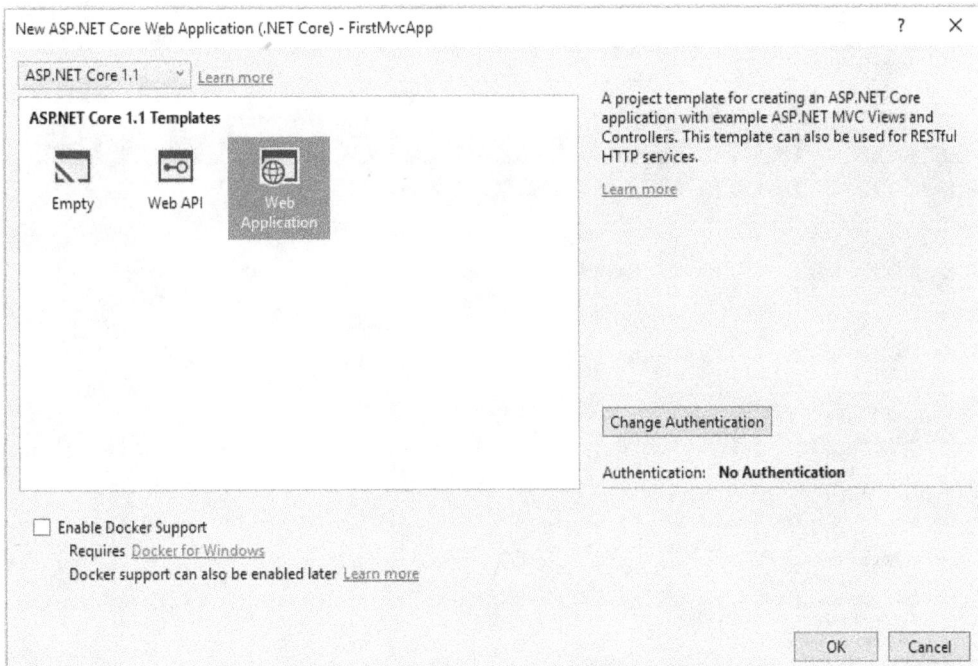

Figure 1-2. New ASP.NET Core Web Application dialog.

You can run the application in the debug mode by pressing F5 or in non-debug model by pressing CTRL+F5. When you do this, Visual Studio compiles the application, uses an application server called IIS Express to run it, and opens a web browser to request the application content. Figure 1-4 shows the result.

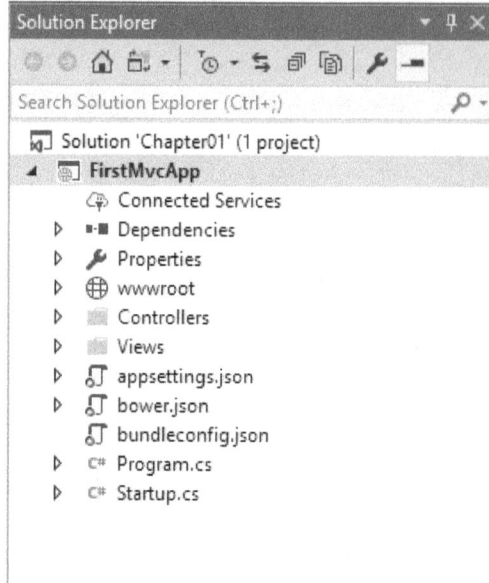

Figure 1-3. The initial file and folder structure of an ASP.NET Core MVC Application.

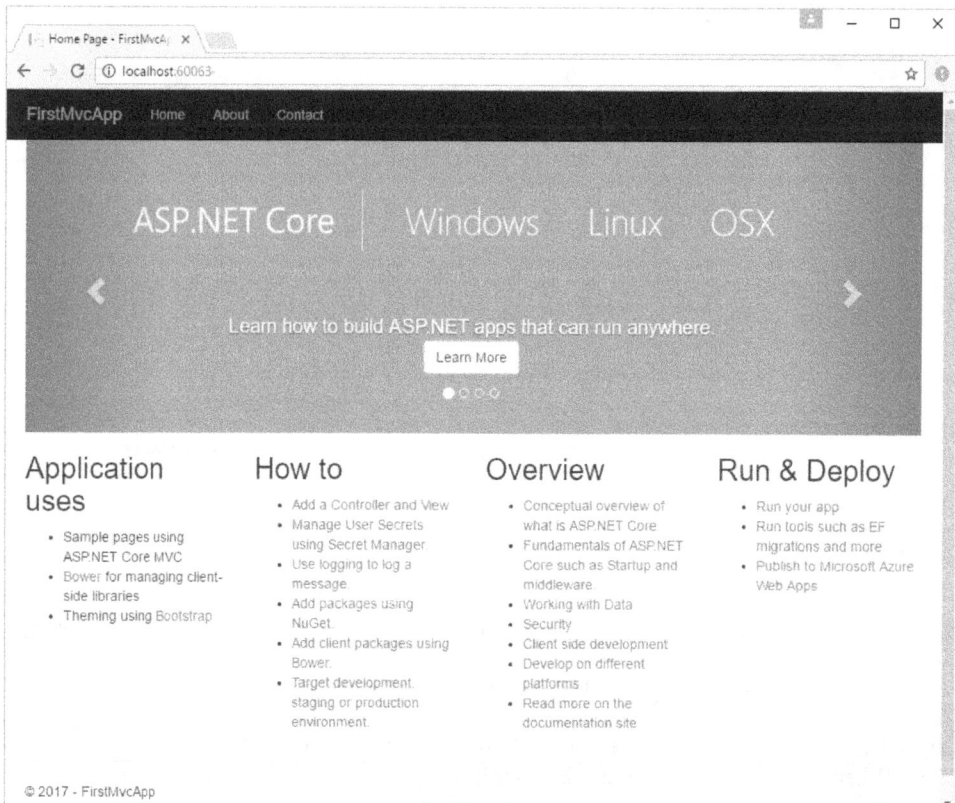

Figure 1-4. Running the example project.

When Visual Studio creates a project with the Web application template, it adds some basic code and content, which is what you see when you run the application. Now, you have a working application by simply entering a project name and selecting a few options. This is a simple starter project, and it is a good place to start. Notice that the address bar shows *localhost:port#* and not something like *example.com*. This is because *localhost* is the standard hostname for your local computer. When Visual Studio creates a web project, a random port is used for the web server. In our example, the port number is 60063. When you run the application on your own computer, you may see a different port number.

Note that launching the application with Ctrl+F5 in non-debug mode allows you to make code changes, save files, refresh the browser, and see the code changes. Many developers prefer to use the non-debug mode to quickly launch the application and view changes.

Creating Database Model

In order to use Entity Framework (EF) Core in your web applications, you need to install the package of the database provider you want to target. This example will use the SQL Server.

Right click *Dependencies* in the Solution Explorer and select *Manage NuGet Packages…*

In the *NuGet Package Manager* window, search for and install the following packages:

- Microsoft.EntityFrameworkCore.SqlServer
- Microsoft.EntityFrameworkCore.Tools

Here, we will use the so-called code first approach to create database. In the code first method, we first create entity classes with properties defined in it. Entity Framework will create the database and tables based on the entity classes defined. So database is generated from the code. The database will be created when you run the application.

Now it is time to define a context and entity classes that make up our stock price database model. Right-click on the project in Solution Explorer and select *Add > New Folder*. Enter *Models* as the name of the folder. Add four new classes, *Symbol*, *Price*, *IndexData*, and *StockPriceContext*, to the *Models* folder and replace the content of the files with the following code:

```
using System.Collections.Generic;
namespace FirstMvcApp.Models
{
    public class Symbol
    {
        public int SymbolID { get; set; }
        public string Ticker { get; set; }
        public string Region { get; set; }
        public string Sector { get; set; }

        public virtual ICollection<Price> Prices { get; set; }
    }
}

using System;
namespace FirstMvcApp.Models
{
    public class Price
    {
        public int PriceID { get; set; }
```

```csharp
        public int SymbolID { get; set; }
        public DateTime Date { get; set; }
        public double Open { get; set; }
        public double High { get; set; }
        public double Low { get; set; }
        public double Close { get; set; }
        public double CloseAdj { get; set; }
        public double Volume { get; set; }
    }
}

using System;
namespace FirstMvcApp.Models
{
    public class IndexData
    {
        public int ID { get; set; }
        public DateTime Date { get; set; }
        public double IGSpread { get; set; }
        public double HYSpread { get; set; }
        public double SPX { get; set; }
        public double VIX { get; set; }
    }
}


using Microsoft.EntityFrameworkCore;
namespace FirstMvcApp.Models
{
    public class StockPriceContext : DbContext
    {
        public StockPriceContext(DbContextOptions<StockPriceContext> options)
            : base(options)
        { }

        public DbSet<Symbol> Symbols { get; set; }
        public DbSet<Price> Prices { get; set; }
        public DbSet<IndexData> IndexDatas { get; set; }

        protected override void OnModelCreating(ModelBuilder modelBuilder)
        {
            modelBuilder.Entity<Symbol>().ToTable("Symbol");
            modelBuilder.Entity<Price>().ToTable("Price");
            modelBuilder.Entity<IndexData>().ToTable("IndexData");
        }
    }
}
```

We will use the classes, *Symbol* and *Price*, to store stock tickers and the stock data from Yahoo Finance. The *IndexData* class will be used to store the market data from a CSV file for some indices, including SPX 500, VIX (volatility index), HY (high-yield CDX index), and IG (investment-grade CDX index). The properties with ID, such as *ID*, *SymbolID*, and *PriceID*, will be the primary keys. By default, the Entity Framework interprets a property that is named *ID* or *classnameID* as the primary key. The *Prices* property in the *Symbol* class is a navigation property, which holds *Price* entities that are related to the *Symbol* entity.

Navigation properties are typically defined as *virtual* so that they can take advantage of certain Entity Framework functionality such as *lazy loading*. If a navigation property can hold multiple entities, its type must be a list or collection, in which entries can be added, deleted, and updated, such as *ICollection*.

The *StockPriceContext* class coordinates Entity Framework functionality for our stock price model. When database is created, Entity Framework creates tables that have names the same as the *DbSet* property names. Property names for collection are typically plural, but developers disagree about whether table names should be pluralized or not. Here, we override the default behavior by specifying singular table names in the *StockPriceContext* class. We create this class by deriving from the *DbContext* class. Here, we specify which entities are included in the data model. The code creates a *DbSet* property for each entity set. In Entity Framework terminology, an entity set typically corresponds to a database table, while an entity corresponds to a row in the table.

Register Context with Dependency Injection

The concept of dependency injection is central to ASP.NET Core. Services, such as *StockPriceContext*, are registered with dependency injection during application startup. Components that require these services (such as MVC controllers) are then provided these services via constructor parameters or properties. In order for our MVC controllers to make use of *StockPriceContext*, we need to register it as a service.

Open the *Startup.cs* file, add the following *using* statements at the start of the file:

```
using Microsoft.Extensions.DependencyInjection;
using Microsoft.Extensions.Logging;
```

New we can use the *AddDbContext*(...) method to register the context as a service. Replace the *ConfigureServices* method with the following code:

```
// This method gets called by the runtime. Use this method to add services
// to the container.
public void ConfigureServices(IServiceCollection services)
{
    // Add framework services.
    services.AddMvc();
    var connection = "Server=(localdb)\mssqllocaldb;Database
        =StockPriceDb;Trusted_Connection=True;";
    services.AddDbContext<StockPriceContext>(options =>
        options.UseSqlServer(connection));
}
```

In a real-world application, you would typically put the connection string in a configuration file, such as the *appsettings.json* file. Here, for sake of simplicity, we are defining it in code. The connection string in our example specifies a SQL Server LocalDB database. LocalDB is a lightweight version of the SQL Server Express Database Engine and is intended for application development, not production use. LocalDB starts on demand and runs in user mode, so there is no complex configuration. By default, LocalDB creates *.mdf* database files in the *C:/users/<user>* director.

Initializing Database

The Entity Framework will create an empty database. We will write a method that is called after database is created in order to populate it with test data. Add a new class named *DbInitializer.cs* to the *Models*

folder and replace the template code with the following code, which causes a database to be created
when needed and loads the test data into the new database:

```
using System;
using System.Linq;
using System.Text.RegularExpressions;

namespace FirstMvcApp.Models
{
    public static class DbInitializer
    {
        public static void Initialize(StockPriceContext context)
        {
            context.Database.EnsureCreated();

            string path = AppContext.BaseDirectory;
            string[] ss = Regex.Split(path, "bin");
            string filePath = ss[0] + @"Data\";

                // look for any symbol
            if (context.Symbols.Any())
            {
                return;  // DB has been seeded
            }

            var symbols = ModelHelper.CsvToSymbolList(
                    filePath + "StockTickers.csv");
            foreach (Symbol s in symbols)
                context.Symbols.Add(s);
            context.SaveChanges();

        //look for any index data
            if (context.IndexDatas.Any())
            {
                return;  //DB has been seeded
            }

            var data = ModelHelper.CsvToIndexData(filePath + "indices.csv");
            foreach (IndexData d in data)
                context.IndexDatas.Add(d);
            context.SaveChanges();
        }
    }
}
```

The code checks if there are any symbols and index data in the database, and if not, it assumes the
database is new and needs to be seeded with the test data.

Here, we use the *EnsureCreated* method to automatically create the database. When we develop a new
application, our data model may change, and each time the model changes, it gets out of sync with the
database. We use the *EnsureCreated* method for the Entity Framework to create the database if it does
not exist. Then each time you change the data model – add, remove, or change entity classes or change
the *DbContext* class – we can delete the database and Entity Framework creates a new one that matches
the model, and seeds it with the test data.

The approach of keeping the database in sync with the data model works well until you deploy the application to production. When the application is running in production, it is usually storing data that you want to keep, and you do not want to lose everything each time you make a change such as adding a new column. In this case, you need to use the Entity Framework Core migrations feature to solve this problem by enabling Entity Framework to update the database schema instead of creating a new database. For the stock price database in this example, our data model is fixed. Therefore, the *EnsureCreated* method should work just fine.

In *Startup.cs*, modify the *Configure* method to call this *seed* method on application startup. First, add the context to the method signature so that ASP.NET dependency injection can provide it to our *DbInitializer* class, and then call the *DbInitializer.Initialize* method at the end of the *Configure* method as shown in the following highlighted code snippet:

```
// This method gets called by the runtime. Use this method to configure
// the HTTP request pipeline.
public void Configure(IApplicationBuilder app, IHostingEnvironment env,
    ILoggerFactory loggerFactory, StockPriceContext context)
{
    loggerFactory.AddConsole(Configuration.GetSection("Logging"));
    loggerFactory.AddDebug();
    ......
    app.UseMvc(routes =>
    {
        routes.MapRoute(
            name: "default",
            template: "{controller=Home}/{action=Index}/{id?}");
    });

    DbInitializer.Initialize(context);
}
```

Now, the first time you run the application the database will be created and seeded with the test data. Whenever you change your data model, you can delete the database, update your seed method, and start afresh with a new database the same way.

Adding Tickers to Database

You can see that inside the *Initialize* method in the *DbInitializer* class, we want to use the CSV files to add the test data to the database. Here, I will show you how to do it.

I have already created a CSV file named *StockTicker.csv* that contains the stock tickers to be inserted into the *Symbol* table. This file is located in the *Models* folder. The following shows the format for this CSV file:

```
Ticker,Region,Sector
A,US,information Technology
AA,US,Materials
ABK,US,Financials
ACE,US,Financials
ACGL,US,Financials
ACN,US,Information Technology
ADI,US,Information Technology
ADP,US,Information Technology
AFG,US,Financials
```

```
AFL,US,Financials
......
```

The first line in the file is the header, and the comma is used to separate data fields. In the *ModelHelper.cs* class located in the *Models* folder, I implemented a *CsvToSymbolList* method, which can be used to convert a CSV file into a *Symbol* list. Here is the code snippet for this method:

```
public static List<Symbol> CsvToSymbolList(string csvFile)
{
    FileStream fs = new FileStream(csvFile, FileMode.Open, FileAccess.Read,
        FileShare.ReadWrite);
    StreamReader sr = new StreamReader(fs);
    List<String> lst = new List<string>();
    while (!sr.EndOfStream)
        lst.Add(sr.ReadLine());
    string[] fields = lst[0].Split(new char[] { ',' });
    var res = new List<Symbol>();
    for (int i = 1; i < lst.Count; i++)
    {
        fields = lst[i].Split(',');
        res.Add(new Symbol
        {
            Ticker = fields[0],
            Region = fields[1],
            Sector = fields[2]
        });
    }
    return res;
}
```

We will use this method to add the stock tickers to database.

Adding Index Data to Database

Inside the *Initialize* method in the *DbInitializer* class, we also want to use a CSV file to add the test data to the *IndexData* table. I have already created a CSV file named *indices.csv* that contains over 10 years of market data for different indices starting from 9/21/2004 to 5/15/2015. This file is located in the *Models* folder. The following shows the format for this CSV file:

```
Date,IGSpread,HYSpread,SPX,VIX
9/21/2004,53.93,363,1129.3,13.66
9/22/2004,55.18,367.5,1113.56,14.74
9/23/2004,54.69,371.2,1108.36,14.8
9/24/2004,55.11,374.5,1110.11,14.28
9/27/2004,54.59,370.5,1103.52,14.62
......
5/8/2014,64.13226232,342.939195,1875.63,13.43
5/9/2014,63.77962727,342.2512993,1878.48,12.92
5/12/2014,62.54275824,337.9057833,1896.65,12.23
5/13/2014,62.48443231,337.2766355,1897.45,12.13
5/14/2014,63.24887055,338.1121574,1888.53,12.17
5/15/2014,65.21262904,346.5008667,1870.85,13.17
```

The first line in the file is the header, and the comma is used to separate data fields. In the *ModelHelper.cs* class located in the *Models* folder, I implemented a *CsvToIndexData* method, which can be used to convert a CSV file into an *IndexData* list. Here is the code snippet for this method:

```
public static List<IndexData> CsvToIndexData(string csvFile)
{
    FileStream fs = new FileStream(csvFile, FileMode.Open,
    FileAccess.Read, FileShare.ReadWrite);
    StreamReader sr = new StreamReader(fs);
    List<String> lst = new List<string>();
    while (!sr.EndOfStream)
        lst.Add(sr.ReadLine());

    string[] fields = lst[0].Split(new char[] { ',' });
    var res = new List<IndexData>();
    for (int i = 1; i < lst.Count; i++)
    {
        fields = lst[i].Split(',');
        res.Add(new IndexData
        {
            Date = DateTime.Parse(fields[0]),
            IGSpread = double.Parse(fields[1]),
            HYSpread = double.Parse(fields[2]),
            SPX = double.Parse(fields[3]),
            VIX = double.Parse(fields[4])
        });
    }
    return res;
}
```

We will use this method to add the index data to database. Now, press F5 to run the application and check if the new database named *StockPriceDb* is created.

Checking Database

If everything goes smoothly, the database named *StockPriceDb* should have been created in the *localdb* server. Now, inside the Visual Studio, go to the *View* menu and select SQL Server Object Explorer. You should see the *StockPriceDb* database in there, which contains three tables: *Symbol*, *Price*, and *IndexData*, as shown in Figure 1-5.

We can also examine if *Symbol* and *IndexData* tables contain the test data. Right-clicking on the *dbo.Symbol* table and choosing *View Data*, you should see the results on your screen, as shown in Figure 1-6. There should be more than 180 tickers in the *Symbol* table. If you could not add those tickers to this table, you need to redo it by closely following the instruction provided in this example. You will need the tickers in the *Symbol* table in the following chapters of this book.

We can also check the *IndexData* table to see if it contains the test data. Right-clicking on the *dbo.IndexData* table and choosing *View Data*, you should see the results on your screen, as shown in Figure 1-7. There should be about 1000 records of the test data in this table.

The *Price* table should contains no data because we did not provide any initial data to it yet. We will populate this table with the market data from Yahoo Finance later.

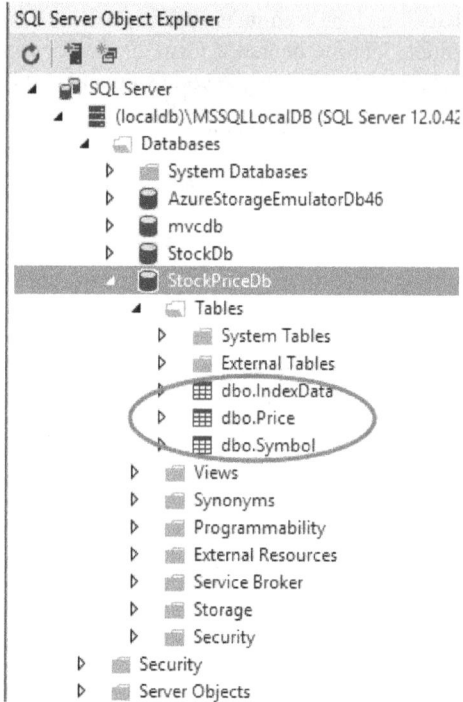

Figure 1-5. New StockPriceDb database in LocalDB.

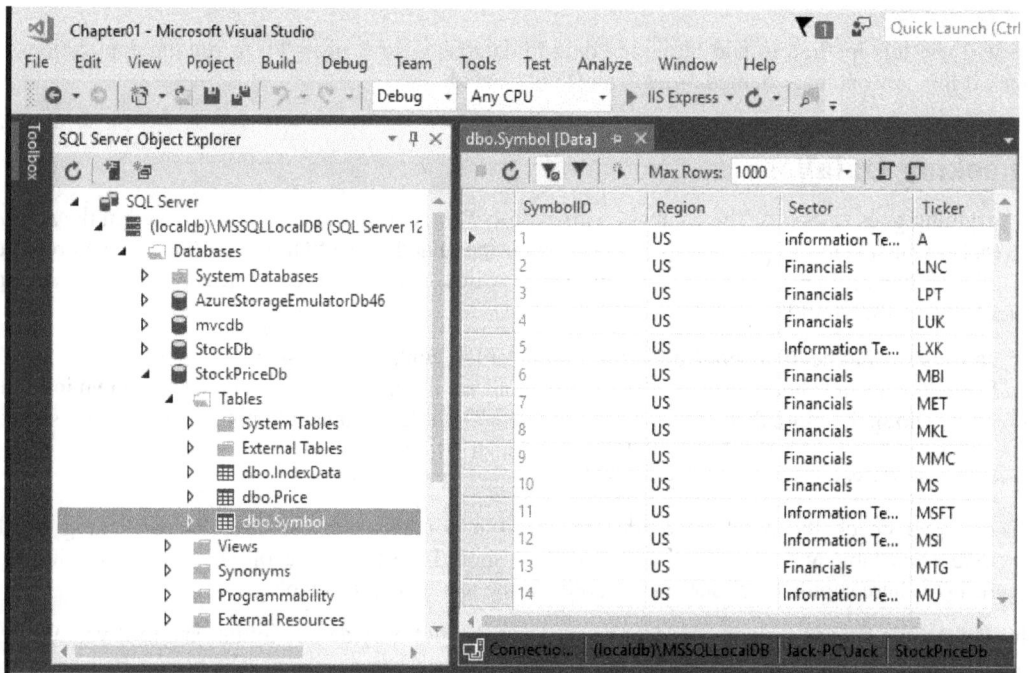

Figure 1-6. Stock tickers in the Symbol table.

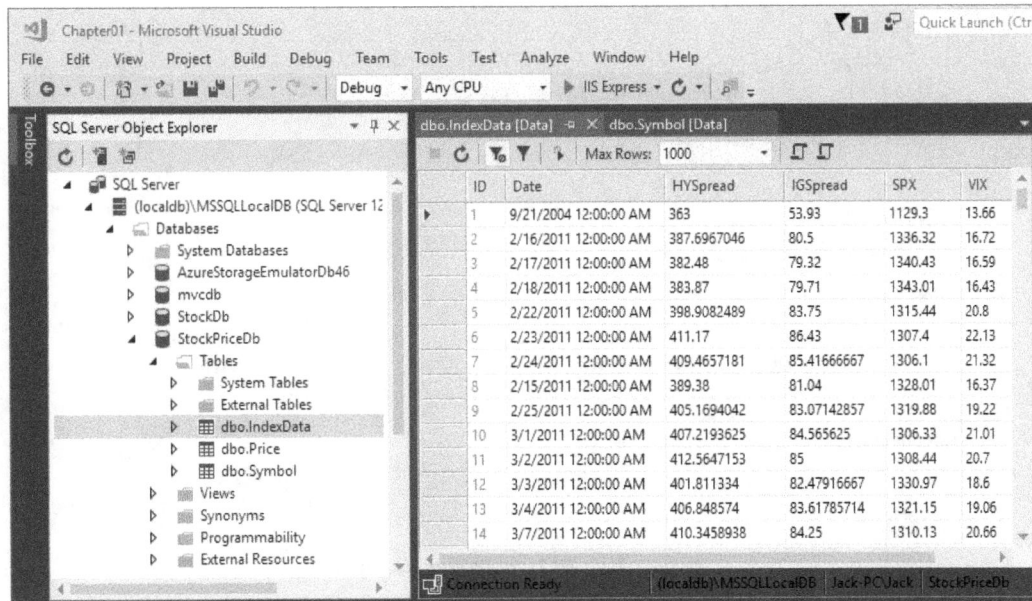

Figure 1-7. Test data in the IndexData table.

Creating a Controller and Views

Next, we will use the scaffolding engine in Visual Studio to add an MVC controller and views that will use Entity Framework to query and save data. We usually call the automatic creation of CRUD (Create, Read, Update, and Delete) action methods and views as scaffolding. Scaffolding is different from code generation in that the scaffolded code is a starting point that you can modify to suite your own requirements, whereas you typically do not modify the generated code. When you need to customize the generated code, you use partial classes or you regenerate the code when things change.

- Right-click the *Controllers* folder in Solution Explorer and select *Add > Controller...*

- In the Add Scaffold dialog box: select *MVC controller with views, using Entity Framework*. Click Add.

- In the *Add Controller* dialog box: Enter corresponding fields as shown in Figure 1-8. Click *Add*.

After this process, the Visual Studio scaffolding engine creates a *StockDataController.cs* file in the *Controllers* folder and a set of views (*.cshtml* files in the *StockData* folder) that work with the controller.

You may notice that the controller takes a *StockPriceContext* as a constructor parameter:

```
namespace FirstMvcApp.Controllers
{
    public class StockDataController : Controller
    {
        private readonly StockPriceContext _context;

        public StockDataController(StockPriceContext context)
        {
            _context = context;
        }
```

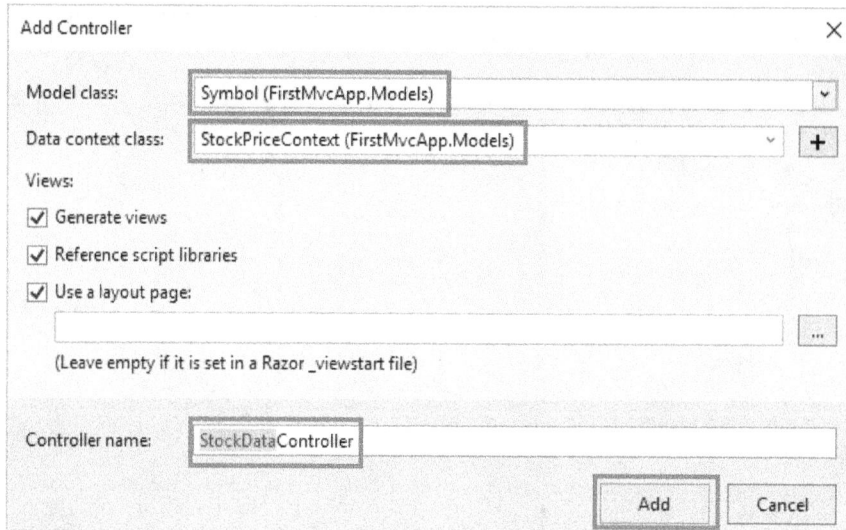

Figure 1-8. Add Controller dialog.

ASP.NET Core dependency injection will take care of passing an instance of *StockPriceContext* into the controller as you configured that in the *Startup.cs* file earlier. The controller contains an *Index* action method, which displays all tickers in the *Symbol* table. The method gets a list of symbols from the *Symbols* entity set by reading the *Symbols* property of the database context instance:

```
// GET: StockData
public async Task<IActionResult> Index()
{
    return View(await _context.Symbols.OrderBy(s => s.Ticker).ToListAsync());
}
```

Here, we use the *async-await* programming to avoid performance bottlenecks and enhance the overall responsiveness of your application. Traditional techniques for writing asynchronous applications can be complicated, making them difficult to write, debug, and maintain. The *async* programming introduced first in Visual Studio 2012 leverages asynchronous support in the .NET applications. The compiler does the difficult work that developers used to do, and your application retains a logical structure that resembles synchronous code. As a result, you get all the advantages of asynchronous programming with a fraction of the effort.

Asynchronous programming is the default mode for ASP.NET Core and Entity Framework Core. A web server has a limited number of threads available, and in high load situations, all of the available threads might be in use. When that happens, the server cannot process new requests until the threads are freed up. With synchronous code, many threads may be tied up while they are not actually doing any work because they are waiting for I/O to complete. With asynchronous code, when a process is waiting for I/O to complete, its thread is freed up for the server to use for processing other requests. As a result, asynchronous code enables server resources to be use more efficiently, and the server is enabled to handle more traffic without delays.

Asynchronous code does introduce a small amount of overhead at run time, but for low traffic situations, the performance hit is negligible, while for high traffic situations, the potential performance improvement is substantial.

The view file *Index.cshtml* in the *Views/StockData* directory displays the list of symbols in a table:

```
@model IEnumerable<FirstMvcApp.Models.Symbol>

@{
    ViewData["Title"] = "Index";
}

<h2>Index</h2>

<p>
    <a asp-action="Create">Create New</a>
</p>
<table class="table">
    <thead>
        <tr>
            <th>
                @Html.DisplayNameFor(model => model.Ticker)
            </th>
            <th>
                @Html.DisplayNameFor(model => model.Region)
            </th>
            <th>
                @Html.DisplayNameFor(model => model.Sector)
            </th>
            <th></th>
        </tr>
    </thead>
    <tbody>
@foreach (var item in Model) {
        <tr>
            <td>
                @Html.DisplayFor(modelItem => item.Ticker)
            </td>
            <td>
                @Html.DisplayFor(modelItem => item.Region)
            </td>
            <td>
                @Html.DisplayFor(modelItem => item.Sector)
            </td>
            <td>
                <a asp-action="Edit" asp-route-id="@item.SymbolID">Edit</a> |
                <a asp-action="Details"
                    asp-route-id="@item.SymbolID">Details</a> |
                <a asp-action="Delete" asp-route-id="@item.SymbolID">Delete</a>
            </td>
        </tr>
}
    </tbody>
</table>
```

Press CTRL + F5 to run the project in non-debug mode. Click the *Stock Database* tab to see the test data. Depending on how narrow your browser window is, you will see the *Stock Database* tab link at the top of the page or you will have to click the navigation icon in the upper right corner to see the link. As shown in the top of Figure 1-9. The test data is displayed in the bottom of the figure.

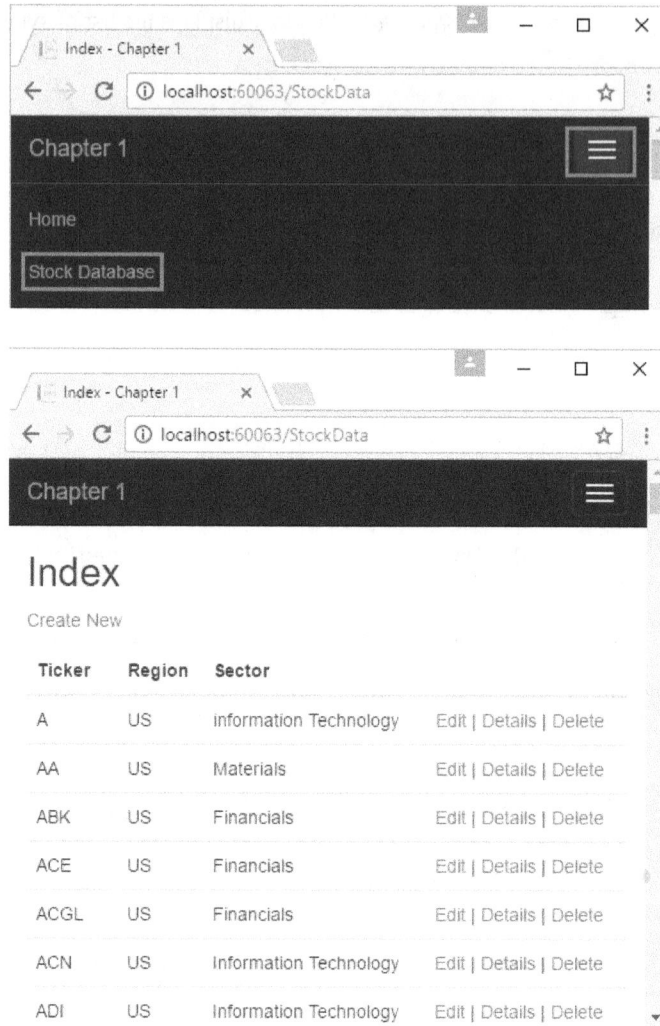

Figure 1-9. Tickers in the Symbol table.

CRUD Operations

In the preceding sections, we demonstrated how to create your first ASP.NET Core MVC web application using Entity Framework Core and Visual Studio 2017. The application can store and display test data using EF and SQL Server LocalDB. In this section, we will discuss and customize the CRUD code that the MVC scaffolding automatically creates for us in controllers and views.

The Details Page

The scaffolded code for the *StockData Index* page left out the *Prices* property, because that property holds a collection of the *Price* entity. In the *Details* page, we will display the contents of the collection in an HTML table if the price data is available in database.

In the *Controllers/StockDataController.cs* file, the action method for the *Details* view uses *SingleOrDefaultAsync* method to retrieve a single *Symbol* entity. Add code that calls *Include* and *AsNoTracking* methods, as shown in the following highlighted code:

```
// GET: StockData/Details/5
public async Task<IActionResult> Details(int? id)
{
    if (id == null)
    {
        return NotFound();
    }

    var symbol = await _context.Symbols
        .Include(s => s.Prices)
        .AsNoTracking()
        .SingleOrDefaultAsync(m => m.SymbolID == id);

    if (symbol == null)
    {
        return NotFound();
    }

    return View(symbol);
}
```

The *Include* method causes the context to load the *Symbol.Prices* navigation property. The *AsNoTracking* method improves performance in scenarios where the entities will not be updated in the current context's lifetime. When a database context retrieves records and creates entity objects, by default it keeps track of whether the entities in memory are in sync with what is in the database. The data in memory acts as a cache and is used when you update an entity. This caching is often unnecessary in a web application because context instances are typically short-lived (a new one is created and disposed for each request) and the context that reads an entity is typically disposed before that entity is used again. We can then disable tracking of entity objects in memory by calling the *AsNoTracking* method.

Using the above code to query all the records for the *Prices* entity from LocalDB, you will find the process will become very slow. In our example, we will use the LINQ to query the top 30 records for the *Prices* entity. Here is the LINQ version of the *Details* method:

```
// GET: StockData/Details/5
public async Task<IActionResult> Details(int? id)
{
    if (id == null)
    {
        return NotFound();
    }

    var symbol = await _context.Symbols.SingleAsync(m => m.SymbolID == id);
    symbol.Prices = await _context.Prices.Where(
        x => x.SymbolID == id).Take(30).ToListAsync();

    if (symbol == null)
    {
        return NotFound();
    }
}
```

```
        return View(symbol);
    }
```

Now, open *Views/StockData/Details.cshtml*. Replace the template content with the following code:

```
@model FirstMvcApp.Models.Symbol

@{
    ViewData["Title"] = "Details";
}

<h2>Details</h2>

<div>
    <h4>Symbol</h4>
    <hr />
    <dl class="dl-horizontal">
        <dt>
            @Html.DisplayNameFor(model => model.Ticker)
        </dt>
        <dd>
            @Html.DisplayFor(model => model.Ticker)
        </dd>
        <dt>
            @Html.DisplayNameFor(model => model.Region)
        </dt>
        <dd>
            @Html.DisplayFor(model => model.Region)
        </dd>
        <dt>
            @Html.DisplayNameFor(model => model.Sector)
        </dt>
        <dd>
            @Html.DisplayFor(model => model.Sector)
        </dd>

        <dt>
            @Html.DisplayNameFor(model => model.Prices)
        </dt>
        <dd>
            <table class="table">
                <tr>
                    <th>Date</th>
                    <th>Open</th>
                    <th>High</th>
                    <th>Low</th>
                    <th>Close</th>
                    <th>CloseAdj</th>
                    <th>Volume</th>
                </tr>
                @if (Model.Prices != null)
                {
                    @foreach (var item in Model.Prices)
                    {
                        <tr>
                            <td>@Html.DisplayFor(modelItem => item.Date)</td>
```

```
                <td>@Html.DisplayFor(modelItem => item.Open)</td>
                <td>@Html.DisplayFor(modelItem => item.High)</td>
                <td>@Html.DisplayFor(modelItem => item.Low)</td>
                <td>@Html.DisplayFor(modelItem => item.Close)</td>
                <td>@Html.DisplayFor(modelItem =>
                                    item.CloseAdj)</td>
                <td>@Html.DisplayFor(modelItem => item.Volume)</td>
            </tr>
        }
    }
    </table>
    </dd>
    </dl>
</div>
<div>
    <a asp-action="Edit" asp-route-id="@Model.SymbolID">Edit</a> |
    <a asp-action="Index">Back to List</a>
</div>
```

The highlighted code loops through the entities in the *Prices* navigation property. For each price entity, it displays information for the date, open, high, low, close, adjusted close, and volume. Now, run the application, select the *Stock Database* tab, and click the *Details* link for a stock ticker, i.e., IBM. Figure 1-10 shows the results. You can see that the list for *Prices* only shows the header because we have not added any stock price data for IBM to database yet. We will add the price data to database from Yahoo Finance in later sections.

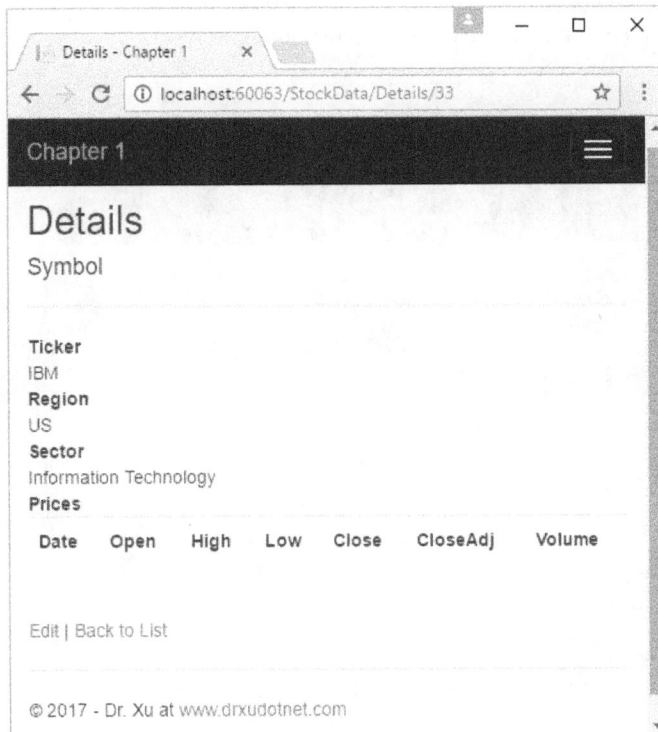

Figure 1-10. The details for IBM.

The Create Page

In the *Controllers/StockDataController.cs* file, we need to modify the *HttpPost Create* method by removing *SymbolID* from the *Bind* attribute:

```
[HttpPost]
[ValidateAntiForgeryToken]
public async Task<IActionResult> Create(
    [Bind("Ticker,Region,Sector")] Symbol symbol)
{
    if (ModelState.IsValid)
    {
        _context.Add(symbol);
        await _context.SaveChangesAsync();
        return RedirectToAction("Index");
    }
    return View(symbol);
}
```

This code adds the *Symbol* entity created by the ASP.NET MVC model binder to the *Symbols* entity set and then saves the changes to the database. We removed *SymbolID* from the *Bind* attribute because *SymbolID* is the primary key value, which the SQL Server will set automatically when the row is inserted. Users do not need to set the *SymbolID* value. The *Bind* attribute that the scaffolded code includes on the *Create* method is one way to protect against overposting in the create scenarios.

We do not need to make any changes to the *Create.cshtml* view. Click CTRL + F5 to run the application. Selecting the *Stock Database* tab and clicking the *Create New* link. Enter *SPY* in the *Ticker* field, *US* in the *Region* field, and *ETF* in the *Sector* field, as shown in Figure 1-11.

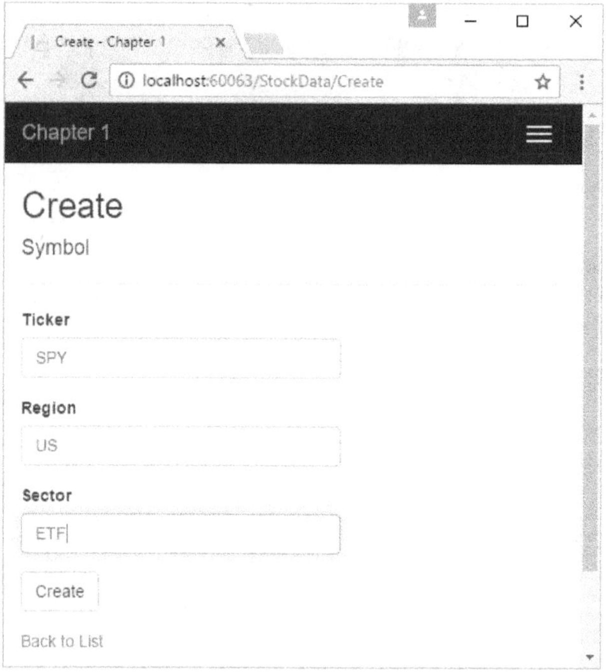

Figure 1-11. Add a new Symbol entity to the database.

Click *Create* to add the new symbol SPY to the database. You can check if it appears in the *Index* page.

The Edit Page

In *StockDataController.cs*, the *HttpGet Edit* method uses the *SingleOrDefaultAsync* method to retrieve the selected *Symbol* entity, as you saw in the *Details* method. You do not need to change this method.

Replace the *HttpPost Edit* action method with the following code:

```
[HttpPost, ActionName("Edit")]
[ValidateAntiForgeryToken]
public async Task<IActionResult> EditPost(int? id)
{
    if (id == null)
    {
        return NotFound();
    }

    var symbolToUpdate = await _context.Symbols.SingleOrDefaultAsync(
        s => s.SymbolID == id);
    if (await TryUpdateModelAsync<Symbol>(symbolToUpdate, "", s => s.Ticker,
        s => s.Region, s => s.Sector))
    {
        try
        {
            await _context.SaveChangesAsync();
            return RedirectToAction("Index");
        }
        catch
        {
            //Log the error (uncomment ex variable name and write a log.)
            ModelState.AddModelError("", "Unable to save changes. Try again,
                and if the problem persists, see your system administrator.");
        }
    }
    return View(symbolToUpdate);
}
```

These changes implement a security best practice to prevent overposting. The scaffolder generated a *Bind* attribute and added the entity created by the model binder to the entity set with a modified flag. That code is not recommended for many scenarios because the *Bind* attribute clears out any pre-existing data in fields out listed in the *Include* parameter.

The new code reads the existing entity and calls *TryUpdateModel* to update fields in the retrieved entity based on user input in the posted form data. The Entity Framework's automatic change tracking sets the *Modified* flag on the fields that are changed by form input. When the *SaveChanges* method is called, the Entity Framework creates SQL statements to update the database row. Concurrency conflicts are ignored, and only the table columns that were updated by the user are updated in the database.

As a best practice to prevent overposting, the fields that you want to be updateable by the *Edit* page are whitelisted in the *TryUpdateModel* parameters. (The empty string preceding the list of fields in the parameter list is for a prefix to use with the form fields names.) Currently there are no extra fields that you are protecting, but listing the fields that you want the model binder to bind ensures that if you add fields to the data model in the future, they are automatically protected until you explicitly add them here.

As a result of these changes, the method signature of the *HttpPost Edit* method is the same as the *HttpGet Edit* method; therefore you need to rename the method *EditPost*.

Now, run the application and select the *Stock Database* tab, then click the *Edit* link for the first row (*Ticker = A*) to bring up the Edit window, as shown in Figure 1-12. Change some of the data (here we change from *US* to *JAPAN* in the *Region* field) and click Save. The *Index* page opens and you can see the changed data. Please do not forget change it back to *US* because Agilent Technologies Inc. (stock ticker: *A*) is really a US company.

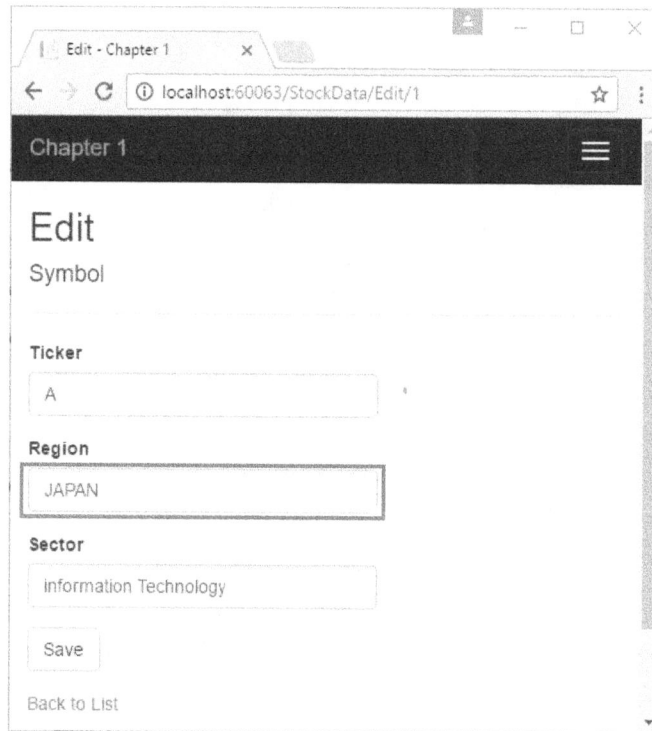

Figure 1-12. The Edit window for selected Symbol entity.

The Delete Page

In the *StockDataController* class, the scaffolded code for the *HttpGet Delete* method uses the *SingleOrDefaultAsync* method to retrieve the selected Symbol entity. As you saw for *update* and *create* operations, *delete* operations require two action methods. The *HttpGet* method displays a view that gives the user a chance to approve or cancel the delete operation. If the user approves it, a *POST* request is created. When that happens, the *HttpPost Delete* method is called and then that method actually performs the delete operation.

We will add a try-catch block to the *HttpPost Delete* method to handle any errors that might occur when the database is updated. If an error occurs, the *HttpPost Delete* method calls the *HttpGet Delete* method, passing it a parameter that indicates that an error has occurred. The *HttpGet Delete* method then redisplays the confirmation page along with the error message, giving the user an opportunity to cancel or try again.

Replace the *HttpGet Delete* action method with the following code, which manages error reporting.

```
public async Task<IActionResult> Delete(int? id, bool? saveChangesError = false)
{
    if (id == null)
    {
        return NotFound();
    }

    var symbol = await _context.Symbols
        .AsNoTracking()
        .SingleOrDefaultAsync(m => m.SymbolID == id);
    if (symbol == null)
    {
        return NotFound();
    }

    if (saveChangesError.GetValueOrDefault())
    {
        ViewData["ErrorMessage"] = "Delete failed. Try again, and if the problem
        persists see your system administrator.";
    }

    return View(symbol);
}
```

This code accepts an optional parameter that indicates whether the method was called after a failure to save changes. This parameter is false when the *HttpGet Delete* method is called without a previous failure. When it is called by the *HttpPost Delete* method in response to a database update error, the parameter is true and an error message is passed to the view.

Replace the *HttpPost Delete* action method named *DeleteConfirmed* with the following code, which performs the actual delete operation and catches any database update error:

```
[HttpPost, ActionName("Delete")]
[ValidateAntiForgeryToken]
public async Task<IActionResult> DeleteConfirmed(int id)
{
    var symbol = await _context.Symbols
        .AsNoTracking()
        .SingleOrDefaultAsync(m => m.SymbolID == id);
    if (symbol == null) return Redirect("Index");

    try
    {
        _context.Symbols.Remove(symbol);
        await _context.SaveChangesAsync();
        return RedirectToAction("Index");
    }
    catch (DbUpdateException /* ex */)
    {
        //Log the error (uncomment ex variable name and write a log.)
        return RedirectToAction("Delete", new { id = id,
            saveChangesError = true });
    }
}
```

This code retrieves the selected entity, and then calls the *Remove* method to set the entity's status to *Deleted*. When *SaveChanges* is called, a SQL DELETE command is generated.

In *Views/StockData/Delete.cshtml*, add an error message between the *h2* heading and the *h3* heading, as shown in the following code snippet:

```
<h2>Delete</h2>
<p class="text-danger">@ViewData["ErrorMessage"]</p>
<h3>Are you sure you want to delete this?</h3>
```

Run the page by selecting *Stock Database* tab and clicking a *Delete* link. This will bring up the *Delete* window for a specified *Symbol* entity, as shown in Figure 1-13.

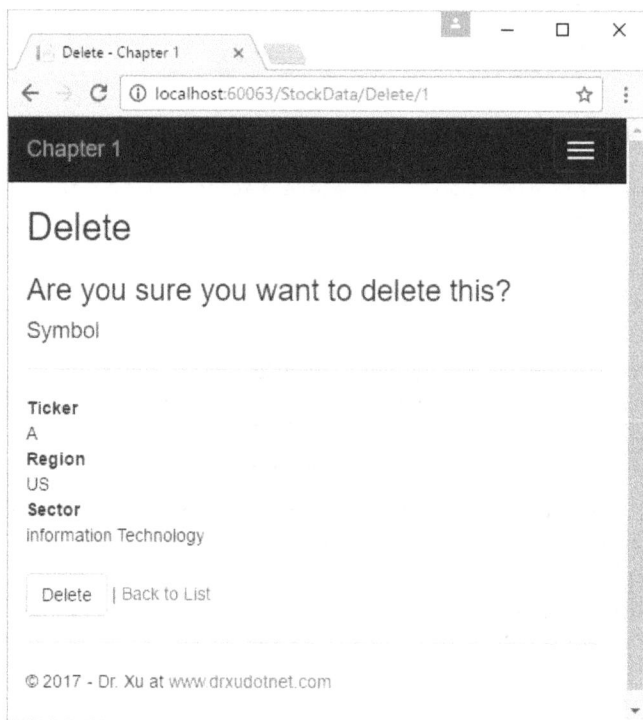

Figure 1-13. The Delete window for selected Symbol entity.

Click *Delete*. The *Index* page is displayed without the deleted *Symbol* entity.

Stock Data from Yahoo Finance

We have added stock tickers and index data to the database in preceding sections. In this section, I will show you how to download stock data from Yahoo Finance and store the data into the *Price* table in database.

Helper Method

First, we need add a helper method named *GetYahooStockData* to the *ModelHelper* class located in the *Models* directory. Here is the code for this method:

```
public static List<Price> GetYahooStockData(string ticker, DateTime? startDate,
    DateTime? endDate, StockPriceContext context)
{
    int symbolId = TickerToId(ticker, context);
    string urlTemplate = @"http://ichart.finance.yahoo.com/table.csv?
        s=[symbol]&a=[startMonth]&b=[startDay]&c=[startYear]&d=[endMonth]&
        e=[endDay]&f=[endYear]&g=d&ignore=.csv";
    if (!endDate.HasValue) endDate = DateTime.Now;
    if (!startDate.HasValue) startDate = DateTime.Now.AddYears(-5);
    if (ticker == null || ticker.Length < 1)
        throw new ArgumentException("Symbol invalid: " + ticker);

    // NOTE: Yahoo's scheme uses a month number 1 less than actual e.g. Jan. ="0"
    int strtMo = startDate.Value.Month - 1;
    string startMonth = strtMo.ToString();
    string startDay = startDate.Value.Day.ToString();
    string startYear = startDate.Value.Year.ToString();

    int endMo = endDate.Value.Month - 1;
    string endMonth = endMo.ToString();
    string endDay = endDate.Value.Day.ToString();
    string endYear = endDate.Value.Year.ToString();

    urlTemplate = urlTemplate.Replace("[symbol]", ticker);
    urlTemplate = urlTemplate.Replace("[startMonth]", startMonth);
    urlTemplate = urlTemplate.Replace("[startDay]", startDay);
    urlTemplate = urlTemplate.Replace("[startYear]", startYear);
    urlTemplate = urlTemplate.Replace("[endMonth]", endMonth);
    urlTemplate = urlTemplate.Replace("[endDay]", endDay);
    urlTemplate = urlTemplate.Replace("[endYear]", endYear);

    var res = new List<Price>();
    using (HttpClient hc = new HttpClient())
    {
        var response = hc.GetAsync(urlTemplate).Result;
        response.EnsureSuccessStatusCode();
        string history = response.Content.ReadAsStringAsync().Result;

        history = history.Replace("\r", "");
        string[] rows = history.Split('\n');
        for (int i = rows.Length - 1; i > 0; i--)
        {
            if (rows[i].Replace("\n", "").Trim() == "") continue;
            string[] cols = rows[i].Split(',');
            res.Add(new Price
            {
                SymbolID = symbolId,
                Date = DateTime.Parse(cols[0]),
                Open = double.Parse(cols[1]),
                High = double.Parse(cols[2]),
```

```
                    Low = double.Parse(cols[3]),
                    Close = double.Parse(cols[4]),
                    Volume = double.Parse(cols[5]),
                    CloseAdj = double.Parse(cols[6])
                });
        }
    }
    return res;
}

public static int TickerToId(string ticker, StockPriceContext context)
{
    int id = 0;
    Symbol symbol = new Symbol();
    var query = from s in context.Symbols
                where (s.Ticker == ticker)
                select s.SymbolID;
    foreach (var q in query)
        id = q;
    return id;
}
```

The *GetYahooStockData* method takes ticker, date range, and *StockPriceContext* as its input arguments. The context parameter is used to convert the ticker into *SymbolID* through the *TickerToId* method. The key step for accessing the Yahoo Finance data is to construct the *urlTemplate* address with a suitable template. Note that Yahoo Finance API uses a month number 1 less than actual month number (e.g., January = "0"), which is why we need to subtract one from the month number in creating *urlTemplate*. Using this method, we can download the stock data with historical prices from Yahoo Finance's website. We construct the URL address from variables inside the method, so that it changes for each value of the stock ticker and date range required.

Creating ViewModel

In order to use the helper method discussed in the preceding section to download stock data from Yahoo Finance, we need to specify the input parameters: ticker and date range. We will create a view model class to bind these input parameters to a model. Add the following *using* statement to the top of the *ModelHelper.cs*:

```
using System.ComponentModel.DataAnnotations;
```

Then, add a new class named *StockPriceViewModel* to this file with the following code:

```
public class StockPriceViewModel
{
    public string Ticker { get; set; }

    [DataType(DataType.Date)]
    [DisplayFormat(DataFormatString = "{0:dd/MM/yyyy}")]
    public DateTime StartDate { get; set; }

    [DataType(DataType.Date)]
    [DisplayFormat(DataFormatString = "{0:dd/MM/yyyy}")]
    public DateTime EndDate { get; set; }
```

```
    public List<Price> Prices { get; set; }
}
```

The code for this view model is very simple. Here, we use the data annotation to format the *StartDate* and *EndDate* fields.

DownloadPrice Action Method

In *StockDataController.cs*, add the *HttpGet* and *HttpPost DownloadPrice* method with the following code:

```
//GET: Specify parameters
public IActionResult DownloadPrice()
{
    StockPriceViewModel model = new StockPriceViewModel();
    model.Ticker = "IBM";
    model.StartDate = DateTime.Parse("1/1/2010");
    model.EndDate = DateTime.Parse("3/1/2017");
    model.Prices = new List<Price>();
    return View(model);
}

//Download stock data
[HttpPost]
[ValidateAntiForgeryToken]
public async Task<IActionResult> DownloadPrice(StockPriceViewModel model,
    string submitButton)
{
    model.Prices = await Task.Run(() => ModelHelper.GetYahooStockData(
        model.Ticker, model.StartDate, model.EndDate, _context));
    if (submitButton == "Download to Save")
    {
        if (ModelState.IsValid && model.Prices.Count > 0)
        {
            foreach (Price p in model.Prices)
                _context.Prices.Add(p);
            await _context.SaveChangesAsync();
            ViewBag.Message = model.Prices.Count.ToString() +
                " records have been Successfully Updated.";
        }
        else
        {
            ViewBag.Message = "Failed ! Please try again.";
        }
    }
    else if (submitButton == "Download to View")
    {
        ViewBag.Message = model.Ticker + "(" + model.Prices.Count.ToString() +
            " rows) - stock prices from " + model.StartDate + " to " +
            model.EndDate + ":";
    }
    return View(model);
}
```

The *HttpGet DownloadPrice* method displays a download page with default parameters, and the *HttpPost DownloadPrice* method takes the user input from the view model and then download the price data from Yahoo Finance by calling the *GetYahooStockData* method. There are two buttons in the view, which provide you two options: view the price data and save the data to database.

DownloadPrice View

Add a new empty view named *DownloadPrice.cshtml* to the *Views* folder with the following code:

```
@model FirstMvcApp.Models.StockPriceViewModel

@{
    ViewData["Title"] = "Download Prices";
}

<h2>Download Prices 2</h2>

<form asp-action="DownloadPrice">
    <div class="form-horizontal">
        <div asp-validation-summary="ModelOnly" class="text-danger"></div>
        <div class="form-group">
            <label asp-for="Ticker" class="col-md-2 control-label"></label>
            <div class="col-md-10">
                <input asp-for="Ticker" class="form-control" />
                <span asp-validation-for="Ticker" class="text-danger" />
            </div>
        </div>
        <div class="form-group">
            <label asp-for="StartDate" class="col-md-2 control-label"></label>
            <div class="col-md-10">
                <input asp-for="StartDate" class="form-control" />
                <span asp-validation-for="StartDate" class="text-danger" />
            </div>
        </div>
        <div class="form-group">
            <label asp-for="EndDate" class="col-md-2 control-label"></label>
            <div class="col-md-10">
                <input asp-for="EndDate" class="form-control" />
                <span asp-validation-for="EndDate" class="text-danger" />
            </div>
        </div>
        <div class="form-group">
            <div class="col-md-offset-2 col-md-10">
                <input type="submit" value="Download to View"
                    name="submitButton" class="btn btn-default" />
                <input type="submit" value="Download to Save"
                    name="submitButton" class="btn btn-default" />
            </div>
        </div>
        <hr />
        <h4>@ViewBag.Message</h4>
    </div>
</form>
```

```
<table class="table">
    <thead>
        <tr>
            <th>
                @Html.DisplayNameFor(model => model.Prices[0].SymbolID)
            </th>
            <th>
                @Html.DisplayNameFor(model => model.Prices[0].Date)
            </th>
            <th>
                @Html.DisplayNameFor(model => model.Prices[0].Open)
            </th>
            <th>
                @Html.DisplayNameFor(model => model.Prices[0].High)
            </th>
            <th>
                @Html.DisplayNameFor(model => model.Prices[0].Low)
            </th>
            <th>
                @Html.DisplayNameFor(model => model.Prices[0].Close)
            </th>
            <th>
                @Html.DisplayNameFor(model => model.Prices[0].CloseAdj)
            </th>
            <th>
                @Html.DisplayNameFor(model => model.Prices[0].Volume)
            </th>
            <th></th>
        </tr>
    </thead>
    <tbody>

        @for (int i = 0; i < Model.Prices.Count; i++)
        {
            <tr>
                <td>
                    @Html.DisplayFor(modelItem => modelItem.Prices[i].SymbolID)
                </td>
                <td>
                    @Html.DisplayFor(modelItem => modelItem.Prices[i].Date)
                </td>
                <td>
                    @Html.DisplayFor(modelItem => modelItem.Prices[i].Open)
                </td>
                <td>
                    @Html.DisplayFor(modelItem => modelItem.Prices[i].High)
                </td>
                <td>
                    @Html.DisplayFor(modelItem => modelItem.Prices[i].Low)
                </td>
                <td>
                    @Html.DisplayFor(modelItem => modelItem.Prices[i].Close)
                </td>
                <td>
                    @Html.DisplayFor(modelItem => modelItem.Prices[i].CloseAdj)
```

```
                </td>
                <td>
                    @Html.DisplayFor(modelItem => modelItem.Prices[i].Volume)
                </td>
            </tr>
        }
    </tbody>
</table>

<div>
    <a asp-action="Index">Back to List</a>
</div>

@section Scripts {
    @{await Html.RenderPartialAsync("_ValidationScriptsPartial");}
}
```

This view allows the user to specify the ticker and date range. The price data will be displayed on the screen by clicking the *Download to View* button, and the data will be displayed and saved to database if the *Download to Save* button is clicked.

Add a link to the *Index* page:

```
<h2>Index</h2>

<p>
    <a asp-action="Create">Create New</a>
    | <a asp-action="DownloadPrice"> Download Stock Prices</a>
</p>
```

Run this application, select the *Stock Database* tab, and click the *Download Stock Prices* link to bring up the *Download Prices* window. Click the *Download to View* button with the default parameters, and you will see the price data on the screen, which are downloaded from IBM from Yahoo Finance, as shown in Figure 1-14.

Now, click the *Download to Save* button, the data will be displayed on screen and saved to the database. Please download and save the stock price data for several other stock tickers, MSFT, AAPL, SPY, and A, we will use these data in later chapters. You can also download more data as you like. If a ticker (such as AAPL) is not in database, you should add ticker first before downloading and saving data to database.

Here, we have added some stock price data to database for several stock tickers. You can check the price data from the *Details* page. Select the *Stock Database* tap and click the *Details* link for ticker A. Now you see the stock price data that are displayed on the *Details* page, as shown in Figure 1-15.

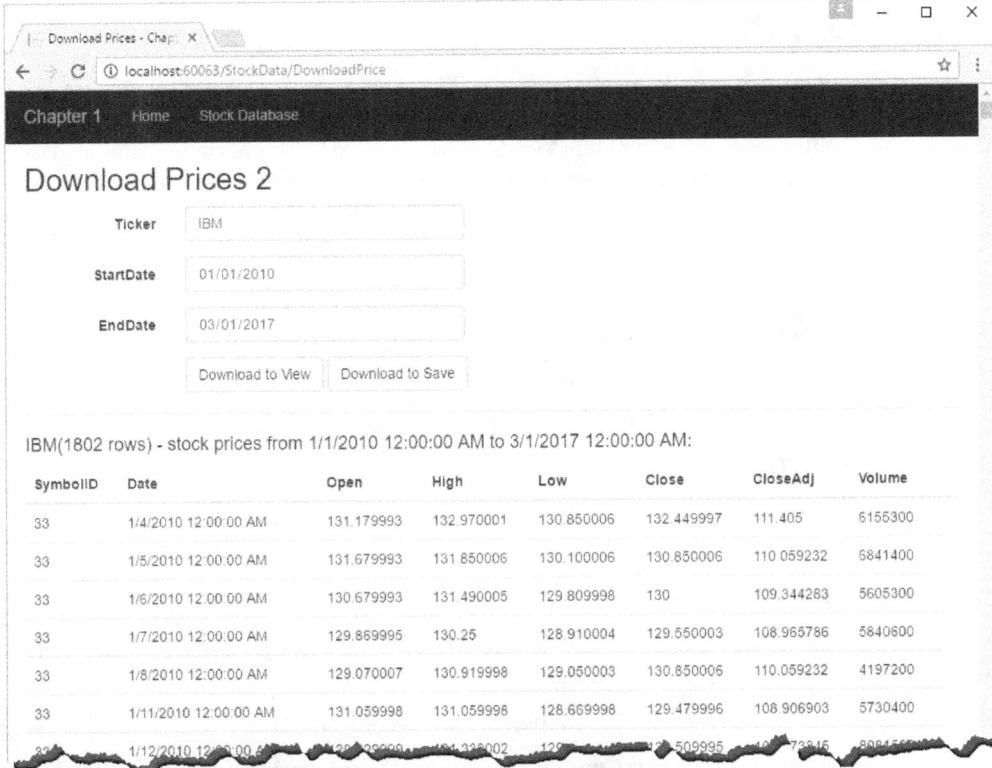

Figure 1-14. Stock price data for IBM.

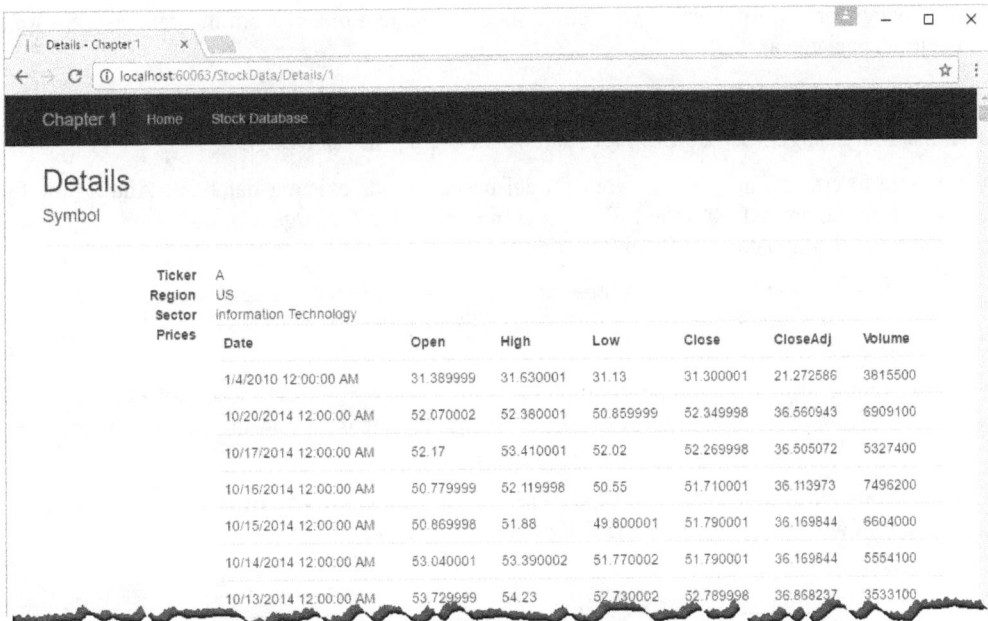

Figure 1-15. The Details page for specified Symbol entity.

Existing Database

In the previous sections, you learned how to create an ASP.NET Core MVC application with the code first approach, which creates the database from our model and performs basic data access using Entity Framework Core. In this section, we will build an ASP.NET Core MVC application with the database-first approach. We will use reverse engineering to create an Entity Framework model based on an existing database. The database we are going to use is just the *StockPriceDb* created in the previous example.

Open the *Chapter01* solution in Visual Studio 2017.

- Right click the Solution *Chapter01* in the Solution Explorer, select *Add > New Project…*
- From the left menu select *Installed >Visual C# > .NET Core*
- Select the ASP.NET Core Web Application (.NET Core) project template
- Enter *DatabaseFirst* as the name and click OK
- Under ASP.NET Core Template 1.1 select the *Web Application* and click OK

Creating Model from Database

In order to create data model from database, we need to install the packages for the database provider we want to target. In our case, it is the SQL Server.

- Select Tools > NuGet Package Manager > Package Manager Console.
- Make sure in the Package Manager Console window, set Default project to DatabaseFirst.
- Run *Install-Package Microsoft.EntityFrameworkCore.SqlServer.*

We will be using some Entity Framework commands to create a model from the database. So we will install the tools package as well.

- Run *Install-Package Microsoft.EntityFrameworkCore.Tools -Version 1.1.0-msbuild3-final*
- Run *Install-Package Microsoft.EntityFrameworkCore.SqlServer.Design*

Now it is time to create Entity Framework model based on our existing database. Add a new folder named *Models* to the project. Run the following command in the *Package Manager Console* to create a model from our existing database: *StockPriceDb*.

```
Scaffold-DbContextt "Server=(localdb)\mssqllocaldb;Database=StockPriceDb;
    Trusted_Connection =True;" Microsoft.EntityFrameworkCore.SqlServer
    -OutputDir Models
```

The reverse engineering process creates entity classes *System.cs*, *Price.cs*, and *IndexData.cs*, as well as a derived context *StockPriceDbContext.cs* in the *Models* folder based on the schema of the existing database.

The entity classes are simple C# objects that represent the data you will be querying and saving. For example, the following is the code for *Symbol.cs* and *StockPriceDbContext.cs*:

```
using System;
using System.Collections.Generic;

namespace DatabaseFirst.Models
```

```
{
    public partial class Symbol
    {
        public Symbol()
        {
            Price = new HashSet<Price>();
        }

        public int SymbolId { get; set; }
        public string Region { get; set; }
        public string Sector { get; set; }
        public string Ticker { get; set; }

        public virtual ICollection<Price> Price { get; set; }
    }
}

using System;
using Microsoft.EntityFrameworkCore;
using Microsoft.EntityFrameworkCore.Metadata;

namespace DatabaseFirst.Models
{
    public partial class StockPriceDbContext : DbContext
    {
        public virtual DbSet<IndexData> IndexData { get; set; }
        public virtual DbSet<Price> Price { get; set; }
        public virtual DbSet<Symbol> Symbol { get; set; }

        protected override void OnConfiguring(DbContextOptionsBuilder
            optionsBuilder)
        {
            #warning To protect potentially sensitive information in your
             connection string, you should move it out of source code. See
             http://go.microsoft.com/fwlink/?LinkId=723263 for guidance on
             storing connection strings.

            optionsBuilder.UseSqlServer(@"Server=(localdb)\mssqllocaldb;
                Database=StockPriceDb;Trusted_Connection=True;");
        }

        protected override void OnModelCreating(ModelBuilder modelBuilder)
        {
            modelBuilder.Entity<IndexData>(entity =>
            {
                entity.Property(e => e.Id).HasColumnName("ID");
                entity.Property(e => e.Hyspread).HasColumnName("HYSpread");
                entity.Property(e => e.Igspread).HasColumnName("IGSpread");
                entity.Property(e => e.Spx).HasColumnName("SPX");
                entity.Property(e => e.Vix).HasColumnName("VIX");
            });

            modelBuilder.Entity<Price>(entity =>
            {
                entity.HasIndex(e => e.SymbolId)
```

```
                              .HasName("IX_Price_SymbolID");
                  entity.Property(e => e.PriceId).HasColumnName("PriceID");
                  entity.Property(e => e.SymbolId).HasColumnName("SymbolID");
                  entity.HasOne(d => d.Symbol)
                      .WithMany(p => p.Price)
                      .HasForeignKey(d => d.SymbolId);
              });

              modelBuilder.Entity<Symbol>(entity =>
              {
                  entity.Property(e => e.SymbolId).HasColumnName("SymbolID");
              });
          }
      }
  }
```

You can see the scaffolded code for *Symbol.cs* is almost identical to our model created in the preceding code-first example.

Registering Context

In ASP.NET Core application, configuration is generally performed in *Startup.cs*. To conform to this pattern, we will move configuration of the database provider to *Startup.cs*. Open *Models\StockPriceDbContext.cs*, delete the *OnConfiguring(...)* method

```
protected override void OnConfiguring(DbContextOptionsBuilder optionsBuilder)
{
    optionsBuilder.UseSqlServer(@"Server=(localdb)\mssqllocaldb;
        Database=StockPriceDb;Trusted_Connection=True;");
}
```

Add the following constructor, which will allow configuration to be passed into the context by dependency injection:

```
public StockPriceDbContext(DbContextOptions<StockPriceDbContext> options)
    : base(options)
{ }
```

In order for our MVC controllers to make use of *StockPriceDbContext* we need to register it as a service. Open the *Startup.cs* file and add the following *using* statement at the start of the file

```
using DatabaseFirst.Models;
using Microsoft.EntityFrameworkCore;
```

Now we can use the *AddDbContext* method to register it as a service. Locate the *ConfigureService* method and add the following code to register the context as a service:

```
// This method gets called by the runtime. Use this method to add services
// to the container.
public void ConfigureServices(IServiceCollection services)
{
    // Add framework services.
    services.AddMvc();

    var connection = @"Server=(localdb)\mssqllocaldb;Database=StockPriceDb;
        Trusted_Connection=True;";
```

```
services.AddDbContext<StockPriceDbContext>(options =>
    options.UseSqlServer(connection));
}
```

Creating a Controller

Now we need to enable scaffolding in our project.

- Right-click on the *Controllers* folder in Solution Explorer and select *Add > Controller…*
- Select *Full Depedencies* and click *Add*
- You can ignore the instructions in the *ScaffoldingReadMe.txt* file that opens

Now that scaffolding is enabled, we can scaffold a controller for the *Symbol* entity.

- Right-click on the *Controllers* folder in Solution Explorer and select *Add > Controller…*
- Select *MVC Controller with views, using Entity Framework* and click *Add*
- Select *Model* class to *Symbol* and *Data context* class to *StockPriceDb*
- Se*t Controller* name *to StockDataController,* click *Add*
- Now add a link of *StockData* to the *Views/Shared/_Layout.cshtml* file:

```
<div class="navbar-collapse collapse">
    <ul class="nav navbar-nav">
        <li><a asp-area="" asp-controller="Home"
            asp-action="Index">Home</a></li>
        <li><a asp-area="" asp-controller="StockData" asp-action="Index">
        Stock Database</a></li>
    </ul>
</div>
```

Run the application and select the *Stock Database* tab. Figure 1-16 shows the results.

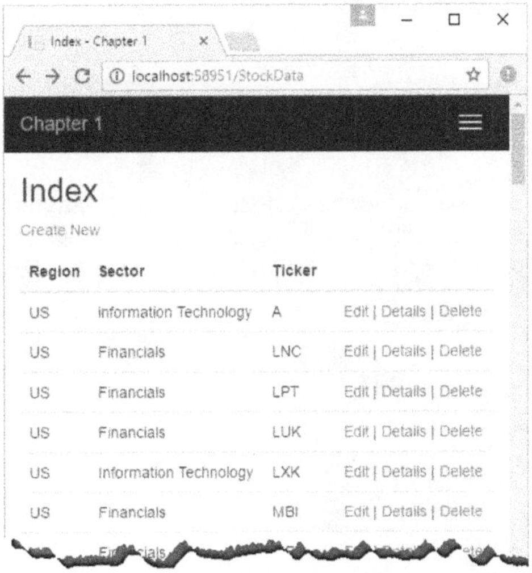

Figure 1-16. The Symbol entities from database.

By default, the scaffolded code creates the CRUD operations. As shown in the previous example, if you click the *Details* link, the content for the *Prices* entity is empty. You need to modify the controller and views in order to display the *Price* data.

Here, we will not try to add data to or update database because these operations can be achieved in the previous example. What we are going to do is to retrieve data from database and display the data on the screen.

Now, we update *StockDataController.cs* with the following code:

```
using DatabaseFirst.Models;
using Microsoft.AspNetCore.Mvc;
using Microsoft.EntityFrameworkCore;
using System.Linq;
using System.Threading.Tasks;

namespace DatabaseFirst.Controllers
{
    public class StockDataController : Controller
    {
        private StockPriceDbContext _context;

        public StockDataController(StockPriceDbContext context)
        {
            _context = context;
        }

        public async Task<IActionResult> Index()
        {
            return View(await _context.Symbol.OrderBy(
                s => s.Ticker).ToListAsync());
        }

        public async Task<IActionResult> Details(int? id)
        {
            if (id == null)
            {
                return NotFound();
            }

            var symb = await _context.Symbol.SingleAsync(m => m.SymbolId == id);
            symb.Price = await _context.Price.Where(
                x => x.SymbolId == id).Take(30).ToListAsync();

            if (symb == null)
            {
                return NotFound();
            }

            return View(symb);
        }


        public IActionResult SingleTicker()
        {
            Symbol symbol = new Symbol();
```

```
        symbol.Ticker = "IBM";
        return View(symbol);
    }


    [HttpPost]
    [ValidateAntiForgeryToken]
    public async Task<IActionResult> SingleTicker(Symbol model)
    {
        var symb = await _context.Symbol.SingleAsync(
            m => m.Ticker == model.Ticker);
        symb.Price = await _context.Price.Where(
            x => x.Symbol.Ticker == model.Ticker).Take(30).ToListAsync();

        if (symb == null)
        {
            return NotFound();
        }

        return View(symb);
    }

    public async Task<IActionResult> GetIndexData()
    {
        return View(await _context.IndexData.Take(30).ToListAsync());
    }
    }
}
```

The code for *Index* action displays the *Symbol* entity list. The *Details* method is used to display the price data for specified *Symbol* entity. We also add a *SingleTicker* method, which can be used to display the detailed information for the stock ticker specified by the user. Finally, we implement a method named *GetIndexData* that displays market data for indices from database.

Configure and Update Views

We first remove the views, *Create.cshtml*, *Delete.cshtml*, and *Edit.cshtml* from the *Views/StockData* folder. We then need to update the *Views/StockData/Index.cshtml* file with the following code:

```
@model IEnumerable<DatabaseFirst.Models.Symbol>

@{
    ViewData["Title"] = "Stock Data";
}

<h2>Index</h2>

<p>
    <a asp-action="SingleTicker">Single Ticker</a> |
    <a asp-action="GetIndexData">Get Index Data</a>
</p>
<table class="table">
    <thead>
        <tr>
            <th>@Html.DisplayNameFor(model => model.Ticker)</th>
```

```
            <th>@Html.DisplayNameFor(model => model.Region)</th>
            <th>@Html.DisplayNameFor(model => model.Sector)</th>
            <th></th>
        </tr>
    </thead>
    <tbody>
        @foreach (var item in Model)
        {
            <tr>
                <td>@Html.DisplayFor(modelItem => item.Ticker)</td>
                <td>@Html.DisplayFor(modelItem => item.Region)</td>
                <td>@Html.DisplayFor(modelItem => item.Sector)</td>
                <td><a asp-action="Details"
                        asp-route-id="@item.SymbolId">Details</a></td>
            </tr>
        }
    </tbody>
</table>
```

Next, we update *Views/StockData/Details.cshtml* with the following code:

```
@model DatabaseFirst.Models.Symbol

@{
    ViewData["Title"] = "Details";
}

<h2>Details</h2>

<div>
    <h4>Stock Data</h4>
    <hr />
    <dl class="dl-horizontal">
        <dt>@Html.DisplayNameFor(model => model.Ticker)</dt>
        <dd>@Html.DisplayFor(model => model.Ticker)</dd>
        <dt>@Html.DisplayNameFor(model => model.Region)</dt>
        <dd>@Html.DisplayFor(model => model.Region)</dd>
        <dt>@Html.DisplayNameFor(model => model.Sector)</dt>
        <dd>@Html.DisplayFor(model => model.Sector)</dd>
        <dt>@Html.DisplayNameFor(model => model.Price)</dt>
        <dd>
            <table class="table">
                <tr>
                    <th>Date</th>
                    <th>Open</th>
                    <th>High</th>
                    <th>Low</th>
                    <th>Close</th>
                    <th>CloseAdj</th>
                    <th>Volume</th>
                </tr>
                @foreach (var item in Model.Price)
                {
                    <tr>
                        <td>@Html.DisplayFor(modelItem => item.Date)</td>
                        <td>@Html.DisplayFor(modelItem => item.Open)</td>
```

```
                <td>@Html.DisplayFor(modelItem => item.High)</td>
                <td>@Html.DisplayFor(modelItem => item.Low)</td>
                <td>@Html.DisplayFor(modelItem => item.Close)</td>
                <td>@Html.DisplayFor(modelItem => item.CloseAdj)</td>
                <td>@Html.DisplayFor(modelItem => item.Volume)</td>
            </tr>
        }
        </table>
    </dd>
  </dl>
</div>
```

Add a new view *Views/StockData/SingleTicker.cshtml* and replace the template content with the following code:

```
@model DatabaseFirst.Models.Symbol

@{
    ViewData["Title"] = "Single Ticker";
}

<h2>Single Ticker</h2>

<form asp-action="SingleTicker">
    <div class="form-horizontal">
        <h4>Stock Data from Database</h4>
        <hr />
        <div asp-validation-summary="ModelOnly" class="text-danger"></div>
        <div class="form-group">
            <label asp-for="Ticker" class="col-md-2 control-label"></label>
            <div class="col-md-10">
                <input asp-for="Ticker" class="form-control" />
                <span asp-validation-for="Ticker" class="text-danger"></span>
            </div>
        </div>
        <div class="form-group">
            <div class="col-md-offset-2 col-md-10">
                <input type="submit" value="Get Data for Single Ticker"
                    class="btn btn-default" />
            </div>
        </div>
    </div>
</form>

<hr />
<dl class="dl-horizontal">
    @if (Model.Price != null)
    {
        <dt>@Html.DisplayNameFor(model => model.Ticker)</dt>
        <dd>@Html.DisplayFor(model => model.Ticker)</dd>
        <dt>@Html.DisplayNameFor(model => model.Region)</dt>
        <dd>@Html.DisplayFor(model => model.Region)</dd>
        <dt>@Html.DisplayNameFor(model => model.Sector)</dt>
        <dd>@Html.DisplayFor(model => model.Sector)</dd>
        <dt>@Html.DisplayNameFor(model => model.Price)</dt>
    }
```

```
    <dd>
        <table class="table">
            <tr>
                <th>Date</th>
                <th>Open</th>
                <th>High</th>
                <th>Low</th>
                <th>Close</th>
                <th>CloseAdj</th>
                <th>Volume</th>
            </tr>
            @if (Model.Price != null)
            {
                foreach (var item in Model.Price)
                {
                    <tr>
                        <td>@Html.DisplayFor(modelItem => item.Date)</td>
                        <td>@Html.DisplayFor(modelItem => item.Open)</td>
                        <td>@Html.DisplayFor(modelItem => item.High)</td>
                        <td>@Html.DisplayFor(modelItem => item.Low)</td>
                        <td>@Html.DisplayFor(modelItem => item.Close)</td>
                        <td>@Html.DisplayFor(modelItem => item.CloseAdj)</td>
                        <td>@Html.DisplayFor(modelItem => item.Volume)</td>
                    </tr>
                }
            }
        </table>
    </dd>
</dl>
<div>
    <a asp-action="Index">Back to List</a>
</div>
```

Add a new view *Views/StockData/GetIndexData.cshtml* and replace the template content with the following code:

```
@model IEnumerable<DatabaseFirst.Models.IndexData>

@{
    ViewData["Title"] = "Stock Data";
}

<h2>Index Data</h2>

<table class="table">
    <thead>
        <tr>
            <th>@Html.DisplayNameFor(model => model.Date)</th>
            <th>@Html.DisplayNameFor(model => model.Igspread)</th>
            <th>@Html.DisplayNameFor(model => model.Hyspread)</th>
            <th>@Html.DisplayNameFor(model => model.Spx)</th>
            <th>@Html.DisplayNameFor(model => model.Vix)</th>
        </tr>
    </thead>
    <tbody>
        @foreach (var item in Model)
```

```
        {
            <tr>
                <td>@Html.DisplayFor(modelItem => item.Date)</td>
                <td>@Html.DisplayFor(modelItem => item.Igspread)</td>
                <td>@Html.DisplayFor(modelItem => item.Hyspread)</td>
                <td>@Html.DisplayFor(modelItem => item.Spx)</td>
                <td>@Html.DisplayFor(modelItem => item.Vix)</td>
            </tr>
        }
    </tbody>
</table>
```

Finally, add links for *SingleTicker* and *GetIndexData* to the *Views/Shared/_layout.cshtml* file:

```
<div class="navbar-collapse collapse">
    <ul class="nav navbar-nav">
        <li><a asp-area="" asp-controller="Home"
            asp-action="Index">Home</a></li>
        <li><a asp-area="" asp-controller="StockData"
            asp-action="Index">Stock Database</a></li>
        <li><a asp-area="" asp-controller="StockData"
            asp-action="SingleTicker">Single Ticker</a></li>
        <li><a asp-area="" asp-controller="StockData"
            asp-action="GetIndexData">Index Data</a></li>
    </ul>
</div>
```

Run the application, select the *Stock Database* tab, and click the *Details* link for ticker *A*. Figure 1-17 shows the *Details* page for ticker *A*.

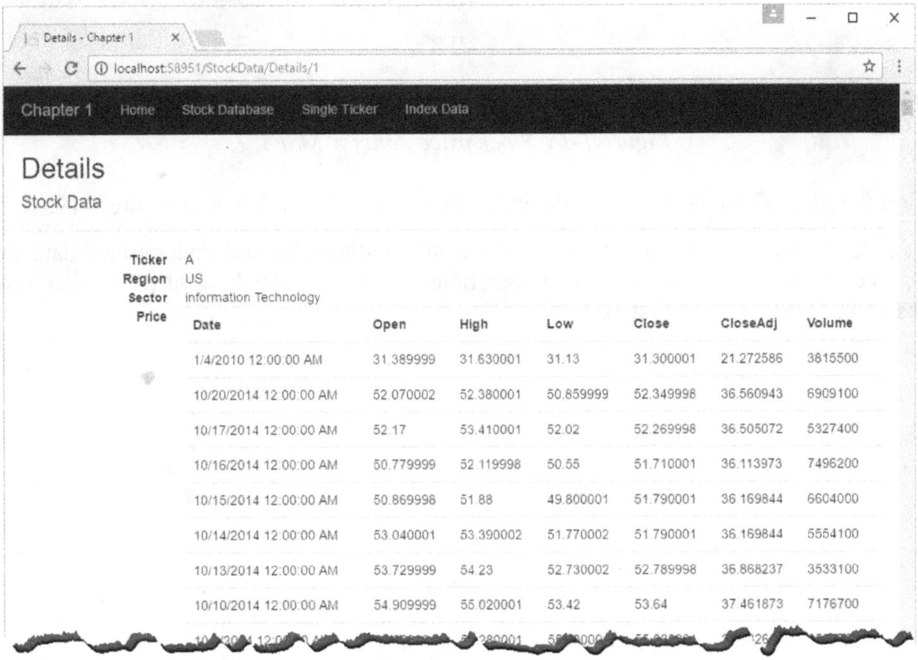

Figure 1-17. The Details page for stock ticker A.

Select the *Single Ticker* tab, set the *Ticker* field to *MSFT*, and click the *Get Data for Single Ticker* button to retrieve stock price data for *MSFT*, as shown in Figure 1-18.

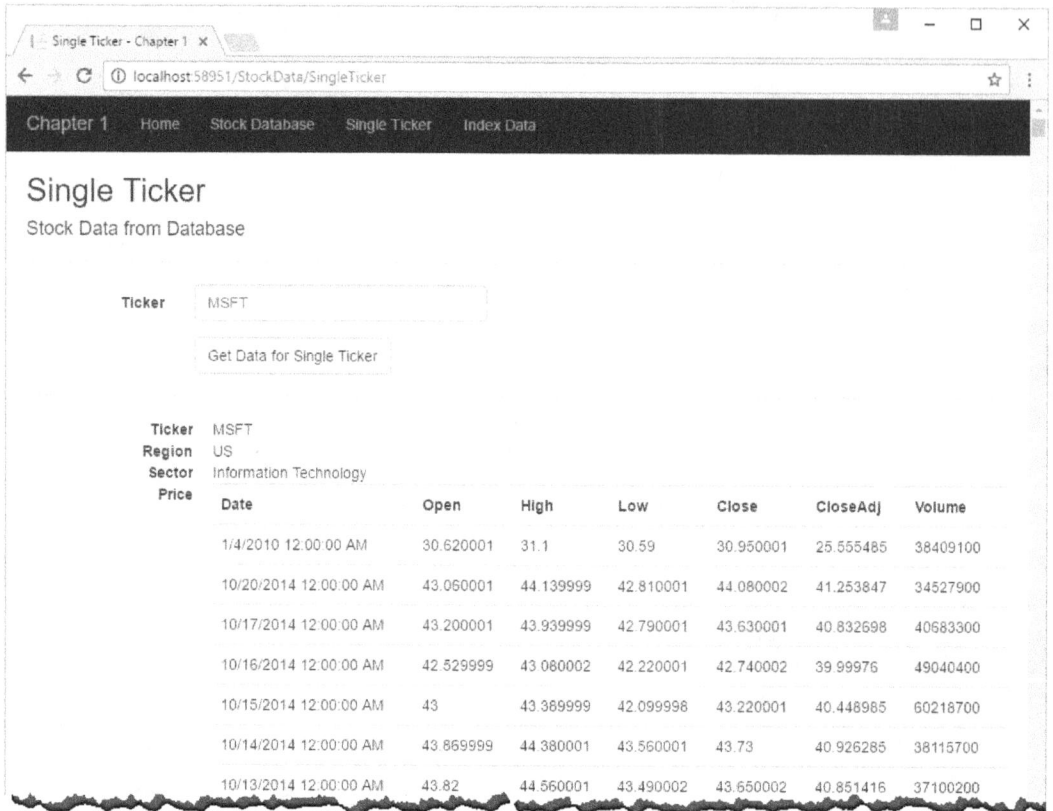

Figure 1-18. Stock price data for MSFT.

Now select the *Index Data* tab to display the index data on screen, as shown in Figure 1-19.

This example shows that we can extract model from existing database and retrieve data from the database. We can also perform the CRUD operations for existing database in the similar fashion as discussed in the previous code-first example.

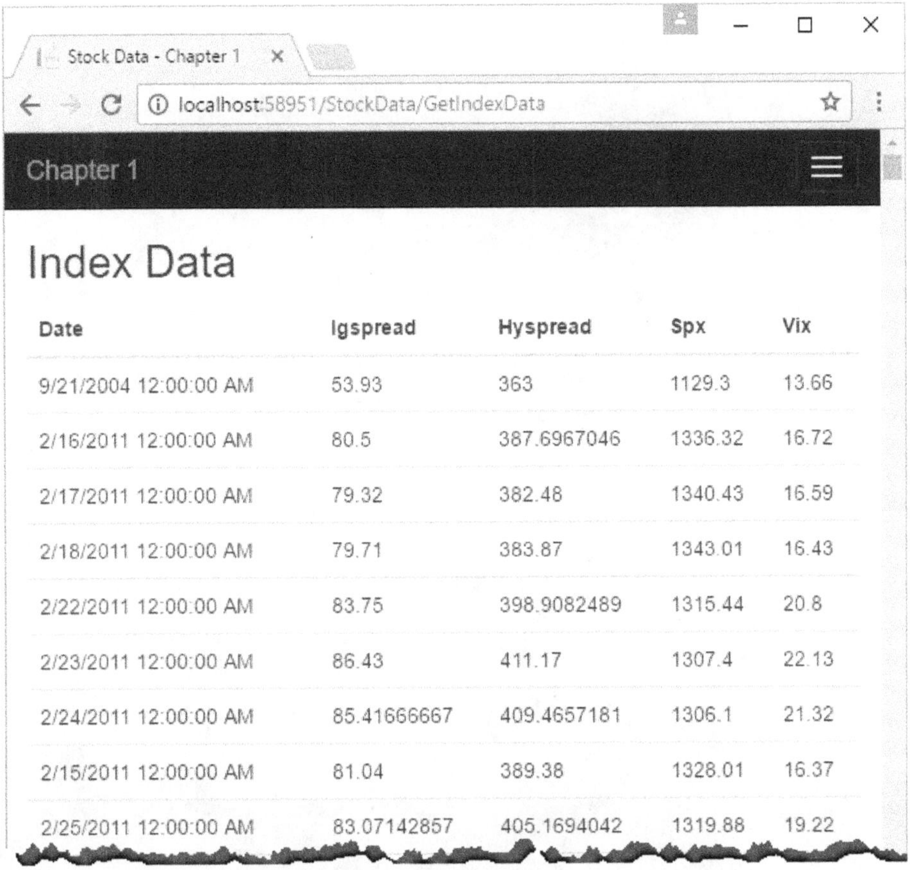

Figure 1-19. Market data for indices.

Chapter 2
Graphics Basics in SVG

Scalable Vector Graphics (SVG) is a language for creating two-dimensional (2D) graphics in XML. SVG allows for three types of graphics objects: vector graphic shapes, images, and text. The XML is then rendered by an SVG viewer. Today most modern web browsers can display SVG elements just as if they can display PNG, GIF, and JPG images, and most vector drawing software packages can export SVG graphics.

There are two major frameworks for representing graphic information on computers: raster and vector graphics. In raster graphics, an image is represented as a rectangular array of picture elements or pixels. Each pixel is represented either by its RGB color values or as an index into a list of colors. We call this series of pixels as bitmap, which is often stored in a compressed format. Because most modern display devices are also raster devices, displaying in image requires a viewer program to do little more than uncompressing the bitmap and transferring it to the screen.

In a vector graphics system, an image is described as a series of geometric shapes. Rather than receiving a finished set of pixels, a vector-viewing program receives commands to draw shapes at specified sets of coordinates. We often describe vector graphics as a set of instructions for a drawing, while bitmap graphics (raster) are points of color in specific places. Because vector graphics are objects rather than a series of pixels, they can easily change their shape and color, whereas bitmap graphics cannot.

In this chapter, we will discuss the graphics coordinate systems used in SVG and show you how to use SVG to create basic 2D shapes. We will also discuss the colors, pains, colormaps, tiles, and textures.

2D Coordinate System in SVG

The world of SVG is an infinite canvas. We need to find out how to tell a viewer program which part of this canvas you are interested in, what its dimensions are, and how to locate points within that area. That is, when you create a graphic object in SVG, you must determine where the graphic object or drawing will be displayed. To do this, you need to understand how SVG measures coordinates of the graphic object. Each point on a SVG viewer has an X and a Y coordinate.

ViewPort

In SVG, the area of the canvas you want to use is called the viewport. You define the size of this viewport with the *width* and *height* attributes on an *<svg>* element. Each attribute's value can be simply a number, which is presumed to be in pixels; which is specified in user coordinate system. You can also specify *width* and *height* as a number followed by a unit identifier, which can be one of the following:

- **em**: The font size of the default font, usually equivalent to the height of a line of text.
- **ex**: The height of the letter *x*.
- **px**: Pixels (1/96 of an inch).
- **pt**: Points (1/72 of an inch).
- **pc**: Picas (1/6 of an inch).
- **cm**: Centimeters.
- **mm**: Millimeters.
- **in**: Inches.

For example, the followings are all valid SVG viewport declarations:

```
<svg width="600" height="400">
<svg width="600px" height="400px">
```

Both of these specify an area 600 pixels wide and 400 pixels high.

```
<svg width="4cm" height="3cm">
```

This specifies an area 4 centimeters wide and 3 centimeters high.

It is also possible to mix units. The following statement specifies an area of 4 inches width and 70 points high:

```
<svg width="4in" height="70pt">
```

An *<svg>* element can also specify its *width* and *height* as a percentage. When the element is nested within another *<svg>* element, the percentage is measured in terms of the enclosing element. If the *<svg>* is the root element, the percentage is in terms of the window size.

Default User Coordinates

The viewer sets up a coordinate system where the origin is in the upper-left corner of the rendering area. In the 2D space, the positive *X* axis points to the right, and the positive *Y* axis points downward, as shown in Figure 2-1. All coordinates and sizes in the default SVG system are measured in units of pixels.

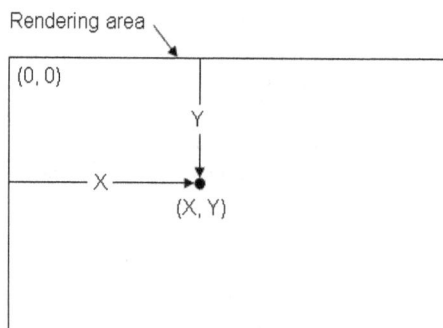

Figure 2-1. Default coordinate system in SVG.

Let us look at an example. Open Visual Studio 2017 and create an ASP.NET Core MVC web application named *Chapter02*. Make some modifications to *Views/Shared/_Layout.cshtml* and *Views/Home/Index.cshtml*. You can review these two files to see the corresponding changes.

Add a new MVC controller named *BasicShapesController* to the *Controllers* folder with the following simple code:

```
using Microsoft.AspNetCore.Mvc;

namespace Chapter02.Controllers
{
    public class BasicShapesController : Controller
    {
        public IActionResult Index()
        {
            ViewBag.Title = "Basic Shapes: Home";
            return View();
        }

        public IActionResult Coordinates()
        {
            ViewBag.Title = "Basic Shapes: Coordinates";
            return View();
        }
    }
}
```

Add a new folder named *BasicShapes* to the *Views* folder. Add *Index.cshtml*, *_Links.cshtml*, and *Coordinates.cshtml* to the *Views/BasicShapes* folder. The first two files are simple home page for the basic shapes and the hyperlinks for navigating to different pages. You can views the content of these files.

In order to see how the default coordinate works in SVG, we create a background with gridlines for an SVG element:

```
@{
    ViewData["Title"] = ViewBag.Title;
}
<h3>@ViewBag.Title</h3>
@Html.Partial("_Links")
<hr />

<div class="container">
    <div class="row">
        <div class="col-sm-3">
            <p>Grid units: pixels</p>
            <svg width="200" height="200">
                <defs>
                    <pattern id="minorGrid" width="10" height="10"
                        patternUnits="userSpaceOnUse">
                        <path d="M 10 0 L 0 0 0 10" fill="none" stroke="gray"
                            stroke-width="0.5" />
                    </pattern>
                    <pattern id="pxGrid" width="50" height="50"
                        patternUnits="userSpaceOnUse">
                        <rect width="50" height="50" fill="url(#minorGrid)" />
```

```
                    <path d="M 50 0 L 0 0 0 50" fill="none" stroke="gray"
                        stroke-width="1" />
                </pattern>
            </defs>
            <rect width="100%" height="100%" fill="url(#pxGrid)"
                stroke="gray" stroke-width="1" />

            <line x1="0" y1="0" x2="100" y2="100" stroke="red"
                stroke-width="3" />
        </svg>
    </div>

    <div class="col-sm-3">
        <p>Grid units: pixels</p>
        <svg width="200" height="200">
            <rect width="100%" height="100%" fill="url(#pxGrid)"
                stroke="gray" stroke-width="1" />

            <line x1="0.5in" y1="1.5cm" x2="150" y2="120pt" stroke="red"
                stroke-width="3" />
        </svg>
    </div>
</div>
<!-- more code will be added here -->

</div>
```

Here, we first establish a viewport 200 pixels wide and 200 pixels high, and then define gridlines using the pattern. The minor grid spacing is 10 pixels and the major grid spacing is 50 pixels. We then create a rectangle with the gridlines as its background through the *fill* attribute.

Now, we can draw a line from point (0, 0) to point (100, 100) on the SVG using the default units of pixels:

```
<line x1="0" y1="0" x2="100" y2="100" stroke="red" stroke-width="3" />
```

Run this application, select the *Basic Shapes* tab, and click the *Coordinates* link to generate the result shown in Figure 2-2.

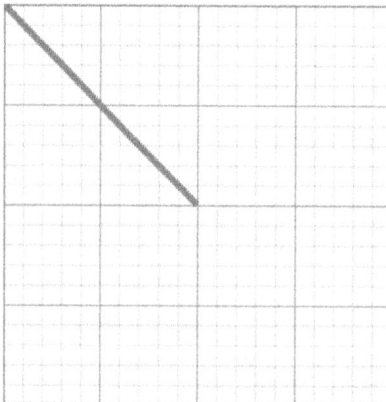

Figure 2-2. Drawing a line from (0, 0) to (100, 100) using default coordinates.

We can also create graphics objects using other units of measure as listed previously. For example, the coordinates for the starting and ending points of a line segment can be specified in different units. If you omit the unit, the default pixels will be used.

The code

```
<line x1="0.5in" y1="1.5cm" x2="150" y2="120pt" stroke="red" stroke-width="3"/>
```

uses the mixed units, which produces results shown in Figure 2-3.

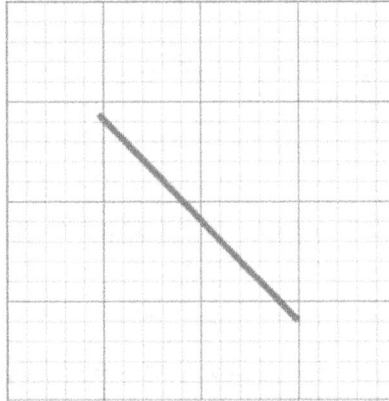

Figure 2-3. Drawing a line using different units of measure.

Custom Coordinates

The default coordinates in SVG uses the pixels as units of measure. In fact, you can define your own coordinates to meet the requirement of your applications. As an example, we will define a coordinates with units of millimeters. In particular, we want to create gridlines with major grid spacing of 10mm and the minor grid spacing of 2mm, and then we can draw lines on these gridlines. For rectangles and lines, it is very simple: you simply specify the point with the units of millimeters, e.g. point (10mm, 15mm). However, the *path* element can use only the units of pixels. In this case, we will use a scale transformation to convert the pixels into millimeters because we know that 1 millimeter = 3.779528 pixels.

Add the following code to the place of <!--*more code will be added here* --> in the *Coordinates.cshtml* file:

```
<div class="row">
    <div class="col-sm-3">
        <p style="margin-top:30px">Grid units: millimeters</p>
        <svg width="50mm" height="50mm">
            <defs>
                <pattern id="smallGrid" width="2mm" height="2mm"
                    patternUnits="userSpaceOnUse">
                    <g transform="scale(3.779528)">
                        <path d="M 2 0 L 0 0 0 2" fill="none" stroke="gray"
                            stroke-width="0.132292" />
                    </g>
                </pattern>
```

```
                    <pattern id="mmGrid" width="10mm" height="10mm"
                        patternUnits="userSpaceOnUse">
                        <rect width="10mm" height="10mm" fill="url(#smallGrid)" />
                        <g transform="scale(3.779528)">
                            <path d="M 10 0 L 0 0 0 10" fill="none" stroke="gray"
                                stroke-width="0.264583" />
                        </g>
                    </pattern>
                </defs>
                <rect width="100%" height="100%" fill="url(#mmGrid)" stroke="gray"
                    stroke-width="1" />

                <line x1="0" y1="0" x2="30mm" y2="30mm" stroke="red"
                    stroke-width="3" />
            </svg>
        </div>

        <div class="col-sm-3">
            <p style="margin-top:30px">Grid units: millimeters</p>
            <svg width="50mm" height="50mm">
                <rect width="100%" height="100%" fill="url(#mmGrid)"
                    stroke="gray" stroke-width="1" />

                <line x1="0.5in" y1="1.5cm" x2="150" y2="120pt" stroke="red"
                    stroke-width="3" />
            </svg>
        </div>
    </div>
```

The key step to create the coordinates with units of millimeters is the scale transformation for the *path* element:

```
<pattern id="smallGrid" width="2mm" height="2mm" patternUnits="userSpaceOnUse">
    <g transform="scale(3.779528)">
        <path d="M 2 0 L 0 0 0 2" fill="none" stroke="gray"
            stroke-width="0.132292" />
    </g>
</pattern>
```

Note that the *stroke-width* also needs to be scaled properly when you use the units of millimeters.

Run this application, select the *Basic Shapes* tab, and click the *Coordinates* link to produce the results based on the units of millimeters, as shown in Figure 2-4.

We can also use the different units of measure to create graphics. For example,

```
<line x1="0.5in" y1="1.5cm" x2="150" y2="120pt" stroke="red" stroke-width="3"/>
```

This code produces results shown in Figure 2-5 in a coordinate system with units of millimeters.

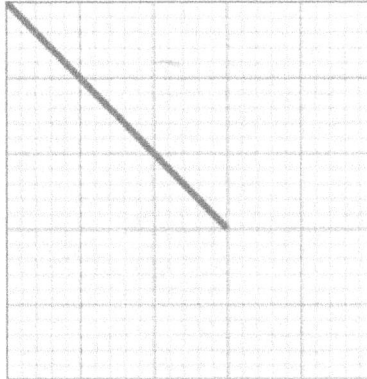

Figure 2-4. Drawing a line from (0, 0) to (30mm, 30mm) in custom coordinate system.

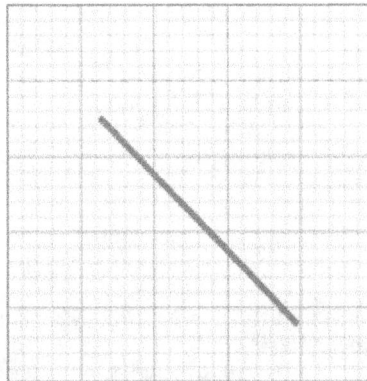

Figure 2-5. Drawing a line using different units on a custom coordinate system.

Basic Shapes in SVG

Once a coordinate system is established in SVG, we are ready to begin drawing. In this section, I will describe the basic geometric shapes in SVG that you can use to create the major elements of most drawings, including: lines, rectangles, polygons, circles, ellipses, paths, curves, and fill rules. These shapes are drawing primitives, which can be combined to create more complex graphics.

Lines

You can use the *<line>* element in SVG to draw a straight line between two ending points. The $x1$ and $y1$ attributes specify the starting point; the $x2$ and $y2$ attributes represent the ending points. The ending points may be specified without units, in which case they are considered to be the default coordinates (pixels), or with units such as *in, cm, em*, etc, as described in the preceding sections.

Let us consider an example. Add *Views/BasicShapes/Lines.cshtml* to the *Chapter02* project in Visual Studio 2017, and replace its content with the following code:

```
@{
    ViewData["Title"] = ViewBag.Title;
}

<h3>@ViewBag.Title</h3>
@Html.Partial("_Links")
<hr />

<div class="container">
    <div class="row">
        <div class="col-sm-3">
            <p>Basic lines</p>
            <svg width="200" height="200">
                <defs>
                    <pattern id="minorGrid" width="10" height="10"
                        patternUnits="userSpaceOnUse">
                        <path d="M 10 0 L 0 0 0 10" fill="none" stroke="gray"
                            stroke-width="0.5" />
                    </pattern>
                    <pattern id="pxGrid" width="50" height="50"
                        patternUnits="userSpaceOnUse">
                        <rect width="50" height="50" fill="url(#minorGrid)" />
                        <path d="M 50 0 L 0 0 0 50" fill="none" stroke="gray"
                            stroke-width="1" />
                    </pattern>
                </defs>
                <rect width="100%" height="100%" fill="url(#pxGrid)"
                    stroke="gray" stroke-width="1" />

                <line x1="50" y1="20" x2="150" y2="20" stroke="black"
                    stroke-width="1" />
                <line x1="0.5cm" y1="0.5cm" x2="0.5cm" y2="2cm" stroke="red"
                    stroke-width="2" />
                <line x1="40" y1="40" x2="150" y2="150" stroke="green"
                    stroke-width="3" />
                <line x1="30" y1="175" x2="170" y2="175" stroke="blue"
                    stroke-width="5" />
            </svg>
        </div>
    </div>
</div>
```

The most part of the code is the same as in previous example, which was used to create the gridlines. The highlighted code creates four basic straight line with different widths and colors.

Add the following code to *BasicShapesController*.cs:

```
public IActionResult Lines()
{
    ViewBag.Title = "Basic Shapes: Lines";
    return View();
}
```

Run the application, select the *Basic Shapes* tab, and click the *Lines* link to produce the results shown in Figure 2-6.

Basic lines

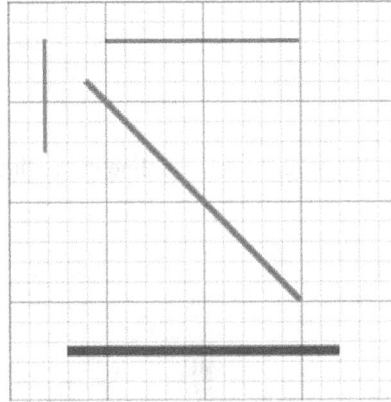

Figure 2-6. Basic back lines with different stroke widths.

SVG represents lines as strokes of a pen that draws on the canvas. The size, color, and style of the pen stroke are part of the line's presentation. In our example, we draw four straight lines with different stroke widths: 1*px*, 2*px*, 3*px*, and 5*px*, as well as different colors: *black*, *red*, *green*, and *blue*, respectively.

In SVG, you can specify the stroke color in a variety of ways, including color names, such as *black*, and hexadecimal specifier in the form *#rrggbb* or *#rgb*. We will discuss more details about color in later sections.

You may notice that all lines in our example are solid, obscuring anything beneath them. SVG allows you to control the opacity of a line by specifying the stroke-opacity a value from 0.0 to 1.0, where 0 is completely transparent and 1 is completely opaque. In the following example, we vary the opacity from 0.1 to 1.0 in steps of 0.1. Add the following code to *Views/BasicShapes/Lines.cshtml*:

```
<div class="col-sm-3">
    <p>Stroke opacity</p>
    <svg width="200" height="200">
        <rect width="100%" height="100%" fill="url(#pxGrid)" stroke="gray"
            stroke-width="1" />
        <line x1="100" y1="20" x2="100" y2="180" stroke="#00f" stroke-width="10"
            stroke-opacity="1.0" />
        <line x1="30" y1="50" x2="170" y2="50" stroke="red" stroke-width="5"
            stroke-opacity="0.1" />
        <line x1="30" y1="60" x2="170" y2="60" stroke="red" stroke-width="5"
            stroke-opacity="0.2" />
        <line x1="30" y1="70" x2="170" y2="70" stroke="red" stroke-width="5"
            stroke-opacity="0.3" />
        <line x1="30" y1="80" x2="170" y2="80" stroke="red" stroke-width="5"
            stroke-opacity="0.4" />
        <line x1="30" y1="90" x2="170" y2="90" stroke="red" stroke-width="5"
            stroke-opacity="0.5" />
        <line x1="30" y1="100" x2="170" y2="100" stroke="red" stroke-width="5"
            stroke-opacity="0.6" />
        <line x1="30" y1="110" x2="170" y2="110" stroke="red" stroke-width="5"
            stroke-opacity="0.7" />
        <line x1="30" y1="120" x2="170" y2="120" stroke="red" stroke-width="5"
```

```
                    stroke-opacity="0.8" />
          <line x1="30" y1="130" x2="170" y2="130" stroke="red" stroke-width="5"
                    stroke-opacity="0.9" />
          <line x1="30" y1="140" x2="170" y2="140" stroke="red" stroke-width="5"
                    stroke-opacity="1.0" />
      </svg>
  </div>
```

This produces the results shown in Figure 2-7. The blue line in the figure lets you see the transparency effect more clearly.

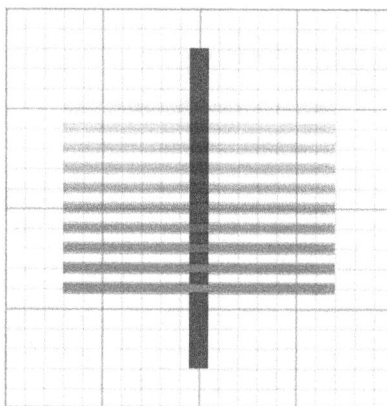

Figure 2-7. Demonstration of stroke opacity.

If you want dotted or dashed lines, you can use the *stroke-dasharray* attribute, whose value consists of an array of numbers, separated by comma or whitespace, specifying dash length and gaps. The array should contain an even number of entries, but if you give an old number of entries, SVG will repeat the array so the total number of entries is even.

Add the following code to *Views/BasicShapes/Lines.cshtml*:

```
<div class="col-sm-3">
    <p>Stroke dash style</p>
    <svg width="200" height="200">
        <text x="0" y="10">solid line</text>
        <line x1="0" y1="20" x2="200" y2="20" stroke="black" stroke-width="2"/>
        <text x="0" y="50">stroke-dasharray = "5,5"</text>
        <line x1="0" y1="60" x2="200" y2="60" stroke="black" stroke-width="2"
            stroke-dasharray="5,5"/>
        <text x="0" y="90">stroke-dasharray = "10,5"</text>
        <line x1="0" y1="100" x2="200" y2="100" stroke="black" stroke-width="2"
            stroke-dasharray="10,5" />
        <text x="0" y="130">stroke-dasharray = "5,5,1,5"</text>
        <line x1="0" y1="140" x2="200" y2="140" stroke="black" stroke-width="2"
            stroke-dasharray="5,5,1,5" />
        <text x="0" y="180">stroke-dasharray = "5,1"</text>
        <line x1="0" y1="190" x2="200" y2="190" stroke="black" stroke-width="2"
            stroke-dasharray="5,1" />
```

```
    </svg>
</div>
```

This code produces the results shown in Figure 2-8.

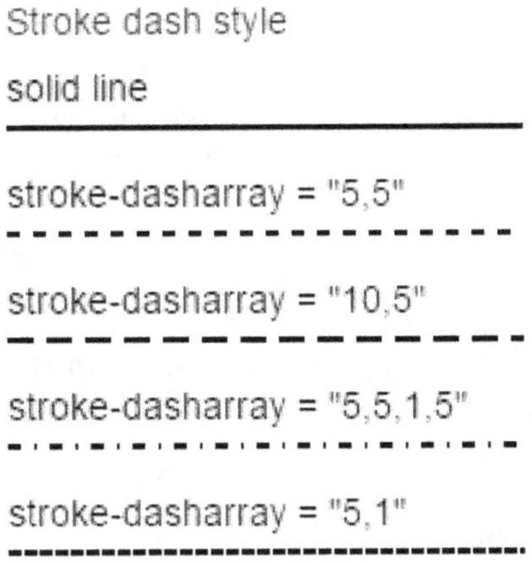

Stroke dash style

solid line

stroke-dasharray = "5,5"

stroke-dasharray = "10,5"

stroke-dasharray = "5,5,1,5"

stroke-dasharray = "5,1"

Figure 2-8. Demonstration of stroke-dasharray.

Rectangles

The rectangle is the simplest of the basic shapes. You specify the *x*- and *y*-coordinates of the upper-left corner of the rectangle, its *width*, and its *height*. The interior of the rectangle is filled with the *fill* attribute you specify and the default *fill* color is *black*. If you set the *fill* attribute to *none*, the interior of the rectangle will be transparent. You can also specify a *fill-opacity* in the same way as you did for the *stroke-opacity*.

After the interior is filled, the outline of the rectangle is drawn with strokes, whose characteristics you may specify as you did for lines. If you do not specify a stroke, the default value *none* is used, and no outline is drawn.

Add *Views/BasicShapes/Shapes.cshtml*, and replace the content of the template with the following code:

```
@{
    ViewData["Title"] = ViewBag.Title;
}

<h3>@ViewBag.Title</h3>
@Html.Partial("_Links")
<hr />

<div class="container">
    <div class="row">
        <div class="col-sm-3">
            <p>Rectangles</p>
            <svg width="200" height="200">

    .....

        <rect width="100%" height="100%" fill="url(#pxGrid)"
```

```
                    stroke="gray" stroke-width="1" />

                <rect x="10" y="10" width="80" height="50" />
                <rect x="110" y="10" width="80" height="50" fill="none"
                    stroke="black" />
                <rect x="10" y="100" width="80" height="80" fill="green"
                    stroke="red" stroke-width="10" stroke-opacity="0.5" />
                <rect x="110" y="100" width="80" height="80" fill="green"
                    fill-opacity="0.5" stroke="red" stroke-width="2"
                    stroke-dasharray="5,5" />
            </svg>
        </div>
    </div>
</div>
```

Here, we omit the part of code for creating the gridlines, which is the same as what we used in the previous example. Add the following code to *Controllers/BasicShapes.cs*:

```
public IActionResult Shapes()
{
    ViewBag.Title = "Basic Shapes: Shapes";
    return View();
}
```

This code produces the results shown in Figure 2-9.

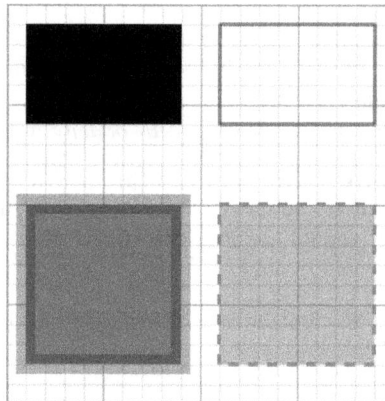

Figure 2-9. Rectangles created in SVG.

Note that the strokes are half inside the shape and half outside the shape. If you do not specify a starting *x* or *y* value, it is presumed to be 0. If you specify a width or height of 0, then the rectangle will not be displayed.

If you wish to have rectangles with rounded corners, you can specify the *x*- and *y*-radius of the corner curvature. Add the following code snippet to *Views/BasicShapes/Shapes.cshtml*:

```
<div class="col-sm-3">
    <p>Rounded rectangles</p>
    <svg width="200" height="200">
        <rect width="100%" height="100%" fill="url(#pxGrid)" stroke="gray"
            stroke-width="1" />
```

```
<rect x="10" y="10" width="80" height="50" fill="none" stroke="black"
    stroke-width="3" rx="5" ry="5" />
<rect x="110" y="10" width="80" height="50" fill="none" stroke="black"
    stroke-width="3" rx="10" ry="10"/>
<rect x="10" y="100" width="80" height="80" fill="none" stroke="black"
    stroke-width="3" rx="20" ry="20" />
<rect x="110" y="100" width="80" height="80" fill="none" stroke="black"
    stroke-width="3" rx="40" ry="40" />
</svg>
</div>
```

This code produces the results shown in Figure 2-10.

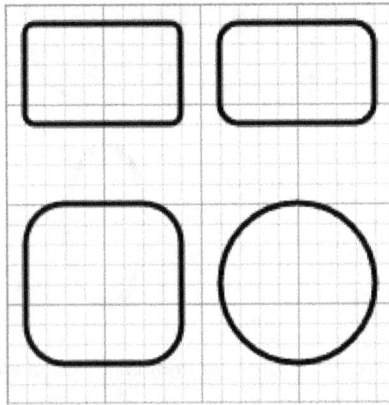

Figure 2-10. Demonstration of rounded rectangles.

Note that the maximum value you may specify for *rx* (*ry*) is one-half the *width* (*height*) of the rectangle. In particular, a square shape becomes a circle when you set the *rx* and *ry* to the one-half of side length, as shown in the figure.

Circles and Ellipses

In SVG, you can use *<circle>* element to create a circle by specifying the center *x*- and *y*-coordinates, and radius with *cx*, *cy*, and *r* attributes. As with a rectangle, the default is to fill the circle with black and draw no outline unless you specify some other combination of *fill* and *stroke*.

An ellipse needs both an *x*-radius (*rx*) and a *y*-radius (*ry*) in addition to *cx* and *cy* attributes. In both circles and ellipses, if *cx* or *cy* is omitted, it is presumed to be 0. If radius is zero, no shaped will be draw on your screen.

Add the following code snippet to *Views/BasicShapes/Shapes.cshtml*:

```
<div class="col-sm-3">
    <p style="margin-top:30px">Circle and Ellipses</p>
    <svg width="200" height="200">
        <rect width="100%" height="100%" fill="url(#pxGrid)" stroke="gray"
            stroke-width="1" />
```

```
<circle cx="50" cy="50" r="40" fill="red" fill-opacity="0.5"/>
<circle cx="150" cy="50" r="40" fill="red" fill-opacity="0.5"
    stroke="black" stroke-width="3" />
<ellipse cx="50" cy="150" rx="40" ry="20" fill="none" stroke="black"/>
<ellipse cx="150" cy="150" rx="20" ry="40" fill="none" stroke="black"
    stroke-width="5"/>
    </svg>
</div>
```

This code produces the results shown in Figure 2-11.

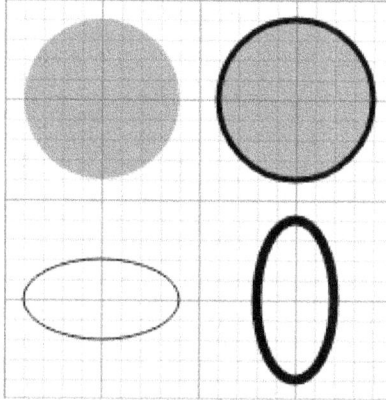

Figure 2-11. Demonstration of circles and ellipses.

Polygons

In addition to rectangles, circles, and ellipses, SVG also allows you to draw arbitrary closed shapes using the *<polygon>* element. This element lets you specify a series of *points* that describe a geometric area to be filled and outlined. The *points* attribute consists of a series of *x*- and *y*-coordinate pairs separated by commas or whitespaces. You do not have to return to the starting point; the polygon will automatically be closed.

Add the following code snippet to *Views/BasicShapes/Shapes.cshtml*:

```
<div class="col-sm-3">
    <p style="margin-top:30px">Polygons</p>
    <svg width="200" height="200">
        <rect width="100%" height="100%" fill="url(#pxGrid)" stroke="gray"
            stroke-width="1" />

        <polygon points="50,10 150,10 110,60 10,60"  fill="red"
            fill-opacity="0.5" stroke="black" />
        <polygon points="50 0,60.7 35.3,97.6 34.5,67.3 55.6,79.4 90.5,50
            68.2,20.6 90.5,32.7 55.6,2.4 34.5,39.3 35.3" fill="yellow"
            fill-opacity="0.5" stroke="black" stroke-width="3"
            transform="translate(50,90)" />
    </svg>
</div>
```

In the above code, we set an attribute for *translate* transformation, which is simply used to place the shape at the correct location on the viewport. This code draws a parallelogram and a star, as shown in Figure 2-12.

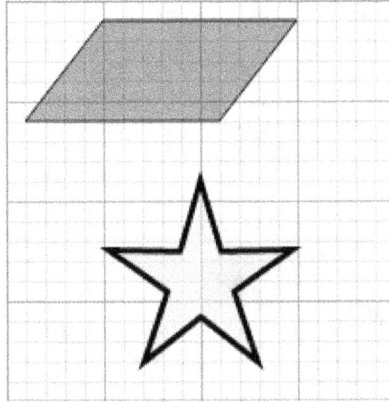

Figure 2-12. Demonstration of polygons.

Polylines

Sometimes, you may want a series of line segments that does or does not make a closed shape. In this case, you can use multiple *<line>* elements, but if there are many lines, it might be easier to use the *<polyline>* element. It has the same *points* attribute as *<polygon>*, except that the shape is not closed (it can be also a closed shape if you add the starting point to the *points* attribute at the end).

Add the following code snippet to *Views/BasicShapes/Shapes.cshtml*:

```
<div class="col-sm-3">
    <p style="margin-top:30px">Polylines</p>
    <svg width="200" height="250">
        <rect width="100%" height="100%" fill="url(#pxGrid)" stroke="gray"
            stroke-width="1" />

        <polyline points="20,50 60,0 100,40 140,0 180,50" stroke="black"
            stroke-width="3" fill="none" transform="translate(0,10)" />
        <polyline points="20,50 60,0 100,40 140,0 180,50 20,50" stroke="black"
            stroke-width="3" fill="none" transform="translate(0,80)" />
        <polyline points="0 100,10 117,20 132,30 143,40 149,50 149,60 143,70
            132,80 117,90 100,100 83,110 68,120 57,130 51,140 51,150 57,160
            68,170 83,180 100" fill="none" stroke="black" stroke-width="3.75"
        transform="translate(27,120) scale(0.8)" />
    </svg>
</div>

<div class="col-sm-3">
    <p style="margin-top:30px">Filled polylines</p>
    <svg width="200" height="250">
        <rect width="100%" height="100%" fill="url(#pxGrid)" stroke="gray"
            stroke-width="1" />
```

```
<polyline points="20,50 60,0 100,40 140,0 180,50" stroke="black"
    stroke-width="3" fill="red" fill-opacity="0.5"
    transform="translate(0,10)" />
<polyline points="20,50 60,0 100,40 140,0 180,50 20,50" stroke="black"
    stroke-width="3" fill="red" fill-opacity="0.5"
    transform="translate(0,80)" />
<polyline points="0 100,10 117,20 132,30 143,40 149,50 149,60 143,70
    132,80 117,90 100,100 83,110 68,120 57,130 51,140 51,150 57,160
    68,170 83,180 100" fill="red" fill-opacity="0.5" stroke="black"
    stroke-width="3.75" transform="translate(27,120) scale(0.8)" />
    </svg>
    </div>
```

This code produces the results shown in Figure 1-13.

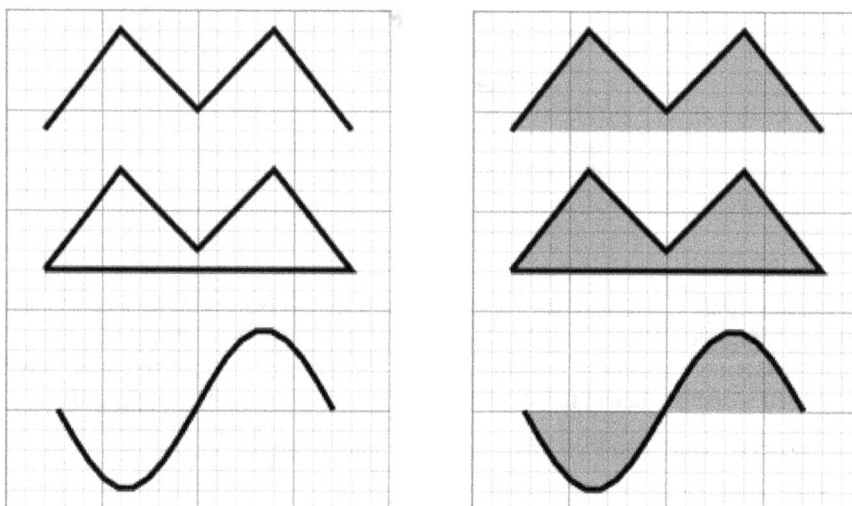

Figure 2-13. Demonstration of polylines (left) and filled polylines.

Fill Rules

In a simple polygon or polyline shape whose lines never cross, it is easy to fill the interior. Sometimes, however, you will have a more complex polygon in which it is not necessarily obvious which portions should be filled and which portions should not.

Let us consider an example, which shows a line cross more than one other line, leaving an irregular region at the center that may or may not be filled.

Add the following code to the *BasicShapesController.cs* file:

```
public IActionResult FillRule()
{
    ViewBag.Title = "Basic Shapes: Fill Rule";
    return View();
}
```

Add *Views/BasicShapes/FillRule.cshtml* and replace its content with the following code:

```
@{
    ViewData["Title"] = ViewBag.Title;
}
<h3>@ViewBag.Title</h3>
@Html.Partial("_Links")
<hr />

<style type="text/css">
    polygon {
        stroke: black;
        stroke-width: 3px;
        fill: red;
        opacity: 0.5;
    }
</style>

<div class="container">
    <div class="row">
        <div class="col-sm-3">
            <p>Fill Rule: EvenOdd</p>
            <svg width="200" height="200">
                ......

                <rect width="100%" height="100%" fill="url(#pxGrid)"
                    stroke="gray" stroke-width="1" />
                <polygon points="0 0,0 150,100 150,100 50,50 50,50 100,150
                    100,150 0" fill-rule="evenodd"
                    transform="translate(20,20)" />
            </svg>
        </div>
        <div class="col-sm-3">
            <p>Fill Rule: NoneZero </p>
            <svg width="200" height="200">
                <rect width="100%" height="100%" fill="url(#pxGrid)"
                    stroke="gray" stroke-width="1" />
                <polygon points="0 0,0 150,100 150,100 50,50 50,50 100,150
                    100,150 0" fill-rule="nonzero"
                    transform="translate(20,20)" />
            </svg>
        </div>
        <div class="col-sm-3">
            <p>Fill Rule: NonZero</p>
            <svg width="200" height="200">
                <rect width="100%" height="100%" fill="url(#pxGrid)"
                    stroke="gray" stroke-width="1" />
                <polygon points="0 0,0 150,100 150,100 100,50 100,50 50,100
                    50,100 100,150 100,150 0" fill-rule="nonzero"
                    transform="translate(20,20)" />
            </svg>
        </div>
    </div>
</div>
```

Here, we use the *fill-rule* attribute to control the filled regions. Every polygon has a *fill-rule* attribute that allows you to choose between two different methods for filling in regions: *evenodd* (the default value) and *nonzero*. In the *evenodd* case, in order to determine which region will be filled, SVG counts the number of lines that must be crossed to reach the outside of the shape. If this number is odd, the region is filled; if it is even, the region is left empty, as shown in Figure 2-14.

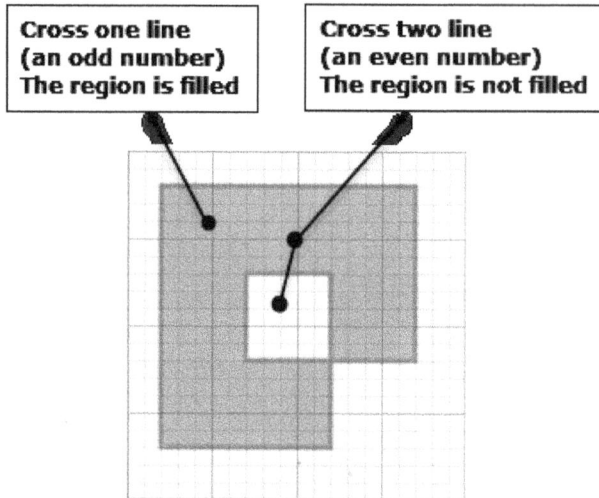

Figure 2-14. Determining filled regions when fill-rule is set to evenodd.

When *fill-rule* is set to *nonzero*, determining which region will be filled becomes trickier. In this case, SVG follows the same line-counting process as *evenodd* but takes into account the line direction. If the number of line going in one direction is equal to the number of lines going in the opposite direction, the region is not filled; if the difference between these two counts is not zero, the region is filled. Figure 2-15 shows the results of running this example.

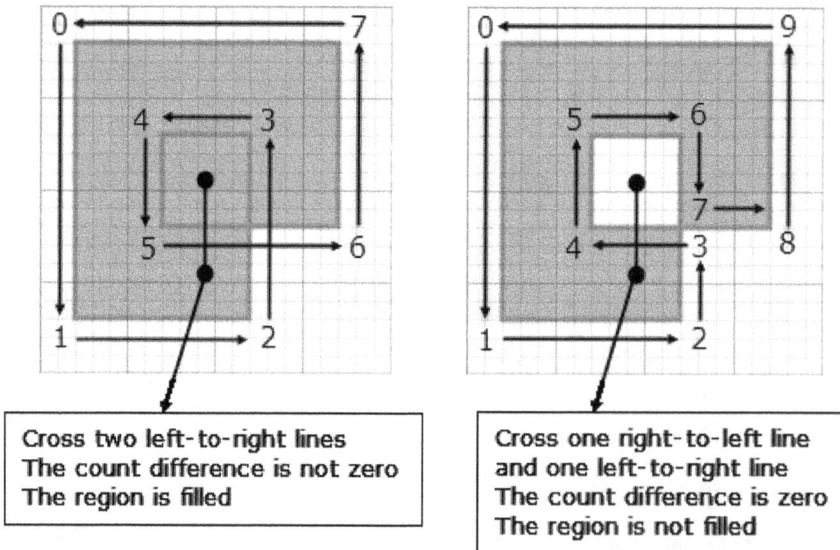

Figure 2-15. Determining filled regions when fill-rule is set to nonzero.

The difference between the two shapes in this figure is that the order of points in the *points* attribute is different, leading to different line directions. This means that in the *nonzero* case, whether a region is filled or not depends on how you draw the shape, not on what the shape itself looks like. Figure 2-15 clearly demonstrates this conclusion.

Paths and Curves

In the preceding section, you learned how to create simple 2D graphics using shapes, including lines, rectangles, circles, ellipses, and polygons. These basic shapes are really shorthand forms for the more general *<path>* element. You can use these shortcuts because they help make your SVG more readable and more structured. The <path> element is more general and has the ability to draw curves and complex shapes by specifying a series of connected lines, arcs, and curves. All of the data describing a path shape is in the *<path>* element's *d* attribute (the *d* stands for data). The path data consists of one-letter commands, such as *M* for *moveto* or *L* for *lineto*, followed by the coordinate information for that particular command.

Let us consider an example. Here, we want to draw some basic shapes using the *<path>* element. Add the following code to the *BasicShapesController.cs* file:

```
public IActionResult Paths()
{
    ViewBag.Title = "Basic Shapes: Paths";
    return View();
}
```

Add a new file *Views/BasicShapes/Paths.cshtml* and replace its content with the following code:

```
@{
    ViewData["Title"] = ViewBag.Title;
}

<h3>@ViewBag.Title</h3>
@Html.Partial("_Links")
<hr />
<div class="container">
    <div class="row">
        <div class="col-sm-3">
            <p>Paths</p>
            <svg width="200" height="200">
                ......

                <rect width="100%" height="100%" fill="url(#pxGrid)"
                    stroke="gray" stroke-width="1" />

                <path d="M10 10 H90 V90 H10" stroke="red" stroke-width="3"
                    fill="none" />
                <path d="M10 10 H90 V90 H10 Z" stroke="red" stroke-width="3"
                    fill="none" transform="translate(100,0)" />
                <path d="M50 10 L90 90 H10 Z" stroke="red" stroke-width="3"
                    fill="none" transform="translate(0,100)" />
                <path d="M50 0 L79.4 90.5 L2.4 34.5 L97.6 34.5 L20.6 90.5 Z"
                    stroke="red" stroke-width="3" fill="none"
                    transform="translate(100,105)" />
            </svg>
```

```
        </div>
     </div>
  </div>
```

For the first path, we have the *d* attribute:

```
d="M10 10 H90 V90 H10"
```

We can examine this path more closely:

- M10 10: Move pen to (10, 10).

- H90: H stands for horizontal. Starting from last point (10, 10), it draws a horizontal line to the *x*-coordinate 90. This puts you at coordinates (90, 10).

- V90: V stands for vertical. Start from the last line drawn and draw a vertical line to *y*-coordinate 90. This puts you at coordinates (90, 90).

- H10: Start from the last coordinates (90, 90) and draw a horizontal line *x*-coordinate 10. This puts you at coordinate (10, 90).

The second path is the same as the first one, except for the *Z* letter at the end of the *d* attribute. Z is a closed path command, and it draws a straight line to the start of the path to form a closed path.

The third path with the following d attribute:

```
d="M50 10 L90 90 H10 Z"
```

This generates a triangle. The code first places move pen to (50, 10), then draws a line to (90, 90), next draws a vertical line to (10, 90), and finally draws a line to the start of the path to form a closed triangle shape.

The last closed path created by the *<path>* element forms a star. The commands we used are simply *M*, *L*, and *Z*.

Running this example produces the results shown in Figure 2-16.

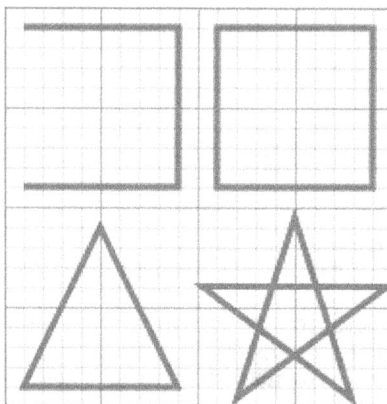

Figure 2-16. Basic shapes created using the <path> element.

You can also create curves in SVG. There are three different commands that you can use to create smooth curves. Two of those are Bezier curves, and the third one is an arc or part of a circle. You might have already gained practical experience with Bezier curves using path tools like Adobe Photoshop. SVG implemented two types of Bezier curves: cubic (called with C letter) and quadratic (called with Q letter).

The cubic Bezier curve, C, is slightly more complex curve. Cubic Beziers take in two control points for each point. Therefore, to create a cubic Bezier curve, you need to specify three sets of coordinates:

```
C x1 y1, x2 y2, x y
```

The last set of coordinates (x, y) are where you want the line to end. The other two sets of coordinates are control points. The control point for the start of your curve is $(x1, y1)$, and $(x2, y2)$ is the ending point of your curve. The control points basically describe the slope of your starting at each point. The Bezier function then creates a smooth curve that transfers you from the slope you established at the beginning of your line, to the slope at the other end.

The quadratic Bezier curve, called with Q, is actually a simpler curve than the cubic one. It requires one control point that determines the slope of the curve at both the starting point and the ending point. It takes two arguments the control point and the ending point of the curve:

```
Q x1 y1, x y
```

We will consider an example, which demonstrates how to create cubic Bezier curves and how to put multiple cubic Bezier pieces together.

Add the following code to *Views/BasicShapes/Paths.cshtml*:

```
<div class="col-sm-3">
    <p>Bezier Curves</p>
    <svg width="200" height="200">
        <rect width="100%" height="100%" fill="url(#pxGrid)" stroke="gray"
            stroke-width="1" />

        <path d="M30 130 C30 10,300 10,300 130" stroke="red" stroke-width="3"
            fill="none" transform="translate(-10,-15) scale(0.68)" />
        <path d="M30 80 C70 30,120 30,160 80 S250 100,290 80" stroke="red"
            stroke-width="3" fill="none" transform="translate(-10,100)
            scale(0.7)" />
    </svg>
</div>
```

The code create the first cubic Bezier curve with the *d* attribute:

```
d="M30 130 C30 10,300 10,300 130"
```

This draws the curve from (30, 30) to (300, 130) with control points at (30, 10) and (300, 10).

The second curve with the following d attribute:

```
d="M30 80 C70 30,120 30,160 80 S250 100,290 80"
```

Here, we want a smooth join between curves by using the *S* command. The above code first draws a cubic Bezier curve from (30, 80) to (160, 80) with control points at (70, 30) and (120, 30). It continues smoothly to (290, 80), using (250, 100) as its ending control point.

Running this example produces the results shown in Figure 2-17.

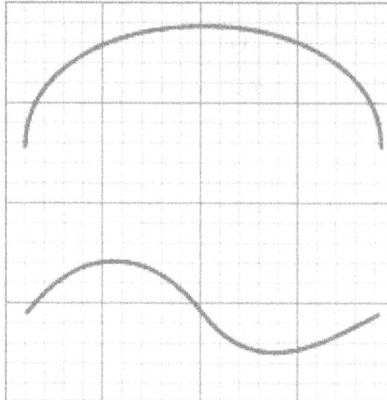

Figure 2-17. Demonstration of cubic Bezier curves.

The other type of curve you can create using SVG is the *arc*, called with *A*. Arcs are sections of circles or ellipses. For a given *x*-radius and *y*-radius, there are two ellipses that can connect any two points. Along either of those circles, there are two possible paths, which you can take to connect the points, so in any situation there are four possible arcs available. Because of that, arcs need to take in more arguments than Bezier curves:

A rx ry x-axis-rotation large-arc-flag sweep-flag x y

At its start, the arc element takes in two arguments for the *x*-radius and *y*-radius, followed by the *x-axis-rotation* of the ellipse. The large-arc-flag takes the zero value if the arc's measure is less than 180 degrees or one if the arc's measure is greater than or equal to 180 degrees. The sweep-flag takes 0 if the arc is drawn in the negative angle direction, or 1 if the arc is drawn in the positive angle direction. The *x* and *y* are the ending *x*- and *y*-coordinates of the ending point (The starting point is determined by the last point drawn or the last *moveto* command).

Add the following code to *Views/BasicShapes/Paths.cshtml*:

```
<div class="row">
    <div class="col-sm-3">
        <p>Arcs</p>
        <svg width="200" height="200">
            <rect width="100%" height="100%" fill="url(#pxGrid)" stroke="gray"
                stroke-width="1" />

            <path d="M0 100 A100 100 0 0 1 200 100 L150 100 A50 50 0 0 0 50 100
                Z" stroke="red" stroke-width="3" fill="none"
                transform="translate(20,10) scale(0.8)" />
            <path d="M0 100 A100 100 0 0 0 200 100 L150 100 A50 50 0 0 1 50 100
                Z" stroke="red" stroke-width="3" fill="none"
                transform="translate(20,30) scale(0.8)" />
        </svg>
    </div>

    <div class="col-sm-3">
        <p>Arcs</p>
        <svg width="200" height="200">
            <rect width="100%" height="100%" fill="url(#pxGrid)" stroke="gray"
```

```
         stroke-width="1" />

    <path d="M0 100 A100 100 0 0 1 100 0 L100 100 Z" stroke="red"
        stroke-width="3" fill="none"
        transform="translate(10,10) scale(0.8)" />
    <path d="M0 100 A100 100 0 1 0 100 0 L100 100 Z" stroke="red"
        stroke-width="3" fill="none"
        transform="translate(30,30) scale(0.8)" />
    </svg>
  </div>
</div>
```

This code generates results shown in Figure 2-18.

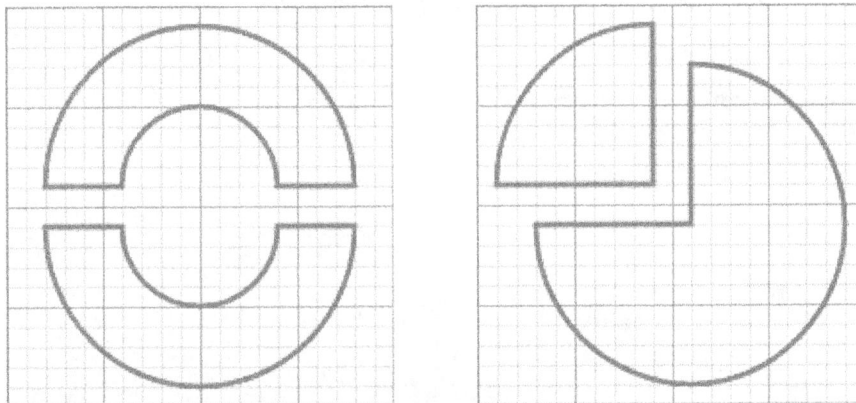

Figure 2-18. Demonstration of the Arcs.

For the arcs shown in the left panel of the figure, the only difference is the sweep-flag in the arc command:

```
d="M0 100 A100 100 0 0 1 200 100 L150 100 A50 50 0 0 0 50 100 Z" (top curve)
d="M0 100 A100 100 0 0 0 200 100 L150 100 A50 50 0 0 1 50 100 Z" (bottom curve)
```

The sweep-flag controls the angle direction when you draw the arc curve. The difference in the sweep-flag results in the different arc shape.

For the arc curves on the right panel, we have:

```
d="M0 100 A100 100 0 0 1 100 0 L100 100 Z"
d="M0 100 A100 100 0 1 0 100 0 L100 100 Z"
```

These two arc curves have different large-arc-flag and different sweep-flag, resulting in different shapes.

2D Transformations in SVG

Up to this point, all graphics have been displayed as is – drawn exactly where and how they are defined in their attributes. Sometimes, you may have a graphic object you would like to rotate, scale, or move to a new location. To accomplish these tasks, you add the *transform* attribute to the appropriate SVG elements. This section examines the details of these transformations.

Group and Use Elements

Before discussing transformations, we introduce two useful elements: the *<g>* and *<use>* elements. These two elements will greatly simplify the process of creating complex shapes. The *<g>* element gathers all of its child elements as a group and often has an *id* attribute to give that group a unique name. Complex graphics often contains repeated elements. The SVG *<use>* element provides you an analogous copy-and-paste ability with a group you define with *<g>* or individual graphic element.

Once you have defined a group of graphics objects, you can display them again with the *<use>* tag. To specify the group you wish to reuse, give its URL in an *xlink:href* attribute, and specify the *x* and *y* location where the group's (0, 0) point should be moved to.

Add a new folder named *Transformation* to the *Views* folder. Add a new controller class *Controllers/TransformationController.cs* and replace its content with the following code:

```
using Microsoft.AspNetCore.Mvc;

// For more information on enabling MVC for empty projects, visit
// https://go.microsoft.com/fwlink/?LinkID=397860

namespace Chapter02.Controllers
{
    public class TransformationController : Controller
    {
        // GET: /<controller>/
        public IActionResult Index()
        {
            return View();
        }

        public IActionResult Groups()
        {
            ViewBag.Title = "Transformations: Groups";
            return View();
        }

        public IActionResult Translation()
        {
            ViewBag.Title = "Transformations: Translation";
            return View();
        }

        public IActionResult Rotation()
        {
            ViewBag.Title = "Transformations: Rotation";
            return View();
        }

        public IActionResult Scaling()
        {
            ViewBag.Title = "Transformations: Scaling";
            return View();
        }

        public IActionResult Skewing()
```

```
        {
            ViewBag.Title = "Transformations: Skewing";
            return View();
        }

        public IActionResult Complex()
        {
            ViewBag.Title = "Transformations: Complex Transformations";
            return View();
        }

        public IActionResult Viewbox()
        {
            ViewBag.Title = "Transformations: View Box in SVG";
            return View();
        }
    }
}
```

Add *Views/Transformation/Groups.cshtml* and replace its content with the following code:

```
@{
    ViewData["Title"] = ViewBag.Title;
}

<h3>@ViewBag.Title</h3>
@Html.Partial("_Links")
<hr />

<div class="container">
    <div class="row">
        <div class="col-sm-3">
            <p>The g and use elements</p>
            <svg width="200" height="200">
                .....

                <rect width="100%" height="100%" fill="url(#pxGrid)"
                    stroke="gray" stroke-width="1" />

                <g id="house" stroke="black" stroke-width="2" fill="red"
                    fill-opacity="0.5">
                    <path d="M50 10 90 40 H10 Z" />
                    <rect x="10" y="40" width="80" height="50" />
                    <rect x="60" y="60" width="20" height="30" fill="none" />
                </g>

                <use xlink:href="#house" x="100" y="0" />
                <use xlink:href="#house" x="0" y="100" />
                <use xlink:href="#house" x="100" y="100" />
            </svg>
        </div>
    </div>
</div>
```

The highlighted code first defines a *house* shape using the *<g>* element, which consists of two rectangles and a path triangle. It then displays this *house* shape three more times at different locations by specifying corresponding *x* and *y* coordinates with the *<use>* element.

Running this example produces the results shown in Figure 2-19.

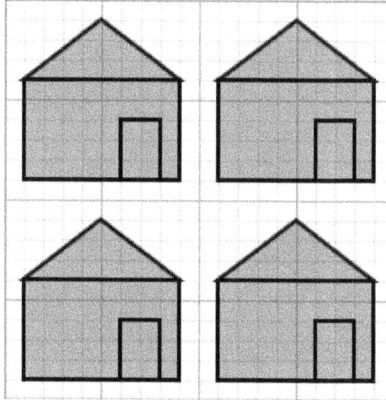

Figure 2-19. Demonstration of the <g> and <use> elements.

Translation

In the preceding section, we create a house object using the *<g>* element and use *x* and *y* attributes with the *<use>* element to place the object at a specific location. In fact, the *x* and *y* values are really shorthand for one form of more general and more powerful *transform* attribute. Specifically, the *x* and *y* values are equivalent to an attribute like *transform="translate(x-value, y-value)"*, where *translate* is just a technical term for *move*.

In order to see the detailed evolution of the transformation in SVG, we will try to animate the process of the transformation. The animation features in SVG are based on W3C's SMIL3 specification. In this system, you simply specify the starting and ending values of the attribute, color, motion, or transformation you wish to animate; the time at which the animation should begin; and the duration of the animation.

Let us consider an example for the translation, where we animate the translation for the original house object. The *animateTransform* element generates animations by setting *transform* attributes on the SVG shape to which it is applied. The animation allows you to visually examine the evolution of the transformation.

Add *Views/Transformation/Translation.cshtml* and replace its content with the following code:

```
@{
    ViewData["Title"] = ViewBag.Title;
}
<h3>@ViewBag.Title</h3>
@Html.Partial("_Links")
<hr />

<div class="container">
    <div class="row">
```

```
<div class="col-sm-3">
    <p>Original</p>
    <svg width="200" height="200">

        .....

            <rect width="100%" height="100%" fill="url(#pxGrid)"
                stroke="gray" stroke-width="1" />

            <g id="house" stroke="black" stroke-width="2" fill="red"
                fill-opacity="0.5">
                <path d="M50 10 90 40 H10 Z" />
                <rect x="10" y="40" width="80" height="50"/>
                <rect x="60" y="60" width="20" height="30" fill="none" />
            </g>
    </svg>
</div>

<div class="col-sm-3">
    <p>Translate in x</p>
    <svg width="200" height="200">
        <rect width="100%" height="100%" fill="url(#pxGrid)"
            stroke="gray" stroke-width="1" />
        <use xlink:href="#house">
            <animateTransform attributeName="transform"
                            type="translate"
                            from="0 0"
                            to="100 0"
                            begin="0s"
                            dur="5s"
                            repeatCount="indefinite" />
        </use>
    </svg>
</div>
</div>

<div class="row" style="margin-top:30px">
    <div class="col-sm-3">
        <p>Translate in y</p>
        <svg width="200" height="200">
            <rect width="100%" height="100%" fill="url(#pxGrid)"
                stroke="gray" stroke-width="1" />
            <use xlink:href="#house">
                <animateTransform attributeName="transform"
                                type="translate"
                                from="0 0"
                                to="0 100"
                                begin="0s"
                                dur="5s"
                                repeatCount="indefinite" />
            </use>
        </svg>
    </div>

    <div class="col-sm-3">
```

```
<p>Translate in both x and y</p>
<svg width="200" height="200">
    <rect width="100%" height="100%" fill="url(#pxGrid)"
        stroke="gray" stroke-width="1" />
    <use xlink:href="#house">
        <animateTransform attributeName="transform"
                        type="translate"
                        from="0 0"
                        to="100 100"
                        begin="0s"
                        dur="5s"
                        repeatCount="indefinite" />
    </use>
</svg>
    </div>
  </div>
</div>
```

The highlight code creates animations for translation of the original house object in the *x-*, *y-* and diagonal-directions, respectively. Running this example produces the output shown in Figure 2-20.

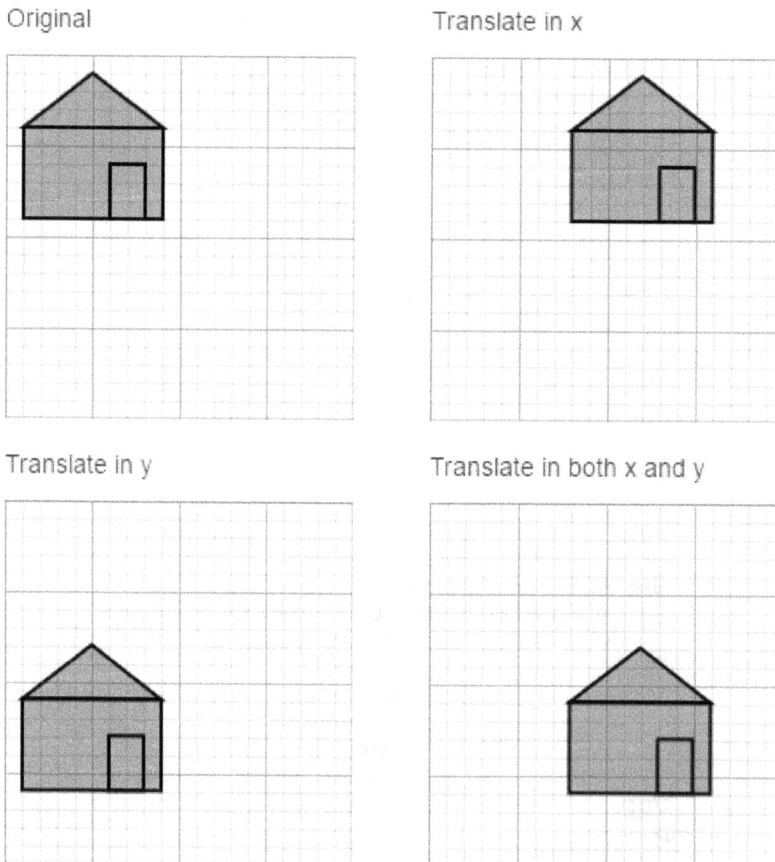

Original

Translate in x

Translate in y

Translate in both x and y

Figure 2-20. Demonstration of translation animations.

Scaling

It is possible to make an object appear larger or smaller than its original size. Such a transformation is specified as follows in SVG:

```
Transform="scale(value)"
```

This scales the *x*- and *y*-coordinates by the given *value*. If you want to scales the *x*- and *y*-coordinates separately with different values, you should use the following code:

```
Transform="scale(x-value, y-value)"
```

This multiplies all *x*-coordinates by a given *x-value* and all *y*-coordinates by a given *y-value*. Here, we will consider an example that illustrates the scaling transformations for the house object, which including the scaling in the *x*-, *y*- and diagonal-directions.

Add *Views/Transformation/Scaling.cshtml* and replace its content with the following code:

```
@{
    ViewData["Title"] = ViewBag.Title;
}

<h3>@ViewBag.Title</h3>
@Html.Partial("_Links")
<hr />

<div class="container">
    <div class="row">
        <div class="col-sm-3">
            <p>Original</p>
            <svg width="200" height="200">

        ......

                <rect width="100%" height="100%" fill="url(#pxGrid)"
                    stroke="gray" stroke-width="1" />

                <g id="house" stroke="black" stroke-width="2" fill="red"
                    fill-opacity="0.5">
                    <path d="M50 10 90 40 H10 Z" />
                    <rect x="10" y="40" width="80" height="50" />
                    <rect x="60" y="60" width="20" height="30" fill="none" />
                </g>
            </svg>
        </div>

        <div class="col-sm-3">
            <p>Scale in x</p>
            <svg width="200" height="200">
                <rect width="100%" height="100%" fill="url(#pxGrid)"
                    stroke="gray" stroke-width="1" />
                <use xlink:href="#house">
                    <animateTransform attributeName="transform"
                                type="scale"
                                from="1 1"
                                to="2 1"
                                begin="0s"
```

```
                                          dur="5s"
                                          repeatCount="indefinite" />
                        </use>
                    </svg>
                </div>
            </div>

            <div class="row" style="margin-top:10px">
                <div class="col-sm-3">
                    <p>Scale in y</p>
                    <svg width="200" height="200">
                        <rect width="100%" height="100%" fill="url(#pxGrid)"
                            stroke="gray" stroke-width="1" />
                        <use xlink:href="#house">
                            <animateTransform attributeName="transform"
                                              type="scale"
                                              from="1,1"
                                              to="1,2"
                                              begin="0s"
                                              dur="5s"
                                              repeatCount="indefinite" />
                        </use>
                    </svg>
                </div>

                <div class="col-sm-3">
                    <p>Scale in both x and y</p>
                    <svg width="200" height="200">
                        <rect width="100%" height="100%" fill="url(#pxGrid)"
                            stroke="gray" stroke-width="1" />
                        <use xlink:href="#house">
                            <animateTransform attributeName="transform"
                                              type="scale"
                                              from="1,1"
                                              to="2,2"
                                              begin="0s"
                                              dur="5s"
                                              repeatCount="indefinite" />
                        </use>
                    </svg>
                </div>
            </div>
        </div>
    </div>
```

The highlight code creates animations for scaling of the original house object in the x-, y- and diagonal-directions, respectively. Running this example produces the output shown in Figure 2-21.

Rotation

You can also rotate the coordinate system by a specified angle. In the default coordinate system, angle measure increases as you rotate clockwise, with a horizontal line having an angle of 0 degrees. Unless you specify otherwise, the center of rotation (or pivot point) is presumed to be (0, 0).

Scale in y   Scale in both x and y

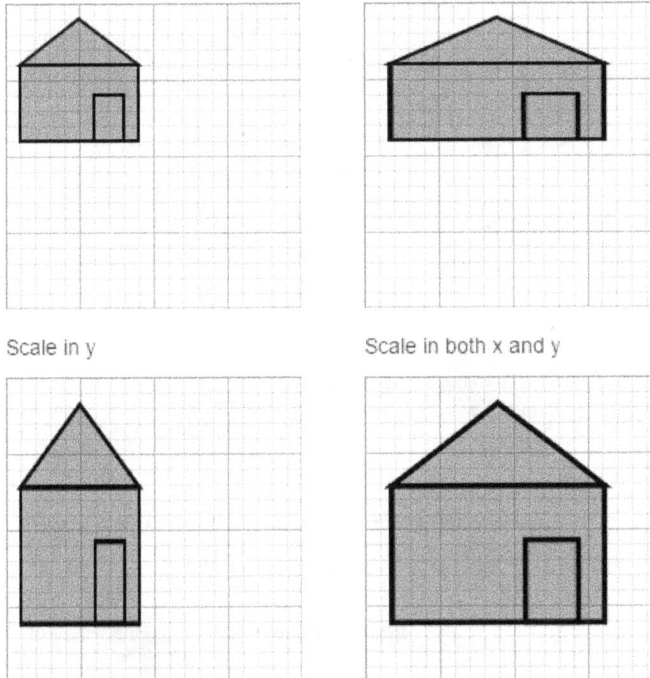

Figure 2-21. Demonstration of the scaling transformations.

Sometimes, you will not want to rotate the entire coordinate system around the origin; you will want to rotate a single object around a point other than the origin. You can do that via a series of transformations: *translate(cx, cy) rotate(angle) translate(-cx, cy)*. SVG provides another version of rotate to make this common task easier. In this case, you simply specify the angle and the center point around which you want to rotate:

`rotate(angle, cx, cy)`

This has the effect of temporarily establishing a new system of coordinates with the origin at the specified center point (*cx, cy*), doing the rotation, and then re-establishing the original coordinates.

Add *Views/Transformation/Rotation.cshtml* and replace its content with the following code:

```
@{
    ViewData["Title"] = ViewBag.Title;
}

<h3>@ViewBag.Title</h3>
@Html.Partial("_Links")
<hr />

<div class="container">
    <div class="row">
        <div class="col-sm-3">
            <p>Original</p>
            <svg width="200" height="200">

            ......
```

```
            <rect width="100%" height="100%" fill="url(#pxGrid)"
                stroke="gray" stroke-width="1" />

            <g id="house" stroke="black" stroke-width="2" fill="red"
                fill-opacity="0.5" transform="translate(50, 50)">
                <path d="M50 10 90 40 H10 Z" />
                <rect x="10" y="40" width="80" height="50" />
                <rect x="60" y="60" width="20" height="30" fill="none" />
            </g>
        </svg>
    </div>


    <div class="col-sm-3">
        <p>Rotate around (0,0)</p>
        <svg width="200" height="200">
            <rect width="100%" height="100%" fill="url(#pxGrid)"
                stroke="gray" stroke-width="1" />
            <use xlink:href="#house">
                <animateTransform attributeName="transform"
                                  type="rotate"
                                  from="-45"
                                  to="45"
                                  begin="0s"
                                  dur="5s"
                                  repeatCount="indefinite" />
            </use>
        </svg>
    </div>
</div>

<div class="row" style="margin-top:10px">
    <div class="col-sm-3">
        <p>Rotate clockwise</p>
        <svg width="200" height="200">
            <rect width="100%" height="100%" fill="url(#pxGrid)"
                stroke="gray" stroke-width="1" />
            <use xlink:href="#house">
                <animateTransform attributeName="transform"
                                  type="rotate"
                                  from="0,100,100"
                                  to="360,100,100"
                                  begin="0s"
                                  dur="5s"
                                  repeatCount="indefinite" />
            </use>
        </svg>
    </div>

    <div class="col-sm-3">
        <p>Rotate counterclosevise</p>
        <svg width="200" height="200">
            <rect width="100%" height="100%" fill="url(#pxGrid)"
                stroke="gray" stroke-width="1" />
            <use xlink:href="#house">
```

```
<animateTransform attributeName="transform"
                  type="rotate"
                  from="360,100,100"
                  to="0,100,100"
                  begin="0s"
                  dur="5s"
                  repeatCount="indefinite" />
            </use>
          </svg>
        </div>
      </div>
    </div>
```

The highlighted code generates three different rotations: the first one rotates the original house object around the origin (0, 0) in the clockwise direction; the second one rotates the house around its own center (100, 100) in the clockwise direction; and the last one rotates the house around its own center (100, 100) in the counterclockwise direction.

Running this example generates the output shown in Figure 2-22.

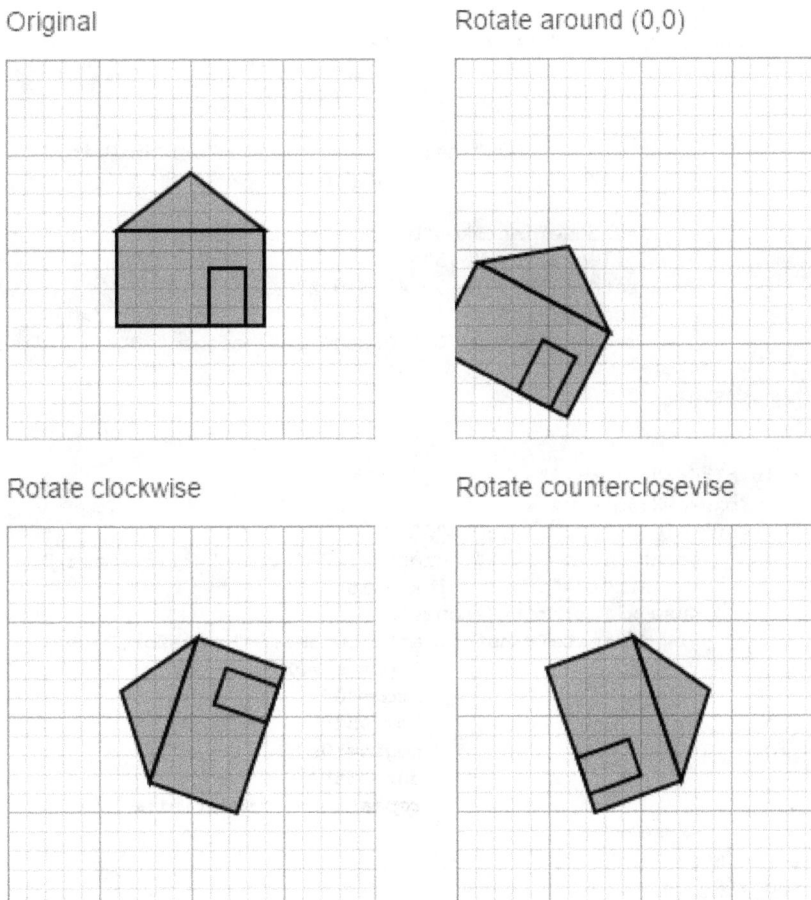

Figure 2-22. Demonstration of rotations.

Skew

The skew transformation stretches the coordinate space of 2D objects in a none-uniform manner. SVG has two skew transformations defined by the *skewX* and *skewY* attributes, which let you skew objects along one of axes. The general form is *skewX(angle)* and *skewY(angle)*. You can also perform the skew transformation along any other direction other than the axes by combining *skewX* with *skewY*.

Add *Views/Transformation/Skewing.cshtml* and replace its content with the following code:

```
@{
    ViewData["Title"] = ViewBag.Title;
}

<h3>@ViewBag.Title</h3>
@Html.Partial("_Links")
<hr />

<div class="container">
    <div class="row">
        <div class="col-sm-3">
            <p>Original</p>
            <svg width="200" height="200">

            .....

                <rect width="100%" height="100%" fill="url(#pxGrid)"
                    stroke="gray" stroke-width="1" />

                <g id="house" stroke="black" stroke-width="2" fill="red"
                    fill-opacity="0.5">
                    <path d="M50 10 90 40 H10 Z" />
                    <rect x="10" y="40" width="80" height="50" />
                    <rect x="60" y="60" width="20" height="30" fill="none" />
                </g>
            </svg>
        </div>

        <div class="col-sm-3">
            <p>skewX(45)</p>
            <svg width="200" height="200">
                <rect width="100%" height="100%" fill="url(#pxGrid)"
                    stroke="gray" stroke-width="1" />
                <use xlink:href="#house">
                    <animateTransform attributeName="transform"
                                type="skewX"
                                from="0"
                                to="45"
                                begin="0s"
                                dur="5s"
                                repeatCount="indefinite" />
                </use>
            </svg>
        </div>
    </div>
```

```
<div class="row" style="margin-top:10px">
    <div class="col-sm-3">
        <p>skewY(45)</p>
        <svg width="200" height="200">
            <rect width="100%" height="100%" fill="url(#pxGrid)"
                stroke="gray" stroke-width="1" />
            <use xlink:href="#house">
                <animateTransform attributeName="transform"
                                  type="skewY"
                                  from="0"
                                  to="45"
                                  begin="0s"
                                  dur="5s"
                                  repeatCount="indefinite" />
            </use>
        </svg>
    </div>

    <div class="col-sm-3">
        <p>skewX(45) + skewY(45)</p>
        <svg width="200" height="200">
            <rect width="100%" height="100%" fill="url(#pxGrid)"
                stroke="gray" stroke-width="1" />
            <use xlink:href="#house">
                <animateTransform attributeName="transform"
                                  type="skewY"
                                  from="0"
                                  to="45"
                                  begin="0s"
                                  dur="5s"
                                  repeatCount="indefinite" additive="sum"/>
                <animateTransform attributeName="transform"
                                  type="skewX"
                                  from="0"
                                  to="45"
                                  begin="0s"
                                  dur="5s"
                                  repeatCount="indefinite" additive="sum"/>
            </use>
        </svg>
    </div>
    </div>
</div>
```

The highlighted code animates three skew transformations: the first one uses *skewX*, the second one uses *skewY*, and the third one uses both *skewX* and *skewY* to perform skew transformation along the diagonal direction. Note that when we animate more than one transformation (*skewX* + *skewY* in this example), you need to use the *additive* attribute. The default value of this attribute is *replace*, which replaces the specified transformation in the object being animated. This would not work in a series of transformations, because the current animation would override the previous one. *By* setting additive to *sum* as we did in this example, SVG will accumulate the transformations.

Running this example produces the results shown in Figure 2-23.

Original

skewX(45)

skewY(45)

skewX(45) + skewY(45)

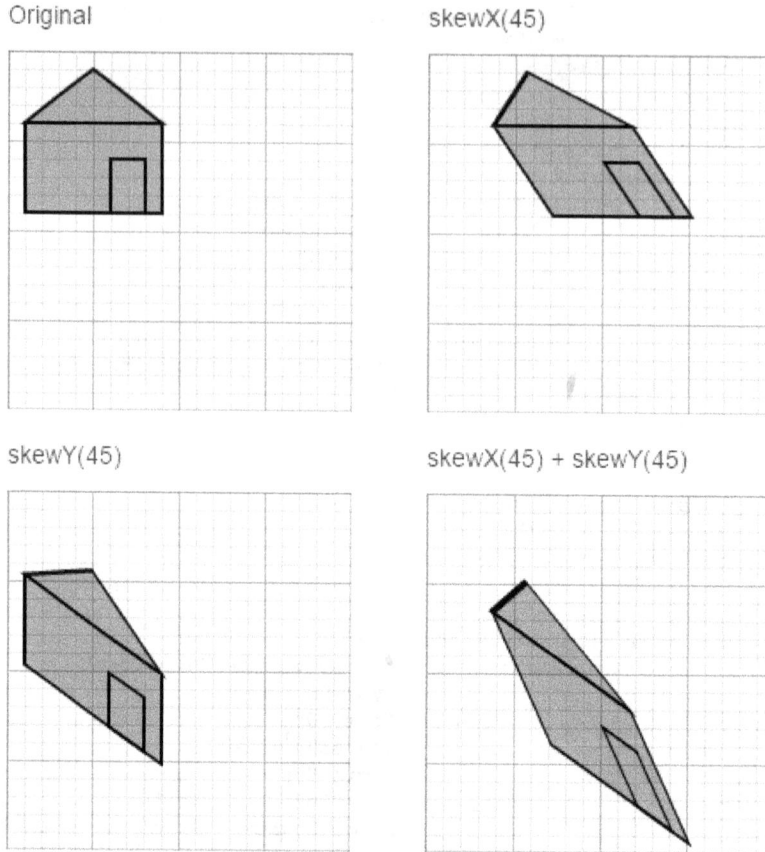

Figure 2-23. Demonstration of skew transformations.

View Box

It is often desirable to specify that a given set of graphics stretch to fit a particular container element. The *viewBox* attribute provides such a capability. You can think of the *viewBox* as the "real" coordinate system because it is the coordinate system used to draw the SVG graphic objects onto canvas. The *viewBox* can be smaller or bigger than the viewport, and it can be fully or partially visible inside the viewport.

Up to this point, we did not specifically define the *viewBox* in our examples. In this case, SVG sets the default *viewBox* to the size of the viewport. This is why all the positioning and drawing in our examples seemed to be done relative to the viewport coordinate system. Because once we created a viewport coordinate system using the *width* and *height* attributes, SVG created a default user coordinate system that is identical to it.

In fact, you can specify your own user coordinate system using the *viewBox* attribute. If the user coordinate system you choose the same aspect ratio (AR) as the viewport coordinate system, it will stretch to fill the viewport area. However, if your user coordinate system does not have the same aspect ratio, you can use the *preserveAspectRatio* attribute to specify whether or not the entire system will be visible inside the viewport or not.

The *viewBox* takes four parameters:

```
viewBox(min-x, min-y, width, height)
```

The *min-x* and *min-y* values determine the upper left corner of the *viewBox*, and the *width* and *height* determine its size.

Add *Views/Transformation/Viewbox.cshtml* and replace its content with the following code:

```
@{
    ViewData["Title"] = ViewBag.Title;
}

<h3>@ViewBag.Title</h3>
@Html.Partial("_Links")
<hr />

<div class="container">
    <div class="row">
        <div class="col-sm-3">
            <p>Viewbox = viewport(200, 200)</p>
            <svg width="200" height="200" viewBox="0,0,200,200">

                ......

                <rect width="100%" height="100%" fill="url(#pxGrid)"
                    stroke="gray" stroke-width="1" />

                <g id="house" stroke="black" stroke-width="2" fill="red"
                    fill-opacity="0.5" >
                    <path d="M50 10 90 40 H10 Z" />
                    <rect x="10" y="40" width="80" height="50" />
                    <rect x="60" y="60" width="20" height="30" fill="none" />
                </g>
            </svg>
        </div>

        <div class="col-sm-3">
            <p>viewBox(0,0,100,100)</p>
            <svg width="200" height="200" viewBox="0,0,100,100">
                <rect width="100%" height="100%" fill="url(#pxGrid)"
                    stroke="gray" stroke-width="1" />
                <use xlink:href="#house" />
            </svg>
        </div>
    </div>

    <div class="row" style="margin-top:10px">
        <div class="col-sm-3">
            <p>viewBox(0,0,150,100)</p>
            <svg width="200" height="200" viewBox="0,0,150,100">
                <rect width="100%" height="100%" fill="url(#pxGrid)"
                    stroke="gray" stroke-width="1" />
                <use xlink:href="#house" />
            </svg>
        </div>
```

```
<div class="col-sm-3">
    <p>viewBox(0,0,150,100): AR=none</p>
    <svg width="200" height="200" viewBox="0,0,150,100"
        preserveAspectRatio="none">
        <rect width="100%" height="100%" fill="url(#pxGrid)"
            stroke="gray" stroke-width="1" />
        <use xlink:href="#house" />
    </svg>
</div>
    </div>
</div>
```

Running this example produces the results shown in Figure 2-24.

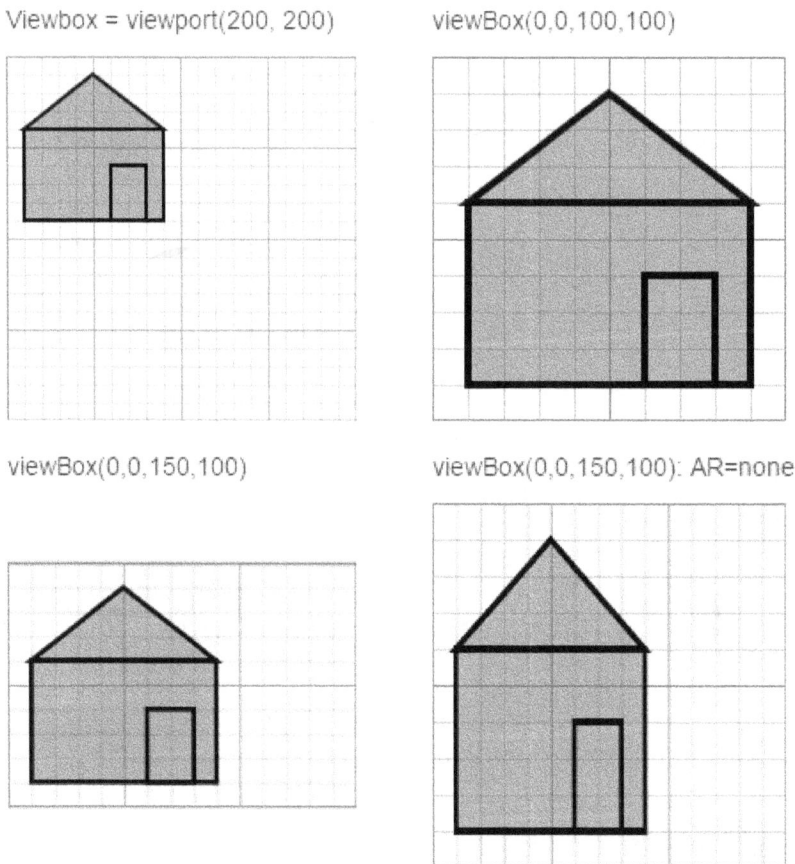

Figure 2-24. Demonstration of the viewBox attribute.

The highlighted code specifies four different *viewBox* attributes. In the first case, we set the *viewBox* to be identical to the viewport, so the resulted graphic object is the original house. In the second case, we have

```
<svg width="200" height="200" viewBox="0,0,100,100">
```

The code specifies a specific region of the canvas spanning from a top left point at (0, 0) to a point at (100, 100). The SVG graphic is then cropped to that region, and the region is scaled up (in a zoom-in-like effect) to fill the entire viewport. In this case, the user coordinate system is mapped to the viewport coordinate system so that one user unit is equal to two viewport units. Thus, anything you draw on the SVG canvas will be drawn relative to the new user coordinate system defined by the *viewBox*.

In the third case, we have

```
<svg width="200" height="200" viewBox="0,0,150,100">
```

In this case, the aspect ratio of height to width is no longer the same as that of the viewport. The entire *viewbox* fits inside the viewport and the aspect ratio of the *viewbox* is preserved. The *viewbox* is not stretched to cover the entire viewport area. It is centered inside the viewport both vertically and horizontally. This is the default behavior in SVG.

We can use the *preserveAspectRatio* attribute to force a uniform scaling for the purpose of preserving the aspect ratio of a graphic object. If we define a user coordinate system with an aspect ratio different from that of the viewport, and if browsers were to stretch the *viewbox* to fit the viewport, the difference in aspect ratios will cause the graphic object to be distorted, as shown in our four case:

```
<svg width="200" height="200" viewBox="0,0,150,100" preserveAspectRatio="none">
```

Here, we set the *preserveAspectRatio* to *none*, resulting in a distorted house object, as shown in Figure 2-24.

Colors and Paints

Almost everything visible on your computer screen is somehow related to colors and paints. For example, you use *stroke* and *fill* attributes to draw graphics and paint the fill of a shape. We have used colors throughout this book, but so far, we have done most of the work with the simple solid color. In fact, you can use colors to paint graphics objects with anything from simple solid colors to complex sets of patterns and images. This section covers the color system and some of the gradient color elements defined in SVG. It also discusses custom colormaps and color shading.

Colors

In SVG, a color is specified in the sRGB color space. This color structure describes a color in terms of alpha (A), red (R), green (G) and blue (B) channels. sRGB is a standard RGB color space created by HP and Microsoft for use in monitors, printers, and internet. It is designed to match typical home and office viewing conditions. sRGB has found wide applications. Software, LCD displays, digital cameras, printers, and scanners all follow the sRGB standard.

Several ways create color are available in SVG, including:

- A RGB color value. You specify each value as an interger in the range [0, 255] or a hex number (#*rgb* or #*rrggbb*).

- A predefined color name. You choose the color name from a list of keyword color names, such as aqua, black, blue, gray, etc. There are 147 keywords for color names available in SVG.

The keyword color names, like most CSS keywords, are case insensitive. Most official references use all lowercase, but you can use all caps or cameCase (i.e. capitalizing the start of subsequent words) to make them easier to read.

Let us consider an example, in which we will shows the resulting colors as an alphabetical patchwork from 147 color names.

Add a new folder named *Models* to the *Chapter02* project in Visual Studio 2017. Add a new class named *ColorNames.cs* to this folder with the following code:

```
using System.Collections.Generic;

namespace Chapter02.Models
{
    public class ColorNames
    {
        public List<string> SvgColors { get; set; }

        public ColorNames()
        {
            SvgColors = GetColorNames();
        }

        private List<string> GetColorNames()
        {
            var colors = new List<string>
            {
                "aliceBlue",
                "antiqueWhite",
                "aqua",
                "aquamarine",

                ......

                "violet",
                "wheat",
                "white",
                "whiteSmoke",
                "yellow",
                "yellowGreen"
            };
            return colors;
        }
    }
}
```

This model returns all of the 147 color names available in SVG.

Add a new controller named *ColorPaintController* to the *Controllers* directory and replace its content with the following code:

```
using Chapter02.Models;
using Microsoft.AspNetCore.Mvc;

namespace Chapter02.Controllers
{
    public class ColorPaintController : Controller
    {
        // GET: /<controller>/
        public IActionResult Index()
        {
```

```
            return View();
        }

        public IActionResult SvgColor(ColorNames model)
        {
            ViewBag.Title = "Colors and Paint: Colors in SVG";
            return View(model);
        }
    }
}
```

Now, add a new folder named *ColorPaint* to the *Views* folder. Add a new file named *SvgColor.cshtml* to this new folder with the following code:

```
@model Chapter02.Models.ColorNames

@{
    ViewData["Title"] = ViewBag.Title;
}
<h3>@ViewBag.Title</h3>
@Html.Partial("_Links")
<hr />

<div class="container">
    <div class="row">
        <div class="col-sm-9">
            <p>SVG colors from 147 color names</p>
            <svg id="svg" width="600" height="200" viewBox="0 0 21 7" />
        </div>
    </div>
</div>

<script>
    var model = @Html.Raw(Json.Serialize(Model));
    var svgNS = "http://www.w3.org/2000/svg";
    var svg = document.getElementById("svg");
    draw();

    function draw() {
        var col = 21;
        for (i = 0; i < model.svgColors.length; i++) {
            var name = model.svgColors[i].trim();
            var rect = document.createElementNS(svgNS, "rect");
            rect.setAttribute("width", 1);
            rect.setAttribute("height", 1);
            rect.setAttribute("x", i % col);
            rect.setAttribute("y", Math.floor(i / col));
            rect.style.setProperty("fill", name);
            var tip = document.createElementNS(svgNS, "title");
            tip.textContent = name;
            rect.insertBefore(tip, null);
            svg.insertBefore(rect, null);
        }
    }
</script>
```

In this view, the model is the *ColorNames* defined in the *Models* folder. The JavaScript variable can access this model using the *Json.Serialize* method

```
var model = @Html.Raw(Json.Serialize(Model));
```

This way, we pass the color names defined in the server-side to the JavaScript variable model. Inside the draw function, a for-loop cycles through each color name in the list, and assigns each rectangle's fill attribute to the color name. The color name is also used as the text content of a *<title>* element, which is then added as a child of each *<rect>* to create the tooltips – you will see the color name when you hover over the colored rectangle in your web browser. Finally, the styled *<rect>* element is added to the SVG.

Running this example produces the results shown in Figure 2-25.

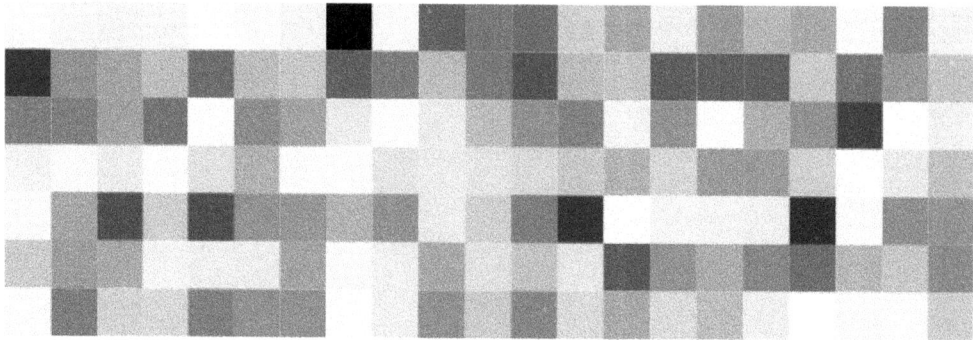

Figure 2-25. The colored rectangles created with all the named colors.

You can also define custom colors using function notation, like *rgb(r, g, b)*, or hexadecimal notation, like *#rrggbb* or *#rgb*. The values used in function notation may be either integers between 0, 255 or percentages. The values in a six-digit hexadecimal format also represent the numbers from 0 to 255, but do so using hexadecimal numbers. The three digit hexadecimal format is a shorthand for colors where both hexadecimal digits in each color are the same.

It is also possible to use HSL (hue-saturation-lightness) color model to describe colors as a mixture of a pure color and black, white, or gray.

Next, we will show you how to specify colors using different approaches. Add the following code to *Views/ColorPaint/SvgColor.cshtml*:

```html
<div class="row" style="margin-top:30px">
    <div class="col-sm-9">
        <p>Colors with different approaches</p>
        <svg id="svg" width="600" height="240">
            <rect x="10" y="10" width="200" height="100" fill="red"
                stroke="green" stroke-width="10"/>
            <text x ="30" y="40" fill="white">color name</text>

            <g transform="translate(220,0)">
                <rect x="10" y="10" width="200" height="100"
                    fill="rgb(255,0,0)" stroke="rgb(0,128,0)"
                    stroke-width="10" />
                <text x="30" y="40" fill="white">rgb(r,g,b)</text>
            </g>
```

```
<g transform="translate(0,120)">
    <rect x="10" y="10" width="200" height="100" fill="#FF0000"
        stroke="#008000" stroke-width="10" />
    <text x="30" y="40" fill="white">Hex number</text>
</g>
<g transform="translate(220,120)">
    <rect x="10" y="10" width="200" height="100"
        style="fill:hsl(0,100%,50%);stroke:hsl(120,100%,25%)"
        stroke-width="10" />
    <text x="30" y="40" fill="white">hsl(h,s,l)</text>
</g>
        </svg>
    </div>
</div>
```

This code generates the output shown in Figure 2-26.

Figure 2-26. Same colors created using different approaches.

For graphics you created in SVG, you may not always want solid regions of color. SVG uses three different attributes to control opacity of graphics: *opacity*, *fill-opacity*, and *stroke-opacity*. All of these can be set with presentation attributes or with CSS style rules. You can also use color functions to specify the opacity property. Partially transparent color can be defined using the *rgba(r, g, b, a)* and *hsla(h, s, l, a)* color functions. Opacity on the web is always expressed as a decimal number between 0.0 and 1. These numbers are also known as *alpha* values. The *a* value in *rgba* and *hsla* functions refers to the *alpha* channel.

Setting *opacity* to less than 1 creates a stacking context, flattening and containing all child content. In contrast, when you set *stroke-opacity* or *fill-opacity*, or when you use *rgba* or *hsla* color functions, the transparent effect is applied at the time each shape is drawn, to that colored section only.

Add the following code to *Views/ColorPaint/SvgColor.cshtml*:

```
<div class="row" style="margin-top:30px">
    <div class="col-sm-9">
        <p>Color opacity</p>
        <svg id="svg" width="450" height="240">
            <defs>
                <pattern id="minorGrid" width="10" height="10"
                    patternUnits="userSpaceOnUse">
```

```
            <path d="M 10 0 L 0 0 0 10" fill="none" stroke="gray"
                stroke-width="0.5" />
        </pattern>
        <pattern id="pxGrid" width="50" height="50"
            patternUnits="userSpaceOnUse">
            <rect width="50" height="50" fill="url(#minorGrid)" />
            <path d="M 50 0 L 0 0 0 50" fill="none" stroke="gray"
                stroke-width="1" />
        </pattern>
    </defs>
    <rect width="100%" height="100%" fill="url(#pxGrid)" stroke="gray"
        stroke-width="1" />

    <rect x="10" y="10" width="200" height="100" fill="red"
        stroke="green" stroke-width="10" opacity="0.8"/>
    <text x="20" y="40">opacity = 0.8</text>

    <g transform="translate(220,0)">
        <rect x="10" y="10" width="200" height="100" fill="red"
            stroke="green" stroke-width="10" opacity="0.5"/>
        <text x="20" y="40">opacity = 0.5</text>
    </g>
    <g transform="translate(0,120)">
        <rect x="10" y="10" width="200" height="100" fill="red"
            stroke="green" stroke-width="10" stroke-opacity="0.5"
            fill-opacity="0.5"/>
        <text x="20" y="40">fill-opacity = 0.5</text>
        <text x="20" y="65">stroke-opacity = 0.5</text>
    </g>
    <g transform="translate(220,120)">
        <rect x="10" y="10" width="200" height="100"
            style="fill:rgba(255,0,0,0.3);stroke:rgba(0,128,0,0.3)"
            stroke-width="10" />
        <text x="20" y="40">rgba(r,g,b,a): a = 0.3</text>
    </g>
</svg>
        </div>
    </div>
```

This code produces the results shown in Figure 2-27. You can see that the top two rectangles show the results by setting opacity = 0.8 and 0.5 respectively, while the rectangles at the bottom show results by setting opacity using *stroke-opacity* and *fill-opacity* (left) or *rgba* colors for the *stroke* and *fill* (right). When the stroke is partially transparent by setting the *stroke-opacity* and *fill-opacity* attributes, this creates a two-toned color effect, with the *fill* visible under the inside part of the *stroke*.

Linear Gradient

Rather than filling a graphic object with a solid color, you can fill it with a gradient, a smooth transition from one shade to another. Linear gradient allows you to paint an area with multiple colors and to create a blended fill effect that changes from one color to another.

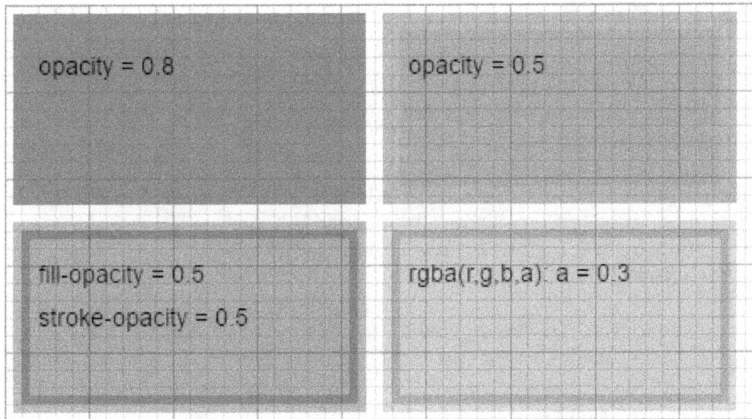

Figure 2-27.Demonstration of opacity.

A linear gradient follows a linear gradient axis. You can define the direction of the axis to obtain vertical, horizontal, or diagonal gradient effects. The gradient axis is defined by two points (*x*1, *y*1) and (*x*2, *y*2), which map to a 1 × 1 matrix. For example, a starting point (0, 0) and an ending point (0, 1) would produce a horizontal gradient, whereas a starting point (0, 0) and an ending point (1, 1) would generate a diagonal gradient. Note that the coordinates you used for the points (*x*1, *y*1) and (*x*2, *y*2) are not real coordinates. Instead, the linear gradient in SVG assigns the (0, 0) to the top-left corner and (1, 1) to the bottom-right corner of the area you want to fill, no matter how high and wide it actually is.

Along the axis, you specify a series of gradient stop colors. The stops are part of the structure of the gradient and the colors are part of the presentation. A stop object has two attributes of interest: *stop-color* and *offset*. The *offset* attribute defines a distance, ranging from 0 to 1, from the starting point of the axis at which the color specified in the *stop-color* property should begin.

Let us look at an example that uses the linear gradient. Add *Views/ColorPaint/LinearGradient.cshtml* and replace its content with the following code:

```
@{
    ViewData["Title"] = ViewBag.Title;
}

<h3>@ViewBag.Title</h3>
@Html.Partial("_Links")
<hr />

<style type="text/css">
    svg rect {
        stroke: black;
        stroke-width: 1px;
    }
</style>

<svg width="100%" height="1">
    <defs>
        <linearGradient id="vertical" x1="0" y1="0" x2="1" y2="0">
            <stop stop-color="green" offset="0" />
            <stop stop-color="yellow" offset="1" />
```

```
        </linearGradient>

        <linearGradient id="horizontal" x1="0" y1="0" x2="0" y2="1">
            <stop stop-color="green" offset="0" />
            <stop stop-color="yellow" offset="1" />
        </linearGradient>

        <linearGradient id="diagonal" x1="0" y1="0" x2="1" y2="1">
            <stop stop-color="green" offset="0" />
            <stop stop-color="yellow" offset="1" />
        </linearGradient>

        <linearGradient id="diagonal1" x1="0" y1="0" x2="1" y2="1">
            <stop stop-color="green" offset="0" />
            <stop stop-color="yellow" offset="0.5" />
        </linearGradient>

        <linearGradient id="vertical1" x1="0" y1="0" x2="1" y2="0">
            <stop stop-color="red" offset="0.2" />
            <stop stop-color="yellow" offset="0.3" />
            <stop stop-color="coral" offset="0.4" />
            <stop stop-color="blue" offset="0.5" />
            <stop stop-color="white" offset="0.6" />
            <stop stop-color="green" offset="0.7" />
            <stop stop-color="purple" offset="0.8" />
        </linearGradient>

        <linearGradient id="diagonal2" x1="0" y1="0" x2="1" y2="1">
            <stop stop-color="red" offset="0.2" />
            <stop stop-color="yellow" offset="0.3" />
            <stop stop-color="coral" offset="0.4" />
            <stop stop-color="blue" offset="0.5" />
            <stop stop-color="white" offset="0.6" />
            <stop stop-color="green" offset="0.7" />
            <stop stop-color="purple" offset="0.8" />
        </linearGradient>
    </defs>
</svg>

<div class="container">
    <div class="row">
        <div class="col-sm-9">
            <svg width="500" height="400">
                <g>
                    <rect x="2" y="2" width="200" height="100"
                        fill="url(#vertical)" />
                    <text x="20" y="40">vertical</text>
                </g>
                <g transform="translate(220,0)">
                    <rect x="2" y="2" width="200" height="100"
                        fill="url(#horizontal)" />
                    <text x="20" y="40">horizontal</text>
                </g>
                <g transform="translate(0,120)">
                    <rect x="2" y="2" width="200" height="100"
```

```
                    fill="url(#diagonal)" />
                <text x="20" y="40">diagonal</text>
            </g>
            <g transform="translate(220,120)">
                <rect x="2" y="2" width="200" height="100"
                    fill="url(#diagonal1)" />
                <text x="20" y="40">diagonal1</text>
            </g>
            <g transform="translate(0,240)">
                <rect x="2" y="2" width="200" height="100"
                    fill="url(#vertical1)" />
                <text x="20" y="40">vertical1</text>
            </g>
            <g transform="translate(220,240)">
                <rect x="2" y="2" width="200" height="100"
                    fill="url(#diagonal2)" />
                <text x="20" y="40">diagonal2</text>
            </g>
        </svg>
    </div>
  </div>
</div>
```

This code produces the results shown in Figure 2-28.

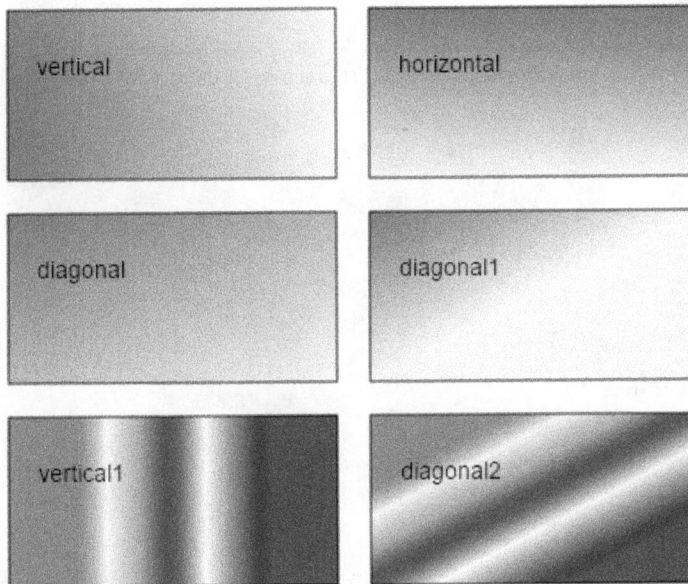

Figure 2-28. Rectangles filled with different linear gradients.

The first rectangle is filled by a linear gradient with a green and yellow gradient along a vertical axis. The second rectangle is filled by a horizontal gradient. Now, look at the third and fourth rectangles, which are filled by a diagonal gradient with green and yellow colors. The stop for the green color has an offset of 0, which means that the green color is placed at the very beginning of the gradient. The stop for the yellow color has an offset of 1 for the third rectangle, which places the yellow color at the end.

For fourth rectangle, however, the offset of the yellow color is set to 0.5, resulting in the much quicker color blend from green (at the top-left corner) to yellow in the middle. You can see from Figure 2-28 that the right side of the fourth rectangle is almost completely yellow. The last two rectangles are filled by a multicolor gradient, the first along a vertical gradient axis and the second along a diagonal gradient axis.

The linear gradient example presented here is simply intended to demonstrate the use of the gradient's basic features in SVG. In real-world applications, you may need to create a custom colormap in order to achieve specific visual effects. I will show you how to create custom colormap later in this chapter.

Radial Gradient

The radial gradient works in a similar way to the linear gradient. Like the linear gradient, it takes a sequence of colors with different offsets, but blends the colors in a radial pattern. A radial gradient is defined as a circle. The axis of the radial gradient starts from the origin, which is specified by (cx, cy), and runs to the outer edge of the circle.

We define the outer circle with the origin or center (cx, cy) and r (radius) attributes. All of these are in terms of percentages of the object's bounding box. The default value for all these attribute is 50%. The 0% stop point, also called the focal point, is by default placed at the center of the circle that defines the 100% stop point. If you wish to have the 0% stop point at some point other than the center of the circle, you need to change the fx and fy attributes. The focal point should be within the circle established for the 100% stop point.

Let us consider an example that demonstrates how to use the radial gradient to fill the shapes in SVG. Add *Views/ColorPaint/RadialGradient.cshtml* and replace its content with the following code:

```
@{
    ViewData["Title"] = ViewBag.Title;
}

<h3>@ViewBag.Title</h3>
@Html.Partial("_Links")
<hr />

<style type="text/css">
    svg rect {
        stroke: black;
        stroke-width: 1px;
    }
</style>

<svg width="100%" height="1">
    <defs>
        <radialGradient id="c1" cx="0.5" cy="0.5" r="1" fx="0.5" fy="0.5">
            <stop stop-color="red" offset="0" />
            <stop stop-color="yellow" offset="0.3" />
            <stop stop-color="green" offset="0.6" />
        </radialGradient>
        <radialGradient id="c2" cx="0.5" cy="0.5" r="1" fx="0" fy="0">
            <stop stop-color="red" offset="0" />
            <stop stop-color="yellow" offset="0.3" />
            <stop stop-color="green" offset="0.6" />
```

```
        </radialGradient>
        <radialGradient id="c3" cx="0.5" cy="0.5" r="0.5" fx="0.5" fy="0.5">
            <stop stop-color="red" offset="0" />
            <stop stop-color="yellow" offset="0.3" />
            <stop stop-color="green" offset="0.6" />
        </radialGradient>
        <radialGradient id="c4" cx="0.5" cy="0.5" r="1" fx="0" fy="0">
            <stop stop-color="red" offset="0" />
            <stop stop-color="yellow" offset="0.3" />
            <stop stop-color="green" offset="0.6" />
        </radialGradient>
        <radialGradient id="c5" cx="0.5" cy="0.5" r="0.4" fx="0.75" fy="0.75"
            spreadMethod="pad">
            <stop stop-color="red" offset="0" />
            <stop stop-color="yellow" offset="0.3" />
            <stop stop-color="green" offset="0.6" />
        </radialGradient>
        <radialGradient id="c6" cx="0.5" cy="0.5" r="0.4" fx="0.75" fy="0.75"
            spreadMethod="reflect">
            <stop stop-color="red" offset="0" />
            <stop stop-color="yellow" offset="0.3" />
            <stop stop-color="green" offset="0.6" />
        </radialGradient>
    </defs>
</svg>

<div class="container">
    <div class="row">
        <div class="col-sm-9">
            <svg width="550" height="400">
                <g>
                    <circle cx="82" cy="82" r="80" fill="url(#c1)" />
                    <text x="60" y="85">circle 1</text>
                </g>
                <g transform="translate(180,0)">
                    <circle cx="82" cy="82" r="80" fill="url(#c2)" />
                    <text x="60" y="85">circle 2</text>
                </g>
                <g transform="translate(360,0)">
                    <circle cx="82" cy="82" r="80" fill="url(#c3)" />
                    <text x="60" y="85">circle 3</text>
                </g>
                <g transform="translate(0,180)">
                    <circle cx="82" cy="82" r="80" fill="url(#c4)" />
                    <text x="60" y="85">circle 4</text>
                </g>
                <g transform="translate(180,180)">
                    <circle cx="82" cy="82" r="80" fill="url(#c5)" />
                    <text x="60" y="85">circle 5</text>
                </g>
                <g transform="translate(360,180)">
                    <circle cx="82" cy="82" r="80" fill="url(#c6)" />
                    <text x="60" y="85">circle 6</text>
                </g>
            </svg>
```

```
            </div>
        </div>
    </div>
```

This code produces the results shown in Figure 2-29.

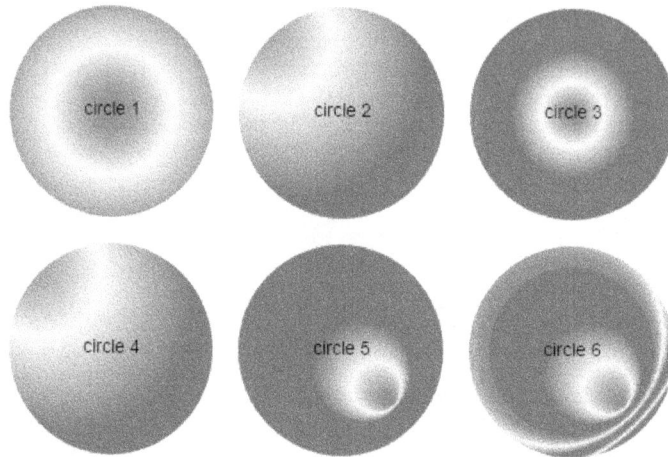

Figure 2-29. Demonstration of radial gradient.

Colormaps

Although SVG implements a variety of colors and gradients that allow you to paint graphic objects with a wide range of visual effects, you may sometimes need to create your own custom colormaps to meet the requirements of your specific applications. In this section, I will show you how to create several custom colormaps.

Colormaps are simply tables or lists of colors that are organized in some desired fashion. There are many ways to create a custom colormap. Here, I present a simple approach: creating a list of colors that you want to include in your colormap, setting these colors as the color stops, and finally interpolating colors using the linear gradient to construct the colormap.

In the following example, we will construct eight commonly used colormaps, including *spring, summer, autumn, winter, gray, jet, hot,* and *cool*. If you have ever used MATLAB, you should be familiar with these colormaps.

Add *Views/ColorPaint/Colormap.cshtml* and replace its content with the following code:

```
@Html.Partial("_Links")
<hr />
<style type="text/css">
    rect {
        stroke: black;
        stroke-width: 1px;
    }
</style>

<svg width="0" height="0">
    <defs>
```

```
<linearGradient id="spring">
    <stop stop-color="#FF00FF" offset="0" />
    <stop stop-color="#FF1CE3" offset="0.111" />
    <stop stop-color="#FF38C7" offset="0.222" />
    <stop stop-color="#FF55AA" offset="0.333" />
    <stop stop-color="#FF718E" offset="0.444" />
    <stop stop-color="#FF8D72" offset="0.556" />
    <stop stop-color="#FFAA55" offset="0.667" />
    <stop stop-color="#FFC639" offset="0.778" />
    <stop stop-color="#FFE21D" offset="0.889" />
    <stop stop-color="#FFFF00" offset="1.0" />
</linearGradient>
<linearGradient id="summer">
    <stop stop-color="#007F66" offset="0" />
    <stop stop-color="#1C8D66" offset="0.111" />
    <stop stop-color="#389B66" offset="0.222" />
    <stop stop-color="#55AA66" offset="0.333" />
    <stop stop-color="#71B866" offset="0.444" />
    <stop stop-color="#8DC666" offset="0.556" />
    <stop stop-color="#AAD466" offset="0.667" />
    <stop stop-color="#C6E266" offset="0.778" />
    <stop stop-color="#E2F066" offset="0.889" />
    <stop stop-color="#FFFF66" offset="1.0" />
</linearGradient>
<linearGradient id="autumn">
    <stop stop-color="#FF0000" offset="0" />
    <stop stop-color="#FF1C00" offset="0.111" />
    <stop stop-color="#FF3800" offset="0.222" />
    <stop stop-color="#FF5500" offset="0.333" />
    <stop stop-color="#FF7100" offset="0.444" />
    <stop stop-color="#FF8D00" offset="0.556" />
    <stop stop-color="#FFAA00" offset="0.667" />
    <stop stop-color="#FFC600" offset="0.778" />
    <stop stop-color="#FFE200" offset="0.889" />
    <stop stop-color="#FFFF00" offset="1.0" />
</linearGradient>
<linearGradient id="winter">
    <stop stop-color="#0000FF" offset="0" />
    <stop stop-color="#001CF0" offset="0.111" />
    <stop stop-color="#0038E2" offset="0.222" />
    <stop stop-color="#0055D4" offset="0.333" />
    <stop stop-color="#0071C6" offset="0.444" />
    <stop stop-color="#008DB8" offset="0.556" />
    <stop stop-color="#00AAAA" offset="0.667" />
    <stop stop-color="#00C69B" offset="0.778" />
    <stop stop-color="#00E28D" offset="0.889" />
    <stop stop-color="#00FF7F" offset="1.0" />
</linearGradient>
<linearGradient id="gray">
    <stop stop-color="#000000" offset="0" />
    <stop stop-color="#1C1C1C" offset="0.111" />
    <stop stop-color="#383838" offset="0.222" />
    <stop stop-color="#555555" offset="0.333" />
    <stop stop-color="#717171" offset="0.444" />
    <stop stop-color="#8D8D8D" offset="0.556" />
```

```
                    <stop stop-color="#AAAAAA" offset="0.667" />
                    <stop stop-color="#C6C6C6" offset="0.778" />
                    <stop stop-color="#E2E2E2" offset="0.889" />
                    <stop stop-color="#FFFFFF" offset="1.0" />
            </linearGradient>
            <linearGradient id="jet">
                    <stop stop-color="#00008F" offset="0" />
                    <stop stop-color="#0000FF" offset="0.111" />
                    <stop stop-color="#006FFF" offset="0.222" />
                    <stop stop-color="#00DFFF" offset="0.333" />
                    <stop stop-color="#4FFFAF" offset="0.444" />
                    <stop stop-color="#BFFF3F" offset="0.556" />
                    <stop stop-color="#FFCF00" offset="0.667" />
                    <stop stop-color="#FF5F00" offset="0.778" />
                    <stop stop-color="#EF0000" offset="0.889" />
                    <stop stop-color="#7F0000" offset="1.0" />
            </linearGradient>
            <linearGradient id="hot">
                    <stop stop-color="#0A0000" offset="0" />
                    <stop stop-color="#550000" offset="0.111" />
                    <stop stop-color="#9F0000" offset="0.222" />
                    <stop stop-color="#E90000" offset="0.333" />
                    <stop stop-color="#FF3500" offset="0.444" />
                    <stop stop-color="#FF7F00" offset="0.556" />
                    <stop stop-color="#FFC900" offset="0.667" />
                    <stop stop-color="#FFFF1F" offset="0.778" />
                    <stop stop-color="#FFFF8F" offset="0.889" />
                    <stop stop-color="#FFFFFF" offset="1.0" />
            </linearGradient>
            <linearGradient id="cool">
                    <stop stop-color="#00FFFF" offset="0" />
                    <stop stop-color="#1CE2FF" offset="0.111" />
                    <stop stop-color="#38C6FF" offset="0.222" />
                    <stop stop-color="#55AAFF" offset="0.333" />
                    <stop stop-color="#718DFF" offset="0.444" />
                    <stop stop-color="#8D71FF" offset="0.556" />
                    <stop stop-color="#AA55FF" offset="0.667" />
                    <stop stop-color="#C638FF" offset="0.778" />
                    <stop stop-color="#E21CFF" offset="0.889" />
                    <stop stop-color="#FF00FF" offset="1.0" />
            </linearGradient>
        </defs>
</svg>

<div class="container">
    <div class="row">
        <div class="col-sm-4">
            <svg width="600" height="400">
                <g>
                    <rect x="2" y="2" width="280" height="50"
                        fill="url(#spring)" />
                    <text x="20" y="30" fill="white">spring</text>
                </g>
                <g transform="translate(300,0)">
                    <rect x="2" y="2" width="280" height="50"
```

```
                          fill="url(#summer)" />
                  <text x="20" y="30" fill="white">summer</text>
          </g>
          <g transform="translate(0,70)">
                  <rect x="2" y="2" width="280" height="50"
                          fill="url(#autumn)" />
                  <text x="20" y="30" fill="white">autumn</text>
          </g>
          <g transform="translate(300,70)">
                  <rect x="2" y="2" width="280" height="50"
                          fill="url(#winter)" />
                  <text x="20" y="30" fill="white">winter</text>
          </g>
          <g transform="translate(0,140)">
                  <rect x="2" y="2" width="280" height="50"
                          fill="url(#gray)" />
                  <text x="20" y="30" fill="white">gray</text>
          </g>
          <g transform="translate(300,140)">
                  <rect x="2" y="2" width="280" height="50"
                          fill="url(#jet)" />
                  <text x="20" y="30" fill="white">jet</text>
          </g>
          <g transform="translate(0,210)">
                  <rect x="2" y="2" width="280" height="50"
                          fill="url(#hot)" />
                  <text x="20" y="30" fill="white">hot</text>
          </g>
          <g transform="translate(300,210)">
                  <rect x="2" y="2" width="280" height="50"
                          fill="url(#cool)" />
                  <text x="20" y="30" fill="white">cool</text>
          </g>
      </svg>
    </div>
  </div>
</div>
```

This code produces the results shown in Figure 2-30.

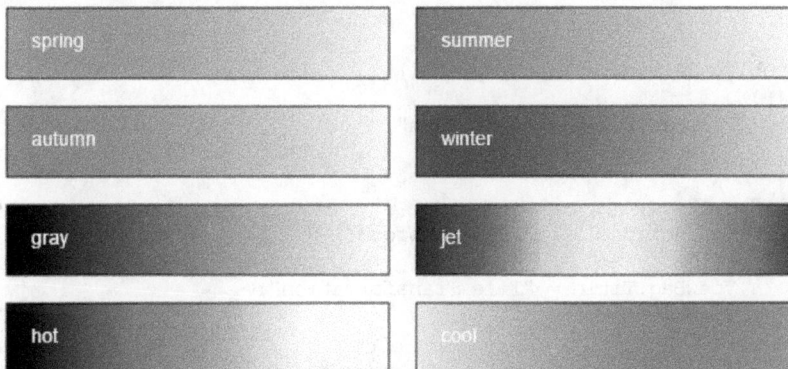

Figure 2-30. Demonstration of custom colormaps.

Tiles and Textures

SVG provides a number of different ways you can use to paint a shape: a single color, one or more gradient, custom colormaps, and repeating patterns etc. An SVG pattern defines a block of SVG graphics that will be used as a paint server for other shapes. Any SVG content can be used, including images, text, and shapes filled with gradients. A pattern is repeated in a rectangular titled layout.

In previous examples, we have used the *<pattern>* element to create the gridlines. In fact, a *<pattern>* element is similar to the gradient elements. The attributes on the element itself define the shape and size of the pattern tile (or repeating unit). The child content of the *<pattern>* element makes up the graphics that are drawn to the screen.

Grid Pattern Tiles

To understand how patterns work, it is best to see one in action. Add a new *TileTextureController.cs* to the *Controllers* folder in the project *Chapter02* and replace its content with the following code:

```
using Microsoft.AspNetCore.Mvc;
namespace Chapter02.Controllers
{
    public class TileTexture : Controller
    {
        // GET: /<controller>/
        public IActionResult Index()
        {
            return View();
        }

        public IActionResult GridTile()
        {
            ViewBag.Title = "Tile and Texture: A Grid Tile";
            return View();
        }

        public IActionResult ResizablePattern()
        {
            ViewBag.Title = "Tile and Texture: Resizable Pattern";
            return View();
        }

        public IActionResult ClipPath()
        {
            ViewBag.Title = "Clip Path";
            return View();
        }

        public IActionResult TileTransform()
        {
            ViewBag.Title = "Tile Transformation";
            return View();
        }
    }
}
```

Add a new folder named *TileTexture* to the project *Chapter02*. Add *GridTile.cshtml* to this folder and replace its content with the following code:

```
@{
    ViewData["Title"] = ViewBag.Title;
}

<h3>@ViewBag.Title</h3>
@Html.Partial("_Links")

<hr />

<svg width="0" height="0">
    <pattern id="p" width="50" height="50" patternUnits="userSpaceOnUse">
        <path d="M0 0 L50 0" stroke="red" />
        <path d="M0 10 L50 10" stroke="lightgreen" />
        <path d="M0 20 L50 20" stroke="lightgreen" />
        <path d="M0 30 L50 30" stroke="lightgreen" />
        <path d="M0 40 L50 40" stroke="lightgreen" />
        <path d="M0 0 L0 50" stroke="red" />
        <path d="M10 0 L10 50" stroke="lightgreen" />
        <path d="M20 0 L20 50" stroke="lightgreen" />
        <path d="M30 0 L30 50" stroke="lightgreen" />
        <path d="M40 0 L40 50" stroke="lightgreen" />
    </pattern>
</svg>

<div class="container">
    <div class="row">
        <div class="col-sm-10">
            <svg width="800" height="800">
                <text x="2" y="10">Unit pattern</text>
                <rect x="0" y="0" width="50" height="50" stroke="none"
                    fill="url(#p)" transform="translate(2,20)"/>

                <g transform="translate(110,0)">
                    <text x="0" y="10">Pattern tile: sqaure</text>
                    <rect x="0" y="0" width="250" height="250" stroke="black"
                        stroke-width="2" fill="url(#p)"
                        transform="translate(0,20)"/>
                </g>

                <g transform="translate(400,0)">
                    <text x="0" y="10">Pattern tile: cirle</text>
                    <circle cx="127" cy="127" r="125" stroke="black"
                        stroke-width="2" fill="url(#p)"
                        transform="translate(0,20)"/>
                </g>

                <g transform="translate(0,330)">
                    <text x="0" y="10">Pattern tile: text</text>
                    <text x="-10" y="200" stroke="black" stroke-width="2"
                        font-family="Arial Black" font-weight="bolder"
                        font-size="270" fill="url(#p)"
                        transform="translate(0,20)">MVC
```

```
                    </text>
                </g>
            </svg>
        </div>
    </div>
</div>
```

Here, we use the *<path>* element to define the grid pattern with the *id* = "*p*". The *id* attribute is required so that the pattern can be used. The *width* and *height* attributes define the size of each repeating tile. We specify the *patternUnits* attribute using *userSpaceOnUse* (i.e., the coordinate system in effect for the shape being filled).

We then set the *fill* attribute using our pattern for several shapes: a rectangle with the same size as the pattern (a unit pattern), a square, a circle and a text object.

Running this example produces the results shown in Figure 2-31.

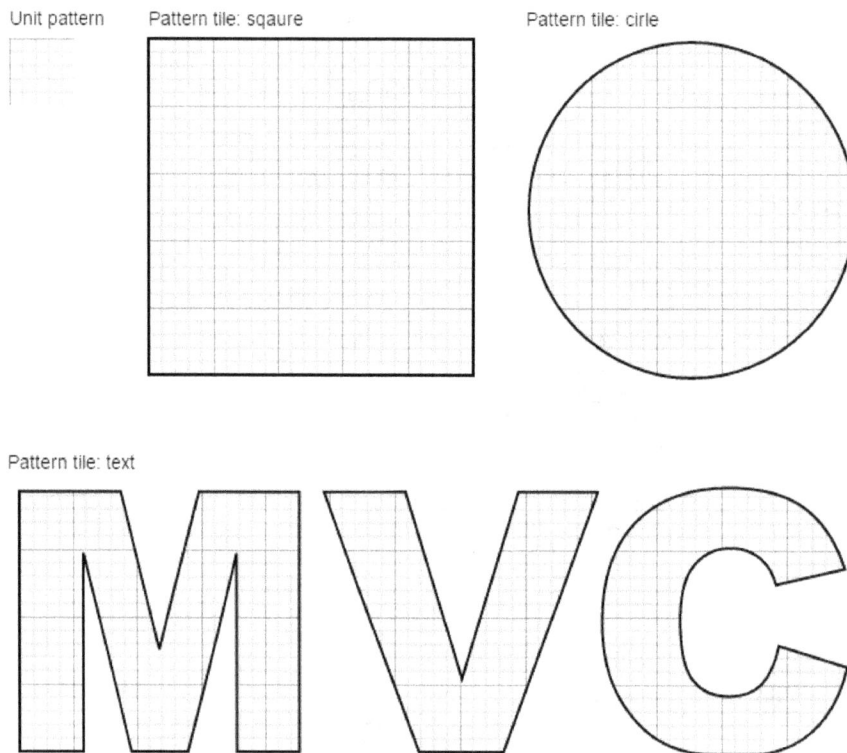

Figure 2-31. Demonstration of grid tiles.

Resizable Pattern Tiles

In the above example, we created a pattern with fixed size (*width* = *50px* and *height* = *50px*). Sometimes, you may want the pattern tiles to scale with the bounding box. Let us consider another example, which uses a pattern to divide a rectangle into a 4 × 4 pieces, each one outlined with a gridline. This type of overlay grid is a common tool in image editing software.

To demonstrate the scaling effect of the pattern titles, a thumbnail version of the image is also included with its own grid. Add *Views/TileTexture/ResizablePattern.cshtml* and replace its content with the following code:

```
@{
    ViewData["Title"] = ViewBag.Title;
}

<h3>@ViewBag.Title</h3>
@Html.Partial("_Links")
<hr />
<div class="container">
    <div class="row">
        <div class="col-sm-8">
            <svg viewBox="0 0 800 550">
                <pattern id="p" width="25%" height="25%">
                    <g stroke="red" stroke-width="5px">
                        <line x2="100%" />
                        <line y2="100%" />
                    </g>
                </pattern>

                <text y="20">Thumbnail</text>
                <image y="30" width="140" height="80"
                    xlink:href="../images/flower.jpg" />
                <rect y="30" width="140" height="80" fill="url(#p)" />

                <text y="160">Full image</text>
                <image y="170" width="700" height="400"
                    xlink:href="../images/flower.jpg" />
                <rect y="170" width="700" height="400" fill="url(#p)" />
            </svg>
        </div>
    </div>
</div>
```

Note that we first define the size of the <*svg*> element using a *viewBox* attribute. Next, we specify the pattern's size using percentages of the bounding box. I also stored an image file named *flower.jpg* in the *wwwroot/images* directory.

Running this example produces the output shown in Figure 2-32. You can play around with the resizable feature of this example to see how it works.

Clip Paths

SVG clip paths, or clipping, are used to clip an SVG graphic object to a certain path. Clipping is a graphical operation that allows you to fully or partially hide portion of an element. The clipped element can be any container or graphics object. A clipping path defines a region where everything on the inside of this region is allowed to show through but everything on the outside is clipped out and does not appear on the canvas. This region is known as the clipping region.

Add *Views/TileTexture/ClipPath.cshtml* and replace its content with the following code:

Thumbnail

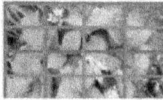

Full image

Figure 2-32. Demonstrateion of resizable pattern tiles.

```
@{
    ViewData["Title"] = ViewBag.Title;
}
<h3>@ViewBag.Title</h3>
@Html.Partial("_Links")

<hr />

<div class="container">
    <div class="row">
        <p>Clip path</p>
        <svg width="600" height="420" viewBox="0,0,600,500">
            <defs>
                <clipPath id="c1">
                    <circle cx="62" cy="62" r="50" />
                </clipPath>
                <clipPath id="p1">
                  <polyline points="5 120,65 60,115 110,165 60,215 120,5 120" />
                </clipPath>
            </defs>

            <g>
                <rect x="52" y="52" width="200" height="100" stroke="black"
                    stroke-width="2" style="fill:red" />
                <circle cx="62" cy="62" r="50" stroke="black" stroke-width="2"
                    fill="lightgreen" opacity="0.5" />
                <rect x="2" y="2" width="280" height="200" fill="none"
                    stroke="black" stroke-width="1" />
```

```
        <text x="120" y="20">Rectangle and circle</text>
    </g>
    <g transform="translate(300,0)">
        <rect x="52" y="52" width="200" height="100" stroke="black"
            stroke-width="2" style="fill:red; clip-path:url(#c1);" />
        <rect x="2" y="2" width="280" height="200" fill="transparent"
            stroke="black" stroke-width="1" />
        <text x="120" y="20">Clipping by circle</text>
    </g>

    <g transform="translate(0,220)">
        <rect x="52" y="52" width="200" height="100" stroke="black"
            stroke-width="2" style="fill:red" />
        <polyline points="5 120,65 60,115 110,165 60,215 120,5 120"
            stroke="black" stroke-width="2" fill="lightgreen"
            opacity="0.5" />
        <rect x="2" y="2" width="280" height="200" fill="transparent"
            stroke="black" stroke-width="1" />
        <text x="120" y="20">Rectangle and polygon</text>
    </g>

    <g transform="translate(300,220)">
        <rect x="52" y="52" width="200" height="100" stroke="black"
            stroke-width="2" style="fill:red; clip-path:url(#p1);" />
        <rect x="2" y="2" width="280" height="200" fill="transparent"
            stroke="black" stroke-width="1" />
        <text x="120" y="20">Clipping by polygon</text>
    </g>
    </svg>
    </div>
</div>
```

This code defines two clip paths: one is a simple circle and the other one is a polygon. These paths are then applied to the rectangle shapes. Running this example produces the results shown in Figure 2-33. On the left are the rectangle shapes with the clip path drawn on top of them. On the right are the resulting shapes after clipping.

By combining the path clipping with the animation, you can create impressive visual effects. Here, I will show you another example, where we create a pattern with *id = p* and will fill circles with it. We want to show one quarter of our circle at a time by creating a wedge like a pizza slice as our clip path. We then animate that clipped shape by spinning it the opposite direction of the pattern's movement. The second circle moving in the opposite direction of the first, and a clip path in the opposite corner rotating just like the first clip path round out the animation for an impressive visual effect.

Add the following code to *Views/TileTexture/ClipPath.cshtml*:

```
<div class="row">
    <p>Clip path animation</p>
    <svg width="400" height="420" viewBox="0,0,400,400">
        <defs>
            <clipPath id="path1">
                <path d="M0,0 200,0 200,200 0,200z" />
            </clipPath>
            <clipPath id="path2">
                <path d="M200,200 400,200 400,400 200,400z" />
            </clipPath>
```

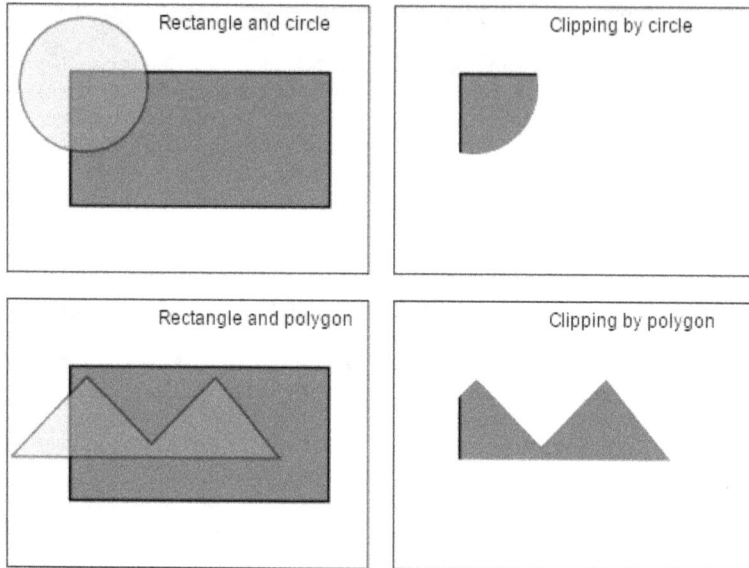

Figure 2-33. Demonstration of path clipping.

```
<linearGradient id="gradient1">
    <stop offset="5%" stop-color="white" />
    <stop offset="95%" stop-color="green" />
</linearGradient>
<linearGradient id="gradient2" x1="0" x2="0" y1="0" y2="1">
    <stop offset="5%" stop-color="red" />
    <stop offset="95%" stop-color="yellow" />
</linearGradient>

<pattern id="p" x="0" y="0" width="0.125" height="0.125">
    <rect x="0" y="0" width="50" height="50" fill="lightgreen" />
    <rect x="0" y="0" width="25" height="25"
        fill="url(#gradient2)" />
    <circle cx="25" cy="25" r="20" fill="url(#gradient1)"
        fill-opacity="0.5" />
</pattern>
</defs>

<rect width="400" height="400" fill="gray" />
<g style="clip-path:url(#path1);">
    <circle cx="200" cy="200" r="200" fill="url(#p)">
        <animateTransform attributeName="transform" begin="0s"
            dur="3s" type="rotate" from="360 200 200" to="0 200 200"
            repeatCount="indefinite" />
    </circle>
    <animateTransform attributeName="transform" begin="0s"
        dur="6s" type="rotate" from="0 200 200" to="360 200 200"
        repeatCount="indefinite" />
</g>

<g style="clip-path:url(#path2);">
```

```
<circle cx="200" cy="200" r="200" fill="url(#p)">
    <animateTransform attributeName="transform" begin="0s"
        dur="6s" type="rotate" from="0 200 200" to="360 200 200"
        repeatCount="indefinite" />
</circle>
<animateTransform attributeName="transform" begin="0s" dur="6s"
    type="rotate" from="0 200 200" to="360 200 200"
    repeatCount="indefinite" />
        </g>
    </svg>
</div>
```

This code produces the results shown in Figure 2-34.

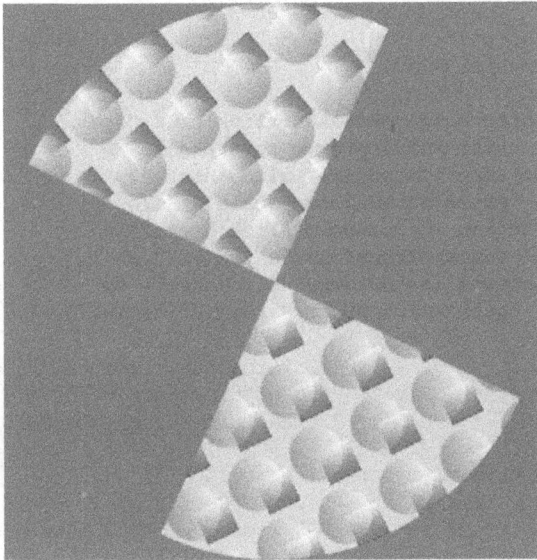

Figure 2-34. Clip path animation.

Pattern Transformation

The *patternTransform* attribute in SVG allows you to rotate, skew, scale, and translate a pattern. The transformation does not only apply to the pattern's contents, but also to the entire pattern tile, and to the repeating pattern of tiles laid end to end.

Let us consider an example, where we will perform the scale, rotate, and skew transformations on a grid pattern we created previously. Add *Views/TileTexture/TileTransform.cshtml* and replace its content with the following code:

```
@{
    ViewData["Title"] = ViewBag.Title;
}
<h3>@ViewBag.Title</h3>
@Html.Partial("_Links")

<hr />
```

```
<div class="container">
    <div class="row">
        <div class="col-sm-10">
            <svg width="800" height="800">
                <pattern id="p" width="50" height="50"
                    patternUnits="userSpaceOnUse">
                    <path d="M0 10 L50 10" stroke="lightgreen" />
                    <path d="M0 20 L50 20" stroke="lightgreen" />
                    <path d="M0 30 L50 30" stroke="lightgreen" />
                    <path d="M0 40 L50 40" stroke="lightgreen" />
                    <path d="M10 0 L10 50" stroke="lightgreen" />
                    <path d="M20 0 L20 50" stroke="lightgreen" />
                    <path d="M30 0 L30 50" stroke="lightgreen" />
                    <path d="M40 0 L40 50" stroke="lightgreen" />
                    <path d="M0 0 L50 0" stroke="red" />
                    <path d="M0 0 L0 50" stroke="red" />
                </pattern>

                <pattern id="pRotate" xlink:href="#p"
                    patternTransform="rotate(45)" />
                <pattern id="pScale" xlink:href="#p"
                    patternTransform="scale(2)" />
                <pattern id="pSkewx" xlink:href="#p"
                    patternTransform="skewX(30)" />
                <pattern id="pSkewxy" xlink:href="#p"
                    patternTransform="skewX(30) skewY(30)" />

                <text x="2" y="10">Original unit pattern</text>
                <rect x="0" y="0" width="50" height="50" stroke="none"
                    fill="url(#p)" transform="translate(2,20)" />

                <g transform="translate(0,100)">
                    <text x="2" y="10">Pattern scale(2)</text>
                    <rect x="2" y="0" width="250" height="250" stroke="black"
                    stroke-width="2" fill="url(#pScale)"
                    transform="translate(0,20)" />
                </g>

                <g transform="translate(270,100)">
                    <text x="2" y="10">Pattern rotate(45)</text>
                    <rect x="2" y="0" width="250" height="250" stroke="black"
                        stroke-width="2" fill="url(#pRotate)"
                        transform="translate(0,20)" />
                </g>

                <g transform="translate(0,400)">
                    <text x="2" y="10">Pattern skewX(30)</text>
                    <rect x="2" y="0" width="250" height="250" stroke="black"
                        stroke-width="2" fill="url(#pSkewx)"
                        transform="translate(0,20)" />
                </g>
                <g transform="translate(270,400)">
                    <text x="2" y="10">Pattern skewX(30) + skewY(30)</text>
                    <rect x="2" y="0" width="250" height="250" stroke="black"
                        stroke-width="2" fill="url(#pSkewxy)"
```

```
                transform="translate(0,20)" />
          </g>
        </svg>
      </div>
    </div>
  </div>
```

Here, we first define the original grid pattern with *id* = *p*, and then create four derived patterns *pRotate*, *pScale*, *pSkewx*, and *pSkewxy* by performing various transformations on the original grid pattern *p*. Finally, we create four squares and set their *fill* attribute to those four derived patterns respectively.

Running this example produces the results shown in Figure 2-35.

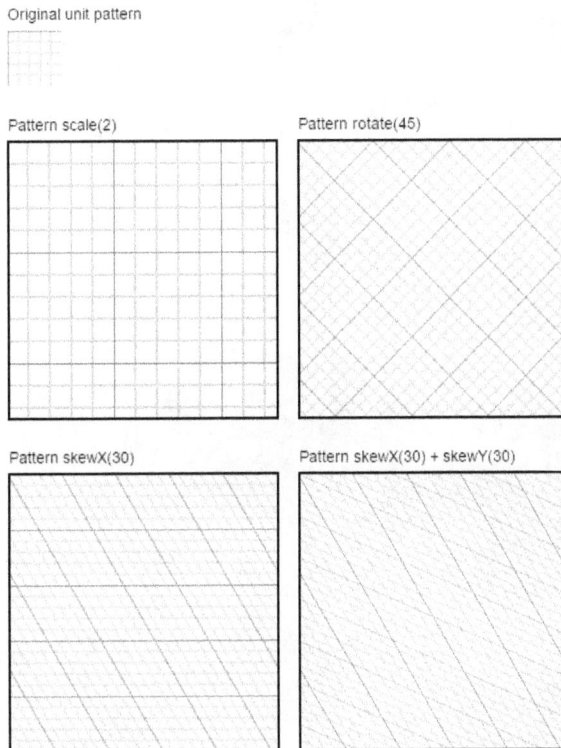

Figure 2-35. Demonstration of tile transformations.

Chapter 3
Dynamic SVG Graphics with D3

In the preceding chapter, we described the basic features of SVG and demonstrated how to create a variety of 2D graphic objects in SVG. All the examples were relatively modest and were written using the standard SVG tags. You may notice that using SVG tags is easy when you are dealing with simple graphics objects. However, when you use this method to create a complex graphics that may consist of hundreds of simple shapes such as rectangles, you have to write hundreds of lines of code for creating those shapes. Clearly, coding by hand using SVG tags for complex graphics becomes extremely difficult. Furthermore, graphics created using SVG tags are usually static, which makes it almost impossible to modify the graphics dynamically because you cannot easily separate the data from the logical decisions you have made upfront.

D3.js is a JavaScript library for manipulating documents based on data. It helps you bring data to life using HTML, SVG and CSS. D3 allows you to create amazing data visualizations using simple data-driven approach by decoupling the data and the logic needed to represent the data. You can use D3 to build any representation, starting from the most basic graphic elements such as circles, lines, rectangles, etc. by manipulating the SVG elements based on data. D3 provides the building blocks and tools to assemble complex graphics structures based on SVG. The result of this approach is the continuous development of new structures, which are graphically rich and open to all sorts of interactions and animations. D3 is the perfect tool for those who want to develop new graphics solutions for aspects not covered by existing frameworks.

In this chapter, I will provide a brief introduction to D3 and demonstrate how to use D3 to create various graphics objects based on SVG.

D3 Basics

In this section, you will learn how to use D3 to create basic SVG elements and how to apply transformations to these graphics elements.

Install D3 Package

First thing you need before using the D3 data visualization tool is to install the package in your ASP.NET Core MVC application. Open Visual Studio 2017, start a new ASP.NET Core MVC project, and name it *Chapter03*.

We will use Bower to install client-side packages. Bower is a package manager for the web. Within the .NET Framework, it fills the void left by NuGet's inability to deliver static content files. For ASP.NET Core MVC projects, these static files are inherent to client-side libraries like jQuery and Bootstrap. The new projects created with the ASP.NET Core project templates set up the client-side build process. jQuerry and Bootstrap are installed, and Bower is supported by default.

Right-click the project in Solution Explorer and select *Manage Bower Packages*. In the *Bower: Chapter03* window, click the *Browse* tab, and then filter the packages list by entering *d3* in the search box, as shown in Figure 3-1. Confirm that the "*Save changes to bower.json*" checkbox is checked. Select a version (here, the latest version of v4.7.3 will be selected) from the drop-down list and click the *install* button.

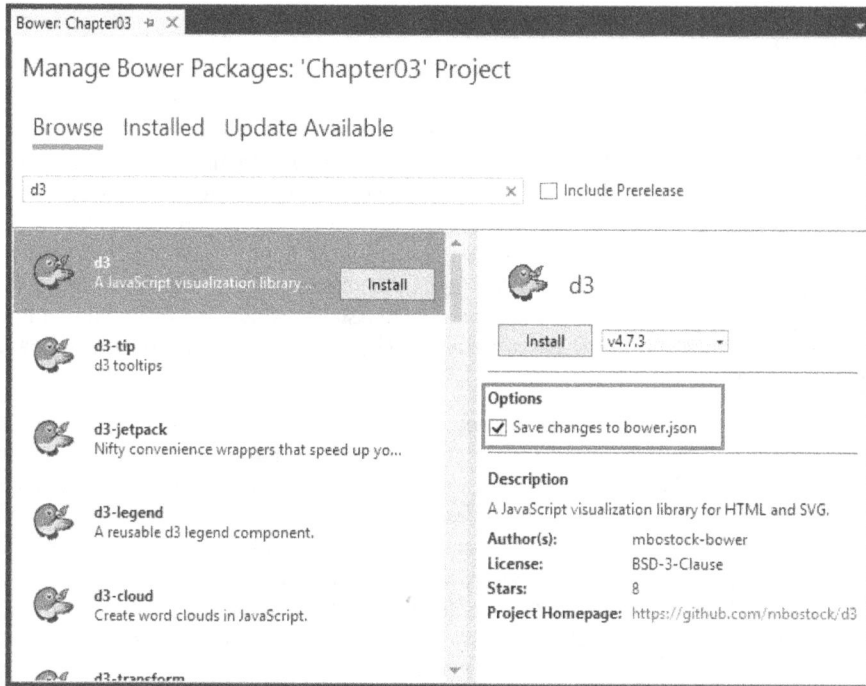

Figure 3-1. Install d3.js package using Bower.

The d3.js package should be installed to the wwwroot/lib folder, as shown in Figure 3-2.

You can then use the package in your project by referencing it in your view pages (.cshtml files):

```
<script src="~/lib/d3/d3.min.js"></script>
```

You can also place this reference to the *Views/Shared/_Layout.cshtml* file to avoid its appearance on every view page.

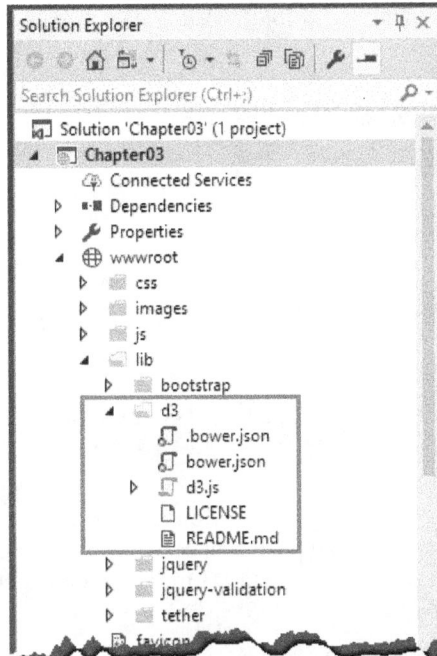

Figure 3-2. d3.js package installed to the lib folder.

Creating SVG Elements

Here, you will learn how to create an SVG element and how to nest it in a group using <g> tag. We then apply the transformations to groups of elements. Add *Controllers/ShapesController.cs* and replace its content with the following code:

```
using Microsoft.AspNetCore.Mvc;

namespace Chapter03.Controllers
{
    public class ShapesController : Controller
    {
        // GET: /<controller>/
        public IActionResult Index()
        {
            ViewBag.Title = "Shapes: Home";
            return View();
        }

        public IActionResult BasicShapes()
        {
            ViewBag.Title = "Shapes: Basic Shapes";
            return View();
        }
    }
}
```

Add a new folder named *Shapes* to the *Views* folder. Add *Views/Shapes/BasicShapes.cshtml* and replace its content with the following code:

```
@{
    ViewData["Title"] = ViewBag.Title;
}

<h3>@ViewBag.Title</h3>
@Html.Partial("_Links")

<hr />
<script src="~/lib/d3/d3.min.js"></script>

<div class="container">
    <div class="col-sm-2">
        <svg width="150" height="150" id="svg1" />
    </div>
</div>
```

Here, we first add the reference of D3 library to the views so that we can access D3 functions. We then add a *<svg>* tag with specified *width* and *height* attributes, which will be used as a container for the SVG graphics objects. Now, we can use JavaScript and D3 to create a SVG circle. Add the following code snippet to the *BasicShapes.cshtml* file:

```
<script type="text/javascript">
    var svg = d3.select("#svg1");
    svg.append("circle")
        .attr("cx", 55)
        .attr("cy", 55)
        .attr("r", 50)
        .style("fill", "lightgray")
        .style("stroke", "black")
        .style("stroke-width", "2");
</script>
```

This code consists of several D3 commands, including *select, append, attr,* and *style*. Selection in D3 is probably the most fundamental task that you need to perform with any data visualization application. To extract a selection from a document, D3 provides two methods: *select* and *selectAll*.

```
d3.select("selector")
```

selects the first element that matches the selector, returning a selection with only one element.

```
d3.selectAll("selector")
```

selects all elements that match the selector, returning a selection with all these elements. In our example, we select only one element and the selector is an *<svg>* element with *id* of *svg1*.

The *append* method in D3 is another popular method for adding elements. It adds a new element, passed as its argument, to the end of all the existing elements contained in the selected tag. Here, we use this method to add a circle to the selected *svg* element.

Next, we use the operator, *attr*, to define the attributes for the appended element, or modifying existing attributes.

If you look at the preceding code again, you may notice a period in front of every method and operator. This syntax is called chain syntax, which is the similar to the syntax in jQuery.

Another method, *style*, is used to specify or change a CSS style for the appended element. Once you understand this principle, it is very simple to create other shapes. Running this example produces the output shown in Figure 3-3.

Figure 3-3. A circle created using D3.

We can use D3 to create a reusable graphics block with the *groups* of element and *defs* commands, as we did using *<g>* tags in the preceding chapter. Here, we want to recreate the *house* object used in the examples of Chapter 2. In order to reuse the function, we add a JavaScritp function to the *wwwroot/js/site.js* file. Here is the code for this function:

```
function creatHouse(svg) {
    var house = svg.append("defs").append("g")
        .attr("id", "house")
        .style("fill", "red")
        .style("fill-opacity", 0.5)
        .style("stroke", "black")
        .style("stroke-width", "2");

    house.append("path")
        .attr("d", "M50 10 90 40 H10 Z")

    house.append("rect")
        .attr("x", 10)
        .attr("y", 40)
        .attr("width", 80)
        .attr("height", 50);

    house.append("rect")
        .attr("x", 60)
        .attr("y", 60)
        .attr("width", 20)
        .attr("height", 30)
        .style("fill", "none");
}
```

This function takes *svg* selector variable as input argument. To define the house object for reuse purpose, we add a new *<defs>* and *<g>* tags to svg selector. The *<g>* tag is a group operator, which groups several elements together. Note that we assign an *id* of *house* to this *<g>* tag, which will be used to create the house objects. We then add a path and two rectangles to this group to construct the house object. You should compare this function with the code used for creating the same house object in Chapter 2 and try to understand how we convert the code based on SGV tags into a D3 script.

Now add the following code snippet to the *Views/Shapes/BasicShapes.cshtml* file:

```
<div class="row">
```

```
<div class="col-sm-2">
    <svg width="150" height="150" id="svg1" />
</div>

<div class="col-sm4">
    <svg width="250" height="250" id="svg2" />
</div>
</div>
```

Here, the new *<svg>* tag with *id* = *svg2* is used to host the house objects. We will use the following JavaScript code to create fifteen house objects:

```
@section scripts{
    <script type="text/javascript">

        // circle
        var svg1 = d3.select("#svg1");
        svg1.append("circle")
            .attr("cx", 55)
            .attr("cy", 55)
            .attr("r", 50)
            .style("fill", "lightgray")
            .style("stroke", "black")
            .style("stroke-width", "2");

        // house objects
        var svg2 = d3.select("#svg2");
        creatHouse(svg2);

        var w = 100;
        var h = 100;
        for (var i = 0; i < 5; i++) {
            for (var j = 0; j < 3; j++) {
                svg2.append("g")
                    .attr("class", "house")
                    .append("use")
                    .attr("xlink:href", "#house");
                    .attr("x", i * w)
                    .attr("y", j * h);
            }
        }
    </script>
}
```

Note that we add a *@section scripts* to enclose our JavaScript in order to use the JavaScript libraries at the bottom of the *_Layout.cshtml* file. If you put the script libraries at the top of the page, there will be page-loading issues because the page may stop or take a long time to load. Putting the script libraries at the bottom allows the page renders fully before script libraries loaded.

The code first selects the SVG tag and then calls the *createHouse* function to define the house object. As long as the house object is defined on the selected SVG tag, we can use *for* loops to create fifteen house objects with the *use* command and corresponding *xlink* to the *house* (*id*). Here, we use the *x* and *y* attributes to position the objects in the right location. In fact, you can use the same code to create thousands of *house* objects without any addition coding, which demonstrates the power of D3 in manipulating SVG elements.

Running this code produces the results shown in Figure 3-4.

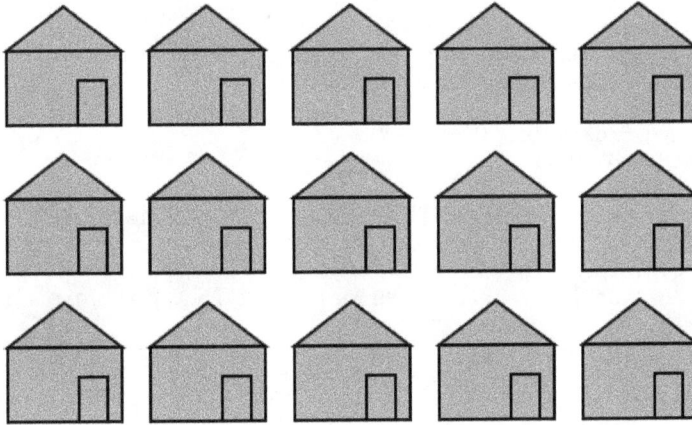

Figure 3-4. House objects created using D3.

Transformations

We can also use D3 to perform transformations on graphics objects. To accomplish these tasks, we add the *transform* attribute to the appropriate SVG elements. This section examines the details of these transformations based on D3.

In the preceding section, we defined a house object as a group element, and created and placed the houses at different location by changing their x- and y-coordinates. You can also achieve this using a translate transformation. Here, we will discuss other types of transformations, including *scale*, *rotate*, and *skew*.

Add *Views/Shapes/Transform.cshtml* and replace its content with the following code:

```
@{
    ViewData["Title"] = ViewBag.Title;
}

<h3>@ViewBag.Title</h3>
@Html.Partial("_Links")

<hr />
<script src="~/lib/d3/d3.min.js"></script>

<div class="container">
    <div class="row">
        <p>Scale</p>
        <svg width="700" height="250" id="scale" />
    </div>
    <div class="row">
        <p>Rotate</p>
        <svg width="700" height="150" id="rotate" />
    </div>
    <div class="row">
        <p>Skew</p>
        <svg width="700" height="300" id="skew" />
```

```
        </div>
    </div>

@section scripts{
    <script type="text/javascript">

        // scale
        var svg = d3.select("#scale");
        creatHouse(svg);
        var w = [0, 100, 300, 400];
        var ts = ["", "scale(2,1)", "scale(1,2)", "scale(2,2)"];
        for (var i = 0; i < 4; i++) {
            svg.append("g")
                .attr("transform", "translate(" + w[i] + ",0)" + ts[i])
                .attr("class", "house")
                .append("use")
                .attr("xlink:href", "#house");
        }

        /* more code will be added here. */

    </script>
}
```

Here, we first creates three *<svg>* tags with *ids*: *scale*, *rotate*, and *skew*. It then adds script for the *scale* transformation, where we select the *<svg>* tag as the container for houses after scale transformation and call the *createHouse* function to define the house object. Next, we define an array variable *ts* using four different *scales*: original shape (no scale), scale 2× in the *x*-direction, scale 2× in the *y*-direction, and scale 2× in both the *x*- and *y*-directions (i.e., the diagonal direction) with the code:

```
var ts = ["", "scale(2,1)", "scale(1,2)", "scale(2,2)"];
```

Finally, we use the *for*-loop to create the scaled houses and place them at the right positions using translate transformation.

Running this code generates the output shown in Figure 3-5.

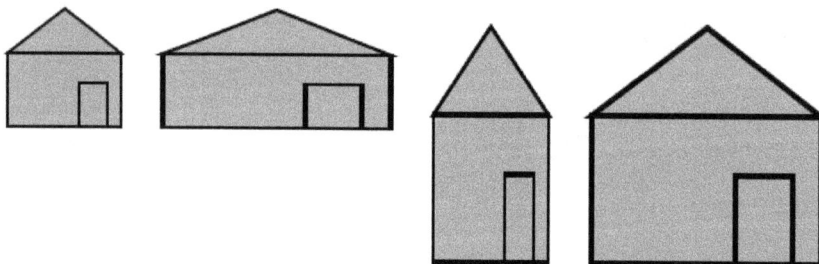

Figure 3-5. Demonstration of scale transformation using D3.

We now consider the rotate transformation. Add the following script to the *Transform.cshtml* view:

```
// rotate
svg = d3.select("#rotate");
creatHouse(svg);
var w = 120;
```

```
var ts = ["", "rotate(20,50,50)", "rotate(40,50,50)", "rotate(60,50,50)",
         "rotate(80,50,50)"];
for (var i = 0; i < 5; i++) {
    svg.append("g")
        .attr("transform", "translate(" + i * w + ",0)" + ts[i])
        .attr("class", "house")
        .append("use")
        .attr("xlink:href", "#house");
}
```

Here, we create five house objects with *rotate* transformations by 0, 20, 40, 60, and 80 degrees. Running this example produces the results shown in Figure 3-6.

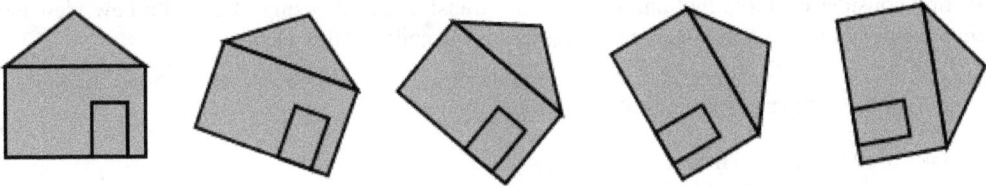

Figure 3-6. Demonstration of rotate transformations using D3.

Finally, we consider the *skew* transformation. Add the following script to the view:

```
// skew
var svg = d3.select("#skew");
creatHouse(svg);
var w = [0, 80, 280, 350];
var ts = ["", "skewX(45)", "skewY(45)", "skewX(45) skewY(45)"];
for (var i = 0; i < 4; i++) {
    svg.append("g")
        .attr("transform", "translate(" + w[i] + ",0)" + ts[i])
        .attr("class", "house")
        .append("use")
        .attr("xlink:href", "#house");
}
```

Here, we create four house objects with *skew* transformations: the original house, *skewX*, *skewY*, and *skewX + skewY*. Running this example produces the results shown in Figure 3-7.

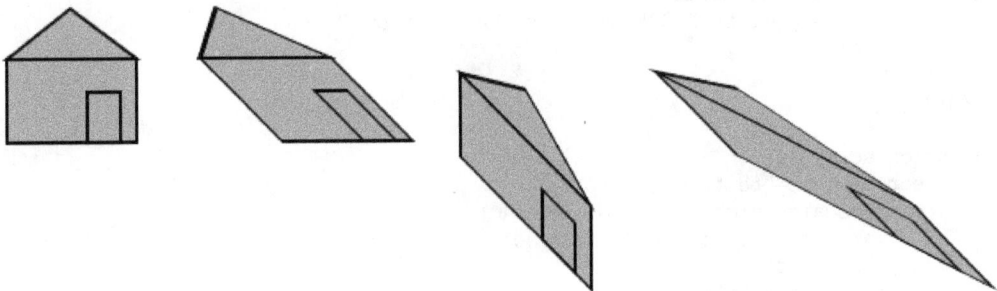

Figure 3-7. Demonstration of skew transformation using D3.

Animations

You have seen that values of attributes, styles, and transforms can be dynamically defined and modified using D3. But, D3 offers more – you can even animate your graphics objects. D3 provides three functions to this purpose: *transition*, *delay*, and *duration*.

You can apply these functions to the SVG elements, and D3 can recognize any kind of values and interpolate them to provide you a smooth animation effect.

We define a transition when an SVG shape passes from one state to another. Both the starting state and the final state are characterized by several parameters that define the color, the shape, the size, and the position of an object.

Let us first consider example that animates several transformations using D3. Add a new view named *Animation.cshtml* to the *Views/Shapes* folder. Here is the code for this view:

```
@{
    ViewData["Title"] = ViewBag.Title;
}
<h3>@ViewBag.Title</h3>
@Html.Partial("_Links")
<hr />
<script src="~/lib/d3/d3.min.js"></script>

<div class="container">
    <div class="row">
        <div class="col-sm-3">
            <p>Scale Animation: one time</p>
            <svg width="200" height="200" id="scale" />
        </div>
        <div class="col-sm-3">
            <p>Scale Animation: repeat</p>
            <svg width="200" height="200" id="scale1" />
        </div>
     </div>
    <div class="row">
        <div class="col-sm-3">
            <p>Rotate Animation</p>
            <svg width="200" height="200" id="rotate" />
        </div>
        <div class="col-sm-4">
            <p>Skew Animation</p>
            <svg width="300" height="200" id="skew" />
        </div>
    </div>
</div>

@section scripts{
    <script type="text/javascript">
        // scale animation: one time
        var svg = d3.select("#scale");
        creatHouse(svg);
        svg.append("g")
            .attr("class", "house")
            .append("use")
```

```
        .attr("xlink:href", "#house")
        .transition()
        .duration(5000)
        .delay(100)
        .attr("transform", "scale(2)");

 // scale animation: repeat
var svg = d3.select("#scale1");
 creatHouse(svg);
 scaleAnimate();
 function scaleAnimate() {
     var ts = svg.append("g")
         .attr("class", "house")
         .append("use")
         .attr("xlink:href", "#house");
     repeat();
     function repeat() {
         ts.transition()
             .duration(2000)
             .attr("transform", "scale(2)")
             .transition()
             .duration(2000)
             .attr("transform", "scale(1)")
             .on("end", repeat);
     };
 };

 // rotate animation: repeat
 var svg = d3.select("#rotate");
 creatHouse(svg);
 rotateAnimate();
 function rotateAnimate() {
     var ts = svg.append("g")
         .attr("class", "house")
         .append("use")
         .attr("xlink:href", "#house")
         .attr("x", 50)
         .attr("y", 50);
     repeat();
     function repeat() {
         ts.transition()
             .duration(5000)
             .ease(d3.easeLinear)
             .attrTween("transform", rotTween)
             .on("end", repeat);
     };
 };

 function rotTween() {
     var i = d3.interpolate(0, 360);
     return function (t) {
         return "rotate(" + i(t) + ",100,100)";
     };
 };
```

```
// skew animation: repeat
var svg = d3.select("#skew");
creatHouse(svg);
skewAnimate();
function skewAnimate() {
    var ts = svg.append("g")
        .attr("class", "house")
        .append("use")
        .attr("xlink:href", "#house");
    repeat();
    function repeat() {
        ts.transition()
            .duration(2000)
            .attr("transform", "skewX(45)skewY(45)")
            .transition()
            .duration(2000)
            .attr("transform", "skewX(0)skewY(0)")
            .on("end", repeat);
    };
};
</script>
}
```

This code animates three different transformations, including *scale*, *rotate*, and *skew*. We use two different approaches to animate the scale transformation: the first one we specify the *duration* and *delay* attributes. The animation will stops after the duration ends. In the second approach, we implement a *repeat* function to continue the animation without stopping. For the *rotate* and *skew* transformations, we also use the *repeat* function to create continuous animations. In particular, for the rotate animation, we create a custom tween function named *rotTween*, which is necessary for a continuous *rotate* animation. This is because D3 normalizes the SVG transformations: i.e., D3 sees that the house object at beginning (0 degree) is the same as at the end (360 degrees). So, if you specify the rotation from 0 to 360, D3 simply takes a shortcut by doing nothing.

Running this example produces the results shown in Figure 3-8.

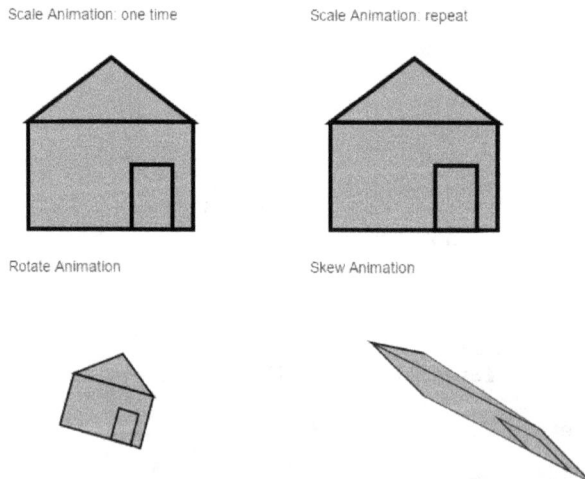

Figure 3-8. Deminstration animations using D3.

Creating Graphics with Data

In this section, we will use D3 to add SVG elements to a web page based on data. This will include binding data to those elements and then using those elements to visualize the data. The question is how can we put the data to graphics elements? This is where the *data* operator in D3 comes in, by passing an array of data as argument. For each elements in the selection, a value will be assigned in the array following the same order of the sequence. This correspondence is indicated by a generic function in which *d* and *i* are passed as arguments:

```
Function(d, i){
    // code with d and i
    // return some elaboration of d;
}
```

This function will be executed as many times as there are elements in the list: *i* is the index of the sequence and *d* is the value in the data array corresponding to that index. In some cases, you are not interested in the value of *i* and use only *d*. The preceding code is equivalent to the following *for*-loop:

```
For(i = 0; i < data.length; i++){
    d = input_array[i];
    // code with d and i
    // return out_array[i];
}
```

Data Array

One of the most common and popular ways to define data in D3 is through the use of JavaScript arrays. For example, if you have multiple data elements stored in an array and you want to generate corresponding visual elements to represent the data. In addition, when the data array changes, you want your visualization to reflect such changes.

Add a new controller named *DatasController.cs* to the *Controllers* folder and replace its content with the following code:

```
using Microsoft.AspNetCore.Mvc;

namespace Chapter03.Controllers
{
    public class DatasController : Controller
    {
        // GET: /<controller>/
        public IActionResult Index()
        {
            ViewBag.Title = "Datas: Home";
            return View();
        }

        public IActionResult DataArray()
        {
            ViewBag.Title = "Datas: Data Array";
            return View();
        }
    }
}
```

Add a new folder named *Datas* to the *Views* directory. Add *Views/Datas/DataArray.cshtml* and replace its content with the following code:

```
@{
    ViewData["Title"] = ViewBag.Title;
}

<h3>@ViewBag.Title</h3>
@Html.Partial("_Links")

<hr />
<script src="~/lib/d3/d3.min.js"></script>

<div class="container">
    <div class="row">
        <div class="col-sm-4">
            <p>Vertical bar chart</p>
            <svg width="300" height="300" id="svg1" />
        </div>
        <div class="col-sm-4">
            <p>Horizontal bar chart</p>
            <svg width="300" height="300" id="svg2" />
        </div>
    </div>
    <div class="row">
        <div class="col-sm-4">
            <p>Vertical bar chart: change color</p>
            <svg width="300" height="300" id="svg3" />
        </div>
        <div class="col-sm-4">
            <p>Horizontal bar chart: update</p>
            <svg width="300" height="300" id="svg4" />
        </div>
    </div>
    <div class="row" id="plotdiv">
    </div>
</div>

@section scripts{
<script type="text/javascript">

    // vertical bar chart
    var svg = d3.select("#svg1");
    var data = [27, 50, 80, 65, 30, 81, 49, 94, 40, 100];

    var w = 20;
    var bar = svg.selectAll("rect")
        .data(data)
        .enter()
        .append("rect");
    bar.attr("x", function (d, i) { return i * (w + 5); })
        .attr("y", function (d) { return 240 - 2 * d; })
        .attr("width", w)
        .attr("height", function (d) { return 2 * d; })
        .style("stroke", "black")
```

```
    .style("fill", "red");

// horizontal bar chart
var svg = d3.select("#svg2");

var h = 20;
var bar = svg.selectAll("rect")
    .data(data)
    .enter()
    .append("rect");

bar.attr("x", 10)
    .attr("y", function (d, i) { return i * (h + 5); })
    .attr("height", h)
    .attr("width", function (d) { return 10 + 2 * d; })
    .style("stroke", "black")
    .style("fill", "green");

</script>
}
```

In this example, the data is stored in a simple JavaScript array. Next, we use the *selectAll* method based on CSS3 selector to grab all the elements that match the specified selector string. But, you might wonder what is it actually doing because the HTML body does not contain any *<rect>* element yet. The *selectAll* method tries to select all of *<rect>* available on the page, which is none in this case. So it returns an empty selection. The following two statements of *.data(data)* and *.enter()* will allow you to bind the data to this empty selection.

The *.data* operator joins the array of data with the current selection. In this example, there is no key provided, so each element of the data array is assigned to each element of the current selection. The *.data* operator in D3 returns three virtual selections: *enter*, *update*, and *exit*. The *enter* selection contains placeholders for any missing elements; the *update* selection contains existing elements, and any remaining elements end up in the *exit* selection for removal.

The *.enter* method in D3 returns the virtual *enter* selection from the *.data* operator. This method only works on the *.data* operator because the *.data* operator is the only one that returns three virtual selections. In our example,

```
var bar = svg.selectAll("rect")
        .data(data)
        .enter()
```

This will return a reference to the placeholder elements for each data element that did not have a corresponding existing element. Once we have this reference we can then operates on this selection. This reference allows three chaining operations: *append*, *insert*, and *select*. After these operators have been chained the *.enter* selection, we can treat the selection just like any other selection to modify the content.

Next, we use *.append("rect")* to the *.enter* selection. As a result, for each placeholder element created in the previous step, a *<rect>* element is inserted. Because we had ten data points in our data array and no *<rect>* elements on our *<svg>* tag, the *append("rect")* method creates and adds ten *<rect>* shapes to the *<svg>* selection.

The following code applys our data array to dynamic attributes, *x*, *y*, and *height* of the *<rect>* element. For example, we set the *height* attribute to be two times the integer value in the data array associated with each rectangle, as shown in the following code snippet:

```
bar.attr("x", function (d, i) { return i * (w + 5); })
    .attr("y", function (d) { return 240 - 2 * d; })
    .attr("width", w)
    .attr("height", function (d) { return 2 * d; })
```

All D3 modifier functions accept this type of dynamic function to compute its value on the fly. For the *height* attribute, the dynamic function receive a parameter *d*, which is the datum associated with the current element. In our example, the first rectangle has the value 27 associated as its datum, while the second one has 50, and so on. Therefore, this function computes a numeric value that is two times the datum for each rectangle and returns it as the *height* attribute.

The code creates ten rectangles based on our data array, which actually generates a vertical bar chart! The other part of the code creates horizontal bar charts. Running this example produces the results shown in Figure 3-9.

Vertical bar chart   Horizontal bar chart

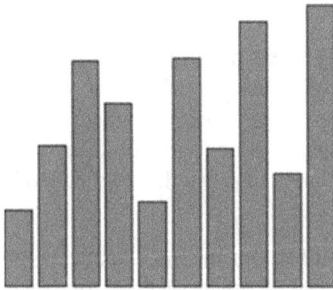

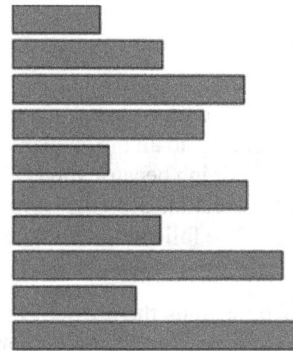

Figure 3-9. Demonstration of bar charts based on data array.

We can also use D3 to modify the styles of SVG elements dynamically. D3 allows you to use a dynamic function inside of the *style* operator. Add the following code snippet to the script section of the view:

```
// Vertical bar chart: change fill
var svg = d3.select("#svg3");
var w = 20;
var bar = svg.selectAll("rect")
    .data(data)
    .enter()
    .append("rect");
bar.attr("x", function (d, i) { return i * (w + 5); })
    .attr("y", function (d) { return 240 - 2 * d; })
    .attr("width", w)
    .attr("height", function (d) { return 2 * d; })
    .style("stroke", "black")
    .style("fill", function (d) {
        var color;
        if (d < 50) {
            return color = "green";
        } else {
            return color = "red";
        }
```

```
    });
```

The highlighted code looks at the data associated for each rectangle to determine the color fill. If the data is less than 50, we then make the *fill* green; otherwise make the *fill* red.

This code generates the results shown in Figure 3-10.

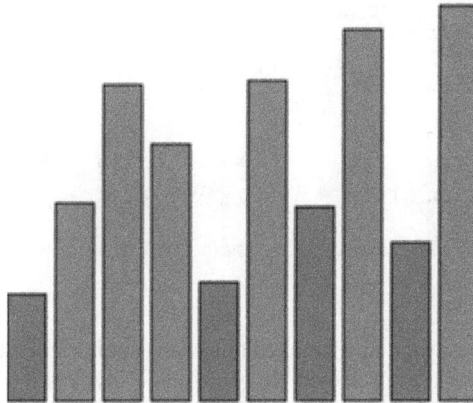

Figure 3-10. Demonstration of bar chart with different color bars.

The bar charts we created in the preceding examples are based on a static data array, i.e., the data array keeps constant during the course of creating the charts. In fact, D3 also allows you to update the graphics objects when your data array is changed or updated. In the next example, I will show you how to use the enter-update-exit pattern in D3 to generate and update SVG elements when data array is changed dynamically.

Add the following code to the script section of the view:

```
// horizontal bar chart: data updated
    var svg = d3.select("#svg4");
    draw(data);

    function draw(data) {
        var h = 20;
        // enter
        svg.selectAll("rect")
            .data(data)
            .enter()
            .append("rect");

        // update
        svg.selectAll("rect")
            .data(data)
            .attr("x", 10)
            .attr("y", function (d, i) { return i * (h + 5); })
            .attr("height", h)
            .attr("width", function (d) { return 10 + 2 * d; })
            .style("stroke", "black")
            .style("fill", function (d) {
                var color;
```

```
                if (d < 50) {
                    return color = "green";
                } else {
                    return color = "red";
                }
            });

        // exit
        svg.selectAll("rect")
            .data(data)
            .exit()
            .remove();
    }

    setInterval(function () {
        data.shift();
        data.push(Math.round(Math.random() * 100));
        draw(data);
    }, 1000);
```

Here, the *draw* function can be repeatedly invoked to update our horizontal bar chart. The *enter* section selects all *<rect>* elements within the selected *<svg>* tag, and invokes the *.data* operator on this initial selection to bind the array. The following *.enter* operator selects all data elements that are not yet visualized. When the draw function is invoked for the first time, it returns all elements in the data array.

In the *update* section, the first two lines are the same as those in the *enter* section. Instead of calling the *enter* and *append* functions as we did in the *enter* section, here, we directly apply *attr* and *style* functions to the selection made by the *data* function. In the update mode, the *data* function returns the intersection between the data elements and visual elements.

In the *exit* section, we call the *exit* function to compute the set difference of all visual elements that are no longer associated with any data. Finally, we call the *remove* function to remove all the elements selected by the *exit* function. This way, as long as we call the draw function after we change the data array, we can always ensure that our visual elements and data are kept synchronized.

The last block of code calls the *setInterval* function, which is a standard JavaScript function that calls a function or evaluates an expression at specified interval (1 second in our example). Here, the *setInterval* function calls *function()* that removes the top element in the data array using the *shift* operator, and appends a random integer to the data array using the *push* function every 1 second. Once the data array is updated, the *draw* function is called again to update our bar chart keeping it synchronized with the new data array. This will gives an animated bar chart, as shown in Figure 3-11.

JSON Data

D3 selections are JavaScript arrays. If you run a simple selection in the JavaScript *console.log*:

```
Console.log(d3.select("body"));
```

You get an array of one element – the HTML body element:

```
dt {_groups: Array[1], _parents: Array[1]}
```

This means that it is important to make sure that the *.data* operator in D3 receives an array of data, regardless of what is inside of the array.

Figure 3-11. Demonstration of dynamic updated bar chart.

The JSON data is a collection of name-value pairs. It is a specific syntax for organizing data as JavaScript objects. So, the data array in D3 can also be an array of JSON objects. JSON structure follows the rules that we have seen for objects and arrays defined in JavaScript. For example:

```
var circles= [
    {"x": 55,  "y": 55, "radius": 50, "color": "red"},
    {"x": 110, "y": 55, "radius": 50, "color": "green"},
    {"x": 165, "y": 55, "radius": 50, "color": "blue"}];
```

This will be very easy to retrieve data from JSON data:

```
circles[0].radius  // returns 50
circles[1].color   // returns green
```

This leads to code with easier comprehension. Add *Views/Datas/JsonData.cshtml* and replace its content with the following code:

```
@{
    ViewData["Title"] = ViewBag.Title;
}

<h3>@ViewBag.Title</h3>
@Html.Partial("_Links")

<hr />
<script src="~/lib/d3/d3.min.js"></script>

<div class="container">
    <div class="row">
        <p>Circles based on JSON</p>
        <svg width="500" height="250" id="svg1" />
    </div>
    <div class="row">
        <p>Circles based on math functions</p>
        <svg width="400" height="400" id="svg2" />
```

```
            </div>
    </div>

    @section scripts{
        <script type="text/javascript">

            // Circles
            var data = [
                { "x": 20,   "radius": 10, "color": "#00008F" },
                { "x": 45,   "radius": 15, "color": "#0000FF" },
                { "x": 75,   "radius": 20, "color": "#006FFF" },
                { "x": 105,  "radius": 25, "color": "#00DFFF" },
                { "x": 145,  "radius": 30, "color": "#4FFFAF" },
                { "x": 190,  "radius": 35, "color": "#BFFF3F" },
                { "x": 240,  "radius": 40, "color": "#FFCF00" },
                { "x": 295,  "radius": 45, "color": "#FF5F00" },
                { "x": 355,  "radius": 50, "color": "#EF0000" },
                { "x": 420,  "radius": 55, "color": "#7F0000" }];

            var svg = d3.select("#svg1");
            var circle = svg.selectAll("circle")
                .data(data)
                .enter()
                .append("circle");

            circle.attr("cx", function (d) { return d.x; })
                .attr("cy", 100)
                .attr("r", function (d) { return d.radius; })
                .style("stroke", "black")
                .style("fill", function (d) { return d.color })
                .style("fill-opacity", 0.8);
        </script>
    }
```

This code uses the dynamic functions and JSON data to specify the *attrr* and *style* operators. We make this code easier to understand what the *return d* is actually returning from the dynamic function.

Running this code produces the results shown in Figure 3-12.

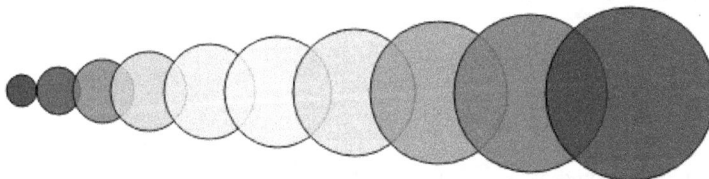

Figure 3-12. Circles created based on JSON data.

Data from Mathematical Functions

One of the benefits of D3 is its support for functional style programming. D3 allows mathematical functions to be treated as data as well. This feature is very powerful when you want to create data from a mathematical function.

In this example, we will use random mathematical function to create 200 circles, whose location (*cx*, *cy*), radius *r*, and *fill* color are all generated from random numbers.

Add a function named *createData* to the *Views/Datas/JsonData.cshtml* file. Here is the code for this function:

```
function createData() {
    var dat = [];
    for (var i = 0; i < 200; i++) {
        var ran = Math.random() * 100;
        var r = Math.round(ran / 3);
        var x = Math.round(400 * Math.random());
        var y = Math.round(400 * Math.random());
        dat.push({ "x": x, "y": y, "radius": r, "color": ran });
    }
    return dat;
}
```

Here, we convert the data generated from the *Math.random* function into the JSON data format. The *color* field in the JSON data represent the integer random number from the range [0, 100], which is associated with the radii of the circles. We will use the following code to convert this color field into a colormap:

```
var colors = ["#00008F", "#0000FF", "#006FFF", "#00DFFF", "#4FFFAF",
              "#BFFF3F", "#FFCF00", "#FF5F00", "#EF0000", "#7F0000"];
var colormap = d3.scaleLinear()
                 .domain([0, 10, 20, 30, 40, 50, 60, 70, 80, 90, 100])
                 .range(colors);
```

We use the *d3.scaleLinear* function to interpolate the colormap for different domains with different colors.

Add the following code to *Views/Datas/JsonData.cshtml*:

```
var svg = d3.select("#svg2");
var data = createData();
draw(data);

function draw(data) {
    // enter
    svg.selectAll("circle")
        .data(data)
        .enter()
        .append("circle");

    // update
    circle = svg.selectAll("circle")
        .data(data)
        .attr("cx", function (d) { return d.x; })
        .attr("cy", function (d) { return d.y; })
        .attr("r", function (d) { return d.radius; })
        .style("stroke", "black")
        .style("fill", function (d) { return colormap(d.color) })
        .style("opacity", 0.5);

    // exit
    svg.selectAll("circle")
```

```
                        .data(data)
                        .exit()
                        .remove();
        }

        setInterval(function () {
            data.shift();
            var ran = Math.random() * 100;
            var r = Math.round(ran / 3);
            var x = Math.round(400 * Math.random());
            var y = Math.round(400 * Math.random());
            data.push({ "x": x, "y": y, "radius": r, "color": ran });
            draw(data);
        }, 100);
```

This code is very similar to that we used for create an animated bar chart in the previous example. Note the last block of the code for the *setInterval* function. It calls *function*() to remove the top element in the JSON data using the *shift* function, and at the same time append a new JSON data entry from the random function using the *push* operator every 100 milliseconds. This will produces animated random circles.

Running this example produces the output shown in Figure 3-13.

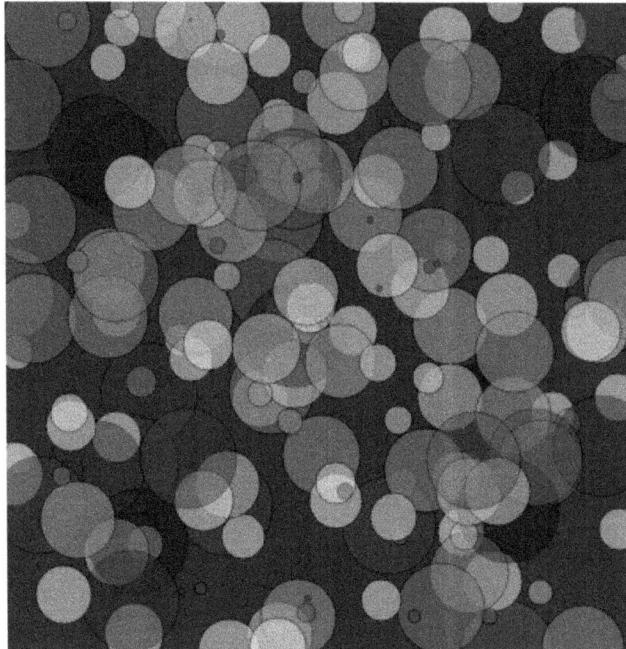

Figure 3-13. Circles created using math functions.

Data from Server

The power of data visualization usually lays on the ability to visualize dynamic data from server-side. The server-side data can be generated by a server-side program or from a database. In ASP.NET Core MVC applications, we have several ways to pass the server-side information from a controller to a view, including as a strongly typed model object, as a dynamic type (using @model dynamic), and using the *ViewBag* or *ViewData*. In Chapter 1, we already demonstrated how to use the strongly typed view and *ViewBag* to pass information. Here, we will use the *JsonResult* type to pass the JSON data to the client-side.

JsonResult is an *ActionResult* type in MVC. It helps send the content in JSON format. Let us consider an example, in which we create a custom shape – a star in the server side and pass the JSON data for 200 stars with random sizes and locations to the view. In the view, we will use D3 to create these random stars.

Add a new folder named *Models* to the *Chapter03* project. Add a new class, *ModelHelper*, to this new folder and replace its content with the following code:

```
using System;
using System.Collections.Generic;

namespace Chapter03.Models
{
    public class ModelHelper
    {
        public static List<Star> Star200()
        {
            List<Star> stars = new List<Star>();
            var ran = new Random();
            for (int i = 0; i < 200; i++)
            {
                var xc = ran.Next(100) * 4;
                var yc = ran.Next(100) * 4;
                var v = ran.Next(100);
                var color = v;
                var r = 10 + v / 3;

                stars.Add(SingleStar(xc, yc, r, color));
            }
            return stars;
        }

        public static Star SingleStar(double xc, double yc, double r,
                                      double color)
        {
            double sn36 = Math.Sin(36.0 * Math.PI / 180.0);
            double sn72 = Math.Sin(72.0 * Math.PI / 180.0);
            double cs36 = Math.Cos(36.0 * Math.PI / 180.0);
            double cs72 = Math.Cos(72.0 * Math.PI / 180.0);

            double x0 = Math.Round(xc, 2);
            double y0 = Math.Round(yc - r, 2);
            double x1 = Math.Round(xc + r * sn36, 2);
            double y1 = Math.Round(yc + r * cs36, 2);
            double x2 = Math.Round(xc - r * sn72, 2);
            double y2 = Math.Round(yc - r * cs72, 2);
            double x3 = Math.Round(xc + r * sn72, 2);
            double y3 = Math.Round(yc - r * cs72, 2);
            double x4 = Math.Round(xc - r * sn36, 2);
            double y4 = Math.Round(yc + r * cs36, 2);
```

```
string data = string.Format("{0},{1} {2},{3} {4},{5} {6},{7}
    {8},{9}", x0, y0, x1, y1, x2, y2, x3, y3, x4, y4);

Star star = new Star
{
    Xc = xc,
    Yc = yc,
    R = r,
    Color = color,
    Data = data
};
return star;
    }
}

public class Star
{
    public double Xc { get; set; }
    public double Yc { get; set; }
    public double R { get; set; }
    public double Color { get; set; }
    public string Data { get; set; }
}
}
```

In the *Star* class, we define several public properties: *Xc* and *Yc* define the central location of the star, *R* defines the size of the star, *Color* defines the fill color of the star, and the *Data* string property contains the point coordinates used to create the star.

We will create the star using the polygon shape in SVG. First, we need to define the coordinates of the star, as illustrated in Figure 3-14.

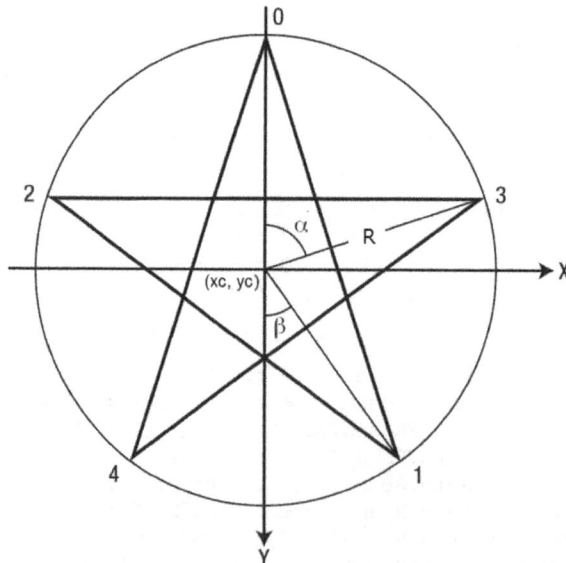

Figure 3-14. Coordinates of the star shape.

Here, we assume the center coordinates of the star are at (*Xc*, *Yc*) and R is the radius of the circle around the star shape. The angle α is equal to 72 degrees and β is equal to 36 degrees. From this figure, we can easily determine the coordinates of points from 0 to 4.

The *SingleStar* method generates the coordinates for these five points with specified the center coordinates, the size, and the color of the star. We also convert these point coordinates into a string so that we can use it to specify the *points* attribute easily when we create the star using the SVG *polygon* shape in D3.

The *Star200* method generates a list of 200 stars with random center coordinates and size. Here, we set the minimum size of the stars to be 10*px*.

Add the following code to *Controllers/DatasController.cs*:

```
public IActionResult ServerData()
{
    ViewBag.Title = "Datas: Data from Server";
    return View();
}

public JsonResult GetStarData()
{
    var star1 = ModelHelper.Star200();
    var star2 = ModelHelper.Star200();
    return Json(new { star1, star2 });
}
```

Inside the *GetStarData* method, we create two list of stars: *star1* and *star2*. We will use the first list to create the initial star shapes, and the second list to update the star shapes when we animate the stars. This method returns these two lists as the JSON data.

Now, we want to use the JSON data in the client-side view. Add *Views/Datas/ServerData.cshtml* and replace its content with the following code:

```
@{
    ViewData["Title"] = ViewBag.Title;
}

<h3>@ViewBag.Title</h3>
@Html.Partial("_Links")

<hr />
<script src="~/lib/d3/d3.min.js"></script>

<div class="container">
    <div class="row">
        <p>Stars based on data from server</p>
        <svg width="400" height="400" id="svg" />
    </div>
</div>

@section scripts{
    <script type="text/javascript">

        $.get("GetStarData", function (d) {
            var data1 = d.star1;
```

```
        var data2 = d.star2;

        var colors = ["#00008F", "#0000FF", "#006FFF", "#00DFFF", "#4FFFAF",
            "#BFFF3F", "#FFCF00", "#FF5F00", "#EF0000", "#7F0000"];
        var colormap = d3.scaleLinear().domain([0, 10, 20, 30, 40, 50, 60,
            70, 80, 90, 100]).range(colors);

        var svg = d3.select("#svg");
        svg.append("rect")
            .attr("width", 400)
            .attr("height", 400)
            .style("fill", "#222");

        draw(data1);

        function draw(data) {
            // enter
            svg.selectAll("polygon")
                .data(data)
                .enter()
                .append("polygon");

            // update
            svg.selectAll("polygon")
                .data(data)
                .attr("points", function (d) { return d.data; })
                .style("fill", function (d) { return colormap(d.color) })
                .style("opacity", 0.5);

            // exit
            svg.selectAll("polygon")
                .data(data)
                .exit()
                .remove();
        }

        setInterval(function () {
            data1.shift();
            var i = Math.round(Math.random() * 199);
            var dat = { "xc": data2[i].xc, "yc": data2[i].yc, "r":
                data2[i].r, "color": data2[i].color, "data": data2[i].data };
            data1.push(dat);
            draw(data1);
        }, 100);
    });

    </script>
}
```

This code uses jQuery AJAX $.*get* method to request data from the server with the HTTP GET request. In our case, you can use either the $.*get* or $.*post* method. The syntax of the $.*get* method looks like the following:

```
$.get(URL, callback);
```

The required URL parameter specifies the URL you wish to request. In this example, it is *GetStarData*, which is defined in our controller. The callback parameter is the name of a function to be executed if the request succeeds.

We then assign the *JSON* data *star1* to the *data1* variable and *star2* to the *data2* variable. These data variables can be used to create the star shapes by D3. You can see in the *draw* function that we set the *points* attribute of the *polygon* to the JSON data's data string field and the *fill* attribute to the JSON data's *color* field. Note that we call the *draw* function with the *data1* variable as its input argument to create the initial star shapes.

In the *setInterval* function, we remove the top element in the *data1* variable using the *shift* function. We then create a random integer as the index of the *data2* variable and append the selected element from *data2* to *data1* using push operator every 100 milliseconds. Once the *data1* variable is updated, we call the *draw* function again to update our visualization keeping it synchronized with the new data.

Running this example, selecting the *Using Data* tab, and clicking the *Data from Server* link, we get the output shown in Figure 3-15.

Figure 3-15. Stars created based on the server-side data.

Scale and Colors

In this section, I will first discuss one of the most important concepts in D3: the *scale*, which maps a dimension of data to a visual variable, and then introduce the colors and colormaps in D3.

D3 Scale

In most of our previous examples, we created various graphics objects within a predefined SVG viewport. For instance, if we set an SVG viewport to be 400*px*×400*px*, the graphics objects will become visible if their dimension is within the viewport. However, anything will be invisible if it is outside of the viewport.

In order to keep visual elements within the predefined viewport, we need to scale our data to fit into this viewport. For this purpose, D3 provides various functions to perform data transformations. These functions are typically used to map data values into visual variables such as position, length, or color.

For example, suppose we have a data array

```
var data = [0, 1000, 2000, 3000, 4000, 5000];
```

This data have an input domain of [0, 5000]. We can map this data within the range of [0, 200] using the following code:

```
var scaledData = d3.scaleLinear().domain([0, 5000]).range([0,200]);
```

D3 creates a function scaledData that accepts input between 0 and 5000 (the *domain*) and maps it to output between 0 and 200 (the *range*). We can then use scaledData to calculate positions based on the data:

```
scaledData(1000);    // returns 40
scaledData(3000);    // returns 120
......
```

D3 comes with quantitative scales and ordinal scales. The quantitative scales have a continuous domain such as dates, times, real numbers, integers, etc, while the ordinal scales are discrete domains – like names, categories, colors, etc. The quantitative scales consists of several different scales: *linear*, *pow*, *sqrt*, *log*, etc. The linear scale is probably the most commonly used scale type.

Let us consider an example, where we will create several curves on the predefined SVG viewports using the linear scale function in D3. Add the following two methods to *Models/modelHelper.cs*:

```
public static object MathData()
{
    // 1/(x*x+1):
    double[] range = new double[] { -5.0, 5.0 };
    Func<double, double> f = (x) => 1.0 / (x * x + 1.0);
    var data1 = MathFunctionData(f, range, 300);

    // sin(x):
    range = new double[] { 0, 2.0 * Math.PI };
    f = (x) => Math.Sin(x);
    var data2 = MathFunctionData(f, range, 300);

    // sqrt(x):
    range = new double[] { 0, 10 };
    f = (x) => Math.Sqrt(x);
    var data3 = MathFunctionData(f, range, 300);

    // x*sin(x*x)+1:
    range = new double[] { -2.0, 3.0 };
    f = (x) => x * Math.Sin(x * x) + 1.0;
    var data4 = MathFunctionData(f, range, 300);

    return new { data1, data2, data3, data4 };
}


private static List<object> MathFunctionData(Func<double, double> f,
    double[] xRange, int numPoints)
```

```
{
    double dx = (xRange[1] - xRange[0]) / numPoints;
    List<object> objs = new List<object>();
    for (var x = xRange[0]; x < xRange[1]; x = x + dx)
    {
        var y = f(x);
        objs.Add(new {x, y});
    }
    return objs;
}
```

The private method *MathFunctionData* takes the *Func*, range for the *x* value, and the number of data points as its input arguments and returns a list of the data points. The public method *MathData* generates data for four different mathematical functions using the *MathFunctionData* method. Note that inside the *MathData* method, we define the mathematical functions using the lambda expression. We will convert these data generated in server-side into the JSON data format.

Add *Controllers/ScaleColorController.cs* and replace its content with the following code:

```
using Chapter03.Models;
using Microsoft.AspNetCore.Mvc;

namespace Chapter03.Controllers
{
    public class ScaleColorController : Controller
    {
        // GET: /<controller>/
        public IActionResult Index()
        {
            return View();
        }

        public IActionResult Scales()
        {
            ViewBag.Title = "ScaleColor: Scales";
            return View();
        }

        public IActionResult CategoricalColors()
        {
            ViewBag.Title = "ScaleColor: CategoricalColors";
            return View(0);
        }

        public IActionResult Colormap()
        {
            ViewBag.Title = "Colormaps";
            return View();
        }

        public JsonResult JsonData()
        {
            var data = ModelHelper.MathData();
            return Json(data);
        }
    }
}
```

```
    }
```

The highlighted code converts the data generated from the mathematical functions into the JSON data, which will be used to create the corresponding curves in the client-side.

Add a new folder named *ScaleColor* to the *Views* folder. Add a new view named *Scales.cshtml* to this new folder. Here is the code for this view:

```
@{
    ViewData["Title"] = ViewBag.Title;
}
<h3>@ViewBag.Title</h3>
@Html.Partial("_Links")
<hr />
<script src="~/lib/d3/d3.min.js"></script>
<div class="container">
    <div class="row">
        <div class="col-sm-4">
            <p>1/(x*x+1)</p>
            <svg id="svg1" width="300" height="200"></svg>
        </div>
        <div class="col-sm-4">
            <p>sin(x)</p>
            <svg id="svg2" width="300" height="200"></svg>
        </div>
    </div>
    <div class="row" style="margin-top:50px">
        <div class="col-sm-4">
            <p>sqrt(x)</p>
            <svg id="svg3" width="300" height="200"></svg>
        </div>
        <div class="col-sm-4">
            <p>x*sin(x*x)+1</p>
            <svg id="svg4" width="300" height="200"></svg>
        </div>
    </div>
</div>

@section scripts{
    <script type="text/javascript">
        d3.json("JsonData", function (data) {
            draw("#svg1", data.data1);
            draw("#svg2", data.data2);
            draw("#svg3", data.data3);
            draw("#svg4", data.data4);
        });

        function draw(svgSelection, data) {
            var svg = d3.select(svgSelection);
            var xmin = d3.min(data, function (d) { return d.x });
            var xmax = d3.max(data, function (d) { return d.x });
            var ymin = d3.min(data, function (d) { return d.y });
            var ymax = d3.max(data, function (d) { return d.y });
            var xscale = d3.scaleLinear().domain([xmin, xmax]).range([10, 280]);
            var yscale = d3.scaleLinear().domain([ymin, ymax]).range([10, 180]);
            var gen = d3.line().x(function (d) { return xscale(d.x);})
```

```
            .y(function (d) { return yscale(d.y); });
        svg.append("path")
            .attr("d", gen(data))
            .attr("stroke", "black")
            .attr("stroke-width", 2)
            .attr("fill", "none");
    }
    </script>
}
```

Instead of using AJAX $.*get* method, here we use the *d3.json* method to retrieve the data from the server. Inside the draw function, we use the *scaleLinear* function to scale the data in the *x*- and *y*-direction to fit the curve inside the SVG viewport. We also use a D3 helper function, *d3.line* to generate data for the path element. For a line curve, we have a sequence of (*x*, *y*) coordinates. The *d3.line* function convert our original JSON data into the SVG path mini-language format. In order to convert our data into the SVG path commands, we need to tell the line path data generator how to access the *x* and *y* coordinates from our data, as shown in the following code snippet:

```
var gen = d3.line().x(function (d) { return xscale(d.x); })
                   .y(function (d) { return yscale(d.y); });
```

Note how we scale our original data using the *xscale* and *yscale* functions.

Running this example, selecting the *Scales and Colors* tab, and clicking the *Scales* link, you will obtain the results shown in Figure 3-16.

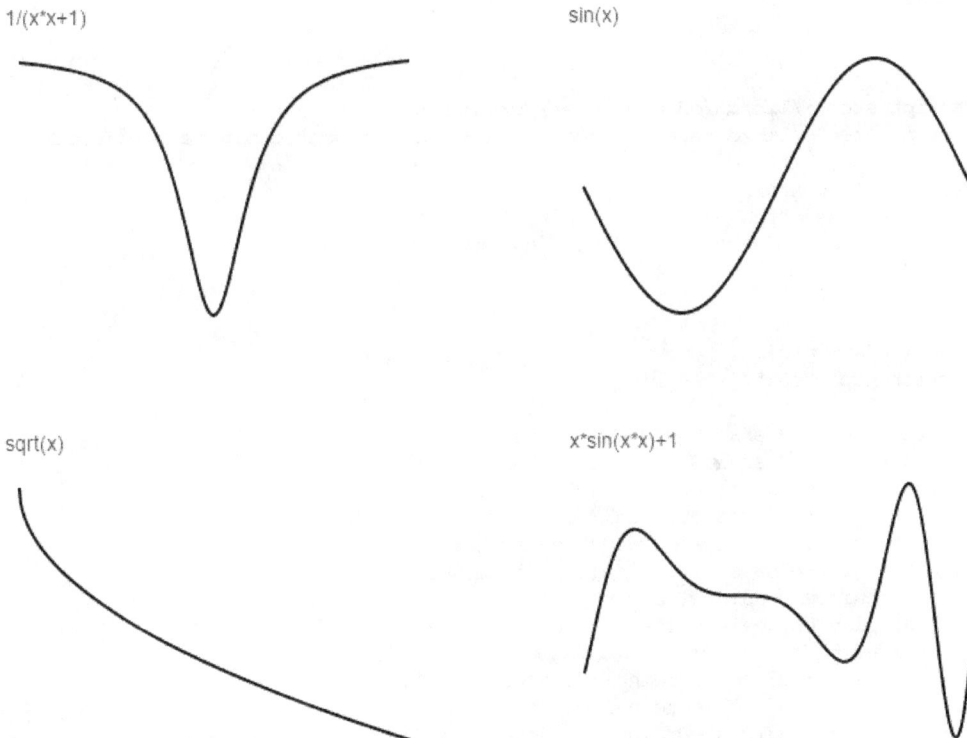

Figure 3-16. Curves created based on linear scale in D3.

Categorical Colors

The linear scale we discussed in the preceding section is the quantitative scales, but how about ordinal scales? The big difference is that ordinal scales have a discrete domain, in other words, they turn a limited number of values into something else, without caring for what is in between those values.

The *scaleOrdinal* function in D3 maps discrete values (usually the categories) to discrete values (usually colors). The domain specifies the possible input values and the range of the output values. The range array will repeat if it is shorter than the domain array. For example:

```
var data = ["Jan", "Feb", "Mar", "Apr", "May", "Jun"];
var scale = d3.scaleOrdinal().domain(data).range(["red", "green", "blue"]);
scale("Feb");    // returns "green"
scale("Apr");    // returns "red"
```

D3 has a plug-in *d3-scale-chromatic* that provides sequential, diverging, and categorical color schemes derived from *ColorBrewer*. Here, we will discuss the categorical color schemes implemented in this plug-in.

Open the *Chapter03* project and install the *d3-scale-chromatic* module using the bower. Add *Views/ScaleColor/CategoricalColors.cshtml* and replace its content with the following code:

```
@{
    ViewData["Title"] = ViewBag.Title;
}

<h3>@ViewBag.Title</h3>
@Html.Partial("_Links")

<hr />
<script src="~/lib/d3/d3.min.js"></script>
<script src="~/lib/d3-scale-chromatic/d3-scale-chromatic.min.js"></script>

<div class="container">
    <div class="row">
        <svg id="svg" width="700", height="800"></svg>
    </div>
</div>

@section scripts{
<script type="text/javascript">

    var c10 = d3.scaleOrdinal(d3.schemeCategory10);
    var c20 = d3.scaleOrdinal(d3.schemeCategory20);;
    var c20b = d3.scaleOrdinal(d3.schemeCategory20b);
    var c20c = d3.scaleOrdinal(d3.schemeCategory20c);
    var accent = d3.scaleOrdinal(d3.schemeAccent);
    var dark2 = d3.scaleOrdinal(d3.schemeDark2);
    var paired = d3.scaleOrdinal(d3.schemePaired);
    var p1 = d3.scaleOrdinal(d3.schemePastel1);
    var p2 = d3.scaleOrdinal(d3.schemePastel2);
    var set1 = d3.scaleOrdinal(d3.schemeSet1);
    var set2 = d3.scaleOrdinal(d3.schemeSet2);
    var set3 = d3.scaleOrdinal(d3.schemeSet3);

    var names = ["Categorical10", "Categorical20", "Categorical20b",
```

```
                    "Categorical20c", "Accent", "Dark2", "Paired", "Pastel",
                    "Paste2", "Set1", "Set2", "Set3"];
        var colors = [c10, c20, c20b, c20c, accent, dark2, paired, p1, p2,
                    set1, set2, set3];
        var rects = [10, 20, 20, 20, 8, 8, 12, 8, 8, 9, 8, 12];

        var w = 30;
        var h = 30;
        var svg = d3.select("svg");

        for (var i = 0; i < names.length; i++) {
            svg.append("text")
                .attr("x", 0)
                .attr("y", 15 + i * (30 + h))
                .text(names[i]);

            svg.selectAll('.rect' + i)
                .attr("class", ".rect" + i)
                .data(d3.range(rects[i]))
                .enter()
                .append("rect")
                .attr("x", d3.scaleLinear().domain([0, rects[i]])
                        .range([0, rects[i] * w]))
                .attr("y", 20 + i * (30 + h))
                .attr("width", w)
                .attr("height", h)
                .style("fill", colors[i]);
        }
    </script>
    }
```

This code first introduces the reference for the *d3* library and *d3-scale-chromatic* module. It then uses the *scaleOridnal* function to set the ordinal scale with twelve categorical color schemes defined in the *d3-scale-chromatic* module. We create different number of rectangles for each color scheme and set its *fill* attribute to the categorical colors.

Running this example produces the results shown in Figure 3-17.

For the first categorical color scheme, *Category10*, which consists of ten different colors. It is an array of ten categorical colors represented as RBG hexadecimal strings. The second one, *Category20*, represents an array of twenty categorical colors based on RGB hexadecimal strings, and so on.

We can use the predefined categorical colors to map a bar chart. Add the following code to the script section of the view – *CategoricalColors.cshtml*:

```
// bar chart
var svg = d3.select("#svg2");
var data = [27, 50, 80, 65, 30, 81, 49, 94, 40, 100];

var w = 20;
var bar = svg.selectAll("rect")
    .data(data)
    .enter()
    .append("rect");
bar.attr("x", function (d, i) { return i * (w + 5); })
    .attr("y", function (d) { return 240 - 2 * d; })
```

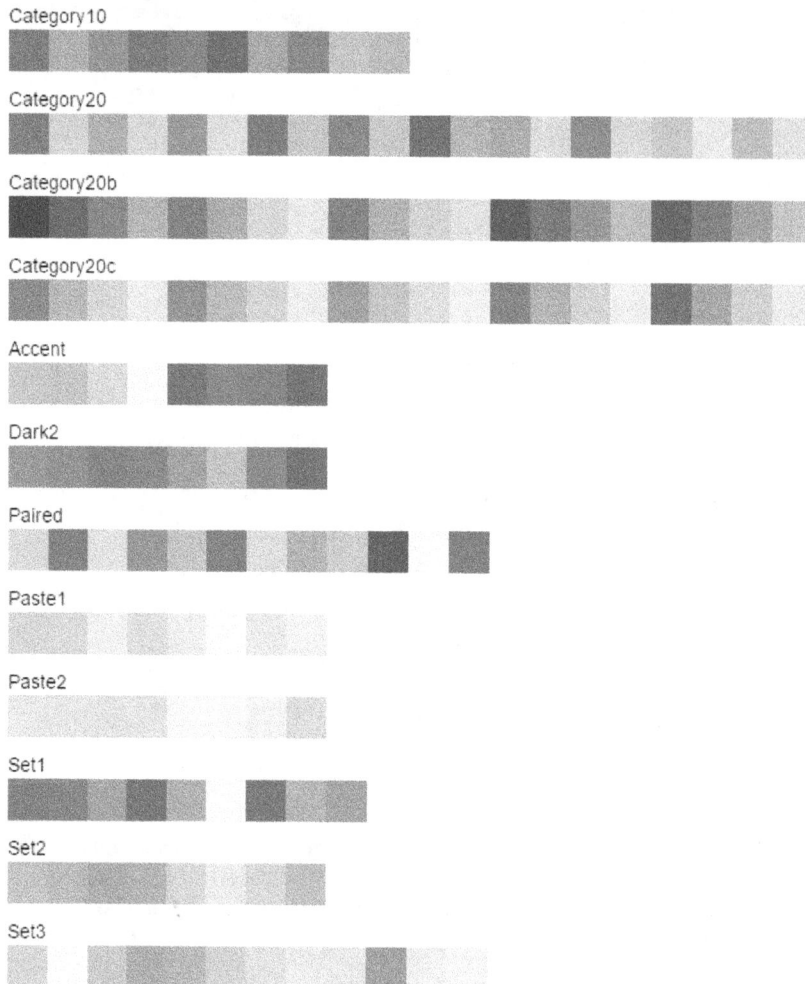

Figure 3-17. Demonstration of categorical color schemes.

```
.attr("width", w)
    .attr("height", function (d) { return 2 * d; })
    .style("stroke", "black")
    .style("fill", c10);
```

Here, we use the *Category10* to specify the *fill* attribute for the bars.

Running this code produces the results shown in Figure 3-18.

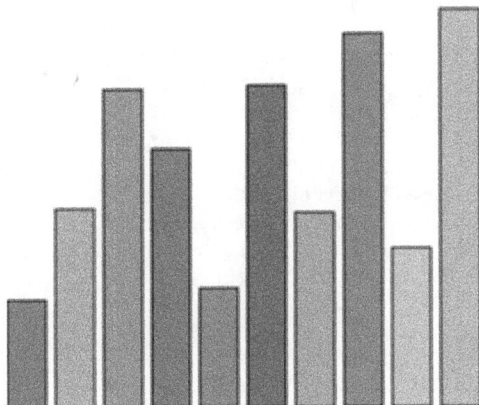

Figure 3-18. Bar chart with categorical colors.

Colormaps

The *d3-scale-chromatic* module also includes over 30 sequential colormaps. The *scaleSequential* function in D3 is used for mapping continuous values to an output range determined by a present interpolator. For example, we can use the *d3.interpolateRainbow* to create a rainbow color scale:

```
var scale = d3.scaleSequential().domain([0, 10])
    .interpolator(d3.interpolateRainbow);
scale(3); // returns  "rgb(225, 120, 71)"
scale(8); // returns  "rgb(35, 171, 216)"
```

Note that the interpolator determines the output range so you do not need to specify the range yourself. Let us consider an example that shows all of the color interpolators provided by the d3-scale-chromatic module.

Add *Views/ScaleColor/Colormap.cshtml* and replace its content with the following code:

```
@{
    ViewData["Title"] = ViewBag.Title;
}
<h3>@ViewBag.Title</h3>
@Html.Partial("_Links")
<hr />
<script src="~/lib/d3/d3.min.js"></script>
<script src="~/lib/d3-scale-chromatic/d3-scale-chromatic.min.js"></script>

<div class="container">
    <div class="row">
        <div class="col-sm-2">
            <span class="label label-info" id="colorname">Color Name:
                Cool</span>
        </div>
        <div class="col-sm-2">
            <div class="dropdown">
                <button class="btn btn-primary dropdown-toggle" type="button"
                    data-toggle="dropdown">
                    Color Maps
```

```html
                            <span class="caret"></span>
                        </button>
                        <ul class="dropdown-menu" id="dm">
                            <li><a href="#">PRGn</a></li>
                            <li><a href="#">PiYG</a></li>
                            <li><a href="#">PuOr</a></li>
                            <li><a href="#">RdBu</a></li>
                            <li><a href="#">RdGy</a></li>
                            <li><a href="#">RdYlBu</a></li>
                            <li><a href="#">RdYlGn</a></li>
                            <li><a href="#">Spectral</a></li>
                            <li><a href="#">Blues</a></li>
                            <li><a href="#">Greenss</a></li>
                            <li><a href="#">Greys</a></li>
                            <li><a href="#">Oranges</a></li>
                            <li><a href="#">Purples</a></li>
                            <li><a href="#">Reds</a></li>
                            <li><a href="#">BuGn</a></li>
                            <li><a href="#">BuPu</a></li>
                            <li><a href="#">GnBu</a></li>
                            <li><a href="#">OrRd</a></li>
                            <li><a href="#">PuBuGn</a></li>
                            <li><a href="#">PuBu</a></li>
                            <li><a href="#">PuRd</a></li>
                            <li><a href="#">RdPu</a></li>
                            <li><a href="#">YlGn</a></li>
                            <li><a href="#">YlOrBr</a></li>
                            <li><a href="#">YlOrRd</a></li>
                            <li><a href="#">Viridis</a></li>
                            <li><a href="#">Inferno</a></li>
                            <li><a href="#">Magma</a></li>
                            <li><a href="#">Plasma</a></li>
                            <li><a href="#">Warm</a></li>
                            <li><a href="#">Cool</a></li>
                            <li><a href="#">Rainbow</a></li>
                            <li><a href="#">CubehelixDefault</a></li>
                        </ul>
                    </div>
                </div>
        </div>
        <div class="row">
            <svg id="svg1" width="600" height="300"></svg>
        </div>
        <div class="row">
            <p>x*sin(x*x)+1</p>
            <svg id="svg2" width="600" height="400"></svg>
        </div>
    </div>
</div>

@section scripts{
<script type="text/javascript">
    d3.json("JsonData", function (data) {
        // Create colormap:
        var width = 600;
        var height = 400;
```

```
var svg = d3.select("#svg1")
    .append("svg")
    .attr("width", width)
    .attr("height", height);
var cs = d3.scaleSequential(d3["interpolateCool"]).domain([0, width]);
var cb = svg.selectAll("rect")
    .data(d3.range(width), function (d) { return d; })
    .enter()
    .append("rect")
    .attr("x", function (d, i) { return i; })
    .attr("y", 30)
    .attr("height", 250)
    .attr("width", 1)
    .style("fill", function (d) { return cs(d); });

 // curve with colormap:
var xmin = d3.min(data.data4, function (d) { return d.x });
var xmax = d3.max(data.data4, function (d) { return d.x });
var ymin = d3.min(data.data4, function (d) { return d.y });
var ymax = d3.max(data.data4, function (d) { return d.y });
var xscale = d3.scaleLinear().domain([xmin, xmax]).range([10, 580]);
var yscale = d3.scaleLinear().domain([ymin, ymax]).range([10, 380]);
var cs1 = d3.scaleSequential(d3["interpolateCool"])
            .domain([yscale(ymin), yscale(ymax)]);
draw("#svg2", data.data4, cs1);
var svg2 = d3.select("#svg2");
$('#dm li a').on('click', function () {
    var text = $(this).text();
    $('#colorname').text("Color Name: " + text);

    // update rectangle
    cs = d3.scaleSequential(d3["interpolate" +$(this).text()])
            .domain([0, width]);
    svg.selectAll("rect")
        .style("fill", function (d) { return cs(d); });

    // update curve
    cs1 = d3.scaleSequential(d3["interpolate" + $(this).text()])
            .domain([yscale(ymin), yscale(ymax)]);
    svg2.selectAll("line")
        .style("stroke", function (d) { return cs1(yscale(d.y)); })
});

function draw(svgSelection, data4, cs1) {
    var svg = d3.select(svgSelection);
    svg.selectAll("line")
        .data(data4)
        .enter()
        .append("line")
        .attr("x1", function (d, i) { return (data4[i - 1] != null) ?
                xscale(data4[i - 1].x) : xscale(d.x); })
        .attr("y1", function (d, i) { return (data4[i - 1] != null) ?
                yscale(data4[i - 1].y) : yscale(d.y); })
        .attr("x2", function (d, i) { return xscale(d.x); })
```

```
                      .attr("y2", function (d, i) { return yscale(d.y); })
                      .style("fill", "none")
                      .style("stroke", function (d) { return csl(yscale(d.y)); })
                      .style("stroke-width", 5);
            }
       });
  </script>
  }
```

This code implements a dropdown menu that consists of all the color interpolators provided by D3. It then create a rectangle and a curve. It updates the *fill* attribute of the rectangle and the *stroke* attribute of the curve with selected color interpolator from the dropdown list. Note that inside the *draw* function, we use a slightly different approach to create the curve: instead of using the *path* element in the preceding sections, here we use the *line* element, because a path curve takes only one colors. In our case, the curve consists of a sequence of line segments with each segment's stroke being colored by the color derived from the *scaleSequential* function of selected interpolator based on data's *y*-value.

Running this example and selecting a color interpolator from the dropdown list generate the results shown in Figure 3-19.

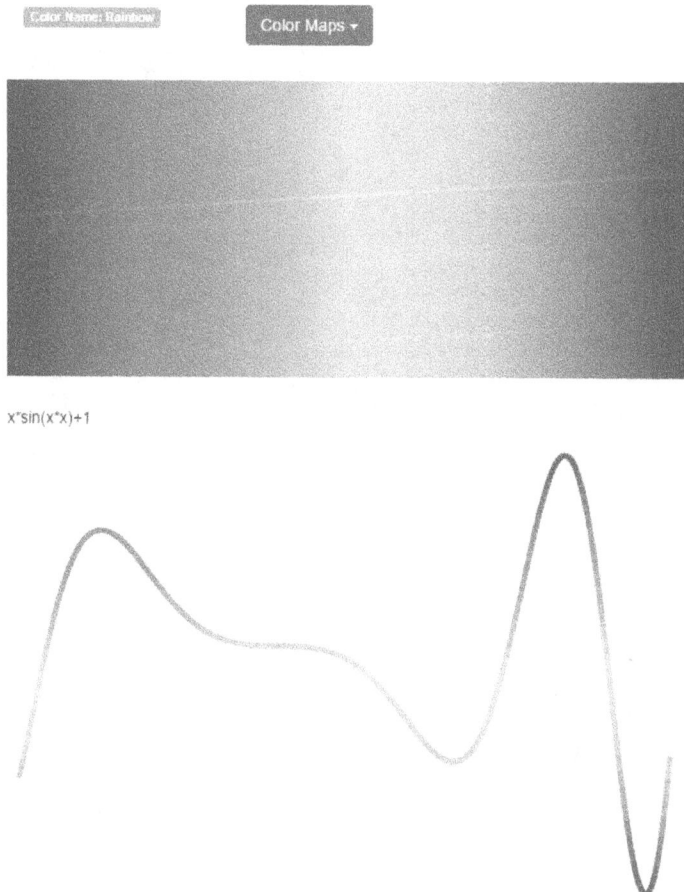

Figure 3-19. Demonstration of colormaps in D3.

Chapter 4
2D Charts with D3

SVG and D3 provide a powerful graphics platform that allows you to easily create a variety of graphics objects in your ASP.NET Core MVC applications. In this chapter, we will turn our attention to the most commonly used data visualization tool – charts. Charts are a well-defined and well-understood graphical representation of data. Nowadays, the use of charts has become common practice in a wide variety of professional fields and in many other aspects of daily life.

I should point out that D3 is not a charting library. It is a library for creating and manipulating the SVG and HTML elements. D3 provides tools to help you visualize and manipulate your data. D3 does not come with a preset array of charts that you can pass your data and then get an output displayed on chart automatically. A few charting libraries built on top of D3 exist, including NVD3, dimple, Google Chart API, etc., in case you want to try out something higher level than D3 in the future.

D3 does, however, enable you to create conventional 2D charts, such as bar, line, pie, polar, etc. Once you understand how to manage your data in proper domain, range, and scales, you can move on to the realization of the chart components, including axes, labels, the title, and the gridline. These components form the basis upon which you will be drawing the chart. Unlike the charting libraries, these components are not readily available but must be developed gradually. This will result in additional work, but it will also allow you to create special features. This means that your D3 charts will be able to respond to particular needs, or at least, they will have a totally original work.

In this chapter, I will show you how to use D3 to create various 2D charts, including line charts and certain special or application-specific charts in ASP.NET Core MVC applications. Some of these are charts that are typically found in commercial charting packages or spreadsheet applications. I will discuss a variety of special charts that display statistical distributions of data or discrete data, including bar, stair-step, stem, error bar, and area charts. You will also learn how to create charts in other coordinate systems, such as pie and polar charts.

Chart Elements

D3 charts can assume a variety forms. In a chart, the data takes on graphic structure through the use of SVG elements specific to the type of chart; there are, however, some features that are common to all charts. The following list quickly overviews the most basic chart elements without getting into details. These elements will often be referred to in this chapter:

- Axes – a graphics object that defines a region of the chart in which the chart is drawn.

- Line and symbols – graphics objects that represent the data you have plotted.
- Text – a graphics object comprising a string of characters.
- Title – the text string object located directly above an axis object.
- Label – the text string object associated with the axis object.
- Legend – the text string array object that represents the color and values of the curves.

The 2D charts use two values to represent each data point. This type of chart is very useful for describing relationships between data and is often involved in the statistical analysis of data, with wide applications in the scientific, mathematics, engineering, and finance communities, as well as daily life.

Chart Layout

Before using D3 to create 2D charts, we need to discuss the chart layout commonly used in the D3 community. The layout convention we are going to use is the one suggested by the creator of D3, Mike Bostock (https://bl.ocks.org/mbostock/3019563), as shown in Figure 4-1.

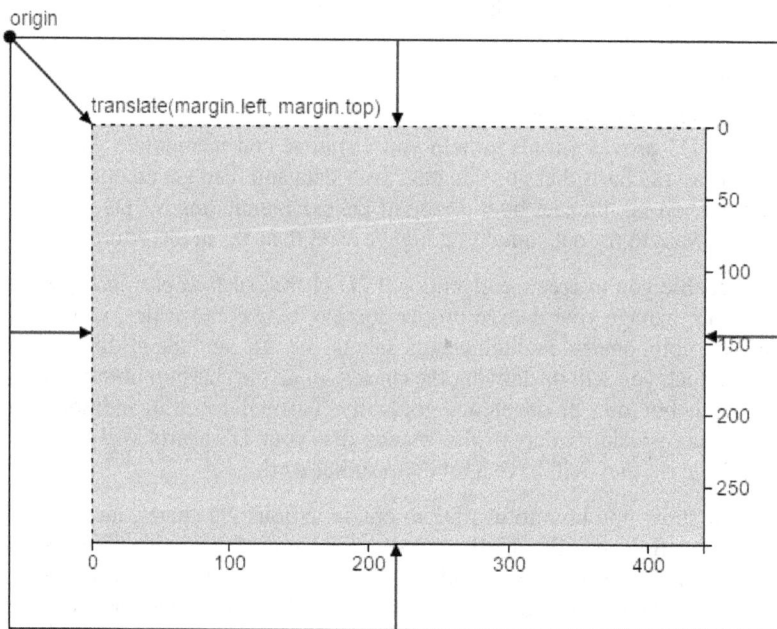

Figure 4-1. D3 chart layout.

You can see from this figure that the origin (0, 0) in the SVG coordinates is at its top-left corner, the chart area (gray colored) is determined by the predefined margins. For each chart, there are four different margin settings: top, right, bottom, and left (clockwise from the top, as in CSS):

```
var margin = { top: 20, right: 20, bottom: 20, left: 20 };
```

A flexible chart implementation should allow its user to set different values for each of these margins.

We then define *width* and *height* as the inner dimensions of the chart area:

```
var width = outWidth - margin.left - margin.right;
var height = outHeight - margin.top - margin.bottom;
```

Next, we define svg as a g element that translates the origin to the top-left corner of the chart area:

```
var svg = d3.select("#svg")
      .attr("width", width + margin.left + margin.right)
      .attr("height", height + margin.top + margin.bottom)
    .append("g")
      .attr("transform", "translate(" + margin.left + "," + margin.top + ")");
```

With this convention, all subsequent code can ignore margins. For example, to create x and y scales, you can simply use the following code:

```
var x = d3.scale.linear().range([0, width]);
var y = d3.scale.linear().range([height, 0]);
```

If you want to add axes to the chart, you can position them correctly by default in the "*left*" and "*top*" orientations. For "*right*" or "*bottom*" orientation, you need to translate the axis g element by the *width* or *height*, respectively. From Figure 4-1, you see that we place axes inside the chart margins instead of being the chart body. This approach has the advantage of treating axes as peripheral elements in a chart, hence not convoluting the chart body implementation and making axes rendering independent of the chart body and easily reusable.

Axes

Charts often have axes – two perpendicular lines that allow the user to refer to the values of the coordinates (x, y) for each data point $P(x, y)$, as shown in Figure 4-2.

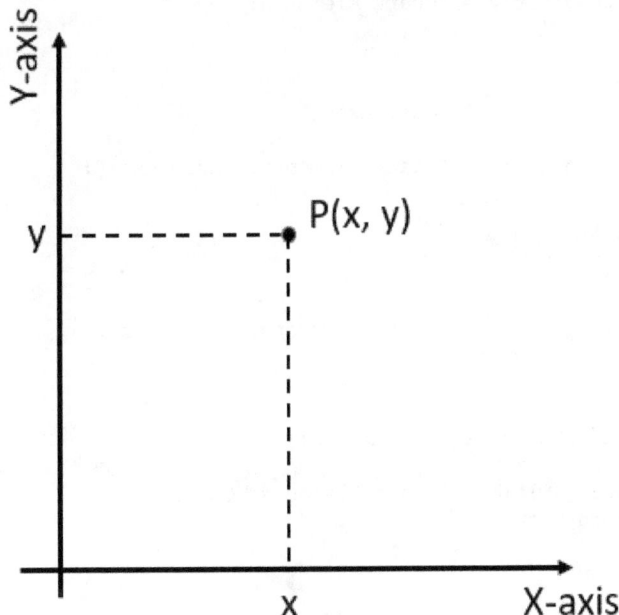

Figure 4-2. Axes in a 2D chart.

The horizontal line usually represents the *x*-axis, and the vertical line, the *y*-axis. A scale can be defined on each axis, which can be either numerical or categorical. Each axis is divided into segments corresponding to the particular range of values represented by the scale. The boundaries between one segment and the next are called ticks. Each tick represents the value of the scale associated with that axis. Generally, we call this tick as tick labels.

Basic Axes

D3 provides various axis elements, including the top, right, bottom, and left axes. Here, I will use an example to illustrate how to create basic axes using D3. Open Visual Studio 2017 and start with a new ASP.NET Core MVC project and name it *Chapter04*. Add *Controllers/ChartElementsControllor.cs* and replace its content with the following code:

```
using Microsoft.AspNetCore.Mvc;

namespace Chapter04.Controllers
{
    public class ChartElementsController : Controller
    {
        // GET: /<controller>/
        public IActionResult Index()
        {
            ViewBag.Title = "Chart Elements: Home";
            return View();
        }

        public IActionResult ChartLayout()
        {
            ViewBag.Title = "Chart Elements: Layout";
            return View();
        }

        public IActionResult BasicAxes()
        {
            ViewBag.Title = "Chart Elements: Basic Axes";
            return View();
        }

        public IActionResult TimeAxes()
        {
            ViewBag.Title = "Chart Elements: Time Axes";
            return View();
        }

        public IActionResult CustomAxes()
        {
            ViewBag.Title = "Chart Elements: Custom Axes";
            return View();
        }
    }
}
```

Add a new folder named *ChartElements* to the *Views* folder. Add a new view named *BasicAxes.cshtml* to this new folder and replace its content with the following code:

```
@{
    ViewData["Title"] = ViewBag.Title;
}
<h3>@ViewBag.Title</h3>
@Html.Partial("_Links")

<hr />

<div class="container">
    <div class="row">
        <p>Basic Axes</p>
        <svg id="svg"></svg>
    </div>
</div>

@section scripts{
<script type="text/javascript">
    var width = 600;
    var height = 450;
    var margin = { top: 50, right: 50, bottom: 50, left: 50 };
    var w = width - margin.left - margin.right;
    var h = height - margin.top - margin.bottom;

    var g = d3.select("#svg")
        .attr("width", width)
        .attr("height", height)
        .append("g")
        .attr("transform", "translate(" + margin.left + "," + margin.top + ")");

    // horizontal bottom axis
    var scale = d3.scaleLinear().domain([-1, 1]).range([0, w]);
    var axis = d3.axisBottom().scale(scale);
    g.append("g")
        .attr("transform", "translate(0," + h + ")")
        .call(axis);

    // horizontal top axis
    scale = d3.scaleLinear().domain([0, 100]).range([0, w]);
    axis = d3.axisTop().scale(scale);
    g.append("g").call(axis);

    // vertical left axis
    scale = d3.scaleLinear().domain([-0.02, 0.04]).range([h, 0]);
    axis = d3.axisLeft().scale(scale);
    g.append("g").call(axis);

    // vertical right axis
    scale = d3.scaleLinear().domain([500, 1000]).range([h, 0]);
    axis = d3.axisRight().scale(scale);
    g.append("g")
        .attr("transform", "translate(" + w + ",0)")
        .call(axis);
</script>
}
```

I assume that you have installed D3 library in your project and referred it in the _Layout.cshtml_ file located in the *Views/Shared* folder. Here, we use the layout convention discussed in the preceding section to define the *g* element (see the highlighted code). We then add four axes to the layout using the *axisBottom*, *axisTop*, *axisLeft*, and *axisRight* functions in D3.

Running this example, selecting the *Chart Elements* tab, and clicking the *Basic Axes* link produce the results shown in Figure 4-3.

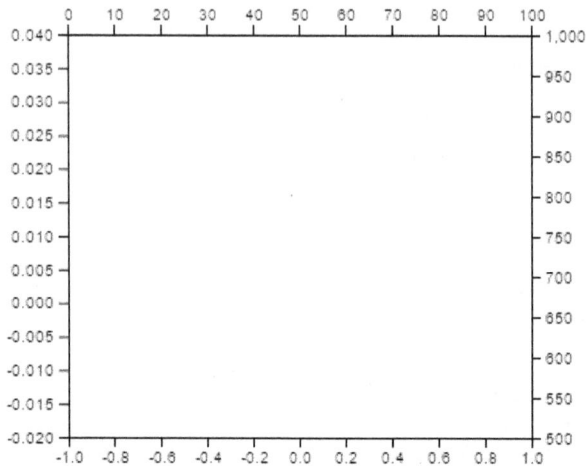

Figure 4-3. Demonstration of basic axes in D3.

Here, we use the *scaleLinear* function to create the *x*- and *y*-axes.

Time Axes

We can also create the time axis using the *scaleTime* function. Add a new view *TimeAxes.cshtml* to the *Views/ChartElements* folder and replace its content with the following code:

```
@{
    ViewData["Title"] = ViewBag.Title;
}
<h3>@ViewBag.Title</h3>
@Html.Partial("_Links")

<hr />

<div class="container">
    <div class="row">
        <p>Time Axes</p>
        <svg id="svg"></svg>
    </div>
</div>

@section scripts{
    <script type="text/javascript">
        var width = 400;
```

```
                var height = 350;
                var margin = { top: 50, right: 50, bottom: 50, left: 50 };
                var w = width - margin.left - margin.right;
                var h = height - margin.top - margin.bottom;

                var g = d3.select("#svg")
                    .attr("width", width)
                    .attr("height", height)
                    .append("g")
                    .attr("transform", "translate(" + margin.left + "," +
                        margin.top + ")");

                // horizontal bottom axis
                var scale = d3.scaleTime().domain([new Date(2016, 1, 1),
                    new Date(2016, 12, 31)]).range([0, w]);
                var axis = d3.axisBottom().scale(scale);
                g.append("g")
                    .attr("transform", "translate(0," + h + ")")
                    .call(axis);

                // horizontal top axis
                scale = d3.scaleTime().domain([new Date(2016, 1, 1),
                    new Date(2016, 1, 31)]).range([0, w]);
                axis = d3.axisTop().scale(scale);
                g.append("g").call(axis);

                // vertical left axis
                scale = d3.scaleTime().domain([new Date(2010, 1, 1),
                    new Date(2017, 1, 1)]).range([h, 0]);
                axis = d3.axisLeft().scale(scale);
                g.append("g").call(axis);

                // vertical right axis
                scale = d3.scaleTime().domain([new Date(2017, 1, 1, 5, 0, 0),
                    new Date(2017, 1, 1, 10, 10, 0)]).range([h, 0]);
                axis = d3.axisRight().scale(scale);
                g.append("g")
                    .attr("transform", "translate(" + w + ",0)")
                    .call(axis);
        </script>
    }
```

This code produces the results shown in Figure 4-4. You can see from this figure that some of the tick labels are overlapped each other along the horizontal axes. There are two ways to solve this problem: one is to reduce the number of ticks along the axis and the other one is to rotate the tick labels by a proper angle.

Custom Axes

You can also customize and format the text used for the tick labels. Let us consider an example, which shows several approaches to modify the tick labels.

Add *Views/ChartElements/CustomAxes.cshtml* and replace its content with the following code:

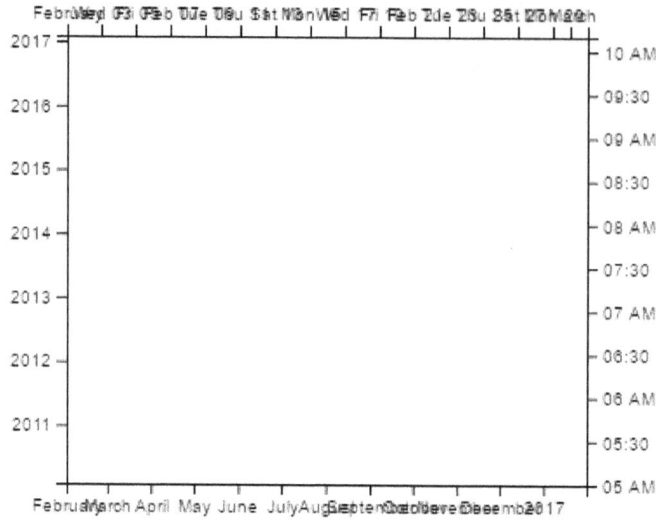

Figure 4-4. Demonstration of time axes.

```
@{
    ViewData["Title"] = ViewBag.Title;
}
<h3>@ViewBag.Title</h3>
@Html.Partial("_Links")
<hr />

<div class="container">
    <div class="row">
        <div class="col-sm-4">
            <p>Bottom time axis</p>
            <br />
            <div id="svg1"></div>
        </div>
        <div class="col-sm-4">
            <p>Top time axis</p>
            <br />
            <div id="svg2"></div>
        </div>
    </div>
    <div class="row">
        <div class="col-sm-4">
            <p>Bottom time axis with fewer ticks</p>
            <br />
            <div id="svg3"></div>
        </div>
        <div class="col-sm-4">
            <p>Top time axis with fewer ticks</p>
            <br />
            <div id="svg4"></div>
        </div>
    </div>
</div>
```

```
    <div class="row">
        <div class="col-sm-4">
            <p>Bottom axis: ticks with %</p>
            <br />
            <div id="svg5"></div>
        </div>
        <div class="col-sm-4">
            <p>Top axis: ticks with unicode character</p>
            <br />
            <div id="svg6"></div>
        </div>
    </div>
</div>

@section scripts{
<script type="text/javascript">

    var width = 340;
    var height = 150;
    var margin = { top: 50, right: 20, bottom: 20, left: 30 }
    var w = width - margin.left - margin.right;
    var h = height - margin.top - margin.bottom;

    var svg = d3.select("#svg1")
        .append("svg")
        .attr("width", width)
        .attr("height", height)
        .append("g")
        .attr("transform", "translate(" + margin.left + "," + margin.top + ")");
    var scale = d3.scaleTime().domain([new Date(2016, 1, 1),
        new Date(2016, 12, 31)]).range([0, w]);
    var axis = d3.axisBottom()
        .scale(scale)
        .tickFormat(d3.timeFormat("%Y-%m-%d"));
    svg.append("g")
        .call(axis)
        .selectAll("text")
        .style("text-anchor", "end")
        .attr("dx", "-0.8em")
        .attr("dy", "0.15em")
        .attr("transform", "rotate(-60)");

    svg = d3.select("#svg2")
        .append("svg")
        .attr("width", width)
        .attr("height", height)
        .append("g")
        .attr("transform", "translate(0," + margin.top + ")");
    scale = d3.scaleTime().domain([new Date(2016, 1, 1),
        new Date(2016, 1, 31)]).range([0, w]);
    axis = d3.axisTop()
        .scale(scale)
        .tickFormat(d3.timeFormat("%m-%d"));
    svg.append("g")
        .call(axis)
```

```
        .selectAll("text")
        .style("text-anchor", "start")
        .attr("dx", "1.0em")
        .attr("dy", "-0.1em")
        .attr("transform", "rotate(-60)");

svg = d3.select("#svg3")
    .append("svg")
    .attr("width", width)
    .attr("height", height)
    .append("g")
    .attr("transform", "translate(0," + margin.top + ")");
scale = d3.scaleTime().domain([new Date(2016, 1, 1),
    new Date(2016, 12, 31)]).range([0, w]);
axis = d3.axisBottom()
    .scale(scale)
    .ticks(6)
    .tickFormat(d3.timeFormat("%Y-%m-%d"));
svg.append("g")
    .call(axis)
    .selectAll("text")
    .style("text-anchor", "end")
    .attr("dx", "-0.8em")
    .attr("dy", "0.15em")
    .attr("transform", "rotate(-60)");

svg = d3.select("#svg4")
    .append("svg")
    .attr("width", width)
    .attr("height", height)
    .append("g")
    .attr("transform", "translate(0," + margin.top + ")");

scale = d3.scaleTime().domain([new Date(2016, 1, 1),
    new Date(2016, 1, 31)]).range([0, w]);
axis = d3.axisTop()
    .scale(scale)
    .ticks(6)
    .tickFormat(d3.timeFormat("%m-%d"));
svg.append("g")
    .call(axis)
    .selectAll("text")
    .style("text-anchor", "start")
    .attr("dx", "1.0em")
    .attr("dy", "-0.1em")
    .attr("transform", "rotate(-60)");

svg = d3.select("#svg5")
    .append("svg")
    .attr("width", width)
    .attr("height", height)
    .append("g")
    .attr("transform", "translate(0," + margin.top + ")");
scale = d3.scaleLinear().domain([0, 100]).range([0, w]);
axis = d3.axisBottom()
```

```
        .scale(scale)
        .ticks(6)
        .tickFormat(function (d) { return d + "%"});
    svg.append("g")
        .call(axis);

    svg = d3.select("#svg6")
        .append("svg")
        .attr("width", width)
        .attr("height", height)
        .append("g")
        .attr("transform", "translate(0," + margin.top + ")");
    scale = d3.scaleLinear().domain([0, 40]).range([0, w]);
    axis = d3.axisTop()
        .scale(scale)
        .ticks(8)
        .tickFormat(function (d) { return d + "\u00B0F"});
    svg.append("g")
        .call(axis);
</script>
}
```

This code produces the results shown in Figure 4-5. Here, we use several ways to modify the tick labels, including rotating tick labels, specifying the number of ticks, and formatting tick labels.

Bottom time axis

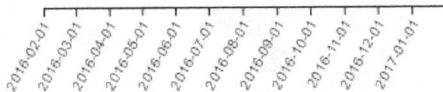

Top time axis

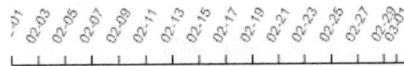

Bottom time axis with fewer ticks

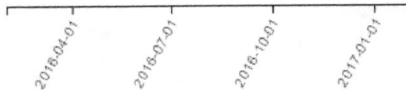

Top time axis with fewer ticks

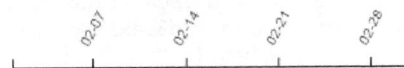

Bottom axis: ticks with %

Top axis: ticks with unicode character

Figure 4-5. Demonstration of custom axes.

Gridlines

In the preceding sections, we demonstrated how to create various chart axes. Here, we will add the gridlines to the axes. Instead writing code directly to the view, we will implement some JavaScript helper functions for the axes with gridlines. These functions can be easily reused in creating 2D charts in D3. Open *wwwroot/js/site.js* file and add the *setAxesGridlines* function to this file:

```
function setAxesGridlines(svgSelection, options) {

    // define default values
    var xdomain = options.xdomain || [0, 100];
    var ydomain = options.ydomain || [0, 100];
    var width = options.width || 400;
    var height = options.height || 300;
    var margin = options.margin || { top: 20, right: 20, bottom: 20, left: 20 };
    var isTimeAxis = options.isTimeAxis || false;
    var isGridline = options.isGridline || true;

    var w = width - margin.left - margin.right;
    var h = height - margin.top - margin.bottom;

    var xscale, yscale;
    var svg = d3.select(svgSelection)
        .attr("width", width)
        .attr("height", height)
        .append("g")
        .attr("transform", "translate(" + margin.left + "," + margin.top + ")");

    // box for chart area
    svg.append("rect")
        .attr("width", w)
        .attr("height", h)
        .style("fill", "none")
        .style("stroke", "black")
        .style("stroke-width", 0.2);

    //X-axis:
    if (!isTimeAxis) {
        xscale = d3.scaleLinear().domain(xdomain).range([0, w]);
        var xaxis = d3.axisBottom().scale(xscale);
        svg.append("g")
            .attr("class", "x-axis")
            .attr("transform", "translate(0," + h + ")")
            .call(xaxis);
    } else {
        xscale = d3.scaleTime().domain(xdomain).range([0, w]);
        var xaxis1 = d3.axisBottom().scale(xscale);
        svg.append("g")
            .attr("class", "x-axis")
            .attr("transform", "translate(0," + h + ")")
            .call(xaxis1)
            .selectAll("text")
            .style("text-anchor", "end")
            .attr("dx", "-0.8em")
            .attr("dy", "0.15em")
```

```
            .attr("transform", "rotate(-60)");
    }

    //Y-axis:
    yscale = d3.scaleLinear().domain(ydomain).range([h, 0]);
    var yaxis = d3.axisLeft().scale(yscale);
    svg.append("g")
        .attr("class", "y-axis")
        .call(yaxis);

    //grid lines:
    if (isGridline) {
        svg.selectAll("line.ygrid")
            .data(yscale.ticks())
            .enter()
            .append("line")
            .attr("class", "ygrid")
            .attr("x1", 0)
            .attr("x2", w)
            .attr("y1", function (d) { return yscale(d); })
            .attr("y2", function (d) { return yscale(d); })
            .attr("stroke", "lightgray")
            .attr("stroke-width", "1px");

        svg.selectAll("line.xgrid")
            .data(xscale.ticks())
            .enter()
            .append("line")
            .attr("class", "xgrid")
            .attr("x1", function (d) { return xscale(d); })
            .attr("x2", function (d) { return xscale(d); })
            .attr("y1", 0)
            .attr("y2", h)
            .attr("stroke", "lightgray")
            .attr("stroke-width", "1px");
    }
    return { xscale, yscale, svg, w, h };
}
```

This code takes the SVG selection as the required input argument. It also includes a key-word *options* argument, which allows you to specify the input parameters for the *x* and *y* value domains (or ranges), viewport size (*width* and *height*), *margin*, *isTimeAxis*, and *isGridline*. If you do not use the key word approach, you have to include all input arguments in your function with most of them being optional. Then the function call will become really terrifying.

Next, we add *x*- and *y*-axes. Depending on the *isTimeAxis* parameter, we create the *x*-axis using the *linearScale* function when the parameter is false, while using the *timeScale* function when the parameter is true.

We use the axis ticks as the data source to draw horizontal and vertical straight lines through the locations of ticks, which forms gridlines for our chart.

Finally, this function returns several variables including *xscale*, *yscale*, *svg*, *w*, and *h*. These variables will be useful when you add more features to your chart.

We can test this function by adding a new view *Gridline.cshtml* to the *Views/ChartElements* folder. Here is the code for this view:

```
@{
    ViewData["Title"] = ViewBag.Title;
}
<h3>@ViewBag.Title</h3>
@Html.Partial("_Links")

<hr />

<div class="container">
    <div class="row">
        <div class="col-sm-4">
            <p style="margin-top:30px">X-Y axes with grid lines</p>
            <svg id="svg1"></svg>
        </div>
        <div class="col-sm-4">
            <p style="margin-top:30px">Time axes with grid lines</p>
            <svg id="svg2"></svg>
        </div>
    </div>
</div>

<div id="showResults"></div>

@section scripts{
<script type="text/javascript">
    var options = {
        xdomain : [0, 10],
        ydomain : [-5, 20],
        margin : { top: 20, right: 20, bottom: 40, left: 50 }
    }
    setAxesGridlines("#svg1", options);

    options = {
        xdomain: [new Date(2016, 1, 1), new Date(2016, 12, 31)],
        margin: { top: 20, right: 20, bottom: 60, left: 50 },
        isTimeAxis: true
    }
    setAxesGridlines("#svg2", options);
</script>
}
```

This code looks very simple. Here, we create two separate gridlines: one is for *x*-axis with double values and the other one for the *x*-axis with the time variable. In the first grid, we define the *options* variable that includes the *x* and *y* value ranges as well as the *margin*, and then call the *setAxesGridlines* function implemented in the *site.js* file to create the gridlines.

The second grid has a time axis. In this case, we set the *isTimeAxis* parameter to *true* right after the *margin* parameter. We expect the tick labels for the time axis may take more space so we set the *margin.bottom* to 60*px*.

Running this example produces the results shown in Figure 4-6.

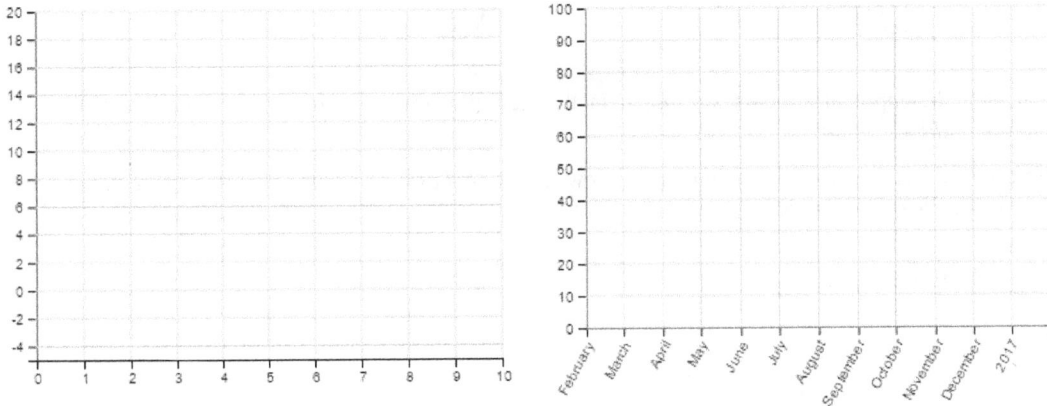

Figure 4-6. Demonstration of gridlines without (left) and with (right) time axis.

Title and Labels

In the preceding section, we implemented a helper function in the *site.js* file for creating axes and gridlines. Based on this function, we can add more features using new functions. This modularized approach allows you to build your own chart library easily in a piece-by-piece manner.

In this section, we will add the title and labels for the axes. Add a new helper function named *addTitleLabel* to the *site.js* file:

```
function addTitleLabel(svg, w, h, options) {
    var title = options.title || "Title";
    var xlabel = options.xlable || "X Axis";
    var ylabel = options.ylabel || "Y Axis";
    var margin = options.margin || { top: 20, right: 20, bottom: 20, left: 20 };

    // title
    svg.append("text")
        .attr("x", (w / 2))
        .attr("y", -margin.top + 15)
        .attr("text-anchor", "middle")
        .style("font-size", "14px")
        .text(title);

    // x label
    svg.append("text")
        .attr("x", w / 2)
        .attr("y", h + margin.bottom - 15)
        .attr("text-anchor", "middle")
        .style("font-size", "12px")
        .text(xlabel);

    // y label
    svg.append("text")
        .attr("text-anchor", "middle")
        .attr("transform", "translate(" + (-margin.left + 15) + "," +
            (h / 2) + ") rotate(-90)")
```

```
        .style("font-size", "12px")
        .text(ylabel);
}
```

Note that the input arguments *svg, w, h* in this function must be the returned variables from the *setAxesGridlines* function.

We can test this function by adding a new view, *TitleLabel.cshtml*, to the *Views/ChartElements* folder. Here is the code for this view:

```
@{
    ViewData["Title"] = ViewBag.Title;
}

<h3>@ViewBag.Title</h3>
@Html.Partial("_Links")

<hr />

<div class="container">
    <div class="row">
        <div class="col-sm-5">
            <p style="margin-top:30px">X-Y axes with grid lines</p>
            <svg id="svg1"></svg>
        </div>
        <div class="col-sm-5">
            <p style="margin-top:30px">Time axes with grid lines</p>
            <svg id="svg2"></svg>
        </div>
    </div>
</div>

<div id="showResults"></div>

@section scripts{
    <script type="text/javascript">
        var options = {
            width: 450,
            height: 400,
            xdomain: [0, 10],
            ydomain: [-5, 20],
            margin: { top: 40, right: 20, bottom: 60, left: 50 },
            title: "Chart One"
        };
        var grid = setAxesGridlines("#svg1", options);
        addTitleLabel(grid.svg, grid.w, grid.h, options);

        options = {
            width: 450,
            height: 400,
            margin: { top: 40, right: 20, bottom: 100, left: 50 },
            xdomain: [new Date(2016, 1, 1), new Date(2016, 12, 31)],
            ydomain: [0, 100],
            isTimeAxis: true,
            title: "Chart Two",
            xlabel:"Date"
```

```
        };
        grid = setAxesGridlines("#svg2", options);
        addTitleLabel(grid.svg, grid.w, grid.h, options);

    </script>
}
```

The code creates two grids with titles and axis labels. Running this example produces the results shown in Figure 4-7.

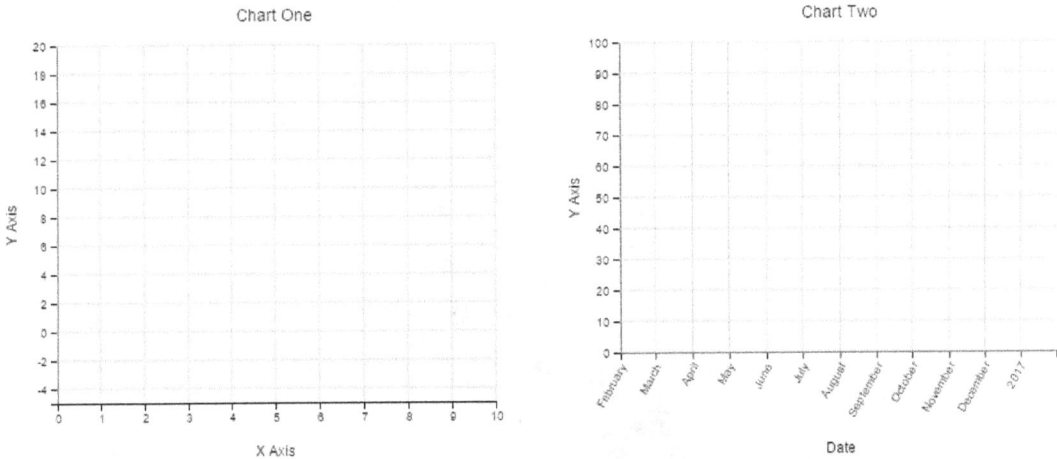

Figure 4-7. Demonstration of title and labels.

Line Charts

In the preceding sections, we have created axes, gridlines, title, and axis labels using the JavaScript helper functions. In this section, we will apply these functions to build 2D line charts.

Simple Line Charts

In fact, the most basic and useful type of chart you can create with D3 is probably a simple 2D line chart of numerical data. It is easy to create a 2D *X-Y* line chart in D3. Let us use an example to illustrate the procedure. Add *Controllers/LineChartsCotroller.cs* and replace its content with the following code:

```
using Chapter04.Models;
using Microsoft.AspNetCore.Mvc;
namespace Chapter04.Controllers
{
    public class LineChartsController : Controller
    {
        // GET: /<controller>/
        public IActionResult Index()
        {
            ViewBag.Title = "Line Charts: Home";
            return View();
        }
```

```
public IActionResult SimpleLine()
{
    ViewBag.Title = "Simple Line Charts";
    return View();
}

public IActionResult MultiLines()
{
    ViewBag.Title = "Multiple Line Charts";
    return View();
}

public IActionResult TwoYAxes()
{
    ViewBag.Title = "Line Charts with Two Y Axes";
    return View();
}

public JsonResult JsonData()
{
    var data = ModelHelper.MathData();
    return Json(data);
}
        }
    }
```

The methods in the above code will be used to generate different types of 2D line charts. Here, we only need the *SimpleLine* and *JsonData* methods to create a simple line chart.

Input Data

In this example, we will use the same data as we did when we created curves in the Chapter 3. Add a new folder named *Models* to the project. Add *Models/ModelHelper.cs* and copy the methods *MathData* and *MathFunctionData* from the same helper file used in the previous chapter, as shown in the following code snippet:

```
using System;
using System.Collections.Generic;

namespace Chapter04.Models
{
    public class ModelHelper
    {
        public static object MathData()
        {
            // 1/(x*x+1):
            double[] range = new double[] { -5.0, 5.0 };
            Func<double, double> f = (x) => 1.0 / (x * x + 1.0);
            var data1 = MathFunctionData(f, range, 300);

            ......

            return new { data1, data2, data3, data4 };
        }
```

```
private static List<object> MathFunctionData(Func<double, double> f,
    double[] xRange, int numPoints)
{
    double dx = (xRange[1] - xRange[0]) / numPoints;
    List<object> objs = new List<object>();
    for (var x = xRange[0]; x < xRange[1]; x = x + dx)
    {
        var y = f(x);
        objs.Add(new { x, y });
    }
    return objs;
}
}
}
```

Chart Function

Add a new JavaScript function *drawLineChart* to the *site.js* file. Here is the code for this function:

```
function drawLineChart(svgSelection, data, options) {
    var width = options.width || 400;
    var height = options.height || 300;
    var margin = options.margin || { top: 20, right: 20, bottom: 20, left: 20 };
    var isTimeAxis = options.isTimeAxis || false;
    var isGridline = options.isGridline || true;

    var xdomain = [d3.min(data, function (d) { return d.x; }),
                   d3.max(data, function (d) { return d.x; })];
    var ydomain = [d3.min(data, function (d) { return d.y; }),
                   d3.max(data, function (d) { return d.y; })];

    options.xdomain = xdomain;
    options.ydomain = ydomain;

    var grid = setAxesGridlines(svgSelection, options);
    var xscale = grid.xscale;
    var yscale = grid.yscale;
    var svg = grid.svg;

    var gen = d3.line()
        .x(function (d) { return xscale(d.x); })
        .y(function (d) { return yscale(d.y); });

    svg.append("path")
        .attr("d", gen(data))
        .attr("stroke", "black")
        .attr("stroke-width", 2)
        .attr("fill", "none");

    return grid;
}
```

This function first defines the default parameters included in the *options* argument. It then calculates the *xdomain* and *ydomain* using the *x*- and *y*-values from the input data (in JSON format). Next, the function calls the *setAxesGridlines* function to perform the *scale* and create axes and gridlines based on the input data. The code then converts the JSON data into the SVG path mini-language format using the *d3.line* function combining with the returned variables, *xscale* and *yscale*, from the *setAxesGridlines* function. Finally, we add the *path* to the same *svg* container as what we used to create axes and gridlines. This method returns the same set of variables as the *setAxesGridlines* function, which will be used when we add the title and labels to the chart.

The *drawLineChart* function requires the input data with the following JSON format:

```
[
    {
        "x": -5,
        "y": 0.038461538461538464
    },
    {
        "x": -4.966666666666667,
        "y": 0.038959352408986625
    },

    ......

    {
        "x": 4.999999999999985,
        "y": 0.038461538461538686
    }
]
```

Otherwise, if your data is a double array, you need to make corresponding modifications to this function: i.e., changing *d.x* and *d.y* to *d*[0] and *d*[1].

Creating a Simple Line Chart

Now, we can use the *drawLineChart* to create a 2D line chart. Add a new folder named *LineCharts* to the *View* folder. Add *Views/LineCharts/SimpleLine.cshtml* and replace its content with the following code:

```
@{
    ViewData["Title"] = ViewBag.Title;
}

<h3>@ViewBag.Title</h3>
@Html.Partial("_Links")

<hr />

<div class="container">
    <div class="row">
        <div class="col-sm-5">
            <svg id="svg1"></svg>
        </div>
        <div class="col-sm-5">
            <svg id="svg2"></svg>
        </div>
```

```
        </div>
        <div class="row">
            <div class="col-sm-5">
                <svg id="svg3"></svg>
            </div>
            <div class="col-sm-5">
                <svg id="svg4"></svg>
            </div>
        </div>
    </div>

    @section scripts{
    <script type="text/javascript">

        d3.json("JsonData", function (data) {
            var options = {
                width: 450,
                height: 400,
                margin: { top: 30, right: 10, bottom: 60, left: 60 },
                xlabel: "X Value",
                ylabel: "Y Value"
            };

            options.title = "1/(x^2+1)"
            var chart = drawLineChart("#svg1", data.data1, options);
            addTitleLabel(chart.svg, chart.w, chart.h, options);

            options.title = "sin(x)"
            var chart = drawLineChart("#svg2", data.data2, options);
            addTitleLabel(chart.svg, chart.w, chart.h, options);

            options.title = "sqrt(x)"
            var chart = drawLineChart("#svg3", data.data3, options);
            addTitleLabel(chart.svg, chart.w, chart.h, options);

            options.title = "x*sin(x^2)+1"
            var chart = drawLineChart("#svg4", data.data4, options);
            addTitleLabel(chart.svg, chart.w, chart.h, options);
        });

    </script>
    }
```

Here, we create four simple line charts for four mathematical functions based on the JSON data, *data.data1*, *data.data2*, *data.data3*, and *data.data4*. Note that we can reuse the parameters defined in the *options* variable and only need to change the *title* parameter for different charts.

From the above code, you can see how easy it is to create simple 2D line charts using our JavaScript helper functions.

Running this code, selecting the *Line Charts* tab, and clicking on the *Simple Line Charts* link produce the results shown in Figure 4-8.

Figure 4-8 shows that you can easily create a professional-like 2D line charts in D3. In the following sections, we will add more features to the 2D line charts.

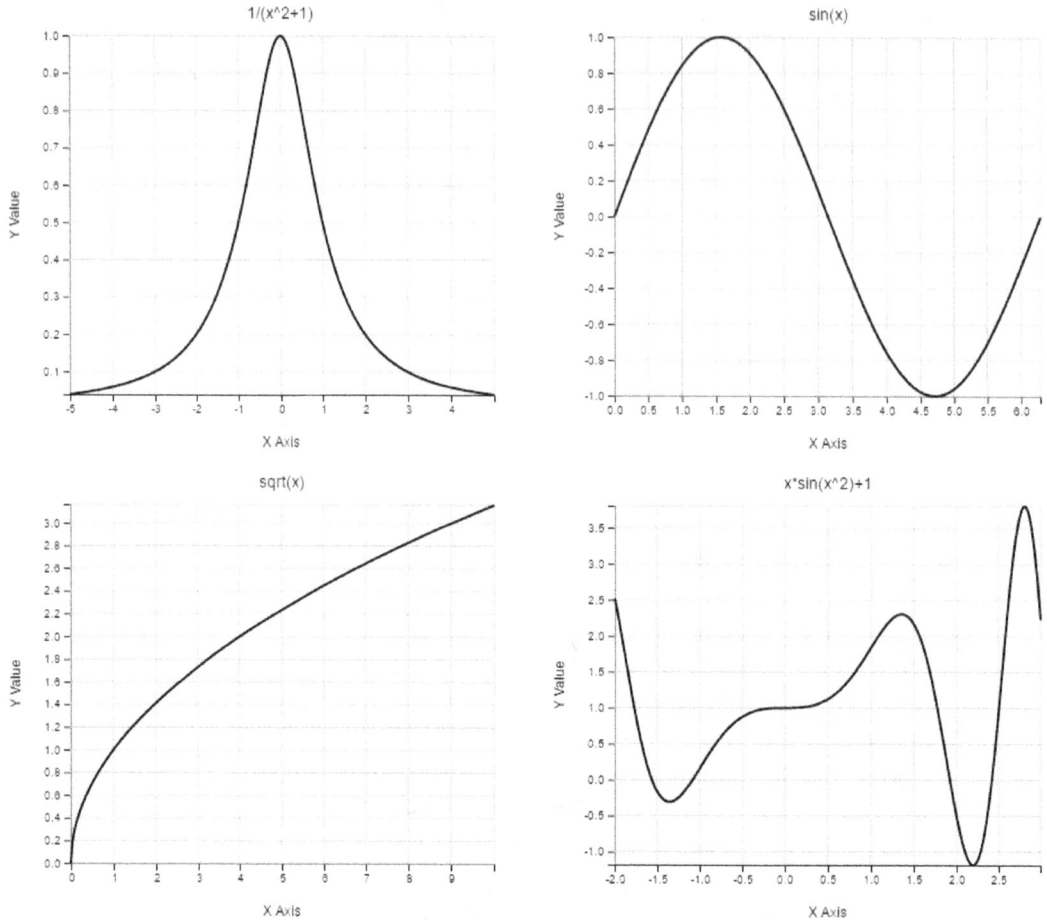

Figure 4-8. Demonstration of simple line charts.

Multiple Line Charts

The *drawLineChart* function is used to create a simple line chart with only a single curve. In some cases, you may want to add multiple curves to a line chart. In this case, for a given *x* value, there are several *y* values that share the same *x* data range. You can easily create such a 2D chart with multiple lines in D3.

Chart Function

Add a new function *drawMultiLineChart* to the *site.js* function:

```
function drawMultiLineChart(svgSelection, data, options) {
    var width = options.width || 400;
    var height = options.height || 300;
    var margin = options.margin || { top: 20, right: 20, bottom: 20, left: 20 };
    var isTimeAxis = options.isTimeAxis || false;
    var isGridline = options.isGridline || true;
    var isLegend = options.isLegend || true;
```

```
var xdomain = [d3.min(data, function (d) { return d.x; }),
               d3.max(data, function (d) { return d.x; })];
var ydomain = [d3.min(data, function (d) { return d.y; }),
               d3.max(data, function (d) { return d.y; })];
options.xdomain = xdomain;
options.ydomain = ydomain;

var grid = setAxesGridlines(svgSelection, options);

var xscale = grid.xscale;
var yscale = grid.yscale;
var svg = grid.svg;
var color = d3.scaleOrdinal(d3.schemeCategory10);

var gen = d3.line()
    .curve(d3.curveBasis)
    .x(function (d) { return xscale(d.x); })
    .y(function (d) { return yscale(d.y); });

var dataGroup = d3.nest().key(function (d) { return d.id; }).entries(data);

dataGroup.forEach(function (d, i) {
    svg.append("path")
        .attr("d", gen(d.values))
        .attr("stroke", function () { return d.color = color(d.key); })
        .attr("stroke-width", 2)
        .attr("fill", "none");

    // Add legend:
    if (isLegend) {
        var lgdspace = width / (dataGroup.length + 1);
        svg.append("text")
            .attr("x", 0.5 * lgdspace + i * lgdspace)
            .attr("y", -10)
            .attr("fill", function () { return d.color = color(d.key); })
            .text(d.key);
    }
});

    return grid;
}
```

This function defines the *x* and *y* domains from the input JSON data. Note that the domains calculated here are for data from all curves. The special format of our input JSON data makes it possible to compute the domains using this simple expression. Otherwise, you may need to loop through the data for each curve in order to calculate the overall domains.

The code then calls the *setAxesGridlines* function to create axes and gridlines based on the data domains. It also uses the *scaleOrdinal* function to color the lines based on the *d3.shemeCategory10*. Next, it converts the JSON data into the SVG path mini-language format using the *d3.line* function. You may notice that we specify the curve interpolation with the *.curve(d3.curveBasis)* command. If we omit this command the default *.curve(d3.curveLinear)* will be used. There are several curve interpolation methods in D3, including:

- *d3.curveLinear*: produces a polyline through the specified points.

- *d3.curveBasis*: produces a cubic basis spline using specified control points.

- *d3.curveStep*: produces a piecewise constant function consisting of alternating horizontal and vertical lines.

- *d3.curveCardinal*: produces a cubic cardinal spline using the specified control points.

- *d3.curveMonotoneX*: produces a cubic spline that preserves monotonicity in y.

- *d3.curveCatmullRom*: produces a cubic *Catmull-Rom* spline.

There are more types of curve interpolations defined in D3. You can specify the type according to your application requirements.

Next, the code uses the *d3.nest* function to group our input data with the *key* (the function name or *id*). The *d3.nest* operation takes a flat data structure and turns it into a nested one. Finally, we apply the *forEach* operator to create each curve and corresponding legend at the top of the chart by looping through all curves included in the *dataGroup*.

Input Data

In order to create 2D multi-line charts using the above function, you need to prepare your input data in a special JSON data format. Here, I generate a sample data from some mathematical functions in the server side to demonstrate the format required by the *drawMultiLineChart* function.

Add a new method *MultiLineData* to the *ModelHelper* class:

```
public static List<object> MultiLineData()
{
    List<object> dat = new List<object>();
    for (int i = 0; i < 101; i++)
    {
        double x = 0.1 * i;
        double y1 = Math.Sin(x);
        double y2 = 1.0 / ((x - 5) * (x - 5) + 1.0);
        double y3 = 0.1 * x * Math.Sin(0.1 * x * x) + 0.1;
        dat.Add(new { id = "Sine", x = x, y = y1 });
        dat.Add(new { id = "1/(x*x+1)", x = x, y = y2 });
        dat.Add(new { id = "x*sin(x*x)", x = x, y = y3 });
    }
    return dat;
}
```

The above method produces the following JSON data format:

```
[
    {
        "id": "Sine",
        "x": 0,
        "y": 0
    },
    {
        "id": "1/(x*x+1)",
        "x": 0,
        "y": 0.038461538461538464
```

```
        },
        {
            "id": "x*sin(x*x)",
            "x": 0,
            "y": 0.1
    },

    ......

    {
            "id": "Sine",
            "x": 10,
            "y": -0.5440211108893698
        },
        {
            "id": "1/(x*x+1)",
            "x": 10,
            "y": 0.038461538461538464
        },
        {
            "id": "x*sin(x*x)",
            "x": 10,
            "y": -0.4440211108893698
        }
]
```

Here, the *id* (or the function name) represents the *key* field and the *x* and *y* represent the *values* field.

Add the following method to the *LineChartsController.cs* file:

```
public JsonResult JsonMultiLineData()
{
    var data = ModelHelper.MultiLineData();
    return Json(data);
}
```

This code converts the data returned by the *MultiLineData* method into the *JSON* data format.

Creating a Chart with Multiple Curves

Now, we can test the *drawMultiLineChart* function by adding a new view named *MultiLines.cshtml* to the *Views/LineCharts* folder and replacing its content with the following code:

```
@{
    ViewData["Title"] = ViewBag.Title;
}
<h3>@ViewBag.Title</h3>
@Html.Partial("_Links")
<hr />
<div class="container">
    <div class="row">
        <div class="col-sm-6">
            <svg id="svg"></svg>
        </div>
    </div>
</div>
```

```
@section scripts{
<script type="text/javascript">
    d3.json("JsonMultiLineData", function (data) {
        var options = {
            width: 600,
            height: 500,
            margin: { top: 50, right: 10, bottom: 60, left: 50 },
            title: "Mutiple-Line Chart",
            xlabel: "X Value",
            ylabel: "Y Value"
        };

        chart = drawMultiLineChart("#svg", data, options);
        addTitleLabel(chart.svg, chart.w, chart.h, options);
    });

</script>
}
```

This code is extremely simple. It uses *d3.json* to retrieve the JSON data from the server and passes it to the *drawMultiLineChart* method. Running the example produces the results shown in Figure 4-9.

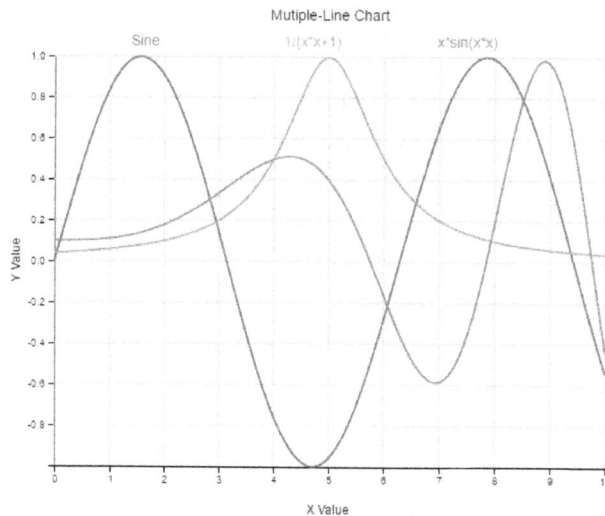

Figure 4-9. Demonstration of 3D chart with multiple lines.

Line Charts with Two Y Axes

In the previous sections, we have implemented powerful 2D line chart functions. In particular, the *drawMultiLineChart* function has no restrictions on the number of lines or curves we could add to a single chart. In this section, we will add another feature, an additional *Y*-axis, to the 2D line chart.

Why You Need Two Y Axes

In some instances, you may have multiple data sets you would like to display on the same chart. However, the *Y*-axis data values for each data set are not within the same range. For example, the two functions implemented in a new method named *MultiLineDataForY2* in the *ModelHelper* class have very different data ranges:

```
public static List<object> MultiLineDataForY2()
{
    List<object> dat = new List<object>();
    for (int i = 0; i < 101; i++)
    {
        double x = i / 3.0;
        double y = 0.1 * x * Math.Cos(x);
        double x1 = x / 3.0;
        double y2 = 0.53 * x1 * x1 * x1 - 5.3 * x1 * x1 + 15.77 * x1;
        dat.Add(new { id = "x*cos(x)", x = x, y = y });
        dat.Add(new { id = "x^3 +...", x = x, y = y2 });
    }
    return dat;
}
```

If you want to display the data from the above method using the same scale on the *Y*-axis, you will get the results shown in Figure 4-10.

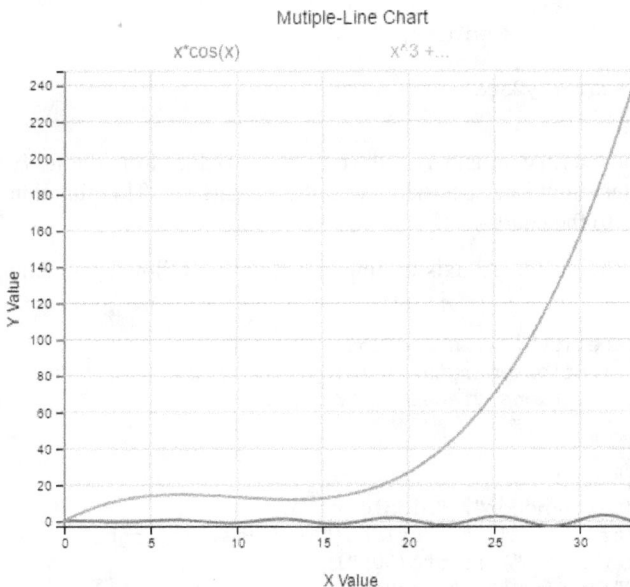

Figure 4-10. A line chart for y1 and y2, whose data values fall in different ranges.

From Figure 4-10, you can see how difficult it is to view the values of the function *x**cos(*x*) because the *Y*-axis limits have been defined to display all of the data points on the same chart; however, the values of the two functions have very different data ranges. This problem can be solved by adding another *Y2*-axis to the chart.

Functions with Two Y Axes

In order to add another *Y*-axis to the chart, you first need to add the *Y2*-axis and corresponding gridlines. Add a new function to the *site.js file* and name it *addY2Gridlines*. Here is the code for this function:

```
function addY2Gridlines(svg, y2domain, w, h, margin, isGridline) {
    isGridline = isGridline || true;

    y2scale = d3.scaleLinear().domain(y2domain).range([h, 0]);
    var yaxis = d3.axisRight().scale(y2scale);
    svg.append("g")
        .attr("transform", "translate(" + w + ",0)")
        .attr("class", "y-axis")
        .call(yaxis);

    if (isGridline) {
        svg.selectAll("line.y2grid")
            .data(y2scale.ticks())
            .enter()
            .append("line")
            .attr("class", "y2grid")
            .attr("x1", 0)
            .attr("x2", w)
            .attr("y1", function (d) { return y2scale(d); })
            .attr("y2", function (d) { return y2scale(d); })
            .attr("stroke", "lightgreen")
            .attr("stroke-width", "1px");
    }
    return { y2scale: y2scale };
}
```

Note that the input arguments *svg*, *w*, and *h* are the returned variables from the *setAxesGridlines* function. The *y2domain* parameter should be specified based the *Y2* data set. This function add the *Y2*-axis and corresponding gridlines to the chart.

You can also add the label to the *Y2*-axis by implementing the following function *addY2Label* in the *site.js* file:

```
function addY2Label(svg, w, h, options) {
    var margin = options.margin || { top: 20, right: 20, bottom: 20, left: 20 };
    var y2label = options.ylabel || "Y2 Axis";

    // y2 label
    svg.append("text")
        .attr("text-anchor", "middle")
        .attr("transform", "translate(" + (w+margin.right - 15) + "," +
            (h / 2) + ") rotate(90)")
        .style("font-size", "12px")
        .text(y2label);
}
```

Finally, we can implement the *drawY2LineChart* function in the *site.js* file:

```
function drawY2LineChart(svgSelection, data, options) {
    var width = options.width || 400;
    var height = options.height || 300;
    var margin = options.margin || { top: 20, right: 20, bottom: 20, left: 20 };
```

```
var isTimeAxis = options.isTimeAxis || false;
var isGridline = options.isGridline || true;

var xdomain =   [d3.min(data, function (d) { return d.x; }),
                 d3.max(data, function (d) { return d.x; })];
var ydomain =   [d3.min(data, function (d) { return d.y; }),
                 d3.max(data, function (d) { return d.y; })];
var y2domain = [d3.min(data, function (d) { return d.y2; }),
                 d3.max(data, function (d) { return d.y2; })];
options.xdomain = xdomain;
options.ydomain = ydomain;

var grid = setAxesGridlines(svgSelection, options);
var xscale = grid.xscale;
var yscale = grid.yscale;
var svg = grid.svg;
var grid2 = addY2Gridlines(svg, y2domain, grid.w, grid.h,
                            margin, isGridline);
var y2scale = grid2.y2scale;

var gen = d3.line()
    .x(function (d) { return xscale(d.x); })
    .y(function (d) { return yscale(d.y); });

var gen2 = d3.line()
    .x(function (d) { return xscale(d.x); })
    .y(function (d) { return y2scale(d.y2); });

svg.append("path")
    .attr("d", gen(data))
    .attr("stroke", "black")
    .attr("stroke-width", 2)
    .attr("fill", "none");

svg.append("path")
    .attr("d", gen2(data))
    .attr("stroke", "green")
    .attr("stroke-width", 2)
    .attr("fill", "none");

    return grid;
}
```

This code is very similar to our *drawLineChart* function except for an additional *Y2* curve.

Input Data

Here, I will use an example to illustrate how to create a line chart with two *Y*-axes. The *drawY2LineChart* function requires the input data in a specific JSON format. Here I will use a sample data generated by two mathematical functions to illustrate the data format.

Add a new C# method named *Y2Data* to the *ModelHelper* class. Here is the code for this method:

```
public static List<object> Y2Data()
{
```

```
List<object> dat = new List<object>();
for (int i = 0; i < 101; i++)
{
    double x = i / 3.0;
    double y = 0.1 * x * Math.Cos(x);
    double x1 = x / 3.0;
    double y2 = 0.53 * x1 * x1 * x1 - 5.3 * x1 * x1 + 15.77 * x1;
    dat.Add(new { x, y, y2 });
}
return dat;
}
```

The output from this method will generate the following JSON data format:

```
[
    {
        "x": 0,
        "y": 0,
        "y2": 0
    },
    {
        "x": 0.3333333333333333,
        "y": 0.03149856487715792,
        "y2": 1.6875171467764059
    },

    ......

    {
        "x": 33.333333333333336,
        "y": -1.1323727080119037,
        "y2": 247.92455418381354
    }
]
```

Creating a Chart with Two Y Axes

Add a new view named *TwoYAxes.cshtml* to the *Views/LineCharts* folder. Here is the code for this view:

```
@{
    ViewData["Title"] = ViewBag.Title;
}

<h3>@ViewBag.Title</h3>
@Html.Partial("_Links")

<hr />

<div class="container">
    <div class="row">
        <div class="col-sm-6">
            <svg id="svg1"></svg>
        </div>
        <div class="col-sm-6">
            <svg id="svg2"></svg>
        </div>
```

```
        </div>
    </div>

@section scripts{
    <script type="text/javascript">
        d3.json("JsonY2MultiLineData", function (data) {
            var options = {
                width: 500,
                height: 450,
                margin: { top: 50, right: 10, bottom: 60, left: 50 },
                title: "Mutiple-Line Chart"
            };
            var chart = drawMultiLineChart("#svg1", data, options);
            addTitleLabel(chart.svg, chart.w, chart.h, options);
        });


        d3.json("JsonY2Data", function (data) {
            var options = {
                width: 500,
                height: 450,
                margin: { top: 30, right: 55, bottom: 60, left: 50 },
                title: "Y2 Chart"
            };
            var chart = drawY2LineChart("#svg2", data, options);
            addTitleLabel(chart.svg, chart.w, chart.h, options);
            addY2Label(chart.svg, chart.w, chart.h, options);
        });
    </script>
}
```

The code creates two charts: the first one is the chart with the same scale for both curves, which has been displayed in Figure 4-10. The other one is our line chart with *Y2* axis.

By running this example, you should obtain the results shown in Figure 4-11.

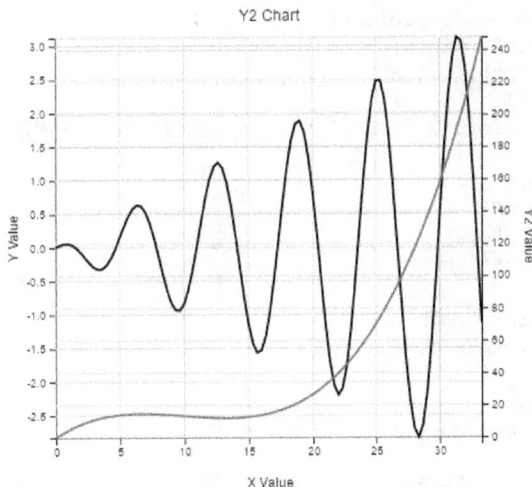

Figure 4-11. A line chart with two Y-axes.

You can see that both sets of data are clearly displayed in Figure 4-11, even though these two sets of data have dramatically different data ranges.

Specialized Charts

In the preceding sections, we discussed 2D line charts, which can be used to visualize data in real-world ASP.NET Core MVC applications. In the following, I will show you how to create certain special or application-specific charts in your applications, including bar, stair-step, and area charts. You will also learn how to create charts in other coordinate systems, such as pie and polar charts.

Bar Charts

The bar chart is useful for comparing classes or groups of data. In a bar chart, a class or group can have a single category of data, or can be broken down further into multiple categories for a greater depth of analysis. A bar chart is often used in exploratory data analysis to illustrate the major features of the data distribution in a convenient form. It displays the data using a number of rectangles of the same width, each of which represents a particular category. The length (and hence area) of each rectangle is proportional to the number of cases in the category it represents, such as, age group, religious affiliation, etc. Previously, we created simple bar charts using the *<rect>* elements. In fact, D3 offers a more efficient approach to create bar charts. In this section, I will show you how to use this new method to create bar charts.

Axes and Gridlines for Bar Charts

As what we did in creating line charts, we first need to build the axes and gridlines for the bar charts. Usually, we only need to add gridlines in the perpendicular direction to the bars. Add a new function *setBarAxesGridlines* to the *site.js* file:

```
function setBarAxesGridlines(svgSelection, xscale, yscale, width, height,
    margin, w, h, isGridline) {

    var svg = d3.select(svgSelection)
        .attr("width", width)
        .attr("height", height)
        .append("g")
        .attr("transform", "translate(" + margin.left + "," + margin.top + ")");

    // box for chart area
    svg.append("rect")
        .attr("width", w)
        .attr("height", h)
        .style("fill", "none")
        .style("stroke", "black")
        .style("stroke-width", 0.2);

    // x-axis
    var xaxis = d3.axisBottom().scale(xscale);
    svg.append("g")
        .attr("class", "x-axis")
        .attr("transform", "translate(0," + h + ")")
```

```
        .call(xaxis);

    // y-axis
    var yaxis = d3.axisLeft().scale(yscale);
    svg.append("g")
        .attr("class", "y-axis")
        .call(yaxis);

    // y grid lines:
    if (isGridline) {
        svg.selectAll("line.ygrid")
            .data(yscale.ticks())
            .enter()
            .append("line")
            .attr("class", "ygrid")
            .attr("x1", 0)
            .attr("x2", w)
            .attr("y1", function (d) { return yscale(d); })
            .attr("y2", function (d) { return yscale(d); })
            .attr("stroke", "lightgray")
            .attr("stroke-width", "1px");
    }
    return svg;
}
```

The input parameters *xscale*, *yscale*, *w*, and *h* are computed in the *drawBarChart* function. This code adds axes and *y* gridlines for vertical bar charts.

Bar Chart Function

Add the *drawBarChart* function to the *site.js* file. Here is the code for this method:

```
function drawBarChart(svgSelection, data, options) {
    var width = options.width || 400;
    var height = options.height || 300;
    var margin = options.margin || { top: 20, right: 20, bottom: 20, left: 20 };
    var isGridline = options.isGridline || true;

    var w = width - margin.left - margin.right;
    var h = height - margin.top - margin.bottom;
    var xscale = d3.scaleBand().domain(data.map(function (d) {
                    return d.x; })).range([0, w]).padding(0.2);
    var ymax = d3.max(data, function (d) { return d.y; });
    var yscale = d3.scaleLinear().domain([0, ymax]).range([h, 0]);

    var svg = setBarAxesGridlines(svgSelection, xscale, yscale, width,
                                height, margin, w, h, isGridline);

    svg.selectAll("bar")
        .data(data)
        .enter()
        .append("rect")
        .attr("fill", "steelblue")
        .attr("x", function (d) { return xscale(d.x); })
        .attr("y", function (d) { return yscale(d.y); })
```

```
        .attr("width", xscale.bandwidth())
        .attr("height", function (d) { return h - yscale(d.y); });
}
```

This code creates a vertical bar chart using the *scaleBand* function in D3 (see the highlighted code). The band scale is similar to ordinal scale, but uses a continuous range instead of a discrete range. Each value in the domain is mapped to an even length of the range, consisting of a length of band and a length of padding. The band length represents the width of the bar and the padding length represents the spacing between the bars.

Input Data

Add the following methods to the *ModelHelper* class:

```
Public  List<object> BarData1()
{
    List<object> dat = new List<object>();
    Random random = new Random();
    for (int i = 0; i < 10; i++)
    {
        dat.Add(new { x = i * i, y = Math.Round(random.NextDouble(), 2) });
    }
    return dat;
}

Public static List<object> BarData2()
{
    List<object> dat = new List<object>();
    string[] letters = new string[] { "A", "D", "C", "B", "G",
                                       "I", "J", "Z", "X", "S" };
    Random random = new Random();
    for (int i = 0; i < 10; i++)
    {
        dat.Add(new { x = letters[i], y = random.Next(100) * random.Next(100) });
    }
    return dat;
}
```

The data from these two methods will be used to create simple bar charts using the *drawBarChart* function.

Creating a Vertical Bar Chart

Now, we will use an example to demonstrate how to create vertical bar charts using the *drawBarChart* function. Add new folder named *SpecializedCharts* to the *Views* folder. Add a view *BarChart.cshtml* to this new folder and replace its content with the following code:

```
@{
    ViewData["Title"] = ViewBag.Title;
}

<h3>@ViewBag.Title</h3>
@Html.Partial("_Links")
```

```
<hr />

<div class="container">
    <div class="row">
        <div class="col-sm-5">
            <p>Bar Chart (numbers in x column)</p>
            <svg id="svg1"></svg>
        </div>
        <div class="col-sm-5">
            <p>Bar Chart (letters in x column)</p>
            <svg id="svg2"></svg>
        </div>
    </div>
    <div class="row">
        <p>Group bar chart</p>
        <svg id="svg3"></svg>
    </div>
</div>

<div id="showResults"></div>

@section scripts{
<script type="text/javascript">

    d3.json("JsonBarData1", function (data) {
        var options = {
            width: 400,
            height: 300,
            margin: { top: 20, right: 20, bottom: 40, left: 30 }
        };
        drawBarChart("#svg1", data, options);
    });

    d3.json("JsonBarData2", function (data) {
        var options = {
            width: 400,
            height: 300,
            margin: { top: 20, right: 20, bottom: 40, left: 50 }
        };
        drawBarChart("#svg2", data, options);
    });
</script>
}
```

The code creates two vertical bar charts: one with numerical *x*-values and the other one with letters.

Running this example produces the results shown in Figure 4-12.

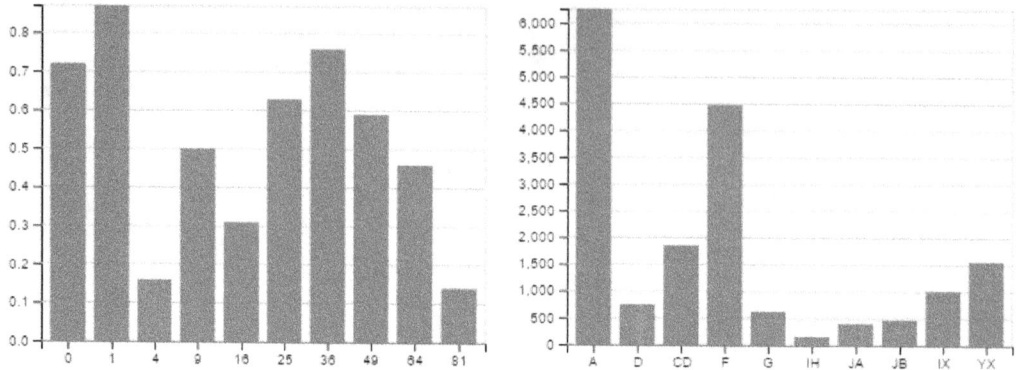

Figure 4-12. Bar charts with numerical values (left) and letters (right) for x.

Creating Group Bar Charts

When we have multiple sets of data with the same X values, we can use D3 and JavaScript function to create a group bar chart. The Y values are distributed along the X-axis, with each Y at a different X drawn at a different location. All of the Y values at the same X are clustered around the same location on the X-axis. In order to create such a bar chart, let us first create the input data. Add the following C# method *BarChartData3* to the *ModelHelper* class:

```
Public static List<object> BarData3()
{
    List<object> dat = new List<object>();
    string[] group = new string[] { "y1", "y2", "y3" };
    Random random = new Random();
    double[] xa = new double[5];
    for (int i = 0; i < group.Length; i++)
    {
        for (int j = 0; j < 5; j++)
        {
            xa[j] = Math.Round(random.NextDouble(), 4);
        }
        dat.Add(new { group = group[i], a = xa[0], b = xa[1],
                  c = xa[2], d = xa[3], e = xa[4] });
    }
    return dat;
}
```

The output from this method generates the following JSON data:

```
[
    {
        "group": "y1",
        "a": 0.1698,
        "b": 0.4452,
        "c": 0.581,
        "d": 0.5579,
        "e": 0.0308
    },
    {
```

```
            "group": "y2",
            "a": 0.1324,
            "b": 0.1154,
            "c": 0.7264,
            "d": 0.5911,
            "e": 0.7473
    },
    {
            "group": "y3",
            "a": 0.8966,
            "b": 0.868,
            "c": 0.1233,
            "d": 0.936,
            "e": 0.5782
    }
]
```

Now, we add the following *drawGroupBarChart* function to the *site.js* file:

```
function drawGroupBarChart(svgSelection, data, options) {
    var width = options.width || 400;
    var height = options.height || 300;
    var margin = options.margin || { top: 20, right: 20, bottom: 20, left: 20 };
    var isGridline = options.isGridline || true;

    var w = width - margin.left - margin.right;
    var h = height - margin.top - margin.bottom;
    var color = d3.scaleOrdinal(d3.schemeCategory10);

    var keys = d3.keys(data[0]).filter(function (key) {
                    return key !== "group"; });
    var xscale = d3.scaleBand().rangeRound([0, w]).paddingInner(0.1)
                    .domain(data.map(function (d) { return d.group; }));
    var x1scale = d3.scaleBand().padding(0.1).domain(keys)
                    .rangeRound([0, xscale.bandwidth()]);
    var ymax = d3.max(data, function (d) { return
                d3.max(keys, function (key) { return d[key]; }); });
    var yscale = d3.scaleLinear().rangeRound([h, 0]).domain([0, ymax]);

    var svg = setBarAxesGridlines(svgSelection, xscale, yscale,
                width, height, margin, w, h, isGridline);

    svg.append("g")
        .selectAll("g")
        .data(data)
        .enter().append("g")
        .attr("transform", function (d) {
            return "translate(" + xscale(d.group) + ",0)"; })
        .selectAll("rect")
        .data(function (d) { return keys.map(function (key) {
                    return { key: key, value: d[key] }; }); })
        .enter().append("rect")
        .attr("x", function (d) { return x1scale(d.key); })
        .attr("y", function (d) { return yscale(d.value); })
        .attr("width", x1scale.bandwidth())
        .attr("height", function (d) { return h - yscale(d.value); })
```

```
                    .attr("fill", function (d) { return color(d.key); });

        var legend = svg.append("g")
            .attr("font-family", "sans-serif")
            .attr("font-size", 12)
            .attr("text-anchor", "end")
            .selectAll("g")
            .data(keys.slice())
            .enter().append("g")
            .attr("transform", function (d, i) {
                    return "translate(0," + i * 22 + ")"; });

        legend.append("rect")
            .attr("x", w + 5)
            .attr("width", 20)
            .attr("height", 20)
            .attr("fill", color);

        legend.append("text")
            .attr("x", w + 35)
            .attr("y", 9.5)
            .attr("dy", "0.32em")
            .text(function (d) { return d; });
    }
```

Pay special attention to the highlighted code, where we first extract the keys by using the code snippet:

```
var keys = d3.keys(data[0]).filter(function (key) { return key !== "group"; });
```

If we use the output data from the *BarData3* method as input data, the above statement generates the following result:

```
a,b,c,d,e
```

which gives the *keys* within the *group*. The *xscale* sets the bar positions according to *group* with the *d3.scaleBand* function, while the *x1scale* represents the bar positions within each *group*. You may wonder how we calculate the *ymax* quantity using the code:

```
var ymax = d3.max(data, function (d) { return d3.max(keys,
    function (key) { return d[key]; }); });
```

This is equivalent to two *for*-loops: we first calculate the maximum values for each group and then the maximum value for all groups, which gives *ymax*.

Next, the code call the *setBarAxesGridlines* function to create the axes and gridlines. We then create the bars by two steps: first set the proper locations for each group with the code:

```
.attr("transform", function (d) {
    return "translate(" + xscale(d.group) + ",0)"; })
```

Here, we use the *translate* transformation along the *x*-axis to determine the locations for each group. We then use the key values within each group as the input data to create the bar rectangles with the following code:

```
.selectAll("rect")
.data(function (d) { return keys.map(function (key)
                    { return { key: key, value: d[key] }; }); })
.enter().append("rect")
```

```
.attr("x", function (d) { return x1scale(d.key); })
.attr("y", function (d) { return yscale(d.value); })
.attr("width", x1scale.bandwidth())
.attr("height", function (d) { return h - yscale(d.value); })
.attr("fill", function (d) { return color(d.key); });
```

The code sets the *x*- and *y*-coordinates for each bar with the *key* and *value* within each group. The width of the bar is determined by *x1scale.bandwidth*, which is different from *xscale.bandwidth* used in creating simple bar chart in the preceding example. Now, you should understand why we use *x1scale.bandwidth* here. Finally, we add the legend to the right of our group bar chart.

We can now test this function. Add the following code to the script section of the *BarChart.cshtml* file:

```
d3.json("JsonBarData3", function (data) {
    width = 600;
    height = 400;
    margin = { top: 20, right: 50, bottom: 40, left: 50 };
    drawGroupBarChart("#svg3", data, width, height, margin, true);
});
```

This code produces the results shown in Figure 4-13.

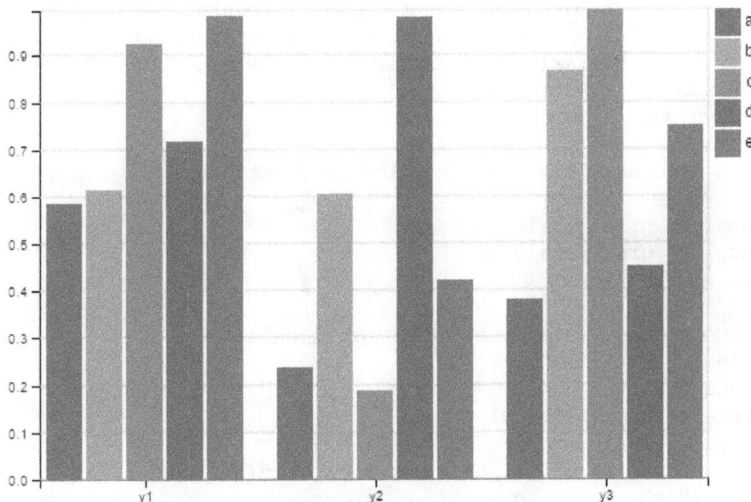

Figure 4-13.Demonstration of group bar chart.

Following the same procedure presented in this section, you should be able to create other types of bar charts without any difficulty, such as horizontal bar charts, overlay bar charts, and stacked bar charts, etc. I will leave these topics for your execises.

Stair-Step Charts

In this section, I will show you how to create a stair-step chart. Instead of creating lines that directly connect your data, you can choose to have your data plotted in a way that emphasizes the discrete nature of the data. Namely, stair-step charts draw horizontal lines at the level specified by the *Y* data. This level will be held constant over the period between the values specified by the *X* data values. Stair-step charts are similar to bar charts except that vertical lines are not dropped down all the way to the zero value point on the *Y*-axis. This type of plot is useful for drawing time-history plots of digitally sampled data systems.

D3 implements three types of step functions, *d3.curveStep*, *d3.curveStepBefore*, and *d3.curveStepAfter*, which can be used to create the stair-step charts. The *d3.curveStep* function produces a piecewise constant function (a step function) consisting of alternating horizontal and vertical lines. The *y*-value changes at the midpoint of each pair of adjacent *x*-values. While the *d3.curveStepBefore* (*d3.curveStepAfter*) function produces a similar step function, but the *y*-value changes before (after) the *x*-value.

Add a function named *drawStairStep* to the *site.js* file. Here is the code for this function:

```
function drawStairStep(svgSelection, data, stepType, options) {
    var width = options.width || 400;
    var height = options.height || 300;
    var margin = options.margin || { top: 20, right: 20, bottom: 20, left: 20 };
    var isTimeAxis = options.isTimeAxis || false;
    var isGridline = options.isGridline || true;

    var xdomain = [d3.min(data, function (d) { return d.x; }),
                   d3.max(data, function (d) { return d.x; })];
    var ydomain = [d3.min(data, function (d) { return d.y; }),
                   d3.max(data, function (d) { return d.y; })];
    options.xdomain = xdomain;
    options.ydomain = ydomain;

    var grid = setAxesGridlines(svgSelection, options);

    var xscale = grid.xscale;
    var yscale = grid.yscale;
    var svg = grid.svg;

    // add dots and dashed line for original data:
    svg.selectAll("circle")
        .data(data)
        .enter().append("circle")
        .attr("r", 4)
        .attr("cx", function (d) { return xscale(d.x); })
        .attr("cy", function (d) { return yscale(d.y); })
        .attr("fill", "red");

    var line = d3.line()
        .x(function (d) { return xscale(d.x); })
        .y(function (d) { return yscale(d.y); });

    svg.append("path")
        .attr("d", line(data))
        .attr("stroke", "red")
        .attr("stroke-width", 1)
        .attr("stroke-dasharray", "3,3")
        .attr("fill", "none");

    // add step path
    var step;
```

```
    if (stepType === "step") {
        step = d3.line().curve(d3.curveStep);
    } else if (stepType === "stepBefore") {
        step = d3.line().curve(d3.curveStepBefore);
    } else if (stepType === "stepAfter") {
        step = d3.line().curve(d3.curveStepAfter);
    }
    step = step.x(function (d) { return xscale(d.x); })
               .y(function (d) { return yscale(d.y); });
    svg.append("path")
        .attr("stroke-width", 2)
        .attr("stroke", "darkgreen")
        .attr("fill", "none")
        .attr("d", step(data));
}
```

This function, similar to the *drawLineChart* function, first creates the axes and gridlines by calling the *setAxesGridlines* function. For comparison, we add a dashed curve to the chart for original data and circles for marking each data points. We then draw the stair-step curve using the D3 step-curve function with specified *stepType* parameter.

Now, we can use the above function to create stair-step charts. Add the following code to the *SpecializedChartsController.cs* file:

```
public JsonResult JsonStepData()
{
    List<object> dat = new List<object>();
    Random random = new Random();
    for (int i = 0; i < 10; i++)
    {
        dat.Add(new { x = i, y = Math.Round(random.NextDouble(), 1) });
    }
    return Json(dat);
}
```

This method returns the JSON data, which will be used in creating our stair-step charts.

Add a new view *StairStep.cshtml* to the *Views/SpecializedCharts* folder, and replace its content with the following code:

```
@{
    ViewData["Title"] = ViewBag.Title;
}
<h3>@ViewBag.Title</h3>
@Html.Partial("_Links")
<hr />

<div class="container">
    <div class="row">
        <div class="col-sm-3">
            <p>Stair-Step Chart</p>
            <svg id="svg1"></svg>
        </div>
        <div class="col-sm-3">
            <p>Stair-Step Chart (Step Before)</p>
            <svg id="svg2"></svg>
        </div>
```

```
                <div class="col-sm-3">
                    <p>Stair-Step Chart (Step After)</p>
                    <svg id="svg3"></svg>
                </div>
        </div>
    </div>

    @section scripts{
    <script type="text/javascript">
        d3.json("JsonStepData", function (data) {
            var options = {
                width: 280,
                height: 250,
                margin: { top: 20, right: 10, bottom: 40, left: 30 }
            };
            drawStairStep("#svg1", data, "step", options);
            drawStairStep("#svg2", data, "stepBefore", options);
            drawStairStep("#svg3", data, "stepAfter", options);
        });
    </script>
    }
```

This code produces the results shown in Figure 4-14.

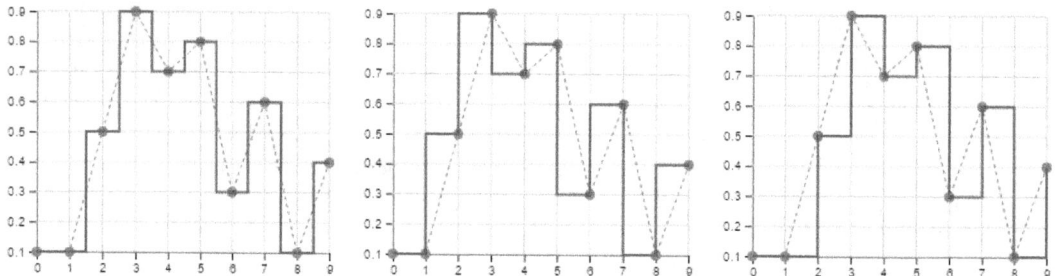

Figure 4-14. Stair-step charts: step (left), step before (middle), and step after (right).

Area Charts

An area chart displays *Y* data values as one or more curves and fills the area beneath each curve. When the data contains more than one line series, the curves are stacked, showing the relative contribution of each line series to the total height of the curve at each *X* value.

In order to create an area chart, we need to add a new function *drawAreaChart* to the *site.js* file. Here is the code for this function:

```
function drawAreaChart(svgSelection, data, options) {
    var ymax = options.ymax || d3.max(data, function (d) { return d.y; });
    var width = options.width || 400;
    var height = options.height || 300;
    var margin = options.margin || { top: 20, right: 20, bottom: 20, left: 20 };
    var isTimeAxis = options.isTimeAxis || false;
    var isGridline = options.isGridline || true;

    options.xdomain = [d3.min(data, function (d) { return d.x; }),
```

```
                         d3.max(data, function (d) { return d.x; })];
    options.ydomain = [0, ymax];

    var grid = setAxesGridlines(svgSelection, options);
    var xscale = grid.xscale;
    var yscale = grid.yscale;
    var svg = grid.svg;

    var area = d3.area()
        .x(function (d) { return xscale(d.x); })
        .y0(yscale(0))
        .y1(function (d) { return yscale(d.y1); });
    svg.append("path")
        .attr("d", area(data))
        .attr("stroke", "black")
        .attr("stroke-width", 1)
        .attr("opacity", 0.5)
        .attr("fill", "red");


    return grid;
}
```

Note that we do not calculate the *ydomain* based on the input data as we usually do for line charts, but preset it to [0, *ymax*] and treat *ymax* as an input parameter included in the *options* argument. This is because we usually start with 0 for most area charts. The input parameter *ymax* allows you to have the flexibility to produce nice-looking area charts.

Next, we use the *d3.area* function to generate the *path* mini-language commands, and finally we draw the area using the *path* element.

You can also create a stacked area chart in a similar manner. Add a new function *drawStackedAreaChart* to the *site.js* file:

```
function drawStackedAreaChart(svgSelection, data, options) {
    var ymax = options.ymax || d3.max(data, function (d) { return d.y; });
    var width = options.width || 400;
    var height = options.height || 300;
    var margin = options.margin || { top: 20, right: 20, bottom: 20, left: 20 };
    var isTimeAxis = options.isTimeAxis || false;
    var isGridline = options.isGridline || true;

    options.xdomain = [d3.min(data, function (d) { return d.x; }),
                       d3.max(data, function (d) { return d.x; })];
    options.ydomain = [0, ymax];

    var grid = setAxesGridlines(svgSelection, options);
    var xscale = grid.xscale;
    var yscale = grid.yscale;
    var svg = grid.svg;

    var keys = d3.keys(data[0]).filter(function (key) { return key !== "x"; });
    var color = d3.scaleOrdinal(d3.schemeCategory10).domain(keys);
    var stack = d3.stack().keys(keys);

    var area = d3.area()
        .x(function (d) { return xscale(d.data.x); })
```

```
            .y0(function (d) { return yscale(d[0]); })
            .y1(function (d) { return yscale(d[1]); });

    var layer = svg.selectAll(".layer")
        .data(stack(data))
        .enter().append("g")
        .attr("class", "layer");

    layer.append("path")
        .attr("class", "area")
        .style("fill", function (d) { return color(d.key); })
        .attr("opacity", 0.5)
        .attr("d", area);

    var legend = svg.append("g")
        .attr("font-family", "sans-serif")
        .attr("font-size", 11)
        .attr("text-anchor", "end")
        .selectAll("g")
        .data(keys.slice())
        .enter().append("g")
        .attr("transform", function (d, i) {
            return "translate(0," + i * 22 + ")"; });

    legend.append("rect")
        .attr("x", grid.w - 19)
        .attr("width", 19)
        .attr("height", 19)
        .attr("fill", color)
        .attr("opacity", 0.5);

    legend.append("text")
        .attr("x", grid.w - 24)
        .attr("y", 9.5)
        .attr("dy", "0.32em")
        .text(function (d) { return d; });

    return grid;
}
```

The beginning of this function is similar to that used in the *drawAreaChart* function. The code then uses the *d3.keys* and *filer* functions to extract the keys from the input data. This approach has been also used previously in creating group bar charts. Next, we draw the areas using the *path* element and add corresponding legend to the chart.

We need the test data to create area charts. Add the following C# method *AreaData* to the *ModelHelper* class:

```
public static List<object> AreaData()
{
    List<object> dat = new List<object>();
    for (int i = 0; i < 41; i++)
    {
        double x = 0.25 * i;
        double sn1 = 2.0 + Math.Sin(x);
        double cs = 2.0 + Math.Cos(x);
```

```
        double sn2 = 3.0 + Math.Sin(x);
        dat.Add(new { x = x, y = sn1, y1 = cs, y2 = sn2 });
    }
    return dat;
}
```

Add a new view *AreaChart.cshtml* to the *Views/SpecializedCharts* folder and replace its content with the following code:

```
@{
    ViewData["Title"] = ViewBag.Title;
}
<h3>@ViewBag.Title</h3>
@Html.Partial("_Links")
<hr />

<div class="container">
    <div class="row">
        <div class="col-sm-5">
            <svg id="svg1"></svg>
        </div>
        <div class="col-sm-5">
            <svg id="svg2"></svg>
        </div>
    </div>
</div>

@section scripts{
<script type="text/javascript">
    d3.json("JsonAreaData", function (data) {
        var options = {
            width: 450,
            height: 400,
            margin: { top: 30, right: 10, bottom: 55, left: 50 },
            ymax: 4.0,
            title: "Area Chart"
        };
        var chart = drawAreaChart("#svg1", data, options);
        addTitleLabel(chart.svg, chart.w, chart.h, options);

        options.ymax = 10.0;
        options.title = "Stacked Area Chart";
        chart = drawStackedAreaChart("#svg2", data, options);
        addTitleLabel(chart.svg, chart.w, chart.h, options);
    });
</script>
}
```

This code create two area charts: one is the simple area chart with a single set of data and the other one is a stacked area chart. Running this example produces the results shown in Figure 4-15.

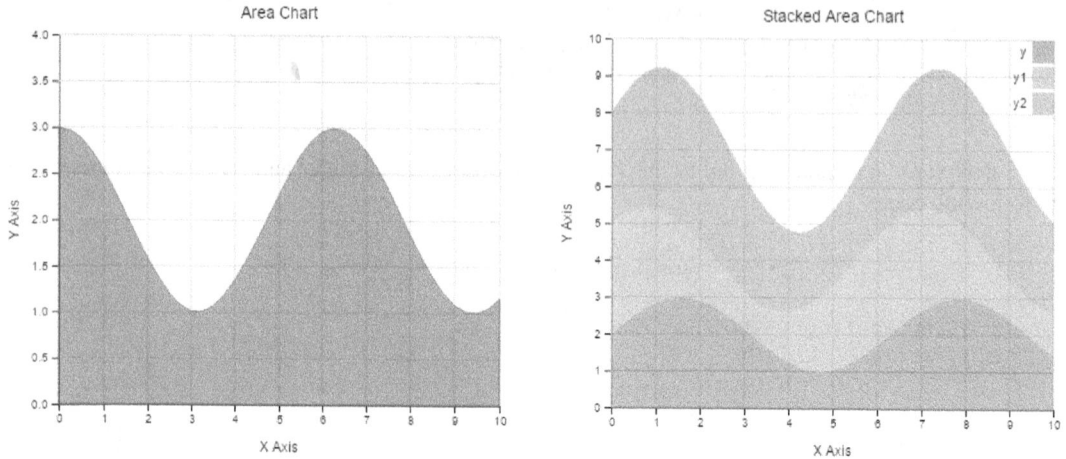

Figure 4-15. Demonstration of area charts.

Polar Charts

So far, we have discussed various chart applications that make use of the Cartesian coordinate system. Now I want to show you how to plot data in polar coordinates (*r*, *theta*).

Add a new JavaScript helper function named *drawPolarChart* to the *site.js* file. Here is the code for this function:

```
function drawPolarChart(svgSelection, data, options) {
    var rmax = options.rmax || d3.max(data, function (d) { return d.r; });
    var width = options.width || 400;
    var height = options.height || 300;
    var numCircles = options.numCircles || 5;

    var r = (Math.min(width, height) - 60) / 2;

    var svg = d3.select(svgSelection)
        .attr("width", width)
        .attr("height", height)
        .append("g")
        .attr("transform", "translate(" + width / 2 + "," + height / 2 + ")");

    var rscale = d3.scaleLinear().domain([0, rmax]).range([0, r]);

    var polar = d3.radialLine().radius(function (d) { return rscale(d.r); })
        .angle(function (d) { return -d.angle + Math.PI / 2; });

    var g1 = svg.append("g")
        .attr("class", "r-axis")
        .selectAll("g")
        .data(rscale.ticks(numCircles).slice(1))
        .enter().append("g");
    g1.append("circle")
        .attr("r", rscale)
        .attr("stroke", "black")
```

```
            .attr("stroke-width", 1)
            .attr("stroke-dasharray", "1,4")
            .attr("fill", "none");
    g1.append("circle")
            .attr("r", rscale(rmax))
            .attr("stroke", "black")
            .attr("stroke-width", 1)
            .attr("fill", "none");
    g1.append("text")
            .attr("y", function (d) { return -rscale(d) - 4; })
            .attr("transform", "rotate(15)")
            .style("text-anchor", "middle")
            .text(function (d) { return d3.format(".2")(d); });

    var g2 = svg.append("g")
            .attr("class", "angle-axis")
            .selectAll("g")
            .data(d3.range(0, 360, 30))
            .enter().append("g")
            .attr("transform", function (d) { return "rotate(" + -d + ")"; });
    g2.append("line")
            .attr("x2", r)
            .attr("stroke", "black")
            .attr("stroke-width", 1)
            .attr("stroke-dasharray", "1,4");
    g2.append("text")
            .attr("x", r + 6)
            .attr("dy", "0.35em")
            .style("text-anchor", function (d) {
                return d < 270 && d > 90 ? "end" : null; })
            .attr("transform", function (d) { return
                d < 270 && d > 90 ? "rotate(180 " + (r + 6) + ",0)" : null; })
            .text(function (d) { return d + "\u00b0"; });

    svg.append("path")
            .attr("class", "line")
            .attr("d", polar(data))
            .attr("stroke", "red")
            .attr("stroke-width", 2)
            .attr("fill", "none");
}
```

Here, the optional parameters include *rmax* and *numCircles*, where *rmax* determines the domain = [0, *rmax*] in the radial direction and *numCircles* represents the number of circles used in the polar gridlines. The code uses *d3.radialLine* function to convert the input data into the *path* mini-language commands.

We then add the polar gridlines by drawing the circles (the *r*-axis) and the radial lines (the *angle*-axis) with a separation of 30 degrees. Finally, we add the curve to the polar chart.

We need some sample data to test the preceding function. Add the following C# method *PolarData* to the *ModelHelper* class. Here is the code for this method:

```
public static object PolarData()
{
    List<object> data1 = new List<object>();
    List<object> data2 = new List<object>();
```

```
        List<object> data3 = new List<object>();
        List<object> data4 = new List<object>();
        for (int i = 0; i < 720; i++)
        {
            double theta = i * Math.PI / 60;
            data1.Add(new { angle = theta, r = Math.Cos(4.0 * theta) });
            data2.Add(new { angle = theta, r = Math.Cos(theta / 6.0) });
            data3.Add(new { angle = theta, r = Math.Cos(5.0 * theta / 6.0) });
            data4.Add(new { angle = theta, r = Math.Cos(7.0 * theta / 2.0) });
        }
        return new { data1, data2, data3, data4 };
    }
```

This method generates four sets of polar data from mathematical functions $r = \cos(a*theta/b)$. These data will generate pretty graphs called polar roses (also known as *rhodonea* curves) in polar coordinates.

Now, add a new view *PolarChart.cshtml* to the *Views/SpecializedCharts* folder and replace its content with the following code:

```
@{
    ViewData["Title"] = ViewBag.Title;
}
<h3>@ViewBag.Title</h3>
@Html.Partial("_Links")
<hr />

<div class="container">
    <div class="row">
        <div class="col-sm-5">
            <p style="margin-left:100px">Polar Rose: r = Cos(4&theta;)</p>
            <svg id="svg1"></svg>
        </div>
        <div class="col-sm-5">
            <p style="margin-left:100px">Polar Rose: r = Cos(&theta;/6)</p>
            <svg id="svg2"></svg>
        </div>
    </div>
    <div class="row">
        <div class="col-sm-5">
            <p style="margin-left:100px">Polar Rose: r = Cos(5&theta;/6)</p>
            <svg id="svg3"></svg>
        </div>
        <div class="col-sm-5">
            <p style="margin-left:100px">Polar Rose: r = Cos(7&theta;/2)</p>
            <svg id="svg4"></svg>
        </div>
    </div>
</div>

@section scripts{
<script type="text/javascript">
    d3.json("JsonPolarData", function (data) {
        var options = {
            width: 400,
            height: 400
        }
```

```
        drawPolarChart("#svg1", data.data1, options);
        drawPolarChart("#svg2", data.data2, options);
        drawPolarChart("#svg3", data.data3, options);
        drawPolarChart("#svg4", data.data4, options);
    });
</script>
}
```

This code produces the results shown in Figure 4-16.

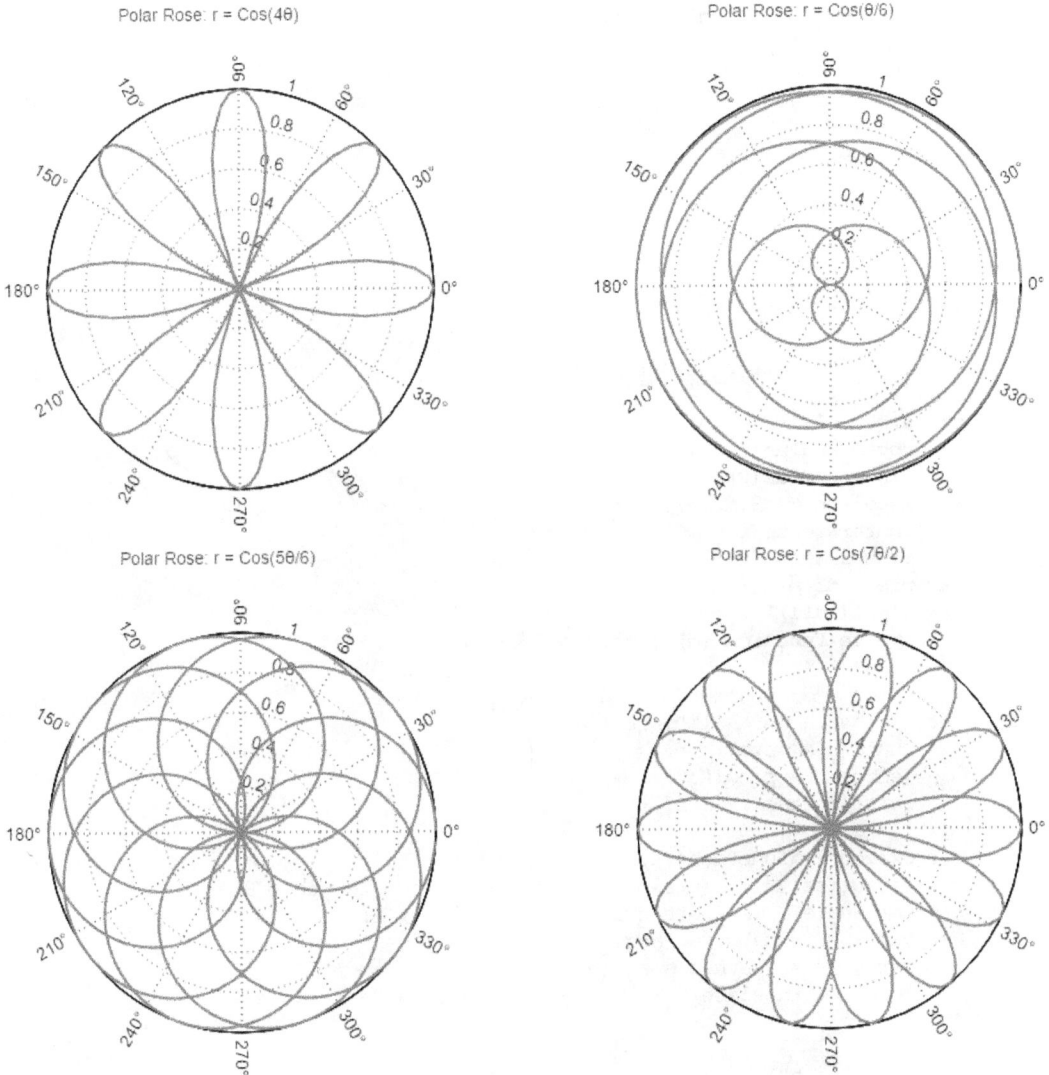

Figure 4-16. Demonstration of polar charts.

Pie Charts

Creating a pie chart in D3 is quite simple, since there are *d3.arc* and *d3.pie* functions available. The *d3.arc* function is an *arc* generator that produces a circular sector, as in a pie or donut chart. While the *d3.pie* function does not produce a shape directly, but instead computes the necessary angles to represent a tabular dataset as a pie or donut chart, these angles can then be passed to the *d3.arc* generator. Thus, we can use the combination of *d3.arc* and *d3.pie* to create pie charts.

Add a new function *drawPieChart* to the *site.js* file. Here is the code for this function:

```
function drawPieChart(svgSelection, data, options) {
    var width = options.width || 400;
    var height = options.height || 400;
    var isRotateLabel = options.isRotateLabel || true;
    var explodedIndex = options.explodedIndex || 0;
    var explodedLength = options.explodedLength || 0;

    var r = (Math.min(width, height) - 2 * explodedLength) / 2;

    var svg = d3.select(svgSelection)
        .attr("width", width)
        .attr("height", height)
        .append("g")
        .attr("transform", "translate(" + width / 2 + "," + height / 2 + ")");

    var arc = d3.arc()
        .outerRadius(r - 10)
        .innerRadius(0);
    var labelArc = d3.arc()
        .outerRadius(r - 70)
        .innerRadius(r - 70);
    var pie = d3.pie()
        .sort(null)
        .value(function (d) { return d.y; });

    var color = d3.scaleOrdinal(d3.schemeCategory10);
    var g = svg.selectAll(".arc")
        .data(pie(data))
        .enter().append("g")
        .attr("class", "arc");

    var explode = function (x, i) {
        var offset = i === explodedIndex ? explodedLength : 0;
        var angle = (x.startAngle + x.endAngle) / 2;
        var xOff = Math.sin(angle) * offset;
        var yOff = -Math.cos(angle) * offset;
        return "translate(" + xOff + "," + yOff + ")";
    };

    g.append("path")
        .attr("d", arc)
        .style("fill", function (d) { return color(d.data.x); })
        .attr("opacity", 0.7)
        .attr("transform", explode);
```

```
        if (!isRotateLabel) {
            g.append("text")
                .attr("transform", function (d) {
                    return "translate(" + labelArc.centroid(d) + ")"; })
                .attr("dy", ".35em")
                .text(function (d) { return d.data.x; });
        } else {
            g.append("text")
                .attr("transform", function (d) {
                    var midAngle = d.endAngle < Math.PI ? d.startAngle / 2 +
                    d.endAngle / 2 : d.startAngle / 2 + d.endAngle / 2 + Math.PI;
                    return "translate(" + labelArc.centroid(d)[0] + "," +
                    labelArc.centroid(d)[1] + ") rotate(-90)
                    rotate(" + midAngle * 180 / Math.PI + ")";
                })
                .attr("dy", ".35em")
                .attr('text-anchor', 'middle')
                .text(function (d) { return d.data.x; });
        }
    }
```

The highlighted code snippet defines the *arc*, *labelArc*, and *pie* variables using the *d3.arc* and *d3.pie* generators. Note that we set the *innerRadius* to zero for the arc element, resulting in a pie chart. Otherwise, if we set it to a finite value, the output will be a donut chart. Next, we create the *arc* element with the *pie* data that determines the size of each pie slice. Finally, we add corresponding labels to each slice for our pie chart.

The *drawPieChart* function also gives you the option of highlighting a particular pie slice by exploding the pieces out from the rest of the pie. To do this we simply need to specify the *explodedIndex* and *explodedLength* optional parameters.

Add a C# method *JsonPieData* to *SpecializedChartsController.cs*:

```
public JsonResult JsonPieData()
{
    List<object> dat = new List<object>();
    string[] xa = new string[] { "Soc. Sec. Tax", "Income Tax",
                                 "Borrowing", "Corp. Tax", "Misc." };
    double[] ya = new double[] { 30, 35, 15, 10, 8 };

    for (int i = 0; i < ya.Length; i++)
    {
        dat.Add(new { x = xa[i], y = ya[i] });
    }
    return Json(dat);
}
```

This method will generate the test data that can be used to create pie charts.

Add a new view *PieChart.cshtml* to the *Views/SpeacializedCharts* folder and replace its content with the following code:

```
@{
    ViewData["Title"] = ViewBag.Title;
}
<h3>@ViewBag.Title</h3>
@Html.Partial("_Links")
```

```
<hr />
<div class="container">
    <div class="row">
        <div class="col-sm-5">
            <p style="margin-left:100px">Pie Chart</p>
            <svg id="svg1"></svg>
        </div>
        <div class="col-sm-5">
            <p style="margin-left:100px">Exploded Pie Chart</p>
            <svg id="svg2"></svg>
        </div>
    </div>
</div>

@section scripts{
<script type="text/javascript">
    d3.json("JsonPieData", function (data) {
        var options = {
            width: 400,
            height: 400,
        }
        drawPieChart("#svg1", data, options);

        options.explodedIndex = 2;
        options.explodedLength = 30;
        drawPieChart("#svg2", data, options);
    });
</script>
}
```

This code creates two pie charts: the first one is a normal pie chart, and the second one is a pie chart with an exploded slice. In the second pie chart, where we want to highlight the pie slice for the *Borrowing*, so we need to explode the third element (*explodedIndex* = 2) out 30 pixels (*explodedLength* = 30) from the center of the pie chart.

Running this example produces the results shown in Figure 4-17.

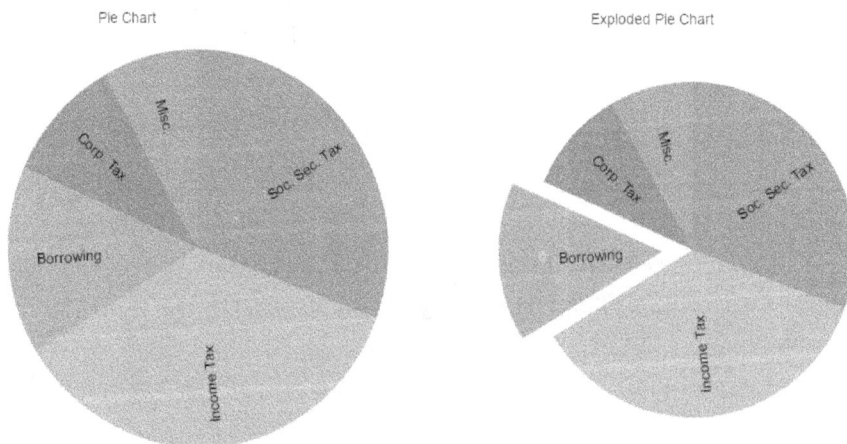

Figure 4-17. Demonstration of pie charts.

Chapter 5
2D Charts with Chart Libraries

In the preceding chapter, we demonstrated how easy and flexible the D3 is to create a variety of 2D charts. You can use D3 to implement JavaScript helper functions that can be reused for creating charts. This way, you can gradually build up your own charting library in a modularized manner. This provides your flexibility for adding more features according to your application requirements. D3 allows you to make your data visualization the way you want. This is not possible in most charting libraries, where you can only create some frequently used charts with predetermined features.

However, as we already pointed out previously, D3 is not a charting library and does not include ready-to-use charts. You cannot simply pass in your dataset, specify the type of the chart you need and get a fancy chart on your screen. D3 is much lower level than that. To implement a powerful chart package in D3, you need to put a lot of effort and hours into it – the learning curve is usually substantial.

If you want to get a quick start with charts in your ASP.NET Core MVC applications, you can go with the JavaScript charting libraries, including Chart.JS, HighCharts, Chartist, Google Charts API, etc. Comparing to D3 where you have to build every axis, label, curve, and bar from scratch, these packages have an easy-to-use API and can be picked up quickly by users. The charting packages cannot create many varieties of graphs and include some special features when compared to D3, but when they can, they usually do it perfectly.

In this chapter, we will discuss two charting libraries: Chart.JS and Google Charts API. These two packages based on different graphics layers: Chart.JS uses HTML5 canvas for rendering charts, while Google Charts is based on SVG and VML for older IE versions. Chart.JS is a small open-source charting library and is perfect for small projects. Google Charts API provides a wide range of charts, for almost any kind of 2D data visualization need. All Google charts are interactive, and some are pannable and zoomable as well. One drawback for using the Google Charts API is that even though it is free, but it is not open-source. Google's licensing does not allow you to host their JavaScript files on your server. This means that you cannot use the Google Charts API offline. If you are with a big enterprise and have some sensitive data, Google Charts might not be the best option.

Charts with Chart.JS

Chart.JS is a small open-source JavaScript charting library. It includes eight chart types including line, bar, horizontal bar, pie, polar, radar, scatter, and bubble. Each type can be animated and customizable. The library uses the HTML5/canvas as its graphic rendering layer, resulting in a great rendering performance across all modern browsers. The charts created using Chart.JS are resized automatically when you change your browser's window size. Unlike Google Charts, Chart.JS can be embedded directly in your server and made available offline.

In the following, I will show you how to use Chart.JS to create various 2D charts.

Installing Chart.JS Library

Before using Chart.JS, you need first to install the package. Open Visual Studio 2017 and start with a new ASP.NET Core MVC project and name it *Chapter05*. Right-click the project in the Solution Explorer, and select *Manage Bower Packages…*Search for Chart.js and install it. After installation, you may notice that Chart.JS provides two different builds. The *Chart.js* or *Chart.min.js* file includes *Chart.js* and the accompanying color-parsing library. If this version is used and you require the use of the time axes, *Moment.js* will need to be included before *Chart.js*.

The *Chart.bundle.js* or *Chart.bundle.min.js* file includes *Moment.js* in a single file. This version should be used if you require time axes and want a single file to include.

Here, we will add the bundle version to the reference on the *Views/Shared/_Layout.cshtml* page:

```
<environment names="Development">
    <script src="~/lib/jquery/dist/jquery.js"></script>
    <script src="~/lib/bootstrap/dist/js/bootstrap.js"></script>
    <script src="~/lib/chart.js/dist/Chart.bundle.min.js"></script>
    <script src="~/js/site.js" asp-append-version="true"></script>
</environment>
```

In order to use the Chart.JS library to create a chart, we need to instantiate the *Chart* class. To do this, we can pass the node, jQuery instance, or 2D context of the canvas of where we want to draw the chart. For example:

```
<canvas id="chart1" width="300" height="200"></canvas>
```

Any of the following formats can be used:

```
var ctx = document.getElementById("chart1");
var ctx = document.getElementById("chart1").getContext("2d");
var ctx = $("#chart1");
var ctx = "chart1";
```

Once you have the element or context, you are ready to instantiate a pre-defined chart-type or create your own.

Line Charts

Creating a line chart with Chart.JS is easy. Here is the basic structure:

```
var myChart = new Chart(ctx, {
    type: "line",
    data: data,
    options: options
});
```

The line chart usually requires an array of labels, which are shown on the *x*-axis. The data for line charts is broken up into an array of datasets with each dataset having a color for the fill, a color for the line, and colors for the points and stroke of the points. These colors are strings just like CSS. You can use RGBA, RGB, HEX, or HSL notation to represent colors.

Let us consider an example that demonstrates how to create a simple line chart. Open the *Chapter05* project. Add a new controller named *CartJSController* to the *Controllers* folder and replace its content with the following code:

```
using Chapter05.Models;
using Microsoft.AspNetCore.Mvc;

namespace Chapter05.Controllers
{
    public class ChartJSController : Controller
    {
        // GET: /<controller>/
        public IActionResult Index()
        {
            return View();
        }

        public IActionResult LineChart()
        {
            ViewBag.Title = "ChartJS: Line Charts";
            return View();
        }
    }
}
```

Add a new folder *ChartJS* to the *Views* folder. Add *Views/ChartJS/LineChart.cshtml* and replace its content with the following code:

```
@{
    ViewData["Title"] = ViewBag.Title;
}

<h3>@ViewBag.Title</h3>
@Html.Partial("_Links")

<hr />

<div class="container">
    <div class="row">
        <div class="col-sm-5">
            <canvas id="chart1" width="300" height="250"></canvas>
        </div>
        <div class="col-sm-5">
            <canvas id="chart2" width="300" height="250"></canvas>
        </div>
    </div>
    <div class="row">
        <div class="col-sm-5">
            <canvas id="chart3"></canvas>
        </div>
        <div class="col-sm-5">
            <canvas id="chart4"></canvas>
        </div>
```

```
        </div>
    </div>

@section scripts{
    <script type="text/javascript">

        var ctx = "chart1";
        new Chart(ctx, {
            type: "line",
            data: {
                labels: ["1", "2", "3", "4", "5", "6", "7", "8", "9", "10"],
                datasets: [{
                    label: "First dataset",
                    data: [2, 3, 5, 7, 11, 13, 17, 19, 23, 29],
                }, {
                    label: "Second dataset",
                    data: [0, 1, 1, 2, 3, 5, 8, 13, 21, 34],
                }]
            },
        });
    </script>
}
```

The data contains a label array and two datasets that used to create a line chart with two curves using the default options. Running this example, selecting the *Chart.JS* tab, and clicking the *Line Charts* link produce the results shown in Figure 5-1.

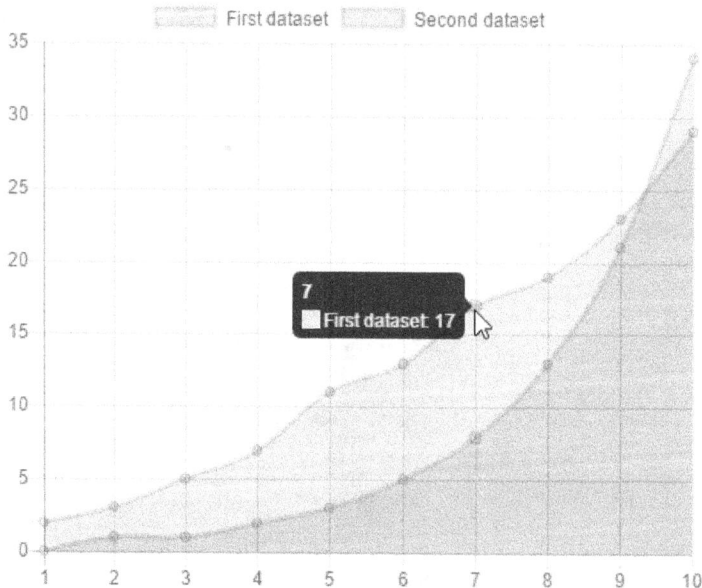

Figure 5-1. Line charts created using Chart.JS with default options.

This gives you an interactive line chart: a tooltip appears when you hover over each data point on the curves. The default line chart looks much like an area chart where the area under the line is filled. You can remove this filled area by setting the *fill* attribute to false.

Chart.JS provides many options you can set to produce the line charts you want. The following code snippet shows an example data object for a line chart using various options attributes:

```
var data = {
    labels: ["Jan", "Feb", "Mar", "Apr", "May", "Jun", "Jul"],
    datasets: [
        {
            label: "My First dataset",
            fill: false,
            lineTension: 0.1,
            backgroundColor: "rgba(75,192,192,0.4)",
            borderColor: "rgba(75,192,192,1)",
            borderCapStyle: 'butt',
            borderDash: [],
            borderDashOffset: 0.0,
            borderJoinStyle: 'miter',
            pointBorderColor: "rgba(75,192,192,1)",
            pointBackgroundColor: "#fff",
            pointBorderWidth: 1,
            pointHoverRadius: 5,
            pointHoverBackgroundColor: "rgba(75,192,192,1)",
            pointHoverBorderColor: "rgba(220,220,220,1)",
            pointHoverBorderWidth: 2,
            pointRadius: 1,
            pointHitRadius: 10,
            data: [65, 59, 80, 81, 56, 55, 40],
            spanGaps: false,
        }
    ]
};
```

Here, I will not discuss the details for each option attribute listed in the preceding code. You can look at the Chart.JS documentation to review definitions for all the chart options (http://www.chartjs.org/docs/). I will use an example to illustrate how to create a line chart with customized option attributes. Add the following code snippet to the script section of the *LineChart.cshtml* view:

```
// chart2
new Chart("chart2", {
    type: "line",
    data: {
        labels: ["January", "February", "March", "April", "May", "June","July"],
        datasets: [{
          label: "First dataset",
                fill: false,
                borderColor: "rgba(220,100,120,1)",
                pointRadius: 0,
                pointHitRadius: 10,
                pointHoverRadius: 10,
                data: [65, 59, 80, 81, 56, 55, 40],
            }, {
                label: "Second dataset",
                fill: false,
                borderColor: "rgba(151,187,205,1)",
                pointRadius: 0,
                pointHitRadius: 10,
                pointHoverRadius: 10,
```

```
            data: [28, 48, 40, 19, 86, 27, 90],
        }]
    },
    options: {
        tooltips: {
            mode: "label"
        }
    }
});
```

This code also create a line chart with two curves using the following specified attributes for each dataset:

- *fill*: *false* – does not fill the area under the line.

- *borderColor*: *color* – specifies the color for the line.

- *pointRadius*: 0 – specifies the radius of the point shape. Zero means that nothing is rendered.

- *pointHitRadius*: 10 – the 10px-radius of the non-displayed point that reacts to mouse events.

- *pointHoverRadius*: 10 – the 10px-radius of the point when hovered by mouse.

In addition, we set the *tooltips* mode to "*label*", indicating that the tooltip displays all of the items at the same *x*-label or (*x*-index). The default mode is *nearest*, meaning that the tooltip will display a single item that is nearest to the point, as shown in Figure 5-1.

Running this example produces the results shown in Figure 5-2.

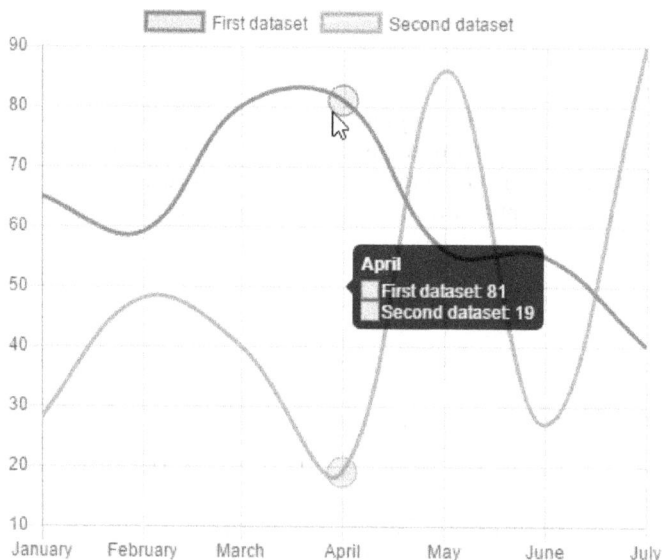

Figure 5-2. Line Charts with customized attributes.

In the preceding examples, we specified the data arrays manually with the script commands at the client-side. In practical chart applications, the data usually comes from databases, data files, or mathematical functions on server. In the following example, I will demonstrate how to use the data from the server to create a line chart.

Add a new folder named *Models* to the *Chapter05* project. Add a new *ModelHelper* class to the *Models* folder and replace its content with the following code:

```
public static object ChartJsData(int numPoints)
{
    List<object> x = new List<object>();
    List<object> y1 = new List<object>();
    List<object> y2 = new List<object>();
    List<object> y3 = new List<object>();

    double dx = 2.0 * Math.PI / numPoints;
    for (double xx = 0; xx < 2.0 * Math.PI; xx+=dx)
    {
        x.Add(Math.Round(xx, 2));
        y1.Add(Math.Sin(xx));
        y2.Add(Math.Cos(xx));
        y3.Add(2 * Math.Sin(xx) * Math.Sin(xx));
    }
    return new { x, y1, y2, y3 };
}
```

This method generates three sets of data lists using different mathematical functions. Add a method named *JsonChartJsData* to the *ChartJSControllor.cs* file:

```
public JsonResult JsonChartJsData(int numPoints)
{
    var data = ModelHelper.ChartJsData(numPoints);
    return Json(data);
}
```

This method converts our data into JSON data format with a specified *numPoints* input argument. We can now use this JSON data to create a line chart using Chart.JS.

Add the following code snippet to the script section of the view *LineChart.cshtml*:

```
// chart3
$.get("JsonChartJsData", { numPoints: 10 }, function (data) {
    new Chart("chart3", {
        type: "line",
        data: {
            labels: data.x,
            datasets: [{
                label: "Sin(x)",
                data: data.y1,
                fill: false,
                borderColor: "red",
            }, {
                label: "Cos(x)",
                data: data.y2,
                fill: false,
                borderColor: "green",
            }, {
                label: "Sin(x)^2",
                data: data.y3,
                fill: false,
                borderColor: "blue",
            }]
```

```
        },
        options: {
            tooltips: {
                mode: "label"
            }
        }
    });
});
```

Here, we use the jQuery AJAX *get* function with the *numPoints* parameter to retrieve our *JsonChartJsData* from server. We then assign *data.x* to the *labels*, and *data.y1*, *data.y2*, and *data.y3* to datasets when specifying the data for our line chart. We also set the label and line color for each dataset. Running this example produces the results shown in Figure 5-3.

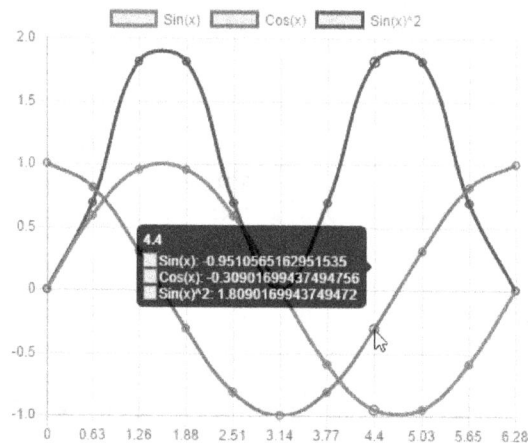

Figure 5-3. Line chart based on JSON data from server.

Note that the interpolation for curves, especially for the $sin(x)^2$ curve, seems not very accurate because we use only ten data points for each curve here. This issue can be solved by increasing the *numPoints* to a big number (say 100), which will produce the results shown in Figure 5-4.

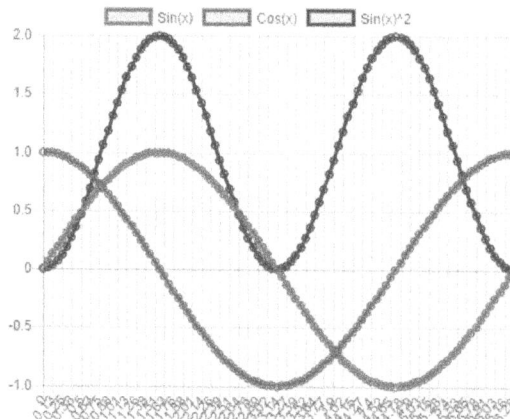

Figure 5-4. Line charts with 100 data points for each curve.

This chart displays the *x*-labels and gridlines for all point points, which looks very unprofessional. In order to avoid this issue, you can specify the *maxTicksLimit* attribute in the *x*-axis with the number of ticks that you want, as shown in the next example.

Add the following code snippet to the *LineChart.cshtml* view:

```
// chart4
$.get("JsonChartJsData", { numPoints: 100 }, function (data) {
    new Chart("chart4", {
        type: "line",
        data: {
            labels: data.x,
            datasets: [{
                label: "Sin(x)",
                data: data.y1,
                fill: false,
                borderColor: "red",
            }, {
                label: "Cos(x)",
                data: data.y2,
                fill: false,
                borderColor: "green",
            }, {
                label: "Sin(x)^2",
                data: data.y3,
                fill: false,
                borderColor: "blue",
            }]
        },
        options: {
            scales: {
                xAxes: [{
                    ticks:{maxTicksLimit:10, maxRotation: 0}
                }]
            },
            tooltips: {
                mode: "label"
            }
        }
    });
});
```

The code retrieves data from server with 100 data points for each dataset. In the *options* section, we specify the *x*-axis ticks with the *maxTicksLimit* being set to 10 rather than 100 (the default value is the number of data points).

Running this example, we obtain a nice-looking line chart, as shown in Figure 5-5.

In fact, the line charts implemented in Chart.JS are more suitable for the categorical rather than continuous variables in the *x*-axis. For the continuous numerical values, you may consider to use the scatter line charts in Chart.JS. In a scatter line chart with a large number of data points, the system will place a proper number of ticks and gridlines automatically, which will be discussed in the following section.

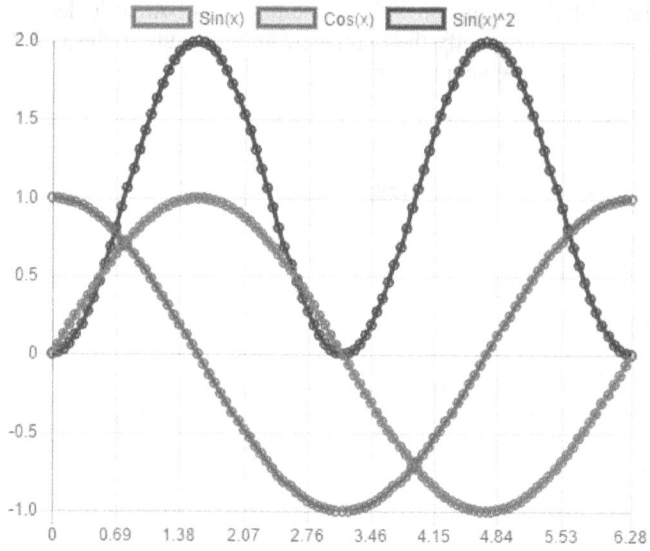

Figure 5-5. Line chart with 100 data points for each curve and 10 x-tick labels.

Scatter Line Charts

You can use the Chart.JS library to create scatter line charts by changing the *x*-axis to a linear axis. To use a scatter chart, you have to pass the data as objects containing *x* and *y* properties. The following code snippet shows the format in creating a scatter chart with three data points:

```
new Chart(ctx, {
    type: 'line',
    data: {
        datasets: [{
            label: 'Scatter Dataset',
            data: [{
                x: -10,
                y: 0
            }, {
                x: 0,
                y: 10
            }, {
                x: 10,
                y: 5
            }]
        }]
    },
    options: {
        scales: {
            xAxes: [{
                type: 'linear',
                position: 'bottom'
            }]
        }
    }
}
```

```
});
```

The highlighted code represents two key steps in creating a scatter chart: the dataset must contain the *x*-and *y*-value pairs; the type for the *x*-axis must be set to *linear* (for numerical values) or *time* (for time axis).

Let us consider an example. Add *Views/ChartJS/ScatterChart.cshtml* and replace its content with the following code:

```
@{
    ViewData["Title"] = ViewBag.Title;
}

<h3>@ViewBag.Title</h3>
@Html.Partial("_Links")

<hr />

<div class="container">
    <div class="row">
        <div class="col-sm-6">
            <canvas id="chart1" width="400" height="350"></canvas>
        </div>
        <div class="col-sm-6">
            <canvas id="chart2" width="400" height="350"></canvas>
        </div>
    </div>
    <div class="row" style="margin-top:30px">
        <div class="col-sm-6">
            <canvas id="chart3" width="400" height="350"></canvas>
        </div>
        <div class="col-sm-6">
            <canvas id="chart4" width="400" height="350"></canvas>
        </div>
    </div>
</div>

@section scripts{
<script type="text/javascript">

    // chart1
    $.get("JsonChartJsData", { numPoints: 100 }, function (data) {
        var xy1 = [], xy2 = [], xy3 = [];
        for (var i = 0; i < data.x.length; i++) {
            xy1.push({ x: data.x[i], y: data.y1[i] });
            xy2.push({ x: data.x[i], y: data.y2[i] });
            xy3.push({ x: data.x[i], y: data.y3[i] });
        }

        new Chart("chart1", {
            type: "line",
            data: {
                datasets: [{
                    label: 'Sin(x)',
                    data: xy1,
                    fill: false,
```

```
                        borderColor: "red",
                        pointRadius: 0
                }, {
                        label: 'Cos(x)',
                        data: xy2,
                        fill: false,
                        borderColor: "green",
                        pointRadius: 0
                }, {
                        label: 'Sin(x)^2',
                        data: xy3,
                        fill: false,
                        borderColor: "blue",
                        pointRadius: 0
                }]
        },
        options: {
            responsive: true,
            title: {
                display: true,
                text: "Math Functions"
            },
            scales: {
                xAxes: [{
                    type: "linear", position: "bottom",
                    display: true,
                    scaleLabel: {
                        display: true,
                        labelString: 'X Axis'
                    }
                }],
                yAxes: [{
                    display: true,
                    scaleLabel: {
                        display: true,
                        labelString: 'Y Values'
                    }
                }]
            }
        }
    }
  });
 });
</script>
}
```

This code uses the same JSON data as what we used in the preceding line chart example. We first convert the original data into three new arrays, *xy1*, *xy2*, and *xy3*, which contain the *x*- and *y*-value pairs. We then assign these arrays to the *datasets* attribute. In the *options* section, we set the *type* for the *xAxes* attribute to *linear*, the *position* attribute to *bottom*; and also specify the title for the chart and labels for the *x*- and *y*-axis.

Running this example produces the results shown in Figure 5-6. You can see that we actually create a nice line chart with the scatter chart format. The Chart.JS library automatically takes care of the creation of the ticks and gridlines in both the *x*- and *y*-axis. In general, if you want to create a line chart with a large number of data points (i.e., time series data), you should use the scatter chart format.

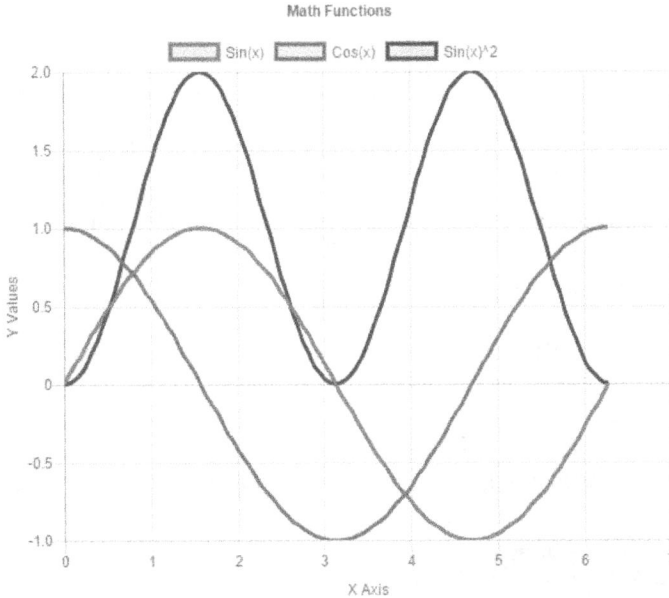

Figure 5-6. Demonstrate the line chart created using the scatter chart format.

In the next example, I will demonstrate how to create a time-series chart with a large amount of data. You can retrieve the time series data from a database. Here, for simplicity's sake, we will use the data from a CSV file. I already included the *indices.csv* data file in the *Models* folder. This file has also been used in Chapter 1 when we created the database using the code-first method. In order to use the data, we need to convert the data file into an object list. Add the following method *CsvToIndexData* to the *ModelHelper* class:

```
public static List<object> CsvToIndexData()
{
    string path = AppContext.BaseDirectory;
    string[] ss = Regex.Split(path, "bin");
    string filePath = ss[0] + @"Models\";
    string csvFile = filePath + "indices.csv";
    FileStream fs = new FileStream(csvFile, FileMode.Open,
        FileAccess.Read, FileShare.ReadWrite);
    StreamReader sr = new StreamReader(fs);
    List<String> lst = new List<string>();
    while (!sr.EndOfStream)
        lst.Add(sr.ReadLine());

    string[] fields = lst[0].Split(new char[] { ',' });
    var res = new List<object>();

    for (int i = 1; i < lst.Count; i++)
    {
        fields = lst[i].Split(',');
        res.Add(new
        {
            Date = DateTime.Parse(fields[0]),
            IGSpread = double.Parse(fields[1]),
```

```
                HYSpread = double.Parse(fields[2]),
                SPX = double.Parse(fields[3]),
                VIX = double.Parse(fields[4])
        });
    }
    return res;
}
```

In Chapter 1, we also used the similar method to convert the CSV data file into a data list. Add a method named *JsonIndexData* to the *ChartJSController.cs* file:

```
public JsonResult JsonIndexData()
{
    var data = ModelHelper.CsvToIndexData();
    return Json(data);
}
```

This method convert the object list into the JSON data. Now we can use this data to create a time-series line chart. Add the following code snippet to the script section of the *ScatterChart.cshtml* view:

```
$.get("JsonIndexData", function (data) {
    var spx = [], hyspx = [], hyvix = [];
    for (var i = 0; i < data.length; i++) {
        spx.push({ x: data[i].date, y: data[i].spx });
        hyspx.push({ x: data[i].spx, y: data[i].hySpread });
        hyvix.push({ x: data[i].vix, y: data[i].hySpread });
    }

    // chart2
    new Chart("chart2", {
        type: "line",
        data: {
            datasets: [{
                label: 'SPX',
                data: spx,
                fill: false,
                borderColor: "red",
                borderWidth: 1,
                pointRadius: 0
            }]
        },
        options: {
            responsive: true,
            title: {
                display: true,
                text: "SPX Time Series"
            },
            legend: {
                display: false,
                labels: {
                    display: false
                }
            },
            scales: {
                xAxes: [{
                    type: "time",
```

```
                display: true,
                scaleLabel: {
                    display: true,
                    labelString: 'Date'
                }
            }],
            yAxes: [{
                display: true,
                scaleLabel: {
                    display: true,
                    labelString: 'SPX',
                }
            }]
        }
    }
  });
});
```

This code first processes the original JSON data and converts it into the data in correct format. The variable *spx* represents the SPX time-series data, *hyspx* represents the HY spread vs SPX data, and *hyvix* represents the HY spread vs VIX data. In this example, we use the SPX time-series data to create a time-series line chart. We will use *hyspx* and *hyvix* in next example to create scatter charts. Note that we remove the legend from the chart by setting its *display* attribute to *false*, and set the *type* for *xAxes* to time, indicating that we want to create a time series chart.

Running this example produces the results shown in Figure 5-7.

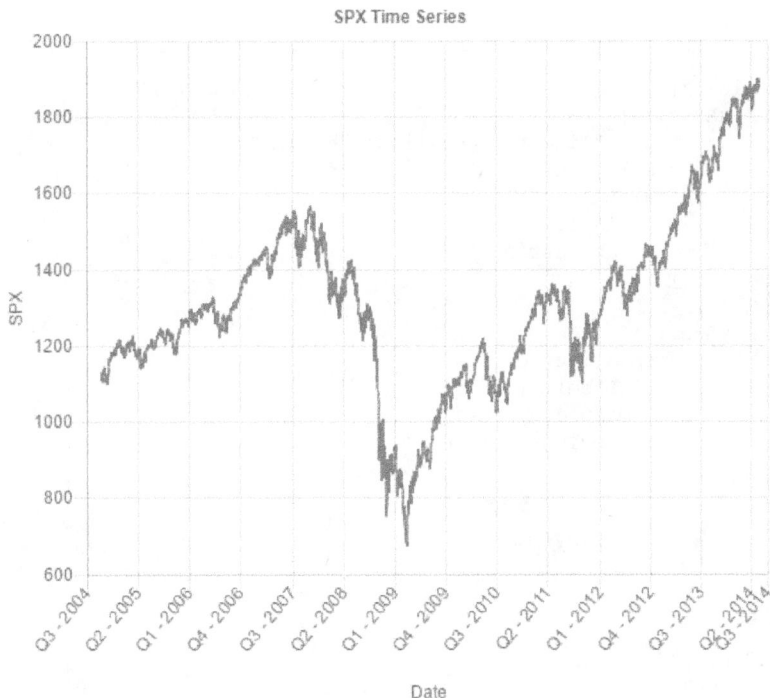

Figure 5-7. Demonstration of time series chart.

We can also create scatter charts for HY spread vs SPX and HY spread vs VIX by the following code snippet:

```
// chart3
new Chart("chart3", {
    type: "line",
    data: {
        datasets: [{
            label: 'HY ~ SPX',
            data: hyspx,
            fill: false,
            borderWidth: 0,
            borderColor: "transparent",
            pointRadius: 2,
            pointBorderColor: "steelblue",
        }]
    },
    options: {
        responsive: true,
        title: {
            display: true,
            text: "HY ~ SPX"
        },
        legend: {
            display: false,
            labels: {
                display: false
            }
        },
        scales: {
            xAxes: [{
                type: "linear", position: "bottom",
                display: true,
                scaleLabel: {
                    display: true,
                    labelString: 'SPX'
                }
            }],
            yAxes: [{
                display: true,
                scaleLabel: {
                    display: true,
                    labelString: 'HY'
                }
            }]
        }
    }
});

// chart4
new Chart("chart4", {
    type: "line",
    data: {
        datasets: [{
```

```
        label: 'HY ~ VIX',
        data: hyvix,
        fill: false,

    ......

});
```

This code generates the results shown in Figure 5-8 (HY ~ SPX) and Figure 5-9 (HY ~ VIX).

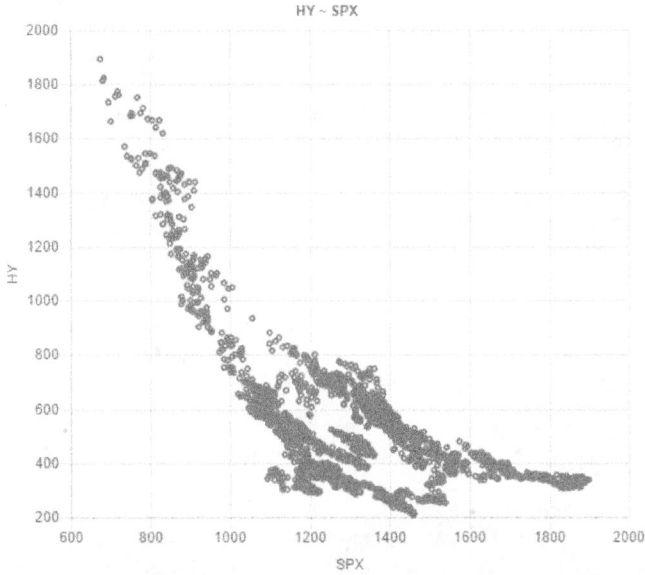

Figure 5-8. Scatter chart for HY ~ SPX.

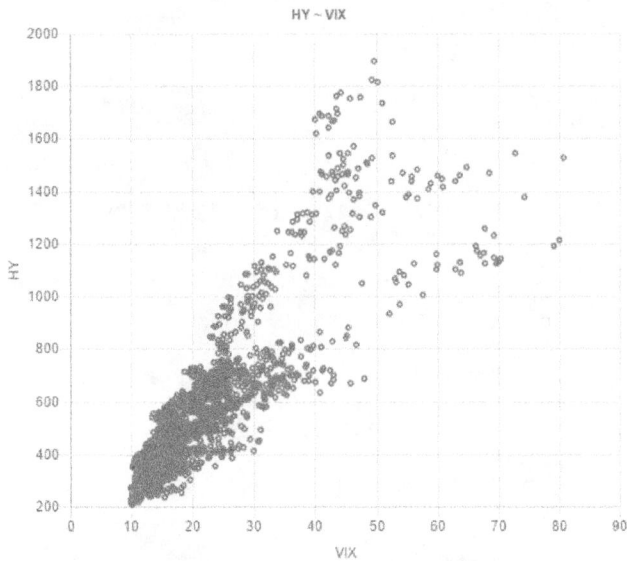

Figure 5-9. Scatter chart for HY ~ VIX.

Polar Area and Pie Charts

You can also use Chart.JS to create polar area and pie charts. A polar area chart is similar to a pie chart, but each segment has the same angle – the radius of the segment differs depending on the value. We often use this type of chart to show a comparison data similar to a pie chart, but also show a scale of values for context. The following code snippet provides a template for creating a polar area chart:

```
new Chart(ctx, {
    type: "polarArea",
    data: data,
    options: options
});
```

Here, I will use an example to demonstrate how to create a simple polar area chart. Add a new view to the *Views/ChartJS* folder and name it *PolarPie.cshtml*. Here is the code for this view:

```
@{
    ViewData["Title"] = ViewBag.Title;
}
<h3>@ViewBag.Title</h3>
@Html.Partial("_Links")
<hr />

<div class="container">
    <div class="row">
        <div class="col-sm-5">
            <canvas id="chart1" width="400" height="400"></canvas>
        </div>
        <div class="col-sm-5">
            <canvas id="chart2" width="400" height="400"></canvas>
        </div>
    </div>
</div>

@section scripts{
    <script type="text/javascript">

        // chart1
        new Chart("chart1", {
            type: "polarArea",
            data: {
                labels: ["Jan", "Feb", "Mar", "Apr", "May", "Jun", "Jul",
                        "Aug", "Sep", "Oct"],
                datasets: [{
                    label: "First dataset",
                    backgroundColor: [
                        "rgba(0,0,143,0.6)",
                        "rgba(0,0,255,0.6)",
                        "rgba(0,111,255,0.6)",
                        "rgba(0,223,255,0.6)",
                        "rgba(79,225,175,0.6)",
                        "rgba(191,225,63,0.6)",
                        "rgba(255,207,0,0.6)",
                        "rgba(255,95,0,0.6)",
                        "rgba(239,0,0,0.6)",
                        "rgba(127,0,0,0.6)",
```

```
            ],
            data: [35, 59, 70, 89, 56, 55, 75, 84, 62, 48],
        }]
    },
    options: {
        title: {
            display: true,
            text: "Polar Area Chart"
        }
    }
});
</script>
}
```

This code passes the chart data in an array of objects, with a value and a color. The value attribute should be a number, while the color attribute should be a string that can be HEX, RGB, RGBA, or HSL notation. We also want to add a *title* to the chart by specifying it in the options section.

Running this example produces the results shown in Figure 5-10.

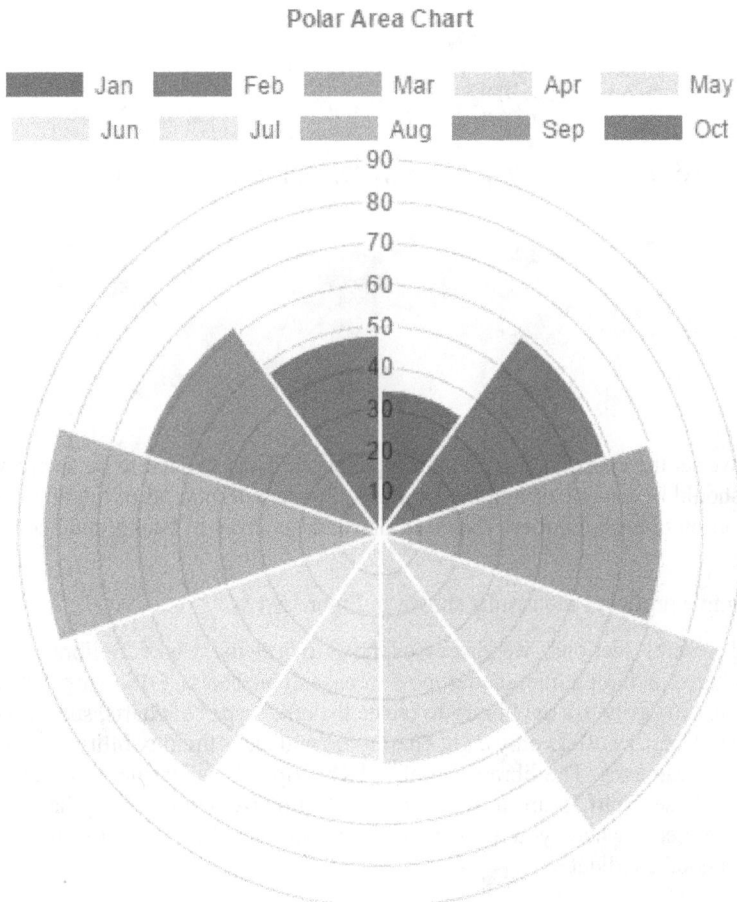

Figure 5-10. Demonstration of a polar area chart.

Using the similar approach, we can also create a pie chart. Pie charts are probably the most commonly used charts. A pie chart is divided into segments, and the arc of each segment shows the proportional value of each piece of data, which shows the relational proportions between data.

Add the following code snippet to the script section of the *PolarPie.cshtml* file:

```
// chart2
new Chart("chart2", {
    type: "pie",
    data: {
        labels: ["Jan", "Feb", "Mar", "Apr", "May", "Jun", "Jul",
                 "Aug", "Sep", "Oct"],
        datasets: [{
            label: "First dataset",
            backgroundColor: [
                "rgb(0,0,143)",
                "rgb(0,0,255)",
                "rgb(0,111,255)",
                "rgb(0,223,255)",
                "rgb(79,225,175)",
                "rgb(191,225,63)",
                "rgb(255,207,0)",
                "rgb(255,95,0)",
                "rgb(239,0,0)",
                "rgb(127,0,0)",
            ],
            data: [35, 59, 70, 89, 56, 55, 75, 84, 62, 48],
        }]
    },
    options: {
        title: {
            display: true,
            text: "Pie Chart"
        }
    }
});
```

As you can see, we set the chart type to *pie*. For a pie chart, datasets need to be an array of data points. The data points should be a number, and the Chart.JS library will total all of the numbers and calculate the relative proportion of each number. The code also adds an array of background colors to distinguish each piece easily.

Running this example produces the results shown in Figure 5-11.

In the preceding several sections, we discussed how to use the Chart.JS library to create several commonly used charts, including line, scatter, polar area, and pie charts. Following the similar procedure presented here, you can easily use the library to create the other types of charts, such as radar and bubble charts. Even though Chart.JS offers only eight chart types and lacks the flexibility offered by the options, it does have some advantages. The library is only 11Kb gzipped, which makes it lightweight and fast. The charts produced use Chart.JS are fully responsive and resize automatically based on the viewport width. For small projects where you want to add charting capability quickly to your applications, Chart.JS may be a good candidate.

Pie Chart

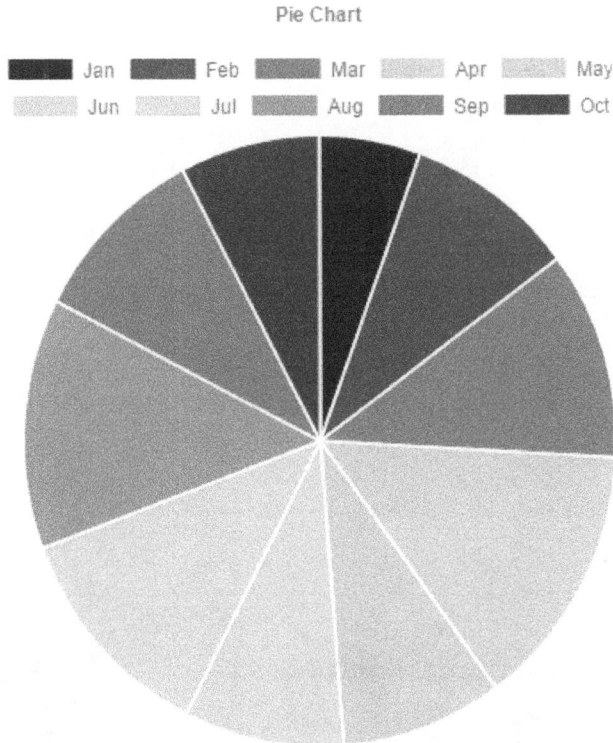

Figure 5-11. Demonstration of a pie chart.

Google Charts API

Google Charts API provides a large number of ready-to-use chart types. It offers sensible default appearance that may usually be all you need, but has flexible options to allow for customization when needed. Better than most other free to use charting libraries, Google Charts has great documentation provided by Google. It uses a predictable API, meaning that once you learn to use it for one chart type, it is easy to begin creating other types of charts.

As mentioned previously, one drawback for using the Google Charts API is that even though it is free, but it is not open-source. Google's licensing does not allow you to host their JavaScript files on your server. This means that you cannot use the Google Charts offline. If you are with a big enterprise and have some sensitive data, Google Charts might not be the best option. It is not suitable for complex charting applications either, such as advanced statistical and financial indicators.

Getting Started

Google Charts is a pure JavaScript based charting library. You can use it to enhance your web applications by adding interactive charting capability. Here, I will use a simple example to show you the basics of Google Charts.

Using DataTable

Before you can use the Google Charts, you need to set up the library by including it in your HTML page using the following script:

```
<script type="text/javascript"
    src="https://www.gstatic.com/charts/loader.js"></script>
```

Add *GoogleChartsController.cs* to the *Controllers* folder and replace its content with the following code:

```csharp
using Microsoft.AspNetCore.Mvc;
using Chapter05.Models;

namespace Chapter05.Controllers
{
    public class GoogleChartsController : Controller
    {
        // GET: /<controller>/
        public IActionResult Index()
        {
            ViewBag.Title = "Google Charts: Home";
            return View();
        }

        public IActionResult DataTableChart()
        {
            ViewBag.Title = "Charts with DataTable";
            return View();
        }

        public IActionResult ArrayChart()
        {
            ViewBag.Title = "Charts with Array";
            return View();
        }

        public IActionResult JsonChart()
        {
            ViewBag.Title = "Charts with Json Data";
            return View();
        }
    }
}
```

Add a new folder named *GoogleCharts* to the *Views* folder. Add a new view *DataTableChart* to the *GoogleCharts* folder and replace its content with the following code:

```
@{
    ViewData["Title"] = ViewBag.Title;
}
<h3>@ViewBag.Title</h3>
@Html.Partial("_Links")
<hr />

<div class="container">
    <div class="row">
```

```html
            <div class="col-sm-4">
                <p style="margin-left:200px">Simple pie chart</p>
                <div id="chart1"></div>
            </div>
            <div class="col-sm-4">
                <p style="margin-left:200px">3D pie chart</p>
                <div id="chart2"></div>
            </div>
        </div>
        <div class="row">
            <div class="col-sm-4">
                <p style="margin-left:200px">Exploded pie chart</p>
                <div id="chart3"></div>
            </div>
            <div class="col-sm-4">
                <p style="margin-left:200px">Exploded 3D pie chart</p>
                <div id="chart4"></div>
            </div>
        </div>
    </div>
</div>

<!--Load the AJAX API-->
<script type="text/javascript"
    src="https://www.gstatic.com/charts/loader.js"></script>

<script type="text/javascript">
    google.charts.load('current', { 'packages': ['corechart'] });
    google.charts.setOnLoadCallback(drawChart);

    function drawChart() {
        var data = new google.visualization.DataTable();
        data.addColumn('string', 'Tax Type');
        data.addColumn('number', 'Tax Percentage');
        data.addRows([
            ['Soc. Sec. Tax', { v: 30, f: '30%' }],
            ['Income Tax', { v: 35, f: '35%' }],
            ['Borrowing', { v: 15, f: '15%' }],
            ['Corp.Tax', { v: 12, f: '12%' }],
            ['Misc', { v: 8, f: '8%' }]
        ]);

        // pie chart:
        var options = {
            'title': 'Tax Structure in US',
            'width': 450,
            'height': 400
        };
        var chart = new google.visualization.PieChart(
            document.getElementById('chart1'));
        chart.draw(data, options);

        // 3D pie chart:
        options.is3D = true;
        chart = new google.visualization.PieChart(
            document.getElementById('chart2'));
```

```
        chart.draw(data, options);

        // Exploded pie chart:
        options.is3D = false;
        options.slices = {
            1: { offset: 0.3 },
            3: { offset: 0.5 },
        };

        chart = new google.visualization.PieChart(
            document.getElementById('chart3'));
        chart.draw(data, options);

        // Exploded 3D pie chart:
        options.is3D = true;
        chart = new google.visualization.PieChart(
            document.getElementById('chart4'));
        chart.draw(data, options);
    }

</script>
```

This code first loads the latest version of *corechart* API using *google.charts.load* method, and implements a JavaScript function named *drawChart*. You can name that function whatever you like, but be sure that it is globally unique and is defined before you reference it in your call to *google.charts.setOnLoadCallback*.

Google Charts requires data to be wrapped in a JavaScript class called DataTable. DataTable is a special 2D collection in Google Charts API that contains the data of the chart. Each column in DataTable has a data type, an optional ID, and an optional label, and each row represents the corresponding data. The code then uses the same data to create four different pie charts: a normal pie chart, a pie chart with 3D effect, an exploded pie chart, and an exploded pie chart with 3D effect. The difference between these charts are specified by configuring the *options* for each chart. Note that we reuse the common parts of options and only need to specify the attributes specific to that chart. This will avoid the repeated code when you set the option parameters for multiple charts. Finally, the code calls the *chart.draw* method to create the charts.

Running this example, selecting the *Google Charts* tab, and clicking the *Charts with DataTable* link produce the results shown in Figure 5-12.

In this example, we set the chart data by directly defining DataTable. In practice, it is almost impossible to use this manual approach to set the chart data when you have a large dataset for charting. Next, I will present several different methods to define the chart data.

Using Data Array

Google Charts offers a helper function *arrayToDataTable* that can be used to create and populate a DataTable using a data array. We will use an example to demonstrate how to use a data array to create charts.

Add a new view named *ArrayChart.cshtml* to the *Views/GoogleCharts* folder and replace its content with the following code:

Simple pie chart

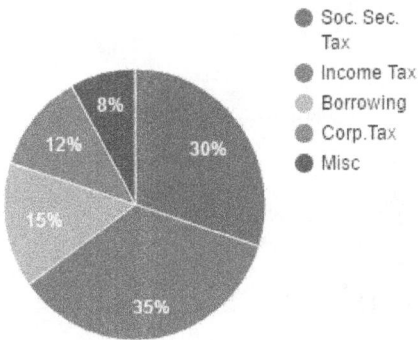

3D pie chart

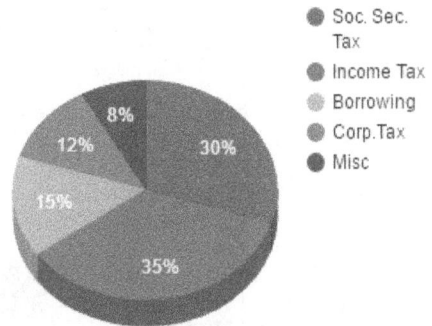

Exploded pie chart

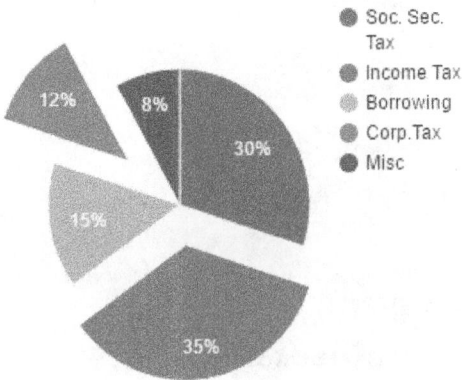

Exploded 3D pie chart

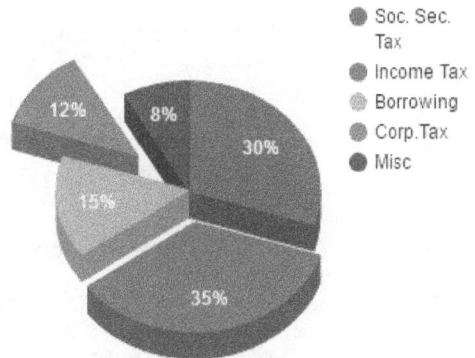

Figure 5-12. Pie charts created using Google Charts.

```
@{
    ViewData["Title"] = ViewBag.Title;
}
<h3>@ViewBag.Title</h3>
@Html.Partial("_Links")
<hr />

<div class="container">
    <div class="row">
        <div class="col-sm-5">
            <p>Simple pie chart</p>
            <div id="chart1"></div>
        </div>
        <div class="col-sm-5">
            <p>Line chart</p>
            <div id="chart2"></div>
        </div>
</div>
```

```
        </div>
    </div>

    <script type="text/javascript"
        src="https://www.gstatic.com/charts/loader.js"></script>

    <script type="text/javascript">
        google.charts.load('current', { 'packages': ['corechart'] });
        google.charts.setOnLoadCallback(drawChart);

        function drawChart() {
            //Pie chart with array data
            var arr = [
                ['Tax Type', 'Tax Percentage'],
                ['Soc. Sec. Tax', { v: 30, f: '30%' }],
                ['Income Tax', { v: 35, f: '35%' }],
                ['Borrowing', { v: 15, f: '15%' }],
                ['Corp.Tax', { v: 12, f: '12%' }],
                ['Misc', { v: 8, f: '8%' }]
            ];
            var data = google.visualization.arrayToDataTable(arr, false);
            var options = {
                'title': 'Tax Structure in US',
                'width': 500,
                'height': 400
            };
            var chart = new google.visualization.PieChart(
                document.getElementById('chart1'));
            chart.draw(data, options);

            // Multiple line chart:
            var arr = [];
            arr[0] = ["X", "Sin(X)", "Cos(X)", "Sin(X)^2"]
            for (var i = 0; i < 70; i++) {
                arr[i + 1] = [0.1 * i, Math.sin(0.1 * i), Math.cos(0.1 * i),
                    Math.sin(0.1 * i) * Math.sin(0.1 * i)];
            }
            data = google.visualization.arrayToDataTable(arr, false);
            chart = new google.visualization.LineChart(
                document.getElementById('chart2'));
            chart.draw(data, options);
        }
    </script>
```

This code creates two charts: a pie chart and a line chart. In the pie chart, we define an array manually, while in the line chart, we create the data array using three mathematical functions: $\sin(x)$, $\cos(x)$, and $\sin(x)^2$. It then calls the *arrayToDataTable* function to define and populate DataTable. The *false* argument in the function call means that the first row in the array contains headers, not data. The headers will be used in the legend.

Running this example, selecting the *GoogleCharts* tab, and clicking the *Charts with Array* link produce the results shown in Figure 5-13.

Tax Structure in US

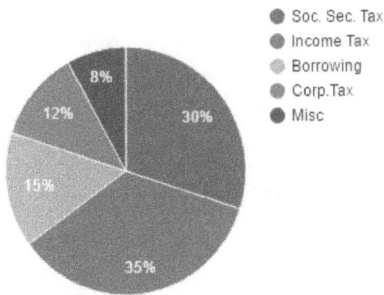

- ● Soc. Sec. Tax
- ● Income Tax
- ● Borrowing
- ● Corp.Tax
- ● Misc

8%

12%

30%

15%

35%

Multiple Line Chart

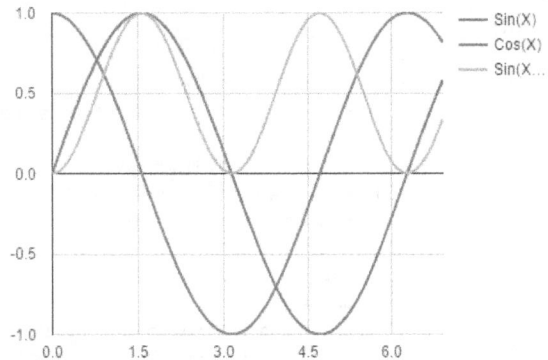

— Sin(X)
— Cos(X)
— Sin(X...

Figure 5-13. Charts created using data arrays.

Using JSON Data

You can also pass the JSON data into your data table constructor, defining the table schema and optionally data as well. This will be very useful when you generate data on your web server. The main advantage of this approach is that it processes much faster than other methods (such as using data array) for larger tables (about 1000 + cells). The disadvantage is its syntax that is tricky to get right, and prone to typos, resulting in a not very readable code. Nevertheless, considering the advantage of performance speed, in the following, we will try to use the JSON data format as much as possible.

Add *Views/GoogleCharts/JsonChart.cshtml* and replace its content with the following code:

```
@{
    ViewData["Title"] = ViewBag.Title;
}
<h3>@ViewBag.Title</h3>
@Html.Partial("_Links")
<hr />

<div class="container">
    <div class="row">
        <div class="col-sm-4">
            <p style="margin-left:150px">Simple pie chart</p>
            <div id="chart1"></div>
        </div>
        <div class="col-sm-4">
            <p style="margin-left:150px">3D pie chart</p>
            <div id="chart2"></div>
        </div>
    </div>
    <div class="row">
        <div class="col-sm-4">
            <p style="margin-left:150px">Exploded pie chart</p>
            <div id="chart3"></div>
        </div>
        <div class="col-sm-4">
            <p style="margin-left:150px">Exploded 3D pie chart</p>
            <div id="chart4"></div>
```

```
            </div>
        </div>
    </div>

<script type="text/javascript"
    src="https://www.gstatic.com/charts/loader.js"></script>

<script type="text/javascript">
    google.charts.load('current', { 'packages': ['corechart'] });
    google.charts.setOnLoadCallback(drawChart);

    function drawChart() {
        var json = {
            cols: [{ id: 'taxType', label: 'Tax Type', type: 'string' },
                   { id: 'percent', label: 'Tax Percent', type: 'number' }],
            rows: [{ c: [{ v: 'Soc. Sec. Tax' }, { v: 30, f: '30%' }] },
                   { c: [{ v: 'Income Tax' }, { v: 35 }] },
                   { c: [{ v: 'Borrowing' }, { v: 15 }] },
                   { c: [{ v: 'Corp. Tax' }, { v: 12 }] },
                   { c: [{ v: 'Misc' }, { v: 8 }] },
            ],
            p: {foo: 'test', bar: 'my bar'}
        };
        var data = new google.visualization.DataTable(json);

        // pie chart:
        var options = {
            'title': 'Tax Structure in US',
            'width': 450,
            'height': 400
        };
        var chart = new google.visualization.PieChart(
            document.getElementById('chart1'));
        chart.draw(data, options);

        // 3D pie chart:
        options.is3D = true;
        chart = new google.visualization.PieChart(
            document.getElementById('chart2'));
        chart.draw(data, options);

        // Exploded pie chart:
        options.is3D = false;
        options.slices = {
            1: { offset: 0.3 },
            3: { offset: 0.5 },
        };

        chart = new google.visualization.PieChart(
            document.getElementById('chart3'));
        chart.draw(data, options);

        // Exploded 3D pie chart:
        options.is3D = true;
        chart = new google.visualization.PieChart(
```

```
            document.getElementById('chart4'));
        chart.draw(data, options);
    }
</script>
```

This code is basically the same as what we used in the *DataTableChart* example, except that we use a JSON string object to populate the DataTable (see the highlighted code snippet). You can see that the JSON data object consists of two required top-level properties, *cols* and *rows*, and an optional *p* property that is a map of arbitrary values. *cols* is an array of objects describing the ID and type of each column. While the *rows* property holds an array of row objects. Each row object has one required property called *c*, which is an array of cells in that row. It also has an optional *p* property that defines a map of arbitrary custom values to assign to the whole row.

The code then puts the JSON object directly into the DataTable's contructor to populate the table.

Running this example produces the same results as shown in Figure 5-12.

Data from Server

You can also use the data from server-side to create charts.

Data Array from Server

Let us consider an example, where we want to create a pie chart and a line chart with data from server. Add two C# methods, *TaskArrayData* and *MultilineArrayData*, to the *ModelHelper* class:

```
public static List<object> TaskArrayData()
{
    List<object> objs = new List<object>();
    objs.Add(new object[] { "Task", "Hours" });
    objs.Add(new object[] { "Work", 11 });
    objs.Add(new object[] { "Eat", 2 });
    objs.Add(new object[] { "Commute", 5 });
    objs.Add(new object[] { "Watch TV", 4 });
    objs.Add(new object[] { "Sleep", 7 });
    return objs;
}

public static List<object> MultilineArrayData()
{
    List<object> objs = new List<object>();
    objs.Add(new object[] { "x", "Sin(x)", "Cos(x)", "Sin(x)^2" });
    for (int i = 0; i < 70; i++)
    {
        double x = 0.1 * i;
        objs.Add(new object[] { x, Math.Sin(x), Math.Cos(x),
                                Math.Sin(x) * Math.Sin(x) });
    }
    return objs;
}
```

These two methods generate two data lists that will be used to create a pie and a line charts in client-side. Add a new method *JsonArrayData* to *GoogleChartsController.cs*:

```
public JsonResult JsonArrayData()
{
    var data1 = ModelHelper.TaskArrayData();
    var data2 = ModelHelper.MultilineArrayData();
    return Json(new { data1, data2 });
}
```

This method returns two arrays: *data1* and *data2*, in JSON format, as shown in the following:

```
{
    "data1": [
        [ "Task", "Hours" ],
        [ "Work", 11 ],
        [ "Eat", 2 ],
        [ "Commute", 5 ],
        [ "Watch TV", 4 ],
        [ "Sleep", 7 ]
    ],
    "data2": [
        [ "x", "Sin(x)", "Cos(x)", "Sin(x)^2" ],
        [ 0, 0, 1, 0 ],
        [ 0.1, 0.09983341664682815, 0.9950041652780258, 0.009966711079379185 ],
        [ 0.2, 0.19866933079506122, 0.9800665778412416, 0.039469502998557456 ],

        ......

        [ 6.9, 0.5784397643882001, 0.8157251001253568, 0.33459256102547646 ]
    ]
}
```

Add a new view named *ServerChart.cshtml* to the *Views/GoogleCharts* folder and replace its content with the following code:

```
@{
    ViewData["Title"] = ViewBag.Title;
}
<h3>@ViewBag.Title</h3>
@Html.Partial("_Links")
<hr />

<div class="container">
    <div class="row">
        <div class="col-sm-5">
            <p>Json array data: pie chart</p>
            <div id="chart1"></div>
        </div>
        <div class="col-sm-5">
            <p>Json array data: line chart</p>
            <div id="chart2"></div>
        </div>
        <div class="col-sm-5">
            <p>Json string data: pie chart</p>
            <div id="chart3"></div>
        </div>
        <div class="col-sm-5">
            <p>Json string data: line chart</p>
            <div id="chart4"></div>
```

```
        </div>
    </div>
</div>

<script type="text/javascript"
    src="https://www.gstatic.com/charts/loader.js"></script>

<script type="text/javascript">
    google.charts.load('current', { 'packages': ['corechart'] });
    google.charts.setOnLoadCallback(drawChart);

    function drawChart() {

        // json array
        $.get('JsonArrayData', function (jsonData) {

            // pie chart
            var data = new google.visualization.arrayToDataTable(
                jsonData.data1, false);
            var options = {
                'title': 'My Daily Activities',
                'width': 500,
                'height': 400,
                is3D: true,
            };
            var chart = new google.visualization.PieChart(
                document.getElementById('chart1'));
            chart.draw(data, options);

            // line chart
            data = new google.visualization.arrayToDataTable(
                jsonData.data2, false);
            options = {
                'title': 'Multiple Line Chart',
                'width': 500,
                'height': 400,
                'chartArea': { right: 100 },
            };
            chart = new google.visualization.LineChart(
                document.getElementById('chart2'));
            chart.draw(data, options);
        });
    }
</script>
```

This code first retrieves the JSON data from server using AJAX *.get* function, and then converts the JSON data into DataTable using the *arrayToDataTable* helper function. It uses *data1* for the pie chart and *data2* for the line chart respectively.

Running this example produces the same results as shown in Figure 5-13, as expected.

JSON String from Server

In the previous example, the JSON string data in client-side was used to create charts. In that example, we defined the JSON string manually. You may notice that this manual approach will soon become unmanageable as the data size increases. We need to find a generic way to convert a list (or array) of objects into the JSON string format that can be used in Google Charts. To achieve this goal, we will implement a class hierarchy that matches the JSON string format required by Google Charts API, and then use the Newtonsoft's *JsonConvert* method to serialize this class.

Add a new class named *JsonString* to the *Models* folder and replace its content with the following code:

```
using Newtonsoft.Json;

namespace Chapter05.Models
{
    public class JsonString
    {
        public static string GetGoogleJson(JsonColumn[] cols, JsonRow[] rows)
        {
            var gc = new GoogleChart();
            gc.cols = new JsonColumn[cols.Length];
            gc.rows = new JsonRow[rows.Length];
            for (int i = 0; i < cols.Length; i++)
            {
                gc.cols[i] = cols[i];
            }
            for (int i = 0; i < rows.Length; i++)
            {
                gc.rows[i] = rows[i];
            }
            return JsonConvert.SerializeObject(gc);
        }
    }

    #region define json structure for google chart
    public class GoogleChart
    {
        public JsonColumn[] cols { get; set; }
        public JsonRow[] rows { get; set; }
    }

    public class JsonColumn
    {
        private string id1 = "";
        private string label1 = "";

        public string id
        {
            get { return id1; }
            set { id1 = value; }
        }
        public string label
        {
            get { return label1; }
            set { label1 = value; }
        }
        public string type { get; set; }
        public string role { get; set; }
    }
```

```
public class JsonRow
{
    public JsonCell[] c { get; set; }
}

public class JsonCell
{
    public object v { get; set; }
    public string f { get; set; }
    public object p { get; set; }
}
#endregion define json struicture for google chart
}
```

Here, we implement four classes, *GoogleChart*, *JsonColumn*, *JsonRow*, and *JsonCell* to mimic the JSON string structure used in Google Charts. In the *JsonColumn* class, it consists of four properties, *id*, *label*, *type*, and *role* (you can add more properties according to the requirement of your applications). This class simulates the *cols* property in the JSON string, such as:

```
cols: [{id: 'A', label: 'A-label', type: 'string'},
       {id: 'B', label: 'B-label', type: 'number'},
       {id: 'C', label: 'C-label', type: 'date'}]
```

The *JsonRow* class holds an array of the *JsonCell* object, and the *JsonCell* class consists of three properties, *v*, *f*, and *p*. These properties simulate the same properties defined in the JSON string used by Google Charts. In JSON string, the *v* property represents the cell value, *f* (optional) represents a string version of the *v* value, formatted for display, and *p* (optional) is an object that is a map of custom value applied to the cell. The *p* value can be any JavaScript type. For example:

```
p:{style: 'border: 1px solid green;'}
```

The *GoogleChart* class consists of an array of *JsonColumn* objects and an array of *JsonRow* objects, which should provide the JSON string required by the Google Charts after serialization. We perform this serialization process using the *GetGoogleJson* method implemented in the *JsonString* class.

Here is a sample JSON string used in Google Charts with three columns, filled with three rows of data:

```
{
  cols: [{id: 'A', label: 'A-label', type: 'string'},
         {id: 'B', label: 'B-label', type: 'number'},
         {id: 'C', label: 'C-label', type: 'date'}
  ],
  rows: [{c:[{v: 'a'},
             {v: 1.0, f: 'One'},
             {v: new Date(2008, 1, 28, 0, 31, 26), f: '2/28/08 12:31 AM'}
        ]},
        {c:[{v: 'b'},
             {v: 2.0, f: 'Two'},
             {v: new Date(2008, 2, 30, 0, 31, 26), f: '3/30/08 12:31 AM'}
        ]},
        {c:[{v: 'c'},
             {v: 3.0, f: 'Three'},
             {v: new Date(2008, 3, 30, 0, 31, 26), f: '4/30/08 12:31 AM'}
        ]}
  ]
}
```

You can see that the structure defined by our classes covers all of the fields that occur in the above sample.

In the preceding example, we created two JSON arrays in the *ModelHelper* class, *TaskArrayData* and *MultilineArrayData*. Now, we can convert this JSON arrays into JSON strings using the *GetGoogleJson* method. Add two new methods, *TaskStringData* and *MultilineStringData*, to the *ModelHelper* class. Here is the code for these two methods:

```
#region Json string data
public static string TaskStringData()
{
    var data = TaskArrayData();
    var cols = new JsonColumn[]
    {
        new JsonColumn{label = "Task", type = "string"},
        new JsonColumn{label = "Hours per Day", type = "number"}
    };

    var rows = new JsonRow[data.Count - 1];
    for (int i = 1; i < data.Count; i++)
    {
        var obj = data[i] as object[];
        rows[i-1] = new JsonRow
        {
            c = new JsonCell[] { new JsonCell { v = obj[0] },
                                 new JsonCell { v = obj[1] } }
        };
    }
    return JsonString.GetGoogleJson(cols, rows);
}

public static string MultilineStringData()
{
    var data = MultilineArrayData();
    var cols = new JsonColumn[]
    {
        new JsonColumn {label = "X", type = "number" },
        new JsonColumn {label = "Sin(X)", type = "number" },
        new JsonColumn {label = "Cos(X)", type = "number" },
        new JsonColumn {label = "Sin(X)^2", type = "number" }
    };

    var rows = new JsonRow[data.Count - 1];
    for (int i = 1; i < data.Count; i++)
    {
        var obj = data[i] as object[];
        rows[i - 1] = new JsonRow
        {
            c = new JsonCell[]
            {
                new JsonCell{ v = obj[0] },
                new JsonCell{ v = obj[1] },
                new JsonCell{ v = obj[2] },
                new JsonCell{ v = obj[3] }
            }
        }
```

```
        };
    }
    return JsonString.GetGoogleJson(cols, rows);
}
#endregion Json string data
```

Here, we first create the *JsonColumn* and *JsonRow* array objects and then convert them into a JSON string. Here is the sample output from the *TaskStringData*:

```
{
    "cols":[{"id":"","label":"Task","type":"string","role":null},
            {"id":"","label":"Hours per Day","type":"number","role":null}
    ],
    "rows":[{"c":[{"v":"Work","f":null,"p":null},
                  {"v":11,"f":null,"p":null}
            ]},
            {"c":[{"v":"Eat","f":null,"p":null},
                  {"v":2,"f":null,"p":null}
            ]},
            {"c":[{"v":"commute","f":null,"p":null},
                  {"v":5,"f":null,"p":null}
            ]},
            {"c":[{"v":"Watch TV","f":null,"p":null},
                  {"v":4,"f":null,"p":null}
            ]},
            {"c":[{"v":"Sleep","f":null,"p":null},
                  {"v":7,"f":null,"p":null}
            ]}
    ]
}
```

This JSON string is exactly what Google Charts requires. We can now create the charts using the preceding methods. Add a new method *JsonStringData* to the *GoogleChartsController.cs* file:

```
public JsonResult JsonStringData()
{
    var string1 = ModelHelper.TaskStringData();
    var string2 = ModelHelper.MultilineStringData();
    return Json(new { string1, string2 });
}
```

This method returns two JSON strings, *string1* and *string2*, which contain the data for creating a pie chart and a line chart respectively. Add the following code snippet to the script section of the *ServerChart* view:

```
// json string
$.get('JsonStringData', function (jsonData) {

    // pie chart
    var data = new google.visualization.DataTable(jsonData.string1);
    var options = {
        'title': 'My Daily Activities',
        'width': 500,
        'height': 400,
        is3D: true,
    };
    var chart = new google.visualization.PieChart(
```

```
            document.getElementById('chart3'));
      chart.draw(data, options);

      // line chart
      data = new google.visualization.DataTable(jsonData.string2);
      options = {
          'title': 'Multiple Line Chart',
          'width': 500,
          'height': 400,
          'chartArea': { right: 100 },
      };
      chart = new google.visualization.LineChart(
          document.getElementById('chart4'));
      chart.draw(data, options);
});
```

The highlighted code shows how to retrieve the JSON string data from the server and how to convert the data into Google Charts DataTable object by directly putting the JSON string to the DataTable constructor.

Running this example produces the same output as shown in Figure 5-13, as expected.

Basic Charts

Up to this point, we already understood the basic data structure of Google Charts and procedure of creating pie and line charts. In this section, we will create several commonly used chart types using the data from server.

Line Charts

Even though we have used the line charts as examples to illustrate the basic structure of Google Charts in the preceding sections, here, we still would like to create several line charts with different customizations. The data we are going to use is the JSON string returned by the *MultilineStringData* method implemented in the *ModelHelper* class.

Add a new view named *LineChart.cshtml* to the *Views/GoogleCharts* folder and replace its content with the following code:

```
@{
    ViewData["Title"] = ViewBag.Title;
}
<h3>@ViewBag.Title</h3>
@Html.Partial("_Links")
<hr />

<div class="container">
    <div class="row">
        <div class="col-sm-6">
            <div id="chart1"></div>
        </div>
        <div class="col-sm-6">
            <div id="chart2"></div>
        </div>
    </div>
</div>
```

```
    <div class="row" style="margin-top:50px">
        <div class="col-sm-6">
            <div id="chart3"></div>
        </div>
        <div class="col-sm-6">
            <div id="chart4"></div>
        </div>
    </div>
</div>

<script type="text/javascript"
    src="https://www.gstatic.com/charts/loader.js"></script>

<script type="text/javascript">
    google.charts.load('current', { 'packages': ['corechart'] });
    google.charts.setOnLoadCallback(drawChart);
    function drawChart() {
        $.get('JsonStringData', {}, function (json) {
            var jsonData = json.string2;
            var data = new google.visualization.DataTable(jsonData);
            var view = new google.visualization.DataView(data);
            view.hideColumns([3]);
            // Lines with different markers:
            options = {
                title: 'Lines with different markers',
                hAxis: { title: "X-Axis" },
                vAxis: { title: "Y Values" },
                width: 600,
                height: 400,
                chartArea: { left: 80, top: 30, width: '70%', height: '80%' },
                pointSize: 10,
                series: {
                    0: { pointShape: 'circle' },
                    1: { pointShape: 'diamond' },
                }
            };
            chart = new google.visualization.LineChart(
                document.getElementById('chart1'));
            chart.draw(view, options);

            // Lines with different dash-styles:
            options = {
                title: 'Lines with different dash-styles',
                hAxis: { title: "X-Axis" },
                vAxis: { title: "Y Values" },
                width: 600,
                height: 400,
                chartArea: { left: 80, top: 30, width: '70%', height: '80%' },
                lineWidth: 4,
                series: {
                    0: { lineDashStyle: [3, 3] },
                    1: { lineDashStyle: [10, 2, 2, 2] }
                }
            };
            chart = new google.visualization.LineChart(
```

```
                document.getElementById('chart2'));
        chart.draw(view, options);

        // Line with two y-axes:
        view = new google.visualization.DataView(data);
        view.hideColumns([2]);
        options = {
            title: 'Lines with two y-axes',
            hAxis: { title: "X-Axis" },
            width: 600,
            height: 400,
            chartArea: { left: 80, top: 60, right: 80, bottom: 60 },
            lineWidth: 4,
            series: { 1: { targetAxisIndex: 1 } }
        };
        chart = new google.visualization.LineChart(
            document.getElementById('chart3'));
        chart.draw(view, options);

        // Multiple line chart:
        options = {
            title: 'Lines with different markers',
            hAxis: { title: "X-Axis" },
            vAxis: { title: "Y Values" },
            width: 600,
            height: 400,
            chartArea: { left: 70, top: 30, width: '70%', height: '80%',
                backgroundColor: { stroke: "gray", strokeWidth: 1 } },
            pointSize: 10,
            series: {
                0: { pointShape: 'circle' },
                1: { pointShape: 'diamond' },
                2: { pointShape: 'triangle' },
            }
        };
        chart = new google.visualization.LineChart(
            document.getElementById('chart4'));
        chart.draw(data, options);
    });
  }
</script>
```

This code creates four line charts. Note that the code first retrieves the JSON string data from server and assign the *string2* (*MultilineStringData*) to a variable *jsonData*. It then converts the data into the DataTable object named *data*. Next, the code introduces a new variable named *view* that is created using the *DataView* function. *DataView* is a read-only view of an underlying *DataTable*. It allows selection of only a subset of the columns and/or rows of DataTable. It also allows reordering columns/rows, and duplicating columns/rows. The following statement returns a view with a subset of the underlying data without column 3

```
view.hideColumns([3]);
```

In our case, the original data has the following columns: column 0: x, column 1: $\sin(x)$, column 2: $\cos(x)$, and column 3: $\sin(x)^2$. This means that we do not want the $\sin(x)^2$ column to be included in our charts.

The first line chart shows the sin(x) and cos(x) curves with different markers: *circle* and *diamond* specified using the *series* option.

The second line charts shows the same sin(x) and cos(x) curves, but each curve has different dash-style specified using an array of numbers.

The third chart shows how to create a line chart with two *y*-axes. In this case, we hide the cos(x) column and display the sin(x) and sin(x)^2 curves on our chart. We use the following code snippet to set the sin(x)^2 curve to the second *y*-axis:

```
series: { 1: { targetAxisIndex: 1 } }
```

That is, the *targetAxisIndex* 0 means the left *y*-axis and 1 the right *y*-axis.

The last line chart uses original data to show a multiline chart. Here, we add a box to the chart area using the following option for the *chartArea*:

```
chartArea: { ......, backgroundColor: { stroke: "gray", strokeWidth: 1 } },
```

This draws a border around the chart area with the specified color of *stroke*. This border will make our chart looks better.

Running this example produces the results shown in Figure 5-14.

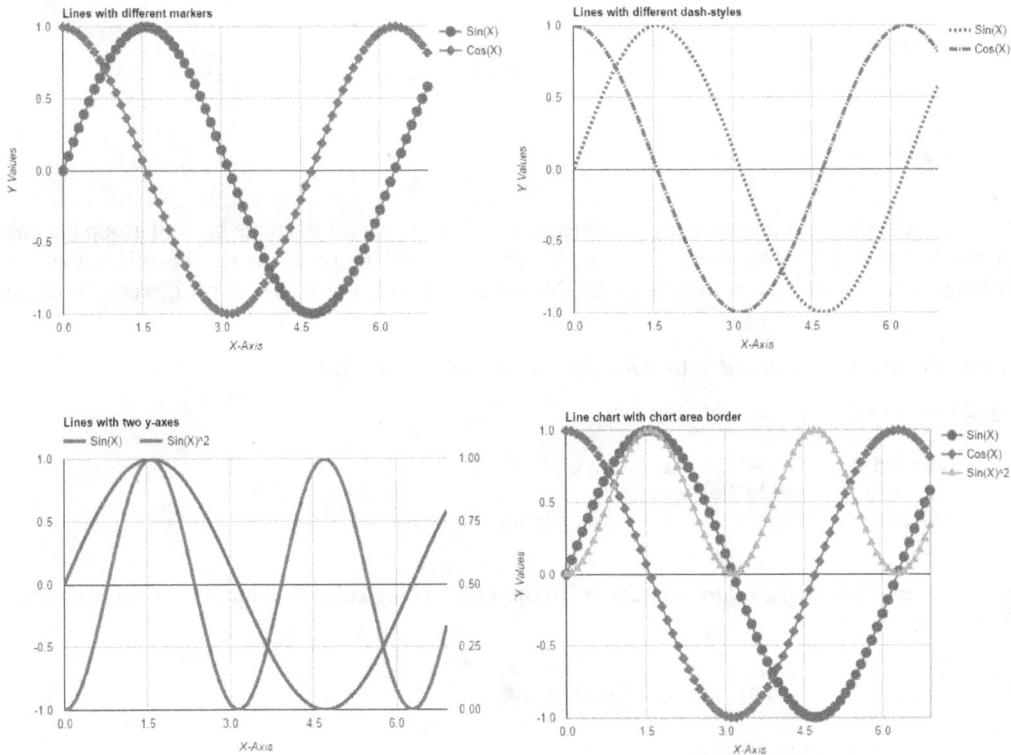

Figure 5-14. Demonstration of customized line charts.

Bar Charts

You can also create various bar charts easily using Google Charts API. First, let us generate some data for bar charts. Add the following two C# methods, *BarArrayData* and *GroupBarArrayData* to the *ModelHelper* class:

```
public static List<object> BarArrayData()
{
    List<object> objs = new List<object>();
    objs.Add(new object[] { "City", "2010 Population" });
    objs.Add(new object[] { "New York City", 8175000 });
    objs.Add(new object[] { "Los Angles", 3792000 });
    objs.Add(new object[] { "Chicago", 2695000 });
    objs.Add(new object[] { "Houston", 2099000 });
    objs.Add(new object[] { "Philadephia", 1526000 });
    return objs;
}

public static List<object> GroupBarArrayData()
{
    List<object> objs = new List<object>();
    objs.Add(new object[] { "Year", "Houston", "Los Angeles",
                            "New York", "Chicago", "Philadephia" });
    objs.Add(new object[] { "1990", 1.70, 3.49, 7.32, 2.78, 1.59 });
    objs.Add(new object[] { "2000", 1.98, 3.70, 8.02, 2.90, 1.51 });
    objs.Add(new object[] { "2005", 2.08, 3.79, 8.21, 2.82, 1.52 });
    objs.Add(new object[] { "2010", 2.10, 3.79, 8.18, 2.70, 1.53 });
    objs.Add(new object[] { "2015", 2.30, 3.97, 8.55, 2.72, 1.57 });
    return objs;
}
```

These two methods generate two arrays of objects, which will be used to create bar and group bar charts respectively. Since these two data arrays are all very small and the performance speed is not an issue. Therefore, rather than convert them into JSON strings, we will use these arrays directly in creating charts.

Add a new method *JsonBarDat* to the *GoogleChartsController.cs* file:

```
public JsonResult JsonBarData()
{
    var data1 = ModelHelper.BarArrayData();
    var data2 = ModelHelper.GroupBarArrayData();
    return Json(new { Bar = data1, GroupBar = data2 });
}
```

Now, add a new view named *BarChart.cshtml* to the *Views/GoogleCharts* folder and replace its content with the following code:

```
@{
    ViewData["Title"] = ViewBag.Title;
}
<h3>@ViewBag.Title</h3>
@Html.Partial("_Links")
<hr />

<div class="container">
    <div class="row">
```

```
        <div class="col-sm-5">
            <div id="chart1"></div>
        </div>
        <div class="col-sm-5">
            <div id="chart2"></div>
        </div>
    </div>
    <div class="row">
        <div class="col-sm-12">
            <div id="chart3"></div>
        </div>
    </div>
    <div class="row">
        <div class="col-sm-12">
            <div id="chart4"></div>
        </div>
    </div>
</div>

<script type="text/javascript"
    src="https://www.gstatic.com/charts/loader.js"></script>

<script type="text/javascript">
    google.charts.load('current', { 'packages': ['corechart'] });
    google.charts.setOnLoadCallback(drawChart);

    function drawChart() {
        $.get('JsonBarData', {}, function (d) {
            var data = new google.visualization.arrayToDataTable(d.bar, false);

            // Horizontal bar chart:
            var options = {
                title: '2010 Population of Largest U.S. Cities',
                width: 500,
                height: 400,
                legend: { position: 'none' },
                chartArea: { width: '60%'},
                hAxis: {
                    title: 'Total Population',
                    minValue: 0
                },
                vAxis: {
                    title: 'City'
                }
            };

            var chart = new google.visualization.BarChart(
                document.getElementById('chart1'));
            chart.draw(data, options);

            // Vertical bar chart:
            var options = {
                title: '2010 Population of Largest U.S. Cities',
                width: 500,
                height: 400,
```

```
                    legend:{position: 'none'},
                    vAxis: {
                        title: 'Total Population',
                        minValue: 0
                    },
                    hAxis: {
                        title: 'City'
                    }
                };

                var chart = new google.visualization.ColumnChart(
                    document.getElementById('chart2'));
                chart.draw(data, options);

                data = new google.visualization.arrayToDataTable(d.groupBar, false);

                // Grouped bar chart:
                var options = {
                    title: 'Population (in millions)',
                    width: 800,
                    height: 500,
                    vAxis: {
                        title: 'Total Population',
                        minValue: 0
                    },
                    hAxis: {
                        title: 'Year'
                    }
                };
                var chart = new google.visualization.ColumnChart(
                    document.getElementById('chart3'));
                chart.draw(data, options);

                // Stacked bar chart:
                options.isStacked = true;

                var chart = new google.visualization.ColumnChart(
                    document.getElementById('chart4'));
                chart.draw(data, options);
            });
        }
    </script>
```

This code first uses the *bar* data array to create horizontal and vertical bar charts, and then uses the *groupBar* data array to create the group and stacked (setting the *isStacked* attribute to *true*) bar charts. Running this example produces bar charts shown in Figure 5-15, a group bar chart shown in Figure 5-16, and a stacked bar chart shown in Figure 5-17.

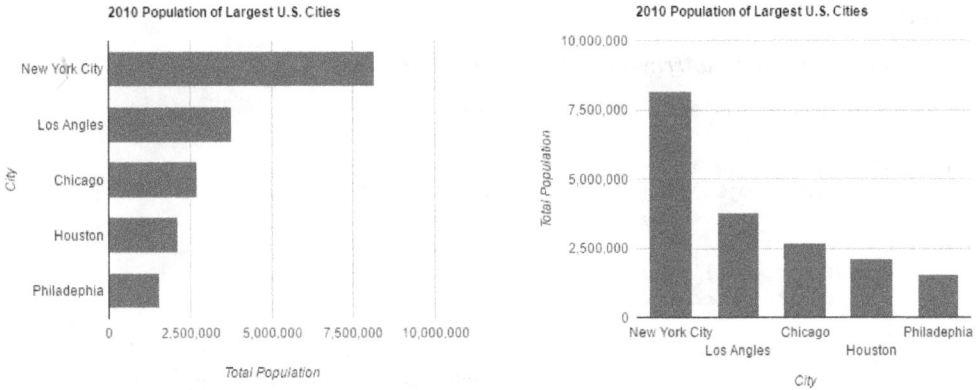

Figure 5-15. Demonstraion of horizontal (left) and vertical (right) bar charts.

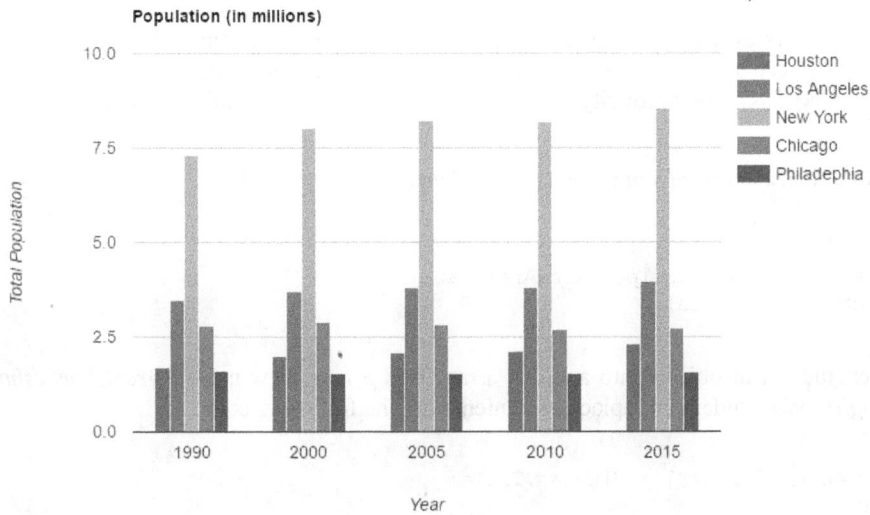

Figure 5-16. Demonstration of a group bar chart.

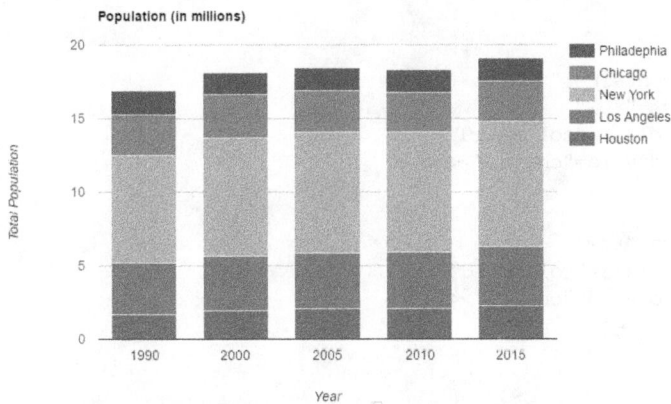

Figure 5-17. Demonstration of a stacked bar chart.

Area Charts

Add a new method named *AreaArrayData* to the *ModelHelper* class:

```
public static List<object> AreaArrayData()
{
    List<object> objs = new List<object>();
    objs.Add(new object[] { "x", "1.2+Sin(x)", "1.2+Cos(x)", "1.2+Sin(x)^2" });
    for (int i = 0; i < 70; i++)
    {
        double x = 0.1 * i;
        objs.Add(new object[] { x,
                            1.2 + Math.Sin(x),
                            1.2 + Math.Cos(x),
                            1.2 + Math.Sin(x) * Math.Sin(x) });
    }
    return objs;
}
```

This method generates a list of objects from three mathematical functions. If you want to improve performance, you can convert the list into a JSON string using the *GetGoogleJson* method implemented in the *JsonString* class. For simplicity's sake, here we will use the list of objects directly to create the area charts.

Add a new method *JsonAreaData* to the *GoogleChartsController.cs* file:

```
public JsonResult JsonAreaData()
{
    var data = ModelHelper.AreaArrayData();
    return Json(data);
}
```

This convert the list of objects into a JSON array. Add a new view named *AreaChart.cshtml* to the *Views/GoogleCharts* folder and replace its content with the following code:

```
@{
    ViewData["Title"] = ViewBag.Title;
}
<h3>@ViewBag.Title</h3>
@Html.Partial("_Links")

<hr />

<div class="container">
    <div class="row">
        <div class="col-sm-10">
            <div id="chart1"></div>
        </div>
    </div>
    <div class="row">
        <div class="col-sm-10">
            <div id="chart2"></div>
        </div>
    </div>
</div>

<script type="text/javascript"
```

```
        src="https://www.gstatic.com/charts/loader.js"></script>

    <script type="text/javascript">
        google.charts.load('current', { 'packages': ['corechart'] });
        google.charts.setOnLoadCallback(drawChart);

        function drawChart() {
            $.get('JsonAreaData', {}, function (d) {
                var data = new google.visualization.arrayToDataTable(d, false);

                // Area chart:
                options = {
                    title: 'Area Chart',
                    width: 700,
                    height: 400,
                    chartArea: { left: 50, top: 30, width: '70%', height: '80%',
                        backgroundColor: { stroke: "gray", strokeWidth: 1 } },
                    vAxis: { minValue: 0 }
                };
                chart = new google.visualization.AreaChart(
                    document.getElementById('chart1'));
                chart.draw(data, options);

                // Stacked area chart:
                options.title = "Stack Area Chart";
                options.isStacked = true;
                chart = new google.visualization.AreaChart(
                    document.getElementById('chart2'));
                chart.draw(data, options);
            });
        }
    </script>
```

This code creates two area charts: one is the normal area chart and the other one is a stacked area chart with the *isStacked* attribute being set to true. To create an area chart, we need to set the *y*-axis *minValue* to 0 because the area chart usually starts with zero *y* value.

Running this example produces the results shown in Figure 5-18.

Interval Charts

Google Charts can display intervals around a series. The intervals can be used to portray confidence intervals, minimum and maximum values around a value, percentile sampling, or anything else that requires a varying margin around a series.

There are six styles of interval: line, bar, box, stick, point, and area. In the following example, we will create several charts with different types of interval, including line, bar, box, and area.

We first need to generate sample data. Add a new method, *IntervalArrayData*, to the *ModelHelper* class:

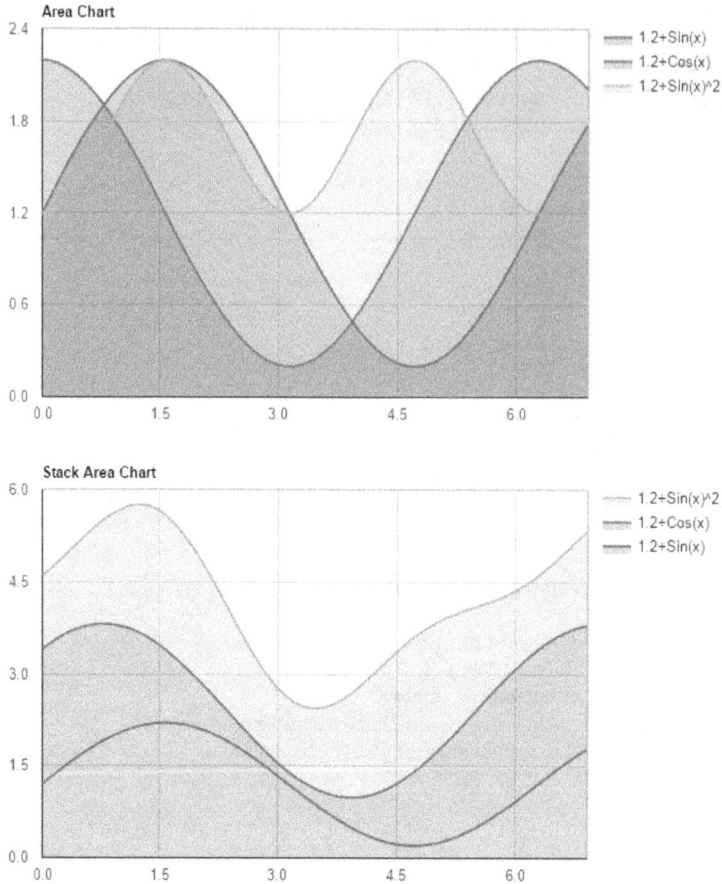

Figure 5-18. Demonstration of area charts.

```
public static List<object> IntervalArrayData()
{
    List<object> objs = new List<object>();
    objs.Add(new object[] { "x", "y", "y1", "y2", "y3", "y4", "y5", "y6" });
    Random random = new Random();
    for (int i = 0; i < 10; i++)
    {
        double ran = random.NextDouble();
        double x = 1.0 * i;
        double y = x * Math.Sin(0.1 * x * x) + 10.0;
        double y1 = y + 1.0 * ran;
        double y2 = y - 1.0 * ran;
        double y3 = y + 2.0 * ran;
        double y4 = y - 2.0 * ran;
        double y5 = y + 3.0 * ran;
        double y6 = y - 3.0 * ran;
        objs.Add(new object[] { x, y, y1, y2, y3, y4, y5, y6 });
    }
    return objs;
}
```

This method generates a list of objects. Next, we need to convert this list into a JSON string. Add a new method named *IntervalStringData* to the *ModelHelper* class:

```
public static string IntervalStringData()
{
    var d = ModelHelper.IntervalArrayData();
    var cols = new JsonColumn[]
    {
        new JsonColumn {label = "X", type = "number" },
        new JsonColumn {label = "X*Sin(X*X)", type = "number" },
        new JsonColumn {id="i0", type = "number", role = "interval" },
        new JsonColumn {id="i0", type = "number", role = "interval" },
        new JsonColumn {id="i1", type = "number", role = "interval" },
        new JsonColumn {id="i1", type = "number", role = "interval" },
        new JsonColumn {id="i2", type = "number", role = "interval" },
        new JsonColumn {id="i2", type = "number", role = "interval" }
    };
    var rows = new JsonRow[d.Count - 1];
    for (int i = 1; i < d.Count; i++)
    {
        var obj = d[i] as object[];
        rows[i - 1] = new JsonRow
        {
            c = new JsonCell[]
            {
                new JsonCell { v = obj[0] },
                new JsonCell { v = obj[1] },
                new JsonCell { v = obj[2] },
                new JsonCell { v = obj[3] },
                new JsonCell { v = obj[4] },
                new JsonCell { v = obj[5] },
                new JsonCell { v = obj[6] },
                new JsonCell { v = obj[7] }
            }
        };
    }
    return JsonString.GetGoogleJson(cols, rows);
}
```

The code attaches three different identifiers to the supplementary series: *i0*, *i1*, and *i3*. It also sets the *role* attribute to *interval* for these supplementary series. We will use the attributes to style those series differently, i.e, we will specify them with different colors and line thickness.

Add a new method named *JsonIntervalData* to the *GoogleChartsController.cs* file:

```
public JsonResult JsonIntervalData()
{
    var data = ModelHelper.IntervalStringData();
    return Json(data);
}
```

Add a new view *IntervalChart.cshtml* to the *Views/GoogleCharts* folder and replace its content with the following code:

```
@{
    ViewData["Title"] = ViewBag.Title;
}
```

```
<h3>@ViewBag.Title</h3>
@Html.Partial("_Links")
<hr />
<div class="container">
    <div class="row">
        <div class="col-sm-6">
            <div id="chart1"></div>
        </div>
        <div class="col-sm-6">
            <div id="chart2"></div>
        </div>
    </div>
    <div class="row" style="margin-top:30px">
        <div class="col-sm-6">
            <div id="chart3"></div>
        </div>
        <div class="col-sm-6">
            <div id="chart4"></div>
        </div>
    </div>
</div>

<script type="text/javascript"
    src="https://www.gstatic.com/charts/loader.js"></script>
<script type="text/javascript">
    google.charts.load('current', { 'packages': ['corechart'] });
    google.charts.setOnLoadCallback(drawChart);
    function drawChart() {
        $.get('JsonIntervalData', {}, function (d) {
            var data = new google.visualization.DataTable(d);

            // Line interval:
            options = {
                title: 'Line interval',
                curveType: 'function',
                lineWidth: 4,
                interval: {
                    i0: { style: 'line', color: '#D3362D', lineWidth: 0.5 },
                    i1: { style: 'line', color: '#F1CA3A', lineWidth: 1 },
                    i2: { style: 'line', color: '#5F9654', lineWidth: 2 }
                },
                width: 600,
                height: 450,
                chartArea: { left: 70, top: 30, width: '80%', height: '80%',
                    backgroundColor: { stroke: "gray", strokeWidth: 1 } },
                legend: 'none'
            };
            chart = new google.visualization.LineChart(
                document.getElementById('chart1'));
            chart.draw(data, options);

            // Error bars:
            options.title = "Error Bars";
            options.interval = {};
            options.intervals = { style: 'bars' };
```

```
        chart = new google.visualization.LineChart(
            document.getElementById('chart2'));
        chart.draw(data, options);

        // Box interval:
        options.title = "Box Interval";
        options.intervals = { style: 'boxes' };
        chart = new google.visualization.LineChart(
            document.getElementById('chart3'));
        chart.draw(data, options);

        // Area interval:
        options.title = "Area Interval";
        options.intervals = { style: 'area' };
        chart = new google.visualization.LineChart(
            document.getElementById('chart4'));
        chart.draw(data, options);
    });
    }
</script>
```

This code create four line charts with different types of interval: line, bar, box, and area. Running this example produces the results shown in Figure 5-19.

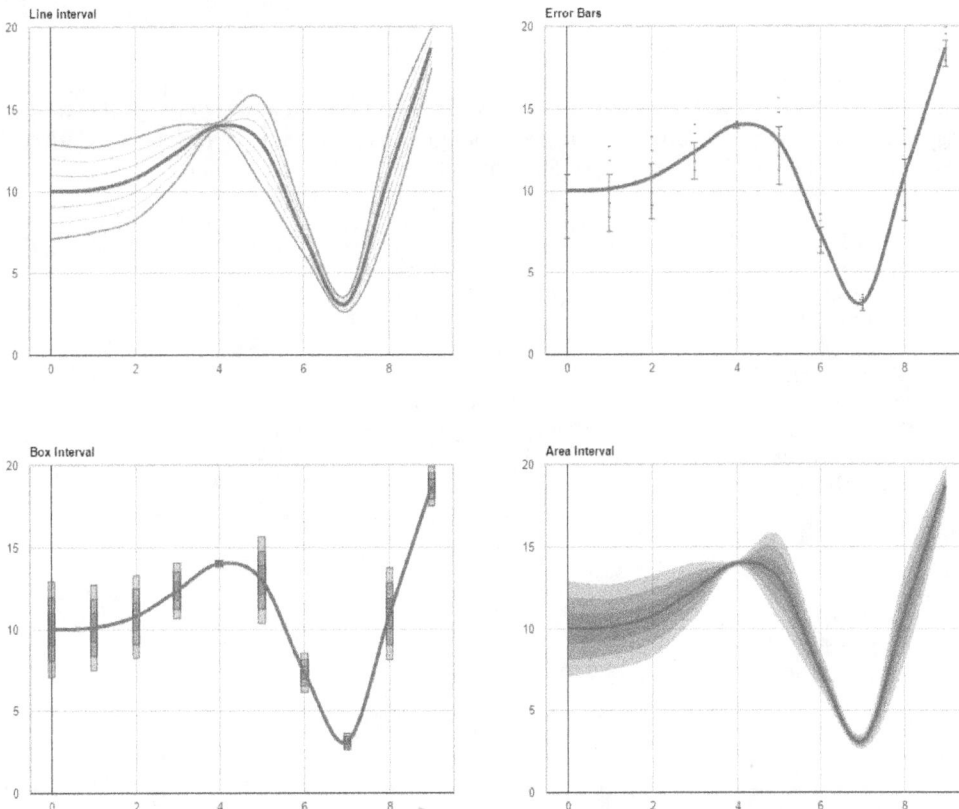

Figure 5-19. Demonstration of line charts with intervals.

This figure shows that we can use the line intervals to depict the variance of multiple experiments. In a line interval chart, we create a primary series and intervals around it. We also customize the line intervals with different colors and thickness.

The bar intervals in the figure create error bars around our data. The first and last columns of the interval are drawn as wide bars parallel to the domain-axis, and inner columns are drawn as short ticks. A stick is added to join the wide bar. The width of the horizontal bars corresponding to the first and last columns is controlled with the *intervals.barWidth* attribute, and the width of the horizontal bars corresponding to the inner columns is controlled with the *intervals.shortBarWidth* attribute.

The figure also consists of a box interval chart. Box intervals rendered columns data table as a set of nested rectangles: the first and last columns form the outermost rectangle, and inner columns render as darker rectangles within their containing box.

Finally, Figure 5-19 includes an area interval chart. An area interval renders interval data as a set of nested shaded areas. Nesting of pairs of columns is similar to that of box intervals, except that an even number of columns is required.

Interacting with Charts

Google Charts provides several ways that allow you to interact with charts in order to help analyze your data. These include resizing, zooming, panning, animation, dashboard, etc.

Resizing

You may notice that the size of charts we created so far is fixed when your window gets resized. It is very easy to use window resize function to resize a Google chart. Add a new view named *Resize.cshtml* to the *Views/GoogleCharts* folder and replace its content with the following code:

```
@{
    ViewData["Title"] = ViewBag.Title;
}
<h3>@ViewBag.Title</h3>
@Html.Partial("_Links")
<hr />
<div class="container">
    <div class="row">
        <div id="chart_wrap_div">
            <div id="chart_div"></div>
        </div>
    </div>
</div>

<style>
    #chart_wrap_div {
        border: 1px solid gray;
        position: relative;
        padding-bottom: 80%;
        height: 0;
        overflow: hidden;
    }
    #chart_div {
        position: absolute;
```

```
            top: 0;
            left: 0;
            width: 100%;
            height: 100%;
        }
    </style>

    <script type="text/javascript"
        src="https://www.gstatic.com/charts/loader.js"></script>
    <script type="text/javascript">
        google.charts.load('current', { 'packages': ['corechart'] });
        google.charts.setOnLoadCallback(drawChart);

        function drawChart() {
            $.get('JsonStringData', function (d) {
                var data = new google.visualization.DataTable(d.string1);
                var options = { is3D: true };
                var chart = new google.visualization.PieChart(
                        document.getElementById('chart_div'));

                function resize() {
                    chart.draw(data, options);
                };
                window.onload = resize();
                window.onresize = resize;
            });
        }
    </script>
```

This code creates two *div* elements for the chart: *chart_wrap_div* and *chart_div*. The *chart_wrap_div* defines the area for our chart – 80% screen from the bottom will be used for the chart. It then defines the width and height for the *chart_div* using percentages, which is important for creating a resizable chart. Next, we define a *resize* function and put the *chart.draw* method inside it. Finally, we let window's *onload* and *onresize* call this *resize* function.

Running this example produces the results shown in Figure 5-20.

Now, your chart will be redraw to fit your screen size when you resize your window. You may worry about its performance: for most chart application, the performance should not an issue. Unless you have large data and many details to draw, then it may become a performance issue to redraw the chart at each resize. In this case, you may need to limit the chart resize frequency with a JavaScript function by a delay or timer.

For example, you can use the following code snippet to redraw your chart:

```
$(window).resize(function () {
    if (this.resizeTO) clearTimeout(this.resizeTO);
    this.resizeTO = setTimeout(function () {
        $(this).trigger('resizeEnd');
    }, 200);
});
$(window).on('resizeEnd', function () {
    chart.draw(data, options);
});
```

This code redraws your chart only when the window resize is completed, and avoids multiple triggers.

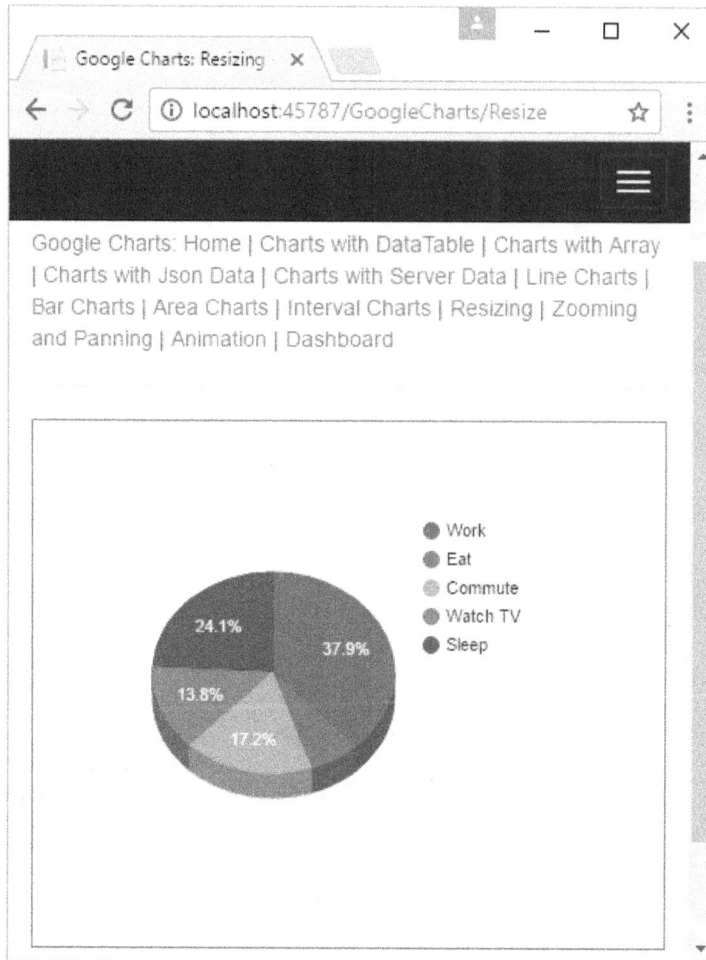

Figure 5-20. Demonstration of a resizable pie chart.

Zooming and Panning

Google Charts has an *explorer* option that allows you to pan and zoom Google charts. *explorer: {}* provides the default explorer behavior, enabling you to pan horizontally and vertically by dragging, and to zoom in and out by scrolling your mouse wheel. The right-clicking will reset the chart to its original state. Note that the *explorer* option only works with continuous axes such as numbers and dates.

The Google Charts explorer also supports three actions

- *dragToPan*: Drag to pan around the chart horizontally and vertically. To pan only along the horizontal axis, use explorer: {*axis*: "*horizontal*"}.

- *dragToZoom*: The explorer's default behavior is to zoom in and out when you scroll. If *explorer*: {*actions*: ["*dragToZoom*", "*rightClickToReset*"]} is used, dragging across a rectangular area zooms into that area.

- *rightClickToReset*: Right clicking on the chart returns it to the original pan and zoom level.

Here, we will use an example to illustrate how to use the Google Charts *explorer* option. Add a new view named *ZoomPan.cshtml* to the *Views/GoogleCharts* folder and replace its content with the following code:

```
@{
    ViewData["Title"] = ViewBag.Title;
}
<h3>@ViewBag.Title</h3>
@Html.Partial("_Links")
<hr />

<div class="container">
    <div class="row">
        <div class="col-sm-6">
            <div id="chart1"></div>
        </div>
        <div class="col-sm-6">
            <div id="chart2"></div>
        </div>
    </div>
    <div class="row">
        <div class="col-sm-6">
            <div id="chart3"></div>
        </div>
        <div class="col-sm-6">
            <div id="chart4"></div>
        </div>
    </div>
</div>


<script type="text/javascript"
    src="https://www.gstatic.com/charts/loader.js"></script>

<script type="text/javascript">
    google.charts.load('current', { 'packages': ['corechart'] });
    google.charts.setOnLoadCallback(drawChart);

    function drawChart() {
        $.get('JsonStringData', {}, function (d) {
            var data = new google.visualization.DataTable(d.string2);

            // chart: zoom and pan
            var options = {
                title: 'Zoom and Pan',
                width: 600,
                height: 450,
                chartArea: { left: 70, top: 30, width: '70%', height: '80%',
                    backgroundColor: { stroke: "gray", strokeWidth: 1 } },
                lineWidth: 3,
```

```
                    pointSize: 10,
                    series: {
                        0: { pointShape: 'circle' },
                        1: { pointShape: 'diamond' },
                        2: { pointShape: 'triangle' },
                    },
                    explorer: {},
                };
                var chart = new google.visualization.LineChart(
                    document.getElementById('chart1'));
                chart.draw(data, options);

                // chart: drag to pan
                options.title = "Drag to Pan";
                options.explorer = { actions: ['dragToPan', 'rightClickToReset'] };
                chart = new google.visualization.LineChart(
                    document.getElementById('chart2'));
                chart.draw(data, options);

                // chart: drag to zoom
                options.title = "Drag to Zoom";
                options.explorer = { actions: ['dragToZoom', 'rightClickToReset'] };
                chart = new google.visualization.LineChart(
                    document.getElementById('chart3'));
                chart.draw(data, options);

                // chart: zoom and pan horizontally
                options.title = "Zoom and Pan Horizontally";
                options.explorer = { axis: 'horizontal' };
                chart = new google.visualization.LineChart(
                    document.getElementById('chart4'));
                chart.draw(data, options);
            });
        }
    </script>
```

This code creates four line charts, and each chart has different zoom and pan behaviors. Running this example produces the results shown in Figure 5-21.

Animation

Google Charts can animate smoothly in two different ways: either on startup when you first draw the chart, or when you redraw a chart after making a change in data or options.

To animate on startup, you need first to set your chart data and options. Be sure to set an animation *duration* and *easing* type. You need then to set *animation: {startup: true}* in the *options* section, which will cause your chart to start with series values drawn at the baseline , and animate out to their final state. On the other hand, if you want to animate a transition, you can start with an already rendered chart and modify the data or options, and then specify the transition behavior using the animation option.

Let us consider an example, where we want to modify its data for animation. Add a new method named *RandomArrayData* to the *ModelHelper* class:

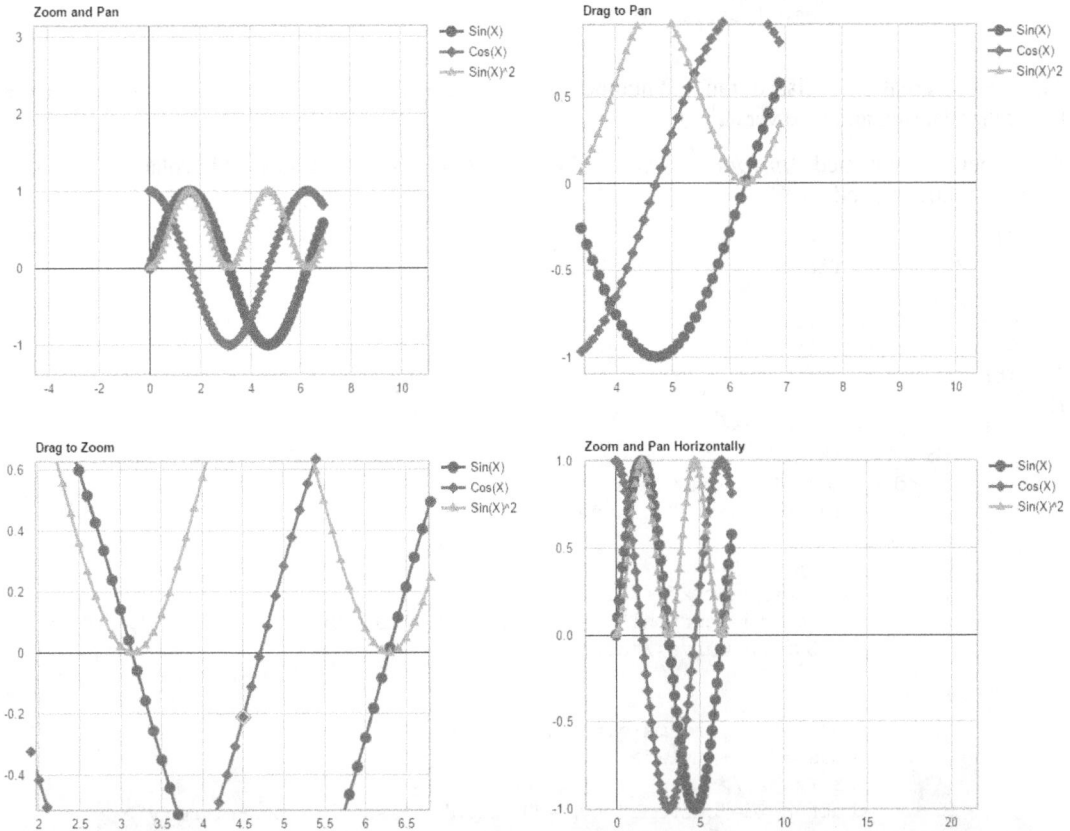

Figure 5-21. Demonstration of line charts with different zoom and pan behaviors.

```
public static List<object> RandomArrayData(Random random)
{
    List<object> objs = new List<object>();
    objs.Add(new object[] { "X", "Y", "Z" });
    for (int i = 0; i < 20; i++)
    {
        var x = random.Next(0, 20);
        var y = random.Next(0, 100);
        var z = random.Next(0, 100);
        objs.Add(new object[] { x, y, z });
    }
    return objs;
}
```

This method returns a list of random number objects, which will be used for our chart animation. Add a new method *JsonRandomArrayData* to the *GoogleChartsController*.cs file:

```
public JsonResult JsonRandomArrayData()
{
    Random random = new Random();
    var data1 = ModelHelper.RandomArrayData(random);
    var data2 = ModelHelper.RandomArrayData(random);
```

```
        return Json(new { data1, data2 });
    }
```

This method creates two lists of random number objects. We will animate the transition from one dataset to another dataset, and vice versa.

Add a new view named *Animation.cshtml* to the *Views/GoogleCharts* folder and replace its contents with the following code:

```
@{
    ViewData["Title"] = ViewBag.Title;
}
<h3>@ViewBag.Title</h3>
@Html.Partial("_Links")
<hr />

<div class="container">
    <div class="row">
        <div class="col-sm-6">
            <div id="chart1"></div>
        </div>
        <div class="col-sm-6">
            <div id="chart2"></div>
            <button id="button1" type="button" class="btn btn-primary">
                Switch Curve</button>
        </div>
    </div>
    <div class="row" style="margin-top:50px">
        <div class="col-sm-12">
            <br /><br />
            <button id="button2" type="button" class="btn btn-primary">
                Change the Chart Size</button>
            <button id="button3" type="button" class="btn btn-primary">
                Slide the Chart</button>
            <div id="chart3"></div>
        </div>
    </div>
</div>

<script type="text/javascript"
    src="https://www.gstatic.com/charts/loader.js"></script>

<script type="text/javascript">
    google.charts.load('current', { 'packages': ['corechart'] });
    google.charts.setOnLoadCallback(drawChart);

    function drawChart() {

        // random animation
        var randomData = $.ajax({
            url: "JsonRandomArrayData",
            dataType: "json",
            async: false
        }).responseJSON;

        var dat = [];
```

```
    dat[0] = new google.visualization.arrayToDataTable(
        randomData.data1, false);
    dat[1] = new google.visualization.arrayToDataTable(
        randomData.data2, false);

    var options1 = {
        height: 450,
        chartArea: {
            width: '85%',
            height: '85%',
            backgroundColor: { stroke: "black", strokeWidth: 0.2 }
        },
        colors: ['#8e0152', '#276419'],
        pointSize: 10,
        animation: {
            duration: 5000,
            easing: 'inAndOut',
            startup: true
        },
        vAxis: {
            ticks: [20, 40, 60, 80, 100],
            gridlines: { color: 'none' }
        },
        hAxis: {
            ticks: [0, 5, 10, 15, 20],
            gridlines: { color: 'none' }
        },
        legend: { position: 'none' },
        enableInteractivity: false
    };

    var chart1 = new google.visualization.ScatterChart(
        document.getElementById('chart1'));
    google.visualization.events.addListener(chart1, 'animationfinish',
        animate);

    var current = 0;
    chart1.draw(dat[current], options1);
    function animate() {
        current = 1 - current;
        chart1.draw(dat[current], options1);
    }

    //...... (more code will be here ...)


    }
</script>
```

The code retrieves the random array data using $.*ajax* method, and then assign those two datasets, *data1* and *data2* to a new JavaScript array *dat*, as described by the code snippet:

```
    dat[0] = new google.visualization.arrayToDataTable(randomData.data1, false);
    dat[1] = new google.visualization.arrayToDataTable(randomData.data2, false);
```

We then specify the *animation* in the options section with parameters – *duration*: 5000 (milliseconds), *easing*: '*inAndOut*', and *startup*: *true*. The *easing* function has the following available options:

- *linear*: Constant spead.
- *in*: Ease in – start slow and speed up.
- *out*: Ease out – start fast and slow down.
- *inAndOut*: Ease in and out – start slow, speed up, and then slow down.

Here, we also set the *startup* to *true*, meaning that the chart will start at the baseline and animate to its final state. When drawing a chart, a *ready* event is fired once the chart is ready for external function calls. The chart will fire the *animationfinish* event when the transition is complete.

In order to animate a transition from *dat*[0] to *dat*[1], we register our *animate* function by calling *google.visualization.events.addListener* with the name of the chart exposing the event, the string name of the event to listen for, and the name of the function to call when that event is fired.

Inside our animate function, we switch the data array and redraw the chart, which will give us a smooth animation for the transition from one dataset to another.

Running this example produces the results shown in Figure 5-22.

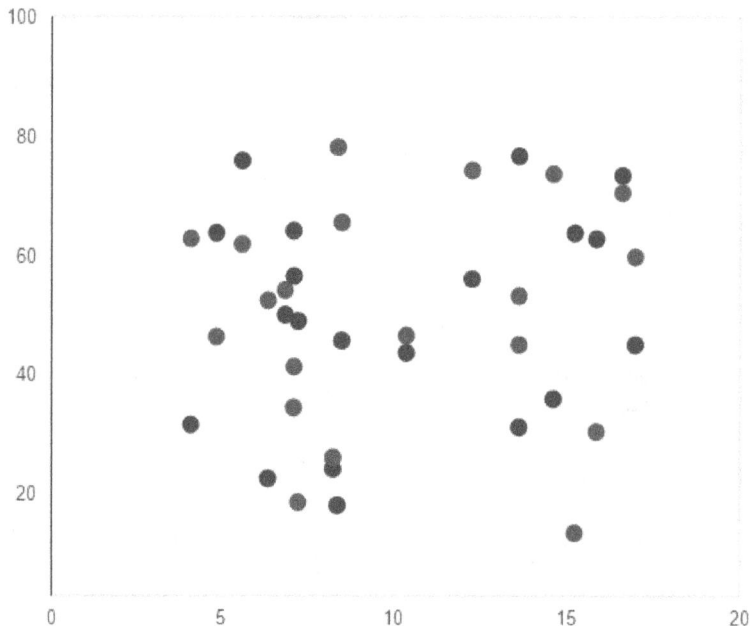

Figure 5-22. Demonstration of animation for data modifications.

Next example shows how to switch from a *sine* curve to a *cosine* curve or vice versa by clicking a function switch button. We will try to animate this transition process.

Add the following code snippet to the script section of the *Animation.cshtml* view:

```
// switch curve
$.get('JsonStringData', {}, function (d) {
    var data = new google.visualization.DataTable(d.string2);
    var views = [];
    var view = new google.visualization.DataView(data);
```

```
        view.setColumns([0, 1]);
        views[0] = view;
        view = new google.visualization.DataView(data);
        view.setColumns([0, 2]);
        views[1] = view;

        var options = {
            title: 'Switch Curve: Sine',
            legend: 'none',
            pointSize: 5,
            width: 500,
            height: 380,
            chartArea: { left: 30, top: 30, width: '90%', height: '85%' },
            lineWidth: 2,
            animation: { duration: 4000, easing: 'out', startup: true },
        };

        var current = 0;
    var chart = new google.visualization.LineChart(
            document.getElementById('chart2'));
        chart.draw(views[current], options);

        var button = document.getElementById('button1');
        button.onclick = function () {
            current = 1 - current;
            options['title'] = 'Switch Curve: ' + (current ? 'Cosine' : 'Sine');
            button.innerText = 'Switch to ' + (current ? 'Sine' : 'Cosine');
            chart.draw(views[current], options);
        }
        //...... (more code will be added here)
    });
```

This code first selects two datasets for sine and cosine functions from the *JsonStringData* created previously using *DataView*, and then assigns them to a new JavaScript array named *views*. The code is basically similar to the preceding example where we switched two datasets with random numbers, except that here we use a button click event to switch the curves.

This code produces the output shown in Figure 5-23.

Now, the curve will be switched when you click the *Switch to Sine* (or *Switch to Cosine*) button.

The next example shows how to animate the changes of the chart size. Add the following code snippet to the script section of the *Animation.cshtml* view:

```
// Change chart size:
var option2 = {
    title: 'Multiline Curve',
    width: 960,
    height: 600,
    pointSize: 5,
    chartArea: { left: '5%', top: '5%', width: '40%', height: '40%' },
    animation: { duration: 1500, easing: 'linear' },
};
```

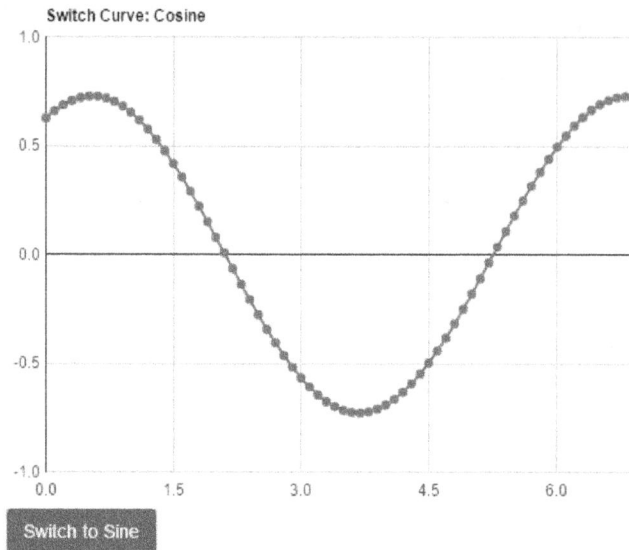

Figure 5-23. Demonstration of animation for curve switching.

```
function increaseSize()
{
    option2.chartArea.height = '80%';
    option2.chartArea.width = '80%';
}
function decreaseSize() {
    option2.chartArea.height = '40%';
    option2.chartArea.width = '40%';
}
function moveTo5() {
    option2.chartArea.left = '5%';
    option2.chartArea.top = '5%';
}
function moveTo50() {
    option2.chartArea.left = '50%';
    option2.chartArea.top = '50%';
}

var chart1 = new google.visualization.LineChart(
    document.getElementById('chart3'));
chart1.draw(data, option2);

var btnSize = document.getElementById('button2');
var btnSlide = document.getElementById('button3');

btnSize.onclick = function () {
    option2.chartArea.height === '40%' ? increaseSize() : decreaseSize();
    chart1.draw(data, option2);
}

btnSlide.onclick = function () {
```

```
        option2.chartArea.left === "5%" ? moveTo50() : moveTo5();
        chart1.draw(data, option2);
    }
```

This code sets the *duration* to 1500 (milliseconds) and *easing* to *linear* for the animation. It then defines four functions: *increaseSize, decreaseSize, moveTo5*, and *moveTo50*. The *increaseSize* function sets the size of the chart area to be 80% of the chart *div* element, while *decreaseSize* sets the chart area to be 40% of the chart *div* element. The *moveTo5* (*moveTo50*) places the top-left corner of the chart area at the 5% (50%) of the chart *div* element. We use two buttons, *btnSize* and *btnSlide*, to control these functions. The chart will increase or decrease its size depending on its current state when you click the *Change the Chart Size* button, while it will slide around on your screen when you click the *Slide the Chart* button.

Running this example produces the results shown in Figure 5-24.

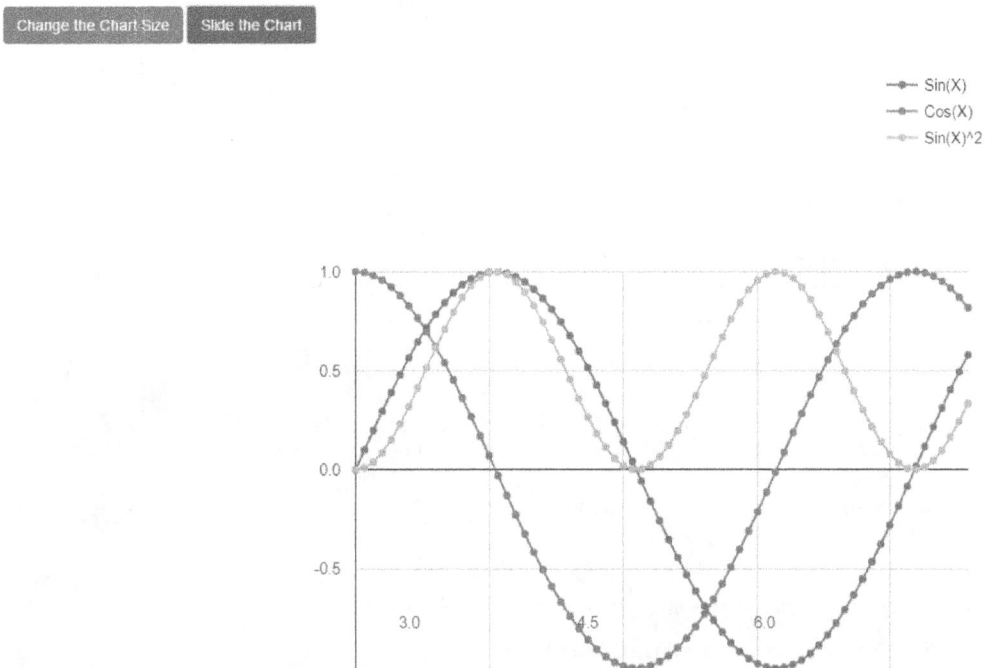

Figure 5-24. Demonstration of animation for changing chart size and sliding the chart.

Dashboard

Dashboard is a simple way to organize together and manage multiple charts that share the same underlying data. Google Charts provides dashboard API via *google.visualization.Dashboard* class, which allows you to wire together and coordinate all the charts that are part of a dashboard. Google dashboard instances receive a DataTable containing the data to visualize and take care of drawing and distributing the data to all the charts that are part of the dashboard.

Google Charts also implemented *google.visualization.ControlWrapper* classes that define the controls. Controls are user interface widgets (such as category pickers, range sliders, autocomleters…) you can interact with in order to drive the data managed by a dashboard and the charts that are part of it. You can add *ControlWrapper* instances to a dashboard to collect user input and use the information to decide which data the dashboard is managing should be made available to the charts that are part of it.

Let us consider a simple dashboard example where a category picker and a range slider are used to drive the data visualized by a pie chart.

The data used in our dashboard example is a list of countries with 2015 population above 1% of world total population (source: United Nations). Add a new method *PopulationArrayData* to the *ModelHelper* class:

```
public static List<object> PopulationArrayData()
{
    List<object> objs = new List<object>();
    objs.Add(new object[] { "Country", "Continent",
        "% of World Population", "Population (Million)" });
    objs.Add(new object[] { "China", "Asia", 19.2, 1401 });
    objs.Add(new object[] { "India", "Asia", 17.5, 1282 });
    objs.Add(new object[] { "United States", "N. America", 4.45, 325 });
    objs.Add(new object[] { "Indonesia", "Asia", 3.49, 256 });
    objs.Add(new object[] { "Brazil", "S. America", 2.79, 204 });
    objs.Add(new object[] { "Pakistan", "Asia", 2.56, 188 });
    objs.Add(new object[] { "Nigeria", "Africa", 2.46, 184 });
    objs.Add(new object[] { "Bangladesh", "Asia", 2.18, 160 });
    objs.Add(new object[] { "Russia", "Europe", 1.97, 142 });
    objs.Add(new object[] { "Japan", "Asia", 1.75, 127 });
    objs.Add(new object[] { "Mexico", "N. America", 1.71, 125 });
    objs.Add(new object[] { "Philippines", "Asia", 1.38, 102 });
    objs.Add(new object[] { "Ethiopia", "Africa", 1.33, 99 });
    objs.Add(new object[] { "Vietnam", "Asia", 1.28, 93 });
    objs.Add(new object[] { "Egypt", "Africa", 1.15, 85 });
    objs.Add(new object[] { "Germany", "Europe", 1.14, 83 });
    objs.Add(new object[] { "Iran", "Asia", 1.08, 79 });
    objs.Add(new object[] { "Turkey", "Asia", 1.05, 77 });
    objs.Add(new object[] { "Congo", "Africa", 0.1, 71 });
    return objs;
}
```

Add a new method *JsonPopulationData* to the *GoogleChartsController.cs* file:

```
public JsonResult JsonPopulationData()
{
    var data = ModelHelper.PopulationArrayData();
    return Json(data);
}
```

Add a new view named *Dashboard.cshtml* to the *Views/GoogleCharts* folder and replace its content with the following code:

```
@{
    ViewData["Title"] = ViewBag.Title;
}
<h3>@ViewBag.Title</h3>
@Html.Partial("_Links")
<hr />

<div class="container">
    <div class="row">
```

```
            <div class="col-sm-12" style="border: 1px solid #ccc; margin-top: 1em">
                <div id="dashboard_div" style="margin-top: 1em">
                    <p style="padding-left: 1em"><strong>
                        Country Population</strong></p>
                    <table class="col-sm-2">
                        <tr>
                            <td>
                                <div id="slider_div"
                                    style="padding-left: 15px"></div>
                            </td>
                            <td>
                                <div id="categoryPicker_div"
                                    style="padding-left: 50px"></div>
                            </td>
                        </tr>
                        <tr>
                            <td>
                                <div id="chart_div" style="padding-top: 15px"></div>
                            </td>
                            <td>
                                <div id="table_div"
                                    style="padding-top: 5px; padding-left:50px"></div>
                            </td>
                        </tr>
                    </table>
                </div>
            </div>
        </div>
    </div>
</div>

<script type="text/javascript"
    src="https://www.gstatic.com/charts/loader.js"></script>

<script type="text/javascript">
    google.charts.load('current', { 'packages': ['corechart', 'controls'] });
    google.charts.setOnLoadCallback(drawDashboard);

    function drawDashboard() {
        $.get('JsonPopulationData', function (d) {
            data = new google.visualization.arrayToDataTable(d, false);

            var dashboard = new google.visualization.Dashboard(
                document.getElementById('dashboard_div'));

            var slider = new google.visualization.ControlWrapper({
                controlType: 'NumberRangeFilter',
                containerId: 'slider_div',
                options: {
                    filterColumnIndex: 2,
                    ui: {
                        labelStacking: 'vertical',
                        label: '% of World Population:'
                    }
                }
            });
```

```
                    var categoryPicker = new google.visualization.ControlWrapper({
                        controlType: 'CategoryFilter',
                        containerId: 'categoryPicker_div',
                        options: {
                            filterColumnIndex: 1,
                            ui: {
                                'labelStacking': 'vertical',
                                'label': 'Continent Selection:',
                                'allowMultiple': false
                            }
                        }
                    });
                    var pie = new google.visualization.ChartWrapper({
                        chartType: 'PieChart',
                        containerId: 'chart_div',
                        options: {
                            width: 600,
                            height: 600,
                            legend: 'none',
                            chartArea: { left: 15, top: 15, right: 10, bottom: 10 },
                            pieSliceText: 'label',
                            is3D: true,
                        },
                        view: { columns: [0, 3] }
                    });

                    var table = new google.visualization.ChartWrapper({
                        chartType: 'Table',
                        containerId: 'table_div',
                        options: {}
                    });

                    dashboard.bind([slider, categoryPicker], [pie, table]);
                    dashboard.draw(data);
                });
            }
        </script>
```

This code first creates an HTML skeleton for our dashboard to hold both the dashboard itself and all the controls and charts. Here, we add several *div* elements with the following IDs: *dashboard_div*, *slider_div*, *categoryPicker_div*, *chart_div*, and *table_div*.

Next, we load Google visualization libraries with the following command:

```
google.charts.load('current', { 'packages': ['corechart', 'controls'] });
```

In addition to the *corechart* package, we also load the *controls* library, which is required to create a dashboard application.

The code then retrieves the JSON data from server and converts it to *DataTable* object using the *arrayToDataTable* function. After loading the data, we instantiate the dashboard object by calling the *google.visualization.Dashboard* function.

Next, we define various control and chart instances using *google.visualization.ControlWrapper* and *google.visualization.ChartWrapper* respectively. Note that when we create *ControlWrapper* and *ChartWrapper* instances, we do not specify either the *dataTable* or the *dataSourceUrl* parameter. The dashboard will take care of feeding each one with the appropriate data. However, we do need to specify the required parameters, including *chartType* and *containerId* for charts, *controlType* and *containerId* for controls.

Note that you must give all controls a *filterColumnIndex* to specify which column of your DataTable the control operates on. For example, in our slider control, it operates on column 2, i.e. the "% *of World Population*" column.

We use the *view* option to configure each *ChartWrapper* instance to define which columns are relevant for the chart. In our pie chart, we use columns [0, 3], i.e. the "*Country*" and "*Population*" columns in DataTable.

Once we have instantiated both the dashboard and all controls and charts, we can use the *bind* method to tell the dashboard about the dependencies that exist between controls and charts. After this binding, the dashboard updates the chart to match the constraints the control enforces over the data.

Running this example produces the results shown in Figure 5-25.

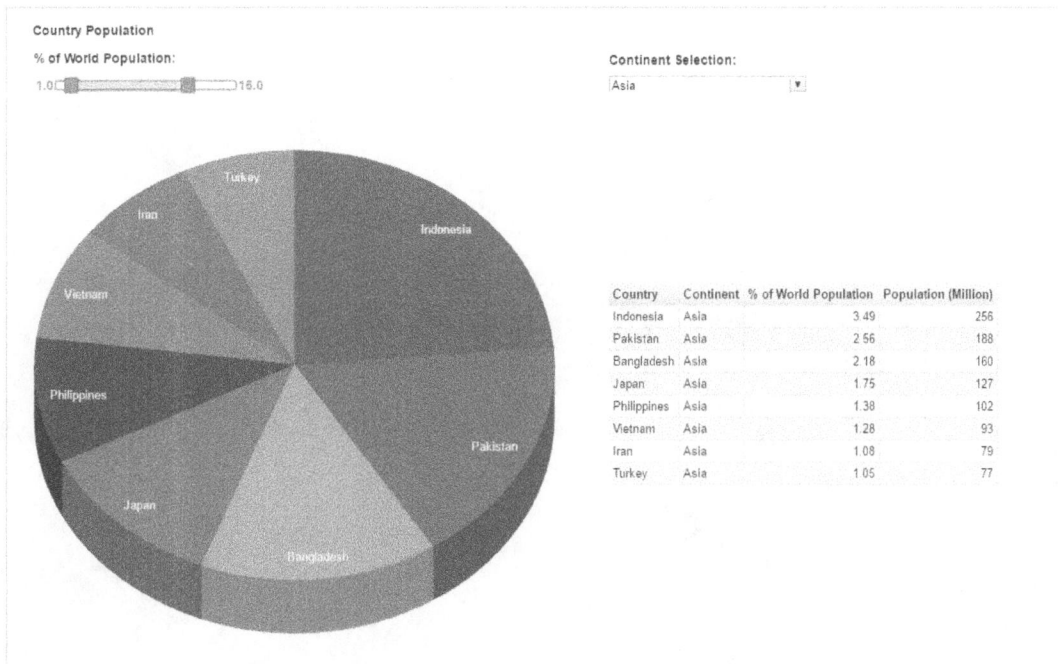

Figure 5-25. Demonstration of a dashboard.

Chapter 6
Stock Charts

Stock charts and technical analysis play an important role in stock market research and analysis. Technical analysis, different from fundamental analysis, usually ignores the actual nature of the company, market, currency, or commodity. It is based solely on the stock charts; namely, the price and volume information. Stock charts usually show the high, low, open, close, and volume data of a security. These charts allow you to plot the change of a stock price over time, analyze the history of stock price changes, and predict the future price of a stock based on prior price history.

In this chapter, I will show you how to create a variety of stock charts using two different JavaScript libraries: Google Charts and TechanJS. As demonstrated in the preceding chapter, Google Charts is a powerful charting package that provides a variety of chart types, including stock candlestick charts. TechanJS is a JavaScript library built on SVG and D3 for creating interactive financial charts.

Get Stock Data

In order to create stock charts, we need to import stock data into our ASP.NET Core MVC applications. In Chapter 1, we implemented a MVC Core application based on existing database where we used reverse engineering to create an Entity Framework model that can be used to perform basic data access. Here, we will use the same approach to retrieve stock data from our existing database named *StockPriceDb* created in Chapter 1, and then generate stock charts using the data.

Open Visual Studio 2017, start with a new ASP.NET Core MVC application, and name it *Chapter06*. Add a new folder named *Models* to the project. Following the same procedure described in the existing database example in Chapter 1, install Entity Framework using the *Package Manager Console* and create the data model with our existing database *StockPriceDb* using reverse engineering based on the *Scaffold-DbContext* method.

The reverse engineering process creates entity classes *Symbol.cs*, *Price.cs*, and *IndexData.cs*, as well as a derived context *StockPriceDbContext.cs* in the *Models* folder based on the schema of the existing database. You need to register context with dependency injection and move configuration of the database provider to *Startup.cs* following the procedure described in Chapter 1.

Now, for better display effect, modify the *Price.cs* with the following code:

```
using System;
using System.ComponentModel.DataAnnotations;
```

```
namespace Chapter06.Models
{
    public partial class Price
    {
        public int PriceId { get; set; }
        [DisplayFormat(DataFormatString = "{0:#,##0.00#}")]
        public double Close { get; set; }
        [DisplayFormat(DataFormatString = "{0:#,##0.00#}")]
        public double CloseAdj { get; set; }

        [DataType(DataType.Date)]
        [DisplayFormat(DataFormatString = "{0:dd/MM/yyyy}")]
        public DateTime Date { get; set; }

        [DisplayFormat(DataFormatString = "{0:#,##0.00#}")]
        public double High { get; set; }
        [DisplayFormat(DataFormatString = "{0:#,##0.00#}")]
        public double Low { get; set; }
        [DisplayFormat(DataFormatString = "{0:#,##0.00#}")]
        public double Open { get; set; }
        public int SymbolId { get; set; }
        public double Volume { get; set; }

        public virtual Symbol Symbol { get; set; }
    }
}
```

Here, we add display format for date and stock price fields.

Now, we need to enable scaffolding in our project. Right click on the *Controllers* folder in Solution Explorer and select *Add > Controller…*, select *Full Dependencies* and click *Add*. The scaffolding is enabled, and we can then scaffold a controller for the *Symbol* entity.

Right click on the *Controllers* folder and select *Add > Controller…*, select *MVC Controller with views, using Entity Framework* and click *OK*. Select Model class to *Symbol* and Data context class to *StockPriceDb*. Set Controller name to *StockDataController*, click *Add*, and replace its content with the following code:

```
using Chapter06.Models;
using Microsoft.AspNetCore.Mvc;
using Microsoft.EntityFrameworkCore;
using System;
using System.Collections.Generic;
using System.Linq;
using System.Threading.Tasks;

namespace Chapter06.Controllers
{
    public class StockDataController : Controller
    {
        private readonly StockPriceDbContext _context;
        public StockDataController(StockPriceDbContext context)
        {
            _context = context;
        }
```

```csharp
// GET: StockData
public async Task<IActionResult> Index()
{
    return View(await _context.Symbol.OrderBy(
        s => s.Ticker).ToListAsync());
}

// GET: StockData/Details/5
public async Task<IActionResult> Details(int? id)
{
    if (id == null)
    {
        return NotFound();
    }

    var symbol = await _context.Symbol.SingleAsync(
        m => m.SymbolId == id);
    symbol.Price = await _context.Price.Where(
        x => x.SymbolId == id).Take(100).ToListAsync();

    if (symbol == null)
    {
        return NotFound();
    }
    return View(symbol);
}

// GET: StockData/Create
public IActionResult Create()
{
    return View();
}

// POST: StockData/Create
[HttpPost]
[ValidateAntiForgeryToken]
public async Task<IActionResult>
    Create([Bind("SymbolId,Region,Sector,Ticker")] Symbol symbol)
{
    if (ModelState.IsValid)
    {
        _context.Add(symbol);
        await _context.SaveChangesAsync();
        return RedirectToAction("Index");
    }
    return View(symbol);
}

// GET: StockData/Edit/5
public async Task<IActionResult> Edit(int? id)
{
    if (id == null)
    {
        return NotFound();
    }
```

```csharp
        var symbol = await _context.Symbol.SingleOrDefaultAsync(
            m => m.SymbolId == id);
        if (symbol == null)
        {
            return NotFound();
        }
        return View(symbol);
    }

    // POST: StockData/Edit/5
    [HttpPost]
    [ValidateAntiForgeryToken]
    public async Task<IActionResult> Edit(int id,
        [Bind("SymbolId,Region,Sector,Ticker")] Symbol symbol)
    {
        if (id != symbol.SymbolId)
        {
            return NotFound();
        }

        if (ModelState.IsValid)
        {
            try
            {
                _context.Update(symbol);
                await _context.SaveChangesAsync();
            }
            catch (DbUpdateConcurrencyException)
            {
                if (!SymbolExists(symbol.SymbolId))
                {
                    return NotFound();
                }
                else
                {
                    throw;
                }
            }
            return RedirectToAction("Index");
        }
        return View(symbol);
    }

    // GET: StockData/Delete/5
    public async Task<IActionResult> Delete(int? id)
    {
        if (id == null)
        {
            return NotFound();
        }

        var symbol = await _context.Symbol
            .SingleOrDefaultAsync(m => m.SymbolId == id);
        if (symbol == null)
```

```
    {
        return NotFound();
    }

    return View(symbol);
}

// POST: StockData/Delete/5
[HttpPost, ActionName("Delete")]
[ValidateAntiForgeryToken]
public async Task<IActionResult> DeleteConfirmed(int id)
{
    var symbol = await _context.Symbol.SingleOrDefaultAsync(
        m => m.SymbolId == id);
    _context.Symbol.Remove(symbol);
    await _context.SaveChangesAsync();
    return RedirectToAction("Index");
}

private bool SymbolExists(int id)
{
    return _context.Symbol.Any(e => e.SymbolId == id);
}

//GET:
public IActionResult DownloadPrice()
{
    StockPriceViewModel model = new StockPriceViewModel();
    model.Ticker = "IBM";
    model.StartDate = DateTime.Parse("1/1/2015");
    model.EndDate = DateTime.Parse("1/1/2016");
    model.Prices = new List<Price>();
    return View(model);
}

//Download stock data
[HttpPost]
[ValidateAntiForgeryToken]
public async Task<IActionResult> DownloadPrice(
    StockPriceViewModel model, string submitButton)
{
    model.Prices = await Task.Run(() => ModelHelper.GetYahooStockData(
        model.Ticker, model.StartDate, model.EndDate, _context));
    if (submitButton == "Download to Save")
    {
        if (ModelState.IsValid && model.Prices.Count > 0)
        {
            foreach (Price p in model.Prices)
                _context.Price.Add(p);
            await _context.SaveChangesAsync();
            ViewBag.Message = model.Prices.Count.ToString() +
                " records have been Successfully Updated.";
        }
        else
        {
```

```
                        ViewBag.Message = "Failed ! Please try again.";
                }
            }
            else if (submitButton == "Download to View")
            {
                ViewBag.Message = model.Ticker + "(" +
                    model.Prices.Count.ToString() + " rows) -
                    stock prices from " + model.StartDate + " to " +
                    model.EndDate + ":";
            }
            return View(model);
        }
    }
}
```

This code is very similar to that we used in Charpter 1. Here we also add the *DownloadPrice* method that allows you to download stock price data from Yahoo Finance. Note that this method takes the *StockPriceViewModel* object as an input argument. This view model is defined in the *Models* folder:

```
using System;
using System.Collections.Generic;
using System.ComponentModel.DataAnnotations;
using System.Linq;
using System.Threading.Tasks;

namespace Chapter06.Models
{
    public class StockPriceViewModel
    {
        public string Ticker { get; set; }
        [DataType(DataType.Date)]
        [DisplayFormat(DataFormatString = "{0:dd/MM/yyyy}")]
        public DateTime StartDate { get; set; }
        [DataType(DataType.Date)]
        [DisplayFormat(DataFormatString = "{0:dd/MM/yyyy}")]
        public DateTime EndDate { get; set; }
        public List<Price> Prices { get; set; }
        public string PriceJson { get; set; }
        public List<object> PriceJsonArray { get; set; }
    }
}
```

This view model will return a list of *Price* object (or stock data in JSON format) for a specified ticker and date period.

Next, we need to update corresponding views as what we did in Chapter 1. To make the views look better and more professional, we will use a table with fixed header and a scrollable content to display the stock price data. To this end, add the following CSS code to the *wwwroot/css/site.css* file:

```
/*my customized css:*/
.well {
    background: none;
    height: 620px;
}

.table-scroll tbody {
```

```
        position: absolute;
        overflow-y: scroll;
        height: 550px;
}

.table-scroll tr {
        width: 100%;
        table-layout: fixed;
        display: inline-table;
}

.table-scroll thead > tr > th {
        border: none;
}
```

Now, running this project and selecting the *Stock Data* tab produce the results shown in Figure 6-1.

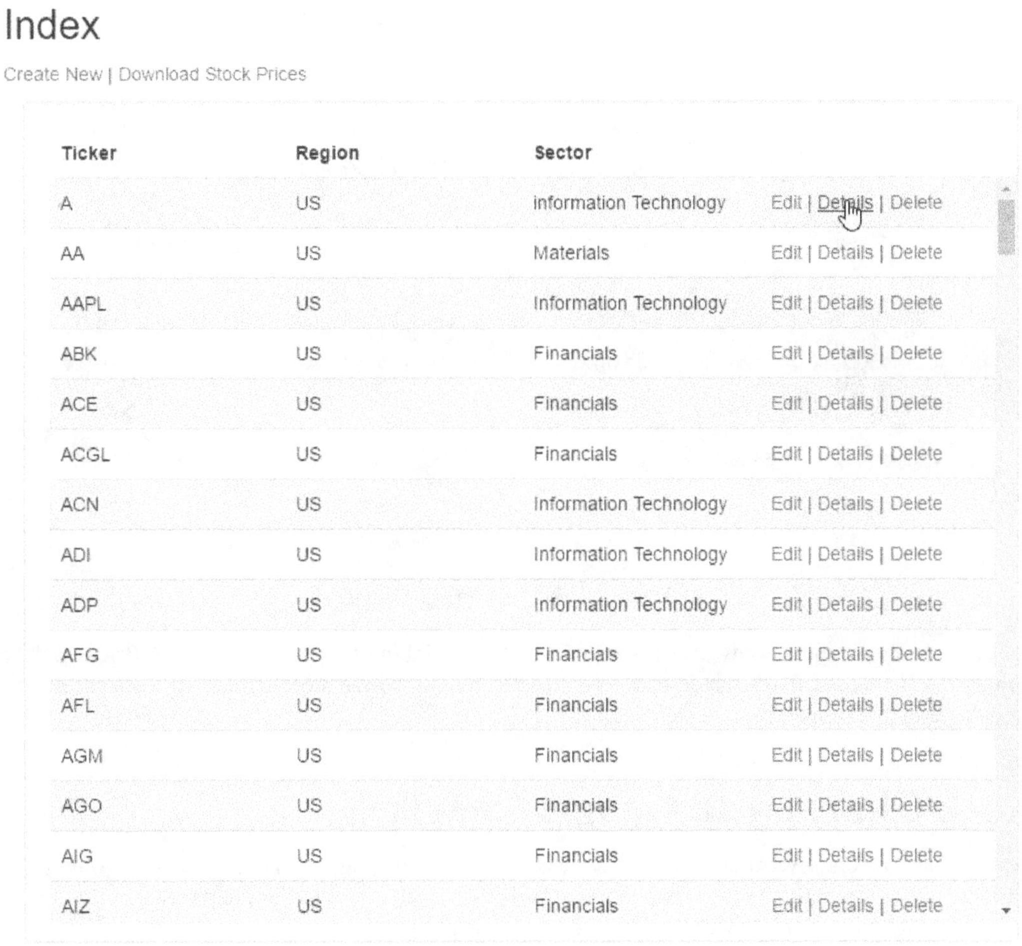

Index

Create New | Download Stock Prices

Ticker	Region	Sector	
A	US	Information Technology	Edit	Details	Delete
AA	US	Materials	Edit	Details	Delete
AAPL	US	Information Technology	Edit	Details	Delete
ABK	US	Financials	Edit	Details	Delete
ACE	US	Financials	Edit	Details	Delete
ACGL	US	Financials	Edit	Details	Delete
ACN	US	Information Technology	Edit	Details	Delete
ADI	US	Information Technology	Edit	Details	Delete
ADP	US	Information Technology	Edit	Details	Delete
AFG	US	Financials	Edit	Details	Delete
AFL	US	Financials	Edit	Details	Delete
AGM	US	Financials	Edit	Details	Delete
AGO	US	Financials	Edit	Details	Delete
AIG	US	Financials	Edit	Details	Delete
AIZ	US	Financials	Edit	Details	Delete

Figure 6-1. Stock symbols displayed in a scrollable table with fixed header.

You can see that the stock ticker information is displayed in a scrollable table with a fixed header. The first row of this table includes the ticker *A* and links to *Edit*, *Details*, and *Delete*. If you click the *Details* link, the stock price data for ticker *A* will be displayed, as shown in Figure 6-2.

Ticker   A
Region   US
Sector   information Technology
Price

Date	Open	High	Low	Close	CloseAdj	Volume
04/01/2010	31.39	31.63	31.13	31.30	21.273	3815500
20/10/2014	52.07	52.38	50.86	52.35	36.561	6909100
17/10/2014	52.17	53.41	52.02	52.27	36.505	5327400
16/10/2014	50.78	52.12	50.55	51.71	36.114	7496200
15/10/2014	50.87	51.88	49.80	51.79	36.17	6604000
14/10/2014	53.04	53.39	51.77	51.79	36.17	5554100
13/10/2014	53.73	54.23	52.73	52.79	36.868	3533100
10/10/2014	54.91	55.02	53.42	53.64	37.462	7176700
09/10/2014	56.28	56.28	55.03	55.03	38.433	3531700
08/10/2014	55.06	56.52	54.80	56.46	39.431	2970300
07/10/2014	56.25	56.33	55.00	55.00	38.412	2117200
06/10/2014	57.06	57.16	56.43	56.57	39.508	1618000
21/10/2014	52.86	54.03	52.86	54.00	37.713	3120100
03/10/2014	56.23	57.01	56.16	56.91	39.746	2205000
01/10/2014	56.85	56.93	56.18	56.20	39.25	3468800

Figure 6-2. Stock price data for ticker A.

From the stock data index view, as shown in Figure 6-1, clicking the *Download Stock Prices* link will open a new *Download Price* window, where you can download the stock prices for a specified ticker and date period, and save the data into database.

Stock Charts with Google Charts

Google Charts offers several chart types that can be used to display the stock price and volume data, including line price charts, volume bar charts, candlestick charts, range filer charts, etc. In this section, I will show you how to create various stock charts using Google Charts API.

Stock Data in JSON Format

In order to create stock charts using the Google Charts API, we need first to convert the stock data from database or Yahoo Finance into a JSON string format. This JSON string can then be used by the Google DataTable object. Add a new method named *StockStringData* to the *ModelHelper* class. Here is the code for this method:

```
public static string StockStringData(StockPriceDbContext db, string ticker,
    DateTime startDate, DateTime endDate, out string dataSource)
{
    dataSource = "Database";
    List<Price> prices = null;
    try
    {
        prices = db.Price.Where(x => x.Symbol.Ticker == ticker &&
            x.Date >= startDate && x.Date <= endDate).OrderBy(
            x => x.Date).ToList();
    }
    catch { }
    finally
    {
        if (prices.Count <= 0)
        {
            prices = GetYahooStockData(ticker, startDate, endDate, db);
            dataSource = "Yahoo Finance";
        }
    }
    if (prices.Count <= 0) return null;

    var cols = new JsonColumn[]
    {
        new JsonColumn {label = "Date", type = "date" },
        new JsonColumn {label = "Open", type = "number" },
        new JsonColumn {label = "High", type = "number" },
        new JsonColumn {label = "Low", type = "number" },
        new JsonColumn {label = "Close", type = "number" },
        new JsonColumn {label = "CloseAdj", type = "number" },
        new JsonColumn {label = "Volume", type = "number" }
    };
    var rows = new JsonRow[prices.Count];
    for (int i = 0; i < prices.Count; i++)
    {
        var date = DateTime.Parse(prices[i].Date.ToString());
        rows[i] = new JsonRow
        {
            c = new JsonCell[]
            {
                new JsonCell { v = "Date(" + date.Year + ", " + (date.Month - 1)
                    + ", " + date.Day + ")" },
                new JsonCell { v = prices[i].Open },
                new JsonCell { v = prices[i].High },
                new JsonCell { v = prices[i].Low },
                new JsonCell { v = prices[i].Close },
                new JsonCell { v = prices[i].CloseAdj },
                new JsonCell { v = prices[i].Volume }
```

```
            }
        };
    }
    return JsonString.GetGoogleJson(cols, rows);
}
```

This code first retrieve stock data from database for a specified ticker and date period using LINQ. If there are no data stored in the database for a specified ticker, we will download the stock data directly from Yahoo Finance using the *GetYahooStockData* method. As long as we have the stock data ready, we then convert the data into a JSON string required by Google Charts DataTable. Note that in order to perform such conversion, you need to import the *JsonString.cs* file from the Chapter05 project and change its namespace to *Chapter06*.

Stock Charts

Now, we can create stock charts using Google Charts API. Add a new controller named *GoogleChartsController* to the *Controllers* folder and replace its content with the following code:

```
using Chapter06.Models;
using Microsoft.AspNetCore.Mvc;
using System;
using System.Threading.Tasks;
namespace Chapter06.Controllers
{
    public class GoogleChartsController : Controller
    {
        private readonly StockPriceDbContext _context;
        public GoogleChartsController(StockPriceDbContext context)
        {
            _context = context;
        }

        // GET: /<controller>/
        public IActionResult Index()
        {
            ViewBag.Title = "Google Stock Charts: Home";
            return View();
        }

        //GET:
        public async Task<IActionResult> StockChart()
        {
            ViewBag.Title = "Stock Charts";
            StockPriceViewModel model = new StockPriceViewModel();
            model.Ticker = "IBM";
            model.StartDate = DateTime.Parse("1/1/2016");
            model.EndDate = DateTime.Parse("3/1/2016");
            string dataSource = string.Empty;
            model.PriceJson = await Task.Run(() => ModelHelper.StockStringData(
                _context, model.Ticker, model.StartDate, model.EndDate,
                out dataSource));
            ViewBag.DataSource ="Data Source: " + dataSource;
            return View(model);
        }
```

```
        [HttpPost]
        [ValidateAntiForgeryToken]
        public async Task<IActionResult> StockChart(StockPriceViewModel model)
        {
            string dataSource = string.Empty;
            model.PriceJson = await Task.Run(() => ModelHelper.StockStringData(
                _context, model.Ticker, model.StartDate, model.EndDate,
                out dataSource));
            ViewBag.DataSource = "Data Source: " + dataSource;
            return View(model);
        }
    }
}
```

Add a new folder named *GoogleCharts* to the *Views* folder. Now, we want to create a partial view named *Views/GoogleCharts/_SpecifyTicker.cshtml*, which can be reused for other views. Here is the code for this partial view:

```
@model Chapter06.Models.StockPriceViewModel

<!--<form asp-action="_SpecifyTicker">-->
<div class="form-horizontal">
    <hr />
    <div asp-validation-summary="ModelOnly" class="text-danger"></div>
    <div class="form-group">
        <label asp-for="Ticker" class="col-md-2 control-label"></label>
        <div class="col-md-10">
            <input asp-for="Ticker" class="form-control" />
            <span asp-validation-for="Ticker" class="text-danger"></span>
        </div>
    </div>
    <div class="form-group">
        <label asp-for="StartDate" class="col-md-2 control-label"></label>
        <div class="col-md-10">
            <input asp-for="StartDate" class="form-control" />
            <span asp-validation-for="StartDate" class="text-danger"></span>
        </div>
    </div>
    <div class="form-group">
        <label asp-for="EndDate" class="col-md-2 control-label"></label>
        <div class="col-md-10">
            <input asp-for="EndDate" class="form-control" />
            <span asp-validation-for="EndDate" class="text-danger"></span>
        </div>
    </div>
    <div class="form-group">
        <div class="col-md-offset-2 col-md-10">
            <input type="submit" value="Create Stock Charts"
                class="btn btn-primary" />
        </div>
    </div>
</div>
<!--</form>-->
```

This partial view simply implements an input form that allows you to specify the ticker and date period. Add a new view named *StockChart.cshtml* to the *Views/GoogleCharts* folder and replace its content with the following code:

```
@model Chapter06.Models.StockPriceViewModel
@{
    ViewData["Title"] = ViewBag.Title;
}
<h3>@ViewBag.Title</h3>
@Html.Partial("_Links")

<form asp-action="StockChart">
    @Html.Partial("_SpecifyTicker", Model)
</form>

<div class="container">
    <p>@ViewBag.DataSource</p>
    <div class="row">
        <div class="col-sm-12">
            <div id="chart1"></div>
        </div>
    </div>
    <div class="row">
        <div class="col-sm-12">
            <div id="chart2"></div>
        </div>
    </div>
    <div class="row">
        <div class="col-sm-12">
            <div id="chart3"></div>
        </div>
    </div>
</div>

<script type="text/javascript"
    src="https://www.gstatic.com/charts/loader.js"></script>

<script type="text/javascript">
        google.charts.load('current', { 'packages': ['corechart'] });
        google.charts.setOnLoadCallback(drawChart);

        function drawChart() {
            var data = new google.visualization
                            .DataTable('@(Html.Raw(Model.PriceJson))');

            //stock price line chart:
            var view = new google.visualization.DataView(data);
            view.hideColumns([6]);
            var options = {
                title: 'Stock Price Line Chart: ' + '@(Model.Ticker)',
                width: 960,
                height: 400,
                chartArea: { left: 100, top: 30, width: '70%', height: '75%' },
                lineWidth: 2,
                pointSize: 5,
```

```
            hAxis: {showTextEvery: 2}
        };
        var chart = new google.visualization.LineChart(
            document.getElementById('chart1'));
        chart.draw(view, options);

        //stock volume bar chart:
        view = new google.visualization.DataView(data);
        view.setColumns([0, 6]);
        options = {
            title: 'Stock Volume Bar Chart: ' + '@(Model.Ticker)',
            width: 960,
            height: 250,
            chartArea: { left: 100, top: 30, width: '70%', height: '65%' },
            lineWidth: 2,
            legend: 'none',
            hAxis: {showTextEvery: 2}
        };
        chart = new google.visualization.ColumnChart(
            document.getElementById('chart2'));
        chart.draw(view, options);

        //stock price candlestick chart:
        view = new google.visualization.DataView(data);
        view.setColumns([0, 3, 1, 4, 2]);
        options = {
            title: 'Stock Price Candlestick Chart: ' + '@(Model.Ticker)',
            legend: 'none',
            width: 960,
            height: 400,
            chartArea: { left: 100, top: 30, width: '70%', height: '75%' },
            explorer: { actions: ['dragToZoom', 'rightClickToReset'] },
            lineWidth: 0.5,
        };
        chart = new google.visualization.CandlestickChart(
            document.getElementById('chart3'));
        chart.draw(view, options);
    }
</script>
```

This is a strong typed view with the *SockPriceViewModel* as its model. The code calls the partial view *_SpecifyTicker* with the action being set to *StockChart*. In the script section, we implement three stock charts: a line stock-price chart, a volumn bar chart, and a candlestick chart. We pass the data from our *Model* to the Google DataTable using the following statement:

```
var data = new google.visualization.DataTable('@(Html.Raw(Model.PriceJson))');
```

We then use the *view* to select relevant columns from *data* according to chart type. Running this example, selecting the *Google Stock Charts* tab, and clicking the *Stock Chart* link generate the results shown in Figure 6-3.

You can see that for IBM, the *Data Source* shows *Database*, meaning that the data we are using in creating the stock charts comes from database because we have saved the stock data for IBM to the database. If you enter a ticker, i.e. COST, whose data is not stored in the database, the *Data Source* will show Yahoo Finance, indicating that the data is downloaded directly from Yahoo Finance.

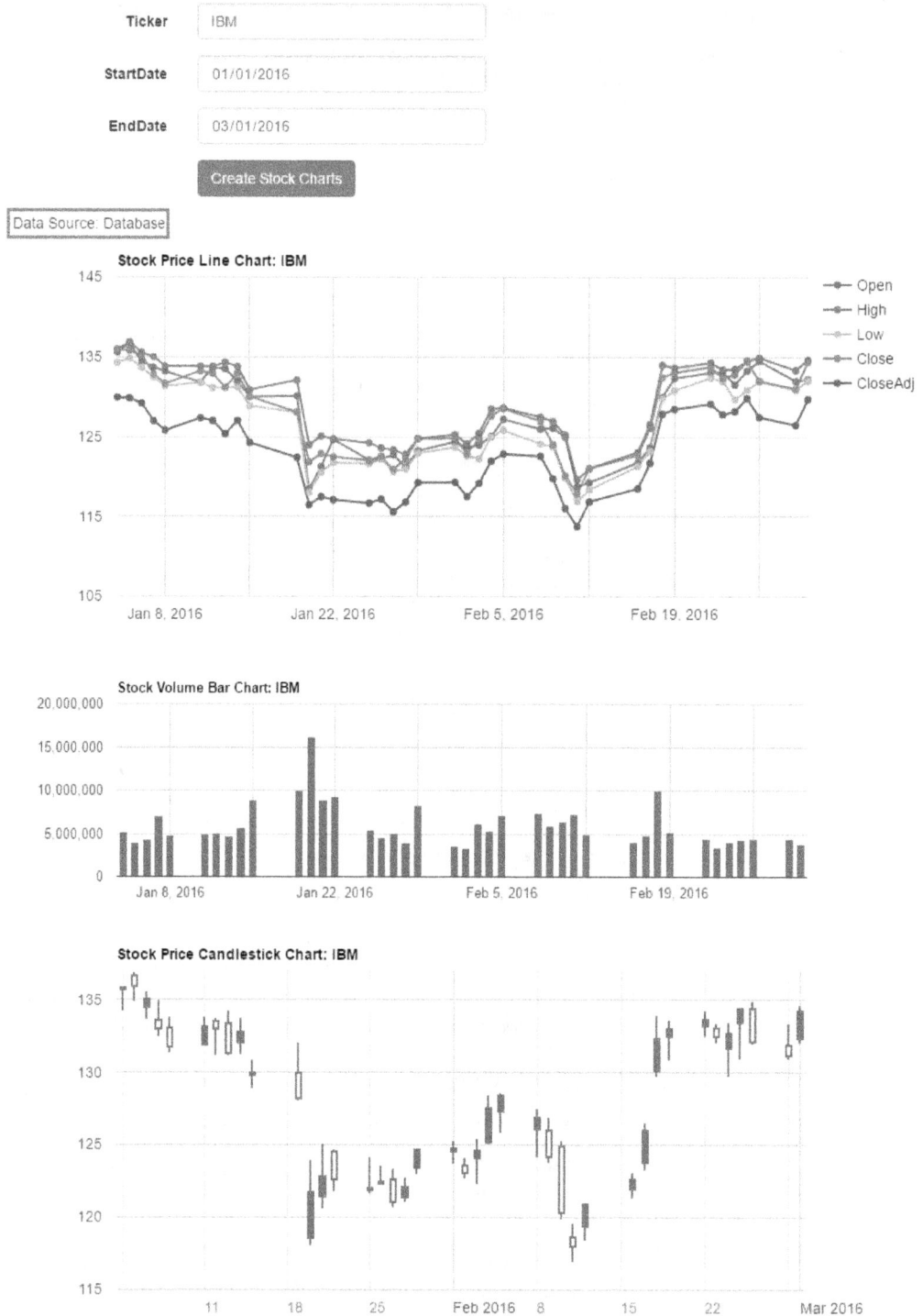

Figure 6-3. Demonstrate stock charts: line (top), volume (middle), and candlestick bottom).

You may notice that the stock charts in Figure 6-3 have some gaps for none trading days (weekends and holidays). You can remove those gaps by setting the type for the date axes to *category*.

Custom Stock Charts

Next, we will create customized stock charts without weekend gaps, and change the default colors for the candlestick chart.

Add *Views/GoogleCharts/CustomChart.cshtml* and replace its content with the following code:

```
@model Chapter06.Models.StockPriceViewModel
@{
    ViewData["Title"] = ViewBag.Title;
}
<h3>@ViewBag.Title</h3>
@Html.Partial("_Links")

<form asp-action="CustomChart">
    @Html.Partial("_SpecifyTicker", Model)
</form>

<div class="container">
    <div class="row">
        <p>@ViewBag.DataSource</p>
        <div class="col-sm-12">
            <div id="chart1"></div>
        </div>
    </div>
    <div class="row">
        <div class="col-sm-12">
            <div id="chart2"></div>
        </div>
    </div>
    <div class="row">
        <div class="col-sm-12">
            <div id="chart3"></div>
        </div>
    </div>
</div>

<script type="text/javascript"
    src="https://www.gstatic.com/charts/loader.js"></script>
<script type="text/javascript">
        google.charts.load('current', { 'packages': ['corechart'] });
        google.charts.setOnLoadCallback(drawChart);
        function drawChart() {
            var data = new google.visualization
                        .DataTable('@(Html.Raw(Model.PriceJson))');

            //stock price line chart:
            var view = new google.visualization.DataView(data);
            view.hideColumns([6]);
            var options = {
                title: 'Stock Price Line Chart: ' + '@(Model.Ticker)',
                width: 960,
```

```
                height: 400,
                chartArea: { left: 100, top: 30, width: '70%', height: '75%' },
                lineWidth: 2,
                pointSize: 5,
                hAxis: { type: 'category', showTextEvery: 6 }
            };
            var chart = new google.visualization.LineChart(
                document.getElementById('chart1'));
            chart.draw(view, options);

            //stock volume bar chart:
            view = new google.visualization.DataView(data);
            view.setColumns([0, 6]);
            options = {
                title: 'Stock Volume Bar Chart: ' + '@(Model.Ticker)',
                width: 960,
                height: 250,
                chartArea: { left: 100, top: 30, width: '70%', height: '65%' },
                lineWidth: 2,
                legend: 'none',
                hAxis: { type: 'category', showTextEvery: 6 }
            };
            chart = new google.visualization.ColumnChart(
                document.getElementById('chart2'));
            chart.draw(view, options);

            //stock price candlestick chart:
            view = new google.visualization.DataView(data);
            view.setColumns([0, 3, 1, 4, 2]);
            options = {
                title: 'Stock Price Candlestick Chart: ' + '@(Model.Ticker)',
                legend: 'none',
                width: 960,
                height: 400,
                candlestick: {
                    fallingColor: { strokeWidth: 0, fill: '#a52714' },
                    risingColor:  { strokeWidth: 0, fill: '#0f9d58' }
                },
                chartArea: { left: 100, top: 30, width: '70%', height: '75%' },
                explorer: { actions: ['dragToZoom', 'rightClickToReset'] },
                lineWidth: 0.5,
                hAxis: { type: 'category', showTextEvery: 6 }
            };
            chart = new google.visualization.CandlestickChart(
                document.getElementById('chart3'));
            chart.draw(view, options);
        }
    </script>
```

This code is similar to that used in the preceding example, except that here we set horizontal axis type to category and change the default colors for candlestick.

Running this example, selecting the *Google Stock Charts* tab, clicking the *Custom Stock Charts* link, entering COST in the *Ticker* field, and clicking the *Create Stock Chart* button produce the results shown in Figure 6-4.

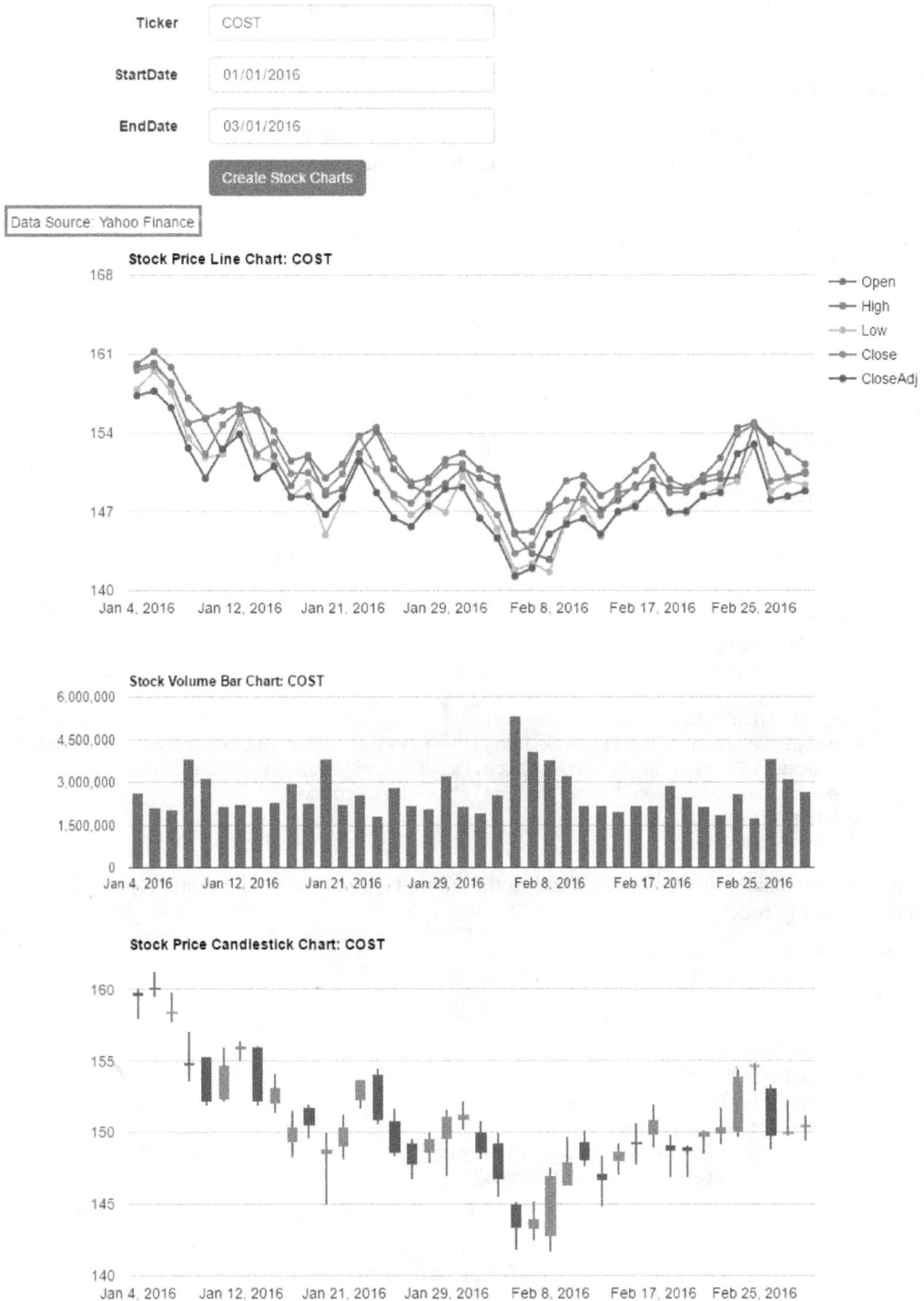

Ticker: COST

StartDate: 01/01/2016

EndDate: 03/01/2016

Create Stock Charts

Data Source: Yahoo Finance

Figure 6-4. Demonstration of custom stock charts.

You can see from the figure that there are no gaps any more in the stock charts.

Chart Range Filter

Google Charts provides a special dashboard-like control: chart range filter. This control consists of a slider with two thumbs superimposed onto a chart, to select a range of values from the horizontal axis of the chart. This will be a good candidate for displaying the stock data.

Add the following method to the *GoogleChartsController.cs* file:

```
public async Task<IActionResult> RangeFilter()
{
    ViewBag.Title = "Chart Range Filter";
    StockPriceViewModel model = new StockPriceViewModel();
    model.Ticker = "SPY";
    model.StartDate = DateTime.Parse("6/1/2015");
    model.EndDate = DateTime.Parse("9/1/2016");
    string dataSource = string.Empty;
    model.PriceJson = await Task.Run(() => ModelHelper.StockStringData(_context,
        model.Ticker, model.StartDate, model.EndDate, out dataSource));
    ViewBag.DataSource = "Data Source: " + dataSource;
    return View(model);
}

[HttpPost]
[ValidateAntiForgeryToken]
public async Task<IActionResult> RangeFilter(StockPriceViewModel model)
{
    string dataSource = string.Empty;
    model.PriceJson = await Task.Run(() => ModelHelper.StockStringData(_context,
        model.Ticker, model.StartDate, model.EndDate, out dataSource));
    ViewBag.DataSource = "Data Source: " + dataSource;
    return View(model);
}
```

Add a new view named *RangeFilter.cshtml* to the *Views/GoogleCharts* folder and replace its content with the following code:

```
<form asp-action="RangeFilter">
    @Html.Partial("_SpecifyTicker", Model)
</form>

<div class="container">
    <div class="row" style="margin-top:30px">
        <p>@ViewBag.DataSource</p>
        <div class="col-sm-10">
            <div id="dashboard_div" style="border: 1px solid #ccc">
                <table class="columns">
                    <tr>
                        <td>
                            <div id="chart_div" style="width: 900px;
                                height: 400px;"></div>
                        </td>
                    </tr>
                    <tr>
```

```
                    <td>
                        <div id="volume_div" style="width: 900px;
                            height: 200px;"></div>
                    </td>
                </tr>
                <tr>
                    <td>
                        <div id="control_div" style="width: 900px;
                            height: 80px;"></div>
                    </td>
                </tr>
            </table>
        </div>
    </div>
</div>
</div>

<script type="text/javascript"
    src="https://www.gstatic.com/charts/loader.js"></script>

<script type="text/javascript">
    google.charts.load('current', { packages: ['corechart', 'controls'] });
    google.charts.setOnLoadCallback(drawChart);

    function drawChart() {
        var dashboard = new google.visualization.Dashboard(
            document.getElementById('dashboard_div'));

        var control = new google.visualization.ControlWrapper({
            controlType: 'ChartRangeFilter',
            containerId: 'control_div',
            options: {
                // Filter by the date axis.
                filterColumnIndex: 0,
                ui: {
                    chartType: 'LineChart',
                    chartOptions: {
                        chartArea: { width: '90%' },
                        hAxis: { baselineColor: 'none' }
                    },
                    // Display a single series that shows the closing
                    // value of the stock.
                    chartView: {
                        columns: [0, 4]
                    },
                    // 1 day in milliseconds = 24 * 60 * 60 * 1000 = 86,400,000
                    minRangeSize: 86400000
                }
            },
            // Initial range:

            state: {
                range: {
                    start: new Date('@Model.StartDate.AddMonths(1).Year',
                                    '@Model.StartDate.AddMonths(1).Month',
```

```
                                 '@Model.StartDate.AddMonths(1).Day'),
                    end: new Date('@Model.StartDate.AddMonths(3).Year',
                                '@Model.StartDate.AddMonths(3).Month',
                                '@Model.StartDate.AddMonths(3).Day')
                }
            }
        });

        var chart = new google.visualization.ChartWrapper({
            chartType: 'CandlestickChart',
            containerId: 'chart_div',
            options: {
                chartArea: { height: '80%', width: '90%' },
                hAxis: { type: 'category', slantedText: false,
                        showTextEvery: 10 },
                legend: { position: 'none' },
                candlestick: {
                    fallingColor: { strokeWidth: 0, fill: '#a52714' },
                    risingColor: { strokeWidth: 0, fill: '#0f9d58' }
                },
                title: 'Candlestick Chart: ' + '@(Model.Ticker)'
            },
            view: { columns: [0, 3, 1, 4, 2] }
        });

        var volume = new google.visualization.ChartWrapper({
            chartType: 'ColumnChart',
            containerId: 'volume_div',
            options: {
                chartArea: { height: '80%', width: '90%' },
                hAxis: { type: 'category', slantedText: false,
                        showTextEvery: 10 },
                legend: { position: 'none' },
                title: 'Volume Chart: ' + '@(Model.Ticker)'
            },
            view: { columns: [0, 6] }
        });

        var data = new google.visualization.DataTable(
            '@(Html.Raw(Model.PriceJson))');
        dashboard.bind(control, [chart, volume]);
        dashboard.draw(data);
    }
</script>
```

Here, we use the close price line chart as the range filter control to control the display range of a candlestick chart and a volume bar chart. We specify an initial range in the *options* section by setting the *range.start* and *range.end* attributes. All the charts that are part of a dashboard share the same underlying DataTable created using the *Model.PriceJson* object.

We use the *view* option while configuring each *ControlWrapper/ChartWrapper* instance to determine which columns are relevant for the chart. For example, for our volume chart, we use the columns [0, 6]. While for our candlestick chart, we use the columns [0, 3, 1, 4, 2], where we not only pick up the relevant columns, but also change the column orders, which is required by our candlestick chart.

Once we have instantiated the dashboard, the chart range filter (the control), and charts, we use the *bind* method to tell the dashboard about the dependencies that exist between the control and charts. After the binding, the dashboard updates the charts to match the constraints the range filter control enforces over the data. Here, our range filter control is bound together with the candlestick and volume charts, so whenever you change the date range using the control, the charts update to display only the data that matches the selected range.

Running this example produces the results shown in Figure 6-5.

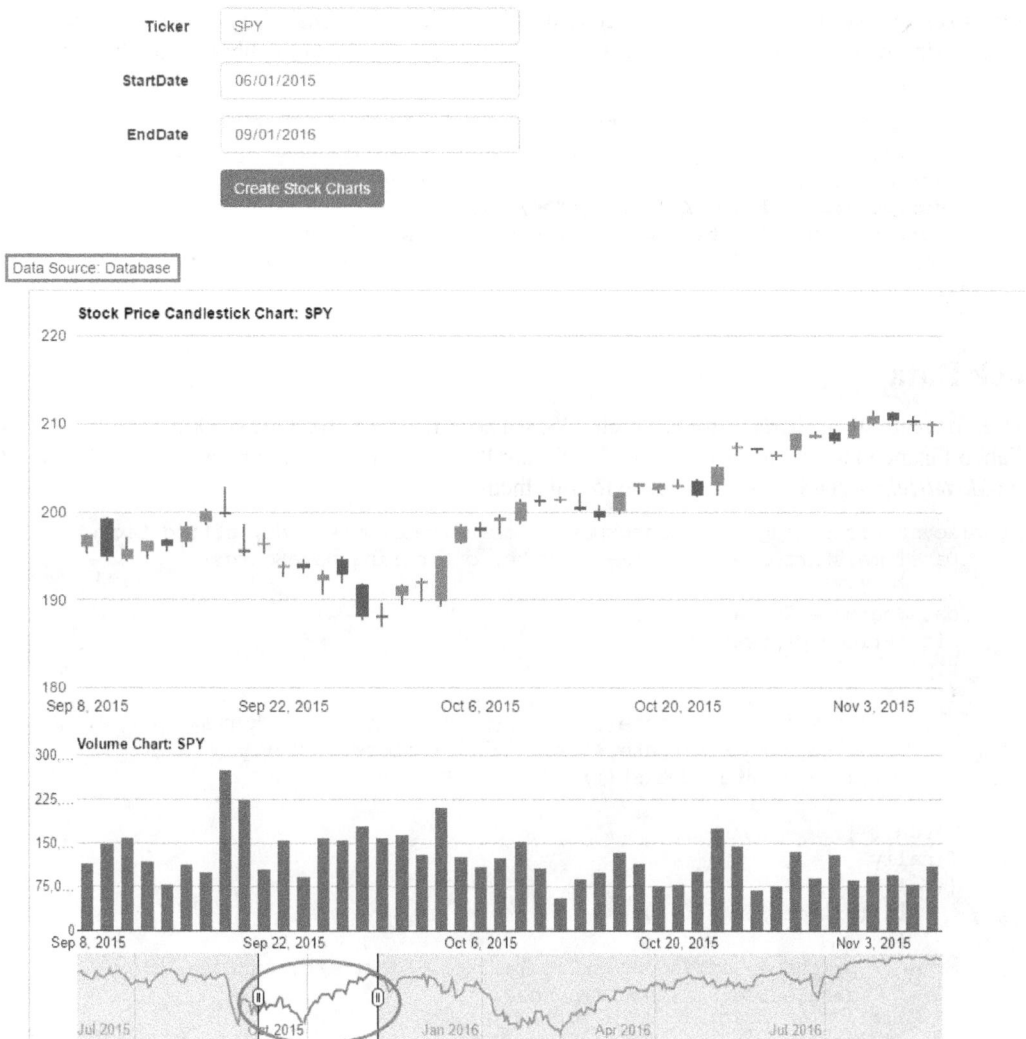

Figure 6-5. Demonstration of a chart range filter control.

Stock Charts with TechanJS

In the preceding sections, we demonstrated how to use Google Charts API to create various stock charts. Even though Google Charts is a powerful charting package with a variety of chart types, it provides limited functionalities for Finance applications. Here, we will consider another charting library TechanJS, which is designed specifically for finance applications. TechanJS is a JavaScript library built on top of SVG and D3 for creating interactive financial charts for modern browsers. The TechanJS API is based on well-established D3 idioms and the reusable chart API.

In order to use the TechanJS library, you need to install both D3 and TechanJS using the *Manager Bower Packages* window in Visual Studio 2017. After installation, we will add the libraries to *Views/Shared/ _Layout.cshtml*:

```
<environment names="Development">
    <script src="~/lib/jquery/dist/jquery.js"></script>
    <script src="~/lib/bootstrap/dist/js/bootstrap.js"></script>
    <script src="~/lib/d3/d3.min.js"></script>
    <script src="~/lib/techan/dist/techan.min.js"></script>
    <script src="~/js/site.js" asp-append-version="true"></script>
</environment>
```

Stock Data

In order to create stock charts using the TechanJS, we need first to convert the stock data from database or Yahoo Finance into the format required by TechanJS. Add a new method named *TechanStockData* to the *ModelHelper* class. Here is the code for this method:

```
public static string TechanStockData(StockPriceDbContext db, string ticker,
    DateTime startDate, DateTime endDate, out string dataSource)
{
    dataSource = "Database";
    List<Price> prices = null;
    try
    {
        prices = db.Price.Where(x => x.Symbol.Ticker == ticker &&
            x.Date >= startDate && x.Date <= endDate).OrderBy(
            x => x.Date).ToList();
    }
    catch { }
    finally
    {
        if (prices.Count <= 0)
        {
            prices = GetYahooStockData(ticker, startDate, endDate, db);
            dataSource = "Yahoo Finance";
        }
    }

    if (prices.Count <= 0) return null;

    List<object> data = new List<object>();
    for (int i = 0; i < prices.Count; i++)
    {
```

```
data.Add(new
{
    Date = (prices[i].Date).ToString("d-MMM-yy"),
    Open = prices[i].Open,
    High = prices[i].High,
    Low = prices[i].Low,
    Close = prices[i].Close,
    Volume = prices[i].Volume,
});
}
return JsonConvert.SerializeObject(data);
}
```

This code first retrieve stock data from database for a specified ticker and date period using LINQ. If there are no data stored in the database for a specified ticker, we will download the stock data directly from Yahoo Finance using the *GetYahooStockData* method. As long as we have the stock data ready, we then convert the data into a list of objects. Finally, we use the *JsonConvert.SerializeObject* method to convert the list into JSON format.

Helper Functions

As mentioned previously, TechanJS is a JavaScript library built on top of D3. It provides tools to help you visualize and manipulate your financial data. It implements several commonly used chart types, including

- *Techan.plot.candlestick*: used to construct a candlestick chart.

- *Techan.plot.ohlc*: used to construct an ohlc chart.

- *Techan.plot.volume*: used to construct a volume chart.

- *Techan.plot.ema*: used to construct an exponential moving average.

- *Techan.plot.sma*: used to construct a simple moving average.

- *Techan.plot.macd*: used to construct a MACD indicator.

- *Techan.plot.rsi*: used to construct an RSI indicator.

- *Techan.plot.bollinger*: used to construct a Bollinger band.

You can use these functions to create your own stock charts and technical indicators. However, TechanJS does not comes with a preset array of charts that you can pass your data and then get an output displayed on chart automatically. You need to understand how to combine TechanJS functions with the other D3 chart components, including axes, labels, title, gridlines, and chart area. These components form the basis upon which you will be drawing the chart. Unlike the ready-to-use charting libraries, these D3 components are not readily available but must be developed gradually. This will result in additional work, but it will also allow you to create special features. This means that your TechanJS charts, much like D3 charts, will be able to respond to particular needs.

In this section, we will implement some common components used in TechanJS charts, including axes, gridlines, chart area, etc. Instead writing code directly to the view, we will implement JavaScript helper functions for these components. These functions can be easily reused in creating stock charts based on TechanJS. Open *wwwroot/js/site.js* file and add the *setChartArea* function to it:

```
function setChartArea(svgSelection, width, height, margin) {
    var w = width - margin.left - margin.right;
```

```
        var h = height - margin.top - margin.bottom;
        var x = techan.scale.financetime().range([0, w]);
        var y = d3.scaleLinear().range([h, 0]);
        var yVolume = d3.scaleLinear().range([y(0), y(0.2)]);

        var svg = d3.select(svgSelection)
            .attr("width", width)
            .attr("height", height)
            .append("g")
            .attr("transform", "translate(" + margin.left + "," + margin.top + ")");

    svg.append("rect")
        .attr("width", w)
        .attr("height", h)
        .style("stroke", "black")
        .style("stroke-width", "0.5px")
        .attr("fill", "none");


        return { svg, x, y, yVolume, w, h };
    }
```

This code simply sets the chart area, which will be used when we create axes and gridlines. Note how we use the *techan.scale.financetime* function to create the *x* scale. This function gives a continuous date axis with the date gaps (due to weekends and holidays) being removed.

Add another function named *setAxesGridlines* to the *site.js* file:

```
function setAxesGridlines(xy, margin, title, ylabel, isGridline) {
    var xAxis = d3.axisBottom(xy.x);
    var yAxis = d3.axisLeft(xy.y);
    xy.svg.append("g")
        .attr("class", "x axis")
        .attr("transform", "translate(0," + xy.h + ")")
        .call(xAxis);
    xy.svg.append("text")
        .attr("transform", "translate(" + (xy.w / 2) + "," +
            (xy.h + 2 * margin.bottom / 3) + ")")
        .style("text-anchor", "middle")
        .text("Date");

    xy.svg.append("g")
        .attr("class", "y axis")
        .call(yAxis);
    xy.svg.append("text")
        .attr("transform", "translate(" + (-margin.left / 1.5) + "," +
            (xy.h / 2) + ") rotate(-90)")
        .style("text-anchor", "middle")
        .text(ylabel);

    xy.svg.append("text")
        .attr("x", xy.w / 2)
        .attr("y", -margin.top / 2)
        .attr("text-anchor", "middle")
        .attr("font-weight", "bold")
        .attr("font-size", "14px")
        .text(title);
```

```
    //grid lines:
    if (isGridline) {
        xy.svg.selectAll("line.ygrid")
            .data(xy.y.ticks())
            .enter()
            .append("line")
            .attr("class", "ygrid")
            .attr("x1", 0)
            .attr("x2", xy.w)
            .attr("y1", function (d) { return xy.y(d); })
            .attr("y2", function (d) { return xy.y(d); })
            .attr("stroke", "lightgray")
            .attr("stroke-width", "1px");

        xy.svg.selectAll("line.xgrid")
            .data(xy.x.ticks())
            .enter()
            .append("line")
            .attr("class", "xgrid")
            .attr("x1", function (d) { return xy.x(d); })
            .attr("x2", function (d) { return xy.x(d); })
            .attr("y1", 0)
            .attr("y2", xy.h)
            .attr("stroke", "lightgray")
            .attr("stroke-width", "1px");
    }
    return { xAxis, yAxis };
}
```

Here, the *xy* input argument is the return values from the *setChartArea* function. This function implement two axes (left and bottom) and corresponding gridlines. The code is basically similar to what we used in Chapter 4.

In some stock charts, we may need four axes (left, bottom, top, and right). Add a new method named *set4Axes* to the *site.js* file:

```
function set4Axes(xy, margin, title, ylabel, isGridline) {
    var xAxis = d3.axisBottom(xy.x);
    var yAxis = d3.axisLeft(xy.y);
    var xTopAxis = d3.axisTop(xy.x);
    var yRightAxis = d3.axisRight(xy.y);
    setAxesGridlines(xy, margin, title, ylabel, isGridline);
    xy.svg.append("g")
        .attr("class", "x axis")
        .call(xTopAxis);
    xy.svg.append("g")
        .attr("class", "y axis")
        .attr("transform", "translate(" + xy.w + ",0)")
        .call(yRightAxis);
}
```

This function simply adds two more axes (top and right) to the original *setAxesGridlines* function, which creates two axes (left and bottom) with gridlines.

You can use CSS style to control the appearance of the stock charts based on TechanJS. Here, I will add the following CSS style code to the *wwwroot/css/site.css* file:

```css
/* style for Techan charts: */
path.ohlc {
    stroke: #000000;
    stroke-width: 1;
}
path.ohlc.up {
    stroke: green;
}

path.ohlc.down {
    stroke: red;
}

path.candle.up {
    fill: green;
    stroke: green;
}

path.candle.down {
    fill: red;
    stroke: red;
}

path.volume.up {
    fill: green;
}

path.volume.down {
    fill: red;
}

rect.pane {
    cursor: move;
    fill: none;
    pointer-events: all;
}

.y.annotation.left path {
    fill: #00AA00;
}

.y.annotation.right path {
    fill: #FF0000;
}

.x.annotation path {
    fill: #DDD80E;
}

.crosshair {
    cursor: crosshair;
}
```

```
.crosshair path.wire {
    stroke: blue;
    stroke-width: 0.5px;
}

.crosshair .axisannotation path {
    fill: lightgray;
}
```

We will use the above code to control the appearance of the stock charts. You can easily change or modify the above code according to your applications' requirement as you like.

Stock Charts

Now, we can create the standard stock charts such as ohlc, candlestick, and volume charts. Add a new JavaScript function named *drawTechanChart* to the *site.js* file:

```
function drawTechanChart(svgSelection, data, options) {
    var chartType = options.chartType || "candlestick";
    var isGridline = options.isGridline || true;
    var width = options.width || 600;
    var height = options.height || 400;
    var margin = options.margin || { top: 40, right: 20, bottom: 60, left: 70 };

    var xy = setChartArea(svgSelection, width, height, margin);
    var parseDate = d3.timeParse("%d-%b-%y");
    var plot, accessor;
    var title, ylabel;

    if (chartType === "ohlc") {
        plot = techan.plot.ohlc().xScale(xy.x).yScale(xy.y);
        accessor = plot.accessor();
        title = options.title || "Stock Price";
        ylabel = options.ylabel || "Price";
    } else if (chartType === "candlestick") {
        plot = techan.plot.candlestick().xScale(xy.x).yScale(xy.y);
        accessor = plot.accessor();
        title = options.title || "Stock Price";
        ylabel = options.ylabel || "Price";
    } else if (chartType === "volume") {
        plot = techan.plot.volume()
                    .accessor(techan.accessor.ohlc())
                    .xScale(xy.x).yScale(xy.y);
        accessor = plot.accessor();
        title = options.title || "Volume";
        ylabel = options.ylabel || "";
    }

    data = data.map(function (d) {
        return {
            date: parseDate(d.Date),
            open: +d.Open,
            high: +d.High,
            low: +d.Low,
```

```
            close: +d.Close,
            volume: +d.Volume
    };
}).sort(function (a, b) { return d3.ascending(accessor.d(a),
                                    accessor.d(b)); });

xy.x.domain(data.map(accessor.d));
if (chartType === "volume") {
    xy.y.domain(techan.scale.plot.volume(data, plot.accessor().v).domain());
} else {
    xy.y.domain(techan.scale.plot.ohlc(data, accessor).domain());
}
setAxesGridlines(xy, margin, title, ylabel, isGridline);

xy.svg.append("g")
    .attr("class", "plot")
    .datum(data)
    .call(plot);
}
```

This code implements three types of stock charts: ohlc, candlestick, and volume. It takes SVG container, data, and optional parameters as input arguments. If you do not specify the optional parameters, the code will use their default values. First, it gets the returned values by calling the *setChartArea* function, and then creates the plot according to the specified chart type. Next, we map the input data into the format required by the TechanTS API, and perform corresponding domain and scale transformations on the data. Finally, we add the axes and gridlines by calling the *setAxesGridlines* function and create the chart using the processed data.

Let us consider an example that demonstrates how to create stock charts using the preceding function. Add a new controller named *TechanChartsController.cs* to the *Controllers* folder and replace its content with the following code:

```
using Chapter06.Models;
using Microsoft.AspNetCore.Mvc;
using System;
using System.Threading.Tasks;

namespace Chapter06.Controllers
{
    public class TechanChartsController : Controller
    {
        private readonly StockPriceDbContext _context;
        public TechanChartsController(StockPriceDbContext context)
        {
            _context = context;
        }

        // GET: /<controller>/
        public IActionResult Index()
        {
            return View();
        }

        //GET:
        public async Task<IActionResult> StockChart()
```

```
        {
            ViewBag.Title = "Techan Stock Charts";
            StockPriceViewModel model = new StockPriceViewModel();
            model.Ticker = "SPY";
            model.StartDate = DateTime.Parse("1/1/2016");
            model.EndDate = DateTime.Parse("3/1/2016");
            string dataSource = string.Empty;
            model.PriceJson = await Task.Run(() => ModelHelper.TechanStockData(
                _context, model.Ticker, model.StartDate, model.EndDate,
                out dataSource));
            ViewBag.DataSource = "Data Source: " + dataSource;
            return View(model);
        }

        [HttpPost]
        [ValidateAntiForgeryToken]
        public async Task<IActionResult> StockChart(StockPriceViewModel model)
        {
            string dataSource = string.Empty;
            model.PriceJson = await Task.Run(() => ModelHelper.TechanStockData(
                _context, model.Ticker, model.StartDate, model.EndDate,
                out dataSource));
            ViewBag.DataSource = "Data Source: " + dataSource;
            return View(model);
        }
    }
}
```

The GET and POST methods simply set up the view model, retrieve data from database, and convert the data into JSON format using the *TechanStockData* method implemented in the *ModelHelper* class.

Add a new folder named *TechanCharts* to the *Views* folder. Add a new view *StockChart.cshtml* to the *Views/TechanCharts* folder and replace its content with the following code:

```
@model Chapter06.Models.StockPriceViewModel
@{
    ViewData["Title"] = ViewBag.Title;
}
<h3>@ViewBag.Title</h3>
@Html.Partial("_Links")
<form asp-action="StockChart">
    @Html.Partial("~/Views/GoogleCharts/_SpecifyTicker.cshtml", Model)
</form>
<hr />

<div class="container">
    <p>@ViewBag.DataSource</p>
    <div class="row">
        <div class="col-sm-12">
            <svg id="svg1"></svg>
        </div>
    </div>
    <div class="row">
        <div class="col-sm-12">
            <svg id="svg2"></svg>
        </div>
    </div>
```

```
        </div>
        <div class="row">
            <div class="col-sm-12">
                <svg id="svg3"></svg>
            </div>
        </div>
    </div>

    @section scripts{
    <script>
        var data = @(Html.Raw(Model.PriceJson));
        var options = {
            chartType: "ohlc",
            title: "Stock Price (ohlc): " + "@Model.Ticker",
            width: 800
        }
        drawTechanChart("#svg1", data, options);
        options.chartType = "candlestick";
        options.title = "Stock Price (candlestick): " + "@Model.Ticker";
        drawTechanChart("#svg2", data, options);
        options.chartType = "volume";
        options.title = "Volume: " + "@Model.Ticker";
        options.isGridline = false;
        drawTechanChart("#svg3", data, options);
    </script>
    }
```

Note that this view also uses the partial view named _SpecifyTicker.cshtml implemented previously in the *Views/GoogleCharts* folder by specifying its full path. You can see how easy it is to create three stock charts (ohlc, candlestick, and volume) using the *drawTechanChart* function implemented in the *site.js* file. You need to simply specify the SVG container, retrieve data from our view model, and set corresponding optional parameters, and you are done. Following the similar procedure presented here, you can gradually build up your own preset charting library that can be used to create various stock charts using a simple function call.

Running this example, selecting the *Techan Stock Charts* tab, and clicking the *Stock Charts* link generate results shown in Figures 6-6, 6-7, and 6-8.

Figure 6-6. Demonstration of an ohlc chart.

Stock Price (candlestick): SPY

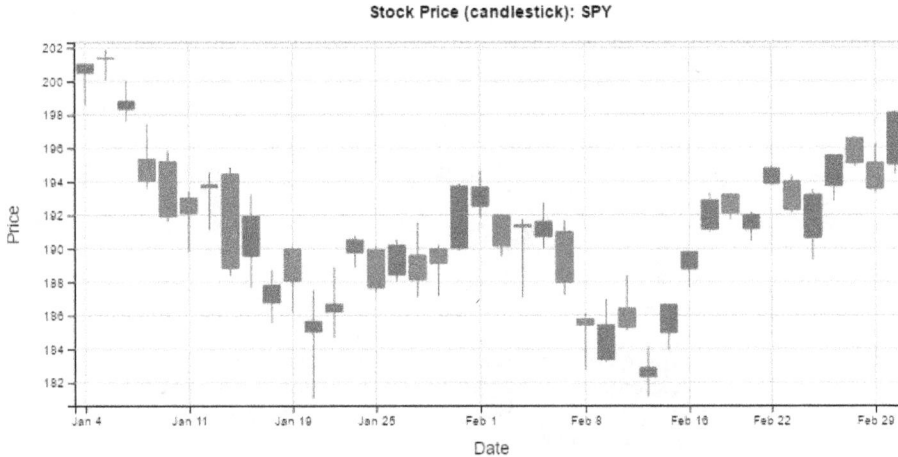

Figure 6-7. Demonstration of a candlestick chart.

Volume: SPY

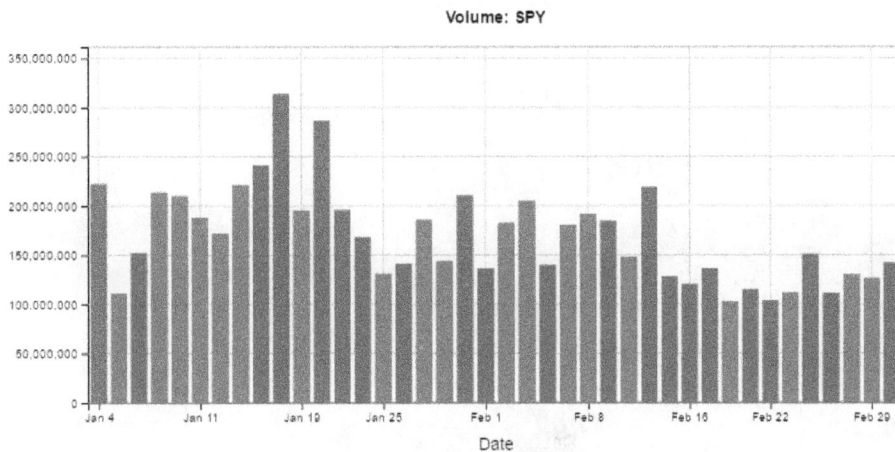

Figure 6-8. Demonstration of a volume chart.

Zooming and Panning Stock Charts

You can interact with the stock charts through zooming and panning. Add a new JavaScript function named *zoomPanChart* to the site.js:

```
function zoomPanChart(svgSelection, data, options) {
    var chartType = options.chartType || "candlestick";
    var width = options.width || 600;
    var height = options.height || 400;
    var margin = options.margin ||
                { top: 60, right: 20, bottom: 60, left: 100 };

    var xy = setChartArea(svgSelection, width, height, margin);
    var parseDate = d3.timeParse("%d-%b-%y");
    var plot, accessor;
```

```
var title, ylabel;

if (chartType === "ohlc") {
    plot = techan.plot.ohlc().xScale(xy.x).yScale(xy.y);
    accessor = plot.accessor();
    title = options.title || "Stock Price";
    ylabel = options.ylabel || "Price";
} else if (chartType === "candlestick") {
    plot = techan.plot.candlestick().xScale(xy.x).yScale(xy.y);
    accessor = plot.accessor();
    title = options.title || "Stock Price";
    ylabel = options.ylabel || "Price";
} else if (chartType === "volume") {
    plot = techan.plot.volume().accessor(techan.accessor.ohlc())
                .xScale(xy.x).yScale(xy.y);
    accessor = plot.accessor();
    title = options.title || "Volume";
    ylabel = options.ylabel || "";
}

var zoom = d3.zoom().on("zoom", zoomed);
var zoomInit;
var xAxis = d3.axisBottom(xy.x);
var yAxis = d3.axisLeft(xy.y);

xy.svg.append("clipPath")
    .attr("id", "clip")
    .append("rect")
    .attr("x", 0)
    .attr("y", xy.y(1))
    .attr("width", xy.w)
    .attr("height", xy.y(0) - xy.y(1));

xy.svg.append("text")
    .attr("x", xy.w / 2)
    .attr("y", (-margin.top / 2))
    .attr("text-anchor", "middle")
    .attr("font-weight", "bold")
    .attr("font-size", "14px")
    .text(title);

xy.svg.append("g")
    .attr("class", "x axis")
    .attr("transform", "translate(0," + xy.h + ")");

xy.svg.append("text")
    .attr("transform", "translate(" + xy.w / 2 + "," +
        (xy.h + 2 * margin.bottom / 3) + ")")
    .style("text-anchor", "middle")
    .text("Date");

xy.svg.append("g")
    .attr("class", "y axis");

xy.svg.append("text")
```

```
            .attr("transform", "translate(" + (-margin.left / 1.5) + "," +
                xy.h / 2 + ") rotate(-90)")
            .attr("y", 6)
            .attr("dy", ".71em")
            .style("text-anchor", "end")
            .text(ylabel);

    xy.svg.append("rect")
        .attr("class", "pane")
        .attr("width", xy.w)
        .attr("height", xy.h)
        .call(zoom);

    data = data.map(function (d) {
        return {
            date: parseDate(d.Date),
            open: +d.Open,
            high: +d.High,
            low: +d.Low,
            close: +d.Close,
            volume: +d.Volume
        };
    }).sort(function (a, b) { return d3.ascending(
        accessor.d(a), accessor.d(b)); });

    xy.x.domain(data.map(accessor.d));
    if (chartType === "volume") {
        xy.y.domain(techan.scale.plot.volume(data, plot.accessor().v).domain());
    } else {
        xy.y.domain(techan.scale.plot.ohlc(data, accessor).domain());
    }

    xy.svg.append("g")
        .attr("class", "plot")
        .attr("clip-path", "url(#clip)")
        .datum(data);
    draw();
    zoomInit = xy.x.zoomable().clamp(false).copy();

    function zoomed() {
        var rescaleY = d3.event.transform.rescaleY(xy.y);
        yAxis.scale(rescaleY);
        plot.yScale(rescaleY);
        xy.x.zoomable().domain(d3.event.transform.rescaleX(zoomInit).domain());
        draw();
    }

    function draw() {
        xy.svg.select("g.plot").call(plot);
        xy.svg.select("g.x.axis").call(xAxis);
        xy.svg.select("g.y.axis").call(yAxis);
    }
}
```

This code uses the *d3.zoom* function to zoom and pan the chart. This function consists of two sub functions: *zoomed* and *draw*. Inside the zoomed function, we rescale *x* and *y* values and redraw the chart by calling the *draw* function.

Running this example produces three stock charts: ohlc, candlestick, and volume. All of these charts allow you to zoom and pan. Figures 6-9 shows an ohlc chart with the zooming- and panning-capability.

Figure 6-9. Zooming and panning an ohlc chart.

Stock Charts with Crosshair

Crosshair is a pair of thin vertical and horizontal lines, moving with the mouse in a chart. It is useful when you need to get the particular data of an action, while the axes contain any other information, such as years/months or any kind of percentage. It makes easy for you to access a specific point and get information about it with the crosshair on a chart.

Add a new JavaScript function named *setCrosshair* to the *site.js* file:

```
function setCrosshair(xy, margin) {
    var xAxis = d3.axisBottom(xy.x);
    var yAxis = d3.axisLeft(xy.y);
    var xTopAxis = d3.axisTop(xy.x);
    var yRightAxis = d3.axisRight(xy.y);

    var yAnnotation = techan.plot.axisannotation()
        .axis(yAxis)
        .orient('left')
        .format(d3.format(',.2f'));

    var yRightAnnotation = techan.plot.axisannotation()
        .axis(yRightAxis)
        .orient('right')
        .format(d3.format(',.2f'))
        .translate([xy.w, 0]);
```

```
var xAnnotation = techan.plot.axisannotation()
    .axis(xAxis)
    .orient('bottom')
    .format(d3.timeFormat('%Y-%m-%d'))
    .width(80)
    .translate([0, xy.h]);

var xTopAnnotation = techan.plot.axisannotation()
    .axis(xTopAxis)
    .orient('top')
    .format(d3.timeFormat('%Y-%m-%d'))
    .width(80);

var coordsText = xy.svg.append('text')
    .style("text-anchor", "end")
    .attr("class", "coords")
    .attr("x", xy.w - 5)
    .attr("y", 15);

var crosshair = techan.plot.crosshair()
    .xScale(xy.x)
    .yScale(xy.y)
    .xAnnotation([xAnnotation, xTopAnnotation])
    .yAnnotation([yAnnotation, yRightAnnotation])
    .on("enter", enter)
    .on("out", out)
    .on("move", move);

xy.svg.append('g')
    .attr("class", "crosshair")
    .datum({ x: xy.x.domain(), y: 0 })
    .call(crosshair)
    .each(function (d) { move(d); });

function enter() {
    coordsText.style("display", "inline");
}

function out() {
    coordsText.style("display", "none");
}

function move(coords) {
    coordsText.text(
        xAnnotation.format()(coords.x) + ", " +
        yAnnotation.format()(coords.y)
    );
}
}
```

This code first creates axis annotation for each of four axes (top, right, bottom, and left) using the *techan.plot.axisannotation* function. It then creates a crosshair by calling the *techan.plot.crosshair* function. Note that the crosshair object connects with the axis annotations and mouse events: *enter*, *out*, and *move*.

Add a new function named *drawCrosshair* to the *site.js* file:

```
function drawCrosshair(svgSelection, data, options) {
    var chartType = options.chartType || "candlestick";
    var isGridline = options.isGridline || true;
    var width = options.width || 600;
    var height = options.height || 400;
    var margin = options.margin ||
                    { top: 60, right: 100, bottom: 60, left: 100 };

    var xy = setChartArea(svgSelection, width, height, margin);
    var parseDate = d3.timeParse("%d-%b-%y");
    var plot, accessor;
    var title, ylabel;

    if (chartType === "ohlc") {
        plot = techan.plot.ohlc().xScale(xy.x).yScale(xy.y);
        accessor = plot.accessor();
        title = options.title || "Stock Price";
        ylabel = options.ylabel || "Price";
    } else if (chartType === "candlestick") {
        plot = techan.plot.candlestick().xScale(xy.x).yScale(xy.y);
        accessor = plot.accessor();
        title = options.title || "Stock Price";
        ylabel = options.ylabel || "Price";
    } else if (chartType === "volume") {
        plot = techan.plot.volume().accessor(
            techan.accessor.ohlc()).xScale(xy.x).yScale(xy.y);
        accessor = plot.accessor();
        title = options.title || "Volume";
        ylabel = options.ylabel || "";
    }

    data = data.map(function (d) {
        return {
            date: parseDate(d.Date),
            open: +d.Open,
            high: +d.High,
            low: +d.Low,
            close: +d.Close,
            volume: +d.Volume
        };
    }).sort(function (a, b) { return d3.ascending(
                            accessor.d(a), accessor.d(b)); });

    xy.x.domain(data.map(accessor.d));
    if (chartType === "volume") {
        xy.y.domain(techan.scale.plot.volume(data, plot.accessor().v).domain());
    } else {
        xy.y.domain(techan.scale.plot.ohlc(data, accessor).domain());
    }

    set4Axes(xy, margin, title, ylabel, isGridline);

    xy.svg.append("g")
        .attr("class", "plot")
```

```
            .datum(data)
            .call(plot);

        setCrosshair(xy, margin);
}
```

This function is very similar to the *drawTechanChart* function, except that here we use four axes by calling the *set4Axes* function and add a crosshair to the chart using the *setCrosshair* function.

We can test this function by adding a new view named *Crosshair.cshtml* to the *Views/TechanCharts* folder. Here is the code for this view:

```
@model Chapter06.Models.StockPriceViewModel
@{
    ViewData["Title"] = ViewBag.Title;
}
<h3>@ViewBag.Title</h3>
@Html.Partial("_Links")

<form asp-action="Crosshair">
    @Html.Partial("~/Views/GoogleCharts/_SpecifyTicker.cshtml", Model)
</form>

<hr />

<div class="container">
    <p>@ViewBag.DataSource</p>
    <div class="row">
        <div class="col-sm-12">
            <svg id="svg1"></svg>
        </div>
    </div>
    <div class="row">
        <div class="col-sm-12">
            <svg id="svg2"></svg>
        </div>
    </div>
    <div class="row">
        <div class="col-sm-12">
            <svg id="svg3"></svg>
        </div>
    </div>
</div>

@section scripts{
<script>
    var data = @(Html.Raw(Model.PriceJson));

    var options = {
        chartType: "ohlc",
        width: 800
    }
    drawCrosshair("#svg1", data, options);
    options.chartType = "candlestick";
    drawCrosshair("#svg2", data, options);
    options.chartType = "volume";
```

```
        drawCrosshair("#svg3", data, options);
    </script>
    }
```

You need also to add corresponding GET and POST methods in the *TechanChartsController.cs* file to make this view work. This view creates three stock charts (ohlc, candlestick, and volume) with crosshair. Figure 6-10 shows a candlestick chart with the crosshair capability.

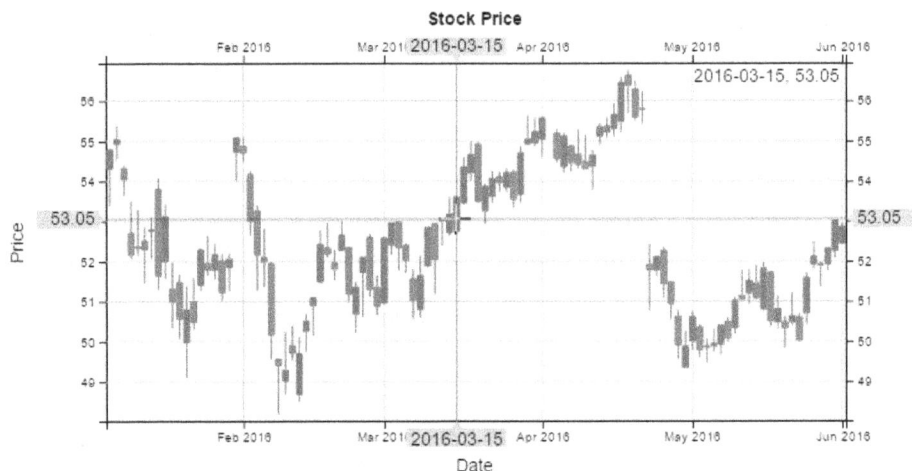

Figure 6-10. Demonstration of a candlestick chart with crosshair.

You can see that a crosshair moves with your mouse inside the chart and the corresponding *x*-, *y*-values are displayed on the corresponding coordinate axes.

Combination Charts and Indicators

In the preceding sections, we created several individual stock charts. You can also create combination charts easily using TechanJS.

Price and Volume Charts

One of the popular stock combination charts is the price and volume chart. Add two new JavaScript functions, *drawPriceVolume* and *setVolumeAxis* to the *site.js* file:

```
function drawPriceVolume(svgSelection, data, options) {
    var title = options.title || "Stock Price";
    var ylabel = options.ylabel || "Price";
    var chartType = options.chartType || "candlestick";
    var width = options.width || 600;
    var height = options.height || 400;
    var margin = options.margin || { top: 40, right: 20, bottom: 60, left: 70 };
    var isGridline = options.isGridline || true;

    var xy = setChartArea(svgSelection, width, height, margin);

    var parseDate = d3.timeParse("%d-%b-%y");
```

```
        var plot, accessor;

        if (chartType === "ohlc") {
            plot = techan.plot.ohlc().xScale(xy.x).yScale(xy.y);
            accessor = plot.accessor();
        } else if (chartType === "candlestick") {
            plot = techan.plot.candlestick().xScale(xy.x).yScale(xy.y);
            accessor = plot.accessor();
        }
        var volume = techan.plot.volume().accessor(accessor)
                            .xScale(xy.x).yScale(xy.yVolume);

        data = data.map(function (d) {
            return {
                date: parseDate(d.Date),
                open: +d.Open,
                high: +d.High,
                low: +d.Low,
                close: +d.Close,
                volume: +d.Volume
            };
        }).sort(function (a, b) { return d3.ascending(
                                accessor.d(a), accessor.d(b)); });

        xy.x.domain(data.map(accessor.d));
        xy.y.domain(techan.scale.plot.ohlc(data, accessor).domain());
        xy.yVolume.domain(techan.scale.plot.volume(data).domain());

        setAxesGridlines(xy, margin, title, ylabel, isGridline);
        setVolumeAxis(xy);

        xy.svg.append("g")
            .attr("class", "plot")
            .datum(data)
            .call(plot);

        xy.svg.append("g")
            .attr("class", "volume")
            .datum(data)
            .call(volume);

        return { xy, data };
    }

    function setVolumeAxis(xy) {
        var volumeAxis = d3.axisRight(xy.yVolume).ticks(3)
                            .tickFormat(d3.format(",.3s"));
        xy.svg.append("g")
            .attr("class", "volume axis")
            .call(volumeAxis);
    }
```

The *setVolumeAxis* function simply creates a volume axis. The *drawPriceVolume* function is similar to the *drawTechChart* function, except that we add the volume to the price chart to produce a price and volume combination chart.

Moving Averages and Bollinger Bands

We can easily add moving averages and Bollinger bands to the price chart. Add the following two JavaScript functions to the *site.js* file:

```
function drawMaChart(svgSelection, data, options) {
    var title = options.title || "Stock Price";
    var ylabel = options.ylabel || "Price";
    var chartType = options.chartType || "candlestick";
    var width = options.width || 800;
    var height = options.height || 400;
    var margin = options.margin || { top: 40, right: 20, bottom: 60, left: 70 };
    var isGridline = options.isGridline || true;
    var xy = drawPriceVolume(svgSelection, data, options);
    var sma0 = techan.plot.sma()
        .xScale(xy.xy.x)
        .yScale(xy.xy.y);
    var ema1 = techan.plot.ema()
        .xScale(xy.xy.x)
        .yScale(xy.xy.y);
    xy.xy.svg.append("g")
        .attr("class", "indicator sma ma0")
        .datum(techan.indicator.sma().period(20)(xy.data))
        .call(sma0);
    xy.xy.svg.append("g")
        .attr("class", "indicator ema ma1")
        .datum(techan.indicator.ema().period(50)(xy.data))
        .call(ema1);
}

function drawBollingerBands(svgSelection, data, options) {
    var title = options.title || "Stock Price";
    var ylabel = options.ylabel || "Price";
    var chartType = options.chartType || "candlestick";
    var width = options.width || 800;
    var height = options.height || 400;
    var margin = options.margin || { top: 40, right: 20, bottom: 60, left: 70 };
    var isGridline = options.isGridline || true;
    var xy = drawPriceVolume(svgSelection, data, options);
    var band = techan.plot.bollinger()
        .xScale(xy.xy.x)
        .yScale(xy.xy.y);
    xy.xy.svg.append("g")
        .attr("class", "bollinger")
        .datum(techan.indicator.bollinger().period(20)(xy.data))
        .call(band);
}
```

The *drawMaChart* function adds two moving averages to the price and volume combination charts: one is the simple moving average (*sma*) with a period of 20 days and the other one is the exponential moving average (*ema*) with a period of 50 days. While the *drawBollingerBands* function adds *Bollinger* bands with a period of 20 days to the price and volume combination chart.

MACD and RSI

We can also create technical indicators, such as MACD and RSI, using TechanJS. Add the following functions to the *site.js* file:

```
function drawMacd(svgSelection, data, options) {
    var title = options.title || "MACD";
    var ylabel = options.ylabel || "Macd Value";
    var width = options.width || 600;
    var height = options.height || 200;
    var margin = options.margin || { top: 20, right: 20, bottom: 60, left: 70 };
    var isGridline = options.isGridline || true;

    var xy = setChartArea(svgSelection, width, height, margin);
    var parseDate = d3.timeParse("%d-%b-%y");

    var macd = techan.plot.macd().xScale(xy.x).yScale(xy.y);
    var accessor = macd.accessor();

    data = data.map(function (d) {
        return {
            date: parseDate(d.Date),
            open: +d.Open,
            high: +d.High,
            low: +d.Low,
            close: +d.Close,
            volume: +d.Volume
        };
    }).sort(function (a, b) { return d3.ascending(
                        accessor.d(a), accessor.d(b)); });
    macdData = techan.indicator.macd()(data);
    xy.x.domain(data.map(accessor.d));
    xy.y.domain(techan.scale.plot.macd(macdData).domain());
    setAxesGridlines(xy, margin, title, ylabel, isGridline);

    xy.svg.append("g")
        .attr("class", "macd")
        .datum(macdData)
        .call(macd);
}

function drawRsi(svgSelection, data, options) {
    var title = options.title || "RSI";
    var ylabel = options.ylabel || "RSI Value";
    var width = options.width || 600;
    var height = options.height || 200;
    var margin = options.margin || { top: 20, right: 20, bottom: 60, left: 70 };
    var isGridline = options.isGridline || true;

    var xy = setChartArea(svgSelection, width, height, margin);
    var parseDate = d3.timeParse("%d-%b-%y");
    var rsi = techan.plot.rsi().xScale(xy.x).yScale(xy.y);
    var accessor = rsi.accessor();

    data = data.map(function (d) {
        return {
```

```
                    date: parseDate(d.Date),
                    open: +d.Open,
                    high: +d.High,
                    low: +d.Low,
                    close: +d.Close,
                    volume: +d.Volume
            };
        }).sort(function (a, b) { return d3.ascending(
                                accessor.d(a), accessor.d(b)); });
        rsiData = techan.indicator.rsi()(data);
        xy.x.domain(data.map(accessor.d));
        xy.y.domain(techan.scale.plot.rsi(rsiData).domain());
        setAxesGridlines(xy, margin, title, ylabel, isGridline);

        xy.svg.append("g")
            .attr("class", "rsi")
            .datum(rsiData)
            .call(rsi);
    }
```

These two functions have the similar code structure, and can be used to create the MACD and RSI indicators.

Creating Charts

In this section, we will use an example to illustrate how to create various combination charts and indicators using the helper functions implemented in the preceding sections.

Add a new view named *CombinedChart.cshtml* to the *Views/TechanCharts* folder and replace its content with the following code:

```
@model Chapter06.Models.StockPriceViewModel
@{
    ViewData["Title"] = ViewBag.Title;
}
<h3>@ViewBag.Title</h3>
@Html.Partial("_Links")

<form asp-action="CombinedChart">
    @Html.Partial("~/Views/GoogleCharts/_SpecifyTicker.cshtml", Model)
</form>
<hr />

<style>
    path.volume.up {
        fill: green;
        opacity: 0.3;
    }

    path.volume.down {
        fill: red;
        opacity: 0.3;
    }

    .indicator path.line {
```

```
        fill: none;
        stroke-width: 2;
}

.ma0 path.line {
        stroke: #1f77b4;
}

.ma1 path.line {
        stroke: #ff7f0e;
}

.bollinger path {
        fill: none;
        stroke-width: 1;
}

.bollinger path.upper {
        stroke: #0000AA;
}

.bollinger path.lower {
        stroke: #0000AA;
}

.bollinger path.middle {
        stroke: green;
}

path {
        fill: none;
        stroke-width: 1;
}

path.macd {
        stroke: blue;
}

path.signal {
        stroke: red;
}

path.zero {
        stroke: gray;
        stroke-dasharray: 0;
        stroke-opacity: 0.5;
}

path.difference {
        fill: gray;
        opacity: 0.5;
}

.rsi path {
        fill: none;
```

```
            stroke-width: 1;
        }

        .rsi {
            stroke: #000000;
        }

        .rsi path.overbought, .rsi path.oversold {
            stroke: #FF9999;
            stroke-dasharray: 5, 5;
        }

        .rsi path.middle, path.zero {
            stroke: #BBBBBB;
            stroke-dasharray: 5, 5;
        }
</style>

<div class="container">
    <p>@ViewBag.DataSource</p>
    <div class="row">
        <div class="col-sm-12">
            <svg id="svg1"></svg>
        </div>
    </div>
    <div class="row">
        <div class="col-sm-12">
            <svg id="svg2"></svg>
        </div>
    </div>
    <div class="row">
        <div class="col-sm-12">
            <svg id="svg3"></svg>
        </div>
    </div>
    <div class="row">
        <div class="col-sm-12">
            <svg id="svg4"></svg>
        </div>
    </div>
    <div class="row">
        <div class="col-sm-12">
            <svg id="svg5"></svg>
        </div>
    </div>
</div>

@section scripts{
<script>
    var data = @(Html.Raw(Model.PriceJson));
    var options = {
        chartType: "candlestick",
        title: "Stock Price + Volume: " + "@Model.Ticker",
        width: 800
    }
```

```
    drawPriceVolume("#svg1", data, options);
    options.title = "Stock Price + Volume + SMA + EMA: " + "@Model.Ticker";
    drawMaChart("#svg2", data, options);
    options.title = "Stock Price + Volume + Bollinger Bands: " +
                    "@Model.Ticker";
    drawBollingerBands("#svg3", data, options);
    options.title = "MACD: " + "@Model.Ticker";
    drawMacd("#svg4", data, options);
    options.title = "RSI: " + "@Model.Ticker";
    drawRsi("#svg5", data, options);
  </script>
}
```

Note that the code includes a CSS style that is used to control the appearance of the various charts we are going to create. Here, we create five stock charts, as shown in Figures 6-11, 6-12, 6-13, and 6-14.

Using the procedure presented here, you can easily build a stock charting library with a variety of preset chart types. You can then pass the data to this library and get a professional stock chart.

Figure 6-11. Demonstration of a price and volume chart.

Figure 6-12. Price and volume chart with SMA and EMA.

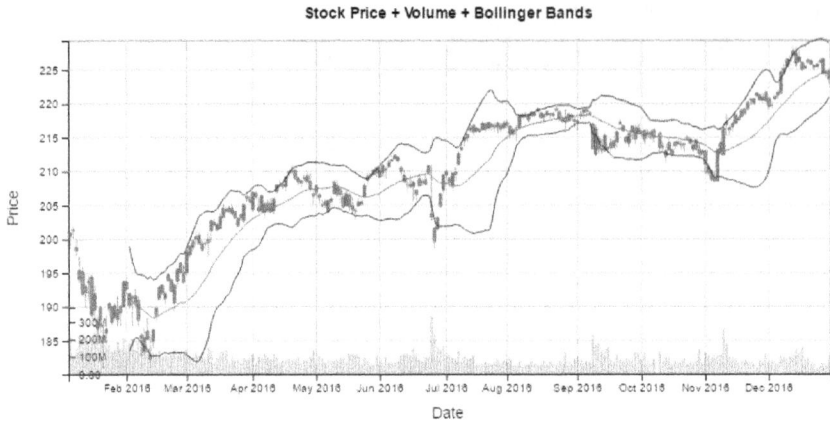

Figure 6-13. A price and volume chart with Bollinger bands.

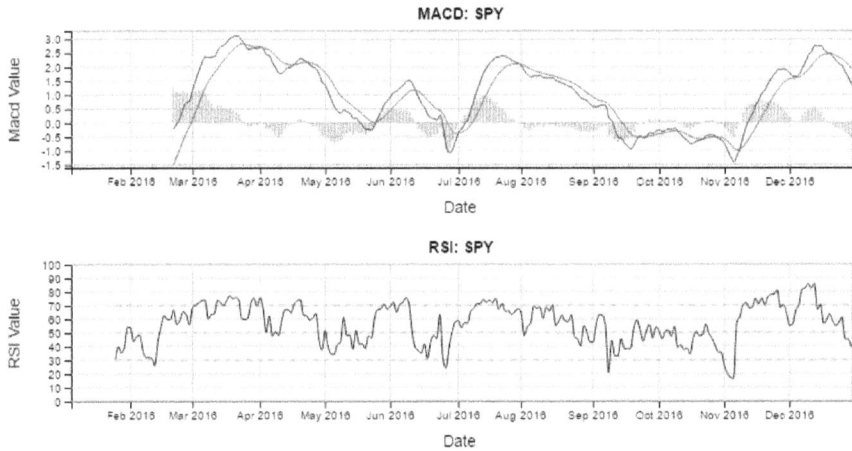

Figure 6-14. Technical indicators: MACD (top) and RSI (bottom).

Chapter 7
3D Graphics with WebGL

WebGL (Web Graphics Library) is a JavaScript API for rendering interactive 3D graphics within modern web browsers without the use of plug-ins. It is based on OpenGL ES 2.0 that can be used in HTML5 *<canvas>* element. WebGL takes advantage of the graphics hardware to accelerate the rendering and enables the display and manipulation of 3D graphics on web pages by using JavaScript. We can use WebGL to create rich user interfaces and 3D games and to use 3D to visualize a variety of information from the internet.

There are several advantages of using WebGL. WebGL applications are written in JavaScript. Using these applications, you can directly interact with other elements of the HTML document. You can also use other JavaScript libraries and HTML technologies to enrich the WebGL application. WebGL also supports mobile browsers, including iOS safari, Android Browser, and Chrome for Android. It is an open source, meaning that you can access the source code of the library and understand how it works and how it was developed. Since WebGL is integrated within HTML5, there is no need for additional set up. To develop a WebGL application, all that you need is a text editor and a web browser.

WebGL Basics

WebGL use both HTML and JavaScript to create and draw 3D graphics on the screen. To do this, WebGL utilizes the new *<canvas>* element, introduced in HTML5, which defines a drawing area on a web page. The *<canvas>* element provides an easy and powerful option to draw graphics using JavaScript.

WebGL is a low-level rasterization API rather than a 3D API. It draws primitives, such as points, lines, and triangles based on code you supply. Getting WebGL to do anything else is up to you to provide code that uses those primitives to accomplish your task. WebGL runs on the GPU on your computer, so you need to provide the code that runs on that GPU. That code should be in the form of pairs of functions. We consider those two functions as a vertex shader and a fragment shader, and they are each written in a very strictly types C/C++ like language called GLSL (GL Shader Language).

The vertex shader's job is to compute vertex positions. WebGL uses the computed vertex positions to rasterize various kinds of primitives including points, lines, and triangles. When rasterizing these primitives, WebGL calls the second fragment shader function whose job is to calculate a color for each pixel of the primitive currently being drawn.

Nearly all of the entire WebGL API is about setting up state for these pairs of functions to run. For each graphics object you want to draw, you setup a bunch of state then execute a pair of functions by calling *gl.drawArray* or *gl.drawElements* that executes your shaders on the GPU.

3D Rendering

WebGL uses the HTML5 canvas element to get 3D graphics into the browser page. In order to render WebGL into a page, your application should at least perform the following steps:

- Create a canvas element.
- Obtain a drawing context for the canvas.
- Initialize the viewport.
- Create buffers containing the data to be rendered.
- Create matrix to define the transformation from vertex buffers to screen space.
- Create shaders to implement the drawing algorithm.
- Initialize the shaders with parameters.
- Draw your graphics.

Canvas and Drawing Context

You can see that the first thing you need in order to use WebGL to render in 3D is a canvas. The following HTML code snippet establishes a canvas:

```
<canvas id="glCanvas" width="300" height="300"></canvas>
```

You can then get the DOM object associated with the canvas using the *document.getElementById* function:

```
var canvas = document.getElementById("glCanvas");
```

The following code snippet shows how to get the WebGL context from a canvas element:

```
function initWebGL(canvas) {
    gl = null;

    // Try to get the standard context. If it fails,
    // fallback to experimental.
    gl = canvas.getContext('webgl') || canvas.getContext('experimental-webgl');

    // If we don't have a GL context, give up now
    if (!gl) {
        alert('Unable to initialize WebGL. Your browser may not support it.');
    }

    return gl;
}
```

The *getContext* function can take one of the following context if string: "2d" for a 2D canvas context, "webgl" for a WebGL context, or "experimental-webgl" to get a WebGL context for earlier-version browsers. To obtain a WebGL context for a canvas, we request the context named "*webgl*" from the canvas. If this fails, we try the name *"experimental-webgl"*. If that, too, fails, we display an alert letting the user know they appear not to have WebGL support. At this point, *gl* is either null (meaning there is no WebGL context available) or is a reference to the WebGL context into which we will be rendering.

Once you have obtained a valid WegGL context from the canvas element, you need to create a *viewport* that is a rectangular bound of where to draw. You can set up a *viewport* easily by calling the context's *viewport* function:

```
function initViewport(gl, canvas) {
    gl.viewport (0, 0, canvas.width, canvas.height);
}
```

Here, we initialize the viewport to take up the entire contents of the canvas's display area. Once we created a viewport, we can start rendering into it. The simplest graphics object we can do is to draw a simple primitive object: a triangle. WebGL uses arrays of data, called buffers, to draw primitives.

Vertex Buffers

The following code snippet defines the vertex buffer data for a triangle object:

```
// vertex data for a triangle
function createObj(gl) {
    var vertexBuffer = gl.createBuffer();
    gl.bindBuffer(gl.ARRAY_BUFFER, vertexBuffer);
    var verts = [
        0.0,  1.0, 0.0,
       -1.0, -1.0, 0.0,
        1.0, -1.0, 0.0,
    ];
    gl.bufferData(gl.ARRAY_BUFFER, new Float32Array(verts), gl.STATIC_DRAW);
    var obj = { buffer: vertexBuffer, vertSize: 3, nVerts: 3,
                primtype: gl.TRIANGLES };
    return obj;
}
```

This function defines the vertex buffer data, the size of a vertex structure, the number of vertices to be drawn, and the triangle primitive type that will be used to draw the triangle object. Note that we use *Float32Array* as a type of *ArrayBuffer*, which is a JavaScript type that stores binary data. You can access typed arrays using the same syntax as ordinary arrays, but they are much faster and consume less memory.

Transform Matrices

In order to display 3D objects on a 2D screen, we must perform a series of transformations on the 3D objects. We usually use two transformation matrices: *modelView* and *projection*. The *modelView* matrix controls the transition between the model and the camera. In our case, we are transforming the triangle object by translating it by 5 units along the negative *z*-axis. While the *projection* matrix changes the geometry of 3D objects from the camera space into the 2D *viewport* and applies perspective distortion to the objects.

However, JavaScript does not have any built-in support to handle matrices and vectors. The JavaScript data type that is closest to a matrix or a vector is the array object. You can either write your own functionality to handle matrices and vectors in JavaScript or you can use one of the open source libraries that are available. The following three open source JavaScript matrix libraries are commonly used in WebGL applications: *Sylvester*, *WebGL-mjs*, and *glMatrix*. These three libraries are all relatively small and have similar functionality. In this book, we will use *glMatrix*, which can be installed by the *bower* package manager in Visual Studio 2017.

The following code snippet shows a sample matrix setup:

```
var projectionMatrix, modelViewMatrix;
function initMatrices(canvas) {
    // model view matrix with object at 0, 0, -5
    modelViewMatrix = mat4.create();
    mat4.translate(modelViewMatrix, modelViewMatrix, [0, 0, -5]);
    // project matrix with 30 degree field of view
    projectionMatrix = mat4.create();
    mat4.perspective(projectionMatrix, Math.PI / 6,
        canvas.width / canvas.height, 1, 1000);
}
```

glMatrices are of type *mat4*, created with the function *mat4.create*. The function *initMatrices* creates the model view and projection matrices and stores them in the global variables *modelViewMatrix* and *projectionMatrix*, respectively.

Shaders

To get a realistic 3D scene, it is not enough to render objects at certain positions. You also need to take into account things like how the objects will look when light sources shines on them. We use *shading* to describe the process of determining the effect of light on different materials. In WebGL, the shading is done using a shader. WebGL requires you to supply a shader for each object. The shader can be used for multiple objects, so in practice it is often sufficient to implement one shader for the whole application, reusing it with different geometry and parameter values each time.

A WebGL shader includes two parts: the *vertex shader* and the *fragment shader*. The vertex *shader* is responsible for transforming the coordinates of the object into 2D display space. While the *fragment shader* is responsible for generating the final color output of each pixel for the transformed vertices, based on input such as color, texture, lighting, and materials. In WebGL, shader setup requires a sequence of steps, including compiling the individual pieces from GLSL source code, then linking them together. The following snippet shows a sample shader code:

```
function createShader(gl, str, type) {
    var shader;
    if (type == "fragment") {
        shader = gl.createShader(gl.FRAGMENT_SHADER);
    } else if (type == "vertex") {
        shader = gl.createShader(gl.VERTEX_SHADER);
    } else {
        return null;
    }
    gl.shaderSource(shader, str);
    gl.compileShader(shader);
    if (!gl.getShaderParameter(shader, gl.COMPILE_STATUS)) {
        alert(gl.getShaderInfoLog(shader));
        return null;
    }
    return shader;
```

```
}

var vertexShaderSource =
    "attribute vec3 vertexPos;\n" +
    "uniform mat4 modelViewMatrix;\n" +
    "uniform mat4 projectionMatrix;\n" +
    "void main(void) {\n" +
    "  gl_Position = projectionMatrix*modelViewMatrix*vec4(vertexPos, 1.0);\n" +
    "}\n";

var fragmentShaderSource =
    "void main(void) {\n" +
    "gl_FragColor = vec4(1.0, 1.0, 1.0, 1.0);\n" +
    "}\n";
```

This code defines a helper function *createShader* that uses WebGL functions to compile the vertex and fragment shaders from source code. The GLSL source code is supplied as JavaScript strings that we define as the global variables *vertexShaderSource* and *fragmentShaderSource*. Once the parts of the shader have been compiled, we need to link them together into a working program using the WebGL function *gl.createProgram*, *gl.attachShader*, and *gl.linkProgram*, as illustrated in the following code for the *initShader* function:

```
var shaderProgram, shaderVertexPositionAttribute, shaderProjectionMatrixUniform,
    shaderModelViewMatrixUniform;
function initShader(gl) {
    // load and compile the fragment and vertex shader
    var fragmentShader = createShader(gl, fragmentShaderSource, "fragment");
    var vertexShader = createShader(gl, vertexShaderSource, "vertex");
    // link them together into a new program
    shaderProgram = gl.createProgram();
    gl.attachShader(shaderProgram, vertexShader);
    gl.attachShader(shaderProgram, fragmentShader);
    gl.linkProgram(shaderProgram);
    // get pointers to the shader params
    shaderVertexPositionAttribute = gl.getAttribLocation(shaderProgram,
                                                         "vertexPos");
    gl.enableVertexAttribArray(shaderVertexPositionAttribute);
    shaderProjectionMatrixUniform = gl.getUniformLocation(shaderProgram,
                                                          "projectionMatrix");
    shaderModelViewMatrixUniform = gl.getUniformLocation(shaderProgram,
                                                         "modelViewMatrix");
    if (!gl.getProgramParameter(shaderProgram, gl.LINK_STATUS)) {
        alert("Could not initialise shaders");
    }
}
```

Drawing a Triangle

Now, we are ready to draw our triangle object. Open Visual Studio 2017 and start a new ASP.NET Core MVC project named *Chapter07*. Right click the project in the Solution Explorer and select *Manage Bower Packges...* to bring up the *Manage Bower Packages* window. Select the *Browse* tab, search for *gl-matrix* and install it. Add the library to the *Views/Shared/_Layout.cshtml* file:

```
<environment names="Development">
```

```html
<script src="~/lib/jquery/dist/jquery.js"></script>
<script src="~/lib/bootstrap/dist/js/bootstrap.js"></script>
<script src="~/lib/gl-matrix/dist/gl-matrix-min.js"></script>
<script src="~/js/site.js" asp-append-version="true"></script>
</environment>
```

Add a new controller named *Basic3DController.cs* to the *Controllers* folder and replace its content with the following code:

```csharp
using Microsoft.AspNetCore.Mvc;

namespace Chapter07.Controllers
{
    public class Basic3DController : Controller
    {
        // GET: /<controller>/
        public IActionResult Index()
        {
            ViewBag.Title = "Basic 3D Shapes: Home";
            return View();
        }

        public IActionResult Triangle()
        {
            ViewBag.Title = "Triangle";
            return View();
        }

        public IActionResult ColorTriangle()
        {
            ViewBag.Title = "Color Triangle";
            return View();
        }

        public IActionResult Square()
        {
            ViewBag.Title = "Square";
            return View();
        }

        public IActionResult TriangleStrip()
        {
            ViewBag.Title = "Triangle Strip";
            return View();
        }

        public IActionResult Cube()
        {
            ViewBag.Title = "Cube";
            return View();
        }
    }
}
```

Add a new folder named *Basic3D* to the *Views* folder. Add a new view named *Triangle.cshtml* to this new folder and replace its content with the following code:

```
@{
    ViewData["Title"] = ViewBag.Title;
}
<h3>@ViewBag.Title</h3>
@Html.Partial("_Links")

<div class="container">
    <div class="row" style="margin-top:50px">
        <div class="col-sm-12">
            <canvas id="glCanvas" width="300" height="300"></canvas>
        </div>
    </div>
</div>

@section scripts{
<script>
    function initWebGL(canvas) {

        ......

        return gl;
    }


    function initViewport(gl, canvas) {
        gl.viewport (0, 0, canvas.width, canvas.height);
    }

    var projectionMatrix, modelViewMatrix;
    function initMatrices(canvas) {

      ......

    }

    // vertex data for a triangle
    function createObj(gl) {

        ......

        return obj;
    }

    function createShader(gl, str, type) {

        ......

        return shader;
    }

    var vertexShaderSource = ......;

    var fragmentShaderSource = ......;

    var shaderProgram, shaderVertexPositionAttribute,
        shaderProjectionMatrixUniform, shaderModelViewMatrixUniform;
    function initShader(gl) {
```

```
        ......

    }

    function draw(gl, obj) {
        // clear the background
        gl.clearColor(0.7, 0.7, 0.7, 1.0);
        gl.clear(gl.COLOR_BUFFER_BIT);

        // set the vertex buffer to be drawn
        gl.bindBuffer(gl.ARRAY_BUFFER, obj.buffer);

        // set the shader to use
        gl.useProgram(shaderProgram);

        // vertex position and projection/model matrices
        gl.vertexAttribPointer(shaderVertexPositionAttribute,
                            obj.vertSize, gl.FLOAT, false, 0, 0);
        gl.uniformMatrix4fv(shaderProjectionMatrixUniform, false,
                        projectionMatrix);
        gl.uniformMatrix4fv(shaderModelViewMatrixUniform, false,
                        modelViewMatrix);

        // draw the object
        gl.drawArrays(obj.primtype, 0, obj.nVerts);
    }

    $(document).ready(
        function () {
            var canvas = document.getElementById("glCanvas");
            var gl = initWebGL(canvas);
            initViewport(gl, canvas);
            initMatrices(canvas);
            var obj = createObj(gl);
            initShader(gl);
            draw(gl, obj);
        }
    );
</script>
}
```

This view first uses the JavaScript functions implemented in the preceding sections to initialize viewport and context, create vertex buffer data, set up the transform matrices, and define the shader. It then implement a *draw* function that takes the WebGL context and our previously created triangle object as input arguments.

The *draw* function first clear the canvas with a gray background color. The method *gl.clearColor* sets the current clear color to gray. This function takes a 4-component RGBA. Note that WebGL's RGBA values are floating-point numbers in the range [0.0, 1.0], which is in contrast to the integer range [0,255] used for web color values. Next, it binds the vertex buffer for the triangle to be drawn, sets the shader that will be executed to draw the primitive, and connect the vertex buffer and matrices to the shader as inputs. Finally, the function calls the WebGL *drawArray* method to draw the triangle.

The code finally uses AJAX to call all of our implemented functions sequentially to draw our triangle object.

Running this example, selecting the *Basic 3D Shapes* tab, and clicking the *Triangle* link produce the result shown in Figure 7-1.

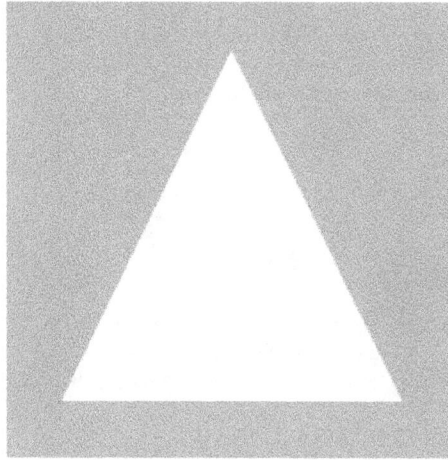

Figure 7-1. Triangle created using WebGL.

Helper Functions

From our triangle example discussed in the preceding section, it is clear that creating 3D objects in WebGL is very complex. To do anything more than the most basic 3D graphics using WebGL requires serious effort and literally thousands of lines of code. Different WebGL applications usually consist of a significant portion of repeated code. We can implement a helper library to avoid the repeated code.

Here, we will implement several commonly used helper functions in WebGL applications, which will be added to the *wwwroot/js/site.js* file.

Drawing Context

Add the following functions to the *site.js* file:

```
function initWebGL(canvas) {
    gl = null;

    // Try to grab the standard context. If it fails, fallback to experimental.
    gl = canvas.getContext('webgl') || canvas.getContext('experimental-webgl');

    // If we don't have a GL context, give up now
    if (!gl) {
        alert('Unable to initialize WebGL. Your browser may not support it.');
    }
    return gl;
}

function initViewport(gl, canvas) {
    gl.viewport(0, 0, canvas.width, canvas.height);
}
```

These two functions are common for almost all of the WebGL applications, so we put them to our JavaScript library.

Transform Matrices

Add a new function named *initMatrices* to the site.js file:

```
function initMatrices(canvas, options) {
    var angle = options.angle || 45;
    var isRotate = options.isRotate || false;
    var distance = options.distance || -3;

    angle = angle * Math.PI / 180;

    // Create a model view matrix with object at 0, 0, z
    var modelViewMatrix = mat4.create();
    mat4.translate(modelViewMatrix, modelViewMatrix, [0, 0, distance]);

    // Create a project matrix with angle:
    var projectionMatrix = mat4.create();
    mat4.perspective(projectionMatrix, angle, canvas.width / canvas.height,
                     1, 1000);

    if (!isRotate) {
        return { modelViewMatrix, projectionMatrix };
    }
    else {
        rotationAxis = vec3.create();
        vec3.normalize(rotationAxis, [1, 1, 1]);
        return { modelViewMatrix, projectionMatrix, rotationAxis };
    }
}
```

This function sets up more general transform matrices with optional parameters: angle, distance in the z-direction, and *isRotate* that is used to define a rotation axis. We also set the default values for these optional parameters.

Shader Functions

In the preceding triangle example, we only consider a black-white color shading. Here, we will define a more general shader.

Add the following shader string functions to the *site.js* file:

```
function shaderString(options) {
    var isColor = options.isColor || false;
    var ss;
    if (!isColor) {
        ss = bwShaderString();
    }
    else {
        ss = colorShaderString();
    }
    return ss;
```

```
}

function bwShaderString() {
    var vertexShaderSource =
        "attribute vec3 vertexPos;\n" +
        "uniform mat4 modelViewMatrix;\n" +
        "uniform mat4 projectionMatrix;\n" +
        "void main(void) {\n" +
        "    gl_Position = projectionMatrix*modelViewMatrix*vec4(
            vertexPos, 1.0);\n" +
        "}\n";
    var fragmentShaderSource =
        "void main(void) {\n" +
        "gl_FragColor = vec4(1.0, 1.0, 1.0, 1.0);\n" +
        "}\n";
    return { vertexShaderSource, fragmentShaderSource };
}

function colorShaderString() {
    var vertexShaderSource =
        " attribute vec3 vertexPos;\n" +
        " attribute vec4 vertexColor;\n" +
        " uniform mat4 modelViewMatrix;\n" +
        " uniform mat4 projectionMatrix;\n" +
        " varying vec4 vColor;\n" +
        " void main(void) {\n" +
        "     gl_Position = projectionMatrix*modelViewMatrix*vec4(
            vertexPos, 1.0);\n" +
        "     vColor = vertexColor;\n" +
        " }\n";

    var fragmentShaderSource =
        " precision mediump float;\n" +
        " varying vec4 vColor;\n" +
        " void main(void) {\n" +
        "     gl_FragColor = vColor;\n" +
        "}\n";
    return { vertexShaderSource, fragmentShaderSource };
}
```

Here, we define the black-white and color shader strings using two different functions: *bwShaderstring* and *colorShaderstring*, respectively. Note that the GLSL source code is supplied as JavaScript strings, where we define them as the variables *vertexShaderSource* and *fragmentShaderSource*. We also implement a common interface function *shaderString* with an *options* argument, and set the default value of *options.isColor* to *false* (i.e. the "black-white" shader string as default).

Next, add the following *createShader* and *initShader* functions to the *site.js* file:

```
function createShader(gl, str, type) {
    var shader;
    if (type == "fragment") {
        shader = gl.createShader(gl.FRAGMENT_SHADER);
    } else if (type == "vertex") {
        shader = gl.createShader(gl.VERTEX_SHADER);
    } else {
        return null;
```

```javascript
    }
    gl.shaderSource(shader, str);
    gl.compileShader(shader);
    if (!gl.getShaderParameter(shader, gl.COMPILE_STATUS)) {
        alert(gl.getShaderInfoLog(shader));
        return null;
    }
    return shader;
}

function initShader(gl, vertexShaderSource, fragmentShaderSource, options) {
    var isColor = options.isColor || false;

    // load and compile the fragment and vertex shader
    var fragmentShader = createShader(gl, fragmentShaderSource, "fragment");
    var vertexShader = createShader(gl, vertexShaderSource, "vertex");

    // link them together into a new program
    var shaderProgram = gl.createProgram();
    gl.attachShader(shaderProgram, vertexShader);
    gl.attachShader(shaderProgram, fragmentShader);
    gl.linkProgram(shaderProgram);

    // get pointers to the shader params
    var shaderVertexPositionAttribute = gl.getAttribLocation(
        shaderProgram, "vertexPos");
    gl.enableVertexAttribArray(shaderVertexPositionAttribute);

    //if color attribue is needed
    if (isColor) {
        var shaderVertexColorAttribute = gl.getAttribLocation(
            shaderProgram, "vertexColor");
        gl.enableVertexAttribArray(shaderVertexColorAttribute);
    }

    var shaderProjectionMatrixUniform = gl.getUniformLocation(
        shaderProgram, "projectionMatrix");
    var shaderModelViewMatrixUniform = gl.getUniformLocation(
        shaderProgram, "modelViewMatrix");

    if (!gl.getProgramParameter(shaderProgram,
        gl.LINK_STATUS)) {
        alert("Could not initialise shaders");
    }

    if (!isColor) {
        return { shaderProgram, shaderVertexPositionAttribute,
            shaderProjectionMatrixUniform, shaderModelViewMatrixUniform };
    } else {
        return { shaderProgram, shaderVertexPositionAttribute,
            shaderProjectionMatrixUniform, shaderModelViewMatrixUniform,
            shaderVertexColorAttribute };
    }
}
```

The *createShader* function uses WebGL functions to compile the vertex and fragment shaders from source code. Once the parts of the shader have been compiled, we need to link them together into a working program using the WebGL function *gl.createProgram*, *gl.attachShader*, and *gl.linkProgram*, as described in the *initShader* function. The *initShader* contains an optional parameter *options.isColor*, which controls whether we want to create a black-white shader or a color shader.

Drawing Functions

Add the following four drawing functions to the *site.js* file:

```
function drawBw(gl, obj, modelViewMatrix, projectionMatrix, shaderProgram,
    shaderVertexPositionAttribute, shaderProjectionMatrixUniform,
    shaderModelViewMatrixUniform) {

    // clear the background
    gl.clearColor(0.7, 0.7, 0.7, 1.0);
    gl.clear(gl.COLOR_BUFFER_BIT);

    // set the shader
    gl.useProgram(shaderProgram);

    // vertex buffer
    gl.bindBuffer(gl.ARRAY_BUFFER, obj.buffer);

    // vertex position and projection/model matrices
    gl.vertexAttribPointer(shaderVertexPositionAttribute,
        obj.vertSize, gl.FLOAT, false, 0, 0);
    gl.uniformMatrix4fv(shaderProjectionMatrixUniform, false, projectionMatrix);
    gl.uniformMatrix4fv(shaderModelViewMatrixUniform, false, modelViewMatrix);

    // draw the object
    gl.drawArrays(obj.primtype, 0, obj.nVerts);
}

function drawColor(gl, obj, modelViewMatrix, projectionMatrix, shaderProgram,
    shaderVertexPositionAttribute, shaderProjectionMatrixUniform,
    shaderModelViewMatrixUniform, shaderVertexColorAttribute) {

    // clear the background
    gl.clearColor(0.7, 0.7, 0.7, 1.0);
    gl.enable(gl.DEPTH_TEST);
    gl.clear(gl.COLOR_BUFFER_BIT | gl.DEPTH_BUFFER_BIT);

    // set the shader
    gl.useProgram(shaderProgram);

    // vertex buffer
    gl.bindBuffer(gl.ARRAY_BUFFER, obj.buffer);

    // vertex position and projection/model matrices
    gl.vertexAttribPointer(shaderVertexPositionAttribute,
        obj.vertSize, gl.FLOAT, false, 0, 0);
    gl.bindBuffer(gl.ARRAY_BUFFER, obj.colorBuffer);
    gl.vertexAttribPointer(shaderVertexColorAttribute, obj.colorSize,
```

```
            gl.FLOAT, false, 0, 0);
        gl.bindBuffer(gl.ELEMENT_ARRAY_BUFFER, obj.indices);
        gl.uniformMatrix4fv(shaderProjectionMatrixUniform, false, projectionMatrix);
        gl.uniformMatrix4fv(shaderModelViewMatrixUniform, false, modelViewMatrix);

        // draw the object
        gl.drawElements(obj.primtype, obj.nIndices, gl.UNSIGNED_SHORT, 0);
    }

    function draw(gl, obj, modelViewMatrix, projectionMatrix, shaderProgram,
        shaderVertexPositionAttribute, shaderProjectionMatrixUniform,
        shaderModelViewMatrixUniform, options) {

        var shaderVertexColorAttribute = options.shaderVertexColorAttribute;
        var isColor = options.isColor || false;
        if (!isColor) {
            drawBw(gl, obj, modelViewMatrix, projectionMatrix, shaderProgram,
                shaderVertexPositionAttribute, shaderProjectionMatrixUniform);
        }
        else {
            drawColor(gl, obj, modelViewMatrix, projectionMatrix, shaderProgram,
                shaderVertexPositionAttribute, shaderProjectionMatrixUniform,
                shaderModelViewMatrixUniform, shaderVertexColorAttribute);
        }
    }

    function drawAll(canvas, gl, obj, options) {
        initViewport(gl, canvas);
        var x = initMatrices(canvas, options);
        var sds = shaderString(options);
        var y = initShader(gl, sds.vertexShaderSource, sds.fragmentShaderSource,
                options);

        if (options.isColor) {
            options.shaderVertexColorAttribute = y.shaderVertexColorAttribute;
        }
        draw(gl, obj, x.modelViewMatrix, x.projectionMatrix, y.shaderProgram,
            y.shaderVertexPositionAttribute, y.shaderProjectionMatrixUniform,
            y.shaderModelViewMatrixUniform, options);
    }
```

Here, we first define *drawBw* and *drawColor* functions, which can be used to draw black-white objects and color objects, respectively. We then introduce a common interface method *draw* with optional parameters, which can be used to draw either the black-white or the color objects depending on the specified optional parameters.

Finally, the *drawAll* function combines several methods together, which make the creation of 3D objects in WebGL easier than calling individual functions.

Creating Objects Using Helper Functions

In this section, we will use the helper functions implemented in the preceding sections to create several simple objects based on WebGL.

Color Triangle

Here, we will create a colored triangle using our helper functions. Add a new view named *ColorTriangle* to the *Views/Basic3D* folder and replace its content with the following code:

```
@{
    ViewData["Title"] = ViewBag.Title;
}
<h3>@ViewBag.Title</h3>
@Html.Partial("_Links")

<div class="container">
    <div class="row" style="margin-top:50px">
        <div class="col-sm-12">
            <canvas id="glCanvas" width="300" height="300"></canvas>
        </div>
    </div>
</div>

@section scripts{
<script>
    function createObj(gl) {
        var vertexBuffer = gl.createBuffer();
        gl.bindBuffer(gl.ARRAY_BUFFER, vertexBuffer);
        var verts = [
            0.0,  1.0, 0.0,
           -1.0, -1.0, 0.0,
            1.0, -1.0, 0.0,
        ];
        gl.bufferData(gl.ARRAY_BUFFER, new Float32Array(verts), gl.STATIC_DRAW);

        var colorBuffer = gl.createBuffer();
        gl.bindBuffer(gl.ARRAY_BUFFER, colorBuffer);
        var vertexColors = [
            1.0, 0.0, 0.0, 1.0,
            0.0, 1.0, 0.0, 1.0,
            0.0, 0.0, 1.0, 1.0
        ];
        gl.bufferData(gl.ARRAY_BUFFER, new Float32Array(vertexColors),
                    gl.STATIC_DRAW);

        var objIndexBuffer = gl.createBuffer();
        gl.bindBuffer(gl.ELEMENT_ARRAY_BUFFER, objIndexBuffer);
        var objIndices = [0, 1, 2];
        gl.bufferData(gl.ELEMENT_ARRAY_BUFFER, new Uint16Array(objIndices),
                    gl.STATIC_DRAW);
        var obj = {
            buffer: vertexBuffer, colorBuffer: colorBuffer,
            indices: objIndexBuffer, vertSize: 3, nVerts: 3, colorSize: 4,
            nColor: 3, nIndices: 3, primtype: gl.TRIANGLES
        };
        return obj;
    }

    var canvas = document.getElementById("glCanvas");
```

```
var gl = initWebGL(canvas);
var obj = createObj(gl);
var options = { isColor: true };
drawAll(canvas, gl, obj, options);
```

```
</script>
}
```

In the script section, we define a *createObj* function, where we first create the triangle's vertex position buffer, and then specify its vertex colors. Note that the values we provide for the colors are in an array, one set of values for each vertex, just like the positions. There is, however, one difference between the two array buffers: while the vertices' positions are specified as three numbers for *x*, *y*, and *z* coordinates, their colors are specified as four elements – red, green, blue, and alpha. In addition, we create a new kind of buffer named *indexBuffer* that holds a set of indices into the vertex buffer data. We do this because the drawing primitive we will use in our *draw* function requires indices into the set of vertices, instead of the vertices themselves, in order to define the triangles.

Once we implemented the *createObj* function, we can create our color triangle using the helper functions. First, we get the DOM object associated with the canvas element and initialize the WebGL context by calling the *initWebGL* helper function. Next, we create the object buffers using the *createObj* function. Next, we specify the optional parameter by setting the *isColor* to *true*. Finally, we call the *drawAll* helper function to create our color triangle. You see how easy it is to create a graphics object in WegGL using our helper functions as long as you define the vertex and color buffers for the object.

Running this example produces the result shown in Figure 7-2.

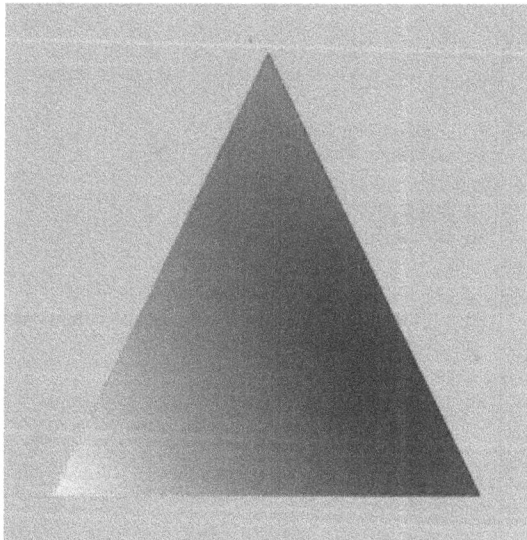

Figure 7-2. Colored triangle created using WebGL.

Squares

In this example, we will use our helper functions to create two square objects: one is a black-white square and the other is a colored one. Add a new view named *Square.cshtml* to the *Views/Basic3D* folder and replace its contents with the following code:

```
@{
    ViewData["Title"] = ViewBag.Title;
}
<h3>@ViewBag.Title</h3>
@Html.Partial("_Links")

<div class="container">
    <div class="row" style="margin-top:50px">
        <div class="col-sm-4">
            <canvas id="glCanvas1" width="300" height="300"></canvas>
        </div>
        <div class="col-sm-4">
            <canvas id="glCanvas2" width="300" height="300"></canvas>
        </div>
    </div>
</div>

@section scripts{
<script>

    // black-white square
    function createObj(gl) {
        var vertexBuffer;
        vertexBuffer = gl.createBuffer();
        gl.bindBuffer(gl.ARRAY_BUFFER, vertexBuffer);
        var verts = [
             1.0,  1.0, 0.0,
            -1.0,  1.0, 0.0,
             1.0, -1.0, 0.0,
            -1.0, -1.0, 0.0
        ];
        gl.bufferData(gl.ARRAY_BUFFER, new Float32Array(verts), gl.STATIC_DRAW);
        var obj = { buffer: vertexBuffer, vertSize: 3, nVerts: 4,
                    primtype: gl.TRIANGLE_STRIP };
        return obj;
    }

    var canvas = document.getElementById("glCanvas1");
    var gl = initWebGL(canvas);
    var obj = createObj(gl);
    drawAll(canvas, gl, obj, {});

    // colored square
    function createObj1(gl) {
        var vertexBuffer = gl.createBuffer();
        gl.bindBuffer(gl.ARRAY_BUFFER, vertexBuffer);
        var verts = [
             1.0,  1.0, 0.0,
            -1.0,  1.0, 0.0,
             1.0, -1.0, 0.0,
            -1.0, -1.0, 0.0
        ];
        gl.bufferData(gl.ARRAY_BUFFER, new Float32Array(verts), gl.STATIC_DRAW);
        var colorBuffer = gl.createBuffer();
        gl.bindBuffer(gl.ARRAY_BUFFER, colorBuffer);
```

```
        var vertexColors = [
            1.0, 0.0, 0.0, 1.0,
            0.0, 1.0, 0.0, 1.0,
            0.0, 0.0, 1.0, 1.0,
            1.0, 1.0, 0.0, 1.0
        ];
        gl.bufferData(gl.ARRAY_BUFFER, new Float32Array(vertexColors),
                    gl.STATIC_DRAW);
        var objIndexBuffer = gl.createBuffer();
        gl.bindBuffer(gl.ELEMENT_ARRAY_BUFFER, objIndexBuffer);
        var objIndices = [0, 3, 1, 0, 3, 2];
        gl.bufferData(gl.ELEMENT_ARRAY_BUFFER, new Uint16Array(objIndices),
                    gl.STATIC_DRAW);
        var obj = {
            buffer: vertexBuffer, colorBuffer: colorBuffer,
            indices: objIndexBuffer, vertSize: 3, colorSize: 4, nIndices: 6,
            primtype: gl.TRIANGLE_STRIP
        };
        return obj;
    }
    canvas = document.getElementById("glCanvas2");
    gl = initWebGL(canvas);
    obj = createObj1(gl);
    var options = { isColor: true };
    drawAll(canvas, gl, obj, options);

</script>
}
```

The *createObj* function is similar to that used in our previous triangle example, except that we use the triangle strip as the primitive type. The triangle strip defines a sequence of triangles using the first three vertices for the first triangle, and each subsequent vertex in combination with the previous two for subsequent triangles. We then create the black-white square using our helper functions, implemented previously, with default options.

Next, the code implements a new function *createObj1* that generates the vertex and color buffers for a colored square object. Finally, we use our helper functions to create the colored square by setting the *options.isColor* parameter to *true*.

Running this example produces the results shown in Figure 7-3.

Figure 7-3. Black-white (left) and colored (right) squares created using WebGL.

Triangle Strip

Here, we want to draw a triangle strip that consists of four triangles with different colors: red, green, blue, and yellow, as shown in Figure 7-4.

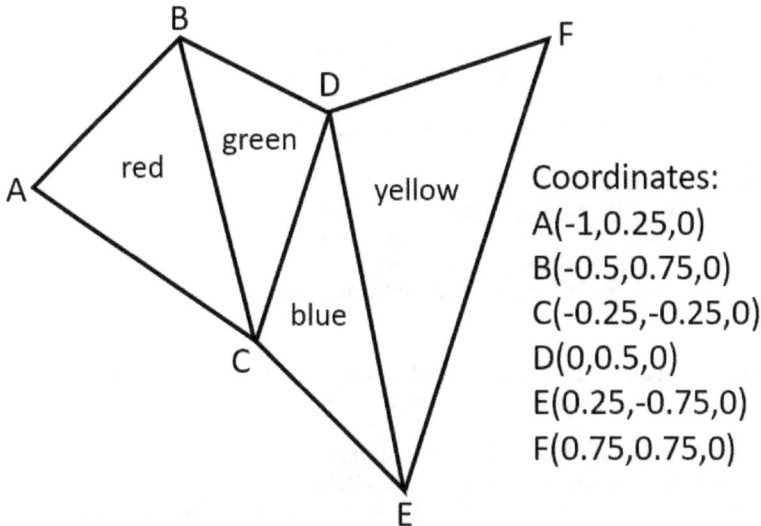

Figure 7-4. Illustration of a triangle strip with vertex coordinates.

Now, we want to realize this triangle strip using WebGL. Add a new view named *TriangleStrip.cshtml* to the *Views/Basic3D* folder and replace its content with the following code:

```
@{
    ViewData["Title"] = ViewBag.Title;
}
<h3>@ViewBag.Title</h3>
@Html.Partial("_Links")

<div class="container">
    <div class="row" style="margin-top:50px">
        <div class="col-sm-12">
            <canvas id="glCanvas" width="500" height="400"></canvas>
        </div>
    </div>
</div>

@section scripts{
<script>

    function createObj(gl) {
        var vertexBuffer = gl.createBuffer();
        gl.bindBuffer(gl.ARRAY_BUFFER, vertexBuffer);
        var verts = [
            -1.0, 0.25, 0.0, -0.25, -0.25, 0.0, -0.5, 0.75, 0.0, //face1 -- ACB
            -0.5, 0.75, 0.0, -0.25, -0.25, 0.0, 0.0, 0.5, 0.0,   //face2 -- BCD
            0.0, 0.5, 0.0, -0.25, -0.25, 0.0, 0.25, -0.75, 0.0,  //face3 -- DCE
```

```
        0.25, -0.75, 0.0, 0.75, 0.75, 0.0, 0.0, 0.5, 0.0    //face4 -- EFD
    ];
    gl.bufferData(gl.ARRAY_BUFFER, new Float32Array(verts), gl.STATIC_DRAW);

    var colorBuffer = gl.createBuffer();
    gl.bindBuffer(gl.ARRAY_BUFFER, colorBuffer);
    var faceColors = [
        [1.0, 0.0, 0.0, 1.0], //face1: Red
        [0.0, 1.0, 0.0, 1.0], //face2: Green
        [0.0, 0.0, 1.0, 1.0], //face3: Blue
        [1.0, 1.0, 0.0, 1.0]  //face4: Yellow
    ];
    var vertexColors = [];
    for (var i in faceColors) {
        var color = faceColors[i];
        for (var j = 0; j < 3; j++) {
            vertexColors = vertexColors.concat(color);
        }
    };
    gl.bufferData(gl.ARRAY_BUFFER, new Float32Array(vertexColors),
                  gl.STATIC_DRAW);

    var objIndexBuffer = gl.createBuffer();
    gl.bindBuffer(gl.ELEMENT_ARRAY_BUFFER, objIndexBuffer);
    var objIndices = [0, 1, 2, 3, 4, 5, 6, 7, 8, 9, 10, 11];
    gl.bufferData(gl.ELEMENT_ARRAY_BUFFER, new Uint16Array(objIndices),
                  gl.STATIC_DRAW);

    var obj = {
        buffer: vertexBuffer, colorBuffer: colorBuffer,
        indices: objIndexBuffer, vertSize: 3, colorSize: 4, nIndices: 12,
        primtype: gl.TRIANGLE_STRIP
    };

    return obj;
}

canvas = document.getElementById("glCanvas");
gl = initWebGL(canvas);
obj = createObj(gl);
var options = {
    isColor: true,
    distance: -2.5
};
drawAll(canvas, gl, obj, options);

</script>
}
```

This code first creates the vertex buffer data and stores it in the variable *vertexBuffer*. Next, we create color data, one four-element color per vertex, and store it in *colorBuffer*. The color values stored in the array *faceColors* are four-component RGBA. We also create an index buffer named *indexBuffer* that holds a set of indices into the vertex buffer data. We do this because the drawing primitive we will use in our *draw* function requires indices into the set of vertices, instead of the vertices themselves, in order to define the triangles. Why? Because 3D geometry often represents contiguous, closed regions where vertex positions are shared among multiple triangles; indexed buffers allow the data to be stored more compactly by avoiding repetition of the vertex data.

Finally, we use the helper functions to draw the triangle strip. Note that we set the *options.distance* parameter to -2.5 instead of default value of -3. This parameter can be used to control the size of our triangle strip.

Running this example produces the results shown in Figure 7-5. You can see that the triangle strip displayed in the figure is exactly what we required.

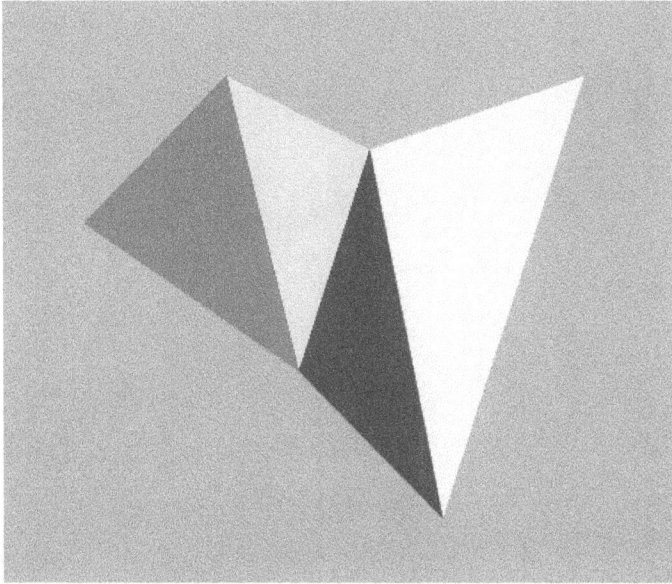

Figure 7-5. Realization of a colored triangle strap in WebGL.

Animated Cube

In the preceding sections, we demonstrated how to create some basic primitive shapes, such as triangle, square, and triangle strip. However, these shapes are not really 3D objects. In this section, we will take our square into 3D by adding five more faces to create a cube.

For a cube, each face requires four vertices to define it, and each vertex is shared by three faces. We can pass a lot less data around by building a list of all 24 vertices, then referring to each vertex by its index into that list instead of passing entire sets of coordinates around. If you wonder why we need 24 vertices, and not just 8, this is because each corner belongs to three faces of different colors, and a single vertex needs to have a single specific color. Therefore, we need to create three copies of each vertex in three different colors, one for each face.

Add a new view named *Cube.cshtml* to the *Views.Basic3D* folder and replace its content with the following code:

```
@{
    ViewData["Title"] = ViewBag.Title;
}
```

```
<h3>@ViewBag.Title</h3>
@Html.Partial("_Links")

<div class="container">
    <div class="row" style="margin-top:50px">
        <div class="col-sm-6">
            <canvas id="glCanvas" width="400" height="400"></canvas>
        </div>
    </div>
</div>

@section scripts{
<script>
    function createObj(gl) {
        var vertexBuffer = gl.createBuffer();
        gl.bindBuffer(gl.ARRAY_BUFFER, vertexBuffer);
        var verts = [
            // front face
            -1.0, -1.0, 1.0, 1.0, -1.0, 1.0, 1.0, 1.0, 1.0, -1.0, 1.0, 1.0,
            // back face
            -1.0, -1.0, -1.0, -1.0, 1.0, -1.0, 1.0, 1.0, -1.0, 1.0, -1.0, -1.0,
            // top face
            -1.0, 1.0, -1.0, -1.0, 1.0, 1.0, 1.0, 1.0, 1.0, 1.0, 1.0, -1.0,
            // bottom face
            -1.0, -1.0, -1.0, 1.0, -1.0, -1.0, 1.0, -1.0, 1.0, -1.0, -1.0, 1.0,
            // right face
            1.0, -1.0, -1.0, 1.0, 1.0, -1.0, 1.0, 1.0, 1.0, 1.0, -1.0, 1.0,
            // left face
            -1.0, -1.0, -1.0, -1.0, -1.0, 1.0, -1.0, 1.0, 1.0, -1.0, 1.0, -1.0
        ];
        gl.bufferData(gl.ARRAY_BUFFER, new Float32Array(verts), gl.STATIC_DRAW);

        var colorBuffer = gl.createBuffer();
        gl.bindBuffer(gl.ARRAY_BUFFER, colorBuffer);
        var faceColors = [
            [1.0, 0.0, 0.0, 1.0], // front face
            [0.0, 1.0, 0.0, 1.0], // back face
            [0.0, 0.0, 1.0, 1.0], // top face
            [1.0, 1.0, 0.0, 1.0], // bottom face
            [1.0, 0.0, 1.0, 1.0], // right face
            [0.0, 1.0, 1.0, 1.0]  // left face
        ];
        var vertexColors = [];
        for (var i in faceColors) {
            var color = faceColors[i];
            for (var j = 0; j < 4; j++) {
                vertexColors = vertexColors.concat(color);
            }
        }
        gl.bufferData(gl.ARRAY_BUFFER, new Float32Array(vertexColors),
                    gl.STATIC_DRAW);

        var objIndexBuffer = gl.createBuffer();
        gl.bindBuffer(gl.ELEMENT_ARRAY_BUFFER, objIndexBuffer);
        var cubeIndices = [
```

```
            0, 1, 2, 0, 2, 3,              // front face
            4, 5, 6, 4, 6, 7,              // back face
            8, 9, 10, 8, 10, 11,           // top face
            12, 13, 14, 12, 14, 15,        // bottom face
            16, 17, 18, 16, 18, 19,        // right face
            20, 21, 22, 20, 22, 23         // left face
        ]
        gl.bufferData(gl.ELEMENT_ARRAY_BUFFER, new Uint16Array(cubeIndices),
                    gl.STATIC_DRAW);

        var obj = {
            buffer: vertexBuffer, colorBuffer: colorBuffer,
            indices: objIndexBuffer, vertSize: 3, colorSize: 4, nIndices: 36,
            primtype: gl.TRIANGLES
        };
        return obj;
    }

    var options = {
        isColor: true,
        isRotate: true,
        distance: -5
    };

    var currentTime = Date.now();
    function animate(x) {
        var now = Date.now();
        var deltat = now - currentTime;
        currentTime = now;
        var angle = Math.PI * 2 * deltat / 5000;
        mat4.rotate(x.modelViewMatrix, x.modelViewMatrix, angle,
            x.rotationAxis);
    }

    function run(gl, obj, x, y) {
        requestAnimationFrame(function () { run(gl, obj, x, y); });
        draw(gl, obj, x.modelViewMatrix, x.projectionMatrix, y.shaderProgram,
            y.shaderVertexPositionAttribute, y.shaderProjectionMatrixUniform,
            y.shaderModelViewMatrixUniform, options);
        animate(x);
    }

    var canvas = document.getElementById("glCanvas");
    var gl = initWebGL(canvas);
    initViewport(gl, canvas);
    var x = initMatrices(canvas, options);
    var obj = createObj(gl);
    var sds = shaderString(options);
    var y = initShader(gl, sds.vertexShaderSource, sds.fragmentShaderSource,
                    options);
    options.shaderVertexColorAttribute = y.shaderVertexColorAttribute;
    run(gl, obj, x, y);
</script>
}
```

This code first build the cube's vertex position buffer. This is pretty much the same as it was for the square, but rather longer since there are 24 vertices (4 per face). Next, we create an array of colors for each of the 24 vertices. The code starts by defining a color for each face, and then uses a for-loop to assemble an array of all the colors for each of the vertices.

Once the vertex arrays are generated, we build an index buffer to avoid repetition of data. The *cubeIndices* array defines each face as a pair of triangles, specifying each triangle's vertices as an index into the cube's vertex array. Thus, the cube is described as a collection of 12 triangles.

Next, we set the optional parameters to be used by our helper functions. Note that we set *options.isRotate* to *true*, indicating that we are going to use the rotation axis implemented in the *initMatrices* helper function. For this cube, this rotation axis will be used to animate its rotation. The *animate* function rotates the cube around the rotation axis over a period of five seconds.

The *animate* function is called repeatedly by another *run* function, which drives continuous animation of the 3D scene using a new browser function called *requestAnimationFrame*. This function asks the browser to call a callback function when it is time to redraw the content of the page. Each time the *animate* function is called, it stores the difference between the current time and the previous time it was called into the variable *deltat*, and uses that to derive an angle for rotating *modelViewMatrix*. The result is a full rotation around the rotation axis every five seconds.

Running this example produces the results shown in Figure 7-6.

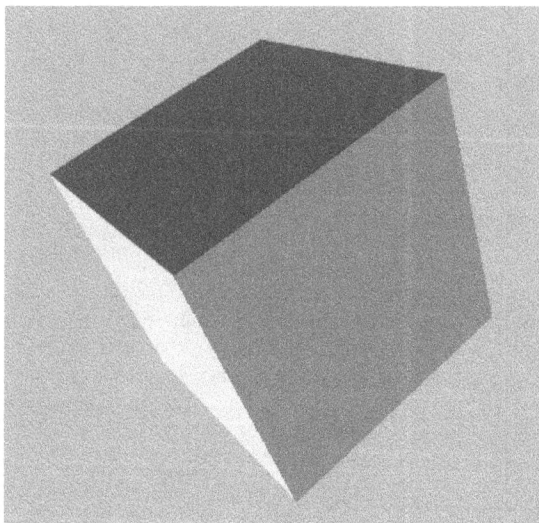

Figure 7-6. Animated cube created using WebGL.

Chapter 8
3D Graphics with Three.js

In the previous chapters, we demonstrated both the power and complexity of creating 3D WebGL graphics applications. WebGL API provides a medium to render interactive 3D graphics on any compatible web browser. The advantage of WebGL lies in the fact that there is no dependency on plug-ins. It does this with the help of control logic implemented with the JavaScript and shader logic that is executed on the GPU. Code implementation for 3D graphics can be written directly in WebGL, but to do anything more than the most basic tasks requires a very high learning curve and literally thousands of lines of code. This is not a recipe for rapidly building applications on web time. Depending on the kind of project you are working on, you are faced with a choice: build your own helper library to ease the pain, as what we did for creating helper functions in the preceding chapter, or use libraries already developed by others.

There are several JavaScript libraries for getting started with your WebGL development, which can handle the complexities of WebGL with ease and provide a user-friendly way of implementing 3D graphics. In this chapter, we will pick Three.js as a 3D framework for developing 3D WebGL applications. Three.js was designed with one goal in mind: to take advantage of web based renders for creating GPU enhanced 3D graphics and animations. As such, this framework employs a very broad approach to web graphics without focusing on any single animation niche. This flexible design makes Three.js a great tool for general-purpose web animations like logos or modeling applications.

Three.js Basics

As mentioned previously, to create WebGL applications, you need to learn a new language (GLSL), understand how vertex and fragment shaders can be used to render your 3D objects, and write a huge amount of code. Three.js gives you the ability to create 3D objects and animations in the web browser while doing all the heavy lifting of WebGL for you.

To use the Three.js library, you need to install it in the ASP.NET Core MVC project. Open Visual Studio 2017 and start with a new ASP.NET Core MVC project and name it *Chapter08*. Install the following libraries using the Bower package manager and refer them in the *Views/Shared/_Layout.cshtml* file:

```
<environment names="Development">
    <script src="~/lib/jquery/dist/jquery.js"></script>
    <script src="~/lib/bootstrap/dist/js/bootstrap.js"></script>
    <script src="~/lib/bootstrap-slider/bootstrap-slider.js"></script>
    <script src="~/lib/three.js/three.js"></script>
```

```
        <script src="~/lib/stats.js/build/stats.js"></script>
        <script src="~/lib/tween.js/src/Tween.js"></script>
        <script src="~/js/site.js" asp-append-version="true"></script>
    </environment>
```

Here, the *three.js* is the main library, *stats.js* provides a simple info box that will help you monitor your code performance, and *tween.js* is for easy animations. The *bootstrap-slider.js* is used to create a bootstrap compatible slider control.

Triangle in Three.js

Let us consider a simple example that creates a colored triangle object using Three.js. We have created such a triangle directly using WebGL in the preceding chapter. The example should make it clear how much value the Three.js library provides over developing to the original WebGL API.

In project *Chapter08*, add *Controllers/Basic3DController.cs* and replace its content with the following code:

```csharp
using Microsoft.AspNetCore.Mvc;

namespace Chapter08.Controllers
{
    public class Basic3DController : Controller
    {
        // GET: /<controller>/
        public IActionResult Index()
        {
            ViewBag.Title = "Basic 3D Shapes: Home";
            return View();
        }

        public IActionResult Triangle()
        {
            ViewBag.Title = "Triangle";
            return View();
        }

        public IActionResult AxisGridline()
        {
            ViewBag.Title = "Axes and Gridlines";
            return View();
        }

        public IActionResult Camera()
        {
            ViewBag.Title = "Camera";
            return View();
        }

        public IActionResult CameraControl()
        {
            ViewBag.Title = "Camera Control";
            return View();
        }
```

```
    public IActionResult Material()
    {
        ViewBag.Title = "Material";
        return View();
    }

    public IActionResult Light()
    {
        ViewBag.Title = "Light Sources";
        return View();
    }
  }
}
```

Add a new folder named *Basic3D* to the *Views* folder. Add *Views/Basic3D/Triangle.cshtml* and replace its content with the following code:

```
@{
    ViewData["Title"] = ViewBag.Title;
}

<h3>@ViewBag.Title</h3>
@Html.Partial("_Links")

<div class="container">
    <div class="row">
        <div class="col-sm-6">
            <div id="webgl" style="width:300px; height:300px;
                margin-top:50px"></div>
        </div>
    </div>
</div>

@section scripts{
<script>

    // create new scene
    var container = document.getElementById('webgl');
    var scene = new THREE.Scene();

    // create a camera
    var camera = new THREE.PerspectiveCamera(45,
        container.clientWidth / container.clientHeight, 1, 100);
    camera.position.z = 3;

    // create triangle
    var geometry = new THREE.Geometry();
    var v1 = new THREE.Vector3(0.0, 1.0, 0.0);
    var v2 = new THREE.Vector3(-1.0, -1.0, 0.0);
    var v3 = new THREE.Vector3(1.0, -1.0, 0.0);

    geometry.vertices.push(v1);
    geometry.vertices.push(v2);
    geometry.vertices.push(v3);

    geometry.faces.push(new THREE.Face3(0, 1, 2));
```

```
        var f = geometry.faces[0];

        f.vertexColors[0] = new THREE.Color("red");
        f.vertexColors[1] = new THREE.Color("green");
        f.vertexColors[2] = new THREE.Color("blue");

        var material = new THREE.MeshBasicMaterial({ color: 0xFFFFFF,
            vertexColors: THREE.VertexColors });
        var mesh = new THREE.Mesh(geometry, material);

        // add Triangle to scene
        scene.add(mesh);

        // setup renderer
        var renderer = new THREE.WebGLRenderer();
        renderer.setSize(container.clientWidth, container.clientHeight);
        container.appendChild(renderer.domElement);

        // render triangle
        renderer.setClearColor("lightgray");
        renderer.render(scene, camera);

    </script>
    }
```

This code produces result shown in Figure 8-1.

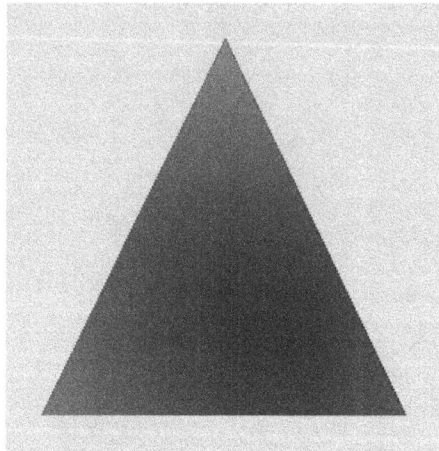

Figure 8-1. Colored triangle created using Three.js.

Let us examine how this example works.

Set the Scene

First, we set a scene by creating a new *THREE.Scene* object. A *Scene* class represents a list of objects that affect what is displayed on the screen, such as 3D models and lights. Each class provided by Three.js is invoked as a property of the global *THREE* variable. The *scene* is the top-level object in the Three.js graphics hierarchy.

A scene is not very useful by itself, so let us put something such as a *camera* and a *mesh* in it. The camera defines where we are viewing the scene from: in this example, we place the camera at a position of $z = 3$. Our camera is of type *THREE.PerspectiveCamera*, which we initialize with a 45-degree field of view, the viewport dimensions, and near and far clipping plane values. Three.js will use these values to create a perspective projection matrix used to render the 3D scene to the 2D viewport.

Next, we add the mesh to the scene. In Three.js, a mesh consists of a geometry object and a material. For the geometry, we use three vectors to create three vertices for our triangle. We need to attach more attributes to each vertex. To add a color to each vertex, we define the triangle's face, and then add the RGB color attribute by specifying a color at each vertex of the face. The GPU will interpolate the colors across the face, giving a blend of these colors in the triangle's interior.

The material tells Three.js how to paint the surface of the object. Here, we use the *MeshBasicMaterial* with vertex colors, which is a simple material without lighting effects.

We then create the triangle mesh. We have constructed the geometry, the material, and vertex colors, now we put them all together into a *THEE.Mesh* object named *mesh* and add it to *scene*.

Rendering the Scene

Up to this point, we have put together what we want to display, so next step is to actually display it. Three.js accomplishes this with renderers, which take the object in a scene, perform corresponding calculation, and then ask the browser to display the result in a specific format like WebGL or the Canvas API. Here we create a new *THREE.WebGLRenderer* object, and initialize its size to be the entire width and height of the container. This is equivalent to calling *gl.viewport* to set the viewport size as we did in the preceding chapter.

Finally, we display our object using the renderer:

```
renderer.render(scene, camera);
```

This is equivalent to our *draw* helper function implemented in the preceding chapter, where we had to set up buffers, render states, shaders, and much more. While using *Three.js*, we simple write one line code and the library does the rest automatically for us.

3D Coordinates and Gridlines

Like OpenGL, Three.js uses a traditional right-hand coordinate system, as shown in Figure 8-2. In this figure, the three axes meet at the origin $(0, 0, 0)$ and the computer screen coincides with the *xy*-plane. The positive z-axis points out or the screen towards the observer's eyes.

When we add a Three.js object, such as sphere, to a scene, the object is added at the origin of the *xyz*-coordinate system. So, if you were adding a camera object and a sphere object to a scene, they would both end up at $(0, 0, 0)$ and you would be looking at the sphere from the inside out. The solution is to move the camera to a reasonable position, such as down the positive z-axis 20 units: *camera.position.z* $= 50$.

Three.js implemented a helper function *THREE.AxisHelper* that can be used to create 3D coordinate axes. Add a new view named *AxisGridline.cshtml* to the *Views/Basic3D* folder and replace its content with the following code:

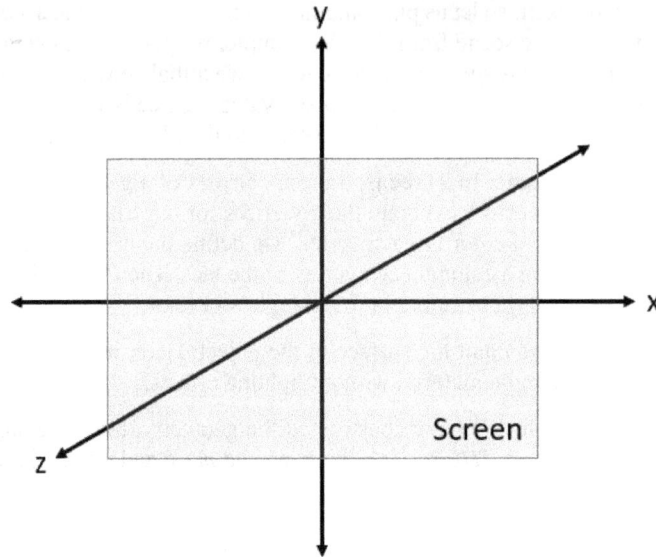

Figure 8-2. 3D coordinate system used in Three.js.

```
@{
    ViewData["Title"] = ViewBag.Title;
}
<h3>@ViewBag.Title</h3>
@Html.Partial("_Links")

<div class="container">
    <div class="row">
        <div class="col-sm-6">
            <p style="margin-top:30px; margin-bottom:5px">
                3D coordinate axes: x - red, y - green, z - blue</p>
            <div id="gl1" style="width:600px; height:480px;
                margin-right:25px;"></div>
        </div>
        <div class="col-sm-6">
            <p style="margin-top:30px; margin-left:25px; margin-bottom:5px">
                3D coordinate system with xz-gridlines</p>
            <div id="gl2" style="width:600px; height:480px;
                margin-left:25px;"></div>
        </div>
    </div>
    <div class="row">
        <div class="col-sm-6">
            <p style="margin-top:30px; margin-bottom:5px">
                3D coordinate system with xz-, xy-, and yz-gridlines</p>
            <div id="gl3" style="width:600px; height:480px;
                margin-right:25px;"></div>
        </div>
        <div class="col-sm-6">
            <p style="margin-top:30px; margin-left:25px; margin-bottom:5px">
                Cube in 3D coordinate system</p>
```

```
            <div id="gl4" style="width:600px; height:480px;
                margin-left:25px;"></div>
        </div>
    </div>
</div>

@section scripts{
<script>
    // 3D coordinate system
    var container = document.getElementById('gl1');
    var scene = new THREE.Scene();
    // add axes and gridlines
    addAxesGrid(scene, "noGrid");
    // add camera and renderer
    addCameraRenderer(container, scene, 0);

    // 3D coordinate system with xz-gridlines
    var container = document.getElementById('gl2');
    var scene = new THREE.Scene();
    // add axes and gridlines
    addAxesGrid(scene, "xzGrid");
    // add camera and renderer
    addCameraRenderer(container, scene, 0);

    // 3D coordinate system with xz-, xy-, and yz-gridlines
    var container = document.getElementById('gl3');
    var scene = new THREE.Scene();
    // add axes and gridlines
    addAxesGrid(scene, "allGrids");
    // add camera and renderer
    addCameraRenderer(container, scene, 90);

    // Cube in 3D coordinate system
    var container = document.getElementById('gl4');
    var scene = new THREE.Scene();
    // add axes and gridlines
    addAxesGrid(scene, "allGrids");
    // add cube:
    var cube = new THREE.BoxGeometry(50, 50, 50);
    var material = new THREE.MeshNormalMaterial();
    var mesh = new THREE.Mesh(cube, material);
    scene.add(mesh);
    addCameraRenderer(container, scene, 90);

    function addAxesGrid(scene, gridType) {
        // add axes
        var axisHelper = new THREE.AxisHelper(150);
        scene.add(axisHelper);
        if (gridType != "noGrid") {
            // add xz grids
            var gridxz = new THREE.GridHelper(160, 16, "black");
            scene.add(gridxz);
        }
        if (gridType ==="allGrids") {
            // add xy grids
```

```
            var gridxy = new THREE.GridHelper(160, 16, "lightgreen");
            gridxy.rotation.x = Math.PI / 2;
            gridxy.position.set(80, 160, 0);
            scene.add(gridxy);
            // add yz grids
            var gridyz = new THREE.GridHelper(160, 16, "lightpink");
            gridyz.rotation.z = Math.PI / 2;
            gridyz.position.set(-160, 0, -80);
            scene.add(gridyz);
        }
    }

    function addCameraRenderer(container, scene, camerayposition) {
        // add camera
        var cameraHeight = 10;
        var camera = new THREE.OrthographicCamera(
            -150, 150, 150, -150, -1000, 1000);
        camera.position.set(cameraHeight, cameraHeight, cameraHeight);
        camera.lookAt(scene.position);
        camera.position.y = camerayposition;
        // add renderer
        var render = new THREE.WebGLRenderer({ antialias: true });
        render.setSize(container.clientWidth, container.clientHeight);
        container.appendChild(render.domElement);
        render.setClearColor("lightgray");
        render.clear();
        render.render(scene, camera);
    }
</script>
}
```

This code adds four *div* elements that hold the Three.js objects: axes, axes with *xz*-gridlines, axes with *xz*- *xy*-, and *yz*-gridlines, and a cube with coordinate axes. In the script section, we implement two helper functions *addAxesGrid* and *addCameraRenderer*. The former adds the coordinate axes and gridlines depending on the specified *gridType* argument. The latter sets camera and creates renderer for rendering the scene. The use of those two functions is to avoid code repetition.

Inside the *addAxesGrid* function, we create coordinate axis using the *THREE.AxisHelper* function, which allows you to visualize the three coordinate axes in a simple way with the red *x*-axis, green *y*-axis, and blue *z*-axis. The function takes an optional *size* or lines (or axis length) parameter representing the axes (the default value is 10). The resulted coordinate axes are shown in Figure 8-3.

Next, we create a 3D coordinate system with gridlines in the *xz*-plane using the *THREE.GridHelper* function that defines grids of 2D arrays of lines. This helper function has four optional parameters: *size*, *divisions*, *colorCenterLine*, and *colorGrid*. The *size* parameter controls the size of the grid (default is 10), *divisions* is the number of divisions across the grid (default is 10), *colorCenterLine* represents the color of the centerline (default is 0x444444), and *colorGrid* represents the color of the gridlines (default is 0x888888). Note that we use the *camerayposition* argument in the *addCameraRenderer* function to control the location of our objects, which makes sure all objects are within the viewport. Figures 8-4 and 8-5 shows the coordinate axes with *xz*-gridlines and coordinate axes with *xz*-, *xy*-, and *yz*-gridlines.

Finally, we add a 50×50×50 cube object to our 3D coordinate system with gridlines using the built-in Three.js object *BoxGeometry*, as shown in Figure 8-6.

Figure 8-3 3D coordinate axes created using Three.js.

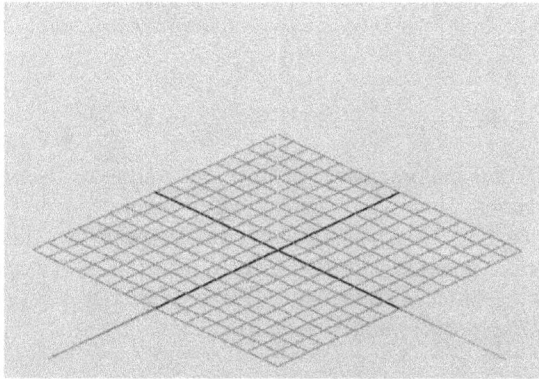

Figure 8-4. 3D coordinate axes with the xz-gridlines created using Three.js.

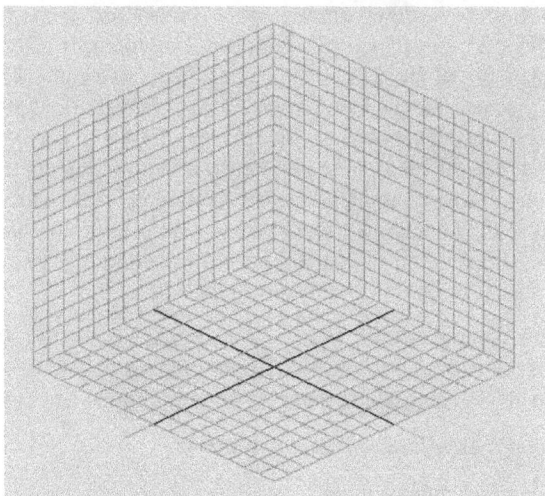

Figure 8-5. 3D coordinate axes with the xz-, xy-, and yz-gridlines.

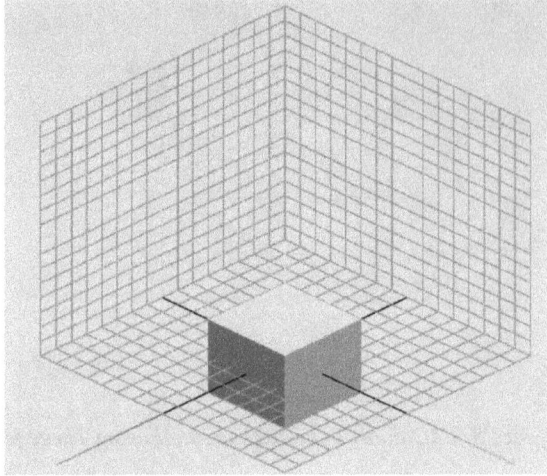

Figure 8-6. A cube in 3D coordinate system created using Three.js.

Camera

When you create a 3D scene, it is important to remember that you are really creating a 2D representation of 3D objects through projection. Since a 3D scene looks different depending on the point of view, you must specify your camera location. This means that in order to see a 3D object you must set a camera at the correct position and orient it in the correct direction. The camera determines how a 3D scene is represented on the 2D viewing surface of a viewport. Three.js introduces several cameras, including the commonly used cameras – *PerspectiveCamera* and *OrthographicCamera*.

Perspective Camera

The perspective projection defines a view volume, called *View Frustrum*, which we use in two ways. The frustrum determines how an object is projected onto the screen. It also defines which objects or portions of objects are clipped out of the final image. The perspective camera specifies a projection that foreshorten the scene. In other worlds, the *perspectiveCamera* renders the scene so that objects that are further away appear smaller. This occurs because the frustrum for a perspective projection is a truncated pyramid whose top has been cut off by a plane parallel to its base. Objects falling within the frustrum are projected toward the apex of the pyramid, where the camera is located. Objects that are closer to the camera appear larger because they occupy a proportionately larger amount of the viewing volume than those that are farther away. This method of projection is also commonly used in 3D computer graphics and visual simulation, because it is similar to how a camera works.

Remember that the viewing volume is used to clip objects that lie outside of it; the four sides of the frustrum, its top and its base correspond to the six clipping planes of the viewing volume, as shown in Figure 8-7. Objects or parts of objects outside these planes are clipped from the final image.

In Three.js, *perspectiveCamera* exposes four input arguments:

- *fov*: Camera frustrum vertical field of view.
- *aspect*: Camera frustrum aspect ratio between the horizontal and vertical size of the area where you render the output.

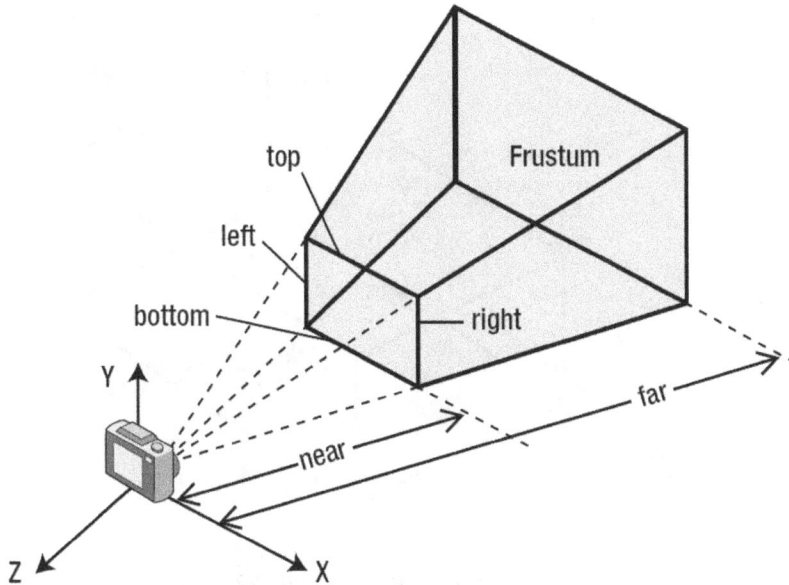

Figure 8-7. View frustrum of a perspective projection.

- *near*: Camera frustrum near plane that defines a minimum distance from the camera in Three.js. Usually, it is a very small value, e.g. 0.1.

- *far*: Camera frustrum far plane that defines a maximum distance we see the scene from the camera. If we set it as too small, a part of our scene might not be rendered; if we set it as too large, in some cases, it might affect the rendering performance. Normal value is between 500 and 2000, e.g. 1000.

The following code snippet shows a sample *perspectiveCamera* setting in Three.js:

```
var container = document.getElementById("gl");
var fov = 45;
var aspect = container.clientWidth / container.clientHeight;
// PerspectiveCamera(fov, aspect, near, far)
var camera = new THREE.PerspectiveCamera(fov, aspect, 0.1, 1000);
camera.position.set(100, 100, 300);
camera.lookAt(scene.position);
```

After setting the camera, we usually need to focus the camera to a certain position, and we can use the *lookAt* function to do it. To make a better perspective, we usually use the perspective camera. This projection mode is designed to mimic the way the human eye sees. It is the most common projection mode used for rendering a 3D scene.

Orthographic Camera

In an orthographic projection mode, an object's size in the rendered image stays constant regardless of its distance from the camera. This can be useful for rendering 2D scene, 3D charts, and UI elements, etc. The viewing volume for an orthographic projection is a rectangular parallelepiped, or a box, as shown in Figure 8-8.

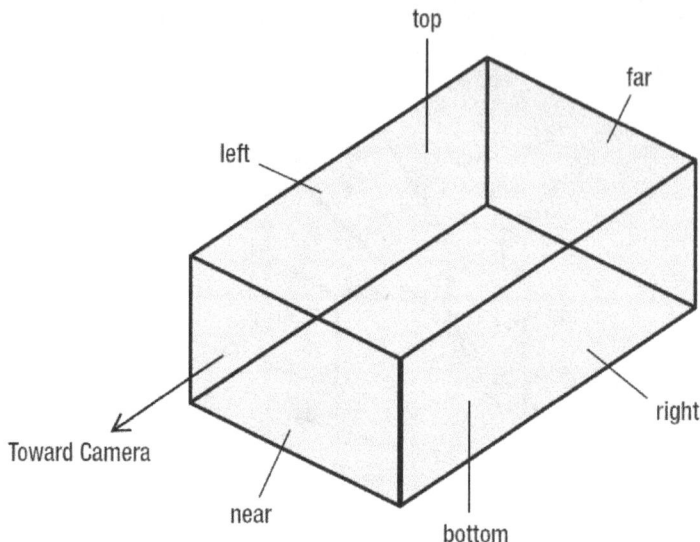

Figure 8-8. Orthographic viewing volume.

Unlike perspective projection, the size of the viewing volume does not change from one end to the other, so the distance from the camera does not affect how large an object appears. Namely, no perspective distortion occurs in orthographic projection. The points in the camera space are always mapped to the projection plane by casting rays that are parallel to the camera's viewing direction. This type of projection can be also used in applications for architecture and computer-aided design (CAD), where it is important to maintain the actual sizes of objects and the angles between them as they are projected.

In Three.js, *orthographicCamera* exposes six input arguments: *left*, *right*, *top*, *bottom*, *near*, and *far*. Anything outside of this rectangular box would not be rendered. The following code snippet shows a sample *orthographicCamera* setting in Three.js:

```
var container = document.getElementById("gl");
var viewSize = container.clientHeight;
var aspect = container.clientWidth / container.clientHeight;
// OrthographicCamera(left, right, top, bottom, near, far)
var camera = new THREE.OrthographicCamera(-aspect * viewSize / 2,
    aspect * viewSize / 2, viewSize / 2, -viewSize / 2, -200, 500);
camera.position.set(100, 100, 300);
camera.lookAt(scene.position);
```

Testing Cameras

In this section, we will test both the orthographic and perspective cameras. Add a new view named *Camera.cshtml* to the *Views/Basic3D* folder and replace its content with the following code:

```
@{
    ViewData["Title"] = ViewBag.Title;}
<h3>@ViewBag.Title</h3>
@Html.Partial("_Links")

<div class="container" >
```

```
        <div class="row" style="margin-top:50px">
            <div class="col-sm-4">
                <div style="margin-top:30px; margin-right:25px">
                    <p style="margin-bottom:5px;">Orthographic camera</p>
                    <input id="slider" type="text" data-slider-min="-100"
                        data-slider-max="1000" data-slider-step="5"
                        data-slider-value="300" />
                    <div id="gl1" style="width:400px; height:350px;
                        margin-top:10px"></div>
                </div>
            </div>
            <div class="col-sm-4">
                <div style="margin-top:30px; margin-left:25px">
                    <p style="margin-bottom:5px;">Perspective camera</p>
                    <input id="slider1" type="text" data-slider-min="1"
                        data-slider-max="1000" data-slider-step="5"
                        data-slider-value="300" />
                    <div id="gl2" style="width:400px; height:350px;
                        margin-top:10px"></div>
                </div>
            </div>
        </div>
    </div>
</div>

@section scripts{
<script>

    // orthographic camera
    var orthographic = setCamera("gl1", "Orthographic");
    $("#slider").slider().on("slide", function (sliderEvt) {
        orthographic.camera.position.z = sliderEvt.value;
        orthographic.render.render(orthographic.scene, orthographic.camera);
    });

    // perspective camera
    var perspective = setCamera("gl2", "Perspective");
    $("#slider1").slider().on("slide", function (sliderEvt) {
        perspective.camera.position.z = sliderEvt.value;
        perspective.render.render(perspective.scene, perspective.camera);
    });

    function setCamera(glCanvas, cameraType) {
        var container = document.getElementById(glCanvas);
        var scene = new THREE.Scene();

        var viewSize = container.clientHeight;
        var aspect = container.clientWidth / container.clientHeight;
        var camera;
        if (cameraType == "Orthographic") {
            // OrthographicCamera(left, right, top, bottom, near, far)
            camera = new THREE.OrthographicCamera(-aspect * viewSize / 2,
                aspect * viewSize / 2, viewSize / 2, -viewSize / 2, -100, 1000);
        } else if (cameraType == "Perspective") {
            // PerspectiveCamera(fov, aspect, near, far)
            camera = new THREE.PerspectiveCamera(45, aspect, 1, 1000);
```

```
        }
        camera.position.set(100, 100, 300);
        camera.lookAt(scene.position);

        // create a cube
        var cube = new THREE.BoxGeometry(100, 100, 100);
        var material = new THREE.MeshNormalMaterial();
        var mesh = new THREE.Mesh(cube, material);
        mesh.name = 'cube';
        scene.add(mesh);

        // Setup renderer
        var render = new THREE.WebGLRenderer();
        render.setSize(container.clientWidth, container.clientHeight);
        container.appendChild(render.domElement);
        render.setClearColor("lightgray");
        render.clear();
        render.render(scene, camera);
        return { render: render, scene: scene, camera: camera }
    }
</script>
}
```

Here, we implement a function *setCamera* that sets the orthographic or perspective camera depending on the specified *cameraType* parameter. Inside this method, we also create a cube object to examine the effect of projection. We then use the AJAX to connect a slider value with the *camera.position.z* property to control the distance between our cube and camera.

Running this example, selecting the *Basic 3D Shapes* tab, and clicking the *Camera* link produce the results shown in Figure 8-9. By moving the slider, you can see the different projection effects of the orthographic (left) and perspective (right) cameras.

Figure 8-9. Projection effects of orthographic (left) and perspective (right) cameras.

In the above example, we only change the distance between the cube and the camera in the *z*-direction using a slider control. In fact, we can use a simple dat.gui.js (https://github.com/dataarts/dat.gui) to change variables in JavaScript. The *dat.gui* is a lightweight graphical user interface for your demos. In the following example, we will use *dat.gui* to add a user interface that allows you to change various camera parameters. In our *Chapter08* project, we have download *dat.gui.js* and put it to the *wwwroot/js/mylib* folder. We can then refer to this file in our view to use this tool.

For simplify our view implementation, we will add some helper functions to the *site.js* file. Add a function named *setOrthographicCameraControl* to the *site.js* file:

```javascript
function setOrthographicCameraControl(gl, glControl, obj) {
    var container = document.getElementById(gl);
    var width = container.clientWidth;
    var height = container.clientHeight;

    var scene = new THREE.Scene();
    // orthographicCamera(left, right, top, bottom, near, far)
    var camera = new THREE.OrthographicCamera(width / -2, width / 2,
        height / 2, height / -2, 0.1, 1500);

    // position and point the camera to the center of the scene
    camera.position.x = -500;
    camera.position.y = 200;
    camera.position.z = 300;
    camera.lookAt(scene.position);

    // create renderer
    var renderer = new THREE.WebGLRenderer();
    renderer.setClearColor("lightgray", 1.0);
    renderer.setSize(width, height);
    container.appendChild(renderer.domElement);

    // add object
    obj.name = "obj";
    scene.add(obj);

    var control = new function () {
        this.rotationSpeed = 0.005;
        this.scale = 1;
        this.left = camera.left;
        this.right = camera.right;
        this.top = camera.top;
        this.bottom = camera.bottom;
        this.far = camera.far;
        this.near = camera.near;
        this.positionz = camera.position.z;
        this.updateCamera = function () {
            camera.left = control.left;
            camera.right = control.right;
            camera.top = control.top;
            camera.bottom = control.bottom;
            camera.far = control.far;
            camera.near = control.near;
            camera.position.z = control.positionz;
            camera.updateProjectionMatrix();
```

```
            };
        };
        addControls();
        renderScene();

        function addControls() {
            var gui = new dat.GUI({ autoPlace: false });
            gui.add(control, 'rotationSpeed', -0.1, 0.1);
            gui.add(control, 'scale', 0.01, 2);
            gui.add(control, 'left', -1000, 0).onChange(control.updateCamera);
            gui.add(control, 'right', 0, 1000).onChange(control.updateCamera);
            gui.add(control, 'top', 0, 1000).onChange(control.updateCamera);
            gui.add(control, 'bottom', -1000, 0).onChange(control.updateCamera);
            gui.add(control, 'far', 100, 2000).onChange(control.updateCamera);
            gui.add(control, 'near', 0, 200).onChange(control.updateCamera);
            gui.add(control, "positionz", 0, 1000).onChange(control.updateCamera);
            var customContainer = $('#' + glControl).append($(gui.domElement));
        }

        function renderScene() {
            renderer.render(scene, camera);
            scene.getObjectByName('obj').rotation.x += control.rotationSpeed;
            scene.getObjectByName('obj').rotation.y += control.rotationSpeed;
            scene.getObjectByName('obj').rotation.z += control.rotationSpeed;
            scene.getObjectByName('obj').scale.set(control.scale, control.scale,
                                            control.scale);
            requestAnimationFrame(renderScene);
        }
    }
```

This function takes the *gl* and *glControl div* elements as well as the 3D object as input arguments. Inside the function, we set the orthographic camera and renderer. The next thing we need to configure is a JavaScript object that will hold the attributes we want to change using *dat.gui*. We add a JavaScript object named *control*, where we define nine attributes, *this.rotationSpreed*, *this.scale*, etc. with their default values. Next, we pass this object into a new *dat.gui* object *gui* and define the range for these attributes inside a new function named *addControls*. You can see from the code that we use the *onChange* feature of data.gui to update camera.

We use the *rotationSpreed* and *scale* attributes to control the rotation and scale of the object. All we need to do now is make sure that in our *renderScene* loop, we reference these two attributes directly so that when we make changes through the *data.gui* user interface, it immediately affects the rotation and scale of our object.

Add a similar function named *setPerspectiveCameraControl* for the perspective camera to the *site.js* file:

```
    function setPerspectiveCameraControl(gl, glControl, obj) {
        var container = document.getElementById(gl);
        var scene = new THREE.Scene();

        // perspectiveCamera(fov, aspect, near, far)
        var camera = new THREE.PerspectiveCamera(45,
            container.clientWidth / container.clientHeight, 0.1, 1000);
        // position and point the camera to the center of the scene
        camera.position.x = 15;
```

```
    camera.position.y = 16;
    camera.position.z = 13;
    camera.lookAt(scene.position);

    // create renderer
    var renderer = new THREE.WebGLRenderer();
    renderer.setClearColor("lightgray", 1.0);
    renderer.setSize(container.clientWidth, container.clientHeight);
    container.appendChild(renderer.domElement);

    // add object
    obj.name = "obj"
    scene.add(obj);

    control = new function () {
        this.rotationSpeed = 0.005;
        this.scale = 1;
        this.aspect = camera.aspect;
        this.far = camera.far;
        this.near = camera.near;
        this.fov = camera.fov;
        this.positionz = camera.position.z;
        this.updateCamera = function () {
            camera.fov = control.fov;
            camera.aspect = control.aspect;
            camera.near = control.near;
            camera.far = control.far;
            camera.position.z = control.positionz;
            camera.updateProjectionMatrix();
        }
    };
    addControls(control, glControl);
    renderScene();
    function renderScene() {
        renderer.render(scene, camera);
        scene.getObjectByName('obj').rotation.x += control.rotationSpeed;
        scene.getObjectByName('obj').rotation.y += control.rotationSpeed;
        scene.getObjectByName('obj').rotation.z += control.rotationSpeed;
        scene.getObjectByName('obj').scale.set(control.scale, control.scale,
                                        control.scale);
        requestAnimationFrame(renderScene);
    }

    function addControls() {
        var gui = new dat.GUI({ autoPlace: false });
        gui.add(control, 'rotationSpeed', -0.1, 0.1);
        gui.add(control, 'scale', 0.01, 2);
        gui.add(control, 'fov', 0, 180).onChange(control.updateCamera);
        gui.add(control, 'aspect', 0, 4).onChange(control.updateCamera);
        gui.add(control, 'near', 0, 40).onChange(control.updateCamera);
        gui.add(control, 'far', 0, 1000).onChange(control.updateCamera);
        gui.add(control, "positionz", 0, 30).onChange(control.updateCamera);
        var customContainer = $('#' + glControl).append($(gui.domElement));
    }
}
```

This function is basically similar to the *setOrthographicCameraControl* function, except that we define seven attributes specific to the perspective camera in the *control* object.

Now, we can test our helper functions. Add a new view named *CameraControl.cshtml* to the *Views/Basic3D* folder and replace its content with the following code:

```
@{
    ViewData["Title"] = ViewBag.Title;
}
<h3>@ViewBag.Title</h3>
@Html.Partial("_Links")

<div class="container">
    <div class="row">
        <div class="col-sm-8">
            <div style="margin-top:30px; margin-right:25px">
                <p style="margin-bottom:5px;">Orthographic camera</p>
                <div id="gl1" style="width:800px; height:600px;"></div>
            </div>
        </div>
        <div class="col-sm-4">
            <div style="margin-top:30px; margin-left:25px">
                <p style="margin-bottom:5px;">Control orthographic camera</p>
                <div id="gl2" style="width:280px; height:600px;
                    margin-top:10px"></div>
            </div>
        </div>
    </div>
    <div class="row">
        <div class="col-sm-8">
            <div style="margin-top:30px; margin-right:25px">
                <p style="margin-bottom:5px;">Perspective camera</p>
                <div id="gl3" style="width:800px; height:600px;"></div>
            </div>
        </div>
        <div class="col-sm-4">
            <div style="margin-top:30px; margin-left:25px">
                <p style="margin-bottom:5px;">Control perspective camera</p>
                <div id="gl4" style="width:280px; height:600px;
                    margin-top:10px"></div>
            </div>
        </div>
    </div>
</div>

@section scripts{
<script language="JavaScript" src="~/lib/mylib/dat.gui.js"></script>
<script>
    // orthographic camera
    var geometry = new THREE.BoxGeometry(300, 300, 300);
    var material = new THREE.MeshNormalMaterial();
    var obj = new THREE.Mesh(geometry, material);
    setOrthographicCameraControl("gl1", "gl2", obj);

    // perspective camera
    var geometry = new THREE.BoxGeometry(10, 10, 10);
```

```
    obj = new THREE.Mesh(geometry, material);
    setPerspectiveCameraControl("gl3", "gl4", obj);
</script>
}
```

Here, we simply create a cube object for both the orthographic and perspective cameras. When you run this example, you will see a simple user interface that you can use to control the various camera properties as well as rotation speed, scale, and distance between the cube and camera. Figures 8-10 and 8-11 shows the screenshots of the cube with a user interface control for orthographic and perspective cameras respectively.

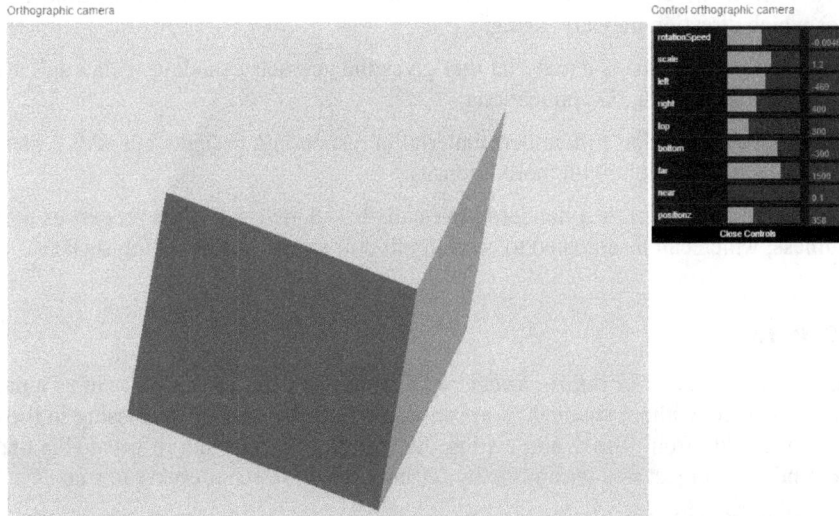

Figure 8-10. Cube with a user interface control for orthographic camera.

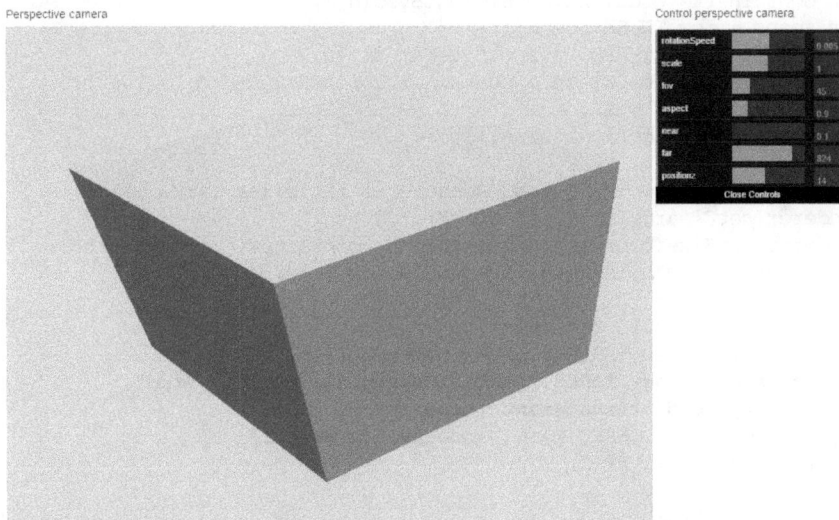

Figure 8-11. Cube with a user interface control for perspective camera.

Materials

The materials in Three.js determine how the surface of our geometry is drawn. If we consider the geometry as our skeleton, which define the shape, the material is then our skin. There are a variety of different types of materials in Three.js, all of which have different properties, like responding to lights, mapping textures, and adjusting opacity, etc. In this section, we will discuss following materials:

- *MeshBasicMaterial*: This is a basic material that passes a color to get a solid colored object without shading, or shows a wireframe of the object.

- *MeshNormalMaterial*: This material colors the faces of the mesh differently based on the face's normal or which direction they are facing.

- *MeshLambertMaterial*: This is a material that gives the geometry shading with a dull surface. It is a common material in most 3D applications.

- *MeshPhongMaterial*: Similar to Lambert material in responding to lights but adds a metallic luster to the surface, reflecting light with more intensity.

- *MeshStandardMaterial*: This is a standard physically based material. It has properties for roughness and metalness, which can be adjusted to create both dull and metallic looking surface.

Basic Materials

The most basic material is the *MeshBasicMaterial*, in which you can pass a *color* in as a parameter to get a solid colored object without shading. You can also adjust the opacity by passing in the *opacity* as a parameter with a value from 0 to 1 and setting the *transparent* attribute to true. This material also allows you to render the object as a wireframe by setting the *wireframe* property to true.

Add a new JavaScript function named *setMeshBasicMaterial* to the *site.js* file:

```
function setMeshBasicMaterial(gl) {
    var container = document.getElementById(gl);
    var scene = new THREE.Scene();
    var camera = new THREE.PerspectiveCamera(45,
        container.clientWidth / container.clientHeight, 0.1, 1000);
    camera.position.z = 12;
    camera.updateProjectionMatrix();

    var renderer = new THREE.WebGLRenderer({ antialias: true });
    renderer.setClearColor("lightgray", 1.0);
    renderer.setSize(container.clientWidth, container.clientHeight);
    container.appendChild(renderer.domElement);

    // sphere with solid red color
    var geometry = new THREE.SphereGeometry(2, 16, 16);
    var material1 = new THREE.MeshBasicMaterial({ color: "red",
        opacity: 0.6, transparent: true });
    var sphere1 = new THREE.Mesh(geometry, material1);
    sphere1.position.x = -2;
    sphere1.position.y = 2;
    scene.add(sphere1);

    // sphere with green wireframe
    var material2 = new THREE.MeshBasicMaterial({ color: "green",
```

```
        wireframe: true });
    var sphere2 = new THREE.Mesh(geometry, material2);
    sphere2.position.x = 2;
    sphere2.position.y = 2;
    scene.add(sphere2);

    // sphere with red solid color + green wireframe
    var sphere3 = new THREE.Mesh(geometry, material1);
    sphere3.position.x = -2;
    sphere3.position.y = -2;
    scene.add(sphere3);
    sphere3 = new THREE.Mesh(geometry, material2);
    sphere3.position.x = -2;
    sphere3.position.y = -2;
    scene.add(sphere3);

    // sphere with combining materials
    var sphere4 = new THREE.SceneUtils.createMultiMaterialObject(geometry,
        [material1, material2]);
    sphere4.position.x = 2;
    sphere4.position.y = -2;
    scene.add(sphere4);

    var render = function () {
        requestAnimationFrame(render);
        scene.traverse(function (e) {
            if (e instanceof THREE.Mesh) {
                e.rotation.x += 0.005;
                e.rotation.y += 0.005;
                e.rotation.z += 0.005;
            }
        });
        renderer.render(scene, camera);
    }
    render();
}
```

This function create four spheres with the *MeshBasicMaterial*. The first one with a red color, named *material1*:

```
var material1 = new THREE.MeshBasicMaterial({ color: "red",
                opacity: 0.6, transparent: true });
```

You can see that we also set opacity to 0.6 for this material. The second sphere is a green wireframe specified using *material2*:

```
var material2 = new THREE.MeshBasicMaterial({ color: "green",
                wireframe: true });
```

The third sphere actually consists of two spheres: one is the red color sphere with *material1* and the other one is a green-wireframe sphere with *material2*. The resulted object is a red sphere with a green wireframe.

The fourth sphere is the same as the third one, except that we use *SceneUtils* helper function:

```
var sphere4 = new THREE.SceneUtils.createMultiMaterialObject(geometry,
            [material1, material2]);
```

This creates a new *sphere4* object with a new mesh for each material defined in the array. This is mostly useful for object that needs a material and a wireframe implementation.

We can test this function by adding a new view named *Material.cshtml* to the *Views/Basic3D* folder. Here is the code for this view:

```
@{
    ViewData["Title"] = ViewBag.Title;
}
<h3>@ViewBag.Title</h3>
@Html.Partial("_Links")

<div class="container">
    <div class="row">
        <div class="col-sm-6">
            <div style="margin-top:30px; margin-right:25px">
                <p style="margin-bottom:5px;">Mesh basic material</p>
                <div id="gl1" style="width:600px; height:480px;"></div>
            </div>
        </div>
        <div class="col-sm-6">
            <div style="margin-top:30px; margin-left:25px">
                <p style="margin-bottom:5px;">Mesh normal material</p>
                <div id="gl2" style="width:600px; height:480px;
                    margin-top:-2px"></div>
            </div>
        </div>
    </div>
    <div class="row">
        <div class="col-sm-6">
            <div style="margin-top:30px; margin-right:25px">
                <p style="margin-bottom:5px;">Mesh lambert material</p>
                <div id="gl3" style="width:600px; height:480px;"></div>
            </div>
        </div>
        <div class="col-sm-6">
            <div style="margin-top:30px; margin-left:25px">
                <p style="margin-bottom:5px;">Mesh phong material</p>
                <div id="gl4" style="width:600px; height:480px;"></div>
            </div>
        </div>
    </div>
    <div class="row">
        <div class="col-sm-6">
            <div style="margin-top:30px; margin-right:25px">
                <p style="margin-bottom:5px;">Mesh standard material</p>
                <div id="gl5" style="width:600px; height:480px;"></div>
            </div>
        </div>
    </div>
</div>

@section scripts{
<script>
    // basic material
    setMeshBasicMaterial("gl1");
```

```
...... (more code goes to here)

</script>
}
```

The HTML code creates six *gl div* elements that will be used to hold our objects with different materials. Here we only use the *gl1 div* element that shows objects with *MeshBasicMaterial* by calling the *setMeshBasicMaterial* helper function implemented in the *site.js* file.

Running this example produces the results shown in Figure 8-12.

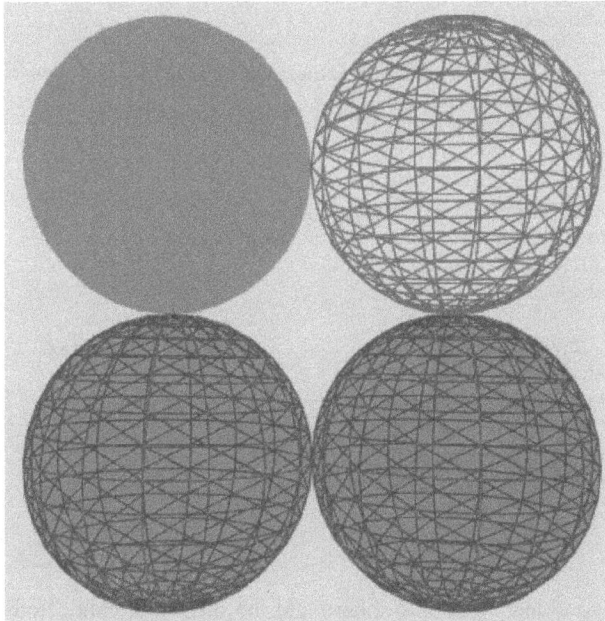

Figure 8-12. Demonstration of spheres with basic materials.

Normal Materials

MeshNormalMaterial maps the normal vectors to RGB colors. It will color the faces of the object differently based on the face's normal or what direction they are facing.

Add a new JavaScript function named *setMaterial* to the *site.js* file:

```
function setMaterial(gl, material) {
    var container = document.getElementById(gl);
    var scene = new THREE.Scene();
    var camera = new THREE.PerspectiveCamera(45,
        container.clientWidth / container.clientHeight, 0.1, 1000);
    camera.position.z = 12;

    var renderer = new THREE.WebGLRenderer({ antialias: true });
    renderer.setClearColor("lightgray", 1.0);
    renderer.setSize(container.clientWidth, container.clientHeight);
```

```
        renderer.shadowMap.enabled = true;
        container.appendChild(renderer.domElement);

        // add ambient lighting
        var ambientLight = new THREE.AmbientLight(0x0c0c0c);
        scene.add(ambientLight);
        // add spotlight for the shadows
        var spotLight = new THREE.SpotLight("white");
        spotLight.position.set(-3, 30, 30);
        spotLight.castShadow = true;
        scene.add(spotLight);

        // sphere with red color
        var geometry = new THREE.SphereGeometry(2, 16, 16);
        var sphere = new THREE.Mesh(geometry, material);
        sphere.position.x = -2.5;
        scene.add(sphere);

        // cube with red color
        geometry = new THREE.BoxGeometry(3, 3, 3);
        var cube = new THREE.Mesh(geometry, material);
        cube.position.x = 2.5;
        scene.add(cube);

        var render = function () {
            requestAnimationFrame(render);
            cube.rotation.x += 0.005;
            cube.rotation.y += 0.005;
            cube.rotation.z += 0.005;
            renderer.render(scene, camera);
        }
        render();
    }
```

This function creates two objects: one is a sphere and the other is a cube. Both are defined using the material specified in the input argument. We can test this function to see how the objects change colors based on their normal directions.

Add the following code snippet to the script section of the *Material.cshtml* file:

```
// normal material
var normalMaterial = new THREE.MeshNormalMaterial({ color: "red" });
setMaterial("gl2", normalMaterial);
```

Here, we define a normal material with red color. The *gl2 div* element was defined in the HTML section in the preceding basic material example. This code will produce the results shown in Figure 8-13.

Lambert Materials

MeshLambertMaterial takes shading into account and is used to create dull non-shiny-looking objects.

Add the following code snippet to the script section of the *Material.cshtml* file:

Figure 8-13. Demonstration of normal materials.

```
// Lambert material
var lambertMaterial = new THREE.MeshLambertMaterial({ color: "red" });
setMaterial("gl3", lambertMaterial);
```

Here, we define a red Lambert material. This produces the results shown in Figure 8-14.

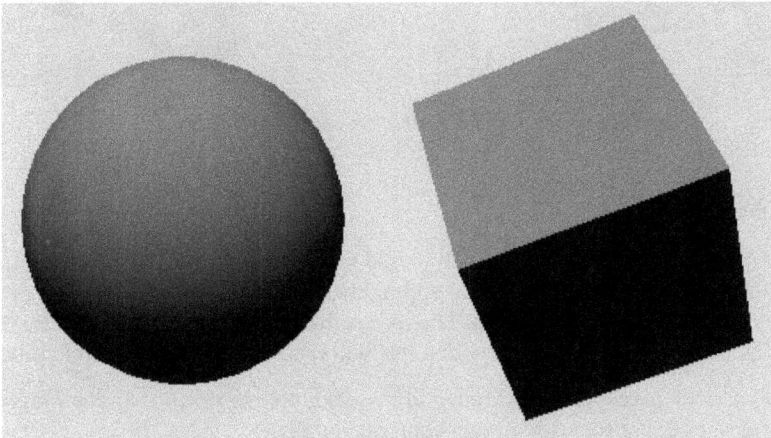

Figure 8-14. Demonstration of Lambert materials.

Phong Materials

Similar to Lambert material, *MeshPhongMaterial* also responds to lights but adds a metallic luster to the surface, reflecting light with more intensity. You can add a specular color and adjust the shininess property of this material to control the intensity of the light reflection.

Add the following code snippet to the *Material.cshtml* file:

```
// phong material
var phongMaterial = new THREE.MeshPhongMaterial({ color: "red",
```

```
        specular: "#222222", shininess: 50 });
    setMaterial("gl4", phongMaterial);
```

Here we define *MeshPhongMaterial*, in which we set its *color* to red, the *specular* color to 0x222222 (dark grey, the default value is a very dark grey color 0x111111), and *shininess* to 50 (default value is 30). Note that a higher shininess value gives a sharper highlight. You can adjust these and other attributes to control the shininess of your objects.

This produces the results shown in Figure 8-15.

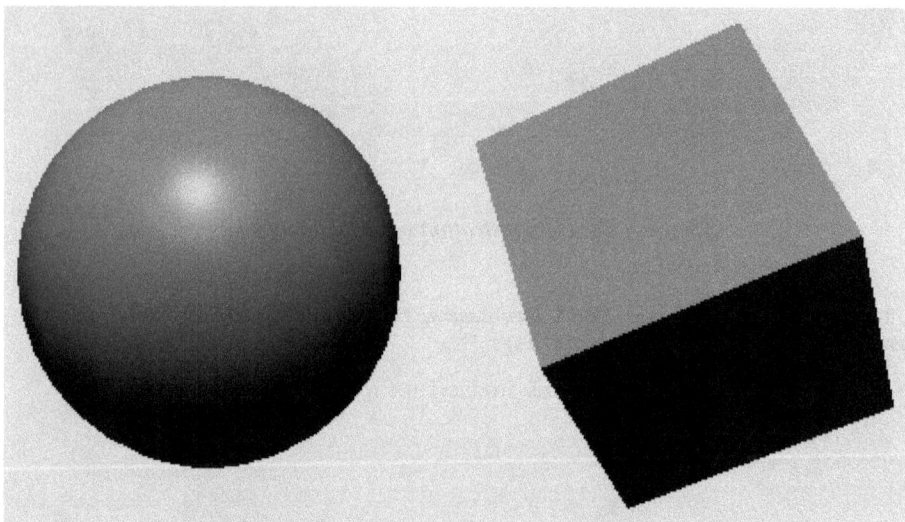

Figure 8-15. Demonstration of phong materials.

Standard Materials

MeshStandardMaterial is a standard physically based material. Physically based rendering is different from older approaches in that instead of using approximations for the way in which light interacts with a surface, a physically correct model is used. The idea is that instead of tweaking materials to look good under specific lighting, a material can be created that will react correctly under all lighting conditions.

In practice, this material gives more accurate and realistic looking result than the Lambert and phong materials, at the cost of being somewhat more computationally expensive.

Add the following code snippet to the *Material.cshtml* file:

```
// standard material
var standardMaterial = new THREE.MeshStandardMaterial({ color: "red",
    metalness: 0.2, roughness: 0.5 });
setMaterial("gl5", standardMaterial);
```

Here we define a standard material where we set its *color* to red, *metalness* to 0.2, and *roughness* to 0.5. The *metalness* attribute controls how much the material is like a metal. Non-metallic materials such as wood or stone use 0.0, metallic use 1.0. A value between 0.0 and 1.0 could be used for a rusty metal look. The *roughness* attribute represents how rough the material appears: 0.0 means a smooth mirror reflection and 1.0 means fully diffuse.

This produces the results shown in Figure 8-16.

Figure 8-16. Demonstration of standard materials.

Lights

Three.js has implemented a variety of lights to apply to materials such as Lambert, phong, and standard materials. The lights affect materials in different ways depending on the type of light and their properties as well as the properties of the materials themselves.

In this section, we will discuss several commonly used light sources, including ambient, point, spot, and directional lights.

Ambient Lights

AmbientLight in Three.js is a basic light that illuminates all objects in the scene globally. This light cannot be used to cast shadows because it does not have a direction. It is often useful for filling parts of your scene not hit by other lights. This is because there is no relevant position or direction, it lights everything equally. You can set the color and the intensity of the ambient light.

Add a new JavaScript function *setLightSource* to the *site.js* file:

```
function setLightSource(gl, lightSources) {
    var container = document.getElementById(gl);
    var scene = new THREE.Scene();
    var camera = new THREE.PerspectiveCamera(45,
        container.clientWidth / container.clientHeight, 0.1, 1000);
    camera.position.x = -20;
    camera.position.y = 15;
    camera.position.z = 12;
    camera.lookAt(new THREE.Vector3(5, 0, 0));

    var renderer = new THREE.WebGLRenderer({ antialias: true });
    renderer.setClearColor("#333333", 1.0);
    renderer.setSize(container.clientWidth, container.clientHeight);
```

```
renderer.shadowMap.enabled = true;
renderer.shadowMap.type = THREE.PCFSoftShadowMap;
container.appendChild(renderer.domElement);

// add a plane
var planeGoemetry = new THREE.PlaneGeometry(35, 15, 1, 1);
var planeMaterial = new THREE.MeshLambertMaterial({ color: 0xffffff });
var plane = new THREE.Mesh(planeGoemetry, planeMaterial);
plane.receiveShadow = true;
plane.rotation.x = -0.5 * Math.PI;
plane.position.set(7.5, 0, 0);
scene.add(plane);

// add an icosahedron
var material = new THREE.MeshLambertMaterial({ color: "#99ff00" });
var geometry = new THREE.IcosahedronGeometry(4, 0);
var obj = new THREE.Mesh(geometry, material);
obj.castShadow = true;
obj.position.y = 4;
var mat = new THREE.LineBasicMaterial({ color: "black"});
var geo = new THREE.EdgesGeometry(obj.geometry);
var wireframe = new THREE.LineSegments(geo, mat);
obj.add(wireframe);
scene.add(obj);

// add subtle ambient lighting
var ambientLight = new THREE.AmbientLight("#404040", 1.2);
scene.add(ambientLight);

for (var i = 0; i < lightSources.length; i++) {
    scene.add(lightSources[i]);
}

var render = function () {
    requestAnimationFrame(render);
    obj.rotation.x += 0.005;
    obj.rotation.y += 0.005;
    obj.rotation.z += 0.005;
    renderer.render(scene, camera);
}
render();
}
```

This function creates an icosahedron and a plane. The plane is used to display the shadow of the icosahedron object. This function also defines an ambient light source (see the highlight code) for the background lightning.

Add a new view named *Light.cshtml* to the *Views/Basic3D* folder and replace its content with the following code:

```
@{
    ViewData["Title"] = ViewBag.Title;
}
<h3>@ViewBag.Title</h3>
@Html.Partial("_Links")
```

```
<div class="container">
    <div class="row">
        <div class="col-sm-4">
            <div style="margin-top:30px; margin-right:25px">
                <p style="margin-bottom:5px;">Ambient light</p>
                <div id="gl1" style="width:400px; height:300px;"></div>
            </div>
        </div>
        <div class="col-sm-4">
            <div style="margin-top:30px; margin-left:25px">
                <p style="margin-bottom:5px;">Spot light</p>
                <div id="gl2" style="width:400px; height:300px;
                    margin-top:-2px"></div>
            </div>
        </div>
    </div>
    <div class="row">
        <div class="col-sm-4">
            <div style="margin-top:30px; margin-right:25px">
                <p style="margin-bottom:5px;">Point light</p>
                <div id="gl3" style="width:400px; height:300px;"></div>
            </div>
        </div>
        <div class="col-sm-4">
            <div style="margin-top:30px; margin-left:25px">
                <p style="margin-bottom:5px;">Drectional light</p>
                <div id="gl4" style="width:400px; height:300px;"></div>
            </div>
        </div>
    </div>
</div>

@section scripts{
<script>
    // ambient light (add spotlight for the shadows)
    var spotLight = new THREE.SpotLight("#222222");
    spotLight.position.set(0, 10, 0);
    spotLight.castShadow = true;
    var ambient = [spotLight];
    setLightSource("gl1", ambient);

    ...... (more code goes to here)

</script>
}
```

For ambient light, we basically use the default background ambient light implemented inside the *setLightSource* function. Here, we add a weak spot-light to show the shadow of our object.

Running this example, selecting the *Basic 3D Shapes* tab, and clicking the *Light Sources* link produces the results shown in Figure 8-17.

Figure 8-17. Demonstration of ambient lights.

Spot Lights

SpotLight in Three.js points in one direction radiating out in a cone shape. This light can cast shadows. It is one of lights, which you will use most often (especially if you want to see shadows). You can compare it with a flashlight or a lantern. *THREE.SpotLight* exposes several parameters that allows you to adjust the color, intensity, cone angle, etc.

Creating a spotlight in Three.js is easy. Just specify the color, set the properties you want, and add it to the scene, and you are done. Add the following code snippet to the script section of the *Light.cshtml* file:

```
// spot light
var spotLight = new THREE.SpotLight("red");
spotLight.position.set(-8, 13, 0);
spotLight.castShadow = true;
spotLight.intensity = 2;
spotLight.angle = Math.PI / 4;
var spotHelper = new THREE.SpotLightHelper(spotLight);
var spots = [spotLight, spotHelper];
setLightSource("gl2", spots);
```

Here, we specify a red spotlight with specified properties: *intensity* (= 2), *angle* (= 45 degrees), and *castShadow* (= *true*). Note that we also create a *spotHelper* object using the *THREE.SpotLightHelper* function, which displays a cone shaped helper object for the specified spotlight and provides the location of the light source and the cone size.

Running this example produces the results shown in Figure 8-18.

Point Lights

Point light is positioned at a specific location and radiates light outwards in all directions from that position. A common use case for this light is to replicate the light emitted from a bare lightbulb. This light can cast shadows.

Add the following code snippet to the *Light.cshtml* file:

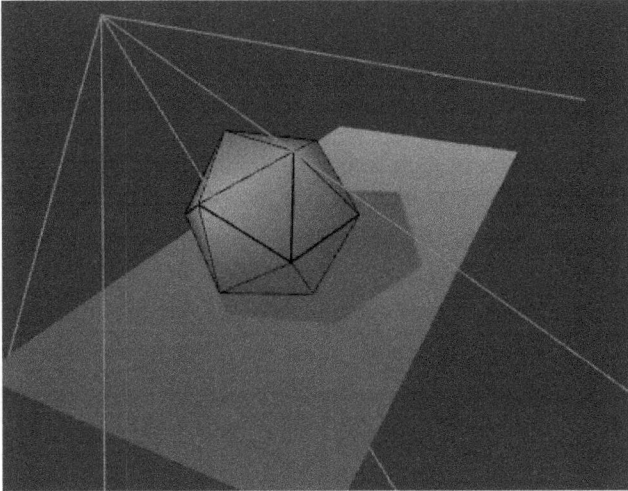

Figure 8-18. Demonstration of spotlights.

```
// point light
var pointLight = new THREE.PointLight("yellow");
pointLight.castShadow = true;
pointLight.position.set(0, 12, 0);
pointLight.intensity = 1;
var pointHelper = new THREE.PointLightHelper(pointLight, 0.3);
var points = [pointLight, pointHelper];
setLightSource("gl3", points);
```

Here, we also add a *pointHelper* object using the *THREE.PointLightHelper* function, which displays a helper object consisting of a spherical mesh for visualizing the specified point light.

Running this example produces the results shown in Figure 8-19.

Figure 8-19. Demonstration of a yellow point light.

Directional Lights

Directional light can be considered as a light that is very far away. All the light rays it sends out are parallel to each other. A good example of this light is the sun. The sun is so far ways that the light rays we receive on earth are almost parallel to each other. The main difference between the spot and directional lights is that the directional light would not diminish the father it gets from the target. The complete area that is lit by the directional light receives the same intensity of light.

To see this light in action, add the following code snippet to the *Light.cshtml* file:

```
// directional light
var directionalLight = new THREE.DirectionalLight("white", 1);
directionalLight.position.set(-8, 13, 0);
directionalLight.castShadow = true;
var directHelper = new THREE.DirectionalLightHelper(directionalLight, 0.2);
var directs = [directionalLight, directHelper];
setLightSource("gl4", directs);
```

Here, we also create a *directHelper* object using the *THREE.DirectionalLightHelper* function, which assists with visualizing a directional light's effect on the scene. This helper object consists of a small plane and a line representing the light's position and direction.

Running this example produces the results shown in Figure 8-20.

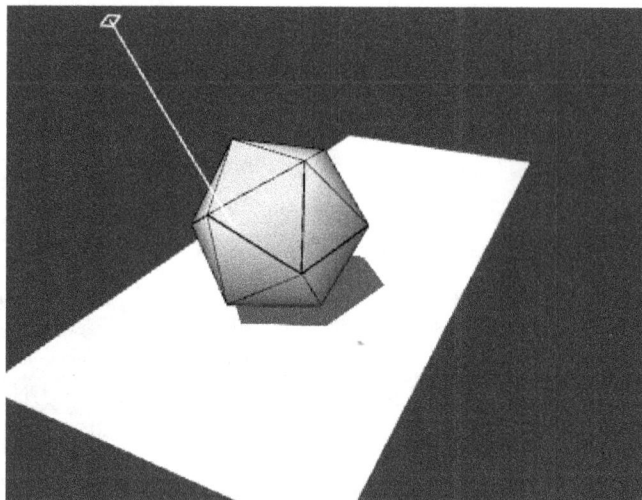

Figure 8-20. Demonstration of a white directional light.

Geometries

In the preceding sections, we demonstrated how to create a basic scene, set camera, add lighting, and configure the materials for your objects in Three.js. In this section, we will walk you through some commonly used geometries available in Three.js. Geometry defines the shapes of the objects you draw on the screen. It consists of a collection of vertices and often faces that combine three vertices into a triangle face. Three.js has a variety of built-in geometries for you to access and set properties of common 3D shapes, but it also allows you to create your own custom geometry by defining the vertices and faces.

Base Geometries

Three.js has two base types of geometries: the first one is *Geometry* and the other one is *BufferGeometry*. *Geometry* is a base class for all geometries (but not for *BufferGeometry*), and can be used directly to build custom geometries. You can use *Geometry* to add vertices by pushing vertices into its vertex array. You can do the same thing for faces by referencing the vertices used in each face and pushing them into the geometry's face array. The following code snippet shows how to create a single triangular face made up of three vertices:

```
var geometry = new THREE.Geometry();
geometry.vertices.push(
    new THREE.Vector3(-1,  1, 0),
    new THREE.Vector3(-1, -1, 0),
    new THREE.Vector3( 1, -1, 0)
);
geometry.faces.push( new THREE.Face3(0, 1, 2));
```

BufferGeometry is more optimized for performance but the vertices are not as directly accessible. In order to add vertices to *BufferGeometry*, you need to create a *Float32Array* of the vertices and then add it to the position attribute of the geometry using *BufferAttribute*, as illustrated in the following code snippet used to create a simple square shape:

```
var geometry = new THREE.BufferGeometry()
var vertices = new Float32Array([
    -1.0, -1.0, 1.0,
     1.0, -1.0, 1.0,
     1.0,  1.0, 1.0,

     1.0,  1.0, 1.0,
    -1.0,  1.0, 1.0,
    -1.0, -1.0, 1.0
]);
geometry.addAttribute("position", new THREE.BufferAttribute(vertices, 3));
var material = new THREE.MeshBasicMaterial({ color: "red" });
var mesh = new THREE.Mesh(geometry, material);
```

You can see that we duplicate the top left and bottom right vertices because each vertex needs to appear per triangle.

BufferGeometry stores all data, including vertex positions, face indices, normal, colors, UVs, and custom attributes within buffers, this reduces the cost of passing all the data to the GPU. This also makes *BufferGeometry* harder to work with than *Geometry*; rather than accessing position data as *Vector3* objects, color data as *Color* objects, and so on, you have to access the raw data from the appropriate attribute buffer.

Built-In Geometries

As mentioned previously, Three.js has a bunch of built-in geometric primitives, including 2D and 3D geometries. In the following subsection, we will first discuss the 2D built-in geometries.

2D Geometries

In this section, we will look at the 2D built-in geometries in Three.js, including *plane*, *circle*, *ring* and *shape* geometries. 2D objects look like flat objects and only have two dimensions. The first 2D geometry is the *THREE.PlaneGeometry* that can be used to create a 2D rectangle, as shown in the following code snippet:

```
var geometry = new THREE.PlaneGeometry(width, height,
                                        widthSegments, heightSegments);
```

THREE.PlaneGeometry takes the *width, height, widthSegments*, and *heightSegments* as input arguments. The *widthSegements* (*heightSegments*) is the number of segments the width (height) should be divided into. The default value is 1.

Another simple 2D geometry in Three.js is *THREE.CircleGeometry*, which allows you to create a simple 2D circle (or partial circle). To use this geometry, you need to define the radius of the circle and the number of segments it is divided into, as well as the start angle and the angle defining the drawn segments, as shown in the following code snippet:

```
var geometry = new THREE.CircleGeometry(radius, segments, thetaStart,
                                        thetaLength);
```

You will get a complete circle if you use the default values for *thetaStart* ($= 0$) and *thetaLength* ($= 2\pi$). Otherwise you will get a partial circle if you set the *thetaLength* $< 2\pi$.

The next 2D geometry is *THREE.RingGeometry*, which allows you to create a 2D ring shape. This geometry specifies the inner and outer radius. The segments broken into around the circumference as well as out from width of the ring. You can also specify the start and end angles for drawing partial sections of the ring. The following code snippet shows how to create a ring shape:

```
var geometry = new THREE.RingGeometry(innerRadius, outerRadius, thetaSegments,
    phiSegments, thetaStart, thetaLength);
```

The 2D plane, circle, and ring geometries we just discussed have limited ways of customizing their appearance. If you want to create custom 2D objects, you can use *THREE.ShapeGeometry*. This geometry has a couple of functions that can be used to create our own shapes. This functionality is very similar to the SVG *path* element discussed in Chapter 2. Next, we will use an example to demonstrate how to create a 2D heart-shape object using *THREE.ShapeGeometry*.

Add a new JavaScript function named *setBuiltIn2DGeometry* to the *site.js* file:

```
function setBuiltIn2DGeometry(gl, geometryType, options) {
    var widthSegments = options.widthSegments || 1;
    var heightSegments = options.heightSegments || 1;
    var thetaStart = options.thetaStart || 0;
    var thetaLength = options.thetaLength || 2 * Math.PI;
    var thetaSegments = options.thetaSegments || 8;
    var phiSegments = options.phiSegments || 8;

    var container = document.getElementById(gl);
    while (container.firstChild) {
        container.removeChild(container.firstChild);
    }
    var scene = new THREE.Scene();
    var camera = new THREE.PerspectiveCamera(45,
        container.clientWidth / container.clientHeight, 0.1, 1000);
    camera.position.x = -10;
```

```
camera.position.y = 15;
camera.position.z = 20;
camera.lookAt(scene.position);

var renderer = new THREE.WebGLRenderer({ antialias: true });
renderer.setClearColor("lightgray", 1.0);
renderer.setSize(container.clientWidth, container.clientHeight);
container.appendChild(renderer.domElement);

var ambientLight = new THREE.AmbientLight("#888888");
scene.add(ambientLight);
var spotLight = new THREE.SpotLight("white", 2);
spotLight.position.set(0, 0, 20);
scene.add(spotLight);

var material1 = new THREE.MeshStandardMaterial({ color: "steelblue",
    metalness: 0.5, roughness: 0.5 });
material1.side = THREE.DoubleSide;
var material2 = new THREE.MeshBasicMaterial({ color: "white",
    wireframe: true });
var geometry, obj;

switch (geometryType) {
    case "PlaneGeometry":
        geometry = new THREE.PlaneGeometry(14, 8, widthSegments,
                                           heightSegments);
        break;
    case "CircleGeometry":
        geometry = new THREE.CircleGeometry(7, thetaSegments, thetaStart,
                                            thetaLength);
        console.log("segments = " + thetaSegments);
        break;
    case "RingGeometry":
        geometry = new THREE.RingGeometry(3, 7, thetaSegments, phiSegments,
                                          thetaStart, thetaLength);
        break;
    case "ShapeGeometry":
        var x = 0, y = 0;
        var heartShape = new THREE.Shape();
        heartShape.moveTo(x + 5, y + 5);
        heartShape.bezierCurveTo(x + 5, y + 5, x + 4, y, x, y);
        heartShape.bezierCurveTo(x - 6, y, x - 6, y + 7, x - 6, y + 7);
        heartShape.bezierCurveTo(x - 6, y + 11, x - 3, y + 15.4, x + 5,
                                 y + 19);
        heartShape.bezierCurveTo(x + 12, y + 15.4, x + 16, y + 11, x + 16,
                                 y + 7);
        heartShape.bezierCurveTo(x + 16, y + 7, x + 16, y, x + 10, y);
        heartShape.bezierCurveTo(x + 7, y, x + 5, y + 5, x + 5, y + 5);
        geometry = new THREE.ShapeGeometry(heartShape)
        break;
}

obj = new THREE.SceneUtils.createMultiMaterialObject(geometry,
    [material1, material2]);
if (geometryType === "ShapeGeometry") {
```

```
                obj.scale.set(0.5, 0.5, 0.5);
        }
        scene.add(obj);
        render();

        function render() {
            requestAnimationFrame(render);
            obj.rotation.x += 0.005;
            obj.rotation.y += 0.005;
            obj.rotation.z += 0.005;
            renderer.render(scene, camera);
        }
    }
```

You should be familiar with the most part of the code, including creating scene, setting camera, specifying materials, and building renderer. The function creates a 2D plane, a circle, a ring, or a custom shape depending on the specified *geometryType* argument. For the *ShapeGeometry*, we create a *heartShape* object using *THREE.Shape*. You can see that we simply create the outline of this shape using several Bezier curve segments and pass in the *heartShape* object as the argument to *THREE.ShapeGeometry*. This gives a geometry that can be used to create a mesh.

Next, we will use an example to demonstrate how to create 2D shapes using this function. Add a new controller named *GeometryController.cs* to the *Controllers* folder and replace its content with the following code:

```
using Microsoft.AspNetCore.Mvc;

namespace Chapter08.Controllers
{
    public class GeometryController : Controller
    {
        // GET: /<controller>/
        public IActionResult Index()
        {
            ViewBag.Title = "Geometry: Home";
            return View();
        }

        public IActionResult BuiltIn2D()
        {
            ViewBag.Title = "Built-In 2D Geometries";
            return View();
        }

        public IActionResult BuiltIn3D()
        {
            ViewBag.Title = "Built-In 3D Geometries";
            return View();
        }

        public IActionResult ParametricGeometry()
        {
            ViewBag.Title = "Parametric Geometries";
            return View();
        }
```

```
        }
    }
```

Add a new folder named *Geometry* to the *Views* folder. Add a new view named *BuiltIn2D.cshtml* to the *Views/Geometry* folder and replace its content with the following code:

```
@{
    ViewData["Title"] = ViewBag.Title;
}
<h3>@ViewBag.Title</h3>
@Html.Partial("_Links")
<hr />

<div class="container">
    <div class="row" style="margin-top:50px">
        <div class="col-sm-2">
            <span class="label label-info" id="geometryname">
                Geometry Name:
                PlaneGeometry
            </span>
        </div>
        <div class="col-sm-2">
            <div class="dropdown">
                <button class="btn btn-primary dropdown-toggle" type="button"
                        data-toggle="dropdown">
                    Built-In 2D Geometries
                    <span class="caret"></span>
                </button>
                <ul class="dropdown-menu" id="dm">
                    <li><a href="#">PlaneGeometry</a></li>
                    <li><a href="#">CircleGeometry</a></li>
                    <li><a href="#">RingGeometry</a></li>
                    <li><a href="#">ShapeGeometry</a></li>
                </ul>
            </div>
        </div>
    </div>
    <div class="row">
        <div id="gl" style="width:500px; height:400px; margin-top:10px"></div>
    </div>
</div>

@section scripts{
<script type="text/javascript">
    var options = {
        widthSegments: 10,
        heightSegments: 6,
        thetaSegments: 32,
        phiSegments: 4
    };
    setBuiltIn2DGeometry("gl", "PlaneGeometry", options);

    $('#dm li a').on('click', function () {
        var text = $(this).text();
        $('#geometryname').text("Geometry Name: " + text);
        setBuiltIn2DGeometry("gl", text, options);
```

```
    });
</script>
}
```

This code defines a dropdown button that lets you select the geometry type. In the script section, we first specify the optional parameters that will be used to create 2D geometry shapes. We then use AJAX click event to call the *setBuiltIn2DGeometry*.

Running this example produces the default plane geometry shape shown in Figure 8-21.

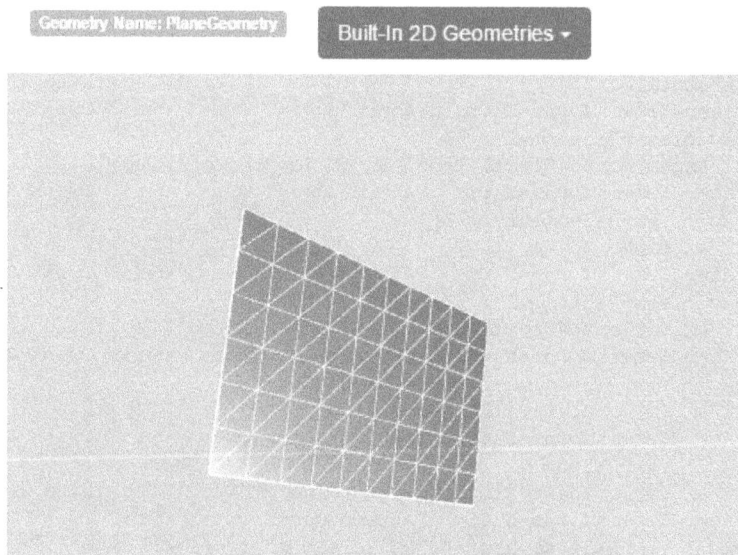

Figure 8-21. Demonstration of a 2D plane.

Selecting the *CircleGeometry* from the dropdown button produces the results shown in Figure 8-22.

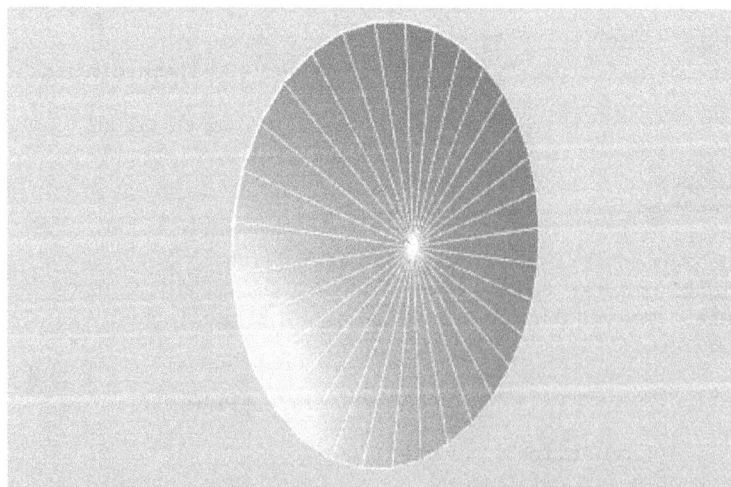

Figure 8-22. Demonstration of a 2D circle.

Selecting the *RingGeometry* from the dropdown button generates the result shown in Figure 8-23.

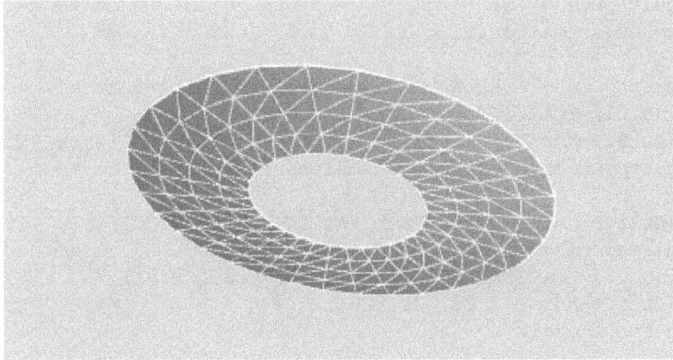

Figure 8-23. Demonstration of a 2D ring shape.

Finally, selecting the *ShapeGeometry* from the dropdown button produces the result shown in Figure 8-24.

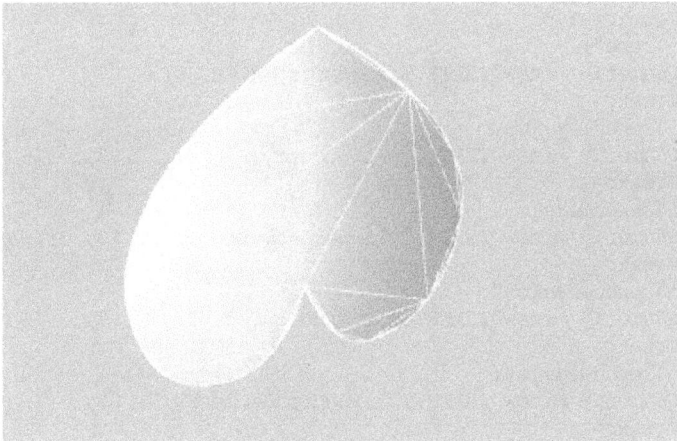

Figure 8-24. Demonstration of a custom heart shape.

3D Geometries

In this section, we will demonstrate how to create 3D shapes using built-in 3D geometries in Three.js. Following the same procedure as what we did for creating 2D shapes in the preceding section, we will first add a new JavaScript helper function named *setBuiltIn3DGeometry* to the *site.js* file:

```
function setBuiltIn3DGeometry(gl, geometryType) {
    var container = document.getElementById(gl);
    while (container.firstChild) {
        container.removeChild(container.firstChild);
    }
    var scene = new THREE.Scene();
    var camera = new THREE.PerspectiveCamera(45,
        container.clientWidth / container.clientHeight, 0.1, 1000);
```

```javascript
camera.position.x = -10;
camera.position.y = 15;
camera.position.z = 20;
camera.lookAt(scene.position);

var renderer = new THREE.WebGLRenderer({ antialias: true });
renderer.setClearColor("lightgray", 1.0);
renderer.setSize(container.clientWidth, container.clientHeight);
container.appendChild(renderer.domElement);

var ambientLight = new THREE.AmbientLight("#707070");
scene.add(ambientLight);
var spotLight = new THREE.SpotLight("#888888", 0.8);
spotLight.position.set(-10, 20, 20);
scene.add(spotLight);

var material1 = new THREE.MeshStandardMaterial({ color: "steelblue",
    metalness: 0.5, roughness: 0.5 });
var material2 = new THREE.MeshBasicMaterial({ color: "white",
    wireframe: true });
var geometry, obj;

switch (geometryType) {
    case "cube":
        geometry = new THREE.BoxGeometry(8, 8, 8);
        break;
    case "cone":
        geometry = new THREE.ConeGeometry(6, 10, 20, 5);
        break;
    case "cylinder":
        geometry = new THREE.CylinderGeometry(5, 5, 10, 15, 3);
        break;
    case "dodecahedron":
        geometry = new THREE.DodecahedronGeometry(7, 0);
        break;
    case "icosahedron":
        geometry = new THREE.IcosahedronGeometry(7, 0);
        break;
    case "octahedron":
        geometry = new THREE.OctahedronGeometry(7, 0);
        break;
    case "sphere":
        geometry = new THREE.SphereGeometry(7, 16, 16);
        break;
    case "tetrahedron":
        geometry = new THREE.TetrahedronGeometry(8, 0);
        break;
    case "torus":
        geometry = new THREE.TorusGeometry(6, 1.7, 10, 20);
        break;
    case "torusknot":
        geometry = new THREE.TorusKnotGeometry(6, 1.5, 50, 8);
        break;
}
```

```
    obj = new THREE.SceneUtils.createMultiMaterialObject(geometry,
        [material1, material2]);
scene.add(obj);
render();

function render() {
    requestAnimationFrame(render);
    obj.rotation.x += 0.005;
    obj.rotation.y += 0.005;
    obj.rotation.z += 0.005;
    renderer.render(scene, camera);
}
}
```

This function creates ten different 3D shapes, including cube, cone, cylinder, etc. We can test this function by adding a new view named *BuiltIn3D.cshtml* to the *Views/Geometry* folder. Here is the code for this view:

```
@{
    ViewData["Title"] = ViewBag.Title;
}
<h3>@ViewBag.Title</h3>
@Html.Partial("_Links")

<div class="container">
    <div class="row" style="margin-top:50px">
        <div class="col-sm-2">
            <span class="label label-info" id="geometryname">
                Geometry Name:
                cube
            </span>
        </div>
        <div class="col-sm-2">
            <div class="dropdown">
                <button class="btn btn-primary dropdown-toggle" type="button"
                        data-toggle="dropdown">
                    Built-In 3D Geometries
                    <span class="caret"></span>
                </button>
                <ul class="dropdown-menu" id="dm">
                    <li><a href="#">cube</a></li>
                    <li><a href="#">cone</a></li>
                    <li><a href="#">cylinder</a></li>
                    <li><a href="#">dodecahedron</a></li>
                    <li><a href="#">icosahedron</a></li>
                    <li><a href="#">octahedron</a></li>
                    <li><a href="#">sphere</a></li>
                    <li><a href="#">tetrahedron</a></li>
                    <li><a href="#">torus</a></li>
                    <li><a href="#">torusknot</a></li>
                </ul>
            </div>
        </div>
    </div>
    <div class="row">
        <div id="gl" style="width:500px; height:400px; margin-top:10px"></div>
```

```
        </div>
    </div>

    @section scripts{
    <script type="text/javascript">
        setBuiltIn3DGeometry("gl", "cube");

        $('#dm li a').on('click', function () {
            var text = $(this).text();
            $('#geometryname').text("Geometry Name: " + text);

            setBuiltIn3DGeometry("gl", text);
        });
    </script>
    }
```

This code implements a dropdown button, which allows you to select the built-in 3D geometry type to create corresponding 3D shape.

The first geometry type is *THREE.BoxGeometry* that is a quadrilateral primitive geometry class. It is typically used to create a cube or irregular quadrilateral of the dimensions specified by *width*, *height*, and *depth* arguments:

```
var geometry = new THREE.BoxGeometry(width, height, depth);
```

Running this example and selecting *cube* from the dropdown button produce the result shown in Figure 8-25.

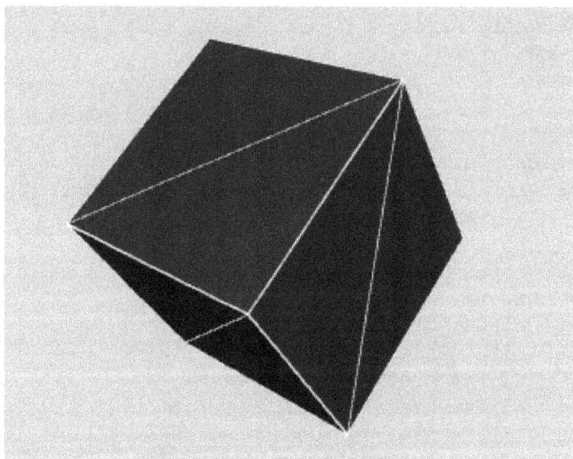

Figure 8-25. A 3D cube.

The next simple 3D geometry type is *THREE.ConeGeometry* that is used to generate 3D cone shapes. The constructor of this geometry has several arguments you can specify, including the *radius*, *height*, *radialSegments*, *heightSegments*, etc, as shown in the following code snippet:

```
var geometry = new THREE.ConeGeometry(radius, height, radialSegments,
                                       heightSegments);
```

Running this example and selecting *cone* from the dropdown button generate the result shown in Figure 8-26.

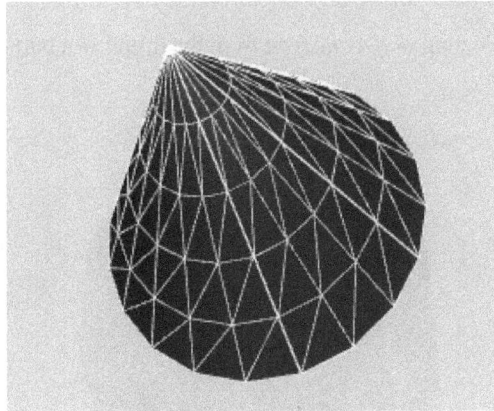

Figure 8-26. A 3D cone.

THREE.CylinderGeometry allows you to create cylinders and cylinder-like objects. This geometry type exposes several arguments that you can specify, including *radiusTop*, *radiusBottom*, *height*, *radiusSegments*, *heightSegments*, etc, as shown in the following code snippet:

```
var geometry = THREE.CylinderGeometry(radiusTop, radiusBottom, height,
                                      radiusSegments, heightSegments);
```

Running this example and selecting *cylinder* from the dropdown button generate the result shown in Figure 8-27.

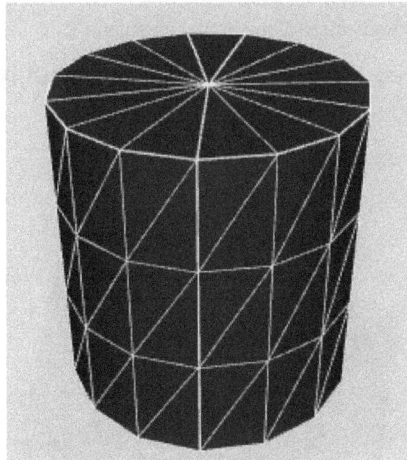

Figure 8-27. A 3D cylinder.

The next geometry type is *THREE.DodecahedronGeometry* that creates dodecahedron geometries. The constructor of this geometry only exposes two input parameters: *radius* and *detail*. The *radius* property defines the size of the geometry. The *detail* attribute should be set to 0, otherwise it will make the shape no longer a dodecahedron. The following code snippet shows how to create a dodecahedron shape:

```
var geometry = THREE.DodecahedronGeometry(radius, 0);
```

Running this example and selecting *dodecahedron* from the dropdown button generate the result shown in Figure 8-28.

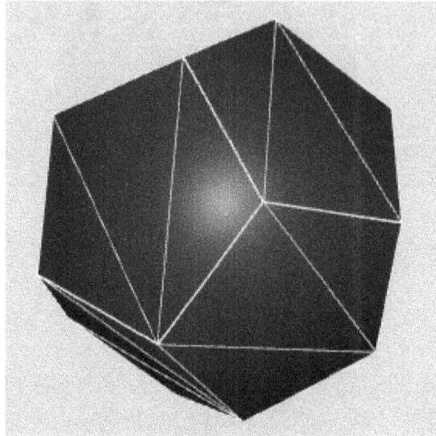

Figure 8-28. A 3D dodecahedron.

The next geometry type is *THREE.IcosahedronGeometry* that creates icosahedron geometries. The constructor of this geometry also exposes two input parameters: *radius* and *detail*. Again, the *radius* property defines the size of the geometry, and the *detail* attribute should be set to 0. The following code snippet shows how to create an icosahedron shape:

```
var geometry = THREE.IcosahedronGeometry(radius, 0);
```

Running this example and selecting *icosahedron* from the dropdown button generate the result shown in Figure 8-29.

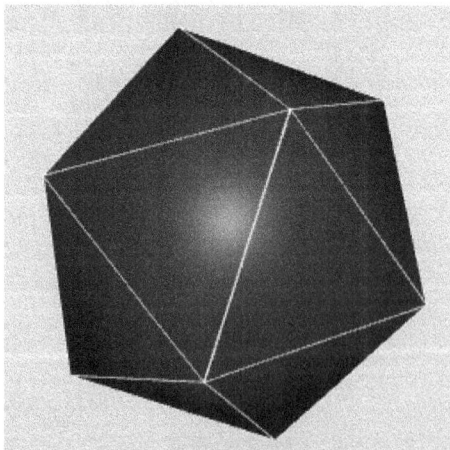

Figure 8-29. A 3D icosahedron.

The next geometry type is *THREE.OctahedronGeometry* that creates octahedron geometries. The constructor of this geometry only exposes two input parameters: *radius* and *detail*. The *radius* property defines the size of the geometry and the *detail* attribute should be set to 0. The following code snippet shows how to create an octahedron shape:

```
var geometry = THREE.OctahedronGeometry(radius, 0);
```

Running this example and selecting *octahedron* from the dropdown button generate the result shown in Figure 8-30.

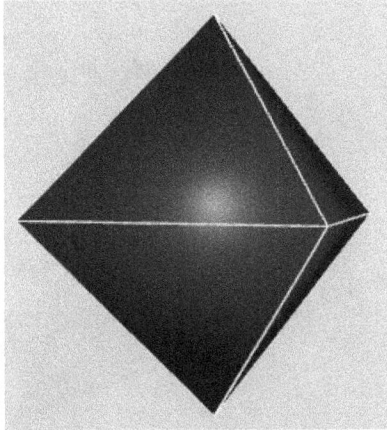

Figure 8-30. A 3D octahedron.

With *THREE.SphereGeometry*, you can create a 3D sphere with the following constructor:

```
var geometry = new THREE.SphereGeometry(radius, widthSegments, heightSegments);
```

The *widthSegments* represents the number of horizontal segments and the *heightSegments* represents the number of vertical segments. This geometry also exposes other properties such as *phiStart*, *phiLength*, *thetaStart*, and *thetaLength*, which can be used to created incomplete spheres.

Running this example and selecting *sphere* from the dropdown button generate the result shown in Figure 8-31.

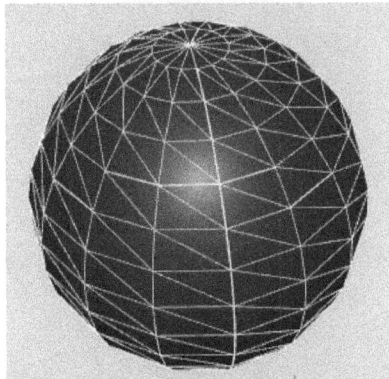

Figure 8-31. A 3D sphere.

THREE.TetrahedronGeometry creates tetrahedron geometries. The constructor of this geometry only exposes two input parameters: *radius* and *detail*. The *radius* property defines the size of the geometry, and the *detail* attribute should be set to 0. The following code snippet shows how to create an octahedron shape:

```
var geometry = THREE.TetrahedronGeometry(radius, 0);
```

Running this example and selecting *tetrahedron* from the dropdown button generate the result shown in Figure 8-32.

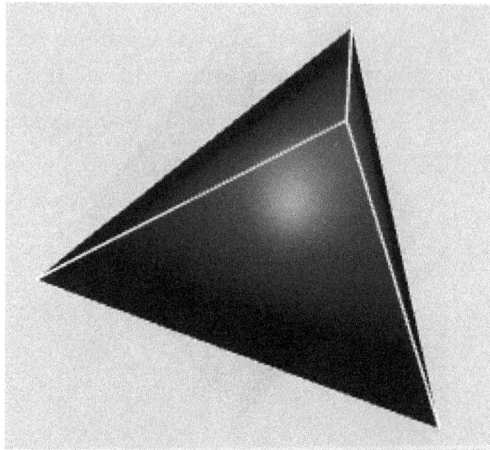

Figure 8-32. A 3D tetrahedron.

THREE.TorusGeometry is a tubular ring. It allows you to specify the radius of the ring, as well as the diameter of the tube. You can then specify the segments along the radius and tube. You can also specify the arc angle of the circumference to draw. The following code snippet creates a standard torus shape:

```
var geometry = new THREE.TorusGeometry(radius, tube, radialSegments,
                                       tubularSegments);
```

Running this example and selecting *torus* from the dropdown button generate the result shown in Figure 8-33.

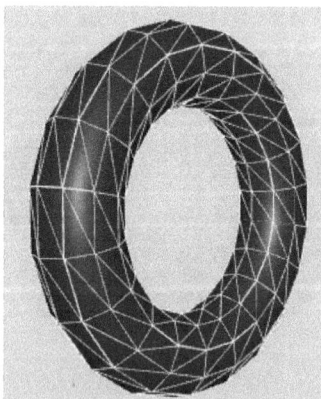

Figure 8-33. A 3D torus.

Finally, *THREE.TorusKnotGeometry* draws a knot shape defined by p and q. It takes in a radius for the whole and the diameter of the tube. Then we define the *tubularSegments* along the tube and *radialSegments* along the radius. The p attribute determines how many times the geometry winds around its axis of rotational symmetry and q determines how many times the geometry winds around a circle in the interior of the torus. The following code snippet create a torus knot shape with default p (= 2) and q (= 3) values:

```
var geometry = new THREE.TorusKnotGeometry(radius, tube, tubularSegments,
                                           radialSegments);
```

Running this example and selecting *torusknot* from the dropdown button generate the result shown in Figure 8-34.

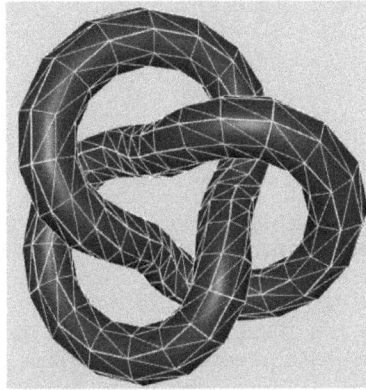

Figure 8-34. A 3D torus knot shape.

Parametric Geometries

Parametric geometry is useful for rendering a flat surface that distorts based on a parametric function. This surface can be described by a set of parametric equations. These equations define the vertex coordinates on the surface in terms of the parametric variables u, and v. Many complex surfaces can be represented using parametric equations. For example, the sphere, the torus, and quadric surfaces are all parametric surfaces.

In this section, I will show you how to create several parametric geometries using the parametric equations.

Add a new helper function named *setParametricGeometry* to the *site.js* file:

```
function setParametricGeometry(gl, geometryType) {
    var container = document.getElementById(gl);
    while (container.firstChild) {
        container.removeChild(container.firstChild);
    }
    var scene = new THREE.Scene();
    var camera = new THREE.PerspectiveCamera(45,
        container.clientWidth / container.clientHeight, 0.1, 1000);
    camera.position.set(-10, 15, 20);
    camera.lookAt(scene.position);
```

```
var renderer = new THREE.WebGLRenderer({ antialias: true });
renderer.setClearColor("lightgray", 1.0);
renderer.setSize(container.clientWidth, container.clientHeight);
container.appendChild(renderer.domElement);

var ambientLight = new THREE.AmbientLight(0x0c0c0c);
scene.add(ambientLight);
var spotLight = new THREE.SpotLight("white", 1.0);
spotLight.position.set(-15, 30, 30);
scene.add(spotLight);

var material1 = new THREE.MeshPhongMaterial({ color: "steelblue",
    side: THREE.DoubleSide, shading: THREE.FlatShading });
var material2 = new THREE.MeshBasicMaterial({ color: "white",
    wireframe: true });
var geometry, obj;

switch (geometryType) {
    case "helicoid":
        var func = function (u, v) {
            var u = 5 * u;
            var v = 5 * Math.PI * (v - 0.5);
            var x = u * Math.cos(v);
            var z = u * Math.sin(v);
            var y = v;
            var vec = new THREE.Vector3(x, y, z);
            return new THREE.Vector3(x, y, z);
        }
        geometry = new THREE.ParametricGeometry(func, 5, 50);
        break;
    case "hyperboloid":
        var func = function (u, v) {
            var u = 2 * Math.PI * u;
            var v = 3 * (v - 0.5);
            var x = 2 * Math.cos(u) * Math.cosh(v);
            var z = 1.5 * Math.sin(u) * Math.cosh(v);
            var y = 3 * Math.sinh(v);
            return new THREE.Vector3(x, y, z);
        }
        geometry = new THREE.ParametricGeometry(func, 20, 10);
        break;
    case "ellipticcone":
        var func = function (u, v) {
            var u = 2 * Math.PI * u;
            var v = 3 * (v - 0.5);
            var x = 2 * v * Math.cos(u);
            var z = 1.5 * v * Math.sin(u);
            var y = 3 * v;
            return new THREE.Vector3(x, y, z);
        }
        geometry = new THREE.ParametricGeometry(func, 20, 20);
        camera.position.set(-7, 9, 13);
        break;
    case "paraboloid":
        var func = function (u, v) {
```

```
                var u = 5 * (u - 0.5);
                var v = 5 * (v - 0.5);
                var x = 0.5 * v * Math.cosh(u);
                var z = 0.4 * v * Math.sinh(u);
                var y = v * v;
                return new THREE.Vector3(x, y, z);
            }
            geometry = new THREE.ParametricGeometry(func, 20, 20);
            break;
    }

    obj = new THREE.SceneUtils.createMultiMaterialObject(geometry,
        [material1, material2]);
    scene.add(obj);
    render();

    function render() {
        requestAnimationFrame(render);
        obj.rotation.x += 0.005;
        obj.rotation.y += 0.005;
        obj.rotation.z += 0.005;
        renderer.render(scene, camera);
    }
}
```

This function creates four parametric geometries: helicoid, hyperboloid, elliptic cone, and paraboloid. You can see that *THREE.ParametricGeometry* takes the value of a function that returns vectors and uses the UV values as parameters. Note that the u and v values will range from 0 to 1 and will be called a large number of times for all the values between 0 and 1. In our example, we use the u and v values to calculate the x, y, and z coordinates of a vector based on parametric equations.

After creating the vector from the parametric function, we can pass it to THREE.ParametricGeometry as shown in the following code snippet:

```
var geometry = new THREE.ParametricGeometry(func, slices, stacks);
```

The *slices* and *stacks* attributes define the number of parts the u and v values should be divided into respectively.

Now, we can test this function by adding a new view named *ParametricGeometry.cshtml* to the *Views/Geometry* folder. Here is the code for this view:

```
@{
    ViewData["Title"] = ViewBag.Title;
}
<h3>@ViewBag.Title</h3>
@Html.Partial("_Links")
<div class="container">
    <div class="row" style="margin-top:50px">
        <div class="col-sm-2">
            <span class="label label-info" id="geometryname">
                Geometry Name:
                kleinbottle
            </span>
        </div>
        <div class="col-sm-2">
```

```
            <div class="dropdown">
                <button class="btn btn-primary dropdown-toggle" type="button"
                        data-toggle="dropdown">
                    Parametric Geometries
                    <span class="caret"></span>
                </button>
                <ul class="dropdown-menu" id="dm">
                    <li><a href="#">helicoid</a></li>
                    <li><a href="#">hyperboloid</a></li>
                    <li><a href="#">ellipticcone</a></li>
                    <li><a href="#">paraboloid</a></li>
                </ul>
            </div>
        </div>
    </div>
    <div class="row">
        <div id="gl" style="width:500px; height:400px; margin-top:10px"></div>
    </div>
</div>
@section scripts{
<script>
    setParametricGeometry("gl", "kleinbottle");
    $('#dm li a').on('click', function () {
        var text = $(this).text();
        $('#geometryname').text("Geometry Name: " + text);
        setParametricGeometry("gl", text);
    });
</script>
}
```

Running this example produces results shown in Figures 8-35.

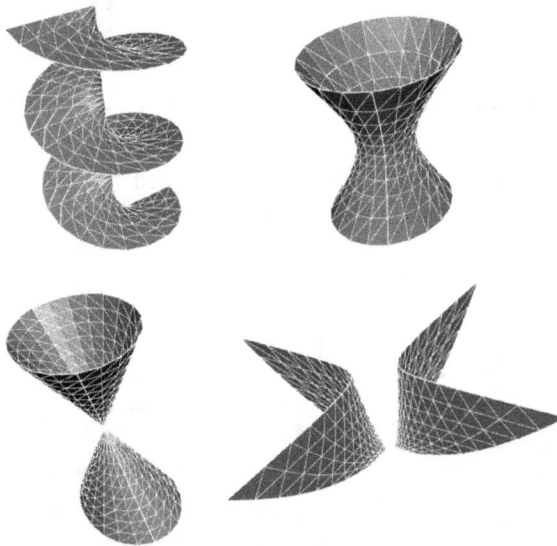

Figure 8-35. 3D parametric shapes: helicoid (top-left), hyperboloid (top-right), elliptic cone (bottom-left), and paraboloid (bottom-right).

Textures

In the preceding sections, we demonstrated how to use various materials to decorate 3D objects. In this section, we will show you how to apply textures to the meshes. Three.js offers many different types of textures. You can use textures to define colors of the mesh, but you can also use them to define shininess, bumps, and reflections.

I have included three *png* files, *crate_grey8.png*, *crate_color8.png*, and *square.png*, for the textures we are going to use in this section. These files are located at *wwwroot/images* folder. Figure 8-36 shows the images from these files.

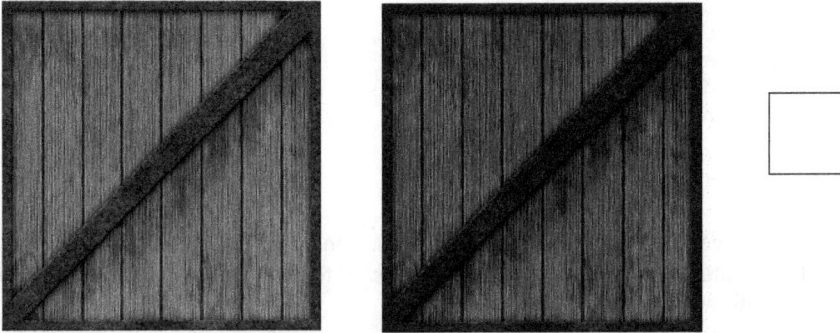

Figure 8-36. Images from texture files: crate_color8.png (left), crate_grey8.png (middle), and square.png (right).

We will apply the first two textures to cube objects, and the third one to create square meshes (instead of default triangular meshes) for a torus object.

Add a new helper function named *set3DTexture* to the *site.js* file:

```
function set3DTexture(gl, geometry, material, options) {
    var isMultipleMaterials = options.isMultipleMaterials || false;

    var container = document.getElementById(gl);
    while (container.firstChild) {
        container.removeChild(container.firstChild);
    }
    var scene = new THREE.Scene();
    var camera = new THREE.PerspectiveCamera(45,
        container.clientWidth / container.clientHeight, 0.1, 1000);
    camera.position.z = 100;
    camera.lookAt(scene.position);

    var renderer = new THREE.WebGLRenderer({ antialias: true });
    renderer.setClearColor("lightgray", 1.0);
    renderer.setSize(container.clientWidth, container.clientHeight);
    container.appendChild(renderer.domElement);

    var ambientLight = new THREE.AmbientLight("#ffffff", 0.4);
    scene.add(ambientLight);
    var light = new THREE.DirectionalLight("#ffffff", 1);
    light.position.set(1, 1, 1);
```

```
        scene.add(light);

        var mesh;
        if (!isMultipleMaterials) {
            mesh = new THREE.Mesh(geometry, material);
        } else {
            mesh = new THREE.SceneUtils.createMultiMaterialObject(
                geometry, material);
        }
        scene.add(mesh);

        render();
        function render() {
            requestAnimationFrame(render);
            mesh.rotation.x += 0.01;
            mesh.rotation.y += 0.01;
            mesh.rotation.z += 0.01;
            renderer.render(scene, camera);
        }
    }
```

This function takes the geometry and material as input arguments. We will use this function to create objects with textures. Add a new view named *Texture.cshtml* to the *Views/Geometry* folder and replace its content with the following code:

```
@{
    ViewData["Title"] = ViewBag.Title;
}
<h3>@ViewBag.Title</h3>
@Html.Partial("_Links")

<div class="container">
    <div class="row">
        <div class="col-sm-4">
            <div style="margin-top:30px; margin-right:25px">
                <div id="gl1" style="width:400px; height:400px;"></div>
            </div>
        </div>
        <div class="col-sm-4">
            <div style="margin-top:30px; margin-right:25px">
                <div id="gl2" style="width:400px; height:400px;"></div>
            </div>
        </div>
    </div>
    <div class="row">
        <div class="col-sm-4">
            <div style="margin-top:30px; margin-right:25px">
                <div id="gl3" style="width:400px; height:400px;"></div>
            </div>
        </div>
        <div class="col-sm-4">
            <div style="margin-top:30px; margin-right:25px">
                <div id="gl4" style="width:400px; height:400px;"></div>
            </div>
        </div>
    </div>
</div>
```

```
</div>

@section scripts{
<script>

    // cube with grey texture
    var loader = new THREE.TextureLoader();
    var texture1 = loader.load("/images/crate_grey8.png");
    var material1 = new THREE.MeshPhongMaterial({ color: "#ffffff",
        map: texture1 });
    var geometry = new THREE.BoxGeometry(40, 40, 40);
    set3DTexture("gl1", geometry, material1, {});

    // cube with color texture
    var texture2 = loader.load("/images/crate_color8.png");
    var material2 = new THREE.MeshPhongMaterial({ color: "#ffffff",
        map: texture2 });
    set3DTexture("gl2", geometry, material2, {});

    //...... (more code goes to here)

</script>
}
```

In the script section, we first load the texture files using *THREE.TextureLoader* and then use them on the meshes for two cube objects respectively. The texture files we are using are in the *png* format, you can also use *gif*, *jpg*, or *tga* images as input.

Running this example, selecting the *Geometry* tab, and clicking the *3D Textures* link produce the results shown in Figure 8-37.

Figure 8-37. Cubes with textures: grey (left) and color (right).

When you apply a texture to a geometry, Three.js will try to apply the texture as optimally as possible. As shown in the preceding example, each side of our cubes will show the complete texture. There are, however, situations where you do not want the texture to spread around a complete face or the complete geometry, but have the texture repeat itself. Three.js provides detailed functionality that allows you to control this. In next example, we will apply texture with the repeat properties.

Add the following code snippet to the script section of the *Texture.cshtml* file:

```
// torus without texture
var material3a = new THREE.MeshPhongMaterial({ color: "steelblue" });
var material3b = new THREE.MeshPhongMaterial({ color: "#444444",
    wireframe: true });
var geometry3 = new THREE.TorusGeometry(25, 6, 20, 30);
var material3 = [material3a, material3b];
set3DTexture("gl3", geometry3, material3, {isMultipleMaterials: true});

// torus with square texture
var wireTexture = loader.load('/images/square.png');
wireTexture.wrapS = wireTexture.wrapT = THREE.RepeatWrapping;
wireTexture.repeat.set(30, 20);
var material4 = new THREE.MeshPhongMaterial({ color: "steelblue",
    map: wireTexture });
var geometry4 = new THREE.TorusGeometry(25, 6, 30, 20);
set3DTexture("gl4", geometry4, material4, {});
```

Here, we first create a torus object with a steel blue color and a wireframe, and we then create another torus decorated with a texture square file. You can see that we set the wrapping of the texture to *THREE.RepeatWrapping*. The *wrapS* property defines how the texture is wrapped horizontally, which corresponds to U in UV mapping, while the *wrapT* property defines how the texture is wrapped vertically, which corresponds to V in UV mapping.

We can set the repeat property as shown in the following code fragment:

```
wireTexture.repeat.set(repeath, repeatv);
```

The *repeath* variable defines how often the texture is repeated horizontally and the *repeatv* variable defines the same vertically.

Running this example produces the results shown in Figure 8-38. You can see that the torus with a square texture does look better.

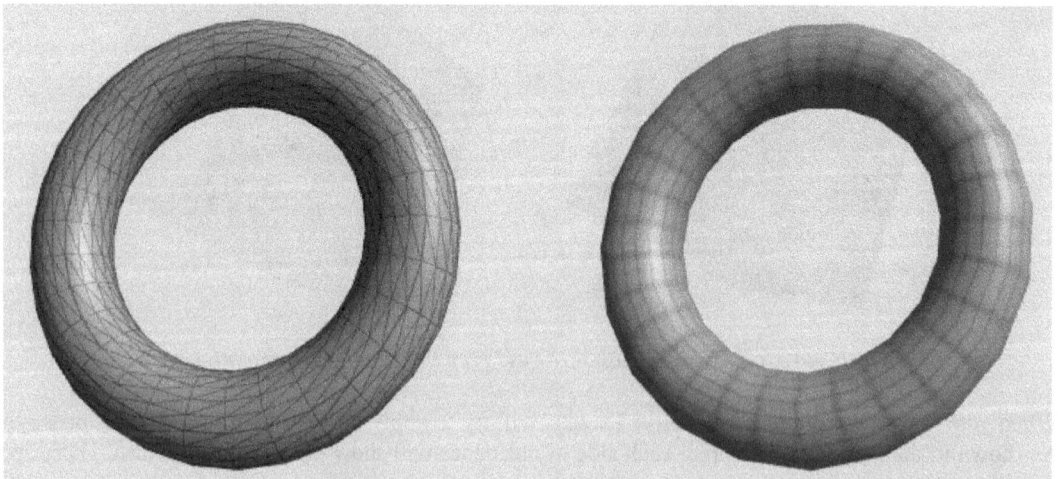

Figure 8-38. A torus with a default triangle mesh (left) and the one with square texture (right).

Chapter 9
3D Charts

In the previous chapter, we demonstrated how to use Three.js to create a variety of 3D graphics objects, including the built-in 3D geometry primitives and parametric surfaces. In this chapter, we will walk you through the detailed procedure on how to create 3D charts. I will skip the mathematical background behind 3D charts; you can refer to my previously published books, *Practical C# Charts and Graphics* and *Practical WPF Charts and Graphics*, for mathematical details.

I will start with creating simple 3D surface charts and parametric charts with a specified colormap and a UV mapped texture in client side, which gives professional-looking 3D charts. Next, I will show you how to use the server-side data to create various custom 3D geometries and UV maps, which can be used to create 3D charts.

Finally, I will introduce a JavaScript 3D charting library named *vis-Graph3d* that is an interactive visualization chart to draw data in a 3D graph. You can freely move and zoom in the chart by dragging and scrolling in the chart window. It is also supports animation of a graph. Note that this library is developed as a 3D module of the Google Visualization Charts in JavaScript.

Client-Side 3D Charts

In this section, I will show you how to create 3D charts at client side using Three.js.

Simple 3D Surfaces

Mathematically, a surface chart draws a Y (not Z because the coordinate system used in Three.js is oriented so that the Y-axis is the "up" direction) function on a surface for each X and Z coordinates in a region of interest. For each X and Z value, a simple surface can have at most on Y value. Complex surfaces can have multiple Y values for each pair of X and Z coordinates; these will be discussed in the following sections.

We can define a simple surface by the Y coordinates of points above a rectangular grid in the X-Z plane. Simple surfaces are useful for visualizing 2D data arrays (matrices) that are too large to display in numerical form and for graphing functions of two variables.

Typically, a surface is formed using rectangular meshes. However, Three.js only provides triangles as a basic unit to represent any surface in 3D. In order to represent a surface using the traditional rectangles, we need to use a square (or rectangle) texture to decorate the surface, as we did for the surface of a torus object in the preceding chapter.

Open Visual Studio 2017 and start a new ASP.NET Core MVC project named *Chapter09*. Add the Three.js library to the project using Bower. We also include several helper JavaScript files that are located in the *wwwroot/lib/mylib* folder.

In order to get a better view of our 3D charts on the screen for specified camera and scene settings, we need to perform a domain or range transformation to our real data, as we did for 2D charts created using D3 in Chapter 4.

Add a helper function named *getNormalize* to the *site.js* file:

```
function getNormalize(vec3, xrange, yrange, zrange) {
    var x = 2 * (vec3.x - xrange[0]) / (xrange[1] - xrange[0]) - 1;
    var y = 2 * (vec3.y - yrange[0]) / (yrange[1] - yrange[0]) - 1;
    var z = 2 * (vec3.z - zrange[0]) / (zrange[1] - zrange[0]) - 1;
    return new THREE.Vector3(x, y, z);
}
```

This function takes the *THREE.Vector3* object and data ranges as input arguments. It converts the X, Y, and Z data ranges into a [−1, 1, −1, 1, −1, 1] cube so that the transformations that are performed on the data point within this cube are independent from the real data ranges. That is, the *getNormalize* function effectively maps the region of our surface into a cube with a fixed side length of 2, which gives us a better view of our charts on the screen.

Next, add a new JavaScript helper function named *setSurface* to the *site.js* file:

```
function setSurface(gl, func, unum, vnum) {
    var container = document.getElementById(gl);
    while (container.firstChild) {
        container.removeChild(container.firstChild);
    }
    var scene = new THREE.Scene();
    var group = new THREE.Group();
    var camera = new THREE.PerspectiveCamera(45,
        container.clientWidth / container.clientHeight, 0.1, 1000);
    camera.position.set(1, 1, 3.5);
    camera.lookAt(scene.position);
    scene.add(camera);

    var renderer = new THREE.WebGLRenderer({ antialias: true });
    renderer.setClearColor("lightgray", 1.0);
    renderer.setSize(container.clientWidth, container.clientHeight);
    renderer.shadowMap.enabled = true;
    container.appendChild(renderer.domElement);

    var loader = new THREE.TextureLoader();
    var wireTexture = loader.load('/images/square.png');
    wireTexture.wrapS = wireTexture.wrapT = THREE.RepeatWrapping;
    wireTexture.repeat.set(unum, vnum);
    var material = new THREE.MeshBasicMaterial({ map: wireTexture,
        vertexColors: THREE.VertexColors, side: THREE.DoubleSide });

    var geometry = new THREE.ParametricGeometry(func, unum, vnum);
```

```
geometry.computeBoundingBox();
ymin = geometry.boundingBox.min.y;
ymax = geometry.boundingBox.max.y;

// add axes
var axes = new THREE.AxisHelper(10);
axes.position.y = ymin;
group.add(axes);

// add xz-grids
var gridxz = new THREE.GridHelper(2, 10);
gridxz.position.y = ymin;
group.add(gridxz);

yrange = ymax - ymin;
var color, point, face, numberOfSides, vertexIndex;
var faceIndices = ['a', 'b', 'c', 'd'];
for (var i = 0; i < geometry.vertices.length; i++) {
    point = geometry.vertices[i];
    color = new THREE.Color(0x0000ff);
    color.setHSL(0.7 * (ymax - point.y) / yrange, 1, 0.5);
    geometry.colors[i] = color;
}
for (var i = 0; i < geometry.faces.length; i++) {
    face = geometry.faces[i];
    numberOfSides = (face instanceof THREE.Face3) ? 3 : 4;
    for (var j = 0; j < numberOfSides; j++) {
        vertexIndex = face[faceIndices[j]];
        face.vertexColors[j] = geometry.colors[vertexIndex];
    }
}

var obj = new THREE.Mesh(geometry, material);
group.add(obj);
scene.add(group);
var control = new THREE.TrackballControls(camera, renderer.domElement);

render();
function render() {
    requestAnimationFrame(render);
    group.rotation.x += 0.005;
    group.rotation.y += 0.005;
    group.rotation.z += 0.005;
    control.update();
    renderer.render(scene, camera);
}
}
```

This function takes *func*, *unum* (or slices), and *vnum* (or stacks) as input arguments. *func* is a parametric function that takes in a *u* and *v* value and returns a *Vector3* object. *unum* (*vnum*) is the count of slices (stacks) to be used for the parametric function.

This function then defines camera and scene settings so that we can get a better view for our 3D charts within a normalized cube with a side length of 2. It loads a *square.png* file using *THREE.TextureLoader*. This file is the same one we have used in the preceding chapter. Here, we will use it as a texture to decorate our surface chart. We repeat the texture with the *unum* and *vnum* along the *u* and *v* directions respectively. The *setSurface* function then defines a material using *THREE.MeshBasicMaterial* that is not affected by lights; this is why we do not need to define the lights in this function. Otherwise, if you use the other materials, such as Lambert, phong, or standard, you need to specify the lights. Note that we define the material using the following code snippet:

```
var material = new THREE.MeshBasicMaterial({ map: wireTexture,
    vertexColors: THREE.VertexColors, side: THREE.DoubleSide });
```

Instead of using a single color as we did for the torus in the preceding chapter, here we use the *THREE.VertexColors*. This means that not only we want a square texture mesh, but we also want a different color for each vertex over the mesh – specifically, we want a colormap based on the data value in the *Y*-direction.

We define the geometry using *THREE.ParametricGeometry*. This geometry can also be used to create a simple 3D surface. In order to specify the colormap, we calculate the data range in the *Y*-direction using the following code snippet:

```
geometry.computeBoundingBox();
ymin = geometry.boundingBox.min.y;
ymax = geometry.boundingBox.max.y;
```

We then add coordinate axes and the *xz*-gridlines at the position of *ymin*, and specify the vertex colors using the HSL:

```
for (var i = 0; i < geometry.vertices.length; i++) {
    point = geometry.vertices[i];
    color = new THREE.Color(0x0000ff);
    color.setHSL(0.7 * (ymax - point.y) / yrange, 1, 0.5);
    geometry.colors[i] = color;
}
```

Here, we fix the *saturation* (= 1, i.e. full color) and *lightness* (= 0.5), while we change the *hue* value from 0 to 0.7 based on the *y* data value for the vertex, which gives a colormap similar to our *jet* colormap defined in Chapter 2. Next, we convert the vertex colors into face colors so that we have a smooth colormap over the mesh with a square texture.

This is just a simple way to specify the colors for vertices. You can also use custom colormaps for this. If you are interested in creating custom colormaps for 3D charts, you can refer to my previously published books, *Practical C# Charts and Graphics* or *Practical .NET Chart Development and Applications*.

Finally, this function defines a *THREE.TrackballControls* object. This control is the most used control in Three.js that allows you to use your mouse (or the trackball) to easily move, pan, and zoom around the scene.

Now, we can test our helper functions. Add a *Surface3DController.cs* file to the *Controllers* folder and replace its content with the following code:

```
using Microsoft.AspNetCore.Mvc;

namespace Chapter09.Controllers
{
    public class Surface3DController : Controller
    {
        // GET: /<controller>/
```

```
public IActionResult Index()
{
    ViewBag.Title = "3D Surfaces: Home";
    return View();
}

public IActionResult SimpleSurface()
{
    ViewBag.Title = "Simple Surfaces";
    return View();
}

public IActionResult ParametricSurface()
{
    ViewBag.Title = "Parametric Surfaces";
    return View();
}
    }
}
```

Add a new folder named *Surface3D* to the *Views* folder. Add a new view named *SimpleSurface.cshtml* to the *Views/Surface3D* folder and replace its content with the following code:

```
@{
    ViewData["Title"] = ViewBag.Title;
}
<h3>@ViewBag.Title</h3>
@Html.Partial("_Links")

<div class="container">
    <div class="row">
        <div class="col-sm-6">
            <div style="margin-top:30px; margin-right:25px">
                <p style="margin-bottom:5px;">Sinc(r) function</p>
                <div id="gl1" style="width:600px; height:480px;
                    margin-top:10px"></div>
            </div>
        </div>
        <div class="col-sm-6">
            <div style="margin-top:30px; margin-left:25px">
                <p style="margin-bottom:5px;">Sinc(x*z) function</p>
                <div id="gl2" style="width:600px; height:480px;
                    margin-top:10px"></div>
            </div>
        </div>
    </div>
    <div class="row">
        <div class="col-sm-6">
            <div style="margin-top:30px; margin-right:25px">
                <p style="margin-bottom:5px;">Peaks function</p>
                <div id="gl3" style="width:600px; height:480px;
                    margin-top:10px"></div>
            </div>
        </div>
        <div class="col-sm-6">
            <div style="margin-top:30px; margin-left:25px">
```

```
                    <p style="margin-bottom:5px;">Monkey saddle function</p>
                    <div id="gl4" style="width:600px; height:480px;
                         margin-top:10px"></div>
                </div>
            </div>
        </div>
    </div>

    @section scripts{
    <script language="JavaScript" src="~/lib/mylib/TrackballControls.js"></script>
    <script>
        // sinc function
        var sinc = function (u, v) {
            var xrange = [-8, 8];
            var zrange = [-8, 8];
            var x = (xrange[1] - xrange[0]) * u + xrange[0];
            var z = (zrange[1] - zrange[0]) * v + zrange[0];
            var r = Math.sqrt(x * x + z * z) + 0.00001;
            var y = Math.sin(r) / r;

            var vec = new THREE.Vector3(x, y, z);
            var vec1 = getNormalize(vec, xrange, [-0.7, 1.5], zrange);
            return vec1;
        }
        setSurface("gl1", sinc, 33, 33);

        //...... (more code goes to here)

    </script>
    }
```

Note that in the script section, we introduce the *TrackballControls.js* helper file that allows you to interact with the chart. We then create a *sinc* parametric function, where we first define the data ranges. Note that the *u* and *v* values are always in the range of [0, 1]. When the *u* and *v* change from 0 to 1, the *x* and *z* will cover all the data range of [−8, 8]. We then call the *getNormalize* to return the normalized *THREE.Vector3* object. Finally, we call the *setSurface* with the *sinc, slices,* and *stacks* as input arguments to create the *sinc* surface chart.

Running this example, selecting the *3D Surfaces* tab, and clicking the *Simple Surfaces* link produce the result shown in Figure 9-1. You can see that the figure indeed gives a professional-looking 3D surface chart.

Next, we will create another *sinc(x*z)* chart. Add the following code snippet to the script section of the *SimpleSurface.cshtml* file:

```
// sinc2 function
var sinc2 = function (u, v) {
    var xrange = [-5, 5];
    var zrange = [-5, 5];
    var x = (xrange[1] - xrange[0]) * u + xrange[0];
    var z = (zrange[1] - zrange[0]) * v + zrange[0];
    var r = x * z + 0.00001;
    var y = Math.sin(r) / r;
    var vec = new THREE.Vector3(x, y, z);
    var vec1 = getNormalize(vec, xrange, [-0.7, 1.5], zrange);
```

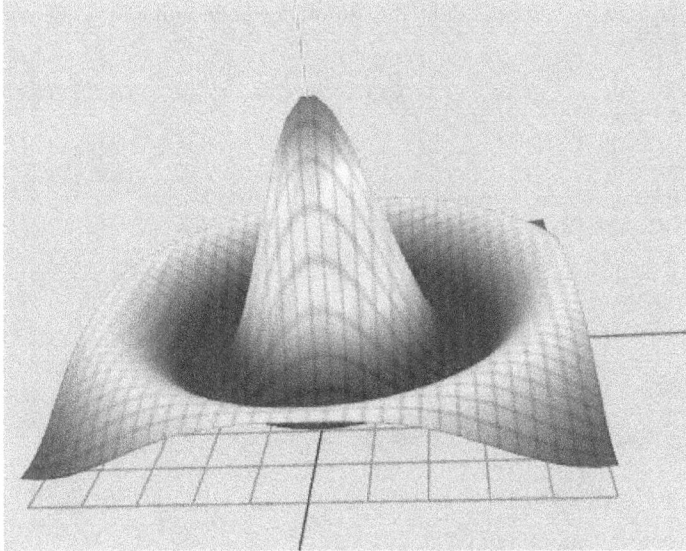

Figure 9-1. A 3D sinc(r) surface chart.

```
    return vec1
}

setSurface("gl2", sinc2, 33, 33);
```

This generates the results shown in Figure 9-2.

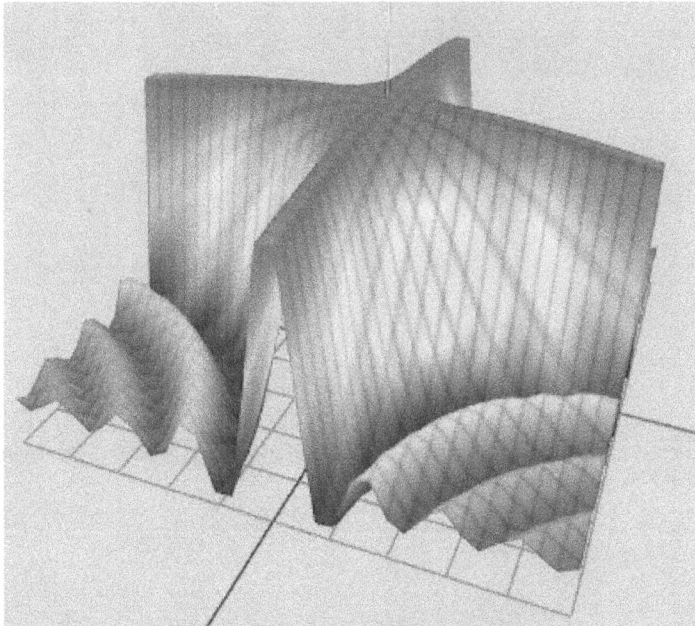

*Figure 9-2. A 3D sinc(x*z) surface chart.*

Next, we will create a *peaks* surface. Add the following code snippet to the script section of the *SimpleSurface.cshtml* file:

```
// peaks function
var peaks = function (u, v) {
    var xrange = [-3, 3];
    var zrange = [-3, 3];
    var x = (xrange[1] - xrange[0]) * u + xrange[0];
    var z = (zrange[1] - zrange[0]) * v + zrange[0];

    var y = 3 * Math.pow((1 - x), 2) * Math.exp(-x * x - (z + 1) * (z + 1)) -
        10 * (0.2 * x - Math.pow(x, 3) - Math.pow(z, 5)) *
        Math.exp(-x * x - z * z) - 1 / 3 * Math.exp(-(x + 1) * (x + 1) - z * z);

        var vec = new THREE.Vector3(x, y, -z);
        var vec1 = getNormalize(vec, xrange, [-10, 10], zrange);
        return vec1;
    }
    setSurface("gl3", peaks, 33, 33);
```

This produces the result shown in Figure 9-3.

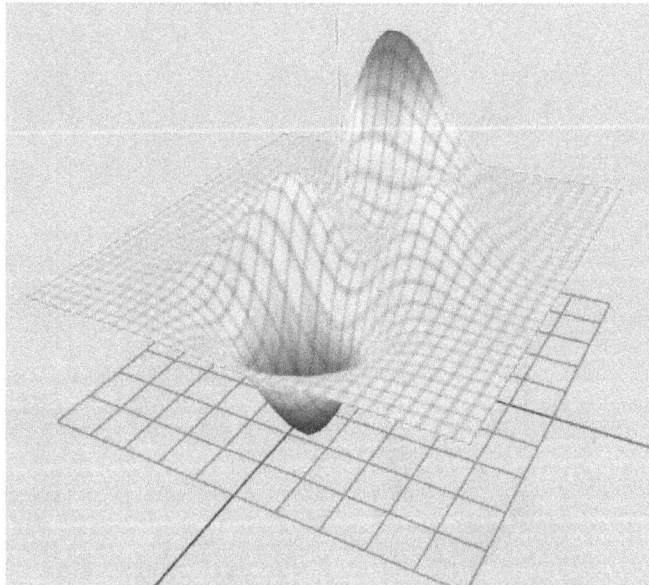

Figure 9-3. A 3D surface chart for the peaks function.

Finally, we want to create a so-called monkey-saddle surface chart. Add the following code snippet to the script section of the *SimpleSurface.cshtml* file:

```
// monkey saddle
var monkey = function (u, v) {
    var umin = 0;
    var umax = 6 * Math.PI;
    var vmin = 0;
    var vmax = 2 * Math.PI;
```

```
        var u = (umax - umin) * u + umin;
        var v = (vmax - vmin) * v + vmin;

        var x = u * Math.cos(v);
        var z = u * Math.sin(v);
        var y = 2 * Math.cos(u);

        var vec = new THREE.Vector3(x, y, z);
        var vec1 = getNormalize(vec, [-umax, umax], [-10, 10], [-umax, umax]);
        return vec1;
    }
    setSurface("gl4", monkey, 31, 31);
```

This generates the output shown in Figure 9-4.

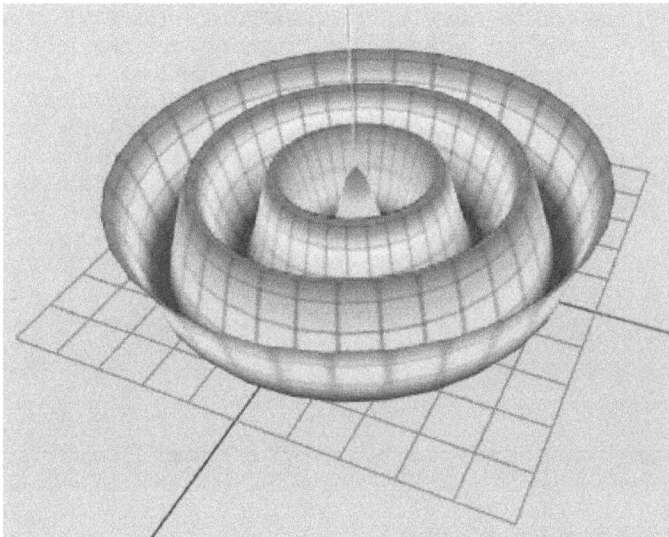

Figure 9-4. A 3D monkey-saddle surface chart.

Following the same procedure presented here, you can easily create your own 3D simple surface charts by defining different mathematical functions.

Parametric Surfaces

In the preceding section, you learned how to create 3D simple surfaces. A key feature of this type of surface is that there is at most one *Y* value for each pair of *X* and *Z* values. However, sometimes you may want to create a complex surface of a certain shape. This kind of complex surface cannot be represented by a simple function. For certain values of *X* and *Z*, this type of surface has more than one *Y* value. This means that you cannot use the approach discussed in the previous section to store and display the data.

One way to represent such a surface is to use a set of parametric equations. These equations define the *X*, *Y*, and *Z* coordinates of points on the surface in terms of the parametric variables *u* and *v*. Many complex surfaces, including the simple surfaces, can be represented using parametric equations. For example, the sphere, the torus, and quadric surfaces are all parametric surfaces.

In this section, I will show how to use the same *setSurface* function to create 3D parametric surfaces. Add a new view named *ParametricSurface.cshtml* to the *Views/Surface3D* folder and replace its content with the following code:

```
@{
    ViewData["Title"] = ViewBag.Title;
}
<h3>@ViewBag.Title</h3>
@Html.Partial("_Links")

<div class="container">
    <div class="row">
        <div class="col-sm-12">
            <div style="margin-top:30px; margin-right:25px">
                <p>Select a chart function:</p>
                <select id="mySelect" class="selectpicker">
                    <option value="sphere">Sphere</option>
                    <option value="torus">Torus</option>
                    <option value="klein">Klein bottle</option>
                    <option value="hyperboloid">Hyper boloid</option>
                    <option value="helicoid">Helicoid</option>
                    <option value="ellipticcone">Elliptic cone</option>
                </select>
                <div id="gl" style="width:600px; height:480px;
                    margin-top:10px"></div>
            </div>
        </div>
    </div>
</div>

@section scripts{
<script language="JavaScript" src="~/lib/mylib/TrackballControls.js"></script>
<script>
    // sphere
    var sphere = function (u, v) {
        var umin = 0;
        var umax = 2 * Math.PI;
        var vmin = -Math.PI / 2;
        var vmax = Math.PI / 2;
        var u = (umax - umin) * u + umin;
        var v = (vmax - vmin) * v + vmin;

        var x = Math.cos(v) * Math.cos(u);
        var z = Math.cos(v) * Math.sin(u);
        var y = Math.sin(v);

        var vec = new THREE.Vector3(x, y, z);
        return getNormalize(vec, [-1, 1], [-1, 1], [-1, 1]);
    }

    // torus
    var torus = function (u, v) {
        var umin = 0;
        var umax = 2 * Math.PI;
        var vmin = 0;
```

```
        var vmax = 2 * Math.PI;
        var u = (umax - umin) * u + umin;
        var v = (vmax - vmin) * v + vmin;
        var a = 1;
        var b = 0.25;

        var x = (a + b * Math.cos(v)) * Math.cos(u);
        var z = (a + b * Math.cos(v)) * Math.sin(u);
        var y = b * Math.sin(v);

        var vec = new THREE.Vector3(x, y, z);
        return getNormalize(vec, [-a - b, a + b], [-1.5, 1.5], [-a - b, a + b]);
    }

// klein bottle
var klein = function (u, v) {
        var umin = 0;
        var umax = 10 * Math.PI;
        var vmin = 0;
        var vmax = 5 * Math.PI;
        var u = (umax - umin) * u + umin;
        var v = (vmax - vmin) * v + vmin;
        var a = 8;
        var n = 3;
        var m = 1;

        var x = (a + Math.cos(n * u / 2.0)
            * Math.sin(v) - Math.sin(n * u / 2.0)
            * Math.sin(2 * v)) * Math.cos(m * u / 2.0);
        var z = (a + Math.cos(n * u / 2.0)
            * Math.sin(v) - Math.sin(n * u / 2.0)
            * Math.sin(2 * v)) * Math.sin(m * u / 2.0);
        var y = Math.sin(n * u / 2.0)
            * Math.sin(v) + Math.cos(n * u / 2.0)
            * Math.sin(2 * v);

        var vec = new THREE.Vector3(x, y, z);
        return getNormalize(vec, [-10, 10], [-6, 6], [-10, 10]);
    }

// hyperboloid
var hyperboloid = function (u, v) {
        var umin = 0;
        var umax = 2 * Math.PI;
        var vmin = -1.5;
        var vmax = 1.5;
        var u = (umax - umin) * u + umin;
        var v = (vmax - vmin) * v + vmin;

        var x = 2 * Math.cos(u) * Math.cosh(v);
        var z = 1.5 * Math.sin(u) * Math.cosh(v);
        var y = 3 * Math.sinh(v);

        var vec = new THREE.Vector3(x, y, z);
        return getNormalize(vec, [-5, 5], [-10, 10], [-5, 5]);
```

```javascript
    }
    // Helicoid
    var helicoid = function (u, v) {
        var umin = 0;
        var umax = 1;
        var vmin = -3 * Math.PI;
        var vmax = 3 * Math.PI;
        var u = (umax - umin) * u + umin;
        var v = (vmax - vmin) * v + vmin;

        var x = u * Math.cos(v);
        var z = u * Math.sin(v);
        var y = v;

        var vec = new THREE.Vector3(x, y, -z);
        return getNormalize(vec, [-1, 1], [-10, 10], [-1, 1]);
    }

    // elliptic cone
    var elliptic = function (u, v) {
        var umin = 0;
        var umax = 2 * Math.PI;
        var vmin = -1.5;
        var vmax = 1.5;
        var u = (umax - umin) * u + umin;
        var v = (vmax - vmin) * v + vmin;

        var x = 2 * v * Math.cos(u);
        var z = 1.5 * v * Math.sin(u);
        var y = 3 * v;

        var vec = new THREE.Vector3(x, y, z);
        return getNormalize(vec, [-3, 3], [-5, 5], [-3, 3]);
    }

    setSurface("gl", sphere, 20, 20);

    $('#mySelect').on('change', function () {
        switch ($(this).val()) {
            case 'sphere':
                setSurface("gl", sphere, 20, 20);
                break;
            case 'torus':
                setSurface("gl", torus, 50, 20);
                break;
            case 'klein':
                setSurface("gl", klein, 300, 100);
                break;
            case 'hyperboloid':
                setSurface("gl", hyperboloid, 30, 10);
                break;
            case 'helicoid':
                setSurface("gl", helicoid, 10, 200);
                break;
        }
```

```
        });
    </script>
    }
```

This code implements six parametric surface charts: sphere, torus, Klein bottle, hyperboloid, helicoid, and elliptic cone. The HTML *selectpicker* element allows you to select a parametric surface to display on the screen, which is achieved using an AJAX on change function. We set the default surface to the sphere chart. You should be familiar with the parametric functions implemented in this view, and we will not discuss them any further.

Running this example produces the results shown in Figures 9-5.

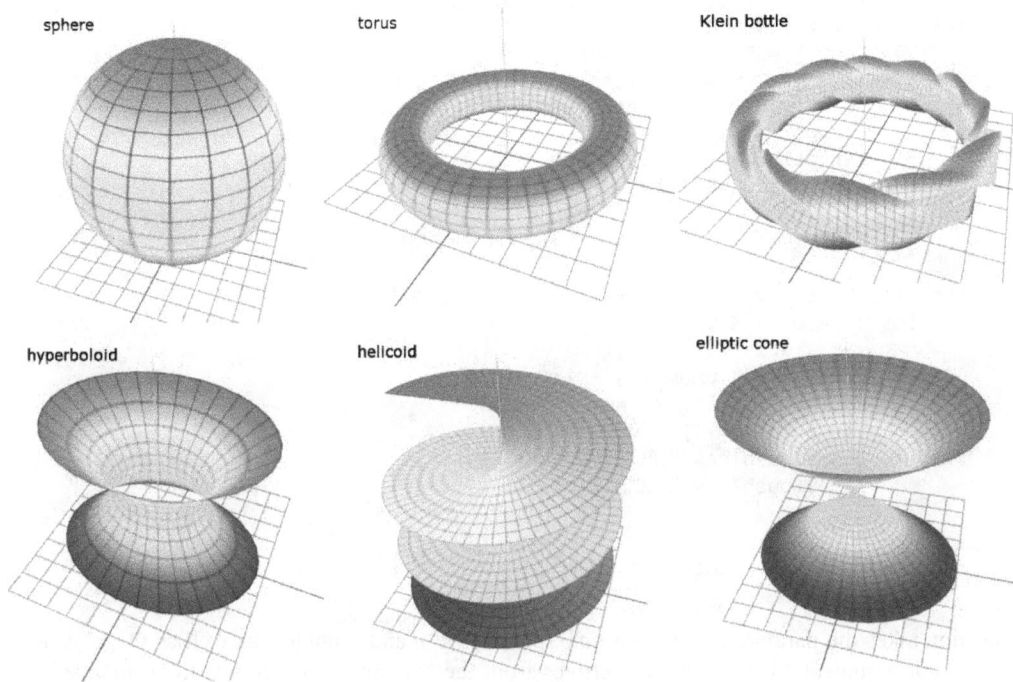

Figure 9-5. 3D parametric surface charts.

Using Server Data

In the preceding sections, we create the 3D charts directly at client side by passing a parametric function defined using JavaScript to our helper function called *setSurface*. In practical applications, we usually create 3D charts using data from database or from mathematical functions at server side. Note that our *setSurface* helper function takes a JavaScript parametric function as an input argument, but it cannot take a C# function directly as input. The best way of taking input from server is to convert it into a data format such as JSON data, instead of an input function. To this end, we need to implement a JavaScript helper function for a custom geometry that takes the data as input.

Custom Geometry

In order to take the data file as input, we need to create a custom geometry. First, we extract the data for vertices and faces from a mathematical function. Add a helper class named *getSurfaceData* to the *site.js* file:

```
function getSurfaceData(func, urange, vrange, unum, vnum,
    xrange, yrange, zrange) {
    du = (urange[1] - urange[0]) / (unum - 1);
    dv = (vrange[1] - vrange[0]) / (vnum - 1);
    var vertices = [];
    var faces = [];
    var i, j;
    for (i = 0; i < vnum; i++) {
        var v = vrange[0] + i * dv;
        for (j = 0; j < unum; j++) {
            var u = urange[0] + j * du;
            var pt = func(u, v);
            var pt1 = getNormalize(pt, xrange, yrange, zrange);
            vertices.push(pt1);
        }
    }

    for (i = 0; i < vnum - 1; i++) {
        for (j = 0; j < unum - 1; j++) {
            var a = i * unum + j;
            var b = i * unum + j + 1;
            var c = (i + 1) * unum + j + 1;
            var d = (i + 1) * unum + j;
            faces.push(new THREE.Face3(a, b, d));
            faces.push(new THREE.Face3(b, c, d));
        }
    }
    return { vertices, faces };
}
```

This function takes the parametric function *func*, parametric *u* and *v* ranges, as well as the *x*, *y*, and *z* ranges as input arguments. It first creates vertices from the parametric function with normalized data points using the *getNormalize* function implemented previously. The code then defines the faces by going over all vertices. Finally, the function returns the data for vertices and faces.

Now, we can use the data returned by this function to create a custom geometry. Add a new JavaScript function named *setCustomGeometry* to the *site.js* file:

```
function setCustomGeometry(gl, data, isServerData) {
    if (isServerData) {
        data = processServerData(data);
    }
    var container = document.getElementById(gl);
    while (container.firstChild) {
        container.removeChild(container.firstChild);
    }
    var scene = new THREE.Scene();
    var group = new THREE.Group();
    var camera = new THREE.PerspectiveCamera(45,
        container.clientWidth / container.clientHeight, 0.1, 1000);
```

```
camera.position.set(1, 1, 3.5);
camera.lookAt(scene.position);
scene.add(camera);

var renderer = new THREE.WebGLRenderer({ antialias: true });
renderer.setClearColor("lightgray", 1.0);
renderer.setSize(container.clientWidth, container.clientHeight);
renderer.shadowMap.enabled = true;
container.appendChild(renderer.domElement);

material1 = new THREE.MeshBasicMaterial({ vertexColors: THREE.VertexColors,
    side: THREE.DoubleSide });
material2 = new THREE.MeshBasicMaterial({ color: 'black',
    side: THREE.DoubleSide, wireframe: true });

var geometry = new THREE.Geometry();
geometry.vertices = data.vertices;
geometry.faces = data.faces;

geometry.computeBoundingBox();
ymin = geometry.boundingBox.min.y;
ymax = geometry.boundingBox.max.y;

// add axes
var axes = new THREE.AxisHelper(10);
axes.position.y = ymin;
group.add(axes);

// add xz-grids
var gridxz = new THREE.GridHelper(2, 10);
gridxz.position.y = ymin;
group.add(gridxz);

yrange = ymax - ymin;
var color, point, face, numberOfSides, vertexIndex;
var faceIndices = ['a', 'b', 'c', 'd'];
for (var i = 0; i < geometry.vertices.length; i++) {
    point = geometry.vertices[i];
    color = new THREE.Color(0x0000ff);
    color.setHSL(0.7 * (ymax - point.y) / yrange, 1, 0.5);
    geometry.colors[i] = color;
}
for (var i = 0; i < geometry.faces.length; i++) {
    face = geometry.faces[i];
    numberOfSides = (face instanceof THREE.Face3) ? 3 : 4;
    for (var j = 0; j < numberOfSides; j++) {
        vertexIndex = face[faceIndices[j]];
        face.vertexColors[j] = geometry.colors[vertexIndex];
    }
}

var obj = new THREE.SceneUtils.createMultiMaterialObject(geometry,
        [material1, material2]);
group.add(obj);
scene.add(group);
```

```
var control = new THREE.TrackballControls(camera, renderer.domElement);

render();
function render() {
    requestAnimationFrame(render);
    group.rotation.x += 0.005;
    group.rotation.y += 0.005;
    group.rotation.z += 0.005;
    control.update();
    renderer.render(scene, camera);
}
}
```

This function is basically similar to the *setSurface* function used in the preceding sections, except that here we use a data file to create a custom geometry. The *isServerData* option will be used in the following section when the data comes from server. Inside this function, we use two materials, one with a vertex colormap and the other one with a black wireframe. Please note that here we cannot use the texture to decorate our surface because the texture requires a proper UV mapping. However, if you try it with a square texture in this function, you will get a black surface. You may ask why the texture mapping works for built-in geometry primitives and the built-in parametric geometries? This is due to the fact that the UV mapping for the built-in geometries and parametric geometries in Three.js has been already calculated internally for us. In the later section, I will show you how to calculate the UV mapping for our custom geometry so that we can apply the texture to it.

We define our custom geometry using *THREE.Geometry* function as shown in following code snippet:

```
var geometry = new THREE.Geometry();
geometry.vertices = data.vertices;
geometry.faces = data.faces;
```

Note that we assign the vertices and faces for our custom geometry with corresponding data components. The rest of the code is standard for creating colormap, defining the mesh using the *SceneUtils* function named *createMultiMaterialObject*, and rendering the scene.

Next, we want to test our custom geometry. Add a new controller named *ServerSurfaceController.cs* to the *Controller* folder and replace its content with the following code:

```
using Chapter09.Models;
using Microsoft.AspNetCore.Mvc;
using System;

namespace Chapter09.Controllers
{
    public class ServerSurfaceController : Controller
    {
        // GET: /<controller>/
        ThreeModel _model = new ThreeModel();
        public IActionResult Index()
        {
            ViewBag.Title = "Use Server Data: Home";
            return View();
        }

        public IActionResult CustomGeometry()
        {
            ViewBag.Title = "Custom Geometry";
```

```
            return View();
        }

        public IActionResult CustomGeometryUv()
        {
            ViewBag.Title = "Custom Geometry with UV Map";
            return View();
        }

        //...... (more code goes to here)


    }
}
```

Add a new folder *ServerSurface* to the *Views* folder. Add a new view named *CustomGeometry.cshtml* to the *Views/ServerSurface* folder and replace its content with the following code:

```
@{
    ViewData["Title"] = ViewBag.Title;
}
<h3>@ViewBag.Title</h3>
@Html.Partial("_Links")

<div class="container">
    <div class="row">
        <div class="col-sm-4">
            <div style="margin-top:30px; margin-right:25px">
                <p style="margin-bottom:5px;">Sinc function</p>
                <div id="gl1" style="width:400px; height:370px;
                    margin-top:10px"></div>
            </div>
        </div>
        <div class="col-sm-4">
            <div style="margin-top:30px; margin-left:25px">
                <p style="margin-bottom:5px;">Peaks function</p>
                <div id="gl2" style="width:400px; height:370px;
                    margin-top:10px"></div>
            </div>
        </div>
    </div>
    <div class="row">
        <div class="col-sm-4">
            <div style="margin-top:30px; margin-right:25px">
                <p style="margin-bottom:5px;">Monkey saddle function</p>
                <div id="gl3" style="width:400px; height:370px;
                    margin-top:10px"></div>
            </div>
        </div>
        <div class="col-sm-4">
            <div style="margin-top:30px; margin-left:25px">
                <p style="margin-bottom:5px;">Torus function</p>
                <div id="gl4" style="width:400px; height:370px;
                    margin-top:10px"></div>
            </div>
        </div>
    </div>
</div>
```

```
</div>

@section scripts{
<script language="JavaScript" src="~/lib/mylib/TrackballControls.js"></script>
<script>
    // sinc function
    function sinc(u, v) {
        var r = Math.sqrt(u * u + v * v) + 0.0001;
        var res = Math.sin(r) / r;
        return new THREE.Vector3(u, res, v);
    }
    var urange = [-8, 8];
    var vrange = [-8, 8];
    var unum = 30;
    var vnum = 30;
    var xrange = urange;
    var yrange = [-0.7, 1.5];
    var zrange = vrange;
    var data = getSurfaceData(sinc, urange, vrange, unum, vnum,
                              xrange, yrange, zrange);
    setCustomGeometry("gl1", data, false);

    // peaks function
    var peaks = function (u, v) {
        var x = u;
        var z = v;

        var y = 3 * Math.pow((1 - x), 2) * Math.exp(-x * x - (z + 1) * (z + 1))
            - 10 * (0.2 * x - Math.pow(x, 3) - Math.pow(z, 5)) *
            Math.exp(-x * x - z * z) - 1 / 3 * Math.exp(-(x + 1) * (x + 1)
            - z * z);

        return new THREE.Vector3(x, y, -z);
    }

    urange = [-3, 3];
    vrange = [-3, 3];
    unum = 31;
    vnum = 31;
    xrange = urange;
    yrange = [-10, 10];
    zrange = vrange;
    data = getSurfaceData(peaks, urange, vrange, unum, vnum,
                          xrange, yrange, zrange);
    setCustomGeometry("gl2", data, false);

    // monkey saddle
    var monkey = function (u, v) {
        var x = u * Math.cos(v);
        var z = u * Math.sin(v);
        var y = 2 * Math.cos(u);
        return new THREE.Vector3(x, y, z);
    }

    urange = [0, 6 * Math.PI];
```

```
        vrange = [0, 2 * Math.PI];
        unum = 31;
        vnum = 31;
        xrange = [-6* Math.PI, 6 * Math.PI];
        yrange = [-10, 10];
        zrange = [-6 * Math.PI, 6 * Math.PI];
        data = getSurfaceData(monkey, urange, vrange, unum, vnum,
                              xrange, yrange, zrange);
        setCustomGeometry("gl3", data, false);

        // torus
        var torus = function (u, v) {
            var a = 1;
            var b = 0.25;

            var x = (a + b * Math.cos(v)) * Math.cos(u);
            var z = (a + b * Math.cos(v)) * Math.sin(u);
            var y = b * Math.sin(v);
            return new THREE.Vector3(x, y, z);
        }

        urange = [0, 2 * Math.PI];
        vrange = [0, 2 * Math.PI];
        unum = 50;
        vnum = 20;
        xrange = [-1.25, 1.25];
        yrange = [-1.5, 1.5];
        zrange = [-1.25, 1.25];
        data = getSurfaceData(torus, urange, vrange, unum, vnum,
                              xrange, yrange, zrange);;
        setCustomGeometry("gl4", data, false);
    </script>
    }
```

This code implements four custom geometry shapes – three with a simple surface: *sinc*, *peaks*, and *monkey saddle*, and one with a complex parametric surface: *torus*. Here, we first create the parametric function, and then define the parametric *u* and *v* ranges as well as the *x*, *y*, and *z* ranges. Next, we call the *getSurfaceData* helper function to generate the data. Finally, we use this data to create our custom surface using the *setCustomGeomtry* function implemented in the *site.js* file.

Running this example, selecting the *Use Server Data* tab, and clicking the *Custom Geometry* link produce the results shown in Figure 9-6. You see from the figure that we have successfully created the 3D surface charts with colormap using our custom geometry function with the input data.

In the next section, we will use the server-side data and the custom geometry to reproduce the 3D surface charts.

3D Charts with Server Data

In this section, I will show you how to recreate 3D charts using the custom geometry with the server data.

Add a new C# class named *ThreeModel.cs* to the *Models* folder and replace its content with the following code:

Sinc function

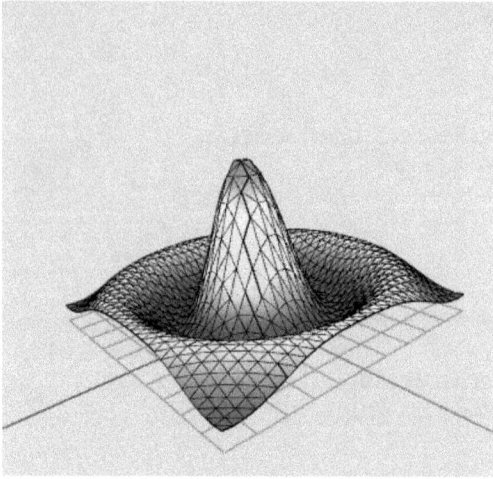

Peaks function

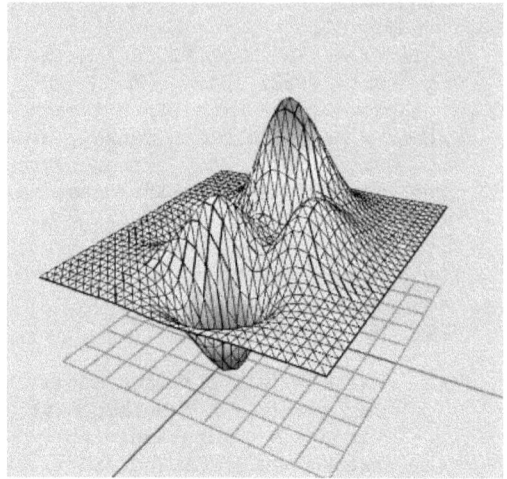

Monkey saddle function

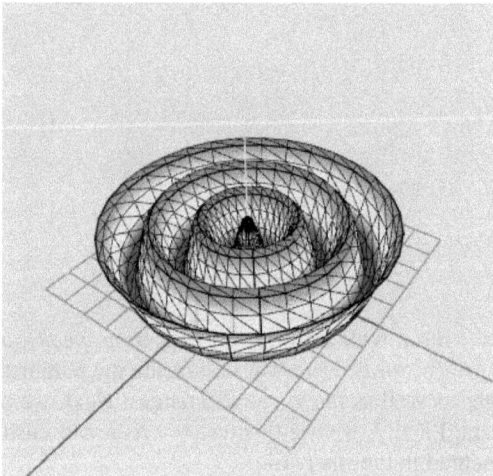

Torus function

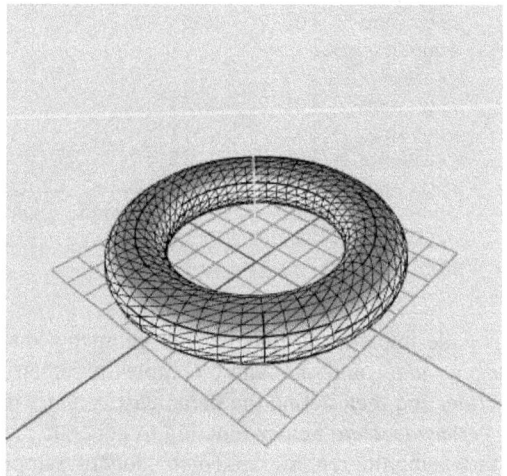

Figure 9-6. 3D surface charts created using custom geometry.

```
using System.Collections.Generic;
using System.Numerics;

namespace Chapter09.Models
{
    public class ThreeModel
    {
        public int[] UvNum { get; set; }
        public List<Vector3> Point3s { get; set; }
        public List<Vector2> Point2s { get; set; }
        public ChartType ChartType { get; set; }
    }
```

```
public enum ChartType
{
    Sinc,
    SincXy,
    SincSin,
    Peaks,
    MonkeySaddle,
    Torus,
    KleinBottle,
    Hyperboloid,
    Hylicoid
}
}
```

The *ThreeModel* class defines several public properties: the *UvNum* array represents the slices (along the *u* direction) and stacks (along the *v* direction). The *Point3s* is a list of *Vector3* (in the *System.Numerics* namespace) objects that is used to hold the vertex data. While the *Point2s* is a list of *Vector2* objects that holds the UV mapping data, which will be used later. The *ChartType* property is an *enum* type of *ChartType* defined in the *ChartType* enumeration. This property allows you to select a chart function and display its 3D surface chart on the screen.

Now, we need to implement parametric functions in C# at the server-side to generate corresponding vertex data.

Add a new method named *VertexData* to the *ModelHelper.cs* file. Here is the code for this method:

```
public static List<Vector3> VertexData(Func<double, double, Vector3> f,
    double[] uvRange, int[] uvNum, double[] xyzRange)
{
    List<Vector3> pts = new List<Vector3>();
    double du = (uvRange[1] - uvRange[0]) / (uvNum[0] - 1);
    double dv = (uvRange[3] - uvRange[2]) / (uvNum[1] - 1);

    for (int i = 0; i < uvNum[1]; i++)
    {
        double v = uvRange[2] + i * dv;
        for (int j = 0; j < uvNum[0]; j++)
        {
            double u = uvRange[0] + j * du;
            pts.Add(NormalizePoint(f(u, v), xyzRange));
        }
    }
    return pts;
}
```

This function takes a *Func<T1, T2, TResult>* method as input. This is a delegate function, which encapsulate a method that has two parameters (in our case, the parameters *u* and *v*) and returns a value type specified by the *TResult* parameter (in our case, it is a *Vector3* object). The *VertexData* function returns a list of *Vector3* objects that holds the vertex data. Note that here we also use a *NormalizePoint* method to normalize the data with the *x*, *y*, and *z* ranges, which is similar to the *getNormalize* JavaScript function implemented previously at the client side. Here is the code for the *NormalizePoint* method located in the *ModelHelper.cs* file:

```
private static Vector3 NormalizePoint(Vector3 pt3, double[] xyzRange)
{
    double x = 2 * (pt3.X - xyzRange[0]) / (xyzRange[1] - xyzRange[0]) - 1;
```

```
        double y = 2 * (pt3.Y - xyzRange[2]) / (xyzRange[3] - xyzRange[2]) - 1;
        double z = 2 * (pt3.Z - xyzRange[4]) / (xyzRange[5] - xyzRange[4]) - 1;
        return new Vector3((float)x, (float)y, (float)z);
}
```

Now, we can create various mathematical functions and then use the *VertexData* method to generate the vertex data. For example, the *sinc* function is implemented using the following *Sinc* method:

```
public static Vector3 Sinc(double u, double v)
{
    double x = u;
    double z = v;
    double r = Math.Sqrt(x * x + z * z) + 0.00001;
    double y = Math.Sin(r) / r;
    return new Vector3((float)x, (float)y, (float)z);
}
```

Following this procedure, we have implemented nine mathematical functions in the *ModelHelper.cs* file, including torus, peaks, hyperboloid, helicoid, etc. I will not list their code here; you can review it by opening the *ModelHelper.cs* file.

Now, we will test our model using a strong typed view and controller. Add the following code to the *ServerSurfaceController.cs* file:

```
public IActionResult UseServer()
{
    ViewBag.Title = "Using Server Data";
    var uvRange = new double[] { -8, 8, -8, 8 };
    var xyzRange = new double[] { -8, 8, -0.7, 1.5, -8, 8 };
    var uvNum = new int[] { 30, 30 };
    _model.UvNum = uvNum;
    _model.Point3s = ModelHelper.VertexData(ModelHelper.Sinc, uvRange,
                                            uvNum, xyzRange);
    return View(_model);
}


[HttpPost]
public IActionResult UseServer(ThreeModel model)
{
    ViewBag.Title = "Using Server Data";

    int[] uvNum;
    var model1 = GetModel(model, out uvNum);
    return View(model1);
}

private ThreeModel GetModel(ThreeModel model, out int[] uvNum)
{
    var selectChart = model.ChartType;
    double[] uvRange, xyzRange;
    uvNum = new int[2];

    switch (model.ChartType)
    {
        case ChartType.Sinc:
        uvRange = new double[] { -8, 8, -8, 8 };
```

```
        xyzRange = new double[] { -8, 8, -0.7, 1.5, -8, 8 };
        uvNum = new int[] { 30, 30 };
        _model.UvNum = uvNum;
        _model.Point3s = ModelHelper.VertexData(ModelHelper.Sinc,
            uvRange, uvNum, xyzRange);
        break;

    case ChartType.SincXy:
        uvRange = new double[] { -5, 5, -5, 5 };
        xyzRange = new double[] { -5, 5, -0.7, 1.5, -5, 5 };
        uvNum = new int[] { 30, 30 };
        _model.UvNum = uvNum;
        _model.Point3s = ModelHelper.VertexData(ModelHelper.SincXy,
            uvRange, uvNum, xyzRange);
        break;

    case ChartType.SincSin:
        uvRange = new double[] { -16, 16, -16, 16 };
        xyzRange = new double[] { -16, 16, 0.6, 1.2, -16, 16 };
        uvNum = new int[] { 50, 50 };
        _model.UvNum = uvNum;
        _model.Point3s = ModelHelper.VertexData(ModelHelper.SincSin,
            uvRange, uvNum, xyzRange);
        break;

    case ChartType.Peaks:
        uvRange = new double[] { -3, 3, -3, 3 };
        xyzRange = new double[] { -3, 3, -10, 10, -3, 3 };
        uvNum = new int[] { 30, 30 };
        _model.UvNum = uvNum;
        _model.Point3s = ModelHelper.VertexData(ModelHelper.Peaks,
            uvRange, uvNum, xyzRange);
        break;

    case ChartType.MonkeySaddle:
        uvRange = new double[] { 0, 6 * Math.PI, 0, 2 * Math.PI };
        xyzRange = new double[] { -6 * Math.PI, 6 * Math.PI, -10, 10,
            -6 * Math.PI, 6 * Math.PI };
        uvNum = new int[] { 30, 30 };
        _model.UvNum = uvNum;
        _model.Point3s = ModelHelper.VertexData(ModelHelper.MonkeySaddle,
            uvRange, uvNum, xyzRange);
        break;

    case ChartType.Torus:
        uvRange = new double[] { 0, 2 * Math.PI, 0, 2 * Math.PI };
        xyzRange = new double[] { -1.25, 1.25, -1.5, 1.5, -1.25, 1.25 };
        uvNum = new int[] { 50, 15 };
        _model.UvNum = uvNum;
        _model.Point3s = ModelHelper.VertexData(ModelHelper.Torus,
            uvRange, uvNum, xyzRange);
        break;

    case ChartType.Hylicoid:
        uvRange = new double[] { 0, 5, -2.5 * Math.PI, 2.5 * Math.PI };
```

```
            xyzRange = new double[] { -5, 5, -10, 10, -5, 5 };
            uvNum = new int[] { 7, 100 };
            _model.UvNum = uvNum;
            _model.Point3s = ModelHelper.VertexData(ModelHelper.Hylicoid,
                uvRange, uvNum, xyzRange);
            break;

        case ChartType.Hyperboloid:
            uvRange = new double[] { 0, 2 * Math.PI, -1.5, 1.5 };
            xyzRange = new double[] { -7, 7, -10, 10, -7, 7 };
            uvNum = new int[] { 30, 30 };
            _model.UvNum = uvNum;
            _model.Point3s = ModelHelper.VertexData(ModelHelper.Hyperboloid,
                uvRange, uvNum, xyzRange);
            break;

        case ChartType.KleinBottle:
            uvRange = new double[] { 0, 10 * Math.PI, 0, 5 * Math.PI };
            xyzRange = new double[] { -10, 10, -6, 6, -10, 10 };
            uvNum = new int[] { 100, 40 };
            _model.UvNum = uvNum;
            _model.Point3s = ModelHelper.VertexData(ModelHelper.KleinBottle,
                uvRange, uvNum, xyzRange);
            break;
    }
    return _model;
}
```

Here, we implement a *GET* and *POST UseServer* method. In the GET UserServer method, we define a default 3D *sinc* surface chart, where we specify the *uvRange*, *xyzrange*, and *uvNum* parameters, calculate the vertex data using the *VertexData* method implemented in the *ModelHelper* class, and pass the data to the *ThreeModel*'s *Point3s* property.

In the *POST UseServer* method, we call the *GetModel* method where we generate the vertex data for a user specified chart type from the view, and return the new model to the view for displaying the corresponding surface chart.

Next, add a view named *UseServer.cshtml* to the *Views/ServerSurface* folder and replace its content with the following code:

```
@using Chapter09.Models
@model ThreeModel
@{
    ViewData["Title"] = ViewBag.Title;
}
<h3>@ViewBag.Title</h3>
@Html.Partial("_Links")

<div class="container">
    <div class="row">
        <div class="col-sm-12">
            <div style="margin-top:30px; margin-right:25px">
                <p>Select a chart type:</p>
                <form method="post" asp-controller="ServerSurface"
                    asp-action="UseServer" asp-antiforgery="true">
                    <div class="form-group">
```

```
            <select class="form-control" asp-for="ChartType"
                    asp-items="@new  SelectList(Enum.GetValues(
                    typeof(ChartType)))" onchange="form.submit();">
            </select>
        </div>
    </form>
    <div id="chart" style="width:700px; height:600px;
        margin-top:20px"></div>
        </div>
    </div>
</div>
</div>

@section scripts{
<script language="JavaScript" src="~/lib/mylib/TrackballControls.js"></script>

<script>
    var data = @Html.Raw(Json.Serialize(Model));
    setCustomGeometry("chart", data, true);
</script>
}
```

This code looks very simple. The first two lines specify the namespace and model (*ThreeModel*). The *using* statement is necessary here because we use not only the *ThreeModel* but also the *ChartType* enum – both of them is under the *Models* namespace. Next, we define a *submit* form that includes a *select* element with its items being filled by the *ChartType* enumeration. In the script section, we convert the *ThreeModel* into JSON data using a *Json.Serialize* function. Finally, we call the *setCustomGeometry* function to create the chart.

Now, get back to the *setCustomGeometry* function in the site.js file:

```
function setCustomGeometry(gl, data, isServerData) {
    if (isServerData) {
        data = processServerData(data);
    }
    ......
}
```

You see that if *isServerData* is *true*, the data from server need to be preprocessed before pass it to our custom geometry using the *processServerData* function. This function is included in the *site.js* file and the following is its code:

```
function processServerData(serverData) {
    var vertices = [];
    var faces = [];
    var i, j;
    for (i = 0; i < serverData.point3s.length; i++) {
        var pt = new THREE.Vector3(serverData.point3s[i].x,
            serverData.point3s[i].y, serverData.point3s[i].z);
        vertices.push(pt);
    }

    var unum = serverData.uvNum[0];
    var vnum = serverData.uvNum[1];
    for (i = 0; i < vnum - 1; i++) {
        for (j = 0; j < unum - 1; j++) {
```

```
                var a = i * unum + j;
                var b = i * unum + j + 1;
                var c = (i + 1) * unum + j + 1;
                var d = (i + 1) * unum + j;
                faces.push(new THREE.Face3(a, b, d));
                faces.push(new THREE.Face3(b, c, d));
            }
        }
        return { vertices, faces };
    }
```

Here, we first convert the *serverData.point3s* into the JavaScript array of *THREE.Vector3* objects, which is the data format for the vertices required by our custom geometry. Next, we also generate the data for the faces by going over all vertices.

Running this example produces the results shown in Figure 9-7.

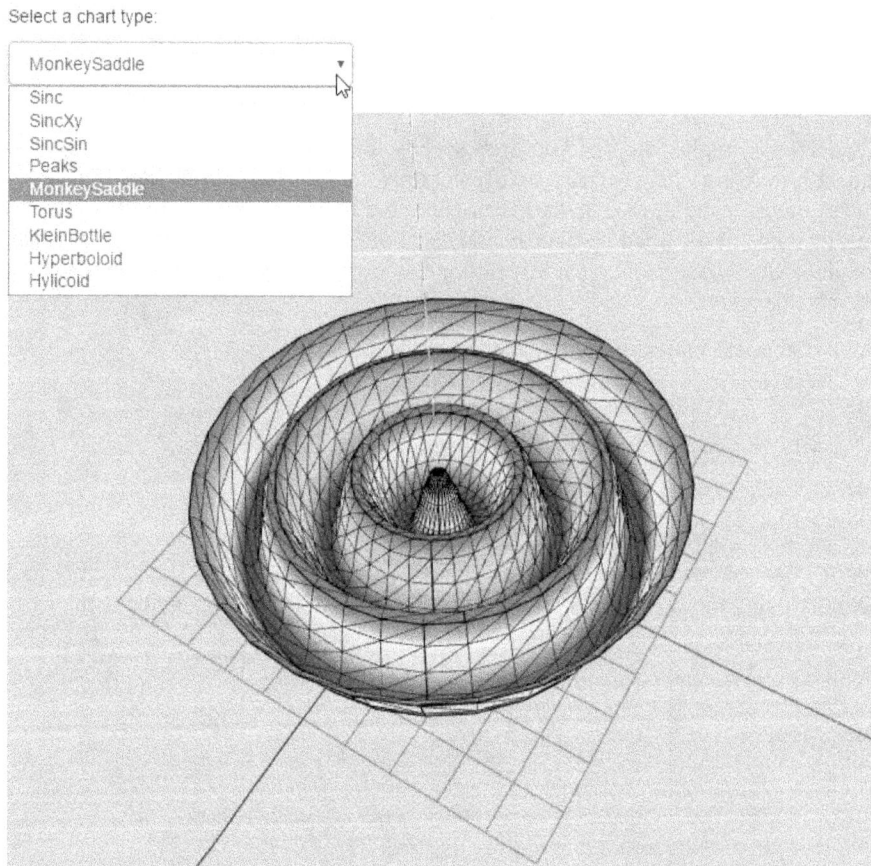

Figure 9-7. A 3D surface chart with the server data.

Here, we have successfully created 3D surface charts using the data from the server side. You can display different chart by selecting a chart type from the dropdown list, as shown in the figure where the *MonkeySaddle* chart type is selected.

Custom Geometry with UV Mapping

As mentioned previously, the *setCustomGeometry* function cannot be used to create 3D charts with texture. In order to use texture to decorate the surfaces, we need to compute the UV mapping. In fact, the UV mapping is a process that projects a texture map onto a 3D object. The letters "U" and "V" denote the axes of the 2D texture because X, Y, and Z are already used to denote the axes of the 3D object. UV texturing permits 3D surface to be decorated with the image.

Now, we want to create a custom geometry with UV mapping. First, we want to extend the original *getSurfaceData* function to include UV mapping. Add a new function named *setSurfaceUvData* to the *site.js* file:

```
function getSurfaceUvData(func, urange, vrange, unum, vnum,
    xrange, yrange, zrange) {
    du = (urange[1] - urange[0]) / (unum - 1);
    dv = (vrange[1] - vrange[0]) / (vnum - 1);
    var vertices = [];
    var faces = [];
    var uvs = [];
    var i, j;
    for (i = 0; i < vnum; i++) {
        var v = vrange[0] + i * dv;
        var v1 = i / vnum;
        for (j = 0; j < unum; j++) {
            var u = urange[0] + j * du;
            var u1 = j / unum;
            var pt = func(u, v);
            var pt1 = getNormalize(pt, xrange, yrange, zrange);
            vertices.push(pt1);
            uvs.push(new THREE.Vector2(u1, v1));
        }
    }

    for (i = 0; i < vnum - 1; i++) {
        for (j = 0; j < unum - 1; j++) {
            var a = i * unum + j;
            var b = i * unum + j + 1;
            var c = (i + 1) * unum + j + 1;
            var d = (i + 1) * unum + j;
            faces.push(new THREE.Face3(a, b, d));
            faces.push(new THREE.Face3(b, c, d));
        }
    }
    return { vertices, faces, uvs };
}
```

The UV mapping or texture coordinate is a 2D vector in the texture space for each vertex. Here, we simply take the unit vector along the *u*- and *v*-direction in the parametric space as our UV mapping coordinate. We can do that because in the *uv* parametric space, the surface is simply a flat plane, which is equivalent to our texture image (also a flat plane). We store the UV mapping data into a JavaScript array called *uvs*.

With this UV mapping data, we can create a custom geometry with texture decoration. Add a new function named *setCustomGeometryUv* to the *site.js* file:

```
function setCustomGeometryUv(gl, data, uvNum, isServerData) {
    if (isServerData) {
        data = processServerUvData(data);
    }
    var container = document.getElementById(gl);
    while (container.firstChild) {
        container.removeChild(container.firstChild);
    }
    var scene = new THREE.Scene();
    var group = new THREE.Group();
    var camera = new THREE.PerspectiveCamera(45,
        container.clientWidth / container.clientHeight, 0.1, 1000);
    camera.position.set(1, 1, 3.5);
    camera.lookAt(scene.position);
    scene.add(camera);

    var renderer = new THREE.WebGLRenderer({ antialias: true });
    renderer.setClearColor("lightgray", 1.0);
    renderer.setSize(container.clientWidth, container.clientHeight);
    renderer.shadowMap.enabled = true;
    container.appendChild(renderer.domElement);

    var loader = new THREE.TextureLoader();
    var wireTexture = loader.load('/images/square.png');
    wireTexture.wrapS = wireTexture.wrapT = THREE.RepeatWrapping;
    wireTexture.repeat.set(uvNum[0], uvNum[1]);
    material = new THREE.MeshBasicMaterial({ map: wireTexture,
        vertexColors: THREE.VertexColors, side: THREE.DoubleSide });

    var geometry = new THREE.Geometry();
    geometry.vertices = data.vertices;
    geometry.faces = data.faces;
    geometry.faceVertexUvs[0] = [];
    geometry.faces.forEach(function (face) {
        var v1 = data.uvs[face.a];
        var v2 = data.uvs[face.b];
        var v3 = data.uvs[face.c];
        geometry.faceVertexUvs[0].push([v1, v2, v3]);
    });
    geometry.uvsNeedUpdate = true;

    geometry.computeBoundingBox();
    ymin = geometry.boundingBox.min.y;
    ymax = geometry.boundingBox.max.y;

    // add axes
    var axes = new THREE.AxisHelper(10);
    axes.position.y = ymin;
    group.add(axes);

    // add xz-grids
    var gridxz = new THREE.GridHelper(2, 10);
    gridxz.position.y = ymin;
    group.add(gridxz);
```

```
        yrange = ymax - ymin;
        var color, point, face, numberOfSides, vertexIndex;
        var faceIndices = ['a', 'b', 'c', 'd'];
        for (var i = 0; i < geometry.vertices.length; i++) {
            point = geometry.vertices[i];
            color = new THREE.Color(0x0000ff);
            color.setHSL(0.7 * (ymax - point.y) / yrange, 1, 0.5);
            geometry.colors[i] = color;
        }
        for (var i = 0; i < geometry.faces.length; i++) {
            face = geometry.faces[i];
            numberOfSides = (face instanceof THREE.Face3) ? 3 : 4;
            for (var j = 0; j < numberOfSides; j++) {
                vertexIndex = face[faceIndices[j]];
                face.vertexColors[j] = geometry.colors[vertexIndex];
            }
        }

        var obj = new THREE.Mesh(geometry, material);
        group.add(obj);
        scene.add(group);
        var control = new THREE.TrackballControls(camera, renderer.domElement);

        render();
        function render() {
            requestAnimationFrame(render);
            group.rotation.x += 0.005;
            group.rotation.y += 0.005;
            group.rotation.z += 0.005;
            control.update();
            renderer.render(scene, camera);
        }
    }
}
```

The highlighted code shows the relevant code snippet for texture mapping. We first load the *square.png* file as our texture file using the *THREE.TextureLoader* and make it to be repeat wrapping, which is identical to what we did for the parametric geometry previously.

The key step in the UV mapping is how we push the *uvs* data into the *geometry.faceVertexUvs[0]* object using a *forEach* loop. After this process, we set the *geometry.uvsNeedUpdate* to *true* to update the texture mapping coordinates.

Now, we can test our new custom geometry with the UV mapping. Add a new view named *CustomGeometryUv.cshtml* and replace its content with the following code:

```
@{
    ViewData["Title"] = ViewBag.Title;
}
<h3>@ViewBag.Title</h3>
@Html.Partial("_Links")

<div class="container">
    <div class="row">
        <div class="col-sm-4">
            <div style="margin-top:30px; margin-right:25px">
                <p style="margin-bottom:5px;">Sinc function</p>
```

```
            <div id="gl1" style="width:400px; height:370px;
                margin-top:10px"></div>
        </div>
    </div>
    <div class="col-sm-4">
        <div style="margin-top:30px; margin-left:25px">
            <p style="margin-bottom:5px;">Peaks function</p>
            <div id="gl2" style="width:400px; height:370px;
                margin-top:10px"></div>
        </div>
    </div>
</div>
<div class="row">
    <div class="col-sm-4">
        <div style="margin-top:30px; margin-right:25px">
            <p style="margin-bottom:5px;">Monkey saddle function</p>
            <div id="gl3" style="width:400px; height:370px;
                margin-top:10px"></div>
        </div>
    </div>
    <div class="col-sm-4">
        <div style="margin-top:30px; margin-left:25px">
            <p style="margin-bottom:5px;">Torus function</p>
            <div id="gl4" style="width:400px; height:370px;
                margin-top:10px"></div>
        </div>
    </div>
</div>
</div>
</div>

@section scripts{
<script language="JavaScript" src="~/lib/mylib/TrackballControls.js"></script>
<script>
    // test sinc
    function sinc(u, v) {
        var r = Math.sqrt(u * u + v * v) + 0.0001;
        var res = Math.sin(r) / r;
        return new THREE.Vector3(u, res, v);
    }
    var urange = [-8, 8];
    var vrange = [-8, 8];
    var unum = 30;
    var vnum = 30;
    var xrange = urange;
    var yrange = [-0.7, 1.5];
    var zrange = vrange;
    var data = getSurfaceUvData(sinc, urange, vrange, unum, vnum,
        xrange, yrange, zrange);
    setCustomGeometryUv("gl1", data, [unum, vnum], false);

    // peaks function
    var peaks = function (u, v) {
        var x = u;
        var z = v;
```

```
    var y = 3 * Math.pow((1 - x), 2) * Math.exp(-x * x - (z + 1) *
        (z + 1)) - 10 * (0.2 * x - Math.pow(x, 3) - Math.pow(z, 5)) *
        Math.exp(-x * x - z * z) - 1 / 3 * Math.exp(-(x + 1) * (x + 1) -
        z * z);

    return new THREE.Vector3(x, y, -z);
}

urange = [-3, 3];
vrange = [-3, 3];
unum = 31;
vnum = 31;
xrange = urange;
yrange = [-10, 10];
zrange = vrange;
data = getSurfaceUvData(peaks, urange, vrange, unum, vnum,
    xrange, yrange, zrange);
setCustomGeometryUv("gl2", data, [unum, vnum], false);

// monkey saddle
var monkey = function (u, v) {
    var x = u * Math.cos(v);
    var z = u * Math.sin(v);
    var y = 2 * Math.cos(u);
    return new THREE.Vector3(x, y, z);
}

urange = [0, 6 * Math.PI];
vrange = [0, 2 * Math.PI];
unum = 31;
vnum = 31;
xrange = [-6 * Math.PI, 6 * Math.PI];
yrange = [-10, 10];
zrange = [-6 * Math.PI, 6 * Math.PI];
data = getSurfaceUvData(monkey, urange, vrange, unum, vnum, xrange,
    yrange, zrange);
setCustomGeometryUv("gl3", data, [unum, vnum], false);

// torus
var torus = function (u, v) {
    var a = 1;
    var b = 0.25;

    var x = (a + b * Math.cos(v)) * Math.cos(u);
    var z = (a + b * Math.cos(v)) * Math.sin(u);
    var y = b * Math.sin(v);
    return new THREE.Vector3(x, y, z);
}

urange = [0, 2 * Math.PI];
vrange = [0, 2 * Math.PI];
unum = 50;
vnum = 20;
xrange = [-1.25, 1.25];
yrange = [-1.5, 1.5];
```

```
    zrange = [-1.25, 1.25];
    data = getSurfaceUvData(torus, urange, vrange, unum, vnum, xrange,
        yrange, zrange);;
    setCustomGeometryUv("gl4", data, [unum, vnum], false);
</script>
}
```

This code is basically similar to the *CustomGeometry.cshtml* file, except that here we generate data using the *getSurfaceUvData* function and create the chart using the *setCustomGeometryUv* function.

Running this example produces the results shown in Figure 9-8.

Sinc function

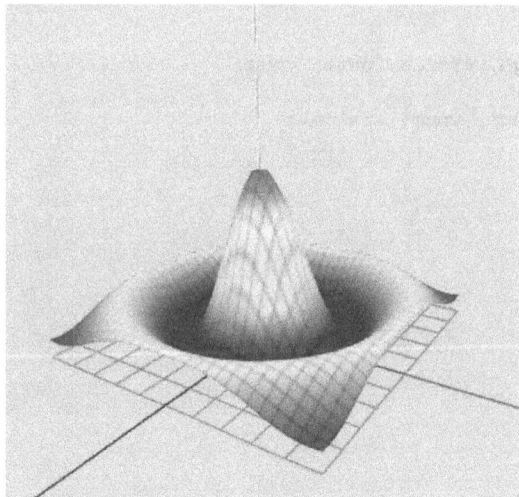

Peaks function

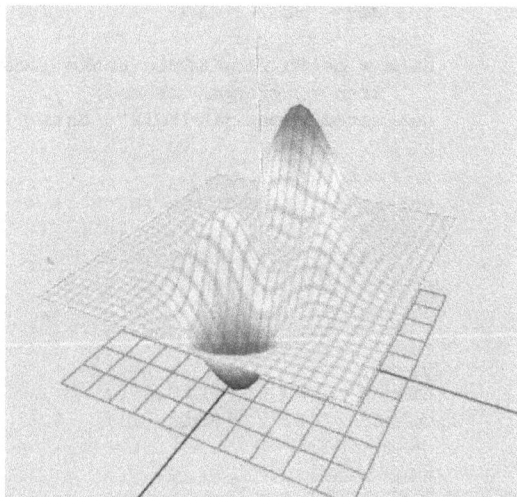

Monkey saddle function

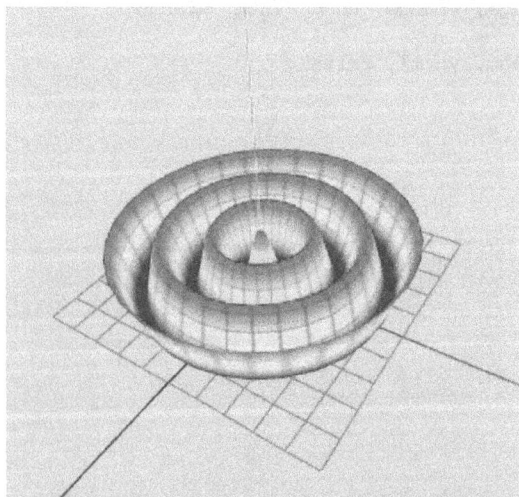

Torus function

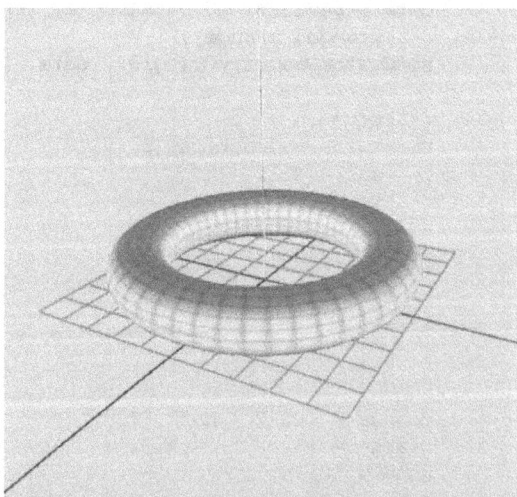

Figure 9-8. A 3D charts with a square texture created with custom geometry with UV mapping.

3D Charts with Server Data and UV Mapping

Now, we want to calculate the UV mapping from the server side. Add a new C# method named *UvData* to the *ModelHelper* class. Here is the code for this method:

```
public static List<Vector2> UvData(int[] uvNum)
{
    List<Vector2> pts = new List<Vector2>();
    for (int i = 0; i < uvNum[1]; i++)
    {
        double v = 1.0 * i / (1.0 * uvNum[1]);
        for (int j = 0; j < uvNum[0]; j++)
        {
            double u = 1.0 * j / (1.0 * uvNum[0]);
            pts.Add(new Vector2((float)u, (float)v));
        }
    }
    return pts;
}
```

This method calculate the *uvs* in the same way as what we did in the client side.

Add the *GET* and *POST* method named *UseServerUv* to the *ServerSurfaceController.cs* file:

```
public IActionResult UseServerUv()
{
    ViewBag.Title = "Using Server Data with UV map";
    var uvRange = new double[] { -8, 8, -8, 8 };
    var xyzRange = new double[] { -8, 8, -0.7, 1.5, -8, 8 };
    var uvNum = new int[] { 30, 30 };
    _model.UvNum = uvNum;
    _model.Point3s = ModelHelper.VertexData(ModelHelper.Sinc, uvRange,
        uvNum, xyzRange);
    _model.Point2s = ModelHelper.UvData(uvNum);
    return View(_model);
}

[HttpPost]
public IActionResult UseServerUv(ThreeModel model)
{
    ViewBag.Title = "Using Server Data with UV map";
    int[] uvNum;
    var model1 = GetModel(model, out uvNum);
    model1.Point2s = ModelHelper.UvData(uvNum);
    return View(model1);
}
```

You can see that in addition to the vertex data, we add the UV mapping data to the model.

Add a new view named *UseServerUv.cshtml* to the *Views/ServerSurface* folder and replace its content with the following code:

```
@using Chapter09.Models
@model ThreeModel
@{
    ViewData["Title"] = ViewBag.Title;
}
```

```
<h3>@ViewBag.Title</h3>
@Html.Partial("_Links")

<div class="container">
    <div class="row">
        <div class="col-sm-12">
            <div style="margin-top:30px; margin-right:25px">
                <p>Select a chart type:</p>
                <form method="post" asp-controller="ServerSurface"
                    asp-action="UseServerUv" asp-antiforgery="true">
                    <div class="form-group">
                        <select class="form-control" asp-for="ChartType"
                            asp-items="@new SelectList(Enum.GetValues(
                            typeof(ChartType)))"
                            onchange="form.submit();"></select>
                    </div>
                </form>
                <div id="chart" style="width:700px; height:600px;
                    margin-top:20px"></div>
            </div>
        </div>
    </div>
</div>

@section scripts{
<script language="JavaScript" src="~/lib/mylib/TrackballControls.js"></script>
<script>
    var data = @Html.Raw(Json.Serialize(Model));
    setCustomGeometryUv("chart", data, data.uvNum, true);
</script>
}
```

This view is similar to the *UseServer.cshtml* file, except that here we use the *setCustomGeometryUv* to create the 3D chart.

Now, get back to the *setCustomGeometryUv* function in the site.js file:

```
function setCustomGeometryUv(gl, data, uvNum, isServerData) {
    if (isServerData) {
        data = processServerUvData(data);
    }
    ......
}
```

You see that if *isServerData* is *true*, the data from server need to be preprocessed before pass it to our custom geometry using the *processServerUvData* function. This function is included in the *site.js* file and the following is its code:

```
Function processServerUvData(serverData) {
    var vertices = [];
    var faces = [];
    var uvs = [];
    var i, j;
    for (i = 0; i < serverData.point3s.length; i++) {
        var pt3 = new THREE.Vector3(serverData.point3s[i].x,
                                    serverData.point3s[i].y,
                                    serverData.point3s[i].z);
```

```
        vertices.push(pt3);
    }

    for (i = 0; i < serverData.point2s.length; i++) {
        var pt2 = new THREE.Vector2(serverData.point2s[i].x,
                                    serverData.point2s[i].y);
        uvs.push(pt2);
    }

    var unum = serverData.uvNum[0];
    var vnum = serverData.uvNum[1];
    for (i = 0; i < vnum - 1; i++) {
        for (j = 0; j < unum - 1; j++) {
            var a = i * unum + j;
            var b = i * unum + j + 1;
            var c = (i + 1) * unum + j + 1;
            var d = (i + 1) * unum + j;
            faces.push(new THREE.Face3(a, b, d));
            faces.push(new THREE.Face3(b, c, d));
        }
    }
    return { vertices, faces, uvs };
}
```

Here, we first convert the *serverData.point3s* into a JavaScript array of *THREE.Vector3* objects, which is the data format for the vertices required by our custom geometry. Next, we convert the *serverData.Point2s* into a JavaScript array of *THREE.Vector2* objects, which is the data format for the UV mapping. Finally, we generate the data for the faces by going over all vertices.

Running this example produces the results shown in Figure 9-9.

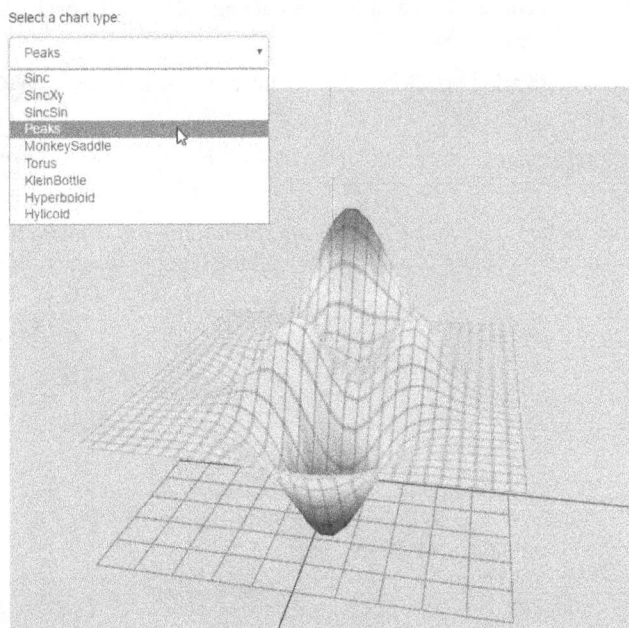

Figure 9-9. A 3D surface chart with a square texture using the server data.

Here, we have successfully created 3D surface charts with a square texture using the data from the server side. You can display different chart by selecting a chart type from the dropdown list, as shown in the figure where the *peaks* chart type is selected.

Up to this point, we have demonstrated how to create various 3D charts using the data from both the client side and server side in Three.js. Following the procedure presented in this chapter, you can add more features to the 3D charts, such as different colormaps, title, ticks, and axis labels. You can also create the other types of 3D charts, such as 3D line charts, 3D scatter charts, contour charts, and 3D combination charts. If you are interested in this topic, you can look at my previously published books, *Practical C# Charts and Graphics*, and *Practical .NET Chart Development and Applications*.

If you do not want to create the 3D charts using Three.js from scratch, you can also use the open source 3D charting libraries. In the following section, I will introduce one of such libraries – *Graph3d*, and show you how to use it to create various 3D charts.

Graph3d Library

Graph3d is an interactive visualization library to draw data in a 3D chart. You can pan and zoom in the chart by dragging and scrolling in the window. Graph3d also supports animation of a chart. This library uses HTML canvas (instead of SVG) to render charts and can render up to a few thousands of data points smoothly.

One limitation of the Graph3d library is that it supports only the simple 3D surface charts, that is, for each X and Y values, the surface can have at most one Z value (The coordinate system in Graph3d is oriented so that the Z axis is the "up" direction). You cannot use Graph3d to create complex 3D charts, such as parametric surfaces with multiple Z values for certain values of X and Y.

You can use the Bower package manager to install the Graph3d package by searching for *vis*. The *Graph3d* is one of the components included in the *vis* package. The *vis.js* package also consists of the other components: *DataSet*, *Timeline*, *Network*, and *Graph2d*.

Graph3d is no built-in visualization of Google. You need to include the old Google API and the following files in your view:

```
<script type="text/javascript" src="http://www.google.com/jsapi"></script>
<script src="~/lib/vis/dist/vis-graph3d.min.js"></script>
```

I have included these files in the *Views/Shared/_Layout.cshtml* file. The Graph3d library uses the Google Visualization format to create 3D charts. You need to load the Google visualization package in order to use DataTable:

```
google.load("visualization", "1");
google.setOnLoadCallback(drawChart);
function drawChart() {
    // load data and create the chart here.
    ……
}
```

You should be familiar with the above code snippet, which is similar to what we have used in creating various 2D charts with the Google Charts API in Chapter 5.

Creating Simple 3D Surfaces

In this section, we will use the Graph3d library to create 3D simple surface charts. Add a new controller named *Graph3dController.cs* to the *Controllers* folder and replace its content with the following code:

```
using Chapter09.Models;
using Microsoft.AspNetCore.Mvc;

namespace Chapter09.Controllers
{
    public class Graph3dController : Controller
    {
        Graph3dModel _model = new Graph3dModel();

        public IActionResult Index()
        {
            ViewBag.Title = "Graph3d: Home";
            return View();
        }

        public IActionResult SimpleSurface()
        {
            ViewBag.Title = "Simple Surfaces";
            return View();
        }

        public IActionResult GraphStyle()
        {
            ViewBag.Title = "Graph3d Style";
            _model.Graph3dStyle = Graph3dStyle.bar;
            return View(_model);
        }

        [HttpPost]
        public IActionResult GraphStyle(Graph3dModel model)
        {
            ViewBag.Title = "Graph3d Style";
            return View(model);
        }
    }
}
```

Add a new folder named *Graph3d* to the *Views* folder. Add a new view named *SimpleSurface.cshtml* to the *Views/Graph3d* folder and replace its content with the following code:

```
@{
    ViewData["Title"] = ViewBag.Title;
}
<h3>@ViewBag.Title</h3>
@Html.Partial("_Links")
<div class="container">
    <div class="row">
        <div class="col-sm-6">
            <div style="margin-top:30px; margin-right:25px">
                <p style="margin-bottom:5px;">Sinc function</p>
                <div id="chart1" style="width:600px; height:480px;
```

```
                          margin-top:10px"></div>
                </div>
            </div>
            <div class="col-sm-6">
                <div style="margin-top:30px; margin-left:25px">
                    <p style="margin-bottom:5px;">Sinc(x*y) function</p>
                    <div id="chart2" style="width:600px; height:480px;
                        margin-top:10px"></div>
                </div>
            </div>
        </div>
        <div class="row">
            <div class="col-sm-6">
                <div style="margin-top:30px; margin-right:25px">
                    <p style="margin-bottom:5px;">Sin*cos function</p>
                    <div id="chart3" style="width:600px; height:480px;
                        margin-top:10px"></div>
                </div>
            </div>
            <div class="col-sm-6">
                <div style="margin-top:30px; margin-left:25px">
                    <p style="margin-bottom:5px;">Peaks function</p>
                    <div id="chart4" style="width:600px; height:480px;
                        margin-top:10px"></div>
                </div>
            </div>
        </div>
    </div>
</div>

@section scripts{
<script>
    google.load("visualization", "1");
    google.setOnLoadCallback(drawChart1);

    var data, graph;
    var options = {
        style: "surface",
        showPerspective: true,
        showGrid: true,
        showShadow: false,
        keepAspectRatio: true,
        verticalRatio: 0.7,
        yCenter: '35%',
    };

    // sinc function
    function sinc(x, y) {
        var r = Math.sqrt(x * x + y * y) + 0.0001;
        return Math.sin(r) / r;
    }

    function drawChart1() {
        var container = document.getElementById("chart1");
        var width = container.clientWidth;
        var height = container.clientHeight;
```

```
        var data = getGraph3dData(sinc, -8, 8, -8, 8, 30, 30);
        graph = new vis.Graph3d(container, data, options);
    }


    // sinc(x*y):
    function sinc2(x, y) {
        var r = x * y + 0.00001;
        return Math.sin(r) / r;
    }


    google.setOnLoadCallback(drawChart2);
    function drawChart2() {
        var container = document.getElementById("chart2");
        var width = container.clientWidth;
        var height = container.clientHeight;
        var data = getGraph3dData(sinc2, -5, 5, -5, 5, 40, 40);
        graph = new vis.Graph3d(container, data, options);
    }


    // sin*cos
    function sinCos(x, y) {
        var z = 1 + Math.sin(3*x) * Math.cos(3*y);
        return z;
    }


    google.setOnLoadCallback(drawChart3);
    function drawChart3() {
        var container = document.getElementById("chart3");
        var width = container.clientWidth;
        var height = container.clientHeight;
        var data = getGraph3dData(sinCos, -1, 1, -1, 1, 40, 40);
        graph = new vis.Graph3d(container, data, options);
    }


    // peaks function
    function peaks(x, y) {
        var z = 3 * Math.pow((1 - x), 2) * Math.exp(-x * x - (y + 1) * (y + 1))

            10 * (0.2 * x - Math.pow(x, 3) - Math.pow(y, 5)) *
            Math.exp(-x * x - y * y) -
            1 / 3 * Math.exp(-(x + 1) * (x + 1) - y * y);
        return z;
    }


    google.setOnLoadCallback(drawChart4);
    function drawChart4() {
        var container = document.getElementById("chart4");
        var width = container.clientWidth;
        var height = container.clientHeight;
        var data = getGraph3dData(peaks, -3, 3, -3, 3, 36, 36);
        graph = new vis.Graph3d(container, data, options);
    }

</script>
}
```

This code creates four surface charts by implementing four mathematical functions. In the script section, we first include the Google visualization package and call the *google.setOnLoadCallback* function to start the chart. The *options* setting is similar to what we did for Google Charts. Here, we set the *style* to *surface*, indicating that we want to create a surface chart. If the *showPerspective* option is set to *true*, the chart is drawn in perspective mode: points and lines which are further away are drawn smaller. The *keepAspectRatio* option controls the *x*-axis and the *y*-axis respect ratio. If it is true, the chart will keep the aspect ratio unchanged; otherwise, the axes will be scaled such that they both have the same, maximum width. The value of the *verticalRatio* is in between 0.1 and 1.0. This scales the vertical size of the chart when *keepAspectRation* is set to false, and *verticalRatio* is set to 1, the chart will be inside a cube.

The function definition is simple: we simply provide the expression for the function and use a helper function named *getGraph3dData* to convert the function into the data format required by Graph3d. Here is the code for the *getGraph3dData* function located in the *site.js* file:

```
function getGraph3dData(func, xmin, xmax, ymin, ymax, nx, ny) {
    var data = new vis.DataSet();
    var dx = (xmax - xmin) / nx;
    var dy = (ymax - ymin) / ny;
    for (var x = xmin; x < xmax; x += dx) {
        for (var y = ymin; y < ymax; y += dy) {
            var z = func(x, y);
            data.add({ x: x, y: y, z: z, style: z });
        }
    }
    return data;
}
```

This function calculates the input function values and put it into a *DataSet* object. Note that here we do not perform any normalization on the original data because Graph3d will do this for us automatically.

Graph3d requires a data table with three to five columns, depending on the specified style and animation. The first three columns must contain the location coordinates for *x*-axis, *y*-axis, and *z*-axis. The fourth column is optional, and can contain a data values. The last column (can be the fourth or fifth column) can contain filter values used for animation.

Running this example, selecting the *3D Chart Package* tab, and clicking the *Simple Surfaces* link produce the results shown in Figure 9-10. You can see that Graph3d offers professional-looking 3D charts, which consists of the axes, tick markers, and axis labels.

Graph Styles

In the preceding section, we set the style to *surface* to create simple 3D surface chart. In fact, Graph3d consists of several graph styles you can set, including *bar*, *bar-color*, *bar-size*, *dot*, *dot-line*, *dot-color*, *dot-size*, *line*, *grid*, and *surface*. In this section, we will examine all of these graph styles.

Add a C# enum named *Graph3dStyle* to the *ThreeModel.cs* file:

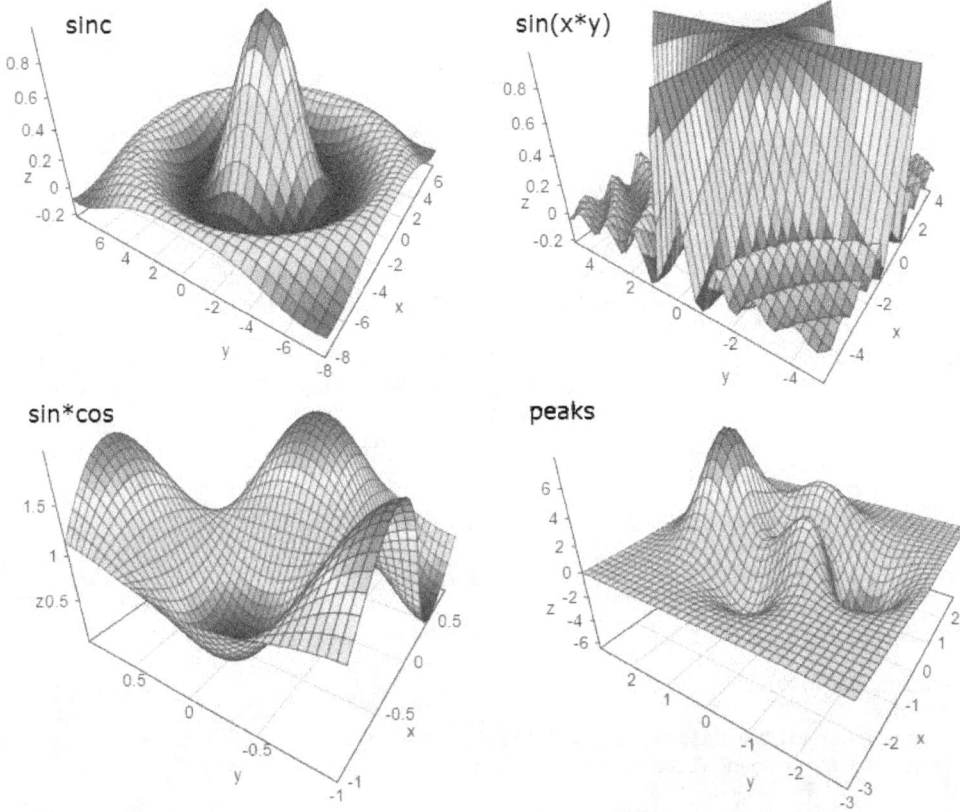

Figure 9-10. Simple 3D surface charts created using Graph3d.

```
public enum Graph3dStyle
{
    bar = 1,
    barcolor = 2,
    barsize = 3,
    dot = 4,
    dotline = 5,
    dotcolor = 6,
    dotsize = 7,
    line = 8,
    grid = 9,
    surface = 0,
}
```

We add ten graph styles to this enumeration and set the default style to *surface.*

Add a new view named *GraphStyle.cshtml* to the *Views/Graph3d* folder and replace its content with the following code:

```
@using Chapter09.Models
@model Graph3dModel
@{
    ViewData["Title"] = ViewBag.Title;
```

```
    }

    <h3>@ViewBag.Title</h3>
    @Html.Partial("_Links")

    <div class="container">
        <div class="row">
            <div class="col-sm-12">
                <div style="margin-top:30px; margin-right:25px">
                    <p>Select a graph type:</p>
                    <form method="post" asp-controller="Graph3d"
                        asp-action="GraphStyle" asp-antiforgery="true">
                        <div class="form-group">
                            <select class="form-control" asp-for="Graph3dStyle"
                                asp-items="@new  SelectList(Enum.GetValues(
                                typeof(Graph3dStyle)))"
                                onchange="form.submit();"></select>
                        </div>
                    </form>
                    <div id="chart" style="margin-top:20px"></div>
                </div>
            </div>
        </div>
    </div>

    @section scripts{
    <script>
        google.load("visualization", "1");
        google.setOnLoadCallback(drawChart);

        var style = '@Model.Graph3dStyle.ToString()'
        if (style === 'barcolor') style = 'bar-color';
        if (style === 'barsize') style = 'bar-size';
        if (style === 'dotcolor') style = 'dot-color';
        if (style === 'dotsize') style = 'dot-size';
        if (style === 'dotline') style = 'dot-line';

        // peaks function
        function peaks(x, y) {
            var z = 3 * Math.pow((1 - x), 2) * Math.exp(-x * x - (y + 1) * (y + 1))
                - 10 * (0.2 * x - Math.pow(x, 3) - Math.pow(y, 5)) *
                Math.exp(-x * x - y * y) - 1 / 3 * Math.exp(-(x + 1) * (x + 1) -
                y * y);
            return z;
        }

        function drawChart() {
            var container = document.getElementById("chart");
            var options = {
                style: style,
                width: '700px',
                height: '600px',
                showPerspective: true,
                showGrid: true,
                showShadow: false,
```

```
                keepAspectRatio: true,
                verticalRatio: 0.7,
                yCenter: '35%',
            };
            var data = getGraph3dData(peaks, -3, 3, -3, 3, 20, 20);
            var graph = new vis.Graph3d(container, data, options);
        }
    </script>
    }
```

This code implements a 3D chart for a *peaks* function. You can select a graph style to change the chart type.

Running this example produces the results shown in Figure 9-11.

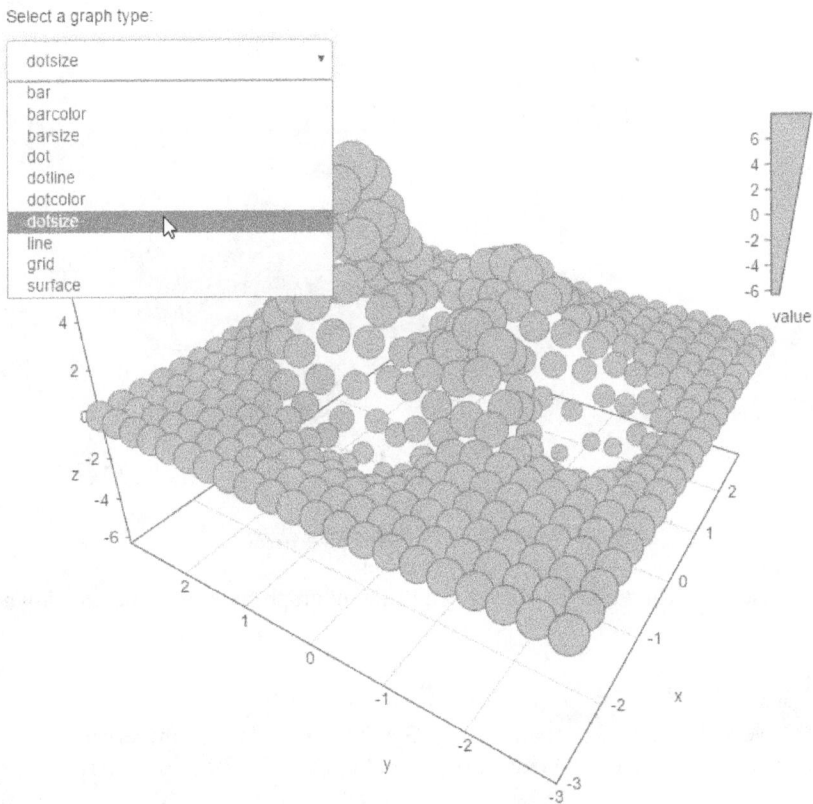

Figure 9-11. 3D chart with different graph styles.

Figure 9-11 shows a 3D chart with a graph style of *dot-size*. You can see that the dot size changes with the z values.

Figure 9-12 shows a 3D chart with a bar-size style.

Select a graph type:

barsize ▾

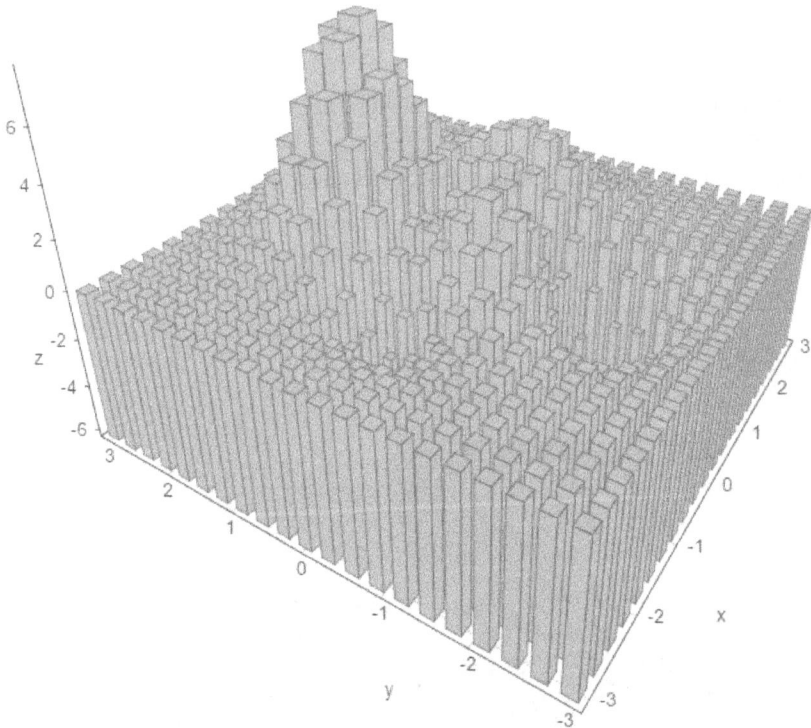

Figure 9-12. A 3D bar-size chart.

You can display the other chart type by selecting a different graph style from the dropdown list.

Using Server Data

In this section, we will create 3D charts using Graph3d with data from server. Add a new class *Graph3dModel* and a new enum *Graph3dChartType* to the *ThreeModel.cs* file. Here is the code for this class:

```
public class Graph3dModel
{
    public List<Vector3> Point3s { get; set; }
    public Graph3dStyle Graph3dStyle { get; set; }
    public Graph3dChartType Graph3dChartType { get; set; }
}

public enum Graph3dChartType
{
    Sinc,
```

```
    SincXy,
    SincSin,
    SinCos,
    Peaks,
}
```

Add the following mathematical functions to the *ModelHelper* class:

```
public static double SincGraph3d(double x, double y)
{
    var r = Math.Sqrt(x * x + y * y) + 0.0001;
    return Math.Sin(r) / r;
}

public static double SincXyGraph3d(double x, double y)
{
    var r = x * y + 0.00001;
    return Math.Sin(r) / r;
}

public static double SinCosGraph3d(double x, double y)
{
    var z = 1 + Math.Sin(3 * x) * Math.Cos(3 * y);
    return z;
}

public static double PeaksGraph3d(double x, double y)
{
    var z = 3 * Math.Pow((1 - x), 2) * Math.Exp(-x * x - (y + 1) * (y + 1)) -
    10 * (0.2 * x - Math.Pow(x, 3) - Math.Pow(y, 5)) *
    Math.Exp(-x * x - y * y) - 1 / 3 * Math.Exp(-(x + 1) * (x + 1) - y * y);
    return z;
}

public static double SincSinGraph3d(double x, double y)
{
    var r = Math.Sin(Math.Pow(Math.Pow(x, 6) + Math.Pow(y, 6), 1.0 / 6.0))
        + 0.00001;
    var z = Math.Sin(r) / r;
    return z;
}
```

Here, we create five mathematical functions that will be used to create 3D charts. We need to convert the above mathematical functions into a data format. Add a new method named *CreateGraph3dData* to the *ModelHelper* class. Here is the code for this method:

```
public static List<Vector3> CreateGraph3dData(Func<double, double, double> f,
    double[] xyRange, int[] xyNum)
{
    List<Vector3> pts = new List<Vector3>();
    var dx = (xyRange[1] - xyRange[0]) / xyNum[0];
    var dy = (xyRange[3] - xyRange[2]) / xyNum[1];

    for (var x = xyRange[0]; x < xyRange[1]; x += dx)
    {
        for (var y = xyRange[2]; y < xyRange[3]; y += dy)
```

```
        {
            var z = f(x, y);
            pts.Add(new Vector3((float)x, (float)y, (float)z));
        }
    }
    return pts;
}
```

Next, we can test these helper methods. Add the following *GET* and *POST* method named *UseServer* to the *Graph3dController.cs*:

```
public IActionResult UseServer()
{
    ViewBag.Title = "Using Server Data";
    var xyRange = new double[] { -8, 8, -8, 8 };
    var xyNum = new int[] { 30, 30 };
    _model.Point3s = ModelHelper.CreateGraph3dData(ModelHelper.SincGraph3d,
        xyRange, xyNum);
    _model.Graph3dStyle = Graph3dStyle.surface;
    return View(_model);
}


[HttpPost]
public IActionResult UseServer(Graph3dModel model)
{
    ViewBag.Title = "Using Server Data";
    double[] xyRange;
    int[] xyNum;

    switch (model.Graph3dChartType)
    {
        case Graph3dChartType.Sinc:
            xyRange = new double[] { -8, 8, -8, 8 };
            xyNum = new int[] { 30, 30 };
            _model.Point3s = ModelHelper.CreateGraph3dData(
                ModelHelper.SincGraph3d, xyRange, xyNum);
            break;
        case Graph3dChartType.SincXy:
            xyRange = new double[] { -5, 5, -5, 5 };
            xyNum = new int[] { 60, 60 };
            _model.Point3s = ModelHelper.CreateGraph3dData(
                ModelHelper.SincXyGraph3d, xyRange, xyNum);
            break;
        case Graph3dChartType.SincSin:
            xyRange = new double[] { -16, 16, -16, 16 };
            xyNum = new int[] { 100, 100 };
            _model.Point3s = ModelHelper.CreateGraph3dData(
                ModelHelper.SincSinGraph3d, xyRange, xyNum);
            break;
        case Graph3dChartType.Peaks:
            xyRange = new double[] { -3, 3, -3, 3 };
            xyNum = new int[] { 50, 50 };
            _model.Point3s = ModelHelper.CreateGraph3dData(
                ModelHelper.PeaksGraph3d, xyRange, xyNum);
            break;
        case Graph3dChartType.SinCos:
```

```
        xyRange = new double[] { -1, 1, -1, 1 };
        xyNum = new int[] { 40, 40 };
        _model.Point3s = ModelHelper.CreateGraph3dData(
            ModelHelper.SinCosGraph3d, xyRange, xyNum);
        break;
    }
    _model.Graph3dStyle = model.Graph3dStyle;
    return View(_model);
}
```

In the *GET UseServer* method, we create a default 3D *surface* chart for the *sinc* function. While the *POST UseServer* method creates five mathematical functions and converts them into data lists of *Vector3* objects using the helper methods implemented in the *ModelHelper* class. The method also updates the graph style that is specified by the user in the view.

Now, add a new view named *UseServer.cshtml* to the *Views/Graph3d* folder and replace its content with the following code:

```
@using Chapter09.Models
@model Graph3dModel
@{
    ViewData["Title"] = ViewBag.Title;
}
<h3>@ViewBag.Title</h3>
@Html.Partial("_Links")

<div class="container">
    <div class="row">
        <div class="col-sm-12">
            <div style="margin-top:30px; margin-right:25px">
                <p>Select a chart type and a style:</p>
                <form method="post" asp-controller="Graph3d"
                    asp-action="UseServer" asp-antiforgery="true">
                    <div class="form-group">
                        <select class="form-control" asp-for="Graph3dChartType"
                                asp-items="@new SelectList(
                                Enum.GetValues(typeof(Graph3dChartType)))"
                                onchange="form.submit();"></select>
                    </div>
                </form>
                <form method="post" asp-controller="Graph3d"
                    asp-action="UseServer" asp-antiforgery="true">
                    <div class="form-group">
                        <select class="form-control" asp-for="Graph3dStyle"
                                asp-items="@new SelectList(
                                Enum.GetValues(typeof(Graph3dStyle)))"
                                onchange="form.submit();"></select>
                    </div>
                </form>
                <div id="chart" style="margin-top:20px"></div>
            </div>
        </div>
    </div>
</div>

@section scripts{
```

```
<script>
    var serverData = @Html.Raw(Json.Serialize(Model));

    google.load("visualization", "1");
    google.setOnLoadCallback(drawChart);

    var style = '@Model.Graph3dStyle.ToString()'
    if (style === 'barcolor') style = 'bar-color';
    if (style === 'barsize') style = 'bar-size';
    if (style === 'dotcolor') style = 'dot-color';
    if (style === 'dotsize') style = 'dot-size';
    if (style === 'dotline') style = 'dot-line';

    function drawChart() {
        var container = document.getElementById("chart");
        var options = {
            style: style,
            width: '700px',
            height: '600px',
            showPerspective: true,
            showGrid: true,
            showShadow: false,
            keepAspectRatio: true,
            verticalRatio: 0.7,
            yCenter: '35%',
        };
        var data = processGraph3dData(mvcData);
        var graph = new vis.Graph3d(container, data, options);
    }
</script>
}
```

This code defines two *submit* forms that consists of *select* elements for chart type and graph style respectively. In the script section, we retrieve the data from server and convert it into a JSON data format using the *Json.Serialize* method. Before using the data by Graph3d, we need to preprocess the data using a JavaScript helper function *processGraph3dData* that is implemented in the *site.js* file. The following is the code for this helper function:

```
function processGraph3dData(serverData) {
    var data = new vis.DataSet();
    for (var i = 0; i < serverData.point3s.length; i++) {
        var x = serverData.point3s[i].x;
        var y = serverData.point3s[i].y;
        var z = serverData.point3s[i].z;
        data.add({ x: x, y: y, z: z, style: z });
    }
    return data;
}
```

This function takes the *serverData* as input argument and converts it into a *DataSet* object that is required by Graph3d. After this preprocessing, we simply call the *vis.Graph3d* library to draw our 3D chart.

Running this example, selecting the *3D Chart Package*, and clicking the *Using Server Data* link produce the results shown in Figure 9-13. Here, we choose the *SincSin* chart type and the *surface* graph style from the dropdown lists to draw the 3D surface chart for the *SincSin* function. You can also draw the chart with the other style for a different mathematical function by selecting different options from the dropdown lists.

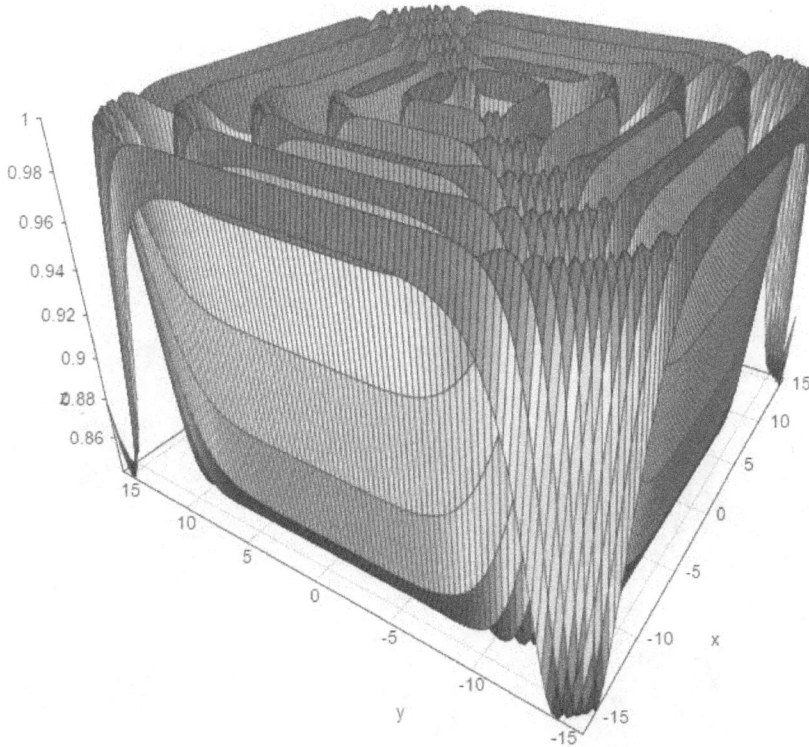

Figure 9-13. 3D surface chart created using the data from server.

Chapter 10
Charts with Web API

In addition to MVC controllers, ASP.NET Core also offers API controllers that can be used to provide access to an application's data. This feature was previously provided through a separate Web API framework but has now integrated into ASP.NET Core MVC. Web API is a framework that makes it easy to build HTTP services that can reach a broad range of clients, including browsers, mobile devices, and traditional desktop applications.

Before ASP.NET Core, MVC and Web API were very similar. Both followed an MVC type pattern with controllers and actions. Web API lacks a view engine like a Razor and instead is designed to be used for Representational State Transfer (REST) API. MVC is designed for standard web page applications with HTML front ends, while ASP.NET Core Web API is an ideal platform for building RESTful applications on the .NET Core Framework.

ASP.NET Core Web API controllers are similar to regular MVC controllers, except that the responses produced by their action methods are data objects that are sent to the client without HTML pages. It allows clients to access the data in an application without also receiving the HTML markup that is required to represent that content to the user. Not all clients are browsers, and not all clients present data to user. The Web API controller makes an application open for supporting new types of clients or clients developed by a third party.

Web API for 3D Charts

In this section, we will use an example to illustrate how to create a Web API application. Here, we will use a Web API to generate the data for some mathematical functions, and then the data will be consumed by a regular MVC application to create 3D charts based on the Graph3d library.

Model and Repository

Open Visual Studio 2017 and start a new ASP.NET Core MVC project, and name it *Chapter10*. First, we need to add support for Entity Framework Core by installing the Entity Framework Core *InMemory* database provider, which allows Entity Framework Core to be used with an in-memory database. You can install the Entity Framework Core *InMemory* database provider by editing the Chapter10.csproj file. In Solution Explorer, right-click the project and select *Edit Chapter10.csproj*. In the *ItemGroup* element, add the highlighted *PackageReference*:

```xml
<Project Sdk="Microsoft.NET.Sdk.Web">

  <PropertyGroup>
    <TargetFramework>netcoreapp1.1</TargetFramework>
  </PropertyGroup>

  <ItemGroup>
    <Folder Include="wwwroot\" />
  </ItemGroup>
  <ItemGroup>
    <PackageReference Include="Microsoft.AspNetCore" Version="1.1.1" />
    <PackageReference Include="Microsoft.AspNetCore.Mvc" Version="1.1.2" />
    <PackageReference Include="Microsoft.EntityFrameworkCore.InMemory"
        Version="1.1.1" />

    ......

  </ItemGroup>
  <ItemGroup>
    <DotNetCliToolReference Include="Microsoft.VisualStudio.Web.CodeGeneration
        .Tools" Version="1.0.0-msbuild3-final" />
  </ItemGroup>

</Project>
```

A model is an object that represents the data in your application. In this example, the model is a *Graph3dModel*.

Add a *Models* folder to the project. Add a new class named Graph3dModel and replace the generated code with the following code:

```csharp
using System.ComponentModel.DataAnnotations;
using System.ComponentModel.DataAnnotations.Schema;

namespace Chapter10.Models
{
    public class Graph3dModel
    {
        [Key]
        [DatabaseGenerated(DatabaseGeneratedOption.Identity)]
        public long DataId { get; set; }
        public double X { get; set; }
        public double Y { get; set; }
        public double Z { get; set; }
    }

    public class Graph3dChartTypeModel
    {
        public FunctionChartType FunctionChartType { get; set; }
    }

    public enum FunctionChartType
    {
        Sinc = 1,
        SincXy = 2,
        SincSin = 3,
```

```
            Peaks = 4,
            SinCos = 5
        }
    }
```

You can see that this file consists of two classes, *Graph3dModel* and *Graph3dChartTypeModel*, as well as an *enum* named *FunctionChartType*. Our main model is the *Graph3dModel* class, where the [*key*] data annotation denotes the property, *DataId*, which is a unique identifier. The [*DatabaseGenerated*] specifies the database will generate the key (rather than the application) and *DatabaseGeneratedOption.Identity* specifies the database should generate integer keys when a row is inserted.

Next, we create the database context that coordinates Entity Framework functionality for a given data model. Add a *FunctionChartContext* class to the *Models* folder and replace its content with the following code:

```
using Microsoft.EntityFrameworkCore;
using System;
using System.Collections.Generic;
using System.Linq;
using System.Threading.Tasks;

namespace Chapter10.Models
{
    public class FunctionChartContext : DbContext
    {
        public FunctionChartContext(DbContextOptions<FunctionChartContext>
            options):base(options)
        { }

        public DbSet<Graph3dModel> Graph3dModels { get; set; }
        public DbSet<FunctionChartItem> FunctionChartItems { get; set; }
    }
}
```

You see that this class is derived from the *Microsoft.EntityFramework.DbContext* class.

Now, we need to add a repository to our project. A repository is an object that encapsulates the data layer. The repository contains logic for retrieving and mapping data to an entity model. First, we define a repository interface named *IFunctionChartRepository* in the *Models* folder:

```
using System.Collections.Generic;

namespace Chapter10.Models
{
    public interface IFunctionChartRepository
    {
        void Add(FunctionChartItem item);
        IEnumerable<FunctionChartItem> GetAll();
        FunctionChartItem Find(long key);
        void Remove(long key);
        void Update(FunctionChartItem item);
    }
}
```

This interface defines basic CRUD operations.

Add a new *FunctionChartRepository* class to the *Models* folder and replace its content with the following code:

```
using System;
using System.Collections.Generic;
using System.Linq;
using System.Threading.Tasks;

namespace Chapter10.Models
{
    public class FunctionChartRepository:IFunctionChartRepository
    {
        private readonly FunctionChartContext _context;

        public FunctionChartRepository(FunctionChartContext context)
        {
            _context = context;

            If(_context.FunctionChartItems.Count() == 0)
            {
                var xyRange = new double[] { -8, 8, -8, 8 };
                var xyNum = new int[] { 30, 30 };
                Add(new FunctionChartItem {
                    FunctionName = "Sinc",
                    Graph3dModels = ModelHelper.CreateGraph3dData(
                        ModelHelper.Sinc,xyRange, xyNum)
                });

                xyRange = new double[] { -5, 5, -5, 5 };
                xyNum = new int[] { 30, 30 };
                Add(new FunctionChartItem
                {
                    FunctionName = "SincXy",
                    Graph3dModels = ModelHelper.CreateGraph3dData(
                        ModelHelper.SincXy, xyRange, xyNum)
                });

                xyRange = new double[] { -16, 16, -16, 16 };
                xyNum = new int[] { 100, 100 };
                Add(new FunctionChartItem
                {
                    FunctionName = "SincSin",
                    Graph3dModels = ModelHelper.CreateGraph3dData(
                        ModelHelper.SincSin, xyRange, xyNum)
                });

                xyRange = new double[] { -3, 3, -3, 3 };
                xyNum = new int[] { 30, 30 };
                Add(new FunctionChartItem
                {
                    FunctionName = "Peaks",
                    Graph3dModels = ModelHelper.CreateGraph3dData(
                        ModelHelper.Peaks, xyRange, xyNum)
                });
```

```
            xyRange = new double[] { -1, 1, -1, 1 };
            xyNum = new int[] { 40, 40 };
            Add(new FunctionChartItem
            {
                FunctionName = "SinCos",
                Graph3dModels = ModelHelper.CreateGraph3dData(
                ModelHelper.SinCos, xyRange, xyNum)
            });
        }
    }

    public IEnumerable<FunctionChartItem> GetAll()
    {
        return _context.FunctionChartItems.ToList();
    }

    public void Add(FunctionChartItem item)
    {
        _context.FunctionChartItems.Add(item);
        _context.SaveChanges();
    }

    public FunctionChartItem Find(long key)
    {
        return _context.FunctionChartItems
            .FirstOrDefault(x => x.ChartId == key);
    }

    public void Remove(long key)
    {
        var item = _context.FunctionChartItems.First(x => x.ChartId == key);
        _context.FunctionChartItems.Remove(item);
        _context.SaveChanges();
    }

    public void Update(FunctionChartItem item)
    {
        _context.FunctionChartItems.Update(item);
        _context.SaveChanges();
    }
    }
}
```

Here, we add five *FunctionChartItem* objects to our *FunctionChartRepository*. Each item contains data for a specific mathematical function. These mathematical functions and the data conversion method *CreateGraph3dData* are implemented in the *ModelHelper* class. Here is the relevant code:

```
public static ICollection<Graph3dModel> CreateGraph3dData(Func<double, double,
    double> f, double[] xyRange, int[] xyNum)
{
    ICollection<Graph3dModel> model = new HashSet<Graph3dModel>();
    var dx = (xyRange[1] - xyRange[0]) / xyNum[0];
    var dy = (xyRange[3] - xyRange[2]) / xyNum[1];

    for (var x = xyRange[0]; x < xyRange[1]; x += dx)
    {
```

```
            for (var y = xyRange[2]; y < xyRange[3]; y += dy)
            {
                var z = f(x, y);
                model.Add(new Graph3dModel { X = x, Y = y, Z = z });
            }
        }
        return model;
    }

    public static double Sinc(double x, double y)
    {
        var r = Math.Sqrt(x * x + y * y) + 0.0001;
        return Math.Sin(r) / r;
    }

    public static double SincXy(double x, double y)
    {
        var r = x * y + 0.00001;
        return Math.Sin(r) / r;
    }

    public static double SinCos(double x, double y)
    {
        var z = 1 + Math.Sin(3 * x) * Math.Cos(3 * y);
        return z;
    }

    public static double Peaks(double x, double y)
    {
        var z = 3 * Math.Pow((1 - x), 2) * Math.Exp(-x * x - (y + 1) * (y + 1)) -
            10 * (0.2 * x - Math.Pow(x, 3) - Math.Pow(y, 5)) *
            Math.Exp(-x * x - y * y) - 1 / 3 * Math.Exp(-(x + 1) * (x + 1) - y * y);
        return z;
    }

    public static double SincSin(double x, double y)
    {
        var r = Math.Sin(Math.Pow(Math.Pow(x, 6) + Math.Pow(y, 6), 1.0 / 6.0))
            + 0.00001;
        var z = Math.Sin(r) / r;
        return z;
    }
```

You should be familiar with the code because we have used the similar code in the preceding chapter. The *CreateGraph3dData* method simply converts the mathematical function into a collection of the *Model3dModel* objects.

By defining a repository interface *IFunctionChartRepository*, we can decouple the repository class from the Web API controller that uses it. Instead of instantiating a *FunctionChartRepository* inside the controller, we will inject an *IFunctionChartRepository* using the built-in support in ASP.NET Core for dependency injection.

In order to inject the repository into the controller, we need to register it with the dependency injection container. Open the *Startup.cs* file. In the *ConfigureServices* method, add the following code snippet:

```
services.AddDbContext<FunctionChartContext>(opt => opt.UseInMemoryDatabase());
```

```
services.AddSingleton<IFunctionChartRepository, FunctionChartRepository>();
```

This code also registers the in-memory database.

Web API Controller

The ASP.NET Core Web API controller uses the repository. In Solution Explorer, right click the *Controllers* folder. Select *Add > New Item*. In the *Add New Item* dialog, select the *Web API Controller Class* template. Name the class *FunctionChartController* and replace its content with the following code:

```
using System.Collections.Generic;
using Microsoft.AspNetCore.Mvc;
using Chapter10.Models;

namespace Chapter10.Controllers
{
    [Route("api/[controller]")]
    public class FunctionChartController : Controller
    {
        private readonly IFunctionChartRepository _repository;
        public FunctionChartController(IFunctionChartRepository repository)
        {
            _repository = repository;
        }

        // GET: api/values
        [HttpGet]
        public IEnumerable<FunctionChartItem> GetAll()
        {
            return _repository.GetAll();
        }

        // GET api/values/5
        [HttpGet("{id}", Name ="GetFunctionChart")]
        public IActionResult GetById(long id)
        {
            var item = _repository.Find(id);
            if (item == null) return NotFound();
            return new ObjectResult(item);
        }

        // POST api/values
        [HttpPost]
        public IActionResult Create([FromBody] FunctionChartItem item)
        {
            if (item == null) return BadRequest();
            _repository.Add(item);
            return CreatedAtRoute("GetFunctionChart",
                new { id = item.ChartId }, item);
        }

        // PUT api/values/5
        [HttpPut("{id}")]
        public IActionResult Update(long id, [FromBody] FunctionChartItem item)
        {
```

```
            if (item == null || item.ChartId != id) return BadRequest();
            var repo = _repository.Find(id);
            if (repo == null) return NotFound();
            repo.FunctionName = item.FunctionName;
            repo.Graph3dModels = item.Graph3dModels;

            _repository.Update(repo);
            return new NoContentResult();
        }

        // DELETE api/values/5
        [HttpDelete("{id}")]
        public IActionResult Delete(long id)
        {
            var item = _repository.Find(id);
            if (item == null) return NotFound();
            _repository.Remove(id);
            return new NoContentResult();
        }
    }
}
```

This class derives from the base class *Controller*. The route to the controller is defined with the *Route* attribute. The route starts with *api* followed by the name of the controller – which is the name of the controller class without the *Controller* postfix. The constructor of this controller requires an object implementing the interface *IFunctionChartRepository*. This object is injected via dependency injection.

This controller implements two *GET* methods: *GET /api/FunctionChart* and *GET /api/FunctionChart/{id}*. The first *GET* method returns the complete collection of type *IEnumerable<FunctionChartItem>*. MVC automatically serializes the object to JSON and writes the JSON into the body of the response message. The response code for this method is 200, assuming there are no unhandled-exceptions.

In contrast, the *GetById* method filters the dictionary of the repository with the *Find* method. The parameter of the filter, *id*, is retrieved from the URL. This method returns a more general *IActionResult* type, which represents a wide range of return types. *GetById* has two different return types: if no item matches the requested *id*, the method returns a 404 error, which is done by returning *NotFound*. Otherwise, the method returns 200 with a JSON response body. This is done by returning an *ObjectResult* object.

In this controller, we also implement the other CRUD operations. We use an HTTP POST method to implement the *Create* operation, indicated by the [*HttpPost*] attribute. The [*FromBody*] attribute tells MVC to get the value of the *FunctionChartItem* from the body of the HTTP request. The *CreateAtRoute* returns a 201 response, which is the standard response for an HTTP POST method that creates a new resource on the server. *CreateAtRoute* also adds a location header to the response. The location header specifies the URL of the newly created *FunctionChartItem*.

The *Update* method is similar to *Create*, but uses HTTP PUT. The response is 204 (No Content). According to the HTTP spec, a PUT request requires the client to send an entire updated entity, not just the deltas. To support partial updates, you need to use HTTP PATCH.

With the HTTP DELETE request, the *FunctionChartItem* is simply removed from the body. The response code for this method is code 204 (No Content).

Testing Web API Services

With the *FunctionChart* Web API controller in place, it is possible to do a first test from the browser. Running this example by pressing F5. Open the link

```
http://localhost:54115/api/functionchart/
```

When you open this link in your browser, you will get a big JSON array with 14422 3D data points, as shown in the following:

```
[
    {
        "chartId": 1,
        "functionName": "Sinc",
        "graph3dModels": [
            {
                "dataId": 1,
                "x": -8,
                "y": -8,
                "z": -0.08394957330744987
            },

            ......

            {
                "dataId": 961,
                "x": 7.999999999999997,
                "y": 7.999999999999997,
                "z": -0.08394957330745006
            }
        ]
    },
    {
        "chartId": 2,
        "functionName": "SincXy",
        "graph3dModels": [
            {
                "dataId": 962,
                "x": -5,
                "y": -5,
                "z": -0.005293671405052932
            },

            ......

            {
                "dataId": 1922,
                "x": 4.999999999999999,
                "y": 4.999999999999999,
                "z": -0.005293671405053216
            }
        ]
    },
    {
        "chartId": 3,
        "functionName": "SincSin",
```

```
            "graph3dModels": [
                {
                    "dataId": 1923,
                    "x": -16,
                    "y": -16,
                    "z": 0.9023325352534788
                },

                ......

                {
                    "dataId": 11922,
                    "x": 15.68000000000002,
                    "y": 15.68000000000002,
                    "z": 0.8565821860476628
                }
            ]
        },
        {
            "chartId": 4,
            "functionName": "Peaks",
            "graph3dModels": [
                {
                    "dataId": 11923,
                    "x": -3,
                    "y": -3,
                    "z": 0.00006746624610283477
                },

                ......

                {
                    "dataId": 12822,
                    "x": 2.800000000000001,
                    "y": 2.800000000000001,
                    "z": 0.00029987258602902334
                }
            ]
        },
        {
            "chartId": 5,
            "functionName": "SinCos",
            "graph3dModels": [
                {
                    "dataId": 12823,
                    "x": -1,
                    "y": -1,
                    "z": 1.139707749099463
                },
                ......

                {
                    "dataId": 14422,
                    "x": 0.9500000000000007,
                    "y": 0.9500000000000007,
```

```
        "z": 0.724657228701183
      }
    ]
  }
]
```

This shows a collection of the function chart items. You can also request a single function chart item by specifying a *ChartId*. For example, the following link

```
http://localhost:54115/api/functionchart/3
```

will return the *FunctionChartItem* with *ChartId* = 3:

```
{
    "chartId": 3,
    "functionName": "SincSin",
    "graph3dModels": [
        {
            "dataId": 1923,
            "x": -16,
            "y": -16,
            "z": 0.9023325352534788
        },
        ......
        {
            "dataId": 11922,
            "x": 15.68000000000002,
            "y": 15.68000000000002,
            "z": 0.8565821860476628
        }
    ]
}
```

In the preceding discussions, we use the web browser to access the data. In fact, there are many ways to access the data provided by the Web API. The simplest way to make sure that the API controller works is to use PowerShell, which makes it easy to create HTTP requests from the Windows command line, which lets you focus on the results of API operations without needing to dig into the details. In the following, I will show you how to use PowerShell to access data generated by our *FunctionChart* API controller.

Open a new PowerShell window by pressing the Windows Key, searching for "powershell", right clicking on the result, and running it as administrator. In the PowerShell window, type the following command:

```
Invoke-RestMethod http://localhost:54115/api/functionChart -Method GET
```

This command uses the *Invoke-RestMethod* PowerShell cmdlet to send a GET request to the *api/functionChart* URL. The result is shown in Figure 10-1.

You can see that the server responds to the GET request with a JSON representation of our *FunctionChart* objects contained in the model, where the *Invoke-RestMethod* cmdlet presents in a table format.

You can also test the POST, PUT, and DELETE operations in the PowerShell. For example, we can send a DELETE request, which will remove a *FunctionChart* item from the repository, as follows:

```
Invoke-RestMethod http://localhost:54115/api/functionChart/3 -Method DELETE
```

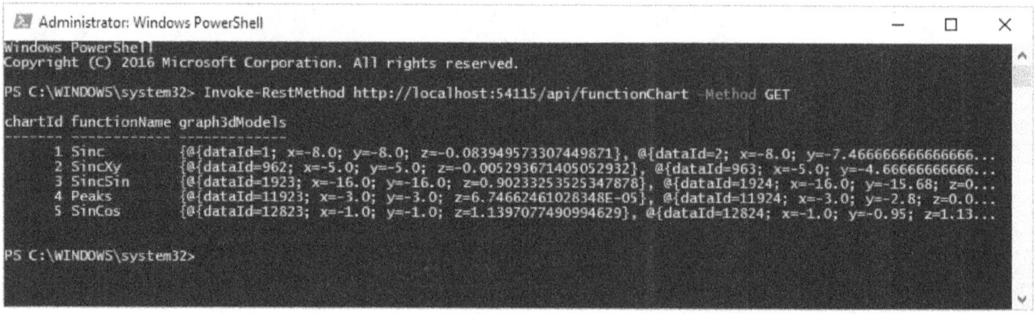

Figure 10-1. Test the GET operation of the FunctionChart controller using PowerShell.

The action that accepts DELETE requests in the *FunctionChart* controller does not return a result, so no data is displayed when the command has completed. To see the effect of the deletion, we request the contents of the repository using the following GET command:

```
Invoke-RestMethod http://localhost:54115/api/functionChart –Method GET
```

In this case, the *FunctionChart* whose *chartId* is 3 was removed from the repository, as shown in Figure 10-2.

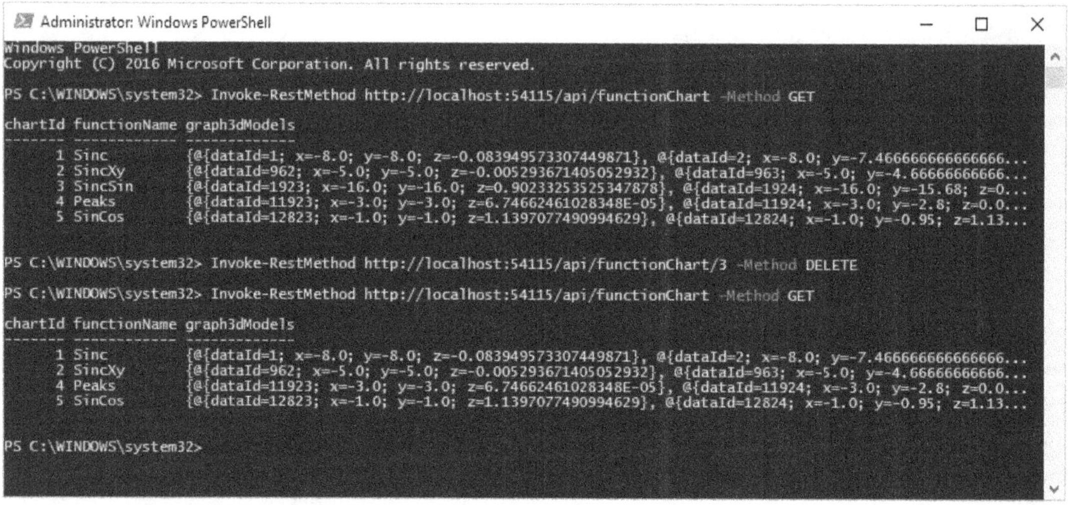

Figure 10-2. Demonstration of the DELETE operation for a Web API controller.

Using API Controller in MVC Applications

As mentioned previously, Web API services can reach a broad range of clients, including browsers, mobile devices, and traditional desktop applications. In this section, I will show you how to consume the services provided by our *FunctionChart* API controller in a standard MVC application.

First, you need install the *vis-Graph3d* library using the bower package manager following the same procedure as what we did in the preceding chapter.

Add a new MVC controller named *Chart3DController* to the *Controllers* folder and replace its content with the following code:

```
namespace Chapter10.Controllers
{
    public class Chart3DController : Controller
    {
        Graph3dChartTypeModel _model = new Graph3dChartTypeModel();

        // GET: /<controller>/
        public IActionResult Index()
        {
            ViewBag.Title = "3D Charts with Graph3d ";
            _model.FunctionChartType = FunctionChartType.Sinc;
            return View(_model);
        }

        [HttpPost]
        public IActionResult Index(Graph3dChartTypeModel model)
        {
            _model = model;
            return View(_model);
        }
    }
}
```

The *Graph3dChartTypeModel* class is implemented in the *Graph3dModel.cs* file. It consists of a property of *FunctionChartType* enumeration type, which allows you to specify the chart type. Add a New folder named *Chart3D* to the *Views* folder. Add a new *Index.cshtml* view to the *Views/Chart3D* folder and replace its content with the following code:

```
@using Chapter10.Models
@model Graph3dChartTypeModel
@{
    ViewData["Title"] = ViewBag.Title;
}
<h3>@ViewBag.Title</h3>

<div class="container">
    <div class="row">
        <div class="col-sm-12">
            <div style="margin-top:30px; margin-right:25px">
                <form method="post" asp-controller="Chart3D" asp-action="Index"
                        asp-antiforgery="true">
                    <div class="form-group">
                        <label>Select a Chart Type</label>
                        <select class="form-control" asp-for="FunctionChartType"
                                asp-items="@new  SelectList(Enum.GetValues(
                                typeof(FunctionChartType)))"
                                onchange="form.submit();"></select>
                    </div>
                </form>
                <div id="chart" style="margin-top:20px"></div>
            </div>
        </div>
    </div>
</div>
```

```
    </div>

    @section scripts{
    <script>
        var chartType = @Html.Raw(Json.Serialize(Model));

        google.load("visualization", "1");
        google.setOnLoadCallback(drawChart);


        function drawChart() {
            $.ajax({
                url: 'api/functionchart/' + chartType.functionChartType,
                method: 'GET',
                dataType: 'json',
                success: function (jsonData) {
                    var data = processJsonDara(jsonData);
                    var container = document.getElementById("chart");
                    var options = {
                        style: 'surface',
                        width: '700px',
                        height: '600px',
                        showPerspective: true,
                        showGrid: true,
                        showShadow: false,
                        keepAspectRatio: true,
                        verticalRatio: 0.7,
                        yCenter: '35%',
                    };
                    var graph = new vis.Graph3d(container, data, options);
                }
            });


            function processJsonDara(jsonData) {
                var data = new vis.DataSet();
                for (var i = 0; i < jsonData.graph3dModels.length; i++) {
                    var x = jsonData.graph3dModels[i].x;
                    var y = jsonData.graph3dModels[i].y;
                    var z = jsonData.graph3dModels[i].z;
                    data.add({ x: x, y: y, z: z, style: z });
                }
                return data;
            }
        }
    </script>
    }
```

This code defines a *submit* form that consists of a *select* element with the *FunctionChartType* enum as its option items. You can select the chart type from this select element. In the script section, we use AJAX to perform the HTTP request, where we set the *url* to our *api/functionchart* link and *datatype* to JSON format. We then process the JSON data and convert it into a data format required by Graph3d using a JavaScript function named *processJsonData*. Finally, we specify options parameter and call the *vis-Graph3d* to create the 3D surface chart.

Running this example, selecting the *3D Charts* tab and selecting *Peaks* from the dropdown list produce the results shown in Figure 10-3.

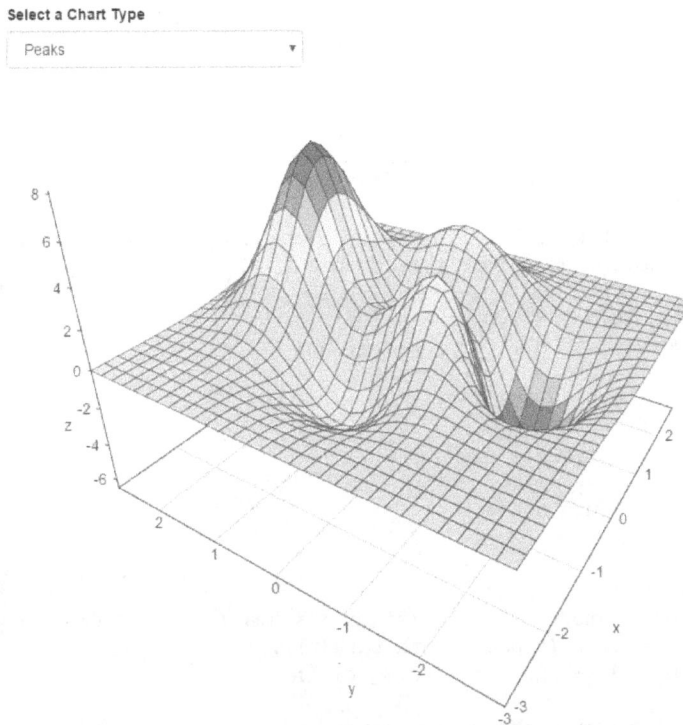

Figure 10-3. 3D surface chart for peaks function using data from Web API controller.

3D Charts for European Options

In this section, we will create an ASP.NET Core Web API application for a real-world financial example – European option pricing. Options are derivative contracts that give the holder the right, but not the obligation, to buy or sell the underlying instrument at a specified price on or before a specified future date. Although the buyer of the option is not obligated to exercise the option, the option seller has an obligation to buy or sell the underlying instrument if the option is exercised.

Options can be categorized into two types: American options and European options according to their exercise characteristics. American options can be exercised at any time between the date of purchase and expiration date. Most exchange-traded options are American options. European options can only be excercised on the expiration date. Both American and European options are standard derivatives or "plain vanilla" options.

Pricing European Options

Here, we will use the generalized Black-Scholes model to price European options. I will omit the mathematical derivations and concentrate on the data generation process. The related formulae for this model can be found in my previously published book: *Practical C# and WPF for Financial Markets*.

Add a new helper class named *OptionHelper* to the *Models* folder. Here is the code for this class:

```
using System;
using System.Collections.Generic;

namespace Chapter10.Models
{
    public static class OptionHelper
    {
        private const double ONEOVERSQRT2PI = 0.39894228;
        private const double PI = 3.1415926;

        public static double[] black_scholes(double t, double s0, double x,
            double sigma, double r, double q, double put)
        {
            double one = 1.0, two = 2.0;
            double d1, d2, temp, temp1, np;
            double EPS = 1.0e-16;
            double PI = 3.14159;

            if (x < EPS || sigma < EPS)
            {
                return null;
            }

            temp = Math.Log(s0 / x);
            d1 = temp + (r - q + (sigma * sigma / two)) * t;
            d1 = d1 / (sigma * Math.Sqrt(t));
            d2 = d1 - sigma * Math.Sqrt(t);

            // Evaluate the option price:
            double value = 0;
            double[] greeks = new double[6];

            // The hedge statistics output as follows: greaks[0] is value,
            // greeks[1] is gamma, greeks[2] is delta, greeks[3] is theta,
            // greeks[4] is rho, and greeks[5] is vega

            if (put == 0)
            {
                value = s0 * Math.Exp(-q * t) * CumNorm(d1) - x *
                    Math.Exp(-r * t) * CumNorm(d2);
            }
            else
            {
                value = (-s0 * Math.Exp(-q * t) * CumNorm(-d1) +
                    x * Math.Exp(-r * t) * CumNorm(-d2));
            }

            greeks[0] = value;

            // Calculate greeks:
            temp1 = -d1 * d1 / two;
            d2 = d1 - sigma * Math.Sqrt(t);
            np = (one / Math.Sqrt(two * PI)) * Math.Exp(temp1);
```

```csharp
        if (put == 0)
        {
            // a call option
            greeks[2] = (CumNorm(d1)) * Math.Exp(-q * t);  // delta

            greeks[3] = -s0 * Math.Exp(-q * t) * np * sigma /
                (two * Math.Sqrt(t))+ q * s0 * CumNorm(d1) *
                Math.Exp(-q * t) - r * x * Math.Exp(-r * t) *
                CumNorm(d2); // theta

            greeks[4] = x * t * Math.Exp(-r * t) * CumNorm(d2); // rho
        }
        else
        {
            // a put option
            greeks[2] = (CumNorm(d1) - one) * Math.Exp(-q * t); // delta
            greeks[3] = -s0 * Math.Exp(-q * t) * np * sigma /
                (two * Math.Sqrt(t)) -
                q * s0 * CumNorm(-d1) * Math.Exp(-q * t) +
                r * x * Math.Exp(-r * t) * CumNorm(-d2); // theta
            greeks[4] = -x * t * Math.Exp(-r * t) * CumNorm(-d2); // rho
        }
        greeks[1] = np * Math.Exp(-q * t)/(s0 * sigma *
            Math.Sqrt(t)); // gamma
        greeks[5] = s0 * Math.Sqrt(t) * np * Math.Exp(-q * t); // vega

        return greeks;
    }


#region Black-Scholes
public static double BlackScholes(string optionType, double spot, double
    strike, double rate, double carry, double maturity, double vol)
{
    double d1, d2, option;
    double sqrtMaturity = Math.Sqrt(maturity);

    d1 = Math.Log(spot / strike) + (carry + vol * vol * 0.5) * maturity;
    d1 /= vol * sqrtMaturity;
    d2 = d1 - vol * sqrtMaturity;

    if (optionType.ToUpper() == "P" || optionType.ToUpper() == "PUT")
        option = strike * CumNorm(-d2) * Math.Exp(-rate * maturity) -
            spot * CumNorm(-d1) * Math.Exp((carry - rate) * maturity);
    else
        option = spot * CumNorm(d1) * Math.Exp((carry - rate) *
            maturity) - strike * CumNorm(d2) * Math.Exp(-rate * maturity);

    return option;
}


public static double BlackScholes_Delta(string optionType, double spot,
    double strike, double rate, double carry, double maturity,
    double vol)
```

```
    {
        double d1, d2, option;
        double sqrtMaturity = Math.Sqrt(maturity);

        d1 = Math.Log(spot / strike) + (carry + vol * vol * 0.5) * maturity;
        d1 /= vol * sqrtMaturity;

        d2 = d1 - vol * sqrtMaturity;

        if (optionType.ToUpper() == "P" || optionType.ToUpper() == "PUT")
            option = (CumNorm(d1) - 1.0) * Math.Exp((carry - rate) *
                    maturity);
        else
            option = CumNorm(d1) * Math.Exp((carry - rate) * maturity);

        return option;
    }

    public static double BlackScholes_Gamma(double spot, double strike,
        double rate, double carry, double maturity, double vol)
    {
        double d1, option;
        double sqrtMaturity = Math.Sqrt(maturity);

        d1 = Math.Log(spot / strike) + (carry + vol * vol * 0.5) * maturity;
        d1 /= vol * sqrtMaturity;

        option = NormDensity(d1) * Math.Exp((carry - rate) * maturity) /
                (spot * vol * sqrtMaturity);

        return option;
    }


    public static double BlackScholes_Vega(double spot, double strike,
        double rate, double carry, double maturity, double vol)
    {
        double d1, option;
        double sqrtMaturity = Math.Sqrt(maturity);

        d1 = Math.Log(spot / strike) + (carry + vol * vol * 0.5) * maturity;
        d1 /= vol * sqrtMaturity;

        option = spot * NormDensity(d1) * Math.Exp((carry - rate) *
                maturity) * sqrtMaturity;

        return option;
    }

    public static double BlackScholes_Theta(string optionType, double spot,
        double strike, double rate, double carry, double maturity,
        double vol)
    {
        double d1, d2, option;
        double sqrtMaturity = Math.Sqrt(maturity);
```

```
        d1 = Math.Log(spot / strike) + (carry + vol * vol * 0.5) * maturity;
        d1 /= vol * sqrtMaturity;
        d2 = d1 - vol * sqrtMaturity;

        if (optionType.ToUpper() == "P" || optionType.ToUpper() == "PUT")
        {
            var p1 = spot * Math.Exp((carry - rate) * maturity) *
                    NormDensity(d1) * vol * 0.5 / sqrtMaturity;
            var p2 = (carry - rate) * spot * Math.Exp((carry - rate) *
                    maturity) * CumNorm(-d1);
            var p3 = rate * strike * Math.Exp(-rate * maturity) *
                    CumNorm(-d2);
            option = p2 + p3 - p1;
        }
        else
        {
            var c1 = spot * Math.Exp((carry - rate) * maturity) *
                    NormDensity(d1) * vol * 0.5 / sqrtMaturity;
            var c2 = (carry - rate) * spot * Math.Exp((carry - rate) *
                    maturity) * CumNorm(d1);
            var c3 = rate * strike * Math.Exp(-rate * maturity) *
                    CumNorm(d2);
            option = -c1 - c2 - c3;
        }

        return option;
    }

    public static double BlackScholes_Rho(string optionType, double spot,
        double strike, double rate, double carry, double maturity,
        double vol)
    {
        double d1, d2, option;
        double sqrtMaturity = Math.Sqrt(maturity);

        d1 = Math.Log(spot / strike) + (carry + vol * vol * 0.5) * maturity;
        d1 /= vol * sqrtMaturity;
        d2 = d1 - vol * sqrtMaturity;

        if (optionType.ToUpper() == "P" || optionType.ToUpper() == "PUT")
        {
            if (carry != 0)
                option = -maturity * strike * Math.Exp(-rate * maturity) *
                        CumNorm(-d2);
            else
                option = -maturity * BlackScholes("P", spot, strike, rate,
                        0, maturity, vol);
        }
        else
        {
            if (carry != 0)
                option = maturity * strike * Math.Exp(-rate * maturity) *
                        CumNorm(d2);
            else
```

```
                option = -maturity * BlackScholes("C", spot, strike, rate,
                    0, maturity, vol);
        }

        return option;
    }


    public static double BlackScholes_ImpliedVol(string optionType,
        double spot, double strike, double rate, double carry,
        double maturity, double price)
    {
        double low = 0.0;
        double high = 4.0;
        double sqrtMaturity = Math.Sqrt(maturity);
        double vol;
        if (BlackScholes(optionType, spot, strike, rate, carry, maturity,
            high) < price)
            vol = high;
        else if (BlackScholes(optionType, spot, strike, rate, carry,
            maturity, low) > price)
            vol = low;
        else
        {
            vol = (high + low) * 0.5;
            int count = 0;
            while (vol - low > 0.0001 && count < 100000)
            {
                if (BlackScholes(optionType, spot, strike, rate, carry,
                    maturity, vol) < price)
                    low = vol;
                else if (BlackScholes(optionType, spot, strike, rate, carry,
                    maturity, vol) > price)
                    high = vol;
                vol = (high + low) * 0.5;
                count++;
            }
        }
        return vol;
    }

    private static double CumNorm(double x)
    {
        if (x < 0)
            return 1.0 - CumNorm(-x);
        else
        {
            double k = 1.0 / (1.0 + 0.2316419 * x);
            return 1.0 - ONEOVERSQRT2PI * Math.Exp(-0.5 * x * x) *
                ((((1.330274429 * k - 1.821255978) * k + 1.781477937) * k -
                0.356563782) * k + 0.319381530) * k;
        }
    }

    private static double NormDensity(double x)
    {
```

```
        return Math.Exp(-x * x * 0.5) / Math.Sqrt(2.0 * PI);
}
public static ICollection<Graph3dModel> CreateOptionData(OptionChartType
    chartType, double strike, double rate, double carry, double vol)
{
    ICollection<Graph3dModel> model = new HashSet<Graph3dModel>();
    double xmin = 0.1;
    double xmax = 3.0;
    double ymin = 10;
    double ymax = 190;
    double dx = 0.1;
    double dy = 5;

    for (var x = xmin; x < xmax; x += dx)
    {
        for (var y = ymin; y < ymax; y += dy)
        {
            double z = double.NaN;
            if (chartType == OptionChartType.PriceCall)
                z = BlackScholes("CALL", y, strike, rate, carry, x,
                    vol);
            else if (chartType == OptionChartType.PricePut)
                z = BlackScholes("PUT", y, strike, rate, carry, x, vol);
            else if (chartType == OptionChartType.DeltaCall)
                z = BlackScholes_Delta("CALL", y, strike, rate, carry,
                    x, vol);
            else if (chartType == OptionChartType.DeltaPut)
                z = BlackScholes_Delta("PUT", y, strike, rate, carry,
                    x, vol);
            else if (chartType == OptionChartType.GammaCall ||
                    chartType == OptionChartType.GammaPut)
                z = BlackScholes_Gamma(y, strike, rate, carry, x, vol);
            else if (chartType == OptionChartType.ThetaCall)
                z = BlackScholes_Theta("CALL", y, strike, rate, carry,
                    x, vol);
            else if (chartType == OptionChartType.ThetaPut)
                z = BlackScholes_Theta("PUT", y, strike, rate, carry,
                    x, vol);
            else if (chartType == OptionChartType.RhoCall)
                z = BlackScholes_Rho("CALL", y, strike, rate, carry,
                    x, vol);
            else if (chartType == OptionChartType.RhoPut)
                z = BlackScholes_Rho("PUT", y, strike, rate, carry,
                    x, vol);
            else if (chartType == OptionChartType.VegaCall ||
                    chartType == OptionChartType.VegaPut)
                z = BlackScholes_Vega(y, strike, rate, carry, x, vol);

            model.Add(new Graph3dModel { X = x, Y = y, Z = z });
        }
    }
    return model;
}

#endregion Black-Scholes
```

```
            }
    }
```

This helper class contains methods that are used to calculate option price and Greeks for European options based on a generalized Black-Scholes model. It also includes a method called *CreateOptionData* that converts the option price and Greeks into a collection of *Graph3dModel* objects. The *Graph3dModel* class was implemented in the *Graph3dModel.cs* file, which has been used in the preceding example.

Model and Repository

Add the following code to the *Graph3dModel.cs* file:

```
public class OptionChartTypeModel
{
    public OptionChartType OptionChartType { get; set; }
}

public enum OptionChartType
{
    PriceCall = 1,
    PricePut = 2,
    DeltaCall = 3,
    DeltaPut = 4,
    GammaCall = 5,
    GammaPut = 6,
    ThetaCall = 7,
    ThetaPut =8,
    RhoCall = 9,
    RhoPut = 10,
    VegaCall = 11,
    VegaPut = 12
}
```

Here, the *OptionChartType* enumeration defines various chart types for the *call* and *put* options, including option price and Greeks. The *OptionChartTypeModel* consists of a property of the *OptionChartType*.

Next, we need to create database context. Add an *OptionChartContext* class to the *Models* folder and replace its content with the following code:

```
using Microsoft.EntityFrameworkCore;

namespace Chapter10.Models
{
    public class OptionChartContext: DbContext
    {
        public OptionChartContext(DbContextOptions<OptionChartContext>
                                    options):base(options)
        { }

        public DbSet<Graph3dModel> Graph3dModels { get; set; }
        public DbSet<OptionChartItem> OptionChartItems { get; set; }
    }
}
```

Define a repository interface named *IOptionChartReposiroty* as shown in the following code:

```
using System.Collections.Generic;

namespace Chapter10.Models
{
    public interface IOptionChartRepository
    {
        void Add(OptionChartItem item);
        IEnumerable<OptionChartItem> GetAll();
        OptionChartItem Find(long key);
        void Remove(long key);
        void Update(OptionChartItem item);
    }
}
```

This interface defines basic CRUD operations.

Add an *OptionChartRepository* class that implements *IOptionChartRepository*:

```
using System.Collections.Generic;
using System.Linq;

namespace Chapter10.Models
{
    public class OptionChartRepository : IOptionChartRepository
    {
        private readonly OptionChartContext _context;

        public OptionChartRepository(OptionChartContext context)
        {
            _context = context;

            if (_context.OptionChartItems.Count() == 0)
            {
                Add(new OptionChartItem
                {
                    OptionChartName = "PriceCall",
                    Graph3dModels = OptionHelper.CreateOptionData(
                        OptionChartType.PriceCall, 100, 0.1, 0.04, 0.3)
                });

                Add(new OptionChartItem
                {
                    OptionChartName = "PricePut",
                    Graph3dModels = OptionHelper.CreateOptionData(
                        OptionChartType.PricePut, 100, 0.1, 0.04, 0.3)
                });

                Add(new OptionChartItem
                {
                    OptionChartName = "DeltaCall",
                    Graph3dModels = OptionHelper.CreateOptionData(
                        OptionChartType.DeltaCall, 100, 0.1, 0.04, 0.3)
                });

                Add(new OptionChartItem
```

```
{
    OptionChartName = "DeltaPut",
    Graph3dModels = OptionHelper.CreateOptionData(
        OptionChartType.DeltaPut, 100, 0.1, 0.04, 0.3)
});

Add(new OptionChartItem
{
    OptionChartName = "GammaCall",
    Graph3dModels = OptionHelper.CreateOptionData(
        OptionChartType.GammaCall, 100, 0.1, 0.04, 0.3)
});

Add(new OptionChartItem
{
    OptionChartName = "GammaPut",
    Graph3dModels = OptionHelper.CreateOptionData(
        OptionChartType.GammaPut, 100, 0.1, 0.04, 0.3)
});

Add(new OptionChartItem
{
    OptionChartName = "ThetaCall",
    Graph3dModels = OptionHelper.CreateOptionData(
        OptionChartType.ThetaCall, 100, 0.1, 0.04, 0.3)
});

Add(new OptionChartItem
{
    OptionChartName = "ThetaPut",
    Graph3dModels = OptionHelper.CreateOptionData(
        OptionChartType.ThetaPut, 100, 0.1, 0.04, 0.3)
});

Add(new OptionChartItem
{
    OptionChartName = "RhoCall",
    Graph3dModels = OptionHelper.CreateOptionData(
        OptionChartType.RhoCall, 100, 0.1, 0.04, 0.3)
});

Add(new OptionChartItem
{
    OptionChartName = "RhoPut",
    Graph3dModels = OptionHelper.CreateOptionData(
        OptionChartType.RhoPut, 100, 0.1, 0.04, 0.3)
});

Add(new OptionChartItem
{
    OptionChartName = "VegaCall",
    Graph3dModels = OptionHelper.CreateOptionData(
        OptionChartType.VegaCall, 100, 0.1, 0.04, 0.3)
});
```

```
            Add(new OptionChartItem
            {
                OptionChartName = "VegaPut",
                Graph3dModels = OptionHelper.CreateOptionData(
                    OptionChartType.VegaPut, 100, 0.1, 0.04, 0.3)
            });
        }
    }

    public IEnumerable<OptionChartItem> GetAll()
    {
        return _context.OptionChartItems.ToList();
    }

    public void Add(OptionChartItem item)
    {
        _context.OptionChartItems.Add(item);
        _context.SaveChanges();
    }

    public OptionChartItem Find(long key)
    {
        return _context.OptionChartItems.FirstOrDefault(
            x => x.ChartId == key);
    }

    public void Remove(long key)
    {
        var item = _context.OptionChartItems.First(x => x.ChartId == key);
        _context.OptionChartItems.Remove(item);
        _context.SaveChanges();
    }

    public void Update(OptionChartItem item)
    {
        _context.OptionChartItems.Update(item);
        _context.SaveChanges();
    }
    }
}
```

Here, we add various data for option price and Greeks in the constructor and implement the basic CRUD operations.

Next, we need to register our repository with the dependency injection container. Open the *Startup.cs* file. In the *ConfigureServices* method, add the following code:

```
services.AddDbContext<OptionChartContext>(opt => opt.UseInMemoryDatabase());
services.AddSingleton<IOptionChartRepository, OptionChartRepository>();
```

This code also registers the in-memory database.

Web API Controller

Add a Web API Controller named *OptionApiController.cs* to the *Controllers* folder and replace its content with the following code:

```
using Chapter10.Models;
using Microsoft.AspNetCore.Mvc;
using System.Collections.Generic;

namespace Chapter10.Controllers
{
    [Route("api/[controller]")]
    public class OptionApiController : Controller
    {
        private readonly IOptionChartRepository _repository;
        public OptionApiController(IOptionChartRepository repository)
        {
            _repository = repository;
        }

        // GET: api/values
        [HttpGet]
        public IEnumerable<OptionChartItem> GetAll()
        {
            return _repository.GetAll();
        }

        // GET api/values/5
        [HttpGet("{id}", Name = "GetOptionChart")]
        public IActionResult GetById(long id)
        {
            var item = _repository.Find(id);
            if (item == null) return NotFound();
            return new ObjectResult(item);
        }

        // POST api/values
        [HttpPost]
        public IActionResult Create([FromBody] OptionChartItem item)
        {
            if (item == null) return BadRequest();
            _repository.Add(item);
            return CreatedAtRoute("GetOptionChart",
                new { id = item.ChartId }, item);
        }

        // PUT api/values/5
        [HttpPut("{id}")]
        public IActionResult Update(long id, [FromBody] OptionChartItem item)
        {
            if (item == null || item.ChartId != id) return BadRequest();
            var repo = _repository.Find(id);
            if (repo == null) return NotFound();
            repo.OptionChartName = item.OptionChartName;
            repo.Graph3dModels = item.Graph3dModels;
```

```
        _repository.Update(repo);
        return new NoContentResult();
    }

    // DELETE api/values/5
    [HttpDelete("{id}")]
    public IActionResult Delete(long id)
    {
        var item = _repository.Find(id);
        if (item == null) return NotFound();
        _repository.Remove(id);
        return new NoContentResult();
    }
  }
}
```

This API controller implements two GET methods as well as the other methods for CRUD operations, which are similar to what we did in the preceding example.

Now, we can use the browser or PowerShell to test our option API controller. Run this example and open the PowerShell window. Type the following command:

```
Invoke-RestMethod http://localhost:54115/api/optionapi -Method GET
```

This command uses the *Invoke-RestMethod* PowerShell cmdlet to send a GET request to the */api/optionapi* URL. The result is parsed and formatted to make the data easy to read, as shown in Figure 10-4.

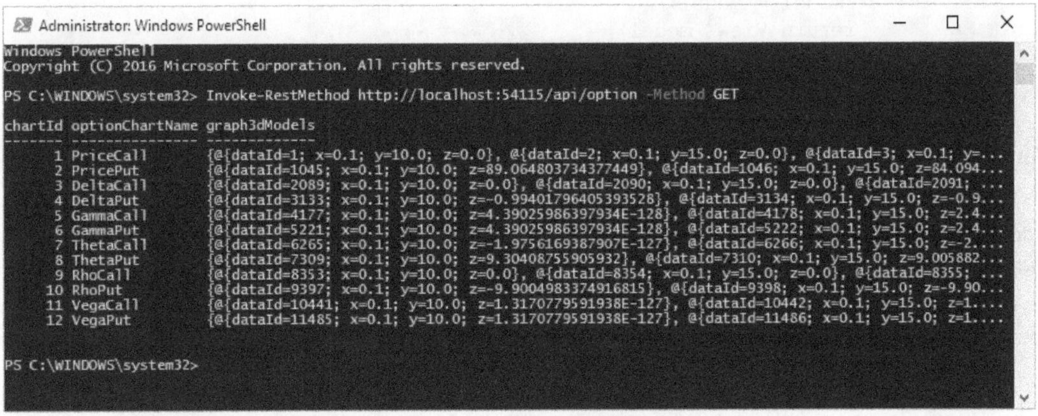

Figure 10-4. Test the GET operation of the option API controller using PowerShell.

The server responds to the GET request with a JSON representation of the *OptionChartItem* object contained in the model, where the *Invoke-RestMethod* cmdlet presents in a table format. You can see there are twelve items in the table, and each item consists of a *chartId*, an *optionChartName*, and a *graph3dModels* collection that contains the data for the 3D chart.

Creating Option Charts

In this section, I will show you how to consume the services provided by our *Option* API controller in a standard MVC application.

Add a new MVC controller named *OptionChartController.cs* to the *Controllers* folder and replace its content with the following code:

```
using Chapter10.Models;
using Microsoft.AspNetCore.Mvc;

namespace Chapter10.Controllers
{
    public class OptionChartController : Controller
    {
        OptionChartTypeModel _model = new OptionChartTypeModel();

        // GET: /<controller>/
        public IActionResult Index()
        {
            ViewBag.Title = "3D Charts with Graph3d ";
            _model.OptionChartType = OptionChartType.PriceCall;
            return View(_model);
        }

        [HttpPost]
        public IActionResult Index(OptionChartTypeModel model)
        {
            _model = model;
            return View(_model);
        }
    }
}
```

This controller is very simple. It only consists of a GET and a POST Index method, which allows you to select a chart type.

Add a new folder named *OptionChart* to the *Views* folder. Add a new view named *Index.cshtml* to the *Views/OptionChart* folder and replace its content with the following code:

```
@using Chapter10.Models
@model OptionChartTypeModel
@{
    ViewData["Title"] = ViewBag.Title;
}
<h3>@ViewBag.Title</h3>

@section scripts{
<div class="container">
    <div class="row">
        <div class="col-sm-12">
            <div style="margin-top:30px; margin-right:25px">
                <form method="post" asp-controller="OptionChart"
                    asp-action="Index" asp-antiforgery="true">
                    <div class="form-group">
                        <label>Select a Chart Type</label>
```

```
                        <select class="form-control" asp-for="OptionChartType"
                                asp-items="@new  SelectList(Enum.GetValues(
                                typeof(OptionChartType)))"
                                onchange="form.submit();"></select>
                    </div>
                </form>
                <div id="chart" style="margin-top:20px"></div>
            </div>
        </div>
    </div>
</div>

<script>
    var chartType = @Html.Raw(Json.Serialize(Model));
    google.load("visualization", "1");
    google.setOnLoadCallback(drawChart);
    function drawChart() {
        $.ajax({
            url: 'api/optionapi/' + chartType.optionChartType,
            method: 'GET',
            dataType: 'json',
            success: function (jsonData) {
                var data = processJsonDara(jsonData);
                var container = document.getElementById("chart");
                var options = {
                    style: 'surface',
                    width: '700px',
                    height: '600px',
                    showPerspective: true,
                    showGrid: true,
                    showShadow: false,
                    keepAspectRatio: false,
                    verticalRatio: 0.7,
                    yCenter: '35%',
                    xLabel: 'Maturity',
                    yLabel: 'Spot',
                    zLabel: jsonData.optionChartName,
                };
                var graph = new vis.Graph3d(container, data, options);
            }
        });

        function processJsonDara(jsonData) {
            var data = new vis.DataSet();
            for (var i = 0; i < jsonData.graph3dModels.length; i++) {
                var x = jsonData.graph3dModels[i].x;
                var y = jsonData.graph3dModels[i].y;
                var z = jsonData.graph3dModels[i].z;
                data.add({ x: x, y: y, z: z, style: z });
            }
            return data;
        }
    }
}
</script>
}
```

This code defines a *submit* form that consists of a *select* element with the *OptionChartType* enum as its option items. You can select the chart type from this select element. In the script section, we use AJAX to perform the HTTP request, where we set the *url* to our *api/optionapi* + *optionChartType* link and *datatype* to JSON format. We then process the JSON data and convert it into a data format required by Graph3d using a JavaScript function named *processJsonData*. Finally, we specify options parameter and call the *vis-Graph3d* to create the 3D surface chart for a selected option chart type. Here, we plot the option price and Greeks as a function of spot and maturity (or time to expiration) for a set of fixed parameters, including strike, interest rate, carry, and volatility.

Price Charts

Running this example, clicking the *Charts for European Options* tab, and selecting the *PriceCall* from the *Select a Chart Type* dropdown menu generate a 3D surface chart for a European call option shown in Figure 10-5.

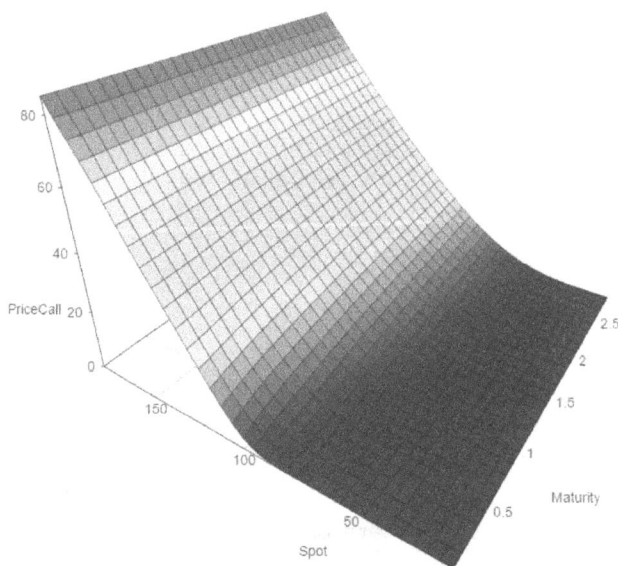

Figure 10-5. Price for a European call option.

If you select the *PricePut* chart type, you will get the results shown in Figure 10-6.

Delta Charts

In options, *Delta* measures the rate of change of the option price with respect to the underlying asset's price. That is, it measures the expected price change of the option given a $1 change in the underlying asset, and can be used in evaluating buying and selling opportunities. Call options have positive deltas with a range of $(0, 1)$ and puts have negative deltas with a range of $(-1, 0)$.

Selecting the *DeltaCall* chart type produces the results shown in Figure 10-7.

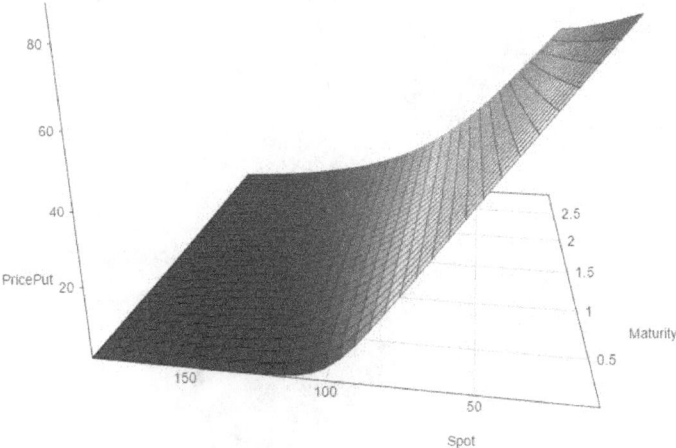

Figure 10-6. Price for a European put option.

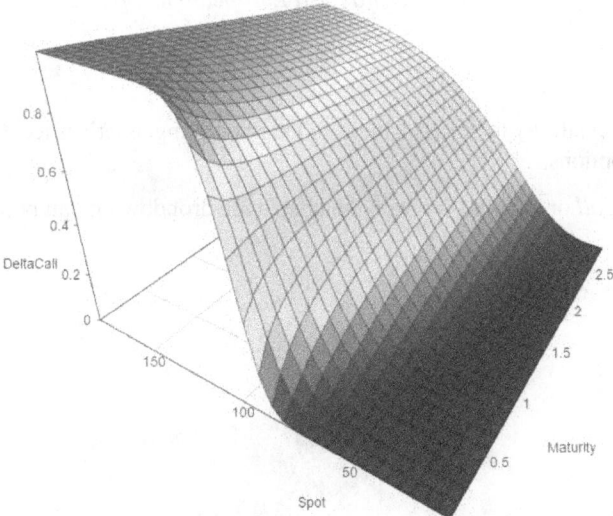

Figure 10-7. Delta for a European call option.

Selecting the *DeltaPut* chart type produces the results shown in Figure 10-8.

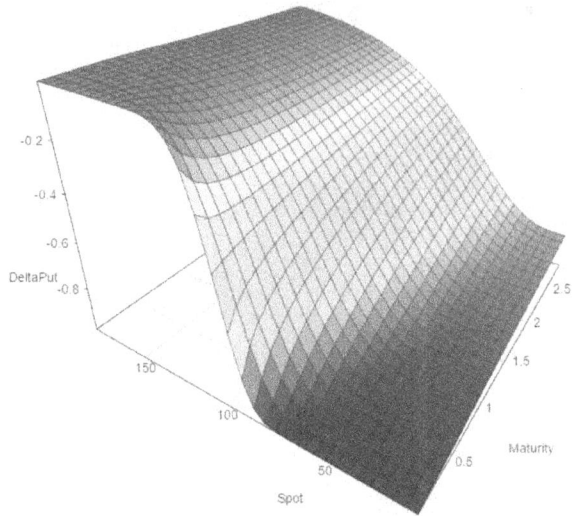

Figure 10-8. Delta for a European put option.

Gamma Charts

Gamma is the delta's sensitivity to small changes in the underlying asset's price. Gamma is identical for both the call and put options.

Selecting the *GammaCall* or *GammaPut* from the chart-type dropdown menu produces results shown in Figure 10-9.

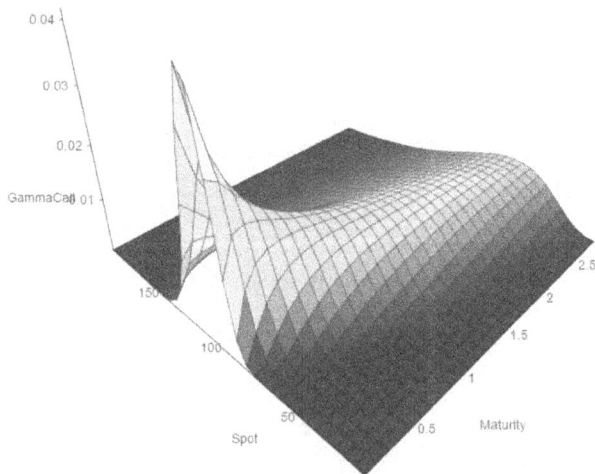

Figure 10-9. Gamma for a European call or put option.

Theta

Theta is the option's sensitivity to a small change in time to expiration, i.e., the time decay.

Selecting the *ThetaCall* chart type produces the results shown in Figure 10-10.

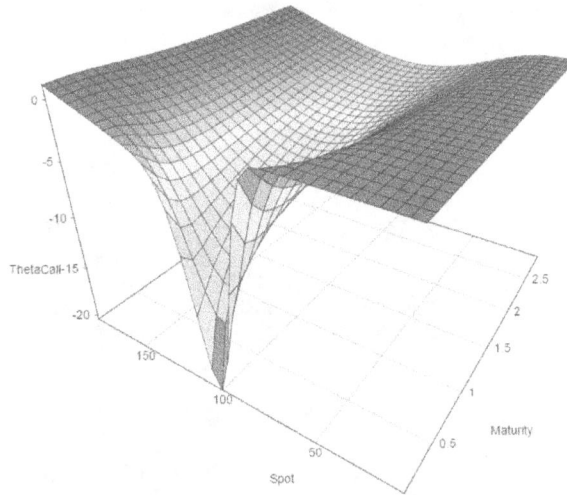

Figure 10-10. Theta for a European call option.

Selecting the *ThetaPut* chart type generates the results shown in Figure 10-11.

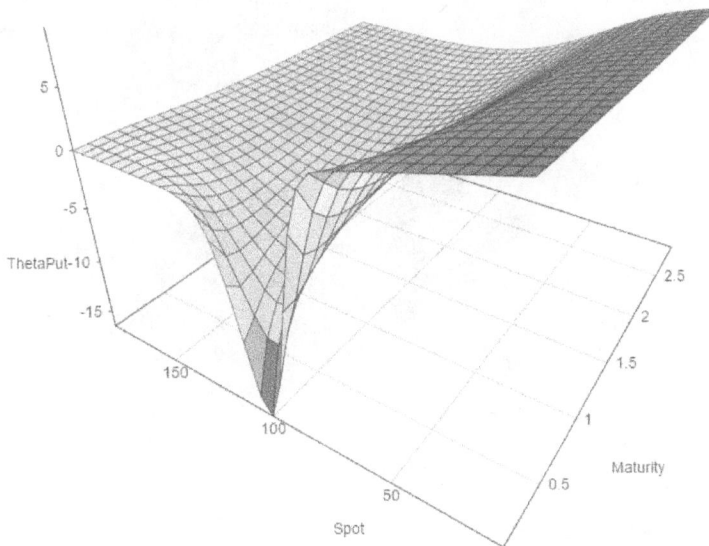

Figure 10-11. Theta for a European put option.

Rho Charts

Rho is the option's sensitivity to small changes in the risk-free interest rate.

Selecting the *RhoCall* chart type produces the results shown in Figure 10-12.

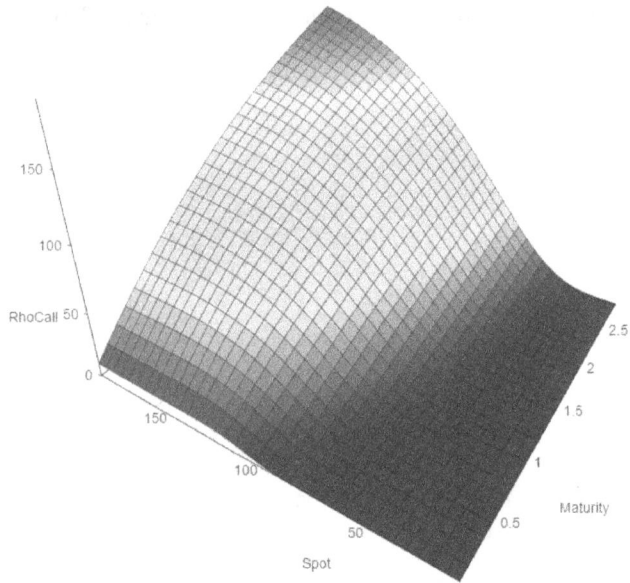

Figure 10-12. Rho for a European call option.

Selecting the *RhoPut* chart type produces the results shown in Figure 10-13.

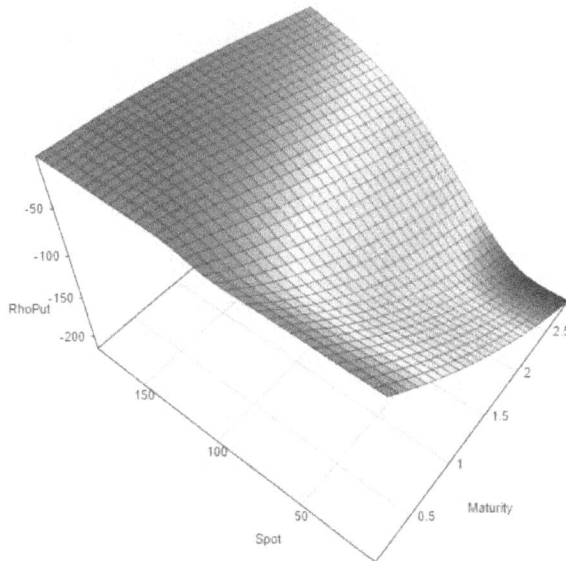

Figure 10-13. Rho for a European put option.

Vega Charts

Vega is the option's sensitivity to a small change in the volatility of the underlying asset. Vega is the same for both the call and put options.

Selecting the *VegaCall* or *VegaPut* chart type produces the results shown in Figure 10-14.

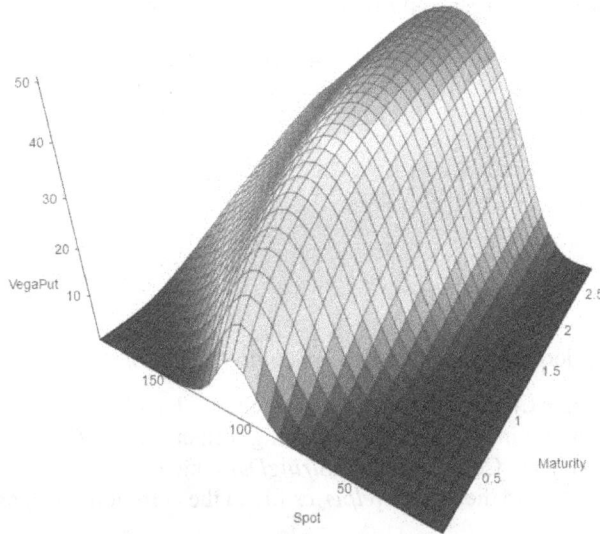

Figure 10-14. Vega for a European call or put option.

Stock Charts

In this section, we will create a web API controller for retrieving stock data from our *StockPriceDb* database implemented in Chapter 1 or Yahoo Finance if the data is not available in the database. In Chapter 1, we implemented a MVC Core application based on existing database where we used reverse engineering to create an Entity Framework model that can be used to perform basic data access. Here, we will use the same approach to retrieve stock data from our existing database named *StockPriceDb* created in Chapter 1 and then generate stock charts using the data.

In the *Chapter10* project, following the same procedure described in the existing database example in Chapter 1, install Entity Framework using the *Package Manager Console* and create the data model based on our existing database *StockPriceDb* using reverse engineering based on the *Scaffold-DbContext* method.

The reverse engineering process creates entity classes *System.cs*, *Price.cs*, and *IndexData.cs*, as well as a derived database context *StockPriceDbContext.cs* in the *Models* folder based on the schema of the existing database. You need to register context with dependency injection and move configuration of the database provider to *Startup.cs* following the procedure described in Chapter 1. After this process, we have created a stock-price entity model in our project.

Model

The database context, *StockPriceDbConext.cs*, generated by reverse engineering coordinates Entity Framework functionality for our stock price model. Here is the code snippet for this context:

```
using Microsoft.EntityFrameworkCore;
```

```
namespace Chapter10.Models
{
    public partial class StockPriceDbContext : DbContext
    {
        public virtual DbSet<IndexData> IndexData { get; set; }
        public virtual DbSet<Price> Price { get; set; }
        public virtual DbSet<Symbol> Symbol { get; set; }

        public StockPriceDbContext(DbContextOptions<StockPriceDbContext>
            options) : base(options) { }

    ......

    }
}
```

You see that this class is derived from the *Microsoft.EntityFramework.DbContext* class.

Here, we will use the Google Charts API to create stock charts. To this end, we need to convert the stock data from database or Yahoo Finance into a JSON string format. This JSON string can then be used by the Google DataTable object. Copy the *StockStringData* method from *ModelHelper* class in the *Chapter06* project and paste it to the *ModelHelper.cs* file in the current project, as shown in the follows:

```
public static string StockStringData(StockPriceDbContext db, string ticker,
    DateTime startDate, DateTime endDate, out string dataSource)
{
    dataSource = "Database";
    List<Price> prices = null;
    try
    {
        prices = db.Price.Where(x => x.Symbol.Ticker == ticker &&
            x.Date >= startDate && x.Date <= endDate).OrderBy(
            x => x.Date).ToList();
    }
    catch { }
    finally
    {
        if (prices.Count <= 0)
        {
            prices = GetYahooStockData(ticker, startDate, endDate, db);
            dataSource = "Yahoo Finance";
        }
    }
    if (prices.Count <= 0) return null;

    var cols = new JsonColumn[]
    {
        new JsonColumn {label = "Date", type = "date" },
        .....
    };
    var rows = new JsonRow[prices.Count];
    for (int i = 0; i < prices.Count; i++)
    {
        var date = DateTime.Parse(prices[i].Date.ToString());
        rows[i] = new JsonRow
        {
            c = new JsonCell[]
```

```
        {
            new JsonCell { v = "Date(" + date.Year + ", " +
                (date.Month - 1) + ", " + date.Day + ")" },
            new JsonCell { v = prices[i].Open },
            ......
        }
    };
}
return GetGoogleJson(cols, rows);
}
```

This code first retrieves stock data from database for a specified ticker and date period using LINQ. If there are no data stored in the database for a specified ticker, we will download the stock data directly from Yahoo Finance using the *GetYahooStockData* method. As long as we have the stock data ready, we then convert the data into a JSON string required by Google Charts DataTable. Note that in order to perform such conversion, you need to copy the content of the *JsonString.cs* file from the *Chapter05* project and paste the content to the *ModelHelper* class in the *Chapter10* project. You need also copy the *GetYahooStockData* method from the *Chapter06* project and paste it to the *ModelHelper* class.

Now, we are ready to create a RESTful Web API by following the standard procedure used in the previous examples – creating Web API with repository pattern and dependency injection. Here, we will bypass this standard process; instead, we will create our Web API directly using the *StockStringData* method implemented in the *ModelHelper* class. The main reason for doing this is that here we are only interested in retrieving stock data from database or Yahoo Finance, and do not need to perform any additional CRUD operations.

Web API Controller

Add a new Web API controller named *StockApiController* to the *Controller* folder and replace its content with the following code:

```
using System.Threading.Tasks;
using Microsoft.AspNetCore.Mvc;
using Chapter10.Models;

namespace Chapter10.Controllers
{
    [Route("api/[controller]")]
    public class StockApiController : Controller
    {
        private readonly StockPriceDbContext _context;
        public StockApiController(StockPriceDbContext context)
        {
            _context = context;
        }

        public async Task<IActionResult> Get(string ticker, DateTime startDate,
            DateTime endDate)
        {
            string dataSource = string.Empty;
            var data = await Task.Run(() => ModelHelper.StockStringData(
                _context, ticker, startDate, endDate, out dataSource));
            return new ObjectResult(data);
        }
}
```

```
        }
    }
```

This API controller is very simple, where we simply inject the *StockPriceDbContex* into the controller. We then define a single *Get* method that takes the stock ticker and date period as input arguments. The method then retrieves stock data from database or Yahoo Finance and converts the data into a JSON string format required by Google Charts API.

With the *StockApi* controller in place, it is possible to test it from the browser. Running this example by pressing F5. Type the following link to your browser

```
http://localhost:54115/api/stockapi?ticker=IWM&startDate=2017-01-01&
    endDate=2017-01-07
```

Note that we specify the parameters after the */api/stockapi* URL with a question mark and a "&" special character in between the parameters.

We know the stock ticker IWM (iShares Russell 2000 ETF) is not in our database, so the stock data should come directly from Yahoo Finance.

When you open this link in your browser, you will get the stock data for IWM in a JSON string format, as shown in the following:

```
{
    "cols": [
        {
            "id": "",
            "label": "Date",
            "type": "date",
            "role": null
        },
        {
            "id": "",
            "label": "Open",
            "type": "number",
            "role": null
        },
        {
            "id": "",
            "label": "High",
            "type": "number",
            "role": null
        },
        {
            "id": "",
            "label": "Low",
            "type": "number",
            "role": null
        },
        {
            "id": "",
            "label": "Close",
            "type": "number",
            "role": null
        },
        {
            "id": "",
```

```
            "label": "CloseAdj",
            "type": "number",
            "role": null
        },
        {
            "id": "",
            "label": "Volume",
            "type": "number",
            "role": null
        }
    ],
    "rows": [
        {
            "c": [
                {
                    "v": "Date(2017, 0, 3)",
                    "f": null
                },
                {
                    "v": 136.490005,
                    "f": null
                },
                {
                    "v": 136.830002,
                    "f": null
                },
                {
                    "v": 134.5,
                    "f": null
                },
                {
                    "v": 135.520004,
                    "f": null
                },
                {
                    "v": 135.130881,
                    "f": null
                },
                {
                    "v": 29792400,
                    "f": null
                }
            ]
        },

        .....

    ]
}
```

We can pass this JSON string (also called the data object) to initialize the DataTable constructor in Google Charts.

Creating Stock Charts

In this section, I will show you how to consume the services provided by our *Stock* API controller in a standard MVC application.

First, add a new class named *StockPriceViewModel.cs* to the *Models* folder and replace its content with the following code:

```
using System;
using System.ComponentModel.DataAnnotations;

namespace Chapter10.Models
{
    public class StockPriceViewModel
    {
        public string Ticker { get; set; }
        [DataType(DataType.Date)]
        [DisplayFormat(DataFormatString = "{0:dd/MM/yyyy}")]
        public DateTime StartDate { get; set; }
        [DataType(DataType.Date)]
        [DisplayFormat(DataFormatString = "{0:dd/MM/yyyy}")]
        public DateTime EndDate { get; set; }
    }
}
```

We can use this view model to specify the stock ticker and date period when we retrieve stock data from database or Yahoo Finance.

Add a new MVC controller named *StockChartController.cs* to the *Controllers* folder and replace its content with the following code:

```
using Chapter10.Models;
using Microsoft.AspNetCore.Mvc;
using System;

namespace Chapter10.Controllers
{
    public class StockChartController : Controller
    {
        // GET: /<controller>/
        public IActionResult Index()
        {
            ViewBag.Title = "Stock Chart";
            StockPriceViewModel model = new StockPriceViewModel();
            model.Ticker = "IBM";
            model.StartDate = DateTime.Parse("1/1/2016");
            model.EndDate = DateTime.Parse("3/1/2016");
            return View(model);
        }

        [HttpPost]
        public IActionResult Index(StockPriceViewModel model)
        {
            ViewBag.Title = "Stock Chart";
            return View(model);
        }
```

```
        }
    }
```

Here, we implement a strong typed MVC controller. In the GET *Index* method, we set the default values of the stock ticker and date period for our stock price view model. In the POST Index method, we simply update the view model with the user's input.

Add a new folder named *StockChart*. Add a new view named *Index.cshtml* to the *Views/StockChart* folder and replace its content with the following code:

```
@model Chapter10.Models.StockPriceViewModel
@{
    ViewData["Title"] = ViewBag.Title;
}
<h3>@ViewBag.Title</h3>

<form asp-action="Index">
    <div class="form-horizontal">
        <hr />
        <div asp-validation-summary="ModelOnly" class="text-danger"></div>
        <div class="form-group">
            <label asp-for="Ticker" class="col-md-2 control-label"></label>
            <div class="col-md-10">
                <input asp-for="Ticker" class="form-control" />
                <span asp-validation-for="Ticker" class="text-danger"></span>
            </div>
        </div>
        <div class="form-group">
            <label asp-for="StartDate" class="col-md-2 control-label"></label>
            <div class="col-md-10">
                <input asp-for="StartDate" class="form-control" />
                <span asp-validation-for="StartDate" class="text-danger"></span>
            </div>
        </div>
        <div class="form-group">
            <label asp-for="EndDate" class="col-md-2 control-label"></label>
            <div class="col-md-10">
                <input asp-for="EndDate" class="form-control" />
                <span asp-validation-for="EndDate" class="text-danger"></span>
            </div>
        </div>
        <div class="form-group">
            <div class="col-md-offset-2 col-md-10">
                <input type="submit" value="Create Stock Charts"
                        class="btn btn-primary" />
            </div>
        </div>
    </div>
</form>
<div class="container">
    <div class="row">
        <div class="col-sm-12">
            <div id="chart1"></div>
        </div>
    </div>
    <div class="row">
```

```
            <div class="col-sm-12">
                <div id="chart2"></div>
            </div>
        </div>
        <div class="row">
            <div class="col-sm-12">
                <div id="chart3"></div>
            </div>
        </div>
    </div>

@section scripts{
<script type="text/javascript"
        src="https://www.gstatic.com/charts/loader.js"></script>
<script type="text/javascript">
    google.charts.load('current', { 'packages': ['corechart'] });
    google.charts.setOnLoadCallback(drawChart);
    var ticker = '@(Model.Ticker)';
    var startDate = '@(Model.StartDate.ToString("yyyy-MM-dd"))';
    var endDate = '@(Model.EndDate.ToString("yyyy-MM-dd"))';
    function drawChart() {
        $.ajax({
            url: 'api/stockapi',
            method: 'GET',
            data: { ticker: ticker, startDate: startDate, endDate: endDate },
            dataType: 'json',
            success: function (jsonData) {
                var data = new google.visualization.DataTable(jsonData);

                //stock price line chart:
                var view = new google.visualization.DataView(data);
                view.hideColumns([6]);
                var options = {
                    title: 'Stock Price Line Chart: ' + ticker,
                    width: 960,
                    height: 350,
                    chartArea: { left: 100, top: 30, width: '70%', height:
                                '80%', backgroundColor: { stroke: 'black',
                                strokeWidth: 0.5 }},
                    lineWidth: 2,
                    pointSize: 5,
                    hAxis: { type: 'category', showTextEvery: 6  },
                };
                var chart = new google.visualization.LineChart(
                    document.getElementById('chart1'));
                chart.draw(view, options);

                //stock volume bar chart:
                view = new google.visualization.DataView(data);
                view.setColumns([0, 6]);
                options = {
                    title: 'Stock Volume Bar Chart: ' + ticker,
                    width: 960,
                    height: 200,
                    chartArea: { left: 100, top: 30, width: '70%',
```

```
                            height: '65%', backgroundColor:
                                { stroke: 'black', strokeWidth: 0.5 } },
                lineWidth: 2,
                legend: 'none',
                hAxis: { type: 'category', showTextEvery: 6 },
            };
            chart = new google.visualization.ColumnChart(
                    document.getElementById('chart2'));
            chart.draw(view, options);

            //stock price candlestick chart:
            view = new google.visualization.DataView(data);
            view.setColumns([0, 3, 1, 4, 2]);
            options = {
                title: 'Stock Price Candlestick Chart: ' + ticker,
                legend: 'none',
                width: 960,
                height: 350,
                candlestick: {
                    fallingColor: { strokeWidth: 0, fill: '#a52714' },
                    risingColor: { strokeWidth: 0, fill: '#0f9d58' }
                },
                chartArea: { left: 100, top: 30, width: '70%',
                            height: '80%', backgroundColor:
                                { stroke: 'black', strokeWidth: 0.5 } },
                explorer: { actions: ['dragToZoom', 'rightClickToReset'] },
                lineWidth: 0.5,
                hAxis: { type: 'category', showTextEvery: 6  },
            };
            chart = new google.visualization.CandlestickChart(
                    document.getElementById('chart3'));
            chart.draw(view, options);
        }
    });
   }
 </script>
 }
```

This code first implements a *submit* form that includes three input elements, which take the user's inputs for the stock ticker and date period defined in our model (*StockPriceViewModel*). It then defines three *div* elements used for creating the line and candlestick charts for stock prices as well as the volume chart.

In the script section, we take the use's inputs from our updated model. Inside the *drawChart* function, we use AJAX to retrieve the stock data from stock API controller using the */api/stockapi* URL. Note how we specify the input arguments required by our API controller in the *data* attribute:

```
data: { ticker: ticker, startDate: startDate, endDate: endDate },
```

This way, we can retrieve stock data for all tickers (over 3000 stock tickers) defined in our database and Yahoo Finance through our stock API controller, and create stock charts for these stocks.

Next, we use the stock data (called *jsonData*) from our stock API controller to create a DataTable object named *data*:

```
var data = new google.visualization.DataTable(jsonData);
```

Note that the DataTable constructor can take *jsonData* directly, because we already converted the original stock data into a JSON data string at the server side.

The code for creating stock charts using Google Charts API is standard, which is similar to what we used in Chapter 6.

Running this example and clicking the *Stock Charts* tab produce the default stock charts for IBM, as shown in Figure 10-15.

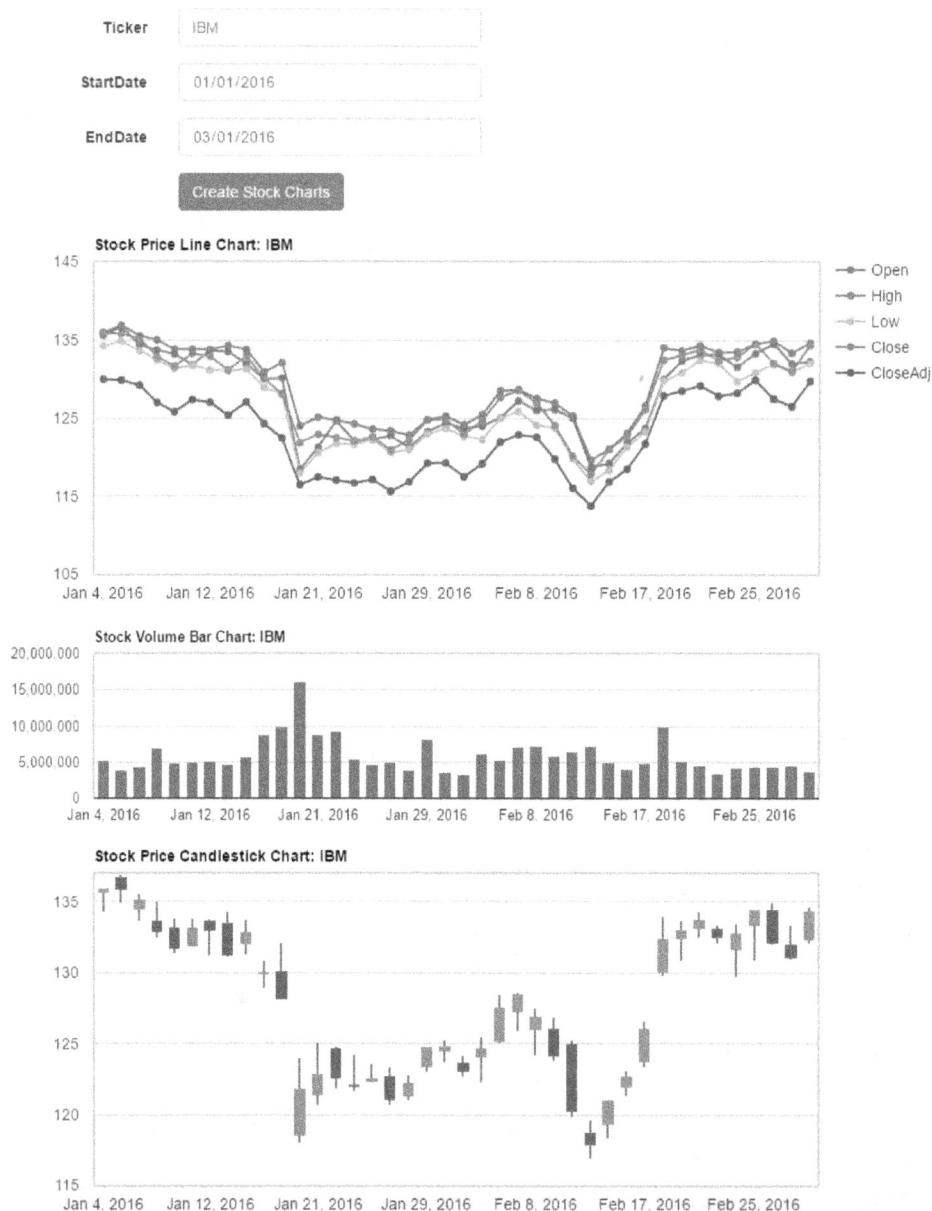

Figure 10-15. Stock charts for IBM created using data from Web API.

In Chapter 1, we already stored the stock data in the database for IBM in the period of 1/1/2016 to 3/1/2016. This means that the data used in creating the stock charts in Figure 10-15 is from our database – *StockPriceDb*.

If the stock data for a specified ticker or period is not in the database, our stock API controller will download the data directly from Yahoo Finance. For example, the stock ticker QQQ (PowerShares ETF for tracking Nasdaq 100 index) is not in our database. We can still create its stock charts. Enter QQQ in the *Ticker* field, and enter 2/1/2017 and 4/1/2017 in the *StartDate* and *EndDate* fields respectively. Clicking the *Create Stock Charts* button generates the output shown in Figure 10-16.

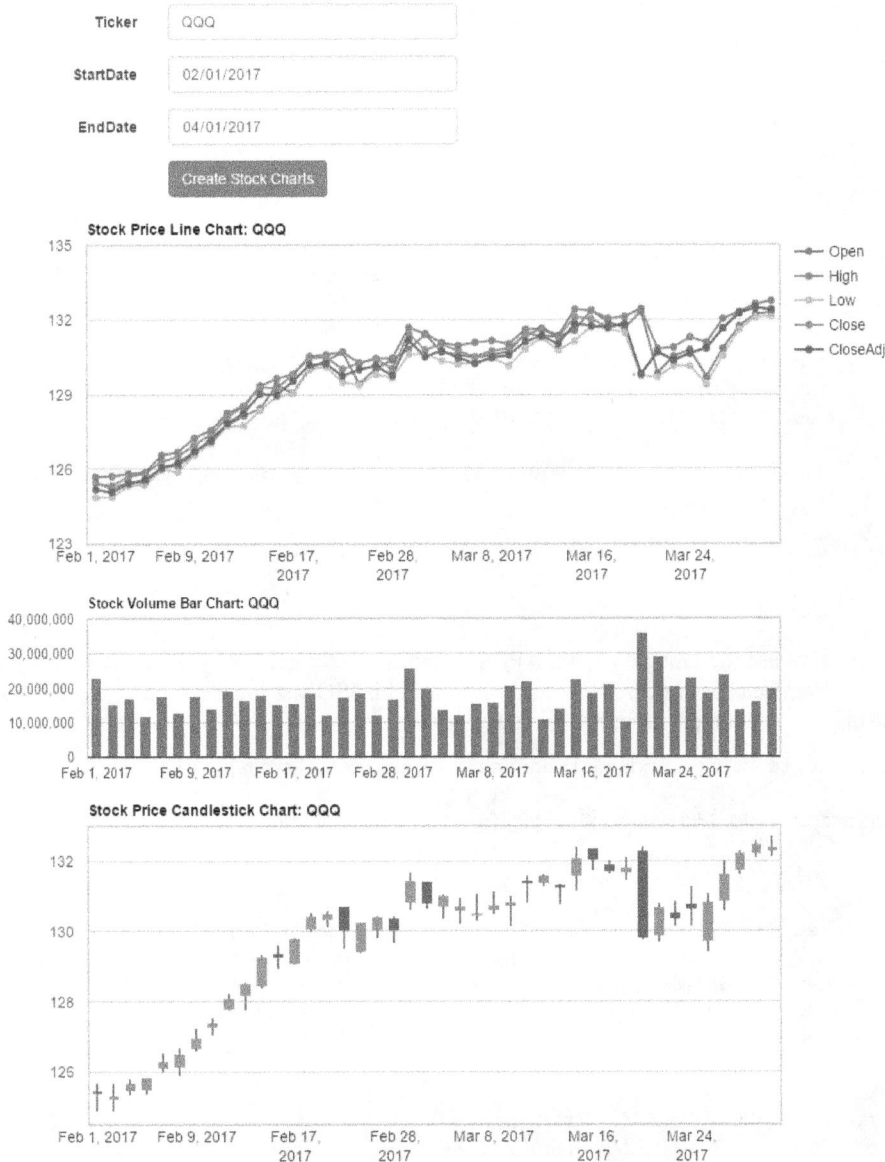

Figure 10-16. Stock charts for QQQ created using data from Web API.

Scatter Charts for Indices

In Chapter 1, we created a database called *StockPriceDb*, which also include an *IndexData* table. The *IndexData* table contains over 10 years of market data for four indices (SPX, VIX, IG, and HY) starting from 9/21/2004 to 5/15/2015.

In this section, we will create a scatter chart for a pair of indices (i.g. HY ~ SPX, IG ~ VIX, etc.). This scatter chart is a visual representation of the correlation between two indices. It ties in with the correlation coefficient as it is used for indicating whether a linear relationship exists or not between two indices.

Model

Here, we can also use the same database context, *StockPriceDbConext.cs*, as we used in the preceding stock chart example, because it consists of a DbSet for IndexData:

```
using Microsoft.EntityFrameworkCore;

namespace Chapter10.Models
{
    public partial class StockPriceDbContext : DbContext
    {
        public virtual DbSet<IndexData> IndexData { get; set; }
        public virtual DbSet<Price> Price { get; set; }
        public virtual DbSet<Symbol> Symbol { get; set; }

        public StockPriceDbContext(DbContextOptions<StockPriceDbContext>
            options) : base(options) { }

        ......
    }
}
```

Here, we will also use the Google Charts API to create scatter charts. To this end, we need to convert the index data from database into a JSON string format. This JSON string can then be used by the Google DataTable object. Add a method named *IndexStringData* to the *ModelHelper.cs* file:

```
public static string IndexStringData(StockPriceDbContext db)
{
    var idx = db.IndexData.OrderBy(s => s.Date).ToList();

    var cols = new JsonColumn[]
    {
        new JsonColumn {label = "Date", type = "date" },
        new JsonColumn {label = "Hyspread", type = "number" },
        new JsonColumn {label = "Igspread", type = "number" },
        new JsonColumn {label = "Spx", type = "number" },
        new JsonColumn {label = "vix", type = "number" },
    };

    var rows = new JsonRow[idx.Count];
    for (int i = 0; i < idx.Count; i++)
    {
        var date = DateTime.Parse(idx[i].Date.ToString());
```

```
        rows[i] = new JsonRow
        {
            c = new JsonCell[]
            {
                new JsonCell { v = "Date(" + date.Year + ", " + (date.Month - 1)
                    + ", " + date.Day + ")" },
                new JsonCell { v = idx[i].Hyspread },
                new JsonCell { v = idx[i].Igspread },
                new JsonCell { v = idx[i].Spx },
                new JsonCell { v = idx[i].Vix },
            }
        };
    }
    return GetGoogleJson(cols, rows);
}
```

This code first retrieves index data from database, and then converts the data into a JSON string required by Google Charts DataTable.

Now, we are ready to create a RESTful Web API. Here, we will create our Web API directly using the *IndexStringData* method. The reason for doing this is that here we are only interested in retrieving the index data from database, and do not need to perform any additional CRUD operations.

Web API Controller

Add a new Web API controller named *IndexApiController* to the *Controllers* folder and replace its content with the following code:

```
using Chapter10.Models;
using Microsoft.AspNetCore.Mvc;
using System.Threading.Tasks;

namespace Chapter10.Controllers
{
    [Route("api/[controller]")]
    public class IndexApiController : Controller
    {
        private readonly StockPriceDbContext _context;
        private string data = string.Empty;
        public IndexApiController(StockPriceDbContext context)
        {
            _context = context;
        }

        public async Task<IActionResult> Get()
        {
            if (string.IsNullOrEmpty(data))
            {
                data = await Task.Run(() =>
                    ModelHelper.IndexStringData(_context));
            }
            return new ObjectResult(data);
        }
    }
}
```

This API controller is very simple. In the constructor, we simply inject the *StockPriceDbContex* into the controller. We then define a single *Get* method that retrieves index data from database and converts the data into a JSON string format required by Google Charts API.

With the *IndexApi* controller in place, it is possible to test it from the browser. Running this example by pressing F5. Type the following link to your browser

```
http://localhost:54115/api/indexapi
```

When you open this link in your browser, you will get the index data a JSON string format, as shown in the following:

```
{
    "cols": [
        {
            "id": "",
            "label": "Date",
            "type": "date",
            "role": null
        },
        {
            "id": "",
            "label": "Hyspread",
            "type": "number",
            "role": null
        },
        {
            "id": "",
            "label": "Igspread",
            "type": "number",
            "role": null
        },
        {
            "id": "",
            "label": "Spx",
            "type": "number",
            "role": null
        },
        {
            "id": "",
            "label": "vix",
            "type": "number",
            "role": null
        }
    ],
    "rows": [
        {
            "c": [
                {
                    "v": "Date(2004, 8, 21)",
                    "f": null
                },
                {
                    "v": 363,
                    "f": null
                },
```

```
            {
                    "v": 53.93,
                    "f": null
            },
            {
                    "v": 1129.3,
                    "f": null
            },
            {
                    "v": 13.66,
                    "f": null
            }
        ]
    },
    ......
    {
        "c": [
            {
                    "v": "Date(2014, 4, 15)",
                    "f": null
            },
            {
                    "v": 346.5008667,
                    "f": null
            },
            {
                    "v": 65.21262904,
                    "f": null
            },
            {
                    "v": 1870.85,
                    "f": null
            },
            {
                    "v": 13.17,
                    "f": null
            }
        ]
    }
    ]
}
```

We can pass this JSON string (also called the data object) to initialize the DataTable constructor in Google Charts.

Creating Scatter Charts

In this section, I will show you how to consume the services provided by our *Index* API controller in a standard MVC application.

First, add a new class named *IndexViewModel.cs* to the *Models* folder and replace its content with the following code:

```
namespace Chapter10.Models
{
```

```
public class IndexViewModel
{
    public string Index1 { get; set; }
    public string Index2 { get; set; }
}
}
```

This model simply define an index pair that will be used in creating our scatter chart.

Add a new MVC controller named *IndexChartController.cs* to the *Controllers* folder and replace its content with the following code:

```
using Chapter10.Models;
using Microsoft.AspNetCore.Mvc;

namespace Chapter10.Controllers
{
    public class IndexChartController : Controller
    {
        // GET: /<controller>/
        public IActionResult Index()
        {
            ViewBag.Title = "Index Scatter Chart";
            IndexViewModel model = new IndexViewModel();
            model.Index1 = "Spx";
            model.Index2 = "HySpread";
            return View(model);
        }

        [HttpPost]
        public IActionResult Index(IndexViewModel model)
        {
            ViewBag.Title = "Index Scatter Chart";
            return View(model);
        }
    }
}
```

Here, we implement a MVC controller. In the GET *Index* method, we set the default index pair to *Spx* and *HySpread* for our index view model. In the POST *Index* method, we simply update the view model with the user's input.

Add a new folder named *IndexChart*. Add a new view named *Index.cshtml* to the *Views/IndexChart* folder and replace its content with the following code:

```
@model Chapter10.Models.IndexViewModel
@{
    ViewData["Title"] = ViewBag.Title;
}
<h3>@ViewBag.Title</h3>

<script type="text/javascript"
    src="https://www.gstatic.com/charts/loader.js"></script>

<form asp-action="Index">
    <div class="form-horizontal">
        <hr />
```

```
        <div asp-validation-summary="ModelOnly" class="text-danger"></div>
        <div class="form-group">
            <label asp-for="Index1" class="col-md-2 control-label"></label>
            <div class="col-md-10">
                <input asp-for="Index1" class="form-control" />
                <span asp-validation-for="Index1" class="text-danger"></span>
            </div>
        </div>
        <div class="form-group">
            <label asp-for="Index2" class="col-md-2 control-label"></label>
            <div class="col-md-10">
                <input asp-for="Index2" class="form-control" />
                <span asp-validation-for="Index2" class="text-danger"></span>
            </div>
        </div>
        <div class="form-group">
            <div class="col-md-offset-2 col-md-10">
                <input type="submit" value="Create Index Charts"
                    class="btn btn-primary" />
            </div>
        </div>
    </div>
</form>

<div class="container">
    <div class="row">
        <div class="col-sm-12">
            <div id="chart"></div>
        </div>
    </div>
</div>

@section scripts{
<script type="text/javascript">
    google.charts.load('current', { 'packages': ['corechart'] });
    google.charts.setOnLoadCallback(drawChart);

    var index1 = '@(Model.Index1)';
    var index2 = '@(Model.Index2)';
    var col1, col2;
    if (index1 === "HySpread") col1 = 1;
    else if (index1 === "IgSpread") col1 = 2;
    else if (index1 === "Spx") col1 = 3;
    else if (index1 === "Vix") col1 = 4;
    if (index2 === "HySpread") col2 = 1;
    else if (index2 === "IgSpread") col2 = 2;
    else if (index2 === "Spx") col2 = 3;
    else if (index2 === "Vix") col2 = 4;

    function drawChart() {
        $.ajax({
            url: 'api/indexapi',
            method: 'GET',
            dataType: 'json',
            success: function (jsonData) {
```

```
                    var data = new google.visualization.DataTable(jsonData);

                    //index scatter chart:
                    var view = new google.visualization.DataView(data);
                    view.setColumns([col1, col2, col2]);

                    var options = {
                        title: 'Index Scatter Chart: (' + index2 + ' ~ ' +
                            index1 + ')',
                        width: 850,
                        height: 600,
                        chartArea: { left: 100, top: 30, width: '80%',
                                    height: '85%', backgroundColor: { stroke:
                                    'black', strokeWidth: 0.5 } },
                        pointSize: 3,
                        legend: 'none',
                        series: { 0: { color: 'steelblue' },
                                1: { color: 'steelblue' } },
                        hAxis: { title: index1, viewWindowMode: 'maximized' },
                        vAxis: { title: index2, viewWindowMode: 'maximized'},
                        trendlines: { 0: { color: 'red' },
                            1: { type: 'polynomial', degree: 2, color: 'green' } },
                    };
                    var chart = new google.visualization.ScatterChart(
                        document.getElementById('chart'));
                    chart.draw(view, options);
                }
            });
        }
    </script>
    }
```

This code first implements a *submit* form that includes two input elements, which take the user's inputs for a pair of indices defined in our model (*IndexViewModel*).

In the script section, we take the use's inputs from our model. Inside the *drawChart* function, we use AJAX to retrieve the index data from our index API controller using the */api/indexapi* URL.

Next, we create a scatter chart for a specified index pair with two trend lines: the first one is the linear trend line and the other one is the second-degree polynomial trend line.

Running this example and clicking the *Index Charts* tab produce the default scatter chart for indices HY ~ SPX, as shown in Figure 10-17. Note from the figure that the quadratic regression fits data better than the linear regression does.

We can also create the scatter chart for the other index pair, i.g., HY ~ VIX. Entering the *Vix* and *HySpread* in the *Index1* and *Index2* fields respectively and then clicking the *Create Index Charts* button generate the results shown in Figure 10-18.

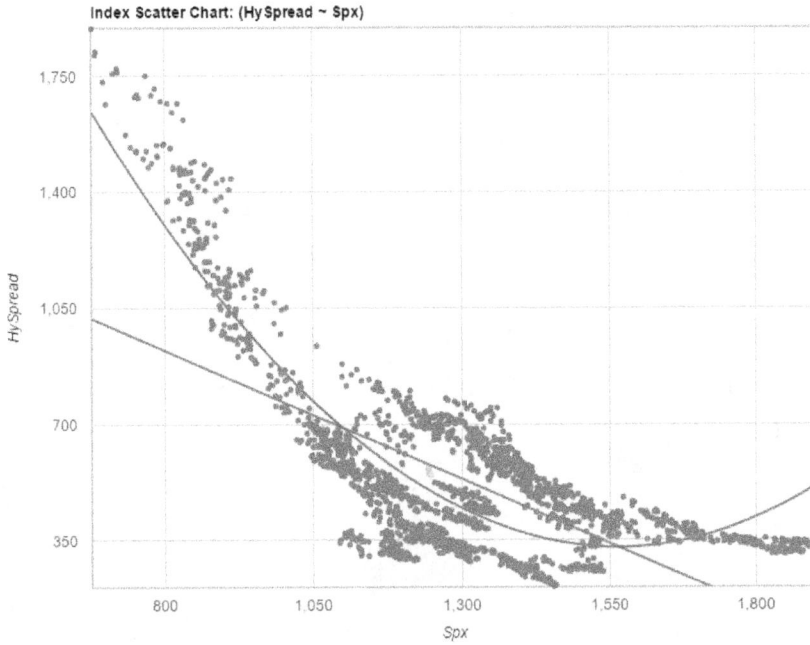

Figure 10-17. A scatter chart for HY vs SPX.

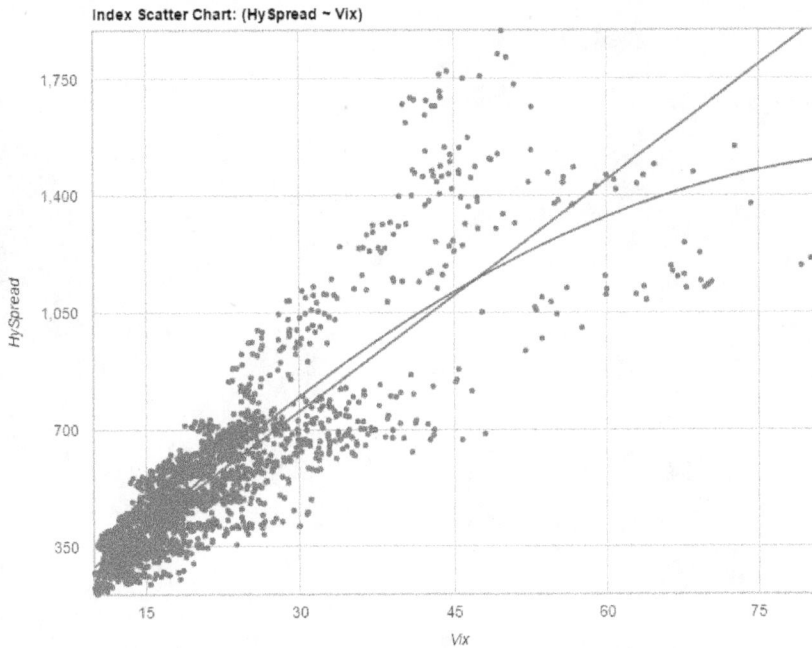

Figure 10-18. A scatter chart for HY vs VIX.

Index